·THE PRO FOOTBALL CHRONICLE

·THE PRO· FOOTBALL CHRONICLE

The Complete (*Well, Almost*)
Record of the Best Players,
the Greatest Photos, the Hardest Hits,
the Biggest Scandals
and the Funniest Stories in Pro Football

■ ■

DAN DALY & BOB O'DONNELL

■

COLLIER BOOKS/MACMILLAN PUBLISHING COMPANY • New York

COLLIER MACMILLAN CANADA • Toronto

MAXWELL/MACMILLAN INTERNATIONAL
New York • Oxford • Singapore • Sydney

Collier Books
Macmillan Publishing Company
866 Third Avenue, New York, NY 10022

Collier Macmillan Canada, Inc.
1200 Eglinton Avenue East, Suite 200
Don Mills, Ontario M3C 3N1

Library of Congress Cataloging-in-Publication Data
Daly, Dan.
    The pro football chronicle: the complete (well, almost) record of the best players, the greatest photos, the hardest hits, the biggest scandals, and the funniest stories in pro football / Dan Daly and Bob O'Donnell.—1st Collier Books ed.
        p. cm.
    Includes bibliographical references and index.
    ISBN 0-02-028300-8
    1. Football—United States—Records. 2. Football—United States—History. 3. Football—United States—Humor. I. Title
GV955.D35 1990   90-39947   CIP
796.332′64′0973—dc20

Macmillan books are available at special discounts for bulk purchases for sales promotions, premiums, fund-raising, or educational use. For details, contact:
    Special Sales Director
    Macmillan Publishing Company
    866 Third Avenue
    New York, NY 10022

First Collier Books Edition 1990

Design by ROBERT BULL DESIGN

10 9 8 7 6 5 4 3 2 1

Printed in the United States of America

To Daniel Richard and Daniel Patrick
            —Dan Daly

To Mom, Pop and Dede
            —Bob O'Donnell

CONTENTS

■ ■ ■

ACKNOWLEDGMENTS

We're grateful to many people for their contributions and assistance. At the top of the list is Joe Horrigan, the curator of the Pro Football Hall of Fame. He gave us the run of the research library for three weeks and never grew impatient with our incessant questions. His assistant, Pete Fierle, was great about digging up old films and photographs.

Special thanks, also, to the staff at the Library of Congress, particularly the folks in the newspaper reading room who fetched us microfilm for a year. The library truly is God's gift to researchers.

Jeanine Bucek, our editor at Macmillan, believed enough in this book to take a chance on two first-time authors. She also gave us extra time at the end so we could get it done the way we wanted. We're lucky to be working with her.

We're indebted, too, to Mike Keating and Mark Green, Dan's bosses at the *Washington Times,* who allowed him not one but two leaves of absence, and to Herb Thatcher, who let Bob work part-time in his painting business when he wasn't writing.

Doug Lang at NFL Alumni was invaluable when it came to tracking down former players. So was Rudy Custer, the ex–business manager of the Chicago Bears, Joe Gordon of the Pittsburgh Steelers and Jim Gallagher of the Philadelphia Eagles.

Farther from home, Debra Anderson, archivist at the University of Wisconsin/ Green Bay; Dorothy Johnson, archivist at the Panhandle Historical Museum in Canyon, Texas; and Minnie Wilson at the Cook County (Ill.) Municipal Court archives provided information we otherwise couldn't have gotten our hands on. The same goes for Seymour Siwoff of the Elias Sports Bureau, who supplied some of the statistics for the back of the book.

The Washington Redskins' public relations staff—Charlie Dayton, Marty Hurney and Jamie Crittenberger—was particularly generous with the team's resources. So was Bob Eller of the Cleveland Browns, from whom we got game-by-game stats for Otto Graham and others. Thanks also to Frank Kleha (Atlanta Falcons), Dave Pelletier (Dallas Cowboys), Jeff Blumb (Green Bay Packers), Craig Kelley (Indianapolis Colts), Greg Gladysiewski (Phoenix Cardinals), Dan Edwards and Pat Hanlon (Steelers), and Steve Sabol and Ann Fisher (NFL Films).

Most of the photos appear courtesy of the Bettmann Archive and NFL Properties. Katherine Bang at Bettmann allowed us a day to rummage through their files for pictures that were out of the ordinary. That was appreciated.

We did scores of interviews, but some people stood out for their cooperation. Jim Fox, the nephew of Benny Friedman, went above and beyond the call of duty to provide valuable information. Tex Coulter is working on a book of his own about his years in the league but shared his unusual insights for hours. Bill Radovich also was generous with his time. Jim Ford, a longtime Packers fan, furnished some of the tidbits in the following pages.

Our gratitude to Dr. Robert O'Donnell, "team" physician; Margaret O'Donnell, "team" legal expert; as well as to Ken Denlinger, Al Kermisch, Bruce Raben, Vito Stellino, Shirley Povich, Lew Atkinson and Bob Oates.

Our families were terrifically supportive, and our wives, Laurel Daly and Dede O'Donnell, absolutely amazing. For more than a year they lived with a book rather than a husband—and they're *still here.* What did we do to deserve them?

■ ■ ■

INTRODUCTION

Pro football, sad to say, doesn't have a very large body of literature. If you want to learn about the history of the game, there are only a few books you can turn to, and they tend to mingle fact with fiction. Most of what happened before 1960—the pre-television era—has been ignored entirely.

We've covered pro football since 1978, most recently for the *Washington Times* and the *Fort Worth Star-Telegram.* And, being history buffs as well as sportswriters, we wanted to know more. What was football really like in the old days? How was it written about? What were the big stories, the major topics of conversation? How has the game evolved?

So we decided to do this book. It was 15 months in the making and much more than either of us had bargained for. We simply weren't prepared for how little research had been done, how little space pro football occupied in newspapers and magazines until the '60s. This, we came to realize, is why mythology abounds.

We read as many worthwhile books as we could get our hands on, but that was only a starting point. Newspaper microfilm was our primary source of information. We virtually lived at the Library of Congress. We also spent three weeks going through the files at the Pro Football Hall of Fame and made shorter trips to Green Bay, New York and Philadelphia to obtain other material. Telephone interviews with players and coaches helped fill in any gaps.

Some of the most interesting items we just happened upon, such as Gus Sonnenberg's wrestling exploits, a locker room speech by Redskins coach Ray Flaherty, Don Hutson's bogus 95-game receiving streak and a new version of how George Halas came to own the Chicago Bears. There was plenty more where those came from, if only we could have browsed a little longer.

The structure of our book was influenced by *The Bill James Historical Baseball Abstract* (Villard, 1986). It's a history written in decade form, a collage of items of various lengths, most less than a page, plus longer essays. We wanted to write a history that was readable, moved along and covered a lot of ground yet also provided some depth on certain subjects—such as the Red Grange tours in 1925–26, the attempt to fix the 1946 NFL championship game, integration, the violence in the '50s and Hardy Brown, the most lethal player the game has known.

Ours is an extremely selective, you might even say idiosyncratic, history. There's plenty that we've left out, particularly in the later, more familiar decades. But we hope we've succeeded in giving you a better understanding of pro football's beginnings, its development and the people who've made it what it is.

This is a kitchen-sink kind of book—part historical, part statistical, part reference. The first and biggest section is a history of the game from the dawn of the NFL in the 1920s to the present day. Each chapter begins with a Decade at a Glance feature, which provides basic information designed to give you more of a feel for the decade. What were the best teams? Who was the highest-paid player? How was pro football changing? If an item is marked with an arrow, it means there's more on the subject elsewhere in the chapter.

The second section contains the game-by-game statistics of 40 famous offensive players. Only in football can a player's entire career—every game he ever played—be reduced to a single page. Players are divided into five categories: quarterbacks, running backs, runner-receivers, wide receivers and tight ends. You'll be able to compare Otto Graham and Roger Staubach, Jim Brown and Walter Payton, Don Hutson and Paul Warfield.

Thirty-nine other players are dealt with more briefly. The game-by-game statistics of only their *best* season are included. Players in this group aren't necessarily on a level below the first group. It's just that stats are hard to come by.

The earlier players, you'll find, stand up surprisingly well against recent stars. They don't always rank very high on the all-time lists because they played shorter seasons and, sometimes, had shorter careers. But their yards-per-game averages are comparable and some of their individual seasons were extraordinary, even by today's standards.

The last section is titled "Stuff You Can Never Lay Your Hands On." In it you'll find such items as the 67 U.S. cities that have had major league football teams (and the teams that represented each), the head-to-head records of famous coaches (e.g. Tom Landry vs. Don Shula) and a list of notable players who wore every number from 0 to 99.

The lack of literature about pro football has created the impression that its history just isn't as compelling as baseball's. We found that to be another myth. You just have to dig a little deeper in football, that's all. We hope our efforts will encourage others to take up the search.

■ ■ ■

THE 1920s

'20s CHALKBOARD

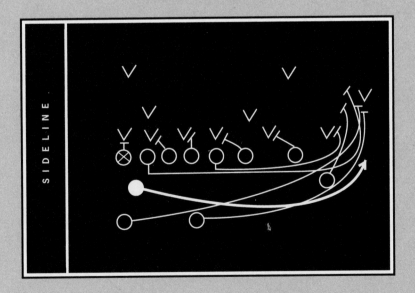

End run by the quarterback from a sideline formation

End Run by the Quarterback from a Sideline Formation

Offenses of the '20s and early '30s considered the sidelines the enemy. There were no hashmarks in those days, so a play began where the previous one ended. If a runner was knocked out of bounds, the ball was spotted one yard in from the line. This called for a special adjustment to the standard single-wing formation—everyone lined up to one side. It also limited the number of plays you could call. "It was possible to run straight ahead but was pretty hard to make it successful," said Hall-of-Fame end and coach Ray Flaherty. "You could run any pass play, but it was usually a much longer throw and harder to complete. The defense had much less area to cover." The choice was usually an end run, as shown here, or an off-tackle play. Even if it didn't gain much, it moved the ball toward the middle of the field. Giants back Tony Plansky made one of the decade's more memorable plays from a sideline formation in 1929. He beat the Chicago Cardinals with a last-second drop kick. Plansky had to kick left-footed because of the severe angle. Fortunately, he was ambidextrous.

THE 1920s AT A GLANCE

Decade Standings

	W	L	T	Pct.		W	L	T	Pct.
New York (1)	44	17	5	.705	Providence (1)	31	24	7	.556
Chi. Bears (1)	84	31	19	.698	Detroit	22	18	9	.541
Frankford (1)	64	26	12	.686	Buffalo	39	37	12	.511
Green Bay (1)	61	25	13	.682	Akron (1)	27	26	11	.508
Canton (2)	38	19	11	.640	Dayton	18	51	8	.286
Rock Island	27	14	12	.623	Columbus	13	44	3	.242
Chi. Cards (1)	56	42	9	.565	Hammond	7	28	4	.231

(Only towns that had a team five or more years included. Figures in parentheses are championships won.)

Best Regular–Season Record   Canton Bulldogs, 1922, 11-0-1

Worst Regular–Season Record   Columbus Tigers, 1925, 0-9

Biggest Crowd   75,000, Red Grange and the Chicago Bears vs. the L.A. Tigers at the Coliseum, 1926.

In	Out
Wilbur "Fats" Henry	Roscoe "Fatty" Arbuckle
brute force	finesse
reserve clause	free agency
18-man rosters	illegal use of college players
season tickets	passing the hat
Red Grange	Jim Thorpe
the three Maras	the seven Nesser brothers
single wing, Notre Dame box	T-formation
punts	field goals
Green Bay, Wis.	Massillon, Ohio
Prohibition	liquor sold at games

Biggest Player   Eddie Keenan, a 6'4", 320-pound guard with the Hartford Blues in 1926. Keenan was 31 when he played his only NFL season. He apparently was no stiff, either. He was singled out in a number of game stories for his defensive play. Of course, it could be that he just blocked out the view of everybody else.

Smallest Player   Jack "Soapy" Shapiro, who played blocking back for one game with the Staten Island Stapletons in 1929, was 5'2", 126.

▶Smallest Real Player   Henry "Two Bits" Homan, the Frankford Yellow Jackets' star back, at 5'5", 145.

Best Athlete   Ernie Nevers

Fastest Player   Fritz Pollard

Slowest Player   We'd put our money on Dayton Triangles lineman Ed "Pud" "Tubby" Sauer, a succinct 5'10" "with nearly 300 pounds of avoirdupois," according to the *Philadelphia Inquirer*.

Most Intimidating Player   Cal Hubbard
The huge (6'2", 250) Hall-of-Fame tackle was the enforcer on the great

Green Bay teams of the late '20s and early '30s. He once told a young teammate: "You see those two holes over the ears in the helmet? Well, they're not to hear through. They're for you to stick your fingers in his helmet and jerk his face down when you raise your knee up."

Most Intimidating Fan   Al "Scarface" Capone, supposedly a regular at Bears games

Best Combination Forearm Shiver/Singing Voice   Paul Robeson

New Stadium   1925--City Stadium, Green Bay (the first one)

Failed Franchises   Too numerous to list

Failed League   The first AFL, 1926

Famous First   Out-of-town training camp, 1929 (Cardinals in Coldwater, Mich.)

Famous Last   Player to lead the NFL in rushing touchdowns and TD passes: Benny Friedman, 1928

Best Championship Race   1926
   Going into December, the Chicago Bears were 11-0-2, Frankford was 12-1-1 and Pottsville 10-1-1. Then the Yellow Jackets beat the Bears, the Bears defeated the Maroons and the Jackets and Maroons played to a scoreless tie, giving Frankford the title.

Owner vs. Owner   The Sternaman brothers owned competing teams in Chicago in 1926. Dutch ran the Bears with George Halas, while Joey jumped the team to be a player/coach/owner with the Bulls of the AFL. Dutch "won." The new league folded after a year.

Player vs. Player   The Packers' Verne Lewellen and Lavie Dilweg both ran in 1928 for Green Bay district attorney. Fortunately they belonged to different parties and never had to face one another in the election. Lewellen, the Republican, won the job; Dilweg didn't survive the Democratic primary.

▸**Best Place to Watch a Game**   The Cycledrome in Providence

Obscenity of the Decade   bunk

Worst Playing Surface   Minersville Park, Pottsville, Pa.
   Opposing players claimed that the field, cut out of the side of a mountain, was covered with more coal slag than grass. "After a rain the minerals from the soil were so toxic that little wounds became infected and were dangerous," Dr. Harry March wrote in *Pro Football: Its Ups and Downs*.

New Position   linebacker

Major Rules Changes   1926--college players can't enter NFL until after they graduate
1927--goal posts moved to back of end zone

New Equipment   nose guards
square-toed kicking shoe

Best Uniforms   Duluth Eskimos
   The players took the field wearing three-quarter length white

mackinaws with lined hoods to give them that authentic Eskimo look. The coats had igloos and the team name on the back. Uniform colors were white with midnight blue numbers and piping.

Worst Uniforms

Any team in the midst of a road trip or playing back-to-back games. Players had only one uniform, and washing often was impossible. Jerseys were usually dark to hide the dirt, but pants were another story. "All we could do was let the mud dry, and then use a wire brush to make the pants lighter in weight," said Hall-of-Fame tackle/coach Steve Owen.

Best Play

The deciding touchdown in Frankford's 13-7 victory over Green Bay in 1925 was scored this way: George Sullivan flipped a 5-yard pass to Two Bits Homan at the Packers 40. When the defense converged on Homan, he lateraled back to Sullivan, trailing the play. Sullivan ran the remaining distance. Under today's rules, the score would read: "Sullivan 45 pass from Sullivan."

▸Hit of the Decade

George Trafton vs. Red Grange, 1927

▸Fight of the Decade

Bears vs. Cardinals, 1922

**Highest–Paid Player
(aside from Red Grange in 1925)**

Ernie Nevers or Benny Friedman
   Nevers supposedly made $15,000 plus a percentage of the gate with Duluth in 1926. Friedman made a well-documented $10,000 a season and as much as $750 a game for exhibitions. He claimed to have grossed $22,000 with the Cleveland Bulldogs in 1927.

Most Unusual Contract

Jim Thorpe's 1925 deal with the Giants
   The team paid him $200 *per half game*. Thorpe couldn't play much more than that. He was 38 and in dreadful shape because of a bad right knee and worsening alcohol problem. The Giants let him go three games into the season after a drunken late-night fight at a local restaurant.

Cheapest Owner

A tough call, because every team struggled to make money. But Duluth's Ole Haugsrud was as tight as they came. He treated adhesive tape as if it were bullion. Nevers, who used rolls of the stuff on his ankles and knees, borrowed what he needed from opponents.

Least Appreciated Players

Two Bits Homan
Cardinals lineman Duke Slater
Pottsville back Tony Latone

▸Best Trade

The Bears picked up Hall-of-Fame lineman Ed Healey from Rock Island in 1922 for $200.

Dumbest Rule

Substitutes weren't allowed to talk when they came into the game. The founding fathers had a mania about coaches sending in plays from the sidelines. The referee actually was charged with watching the new player to ensure his silence. If more than one player came in, the umpire helped out.

**▸Individual Records That
Have Never Been Equaled**

Cub Buck's 19 punts vs. St. Louis, 1923
Ernie Nevers' 40 points vs. the Bears, 1929

THE UNSINKABLE GEORGE HALAS

On July 24, 1915, the excursion boat *Eastland* capsized at its dock on the Chicago River, killing nearly a thousand. On the list of missing published two days later, you'll find the name "Halas, G. S." That is indeed the future owner of the Chicago Bears.

Halas had booked passage on the *Eastland* to get to a baseball game in Michigan City, Indiana. He wasn't on board, though, and there are two stories as to why. One is that he decided to take a later boat, the other that he was delayed at home and arrived at the dock after the *Eastland* had gone down.

Two fraternity brothers from the University of Illinois showed up at the Halas home several days later to pay their respects. They were met at the door by the ghost himself. "I'll never forget the shocked look on their faces," Halas said.

Years later he reflected on his good fortune. "When I missed connections on the ill-fated *Eastland*," he said, "I realized I was a very lucky man. Nothing which has happened since has given me any reason to think otherwise."

...

THE BORING '20s

Almost two-thirds of all NFL games from 1920 to '32 were shutouts. Only four of the 40 games in 1920 *weren't* shutouts. The situation improved gradually until 1933, when rules changes and a more aerodynamic ball tilted the game toward the offense.

The worst year was 1926, when the talent was spread particularly thin because of the founding of the first American Football League. There were 116 NFL games that year; 86 (74.1 percent) were shutouts, 10 were 0–0 ties. An average of 15.3 points was scored in each game.

The worst single day? Take a look at the NFL scoreboard from October 7, 1923:

Buffalo 9, Akron 0
Canton 37, Louisville 0
Chicago Bears 3, Racine 0
Chicago Cards 60, Rochester 0
Cleveland 0, Rock Island 0
Columbus 0, Milwaukee 0
Duluth 10, Minneapolis 0
Hammond 7, Dayton 0
St. Louis 0, Green Bay 0
Toledo 7, Oorang 0

Ten games, 10 shutouts. Three 0–0 ties. This, while baseball was going bonkers with the new lively ball.

Scoring was a chore in the '20s. The ball was fatter and harder to pass. All passes, moreover, had to be thrown from at least five yards behind the line of scrimmage. A team that threw an incompletion in the end zone *lost possession of the ball.*

Penalties were severe—25 yards for clipping and sometimes longer for more serious infractions. There were no hashmarks. When a player was tackled near the sideline or went out of bounds, the next play began at that spot. In 1927, the owners made it even harder to kick a field goal by moving the goal posts from the goal line to the back of the end zone.

One sportswriter referred to pro football in this period as "paid punting." That pretty well sums it up. Field position was the name of the game: Pin your opponent deep in his territory and wait for a mistake. Punting on third down was especially effective, particularly with the rounder ball. With no deep safety, the ball would just roll and roll.

The league finally did something about the situation in February 1933. During meetings at the Fort Pitt Hotel in Pittsburgh, the owners made passes legal from anywhere behind the line, approved hashmarks 10 yards in from the sidelines and returned the goal posts to the goal line.

(All three changes had sprung from the 1932 NFL championship game between the Chicago Bears and Portsmouth Spartans. Snow and cold had forced the game indoors, and some of the rules had to be altered because there was barely enough room at Chicago Stadium for an 80-yard field.)

"We think we have helped overcome the balance held by the defense," president Joe Carr said. "In fact, if we can give the offense a slight edge, it doubtless would improve the game for both players and spectators."

Giving the offense "a slight edge" has been the NFL's philosophy ever since.

"We are primarily interested in developing a spectacular scoring game," Carr explained. "We haven't the pageantry that goes with college games, hence as a substitute we must offer wide open play, with frequent scoring. Then, too, we are not compelled to throw a tight wall of protection around our players. They are more mature, more experienced than collegians, and thus are better able to protect themselves."

Giants owner Tim Mara pushed for two more changes—doing away with the extra point and instituting a 10-minute overtime period to break ties. Mara said only one game the previous season had been decided by an extra point, while there had been 10 ties. The champion Bears had finished with 6 ties, the most in NFL history.

"In every sport but football the authorities have sought to avoid a tie score," Mara said. When the Giants had played the Bears in Chicago the month before, he revealed, the two teams had agreed to experiment with an overtime period if the game ended in a tie. (The Bears needed to win their last two games to pull even with Portsmouth and force the playoff.)

Bringing the goal posts back to the goal line, however, had the same effect as getting rid of the extra point. Field goals increased from 6 to 36 in 1933 and ties decreased from 10 to 5. As for overtime, that was an idea whose time had not yet come.

■ ■ ■
THE '20s PLAYER

BACKS

The ideal backfield would be four men, each about 6 feet in height and weighing 185 to 205 pounds, heavy enough to plunge and block, adroit enough to get passes and know what to do after catching them and fast enough to outrun the opposition.
—Dr. Harry March, from *Pro Football: Its Ups and Downs*

LINEMEN

It was a bruising game. Most teams were "right-handed"—that is, they ran to their right, from an unbalanced line plus a single wingback [five men to the right of the ball]. Thus, almost invariably, the focal point of attack was the defensive left tackle. The result was between seventy to one hundred pile-ups on the line of scrimmage per game. The fourth quarter, when both teams were injured and tired, was often decisive. This kind of play developed a general type of player called variously a "square rigger," a "husky," or a "brick smokehouse." On an average players ran between 5 feet 9 inches and 6 feet tall and weighed from 185 to 200 pounds, though a few went up to 215. Players were chunky and quick rather than fast; they were built "close to the ground," were trained "to get the jump"—that is, spring at their adversary before he got up momentum. A principal qualification was the ability to absorb terrific physical punishment. This macho bravado was a matter of pride. A player would never ask to be relieved; he was expected to "keep going until unconscious," and it never occurred to him to do otherwise.
—Ernie Cuneo, guard, *Orange Tornadoes and Brooklyn Dodgers*. Reprinted from *The American Scholar*. Copyright 1987. By permission of the publisher.

■ ■ ■
'20s MYTHOLOGY

Hall-of-Fame center George Trafton knocked four Rock Island Independents out of a 1920 game in the first dozen plays. One of them was a player the Independents had signed to get Trafton.

A good rule of thumb for any Trafton story: Divide all claims by at least two.

On November 7, 1920, the Independents and Decatur Staleys (soon to be the Chicago Bears) played a brutal 0–0 tie. Four Rock Island players did indeed leave the game with serious injuries.

But a number of Staleys were responsible for the damage, including player/coach George Halas. Trafton put out *one* of the Independents—with a well-placed and exceptionally late knee to the face. This happened in the third quarter, not the first 12 plays.

Trafton himself might be the source of the myth; he certainly never denied the anecdote. In *The Chicago Bears* by Howard Roberts, he went so far as to describe how he knocked Rock Island halfback Fred Chicken out of bounds and into a fence, breaking Chicken's leg. But according to game accounts, Chicken suffered a wrenched knee when tackled by Halas and Huge Blacklock.

That's Trafton for you. He was a master of embellishment (some prefer the term blowhard). In later years he was a favorite of reporters because of his colorful—and exaggerated—stories.

The reality of the Rock Island game is almost as gruesome as the myth. Trafton's victim was center Harry Gunderson, who was about the same size (6'2", over 200 pounds) and apparently giving him a good game. Gunderson had just tackled Decatur back Jimmy Conzelman for a loss when Big George landed on him knees first. Gunderson was carried unconscious from the field with an 11-stitch cut over his eye, a 2-stitch cut in his lip and a broken hand.

"Flagrant is too mild a word to describe such utter lack of sportsmanship," Bruce Copeland of the *Rock Island Argus* wrote. "A cave dweller could have done no better."

Umpire "Stub" Barron immediately ejected Trafton but was overruled by the referee (after much discussion with Halas). The Staleys wound up with a 10-yard penalty for "running into opponents."

Gunderson was supposed to be the thug the Independents contracted to take care of Trafton. Actually, he'd been signed several weeks before and was

a regular in the lineup. Whether that makes him an innocent in the affair is debatable, though.

Trafton found out he was a marked man from a local gambler the night before the game, according to the nearby *Davenport* (Iowa) *Democrat*. The gambler supposedly had a $100 bet that Gunderson would disable George sometime in the first quarter. True or not, the tip put Trafton on red alert. He later claimed to have made his own bet—at 5–2 odds—that he'd be playing at game's end. Take it for what it's worth.

The tip might also account for the Staleys' all-around rough play that day. Their tactics so enraged the 5,000 spectators at Rock Island's Douglas Park that an angry mob chased them to their buses.

. . .

TWO-TIMING IN BUFFALO

Pro football players were the freest of free agents before the NFL was organized in 1920. They routinely jumped teams when they got a better offer. As late as '21, there was even an instance of double-dipping—playing for two teams in the same week.

Eight members of the Buffalo All Americans that year played Saturdays for the Philadelphia Quakers, a non-NFL team, then took the overnight train to Buffalo for Sunday afternoon games. (Monday mornings couldn't have been much fun, but then two paychecks were better than one.)

The Quakers played on Saturdays because Pennsylvania blue laws didn't allow pro football on Sundays. It was a perfect setup for the players.

But Joe Carr, the NFL's new president, didn't see it that way. The league's number-one public relations problem was its mercenary image. And unlike his figurehead predecessor, Jim Thorpe, Carr was determined to do something about it.

He began by instituting the forerunner of the reserve clause (which appeared officially a decade later). It bound a player to the team he'd played for the previous season unless the club released him. A year later, he introduced standardized contracts. He also began enforcing largely ignored rules already on the books. Which brings us back to Buffalo.

In November 1921, the All Americans were bat-

DECADE LEADERS

PASSING
Yards*: Benny Friedman, 4,538; Curly Lambeau, 4,478; Red Dunn, 3,417.
Touchdowns: Friedman, 42; Dunn, 29; Lambeau, 24.
Interceptions*: Lambeau, 78; Dunn, 54; Jack Ernst, 52.

RUSHING
Yards*: Tony Latone, 2,365; Paddy Driscoll, 2,274; Barney Wentz, 1,728.
TDs: Driscoll, 27; Ernie Nevers, 24; Latone and Verne Lewellen, 23.

RECEIVING
Receptions*: Charlie Mathys, 90; Jimmy Conzelman, 89; Eddie Kotal, 74.
Yards*: Mathys, 1,506; Conzelman, 1,344; Guy Chamberlin, 1,201.
TDs: Ray Flaherty, 13; Conzelman, 11; Lewellen, 10.

OTHER CATEGORIES
Scoring: Driscoll, 418; Joey Sternaman, 309; Lewellen, 211.
Field goals: Driscoll, 51; Hank Gillo, 22; Dutch Sternaman, 21.
*Statistics are incomplete.

tling the Chicago Staleys and Akron Pros for the league championship. On Sunday, November 20, they had a big game scheduled with the Canton Bulldogs. But that morning there was a startling story in the *Buffalo Morning Express.* The paper reported that the All Americans' management had forced the cancellation of the Canton–Philadelphia Quakers game in Philadelphia the day before.

The reason? Carr had discovered the double-dipping by the Buffalo players, a violation of league rules, and threatened disciplinary action if it wasn't stopped.

Five of the eight players—back John Scott, end Heinie Miller, center Lud Wray and tackles Butch Spagna and Lou Little—were so incensed that they didn't show up for the All Americans' game against the Bulldogs and played the rest of the season with the Quakers. They claimed the Buffalo management knew all along what was going on and was caving in to the league office.

Indeed the players had been so up front about the double-dipping that they'd used their real names with the Quakers. One Philadelphia newspaper even referred to the team as the "All Americans."

The mass desertion left the Buffalo franchise in a bind. Four of the five players were starters. Carr gave the team an out by approving a hastily reached agreement whereby the All Americans picked up five members of the Detroit Tigers. (The Tigers had completed their season, which made the transaction legal in the eyes of the league.)

The replacement players reported to Buffalo Sunday morning, went through a brief practice and played that afternoon against Canton. The game ended in a nondamaging 7–7 tie.

Buffalo wound up finishing second to the Staleys, but that had less to do with the loss of five key players than with poor scheduling. The new-look All Americans played some of their best football after the Quakers scandal. They got hot and won three straight against key opponents—the Staleys, Dayton and Akron. But their last game was a rematch with the Staleys December 4, less than 24 hours after they'd beaten Akron.

The All Americans literally stepped off the train and played the game that ultimately decided the '21 championship. Chicago won, 10–7. It was Buffalo's only defeat of the season. The All Americans' final record was 9–1–2. The Staleys were 9–1–1. Carr awarded the championship to Chicago.

ANOTHER VICTORY FOR JOE CARR

The effect of Carr's policies could be seen clearly one year later, on November 27, 1922, when the Chicago Bears acquired future Hall-of-Fame tackle Ed Healey from the Rock Island Independents for a measly $100. It wasn't the league's first player transaction—Buffalo paid Akron $300 for Bob "Nasty" Nash in '20. But it's believed to be the first in the era of standardized contracts. Even the press recognized the significance of that.

"A year ago no manager would think of buying a player from another team," the *Rock Island Argus* reported. "That was considered unnecessary. If a manager wanted a player from the other team, he got in touch with the player and made him an offer. If the player accepted, he packed his baggage and hiked, sometimes not even notifying the team that he was playing with that he was leaving."

If nothing else, the deal was the first fleecing in league history. Healey played five-plus seasons with the Bears and was a great player.

In his 1986 biography, owner-coach George Halas took the credit. He claimed Rock Island manager Walter Flanigan owed him $100 and that he agreed to cancel the debt in return for Healey.

But a day-after story in the *Argus* cites Halas' partner, Dutch Sternaman, as the instigator. The paper said Healey and Sternaman talked shortly after the Independents' season ended abruptly in late November. The team was plagued by dissension and financial problems, so Sternaman decided to make an offer for Healey. Rock Island accepted.

The *Argus* also reported that as part of the deal the Independents had the option of buying back Healey for the same price the next year or receiving one of the Bears' three quarterbacks. For some reason they did neither. Healey finished the '22 season and his career as a Bear.

■ ■ ■

Two of the finest kickers in football history, Charlie Brickley and Jim Thorpe, engage in a halftime competition at New York's Polo Grounds in 1921. (UPI/Bettmann Newsphotos)

CLASH OF THE GREAT DROP-KICKERS

New York's first pro football game in December 1921 was upstaged by the halftime show. It was a drop-kicking contest between Jim Thorpe of the Cleveland Tigers and Charlie Brickley, owner-coach of Brickley's Giants.

A Polo Grounds crowd of about 5,000 watched the historic competition between two of the greatest kickers in football history, by then in their 30s. Brickley, who played pro ball only briefly, had established his reputation at Harvard, where he once booted five field goals in a 15–5 victory over Yale. He was generally considered the most accurate drop-kicker ever. Grantland Rice said "he could drop-kick and hit targets [Sammy] Baugh or [Sid] Luckman might miss throwing."

Both men attempted a dozen drop kicks, starting from the 25-yard line and moving back to midfield. Thorpe, competing with two broken ribs, took the early lead, but the final score was 6–6.

Accounts differ on the lengths of the kicks each

made. The *New York Times* said Brickley booted a 60-yarder. According to the *Herald,* Thorpe's longest was 45 yards, while Brickley was good from 48 and 50.

Perhaps in an attempt to break the tie, Thorpe and Brickley tried three place kicks from 55 yards. None was successful, though the *World* reported that Brickley hit the upright on one.

Then, the *Herald* said, "Thorpe booted a drop kick from fifty-five yards. Honest Injun!"

In the game, he kicked a 42-yard field goal as Cleveland beat New York, 17–0. But his drop-kicking duel with Brickley was the day's highlight. It was such a big deal that a newspaper as far away as Milwaukee ran *photos* of the two contestants the next day.

Thorpe and Brickley "were more of an attraction than the game itself," the *Journal* said.

■ ■ ■

A 1922 GAME SUMMARY

Game statistics were hard to come by in 1922. Most newspapers didn't even bother with them. It would be another decade before the league did.

The *Rock Island Argus,* however, did a pretty good job with stats. Here's what the paper ran after an October 8, 1922, game between the hometown Independents and Chicago Bears, won by the Bears, 10–6.

All the figures in the individual statistics are yards gained (or lost) in each category. Total yards was considered the key stat. How far did a player move the ball via running, receiving and kick returning?

The *Argus'* summary tells you not only how many yards a player rushed for, but also *where* he gained them—between the tackles ("Line Smashes") or on sweeps ("End Runs"). Today's statistics aren't that detailed.

Note, too, that the number of incomplete passes is given, but not the number of complete ones. This is probably because incompletions could have such dire consequences. A team that threw incomplete in the end zone lost possession of the ball.

■ ■ ■

HOW THE BEARS WERE REALLY BORN

The records of an obscure lawsuit raise doubts about how George Halas came to own the Chicago Bears. Halas' version of history is that he and partner Dutch Sternaman struck out on their own in 1922 with the blessing of Decatur, Illinois, starch producer A. E. Staley, who had bankrolled the team for two years.

Court records indicate, however, that the parting was less than friendly and that Halas and Sternaman may have simply outmaneuvered Staley for control of the team. They also show that the franchise was far more profitable in the early days than anyone has been led to believe.

The Bears began as the Decatur Staleys in 1920. They were a charter member of the American Professional Football Association, which two years

BEARS 10, INDEPENDENTS 6

Legend: RK = Returning Kickoffs; RP = Returning Punts; LS = Line Smashes; ER = End Runs; FP = Forward Passes; LG = Lost Ground; TOT = Totals.

ROCK ISLAND	RK	RP	LS	ER	FP	LG	TOT
Conzelman	35	31	20	25	0	36	75
Gavin	0	0	25	0	0	0	25
Lauer	70	20	22	16	21	7	142
Johnson	0	0	6	0	19	7	18
Wenig	0	0	0	0	41	0	41
Bridgeford	0	0	4	0	0	0	4
Grand Totals	**105**	**51**	**77**	**41**	**81**	**50**	**305**

CHICAGO BEARS	RK	RP	LS	ER	FP	LG	TOT
D. Sternaman	11	0	29	5	0	3	42
Stinchcomb	20	0	22	52	0	2	92
J. Sternaman	0	21	27	9	0	1	56
Bolan	0	0	10	0	0	0	10
Walquist	0	0	3	1	0	0	4
Halas	0	0	0	0	11	0	11
LaFleur	0	0	12	0	0	3	9
Lanum	0	0	4	0	0	0	4
Grand Totals	**31**	**21**	**107**	**67**	**11**	**9**	**228**

First downs -- Rock Island, 13; Bears, 10.
Passes Incomplete -- Rock Island, 8; Bears, 3.
Passes Intercepted -- By Rock Island, 0; by Bears, 3.
Punts -- Rock Island, 4; Bears, 8.
Penalties -- Rock Island, 2 for 20 yards total; Bears, 2 for 20 yards total.
Fumbles -- Rock Island, 1 (Gavin); Bears, 0.

later changed its name to the NFL. Staley founded the team as a means of advertising his products. He hired Halas as his coach and general manager and gave him free rein.

But Decatur proved too small to support pro football, and the two struck an unusual agreement for 1921: Halas would operate the franchise in Chicago, using $5,000 seed money supplied by the company. In return he'd continue to call the team the Staleys and advertise the company in game programs. Money made or lost was his concern.

"Wonder of wonders," Halas said in his autobiography, "we paid all our bills and still had $7 in the bank."

Or so he claimed. According to court records, the Staleys turned a $21,600 profit! The $7 ($7.70, actually) was interest left over in the team account *after* profits were divvied. So much for the dirt-poor picture Halas always painted of that first year in Chicago.

It was at about this time, too, that Staley supposedly gave up the franchise. But once again court records show there was more to it than Papa Bear ever let on.

Shortly after the 1921 season ended, he and Sternaman began negotiating a new lease for Cubs Park, the Staleys' home field. On January 3, 1922, Staleys superintendent George Chamberlain fired off this telegram to Chicago Cubs president Bill Veeck:

> Understand overtures being made for rental Cubs Park foot ball season nineteen twenty two STOP We expect to place another team in the field if anything stronger than last years and trust that experience of past two years is such that you will wish to continue present arrangement with this company.

Clearly, Staley was still interested in sponsoring a football team.

Chamberlain, who had negotiated and signed the team's 1921 lease, arranged to meet with Veeck in Chicago January 13. Halas and Sternaman were present, too, though it's not clear at whose invitation. According to court records, Chamberlain told Veeck he was the only representative of the Staley Company empowered to do business. Veeck told Chamberlain if he wanted a new lease, Halas and Sternaman would have to be in charge of the football team. Chamberlain said that was a matter for the Staley Company to decide.

Two days later, Chamberlain sent Veeck this letter:

> Since our conference I have been giving very careful consideration to the general condition [that Halas and Sternaman run the team] surrounding the 1922 foot ball situation. The matter has become snarled up in a way that will probably throw it into the courts before the season opens and may very possibly result in the breaking up of the present team. The season is a very short one, the number of games played is extremely limited, the preliminary investment is quite heavy, and the risk of loss from personal injury or in other ways is too serious to be disregarded.
>
> When on top of these various rather pessimistic conditions, we contemplate the considerable increase which you require in the next contract amounting to approximately $5,000 per year, the sum total gives us pause. The writer has discussed these various phases with our interested department heads, and we have come to the conclusion that our best interest will be served by withdrawing our application for the use of your park for 1922.

Halas doesn't mention the meeting or Chamberlain's letter in his autobiography. He says simply that after the '21 season "my obligation to the A. E. Staley Company ceased."

Technically, he was right. His agreement with Staley, which is also in the court records, is for 1921 only.

But did the two have some sort of verbal agreement for 1922? Was this a power play on Halas' part? Or did Staley get wind of the team's profits in '21 and try to move back in?

One thing's for certain: There was antagonism between the two sides. That's a new twist to the tale.

The rest of the story goes pretty much according to form. Staley decided not to renew his franchise. Halas and Sternaman went to the January 28 league meeting and filed an application for it.

"The Chicago Bears were born," Halas proclaimed in his book.

We would have continued to accept his version of the birth had he and Sternaman not been sued later that year. Two brothers named William and Chic Harley accused them of reneging on a deal to share the team's profits. William, one of football's first agents, had delivered three college stars, including Chic, to the Staleys. The Harleys had no case, as it turned out, but the legal proceedings shed light on the business relationship between Halas and Staley.

RUNNING WILD

The difference between good teams and bad was so great in the '20s that huge scores were inevitable, even with the rules stacked so much in favor of the defense. On October 15, 1922, Rock Island defeated visiting Evansville, 60–0, by scoring *nine* rushing touchdowns. No modern team has had more than seven (L.A. Rams vs. Atlanta, December 4, 1976).

The Independents' TD runs ranged from one to 22 yards. Hall-of-Famer Jimmy Conzelman, playing at right halfback instead of his usual quarterback spot, scored five of them.

Rock Island might have had even more points if the second and fourth quarters hadn't been shortened to 12 minutes. Evansville was so badly outmanned that it often punted on first down.

• • •

FIGHT OF THE DECADE

Bears vs. Cards, 1922

Games between Chicago's Bears and Cardinals were always rough and tough, but the one on Thanksgiving Day, 1922 topped them all. That was the time the Bears went after Cards star Paddy Driscoll.

It happened in the third quarter with the home-team Cardinals leading 3–0. On an end run, Driscoll was lifted off his feet by end–co-owner George Halas and defensive back Joey Sternaman and heaved five yards back. When he got up, somewhat shakily, he threw a punch at Sternaman. (This was a wise choice, since Halas was 6', 182 pounds and Sternaman 5'6", 150.)

A free-for-all followed. Players rushed in from the sideline and at least 100 fans and several policemen came out of the Comiskey Park stands. The officials managed to restore order, then restored it by tossing Driscoll from the game. Paddy was led off the field protesting.

The Bears—either fearing for their lives or wanting another shot at Driscoll—offered to let him continue playing, but the officials rejected the proposal. While the argument continued, three Cardinals jumped Halas, one of them knocking him to the ground with a roundhouse right to the chin.

Halas looked up, George Strickler of the *Chicago Daily Tribune* wrote some years later, and saw "a [South Side] policeman . . . bending over him, pressing the cold muzzle of a .35 behind his ear." He was saved by the arrival of patrol wagons.

Halas and Sternaman also left the game—presumably for their own safety. The Cardinals wound up winning, 6–0, effectively killing the Bears' chances of repeating as league champions. The teams played each other again 10 days later without incident. Driscoll drop-kicked three field goals to give the Cards a 9–0 victory.

• • •

THE PRO FOOTBALL "MENACE"

Pro football had no greater opponent in its early years than Amos Alonzo Stagg. The University of Chicago coach once advocated—and the Big Ten adopted—a rule that former college players be asked to give back their varsity letters if they turned pro. On November 1, 1923, he issued a plea to "all friends of the game" to stamp out this clear and present threat to college football. Here are some of the more nauseating parts:

"It seems like a matter of little consequence for one to attend the Sunday professional football games—nothing more than attending any Sunday event—but it has a deeper meaning than you realize, possibly a vital meaning to college football. . . .

"Under the guise of fair play but countenancing rank dishonesty in playing men under assumed names, scores of professional teams have sprung up within the last two or three years, most of them on a salary basis of some kind. These teams are bidding hard for college players in order to capitalize not only on their ability but also, and mostly, upon the name of the colleges they come from. . . .

"Cases of the debauching of high school boys not infrequently have come to notice. Also, recently, one of the well known Sunday professional teams on which several men are said to be regularly playing under assumed names employed a well known conference official who officiated under an assumed name.

"The schools and colleges are struggling to combat the various evils connected with football, which, when played with the amateur spirit, possesses more elements for the development of character and manhood than any other sport I know of.

"To patronize Sunday professional football games is to cooperate with forces which are destructive of the finest elements of interscholastic and intercollegiate football. . . .

"If you believe in preserving interscholastic and intercollegiate football for the upbuilding of the present and future generations of clean, healthy, rightminded and patriotic citizens, you will not lend your appearance to any of the forces which are helping to destroy it."

∎∎∎
PUNT, PUNT AGAIN

John Teltschik of the Philadelphia Eagles is the official NFL record holder for punts in a game with 15, but we know better. On a cold and rainy day in St. Louis in 1923, Green Bay Packers immortal Cub Buck punted 19 times. And he didn't need an overtime period to pad his total. (Teltschik had only 11 in regulation.)

Buck, one of the key players in the Packers' early years, was a rotund 265-pounder who usually played tackle. He was such a good athlete, though, that the Packers left almost all the kicking to him.

On November 4, Green Bay took on the St. Louis All-Stars in ankle-deep mud at Sportsman's Park. Conditions dictated a defensive game. With field position more important than ever, both teams kicked often. Buck punted five times on first down, once on second and eight times on third. The strategy was to avoid costly mistakes deep in your territory.

Buck also showed his versatility by passing from punt formation once. He completed the pass, to player-coach Curly Lambeau, for 13 yards.

It's difficult to determine Buck's exact yardage from play-by-play accounts in the *Green Bay Press-Gazette,* but it was close to 700. That would give him an average of about 31 yards per kick—not bad for those conditions. (Chances are the same ball was used throughout the game, and it must have weighed a couple of pounds by the end of the day.)

One of Buck's better punts led to the only score of the game. In the third quarter, he boomed one 50 yards. Jimmy Simpson of the All-Stars fumbled it,

and the Packers recovered at the St. Louis 16. On third down, Buck booted a 20-yard field goal for the only points in a 3–0 victory.

∎∎∎
1924 WAGE SCALE

(According to Steve Owen, Hall-of-Fame coach and tackle. Figures are per-game salaries.)

$50–75 — Average linemen.
$100 — Your "better" linemen.
$125–150 — Average backs.
$250–400 — "Big stars."

Even then there was no appreciation for the grunts up front.

∎∎∎
REASSESSING THE GRANGE TOURS

Pro football came of age during Red Grange's 1925 tour with the Chicago Bears. Grange was the golden gridder of sport's golden era. When he left the University of Illinois in November of that year and traveled around the country with the Bears, it was like a coast-to-coast ticker-tape parade—bands blaring, crowds cheering, cash registers ringing.

That's what we've been led to believe, at least. In reality, it's just another romantic notion out of the Roaring '20s. Grange's impact on pro football wasn't nearly that great. At best, the pro game might have been nudged ahead half a decade because "The Galloping Ghost" joined up. As Bears end–co-owner George Halas said during the team's travels: "We have been doing well in professional football and making money for several seasons. We were gaining ground steadily but slowly."

It's true Grange rescued the New York Giants from red ink in their first year in 1925 by filling the Polo Grounds with 65,000 people. But he also caused the Giants to *lose* $40,000 the next season when he and manager C. C. Pyle started the American Football League. Naturally, the two aspiring moguls took the New York franchise, the Yankees, for themselves.

Some lean years followed for pro football, during which "the promoters learned that freak attractions, such as the Grange appearance before being awarded his final college letter, hurt the game more than they helped it," the *New York World-Telegram* said in 1938. "They found that the public which followed its games is a fraternity of football fanciers who don't give a hang for college traditions or great names, but dote on perfection in performance. Slowly, but surely, they initiated new customers into this fraternity, and now they have a following of their own that rivals those of the best colleges."

Grange's tour with the Bears, moreover, wasn't the happiest of trails. He injured his left arm against the Giants, was virtually useless for three games, then sat out the next two. Unknowing fans razzed him in Washington and booed him in Boston and Pittsburgh. At Forbes Field, he walked off after only a quarter, clutching his badly swollen arm.

The headline the next day in the *Pittsburgh Press* read: "Grange Fails to Provide a Single Thrill."

There were actually two tours. This was the first, the Eastern swing. Eight games in 12 early-December days. St. Louis, two days off, Philadelphia, New York, a day off, Washington, Boston, Pittsburgh, a day off, Detroit and a rematch against the Giants back in Chicago. That's five games in the last six days.

The Pittsburgh paper said many Chicago players were visibly lame. The Bears had only 10 men on the field at the beginning of the game, Grange recalled years later, and it was several minutes before anyone realized it. They had flipped coins to determine who would start.

"It was laughable at times to see their efforts to protect themselves against hard contact with the frozen ground," the *Press* reported, "and their anger when they were thrown with anything like ordinary roughness."

To undertake such a tour at the end of the season seems almost cruel, especially with an 18-man squad. Not only were the Bears playing virtually every day, they were doing most of their sleeping on trains. And some of the overnight trips—Washington to Boston and Boston to Pittsburgh, for instance—were hardly short hops.

The weather was almost always atrocious. There was torrential rain in Philadelphia, mud in New York and frozen fields in Boston and Pittsburgh. Under such conditions, Grange's speed and cutting ability were severely curtailed. He never broke away for one of his trademark long touchdowns. Four of his seven TDs came in a 39–6 victory over a hastily organized "all-star" team in St. Louis led by Detroit Panthers quarterback-owner Jimmy Conzelman.

The only other mismatch was in Washington, where the Bears won 19–0 against a team made up mostly of sandlot players. Other than that, they had all they could handle. Opponents got up for Grange, up for playing in front of big crowds for a change. They worked him over pretty good, too.

New York was the worst. Grange called it "one of the most bruising battles I had ever been in." Late in the second quarter, after breaking up a pass, he "was slugged with a Firpoesque slam on the back of the headgear by [Joe] Williams of the Giants, who had been sent out to receive the throw," the *Chicago Tribune* reported. "Red stumbled unsteadily, but did nothing about it, and neither did the officials, who were about as hostile to fist fighting as Tex Rickard is."

There were two other incidents in the fourth quarter. "Red was kicked on the forearm by [Tommy] Tomlin of the Giants' front line, and it wasn't long after that till Joe Alexander, the Giants' center, stopped a line play and squatted on the

$$$$	
$1	Amount Ole Haugsrud and Dewey Scanlon paid for Duluth franchise in 1925
$5	What a share of Packers stock cost in August 1923
$17.25	Price of Hartford Blues season ticket in 1926
$25	Fine for breaking training on Canton Bulldogs in 1926 (first offense; second offense resulted in suspension)
$100	Membership fee for NFL's charter teams in 1920
$200	Jimmy Conzelman's per-game salary as player-coach of Milwaukee Badgers in 1923
$290	Expense of outfitting 1920 Rock Island Independents with wool blankets to keep warm on sideline
$500	Fine assessed Pottsville Maroons for playing illegal game in Philadelphia in 1925
$1,800	Maximum allowable team payroll (per game) in 1923
$1,960.05	Bank balance of NFL on July 15, 1929
$3,500	Price Bears paid Cardinals for HB Paddy Driscoll, 1926
$25,000	Purchase price of Cards in 1929
$143,500	Gate receipts for Red Grange's New York debut, 1925

ground with Grange in his lap, trying to twist his head off to see what kind of sawdust he's stuffed with. The officials told Alexander he oughtn't to do that but didn't charge him anything for it."

The kick by Tomlin probably caused Grange's injury. In the next three games he played as if trying to preserve himself, letting punts hit the ground and making tackles only when necessary. "A pitiful failure" in a 9–6 loss to the Providence Steam Roller in Boston, according to the Chicago paper, he swapped coats and hats with end Vern Mullen so he wouldn't be recognized by the press en route to Pittsburgh. The raccoon coat Grange usually wore was too easy to spot.

The Bears, who won four straight to start the tour, lost four in a row to end it. They didn't put up much of a fight at all in the last three games, in which they were outscored 53–0. It's unlikely, in fact, that fans came away from any of the eight games saying, "This was pro football at its best."

But this tour wasn't about establishing the credibility of the National Football League. Any progress made along those lines was purely coincidental. This tour was about money. This tour was about squeezing every last dollar out of the Grange phenomenon. When you schedule eight games in 12 days, you're not overly concerned with the quality of play.

For show, the Bears also signed Grange's blocking back at Illinois, Earl Britton. Britton didn't see a lot of action on the tours, and Grange never rushed for 402 yards in a game, as he had against Michigan in 1924, but it was a brilliant marketing move.

Jimmy Conzelman was upset, and understandably so, when Grange was unable to play in Detroit. At the time the game was booked, he claimed, the Bears hadn't agreed to play in Washington, Boston or Pittsburgh. Their last game was in New York on December 6, six days before they were to meet the Panthers.

Nine thousand of the 15,000 tickets sold in Detroit for the Grange game were turned in for refunds. The Panthers folded after the next season, and it wasn't until 1934 that Detroit was in the NFL permanently. Things might have been different if Grange had played there.

Conzelman wasn't the only one who got screwed. So did the Cleveland Bulldogs, whose game the following week against the Bears was canceled because Grange was hurt (and who later sued him). So did the people who paid inflated prices in Washington,

Boston and Pittsburgh. By then Grange was damaged goods.

The promoters in Washington and (probably) Pittsburgh lost money. But not Grange, Pyle and the Bears. They got guarantees. By contract, Grange had to play a minimum of 25 minutes in each game. He rarely played much more. Why chance it? His usual pattern was to play the first quarter, the first part of the second and the last part of the fourth.

Crowds would get antsy during his long absence and begin chanting, "We want Grange!" (if not something worse). The Bears were careful not to call his number too much, especially against the tougher teams. But they let him score the touchdowns as often as they could. It was good box office.

Grange says he made $125,000 from this tour and the one that began in Coral Gables, Florida, on Christmas Day, after his arm had healed. (Cardinals tailback Paddy Driscoll, previously the highest-paid pro, reportedly pulled down $500 a game.) The second tour was more the barnstorming type, a nine-game, six-week excursion that took the Bears through the South and West.

The schedule was infinitely more sensible. The team played back-to-back games three times, but it had breaks of eight days and a week in between. The roster also was increased to 22. Reinforcements included five players from other clubs: Hall-of-Famer Link Lyman of Frankford, Dutch Vick of Detroit, Paul Goebel of Columbus and Ralph Claypool and Swede Erickson of the Cardinals.

The Bears were better (and better rested), and the competition was considerably worse. They won the game in Portland, their next-to-last stop, 60–3. In the first tour they played most of the NFL's top teams; in the second they faced all-star squads lacking in conditioning, coordination or both. Winning eight of nine wasn't very hard work.

Halfback–co-owner Dutch Sternaman was up front about it. "As a rule," he said, "we prefer to play against all-star teams, for they are seldom finished teams, and it is not difficult to beat them."

Grange played well but not, for the most part, spectacularly. He won the game in Tampa with a 70-yard touchdown run in the fourth quarter, but the crowd had been booing him up to then. He was shown up by Stanford star Ernie Nevers in Jacksonville and by Washington All-American George "Wildcat" Wilson in Los Angeles and San Francisco. Wilson, behind blockers who had hardly

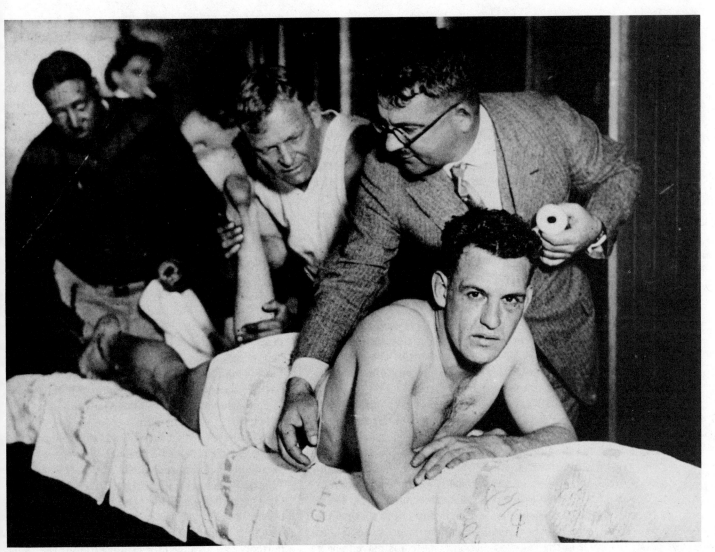

Trainers attend to Red Grange's aches and pains during his 1925 tour. (Pro Football Hall of Fame/NFL Photos)

played together, outrushed him 205 to 74 in the two games.

Joey Sternaman, the Bears' 5′6″, 150-pound quarterback, got better reviews than Grange in many places. Sternaman saw defenses were laying for Grange, so he often faked to him and bootlegged around the other end or threw a pass.

The Bears' offense was something to behold in 1925. They would hurry out of the huddle and snap the ball before the defense could make the necessary adjustments. They also used the T-formation—with lots of deception—long before it became fashionable. Seeing the center hand the ball directly to Sternaman must have been a strange sight to many fans.

Grange was used to playing in the single wing. He also was used to an offense that revolved around him. The Bears took advantage of all their players' talents. Those are two reasons why he didn't run wild on the tours. Another is that, at 5′11″, 175, he might not have been built for the pro game. He continued to take a beating on the second tour. A photo of him arriving in San Francisco shows a cut over the right eye, another beside the left eye and a puffed lower lip.

Then again, maybe pro football wasn't built for *him*. It was an inside, between-the-tackles game then, and Grange was an outside runner. The problem was that hashmarks didn't come along until

1933. The ball was marked where the runner was downed. If the runner went out of bounds, the ball was placed one yard in from the sideline. Being pinned against the sideline was not a position any team wanted to be in.

The criticism Grange received for forsaking college sports—and for his disappointing performance in the pros—was new to him. Finally, in New Orleans, his frustration could be contained no longer.

"I'm tired of being a target," he said. "I want to do a little shooting myself. I've got a few things I want to get off my chest."

Such as: "I never knew there was so much bunk in the world as I have heard since I started to play pro football. . . . I have the same affection for Illinois any decent fellow has for the college where he got his education. But I don't owe the university a cent. I never borrowed a cent from their fund for student aid."

And: "Football is the thing I do best in the world. . . . What's the disgrace of being a professional, I'd like to know? You never heard a howl about Christy Mathewson or Eddie Collins or any other college man playing professional baseball."

Also: "One of my frat brothers . . . worked for a year in business after college. He earned $700. That's one reason I'm playing professional."

The three Florida games on the second tour were said to be losing propositions for the local promoters. Tickets in Coral Gables were priced as high as $18 (the best seats in Chicago went for $2). There were so many empty seats in San Diego that people who bought general admission tickets were able to sit in the reserved section. The teams played short quarters that day. The first quarter was only 12 minutes long, the second 10. They were able to get away with this because the officials kept the time.

Los Angeles was the highlight. A pro-record crowd of 75,000 watched the Bears defeat the L.A. Tigers, 17–7, at the Coliseum. The only other sizable turnout was in San Francisco, where the attendance was 23,000.

But even though the facts don't quite square with the legend, this was a fascinating chapter in pro football history. It would make a great movie, a kind of gridiron *Ragtime.* Along the way, Grange rubbed elbows with Calvin Coolidge, Babe Ruth and Luther Burbank ("the great vegetable coach," the *San Francisco Examiner* called him). Ruth's advice to Grange: Don't pay any attention to the papers, kid, and don't pick up too many checks.

In Boston, Grange played against Four Horsemen Jim Crowley and Don Miller. John Heisman—yes, *that* Heisman—refereed in Coral Gables. The Tampa all-star team was led by 37-year-old Jim Thorpe. (Thorpe fumbled on the second play from scrimmage to hand the Bears a field goal and was "pathetically out of shape," Grange said later.)

A plane piloted by a woman, one Mabel Cody, dropped leaflets advertising the Jacksonville game on surrounding towns. New Orleans held the Red Grange Handicap at the Fair Grounds. The winner was Prickly Heat by a neck. (Grange reportedly wouldn't bet more than $2 at the track or more than 10 cents in poker games with his teammates. They must have loved that.)

The San Francisco paper also reported this story: "It is the custom in the South for each football captain to have a society girl sponsor. According to Jim [Lawson, a Stanford grad who played against Grange in Jacksonville], there was no end of trouble in securing a proper mascot for Harold Grange. He had been an ice man. Negroes carry the ice in Florida, and the inhabitants couldn't figure how any one who carried ice could amount to much."

Said Lawson: "An acceptable lady finally agreed, reluctantly, to act the part."

What happened off the field was every bit as interesting as what happened on it. Like the $50,000 breach-of-contract suit filed against Grange by Wheaton innkeeper A. H. Schatz. Schatz said Grange verbally agreed to be represented by him before the start of his senior season, then changed his mind when Pyle made a better offer. Schatz reportedly had arranged for Grange to tour the country for 32 weeks in a vaudeville sketch at a salary of $2,000 a week.

Then there was the "feud" between Grange and Illinois coach Bob Zuppke. Zuppke had envisioned Grange as another Walter Camp, the "Father of American Football." On the ride back to the hotel in Columbus, Ohio, after Grange's last college game, Zuppke tried to talk him out of turning pro, kept the taxi meter running for almost an hour. At the annual football banquet, he publicly criticized Grange. Grange got up from the head table and walked out.

They didn't see each other again until January, at a dinner given by Illinois alumni in Los Angeles. "The tenseness of the situation," as the *Los Angeles Times* described it, was defused when Grange worked his way across the room and shook his coach's hand.

Zuppke wished him luck. Grange asked him if he had tickets to the game. "If not," he said, "I want you to sit on our bench."

"Thanks just the same," Zuppke replied, "but I've sat on enough benches for some time to come."

They were, indeed, Ten Weeks That Shook the Football World. Such celebrated sportswriters as Grantland Rice, Westbrook Pegler, Damon Runyon and Ford Frick accompanied the Bears on the first tour. Pro football had never had that kind of exposure before. But not every story they filed was flattering. (Pyle once complained to Pegler about one particularly acerbic piece. The columnist replied: "Well, as long as I keep your name singular, don't holler.")

"As a football player heralded as the greatest of all time," *Chicago Tribune* sports editor Don Maxwell wrote at the end of the second tour, "Grange has proved a failure. Little Joe Sternaman has outstarred him in every game they've played. But as a gate attraction Red can be said to have been a winner.

"We're wondering what sort of attraction he'll be next fall."

Not enough of one to keep the AFL afloat. It lasted only a year. The Yankees were admitted to the NFL, but couldn't make a go of it competing against the Giants. Grange suffered a serious knee injury in 1927 that turned him into a straight-line runner. At the end of the next season the team went belly-up.

This idea that the Grange tours put pro football on the path to success is sheer mythology. As Halas said, the game was already walking, slowly, along that path. Grange's financial success undoubtedly encouraged other college stars to go pro, but they had already started to do that—the Four Horsemen, for example. Nevers would have played pro football anyway. He was an athletic machine. In 1926 he played pro baseball and basketball, too.

At the end of the first tour, Frankford Hall-of-Famer Guy Chamberlin said: "The day the former Illinois star stepped on the professional field is one that will be regretted a long time by followers of the commercial game. Grange broke down mentally and physically, because more was asked of him than any human being could perform. The pro players on other teams were affected by the Grange splurge, and the public is disillusioned."

While the first tour was winding up, two controversies arose that exposed the NFL for the rinky-dink operation it still was. First the Pottsville (Penn-sylvania) Maroons defied league rules and played an exhibition against a Four Horsemen–led team in Philadelphia, Frankford's home territory. Then it was discovered that the Milwaukee Badgers, short of bodies, had used four Chicago high school players in a game against the Cardinals.

Commissioner Joe Carr suspended the Pottsville franchise and fined the Milwaukee owner and ordered him to sell the club. He also fined the Cardinals owner and kicked the Cards' Art Folz, who had recruited the boys from his old high school, out of the league for life. The Maroons and Cardinals just happened to be the two best teams that year. As a result, the NFL championship was never officially awarded.

Great league, huh?

But the damage was minimized because the papers were too busy following the exploits of Grange. This might have been his biggest contribution to pro football.

Another thought: Grange may have lent credibility to the NFL because he *didn't* dominate. The public in the '20s tended to view pro ball as inferior to the college game. But if the pros could stop the great Grange, well . . .

To sum up the Grange tours in a sentence: He made a lot of money, and he went over big in New York. We all know the effect the latter can have on the writing of history.

A scene that took place several years later, however, puts things more in perspective. On a visit to Temple University, Grange advised the football team to "stay out of the professional game."

"It's not all it's cracked up to be," he said. "I was glad to get out, and now I'm going to stay out."

This is the man who *made* pro football?

∎∎∎

GAME-BY-GAME WITH "THE GHOST"

Red Grange played two home games with the Bears before taking his show on the road. The first, less than a week after he had closed out his college career at Illinois, was a 0–0 Thanksgiving Day tie against the crosstown Cardinals before 36,000 at Cubs Park (now Wrigley Field). He was held to 36 yards rushing and didn't complete any of the six passes he threw, but he had some nice punt returns and an interception near the goal line to stop the Cards' most serious scoring threat.

Five days later, the Bears hung on to beat the Columbus Tigers, 14–13, in a snowstorm. The attendance was 28,000. Grange gained 140 total yards and threw a 37-yard TD pass to halfback Laurie Walquist.

Then he and the Bears headed to St. Louis to begin the first of the two tours—the first eight games, the second nine—that would bring pro football to the national forefront. Here's how it went:

THE FIRST TOUR

ST. LOUIS—December 2, Bears 39, Donnelly Stars 6, at Sportsman's Park. Attendance: 5,000. On a bitterly cold day, Grange ran for four touchdowns against a quickly assembled "all-star" team sponsored by an undertaker. His longest scoring run was eight yards. He finished with 86 yards rushing, 54 passing and 19 receiving and had a 33-yard punt return that was the longest play of the day. "Grange was not in the lineup as the third quarter started," the *St. Louis Post-Dispatch* reported, "and the crowd put up a yell."

PHILADELPHIA—December 5, Bears 14, Frankford Yellow Jackets 7, at Shibe Park. Attendance: 25,000. In the rain and mud, Grange scored both Chicago touchdowns, the game-winner coming in the fourth quarter. He set up the first TD with a 20-yard reception to the Frankford 12, the second with a 20-yard pass to halfback Johnny Mohardt to the Yellow Jackets 32. The third quarter was shortened to 10 minutes because it was getting dark. By the end, the fans "could not distinguish the players or follow the plays intelligently," the *Philadelphia Inquirer* said.

NEW YORK—December 6, Bears 19, Giants 7, at the Polo Grounds. Attendance: 65,000. Grange's best all-around game in the two tours. He rushed for 53 yards in 11 attempts, caught one pass for 23 yards, completed two of three for 32 yards, threw a key block on one of quarterback Joey Sternaman's two touchdown runs and clinched the win in the final quarter with a 35-yard interception return for a score. It was a sunny day, but recent rains made for another muddy track. "The game was fast and beautifully open," the *New York World* raved. "The widening out of the

game by virtue of the forward pass has put football in the class of fine spectacles so it can be professionalized for profit. Grange was the drawing card, but the game itself was the holding card."

WASHINGTON—December 8, Bears 19, Washington All-Stars 0, at Griffith Stadium. Attendance: 5,000. Grange later described the opposition as "a tough bunch of sandlot players who mauled and roughed us up at every opportunity." Bears halfback–co-owner Dutch Sternaman and Washington lineman Nick Busch were thrown out for fighting. Grange, nursing a badly swollen left arm from the Giants game, limited his activity, particularly when it came to tackling. His major contribution was kicking the extra point after the first touchdown. He gained only eight yards in 11 carries. The crowd "greeted him with several 'raspberries,'" when he came out in the second quarter, the *Washington Post* reported. Promoter Al Stern lost money, which "settled for all time the moot question as to whether or not Capital City fans will support professional football," the *Post* said.

BOSTON—December 9, Providence Steam Roller 9, Bears 7, at Braves Field. Attendance: 18,000. Again, Grange was a nonfactor. He rushed for just 11 yards on the frozen field and threw an interception. Game accounts also indicate he might have been to blame for the blocked punt that resulted in a Providence safety. He was booed when his injured arm forced him out of the game in the third quarter. *Boston Globe* headline: "Professional Exhibition Convinces Boston Fans that Football Is a College and School Game." Charley Coppen, the Steam Roller's manager, had a number 77 jersey made up and asked tailback Cy Wentworth to wear it, but Wentworth wouldn't go along with the gag.

PITTSBURGH—December 10, Pittsburgh All-Stars 24, Bears 0, at Forbes Field. Attendance: 5,000. Grange hit bottom here. He played less than a quarter on the icy turf before the pain in his arm became too great. Once more he was booed as he walked wearily to the dressing room. At first it was thought he had broken his wrist, but the injury was diagnosed as a torn muscle. The arm was put in a splint. The *Pittsburgh Press* said of promoter Barney Dreyfuss: "Chances are that a deficit stares him in the face today. However, it is intimated that he may refuse to pay the Bears their full sum, because Grange didn't play 25 minutes [as required by contract]."

DETROIT—December 12, Panthers 21, Bears 0, at Navin Field. Attendance: 6,000 (9,000 tickets returned for refunds). Grange watched from the sideline with his arm in a sling. To placate the masses, he was brought out on the field at halftime and introduced.

CHICAGO—December 13, Giants 9, Bears 0, at Cubs Park. Attendance: 15,000. Grange sat on the bench in a coonskin coat for part of the game, then went to the clubhouse for treatment on his arm. He was no longer wearing a sling. After the Bears had been shut out for the third time in a row, he was escorted to a taxi by a dozen policemen.

Final record: 4–4. Total attendance: 144,000.

THE SECOND TOUR

CORAL GABLES, FLA.—December 25, Bears 7, Coral Gables Collegians 0. Attendance: 8,000. A temporary 17,000-seat stadium was built for the game. Grange's arm had healed, but now he had a black eye from an elbow in practice. He ran 20 yards the first time he carried the ball and scored the only touchdown in the second quarter on a short run. Late in the game he intercepted a pass and a few plays later broke away for a 52-yard gain. Totals: 8 carries, 89 yards.

TAMPA—January 1, Bears 17, Tampa Cardinals 3. Attendance: 8,000. The opposition was made up mostly of members of the Rock Island Independents, Jim Thorpe among them. Thorpe looked and played as if he was 37, a sad sight. The game was tied 3–3 in the fourth quarter when Grange swept left end and went 70 yards for a score. The *Chicago Tribune* said his run "silenced the boos." In his six other rushing attempts, he netted only 15 yards.

JACKSONVILLE—January 2, Bears 19, Jacksonville All-Stars 6, at Fairfield Stadium. Attendance: 6,700. Grange threw a 30-yard touchdown pass to end Vern Mullen for the first score but didn't do much running. He carried just five times for 29 yards. The star was Stanford great Ernie Nevers, playing for Jacksonville in his first pro game. Nevers had 46 yards rushing, completed 8 of 16 passes, intercepted two passes and twice tackled Grange when he appeared about to

break away. Nevers also punted six times for a 53.3-yard average and had his team's only touchdown, an eight-yard run in the fourth quarter. This game, like the two others in Florida, was reportedly a losing proposition for the promoter. It couldn't have helped that the team representing this southern city had three starters from the University of Pittsburgh and two from Stanford.

NEW ORLEANS—January 10, Bears 14, All-Southerns 0, at Heinemann Park. Attendance: 5,000. Grange gained 120 yards in 16 plays, according to the Chicago paper, but that may have included punt returns. Most of his rushing yardage came between the tackles. "His usual runs were not spectacular in yardage," the *New Orleans Times-Picayune* reported, "but the way he ran and the terrible threat he made were enough." He returned a punt 51 yards to the four-yard line in the last quarter, only to have a holding penalty reduce the runback to 20 yards. He sewed up the victory soon afterward, though, with a two-yard touchdown run.

LOS ANGELES—January 16, Bears 17, Los Angeles Tigers 7, at the L.A. Coliseum. Attendance: 75,000. The first of four games in which Grange faced Washington All-American George "Wildcat" Wilson. Wildcat outrushed him in this one 118–33, prompting Bears chatterbox-center George Trafton to remark: "Wilson is one tough baby to stop." Grange had a 2–0 edge in touchdowns, though, running the ball in from four and six yards out. He caught a 16-yard pass from Walquist to set up the first score and threw a 15-yard completion to Mullen to set up the second.

SAN DIEGO—January 17, Bears 14, California All-Stars 0, at a high school stadium. Attendance: 10,000. The teams played shortened quarters, perhaps because it was the second game in two days for most of the players. Grange carried 12 times for 53 yards and scored a touchdown in the final quarter.

SAN FRANCISCO—January 24, San Francisco Tigers 14, Bears 9, at Kezar Stadium. Attendance: 23,000. Wilson won the battle and the war. He had 87 yards rushing to 41 for Grange, who had only seven attempts. "Red was not called on often enough to satisfy the crowd," the *San Francisco Examiner* said.

PORTLAND—January 30, Bears 60, Longshoremen 3, at the baseball park. Attendance: 6,500. Grange had touchdowns running and receiving and gained 109 yards from scrimmage. He left the game after being hurt in a pileup. From the Chicago paper: "Red lay on the ground a couple of minutes. Tonight it was said he was not hurt."

SEATTLE—January 31, Bears 34, Washington All-Stars 0, at the baseball park. Attendance: 5,000. Grange concluded the second tour in grand style against another overmatched team. Perfect blocking sprung him for two 30-yard touchdown runs. He also threw a 60-yard TD pass. Wilson was injured tackling him in the second quarter and went out of the game. Rollie Corbett, the All-Stars' left end, broke his leg. C. C. Pyle, Grange's manager, gave Corbett $100 for his medical bills, and Wilson chipped in $50. The *Seattle Times* didn't think much of the show. Headline: "No Thrills, Few Frills in Pro Game's Debut Here."

Record: 8–1. Total attendance: 147,200.

Record for both tours: 12–5. Total attendance: 291,200.

■ ■ ■

ON THE RADIO

There is only one way I know to become an athlete. Get lots of sleep and live a normal, regular, healthy life.

Keep away from the bright lights and eat plain food. Don't eat too much meat. Any vegetable is good. Spinach and potatoes are excellent. Chew the food well. Don't smoke. Don't drink liquor. Don't be a loafer on the street. Think, dream and believe that you will come to the top, and you'll get there. Track work is the best way to build up endurance, but hard work of any kind—such as carrying ice on an ice wagon—is first-class training. . . .

Everybody who is physically fit should play some football. Whether he wins or loses doesn't really matter very much. Let him get used to standing up under punishment and stress. Everybody gets kicked around like a football some time during life.

—RED GRANGE's *advice to America's youth, delivered over WEAF Radio in New York after the Bears beat the Giants on December 6.*

■ ■ ■

QUOTATIONS FROM COAST TO COAST

There is only one thing worse than December football. That's January football.

—JAMES C. ISAMINGER, *Philadelphia Inquirer*

Professional baseball is killing the game in the colleges and universities, and pro football will have the same effect on the king of college sports. If professional football continues to grow, then the colleges must find some other sort of games which will fill the large stadiums.

—MAJ. JOHN L. GRIFFITH, *Western Conference commissioner*

Professional football will never replace college football, and we don't want it to.

—GEORGE HALAS

Everyone knows, I guess, the food and health value of malted milk. But of all the various kinds of malted milk, there is none, in my opinion, to compare with Yeast Foam Malted Milk. Delicious tasting; easily digested; a food and drink with "kick" and "pep" that wins.

It may interest you to know that our private dining car (for our big trip south and west) is stocked with Yeast Foam Malted Milk and all of our 22 players will have it constantly available.

—RED GRANGE *in newspaper ad*

Any critic placing Grange upon an All-American team for All Time must judge him solely on the publicity he has received and not upon his all-around work on the field.

—*Stanford coach* POP WARNER

I have played against harder players than Grange, but he *is good.*

—GEORGE "WILDCAT" WILSON

[I'll never marry] unless I meet some girl far more sensible than the flappers who have flocked around since I became a headliner. . . .

I've never been engaged and don't want to be. When you're in the headlines you can't tell a woman

the way to the station without being mentioned as a divorce co-respondent. I've learned that anyone who gets big money out of the public surely earns it.
—RED GRANGE

It's not long since the definition of a pro football player was a "tough guy." Now the pro is a "star who draws more money in one day than a coach makes in a year."
—DON MAXWELL, *Chicago Tribune*

▪ ▪ ▪

DIRTY TRICK

C. C. Pyle, Red Grange's manager, liked to do a party trick with Jim Thorpe. Pyle had two quarters with identical marks on them. He'd get Thorpe to plant one in an orange. Then he'd show people the other quarter and say he was going to use his magical powers to put it in the orange on the table. Pyle would go through all sorts of gyrations, palm the quarter and—presto!

One night Thorpe decided to pull Pyle's chain. When the orange was opened, two dimes and a nickel were found.

"It was the only time I ever saw Pyle get mad at anyone," Grange said.

▪ ▪ ▪

A LOOK INSIDE THE BOOKS

A crowd of 75,000, the biggest ever for a pro game, came out to see Red Grange play in Los Angeles. The estimated receipts were $135,000. Who got what (according to the *L.A. Times*):

▪ Grange received 35 percent of the first $100,000 and 40 percent of the additional $35,000. Total: $49,000.

▪ $25,000 was given to charity.

▪ The remaining $61,000 went to promoter P. H. "Puss" Halbriter. Out of that, Halbriter had to pay the stadium rental, the game expenses and the Los Angeles Tigers players and coaches. Halfback George "Wildcat" Wilson made $5,000, the rest of the players an average of $200 each. Halbriter, who had invested $17,000 in the venture, cleared $10,-000. Two days later he was in bed suffering from exhaustion.

The Bears' salaries came out of Grange's end, but amounted to no more than $10,000, the *Times* said. This left him with about $40,000 to split with manager C. C. Pyle.

Grange has said he and the Bears shared the profits equally. Either way he made a killing. In 1926, remember, you could buy a very nice car for less than $1,000.

▪ ▪ ▪

THE AFTERMATH

On October 30, 1932, Red Grange played in Boston for the first time since his ballyhooed 1925 tour. He was an aging halfback for the Chicago Bears going

NICKNAMES

Carl "Scummy" Storck
Howard "Fungy" Lebengood
Jay "Inky" Williams
Al "Old Pig Iron" Nesser
Russ "Cuss" Method
Reggie "Laughing Gas" Attache
Tom "Goof" Leary
William "Blink" Bedford
Walter "Sneeze" Achui
Adrian "Barrel" Baril
Heartley "Hunk" Anderson
Jim "Big Heavy" Underwood
Dick "Death" Halladay
Roy "Bullet" Baker
Harlan "Whippet" Carr
Frank "Slippery" Seeds
Eddie "Five Yards" Novak
Guy "Champ" Chamberlin
Larry "The Atlantic City Airedale" Conover
Benny "The Purple Streak" Boynton
Eddie Kotal, "The Lawrence Flash"

Garland "Gob" Buckeye
Babe "Gunboat" Connaughton
Clarence "Steamer" Horning
Jack "Butter" Fleischman
Walter "Dinty" Moore
Verne "Moon" Mullen
Casimir "Hippo" Gozdowski
Stancil "Possum" Powell
George "Wildcat" Wilson
Mike "Doggie" Gulian
Herbert "Fido" Kempton
Gilbert "Hawk" Falcon
Erling "Dinger" Doane
Pat "Smoke Screen" Dowling
Maurice "Mush" Dubofsky
Francis "Jug" Earpe
Mark "Spoke" Devlin
Romanus "Peaches" Nadolney
Not Nicknames:
Arrowhead
Woodchuck Welmus
Century Millstead
Baptiste Thunder
J. Bourbon Bondurant
Xavier Downwind

against the hometown Braves. Arthur Sampson of the *Evening Transcript* drew this portrait of him:

"Yesterday Grange attracted some attention, but for the most part he was just another player on the field. On his showing yesterday, he has not much of a career ahead of him. There are many better ball carriers in the league than the former famous Illinois iceman.

"He makes no waste[d] motions. He looks like a far smarter player now than he did when he first joined the ranks of the professionals. But there certainly are better halfbacks . . . and we doubt if he will command much attention in the league from now on."

...
THE FOUR HORSEMEN IN PRO FOOTBALL

The Four Horsemen of Notre Dame *did* play pro football, they just didn't play very long. None of them put in more than two seasons. Which is not to say they didn't have an impact on the game. A team, the Brooklyn Horsemen, was named after them in 1926. And two of them became league commissioners, Elmer Layden of the NFL and Jim Crowley of the All-America Football Conference.

The only time they all played together as pros was when they toured at the end of the 1925 season. They lost to the NFL's Pottsville Maroons (9–7) and Cleveland Bulldogs (13–6) and, on New Year's Day 1926, beat an all-star team made up mostly of former Princeton players (6–0) in Coral Gables, Florida. The Pottsville game caused a controversy because it was played in Philadelphia's Shibe Park, home territory of the Frankford Yellow Jackets. Commissioner Joe Carr suspended the Pottsville franchise for its act of defiance, killing the Maroons' chances of a championship.

After bowing to the Maroons, Horseman Harry Stuhldreher said: "We were showered with praises when we played together at Notre Dame, but I had my doubts just how things might work out in [the] professional ranks. The public should not lose sight of the fact that while we were playing back of former

Notre Dame linemen, some of these boys have been out of college five and six years. Rockne's system of play is not the same from year to year, and they found themselves using different styles."

All the Horsemen took college coaching jobs after graduating from Notre Dame that year. Stuhldreher was the only one who played pro ball full-time. The others were lukewarm about it. College football's most famous backfield wasn't very big. Layden was the heaviest at 180 pounds.

After they had played games on consecutive days against Pottsville and Cleveland, the *Hartford* (Connecticut) *Times* reported: "All four of the Four Horsemen are now on the injured list. Stuhldreher has a wrecked shoulder . . . [Don] Miller a damaged left leg . . . and Jim Crowley is nursing a leg which has been bothering him some weeks." Layden was knocked out of the second game with an unspecified injury but returned later. The Horsemen were so hobbled they had to cancel a rematch with the Bulldogs in Cleveland the next week.

Miller, Crowley and Layden might have been more susceptible to injury because they hadn't been playing all season. But they got out of the pro game so early that we'll never know for sure. A brief summary of each Horseman's pro activities:

HARRY STUHLDREHER, QB

Knute Rockne's coach on the field, Stuhldreher made some enemies in his first year in pro football. He reportedly was all ready to sign a $4,500 contract—plus injury protection—with an independent team in New Britain, Connecticut, when he agreed to play with the NFL's Providence Steam Roller. New Britain's president said he was "double-crossed."

Stuhldreher lasted one game with Providence, a 127–0 exhibition victory over the West Point Field Artillery. Then he got a better offer from the Waterbury (later Hartford) Blues and signed with them. The sum must have been considerable. The Steam Roller, in its first year in the NFL and desirous of a drawing card, had agreed to a deal that "would have made the Notre Dame player the highest paid man in the National league by at least $2,000," the *Providence Journal* reported. "The Roller management ended a very distasteful meeting by wishing him the best of luck in his new field."

Stuhldreher earned his keep with Waterbury. His

quarterbacking and kicking led the Blues to a 9–1 record, including two wins over the NFL's Rochester Jeffersons. (The only loss was to the New Britain club he had spurned, a game in which he fumbled "four or five times," according to the Hartford paper. Sweet revenge!) He coached at Villanova during the week.

In 1926 he took up with the Brooklyn Horsemen of the newly founded AFL—"The one-horse Horsemen," one sportswriter called them. The team won only one of eight games. It merged in November with the NFL's Brooklyn Lions and finished the season in the other league.

The *Brooklyn Eagle* didn't spell Stuhldreher's name right until the fourth game (Stuhdraher and Stuldreher were the earlier versions). He's said to have earned $750 a game, nearly a quarter of the team's payroll, yet failed to score a touchdown. An injury kept him out of the last two games.

JIM CROWLEY, HB

Crowley is generally thought to have begun his pro career in November 1925 with his hometown Green Bay Packers. In fact, he played a game with Stuhldreher's Waterbury team almost seven weeks earlier. He made a real splash, too, scoring three touchdowns on a 65-yard run and passes of 35 and 15 yards from Stuhldreher as the Blues defeated a club from Adams, Massachusetts, 34–0.

Later, after completing his coaching duties at Georgia, Crowley agreed to join the injury-plagued Packers for the last two games of their season. Green Bay coach-tailback Curly Lambeau had been his high school coach. Crowley made only a cameo appearance in the first game, at Frankford, having just traveled 36 hours by train. But in the finale at Providence he caught a TD pass in the fourth quarter to give the Packers a 13–10 victory.

The Steam Roller then signed him for its game against Grange and the Chicago Bears in Boston. The team hoped to have him for its last game, against the Yellow Jackets, but there was more money to be made touring with the Four Horsemen. Crowley received $1,500 a game on tour and played only the first quarter, Miller said. (Miller got $500 and played the whole game.)

Crowley was named AAFC commissioner in 1945. He resigned after the league's first season, however, to become part-owner and coach of the struggling Chicago Rockets franchise. The Rockets posted a 1–13 record in 1947, after which the club was sold and Crowley got out of pro football for good.

DON MILLER, HB

Miller also made his debut with Stuhldreher's Blues in 1925. He came north when he was finished coaching at Georgia Tech and played in Waterbury's last two games. He was phenomenal in the first, rushing 18 times for 130 yards, catching five passes for 100 and scoring two touchdowns in a 28–7 win over New Britain for the state championship.

"Miller proved a true wonder," the *Times* said. "He clicked off spectacular runs with his dazzling speed, caught forward passes with rare skill and proved just the spark that set off the Blues into an eleven of undeniable power and brilliance."

In a 12–0 season-ending victory over the Pere Marquette team from Boston, Miller caught a 10-yard TD pass from Stuhldreher and had a 38-yard punt return. Then he signed on with Providence for the Grange game before touring with the Horsemen.

There was a report in 1947 that Miller, then a U.S. District Attorney, might succeed Crowley as AAFC commissioner, but it didn't happen. He and a New York friend once made an $8 million offer for a controlling interest in the Washington Redskins, he later revealed. George Preston Marshall wasn't interested.

ELMER LAYDEN, FB

Layden never played in the league he became commissioner of. He coached at Columbia (now Loras) College in Dubuque, Iowa, in 1925, toured with the Horsemen in December and January (he scored the only touchdowns against Pottsville and Cleveland), then signed in '26 with the AFL's Rock Island Independents.

He played one game for Rock Island and another for Brooklyn, Stuhldreher's team. That was the extent of his major league career.

Layden was forced out as NFL commissioner in 1946 at the end of his five-year, $100,000 contract. George Preston Marshall reportedly said when he arrived at the league meeting: "Layden will be re-elected over my dead body." What really irritated the owners was Layden's friendship with *Chicago*

Tribune sports editor Arch Ward. Ward had campaigned for Layden's appointment; now he was helping to organize the All-America Football Conference. Marshall even floated the rumor that Layden was about to become coach of the AAFC's Chicago entry. Layden called such speculation "silly," but people in the league wondered how aggressive he'd be against the new competition.

Technically, Layden resigned. In reality, it was because he didn't have enough votes to be rehired. The owners offered him $20,000 to stay on as an advisor to successor Bert Bell for a year, but he walked away.

■ ■ ■

BY CHET YOULL, BUFFALO EXPRESS

Menaced by a yellow juggernaut from the Middle West yesterday, the big Orange and Black football machine of Walter Koppisch turned on full speed ahead and split the juggernaut in two. In a tense struggle between supermen of the gridiron, Columbus's Tigers reeled under a sharp and versatile Buffalo attack and finally staggered to defeat as 4,500 spectators looked down from the stands at Bison stadium. The score was 17 to 6.

—October 19, 1925

■ ■ ■

A rare 1920s action shot featuring the Columbus (Ohio) Panhandles in 1924. Notice the full stands and spread-out players. Football in the '20s is thought of as unpopular and dull. (Pro Football Hall of Fame/NFL Photos)

THE BEST PUNT RETURNER YOU NEVER HEARD OF

The greatest punt returner in NFL history was a 5′5″, 145-pound dynamo named Two Bits Homan, aka Babe Homan. "A manikin in moleskins," the newspapers called him. "A shrimp in armor." "Midget." "Dwarf."

Henry Homan played quarterback (blocking back) and safety for the Frankford Yellow Jackets from 1925 to '30, years when no official records were kept. But the most reliable source on the subject, *The Sports Encyclopedia: Pro Football,* puts him at the top of the punt-return heap with a 13.59-yard average on 82 runbacks. That's almost a yard better than George McAfee (12.78) and Jack Christiansen (12.75), currently ranked 1-2 on the league's "all-time" list.

Homan's style was unique for its time. He used to catch punts going full speed—no easy trick given the size of the ball (not to mention the size of his hands) and the windy conditions common in the days before large stadiums. The Frankford fans immediately took to him. He replaced in their hearts another waif, 5′8″, 145-pound wingback Charlie Way, who left the Yellow Jackets after an all-pro season in 1924.

"Every move Homan makes is colorful," a Philadelphia sportswriter said. "The spectators look for this midget to perform some spectacular feat every time he takes a step whether or not he has the ball."

His size and just as small reputation coming out of college nearly kept him out of the pros. But Frankford tackle Bull Behman, who had played with "Hennie" Homan at Lebanon Valley, got him a tryout, and he won a starting job. On offense, when he wasn't blocking, Homan occasionally ran the ball but was most effective as a receiver. He averaged 22.2 yards a catch in his career, according to incomplete figures.

Defensively Homan picked off passes—five in his

Henry "Two Bits" Homan of the Frankford Yellow Jackets. (Pro Football Hall of Fame/NFL Photos)

In the 1920s, the story of a game was often told in a cartoon. "Two Bits" Homan was the star of this 1926 game between the Bears and the Yellow Jackets that gave Frankford its only NFL title. (Pro Football Hall of Fame)

first two seasons—and, from the sound of things, brought down ball carriers by cutting their legs out from under them. One paper likened him to "a rubber ball," adding, "Homan rebounds almost as soon as he strikes the body of the man carrying the ball. It seems as though the runner strikes the ground about the time Hennie is on his feet."

Homan also deserves much of the credit for Frankford's only NFL championship, in 1926. Coach-end Guy Chamberlin had an outstanding year, as did tailback Hust Stockton and all-pro guard Johnny Budd, but it was Homan who made the biggest plays in the biggest games.

Ironically, his season nearly ended before it began. In an exhibition game against the Atlantic City (New Jersey) Roses, he was trampled trying to stop a running play and had his ribs caved in. He missed the first nine games. But he was back in working order by the time the contending Green Bay Packers and Chicago Bears came to town.

The Yellow Jackets blew a 13–0 lead against the Packers on Thanksgiving Day and were trailing 14–13 in the fourth quarter. The outlook wasn't brilliant, especially after Budd missed a 30-yard field goal attempt. The Jackets, then 10–1–1, simply couldn't afford another loss. The Bears were still unbeaten.

To the rescue came Two Bits. Late in the game he took a short pass from Stockton and scooted down the sideline 38 yards for the game-winning score. Homan's heroics set off "a spectacle of joyful exuberance not witnessed in professional gridiron annals in this dear Quaker city of ours," the *Philadelphia Inquirer* reported. "Oh what a bedlam, as hats and other miscellaneous articles were tossed in the air, and the crowd threatened to break forth in its demonstration in true rabble fashion on the gridiron."

Nine days later, Frankford was in similarly desperate straits. The Bears went ahead 6–0 with six minutes left on a 61-yard run by Bill Senn. But a series of passes moved the Yellow Jackets downfield. Then Stockton, chased back 15 yards by the Chicago rush, let another one fly just as a Bear dove for him.

His throw "looked more like a punt, it had been thrown so high," the *Inquirer* said. Miraculously, it came down into the arms of Homan, who had run nearly out of the end zone. The crowd, some of whom were watching from rooftops outside Shibe Park, went "into a delirium." Tex Hamer's extra point gave the Jackets an all-important 7–6 victory.

The following Saturday against Providence, Homan helped Frankford avenge its only defeat. He had a 50-yard punt return to set up the first Yellow Jackets touchdown and scored the last himself on a short run. Final score: Jackets 24, Steam Roller 0. Frankford won the title with a 14–1–2 record, nosing out the Bears (12–1–3) and Pottsville Maroons (10–2–2).

"It will be a long, long while," the *Philadelphia Bulletin* said, "before the fans . . . are going to forget the last two minutes of play" against the Bears.

Two Bits somehow survived six seasons in the rough-and-tumble NFL. He later coached high school football in Glens Falls, New York, and was inducted posthumously into the Pennsylvania Sports Hall of Fame in 1969.

■ ■ ■

HIT OF THE DECADE
Pop Goes Red Grange's Knee, 1927

Some 30,000 people jammed into Cubs Park on October 16, 1927, to watch Red Grange and the New York Yankees play the Chicago Bears. What they saw was a 12–0 Chicago victory and Grange's last

day as an elusive runner. In the final seconds of the game, the Bears' George Trafton hit Grange and wrecked his right knee.

It's ironic that Grange was hurt against the team he signed and toured with in 1925, and on the same field where he'd begun his pro career two years earlier. But how about Trafton the Terrible's most memorable hit turning out to be legal? That borders on the unbelievable.

Precisely what happened isn't clear. Game accounts fail to include even the yard line where the injury occurred. Behind by two touchdowns, the Yankees were desperate for a score. They threw to Grange near the sideline, and the 220-pound Trafton arrived at about the same time. The pass wasn't even completed.

As Grange later recalled: "I went up for a pass, and when I came down, I caught my cleats in the sod, and George Trafton . . . fell over me."

There's no mention of anything shady about the collision. Big, bad George even helped carry his former teammate off the field and into the locker room. It was a freak thing, really.

Grange had played a decent game to that point. He'd run for a 20-yard gain from scrimmage and for 25 yards after recovering a punt blocked by the Bears. He'd also had an interception and made a saving tackle on an 84-yard kickoff return by Paddy Driscoll.

Driscoll, the star of the game, set up both Bears touchdowns with long runs. He missed the extra-point tries, though, a rarity for one of the game's deadliest drop-kickers. On the first, a fan caught the ball and sprinted out of the stadium. Ever-ex-

> *There was nothing funny about being knocked down and trampled by Cal Hubbard in the afternoon, and then going out and drinking cheap booze at night to ease the pain.*
>
> *The booze hurt you worse than Hubbard, so that ought to give you some idea of the kind of stuff they were peddling in the Loop in those days. Rugged, man, rugged.*
>
> —GEORGE TRAFTON

travagant George Halas made the Yankees supply the replacement ball.

The two teams came into the game undefeated in league play, but Grange was the drawing card. Thousands forced their way through the center-field gate after it appeared they might not be admitted. As he was carried from the field, the huge crowd responded with an ovation.

There were conflicting initial reports about the injury. The *Chicago Tribune* diagnosed it as a "torn tendon" and said the attending physician didn't consider it serious. Grange, it was said, should be able to play next week in Green Bay. Actually, it was a torn ligament, and wire accounts that ran in the New York papers raised the possibility that Grange could be out for the season.

The discrepancy might have been accidental, but we doubt it. Yankees owner C. C. Pyle knew how to make a buck. The Midwest papers were reporting his star would probably play, and that could only help the gate in Green Bay.

Grange didn't, of course. He refused surgery, and when the knee didn't come around he went into semiretirement. After sitting out a year, he came back with the Bears in 1929 and played six more seasons. But he'd lost the stability in his knee, and that affected his ability to cut. He'd also lost considerable speed. He finished his career a better defensive back than runner.

● ● ●

THE CHANGELINGS

In 1928 Providence player-coach Jimmy Conzelman got a tip on a tackle from Southwest (Oklahoma) State named Perry Jackson and invited him to a tryout. Jackson had contracted typhoid, however, and couldn't go, so in his place went college teammate and buddy Arthur Shockley.

Shockley presented himself in Providence as Perry Jackson. Who was to know? Both played tackle. When Shockley impressed Conzelman enough to be offered a contract, he signed it in Jackson's name. He then played the entire '28 season—one in which the Steam Roller won the NFL championship—as someone else.

The plot grew more complicated the following year. The real Perry Jackson was healthy again and wanted a shot at pro ball. So his pal prevailed upon the Providence management to send two contracts west, one for Jackson and one for this new prospect named Shockley. The two men then signed as each other.

The real Perry Jackson didn't turn out to be as good as the fake one. The Steam Roller wound up selling "Arthur Shockley" to the Boston Bulldogs, where he played only the 1929 season. "Perry Jackson," meanwhile, lasted three seasons in Providence.

Playing under an assumed name was common in the '20s. College players did it all the time to pick up a few extra bucks. But this is the only case we've come across of players assuming *identities*.

● ● ●

THE CYCLEDROME

The Providence Steam Roller played in a 10,000-seat stadium built for bicycle racing called the Cycledrome. The field was surrounded by a banked, four-lane track that cut five yards off the corners of one end zone.

Temporary bleachers were set up on the track, putting fans right next to the action. It wasn't unusual for players to crash-land among them.

The public-address system was a megaphone. A man walked the sidelines announcing substitutions, down and yardage, names of players who scored and other pertinent information.

"There was only one locker room and it was very small," says Pearce Johnson, the team's assistant general manager. "After all, it was built for bicycle people and they only had four on the track at one time. The players took their turns going inside and changing. There were only two showers and a limited amount of hot water, so the first ones in were the lucky ones.

"There was no opponent's locker room. They'd dress at their hotel and then we'd bus them to the field."

In 1928 there was no tougher place to play. The Steam Roller was 6–1–1 at home and won its only NFL title.

The Cycledrome was later torn down and replaced by a drive-in theater. That, too, is now dead.

■ ■ ■

The Cycledrome, home field of the Providence Steam Roller. It was built for bicycle racing. Note the fans sitting on the banked track and the clipped end zone. A regulation field didn't quite fit. (Pro Football Hall of Fame/NFL Photos)

GUS SONNENBERG, KING OF THE WRESTLERS

Before Hulk Hogan, there was Gus Sonnenberg. A stumpy all-pro lineman with the Providence Steam Roller, Sonnenberg may be the man most responsible for transforming pro wrestling from a push-and-pull affair into the rock 'em, sock 'em sport it is today.

His wrestling skills were virtually nil when he climbed into the ring for the first time, on a dare, in 1928. So he resorted to football tactics, "inventing" the flying tackle. He would leap at his opponent, wrap his truncated arms around the man's legs and slam him to the mat. One or two of those was usually enough.

Occasionally, of course, he missed. In the first of his epic battles with heavyweight champion Strangler Lewis, he flew out of the ring and landed on his head. He regained consciousness in the hospital.

"To those at ringside," the *Boston Herald* said, "it was unbelievable that the human frame could withstand such a dive."

"The Flying Dutchman," one sportswriter dubbed him. The only problem was that Gustavus Adolphus Sonnenberg had a German father and a Swedish mother. He was 5'6", 200 pounds, and his chest measured 46 inches. As a farmboy in Ewen, Michigan, he used to show off his strength by tipping over Model Ts and pulling signposts out of the cement.

He started college at Dartmouth, dropped out and finished his degree at the University of Detroit. Before coming to Providence in 1927, he had played for the Columbus Tigers, Buffalo All-Americans and Detroit Tigers/Panthers. He also was a kicker, once booting a reported 52-yard field goal.

As a wrestler, "Dynamite Gus" quickly became a star, "possibly the most colorful champion the game has ever had," according to the *Los Angeles*

Gus Sonnenberg (left) of the Columbus Tigers in 1926, with teammate Joe Mulbarger. (Pro Football Hall of Fame/NFL Photos)

Times. The sport had never seen anything quite like him. He was a college graduate, an All-American; he was aggressive; and he fought all comers.

He could talk a good game, too. "I could take Primo Carnera and break him in two," he once bragged. (A feeling of invincibility can come over you when you've survived the airplane whirls of Pat McGill, the forward headlocks of Lithuanian Jack Ganson and the toe holds of Marin Plestina.)

Said the *Boston Evening Globe:* "The old wrestling game has been looking the world in the eye since Gus Sonnenberg catapulted into new fame. It seemed as if the staunch sporting public was just a bit weary of terrible Turks who seemed so tame, and foreign wrestlers whose chief claim to fame was that they refused to brush their teeth, wore celluloid collars, chewed nails and ate half an ox at one sitting."

Sonnenberg's first big match was in May 1928 against former champ Wayne (Big) Munn in Boston. Despite giving away 70 pounds, he pinned Munn in 1:19 and 0:25. The *Evening Globe* described the action:

"There was nothing stylish about Sonnenberg's wrestling, nothing skillful. It was raw savagery. . . . Sonnenberg directed the fury of his attack at his [Munn's] body and long legs. At times, in the whirlwind of action, it seemed that the squat little Sonnenberg intended to make a fight out of the wrestling bout. At other times, it looked like a rough and tumble football game, with Munn representing a live tackling dummy. Only when he had flopped Munn to the floor with his flying tackles did Sonnenberg resort to an orthodox wrestling hold."

His five matches against Lewis from 1928 to '30 were the highlight of his wrestling career. They were "to wrestling what the Follies are to the stage," the *Kansas City Star* said. "It is the *piece de resistance* which no follower of this sort of thing misses." The first three were held in Boston and attracted bigger crowds each time—13,000 at the Arena, 20,000 at the Garden and 25,000 at Fenway Park. The gate for Sonnenberg–Lewis III was reportedly $90,000, a wrestling record.

Dynamite Gus won the title from The Strangler in their second meeting in January 1929 and successfully defended it against him three times. Lewis had never lost more than twice in a row to any man. The consummate defensive wrestler, he'd always been able to figure out something, legal or otherwise.

But he couldn't come up with an answer to the flying tackle. Before the fourth match in Los Angeles, he asked Southern Cal football coach Howard Jones for advice. Jones suggested using a straightarm. Lewis trained for his last go against Sonnenberg, in Kansas City, by having his seconds thrust ramrods with padded dummy heads at him.

But there were suspicions these spectaculars weren't on the up and up. The endings of the last two matches sound particularly stagey. In L.A., one of Sonnenberg's cornermen went to help him after he had missed a flying tackle and landed in press row.

Lewis, assuming his opponent would be disqualified, turned his back. You can guess the rest. In K.C., The Strangler lost on a dubious foul.

Rumors were going around that Lewis had signed a contract "agreeing to be a servile worshipper at the Sonnenberg throne for a period of some three years," the *Star* reported.

Gus' time was running out. The California Athletic Commission had recently outlawed the flying tackle after his match against Everett Marshall in Los Angeles. Marshall had suffered "a serious injury about the groin." It had always been a controversial maneuver because Sonnenberg tended to bury his head in his opponent's belly, which technically was a butt. Thus another of his nicknames: "Gus the Goat."

"Well," Sonnenberg replied, "what if I do tackle low? That's a lot of bunk. Anybody can tackle me who wants to."

Ed "Don" George, "The Wolverine Express," finally knocked him from wrestling's throne in December 1930. George, two years out of Michigan, had just missed a medal in the superheavyweight class at the '28 Olympics. Sonnenberg defeated George in their first match when—are you ready for this?—they hit heads attempting simultaneous flying tackles. Gus recovered more quickly, probably because he had played football without a helmet, and jumped on George for the deciding fall. But in the rematch, George won the third fall with his dreaded Japanese armlock. (For those of you scoring at home, that's a head scissors coupled with a wristlock.)

One estimate put Sonnenberg's ring earnings at as much as $1 million. But the story doesn't have a happy ending. He lost a lot of his money in the Depression, and his big-spending ways took care of much of the rest. He was no luckier in love. He helped his first wife, Judith Allen, get a series of screen tests which led to a Hollywood career. But that marriage and another ended in divorce. Allen later wed a heavyweight boxer.

Health problems also plagued Sonnenberg. He was barred from wrestling in Rhode Island in 1939 because of an irregular heartbeat and soon retired from the ring. While a physical training instructor in the Navy during World War II, he developed leukemia and died in 1944 at 44.

■ ■ ■

PARTYTOWN U.S.A.

NFL players have been dumping on the city of Green Bay for years. It's too small, too cold, and—here comes the kiss of death—too *boring* for today's athletes.

If they only knew.

Green Bay in the '20s was the most popular stop in the league. Visiting players loved the place. Teams made it a point to schedule several days there. It had a bustling bar scene, and its red-light district in the northeast section was famous.

"On Sunday nights after Packer football games . . . two and three bartenders worked at top speed in the Rex, the Office and the National on Pine St., and in Jake Geurtz's place on Cherry St.," R. G. Lynch of the *Milwaukee Journal* wrote in 1928. "Late comers had to stand on the steps and wait for a chance to get in." Prohibition "was just a slight inconvenience" to the city.

Bawdy houses flourished. One of the more popular among the players was known simply as "801 and 803 Reber," which was the duplex-of-ill-repute's address. Its doors were routinely open to visiting teams, and the parties sometimes lasted till dawn.

"The players would go in about 10 at a time," says Bill Swanson, who grew up two doors down and eventually became sheriff of Green Bay. "But no more than 10. That was the limit. The whole neighborhood knew what was going on."

The only team the madam apparently had her doubts about was the Duluth Eskimos, according to Swanson. She once made the mistake of denying them entrance and locking the door. They responded the way you'd expect football players to respond, by breaking it down.

■ ■ ■

The National Football League
GAME CONTRACT

For the purpose of playing a game of football, _____,
party of the first part, and _____, party of the second part, both being members in good standing in **The National Football League,** hereby agree as follows:

That a game of football shall be played in the city of _____, on grounds furnished by the party of the _____part, on the date of _____192____, between the hours of 2 P. M. and 6 P. M.

That the length of each quarter period of said game shall be _____minutes.

That the party of the _____part shall receive as consideration for said game, the guaranteed sum of _____, plus _____for hotel expenses and _____for travel, with the option of taking _____per cent of the entire gross receipts after 15 per cent thereof has been deducted for park rental, not including war tax, to be paid at the conclusion of the game.

That party of the _____part, for the game aforesaid, shall bear their own expense, and party of the _____part shall pay all officials for said game.

That the eligibility of all officials and players participating in said game shall have the approval of the officials of **The National Football League.**

That in case of any dispute regarding plays made during the game _____ Official Football Guide shall govern, and the decision of the President shall be final.

Special Provisions:

_____

_____

_____

_____

_____

_____

That party of the _____part shall have the right to cancel said game in case of inclement weather only, by giving notice to party of the _____part at least five hours before departure of _____party's train. In the event _____party shall fail to give such notice of cancellation to _____party, as above provided, and no game is played, party of the _____ part shall receive only actual expenses (railroad fare, hotel and meals for twenty [20] men).

That if both teams have arrived on the field of play, and it is found that said field is questionable for play, the question of cancellation of said game shall rest solely with the manager of the home team.

Party of _____part shall issue _____passes and party of _____part shall receive _____passes.

In Witness Whereof, the said parties have hereunto set their hands and seals this _____day of _____192____

By _____

By _____

Approved by:
THE NATIONAL FOOTBALL LEAGUE

_____
Secretary and Treasurer

This copy to be held by the party of the second part.

THE CASE FOR BENNY FRIEDMAN

No player ever campaigned harder for election to the Pro Football Hall of Fame than Benny Friedman. Benny was his own biggest booster. He wrote letters to the *New York Times*. He asked Giants owner Wellington Mara to intercede on his behalf. He even sent suspicious-sounding testimonials from his contemporaries to the Hall's director.

These were typed on stationery bearing the letterhead of Friedman's quarterback camp. They read almost like form letters, even though they were signed at the bottom.

He did a great job as a field general as well as being an accurate passer.
—BRONKO NAGURSKI

He was a very accurate passer and . . . was a very able field general.
—RED GRANGE

He was one of the greatest forward passers the game has ever known, and a tremendous field general.
—SID LUCKMAN

He was without doubt the peer of his time, both as a field general and forward passer.
—GEORGE HALAS

As a matter of fact, he is one of the finest passers in football . . . pro football and college ball. And he was always a great field general.
—ERNIE NEVERS

In his own letter to Hall of Fame director Dick McCann, Friedman said he was afraid he was being passed over by the voters. "There was nobody tooting my horn," he wrote, "therefore, I felt I should do it myself."

He tooted away—unsuccessfully—until his death in 1982. But he *did* have a point.

Friedman wasn't much for modesty or tact, but he could sure throw a football. He was the game's first great passer, and in that sense ultimately had more impact on the NFL than Red Grange. He was a superstar in the late '20s and early '30s who commanded an unheard-of base salary of $10,000. He might not have been the gate attraction Grange was, but he certainly was on par with the likes of Hall-of-Famers Ernie Nevers and Ken Strong.

So why no bust in Canton? Good question.

The short answer is that he didn't fare well on surveys the Hall of Fame's old-timers committee sent to players from the early years. The real answer is *why* he didn't.

Friedman's career ran essentially from 1927 to '33, though he came out of retirement to play one game for Brooklyn in '34. Even with the sketchy statistics of the time, it's clear no one came close to him as a passer. He threw for at least 7,400 yards and 68 touchdowns. His nearest competitor, Red Dunn (1924–31), had about 4,700 yards and 48 TDs.

Those numbers are minuscule by today's standards, but keep in mind Friedman was throwing the fat ball that was in use until '33. He also had to deal with Stone Age rules that often made passing a poor proposition.

His 1929 season for the New York Giants was extraordinary. Ten touchdown passes in a season was something back then. He threw *20* (four in one game, which most likely was another mark). His record lasted 13 years, an unusually long time considering the offensive changes the game was undergoing. Put it this way: Friedman's 20 TDs would have been enough to lead the league in 1977.

Giants owner Tim Mara bought the entire Detroit Wolverines franchise for $10,000 in 1929 to get Friedman and several of his teammates. (Contrary to legend, Mara didn't purchase the club *just* to acquire a quarterback. Friedman certainly was the key to the deal—he was a marquee player who would appeal to the large Jewish population in New York—but six other Wolverines wound up starting for the '29 Giants.)

That year the Giants took to the air like no NFL team before them and finished 13–1–1. Only a loss to the unbeaten Green Bay Packers (12–0–1) kept them from winning the title. They also turned a profit of $8,500, just the second time in their five-year history they had made money. Mara had dropped $40,000 on them the season before.

Friedman represented the future of pro football. He showed how a skilled passer could open up the game. He wasn't afraid to throw on any down or from anywhere on the field, even deep in his own territory.

"The time when a ground attack could carry a team to successive victories has gone forever," he wrote in 1931. "A good running game must be backed by a good passing game. To make the run-

Benny Friedman spent hours strengthening and enlarging his hands so he could better throw the fat football used in the 1920s. (UPI/Bettmann Newsphotos)

ning attack successful, a passing attack is needed to spread the defense."

That was two years before the landmark 1933 league meeting, when major rules changes were made to aid the offense. The owners realized early on that more points and more passes meant more fans. Friedman was the proof. The Giants scored an astounding 312 points in 15 games in 1929. It was only the second time the 300 barrier had been broken. They repeated the feat in '30 (308) and finished in the black for the second straight year.

By then Friedman was famous. He'd been named first-team all-pro four straight seasons by the *Green*

Bay Press-Gazette. Gushed writer Paul Gallico in 1930: "In his own game, Friedman is in a class with Babe Ruth and Bobby Jones and Earl Sande and Gallant Fox."

Friedman was known for his accuracy, not his arm strength. His effective range was only about 40 yards, but he was deadly within it. He was fascinated by the mechanics of throwing a football and had spent hours perfecting his technique at the University of Michigan.

His trademark was a unique follow-through. When he delivered the ball, his right leg finished ahead of his left (or lead) leg in a motion similar to a baseball pitcher's. He insisted it gave him greater distance and accuracy while leaving him less susceptible to a crippling knee injury. (With the results he got, who was going to argue?)

He was, in many ways, a self-made quarterback. By lifting weights beginning at an early age, he built himself into a solid 5'10", 180-pounder. He also worked in college on strengthening his forearms and large hands.

"In class we were seated in one-arm chairs," he recalled in his book *The Passing Game.* "I used to spread my fingers over the entire arm. I watched the slow growth. I took pride in the fraction-of-an-inch developments as they appeared."

By the end of his freshman year, he claimed, he could wrap his hand halfway around the rotund ball. This helped him spiral it when few others could, and he developed a touch on his passes that was rare in those days.

"Other players will throw you a pass that will tear your fingers off," Gallico wrote. "Friedman's pass is launched and so calculated that when it reaches the receiver it has gone its route. The ball is dead. The receiver has merely to reach up to take hold of it, like picking a grapefruit from a tree."

Ernie Cuneo, a guard for the Orange Tornadoes and Brooklyn Dodgers (1929–30), said Friedman threw the single greatest pass he'd ever seen during a game in '29. He described it in *The American Scholar:*

"It was a snowy day, the Polo Grounds' lights were on, time was running out, and the Giants, running out of steam on our 25-yard line, had to throw a Hail Mary pass. Everybody knew it, so everybody keyed on Friedman—a blitz. I got through their blockers and so did several others, and we tore at Benny. Benny fell back to the 40-yard line. In the meantime, his end slid across our goal line, slipping as he did so. Then, at 40 yards, in the gathering gloom, with a wet ball, Benny pegged it to the end, who caught it while flat on the ground!"

Now for the bad news about the guy.

Friedman's personality might be the reason he's not in the Hall of Fame. He was an economy-sized prima donna. He had the kind of ego that led him to write a *Sport* magazine article in 1953 entitled "I Could Play Pro Football—And I'm 48." In it he said:

"I . . . have been out of the National Football League for 20 years, but I'm confident I could do the job as well as, if not better than the present-day big-league quarterbacks, most of whom are half my age."

Imagine what the guy was like in his prime! Ray Flaherty was Friedman's teammate in New York for three years and is as diplomatic as possible about that:

"He was opinionated and . . . well, I don't know how to put it. He wasn't a jerk—he was a pretty smart guy. But he thought Benny Friedman was running the show most of the time."

That comes across in everything you read about or by Friedman (he wrote a number of articles for *Collier's* in addition to his book). He was a tireless self-promoter. In an interview with Bob Curran for the book *Pro Football's Rag Days,* he said one of the handicaps for a quarterback in his day was the shortage of good receivers.

"In fact, I can think of only one great one in the pros—Don Hutson," he said. "But for the most part the receivers were quite ordinary."

Friedman's ends with the Giants happened to be Flaherty and Red Badgro, both Hall-of-Famers. It's that kind of arrogance that made him easy to dislike. You have to believe it also made him easy to exclude from the Hall-of-Fame surveys. Friedman didn't have a lot of friends in football, and that included teammates, with whom he didn't socialize. He pre-

DECADE ALL–STAR TEAM

For skill position players, figures under "Data" are their best seasons (except where indicated).

Pos. Player	Years*	Data
E Guy Chamberlin	8	13 catches, 340 yds., 2 TDs; 2 all-NFL
T Ed Healey	8	5 all-NFL
G Gus Sonnenberg	5	3 all-NFL
G Jim McMillen	5	2 all-NFL
C Clyde Smith	3	3 all-NFL
T Duke Slater	8	5-time second-team all-NFL
E Lavie Dilweg	4	25 catches, 429 yds., 3 TDs; 3 all-NFL
B Benny Friedman	3	20 TD passes in 1929; 3 all-NFL
B Paddy Driscoll	10	2,274** career rushing yds.; 6 all-NFL
B Tony Latone	5	593 yds., 4.0, 7 TDs, 0 all-NFL
B Ernie Nevers	3	Almost no statistics available; 3 all-NFL

OTHER SELECTIONS

Returner -- Two Bits Homan		Wild Card Selection -- Charlie Berry
Punter -- Fats Henry		Enforcer -- George Trafton
Kicker -- Paddy Driscoll		Player-coach -- Guy Chamberlin

*Number of years he played in the decade.   **Statistics incomplete.

ferred high society to the hoi polloi and made that condescendingly clear.

In 1932 former Giants teammate Jack McBride allegedly gave up a sure touchdown to throw a punch at Friedman, who was then playing for the Dodgers. In a game at Ebbets Field, McBride burst through a hole and appeared headed for the end zone when he deliberately angled back toward the middle of the field, where Friedman was in pursuit from his safety position. The two collided, and McBride took a swing.

Friedman was also Jewish. While that didn't keep Sid Luckman—no sweetheart himself—out of Canton, Luckman wasn't dependent on the results of player surveys to get in. We didn't find any specific evidence of bigotry in Friedman's case, but all you have to do is count the number of black players from the '20s in the Hall (zero) to appreciate the times.

Friedman also might have suffered in the surveys because he was primarily a passer, a specialist in an era of generalists. He was a decent runner—not much speed but fairly elusive, according to Flaherty—but you don't hear much about his kicking or defense. Versatility was everything in the '20s and '30s. The backs from that period who made the Hall of Fame (Grange, Jimmy Conzelman, Paddy Driscoll, Joe Guyon, Johnny Blood, Nevers and Strong) did everything well.

There's also the longevity argument, but it's not a very strong one. Friedman's seven full seasons were plenty by the standards of the day. Nevers, for example, played only five. While it's true Friedman's performance slipped in his last three years, so did the talent around him. When he left the game, he still was one of its greatest players.

In 1931 he retired to take an assistant coaching job at Yale. It was rumored that an alumnus had promised him a seat on the New York Stock Exchange as part of the agreement. The seat never materialized, and Friedman returned to the Giants for the second half of the season. After losing three of its first four games, the team rallied to finish 7–6–1. He then approached Mara about becoming a part-owner, but his proposal was rejected.

"My timing was off," Friedman said. "If I had asked him in the years when the team was like a plaything to him, I probably would have got what I wanted. But at the time I asked him it was his sole asset. He said, 'No, I'm keeping it all for my sons.'

"That was that. I thought I deserved a piece of the club because I felt I had played a big part in moving it from the red ink to the black ink. And when Tim turned me down I felt I should move along, that I couldn't stay with him."

His career might have been dramatically different had he gone ahead and signed with the Bears. George Halas wanted Friedman badly. He was putting together a powerhouse and the only missing ingredient was a pure passer. (Imagine Friedman, Nagurski and Grange in the same backfield.) The deal was all set, but Friedman's wife, Shirley, squelched it. She wouldn't leave New York. Benny wound up signing as a player-coach with Brooklyn.

Two years later he retired a second time to become head coach at City College of New York. Except for his one-game comeback in '34, that was the end of his NFL career. He was only 29.

He held a variety of jobs during the rest of his life but never put football away. He was athletic director at Brandeis. He played semipro ball on Long Island. He tried officiating in the NFL briefly. He ran successful quarterback schools for years. He wrote a weekly sports column for a New York paper. And, of course, he pushed himself for the Hall of Fame.

As Ernie Cuneo put it: "Benny, in a way, never grew up."

In 1979 Friedman's left leg—the one he bragged was never damaged because of his patented follow-through—developed a blood clot and had to be amputated. Not long afterward he developed shingles. According to his wife, he was in constant pain. On November 23, 1982, he killed himself with a pistol. In notes to his family, he explained that he didn't want to finish life as "the old man on the park bench."

■ ■ ■

FRIEDMAN'S 20 TD PASSES, 1929

No pro passer had ever come close to accomplishing what Benny Friedman did with the New York Giants in 1929. Friedman threw for 20 TDs at a time when 10 was an exceptional number. It was 13 years before another quarterback (Cecil Isbell) cracked the magical 20 mark.

■ **Game 1, September 29**—A slow start. Friedman and the Giants play a scoreless tie against the Orange Tornadoes at Orange, New Jersey. He throws an interception that stops one drive and has a last-second field-goal try blocked. The TD count: 0.

■ **Game 2, October 6**—The Giants manage only one score—a nine-yard run by Led Sedbrook—in a 7–0 victory over the defending NFL champion Providence Steam Roller in Providence. Passes by Friedman account for 43 of the 75 yards on the scoring drive. The count: 0.

■ **Game 3, October 13**—Friedman throws his first two TD passes of the season in his home debut as a Giant. With 30,000 looking on at the Polo Grounds, he hits Sedbrook from 15 yards out in the second quarter and Hap Moran from 20 in the fourth. New York beats Ken Strong and the Staten Island Stapletons, 19–9. The count: 2.

■ **Game 4, October 20**—Another crowd of 30,000 at the Polo Grounds watches as Friedman throws three touchdowns in the second quarter alone in a 32–0 rout of the Frankford Yellow Jackets. The first is an 18-yarder to Moran, the second a 43-yard bomb to Ray Flaherty, the third a 25-yarder to Jack Hagerty. A fourth TD pass is dropped by Snitz Snyder. The count: 5.

■ **Game 5, October 27**—All three Giants touchdowns in a 19–0 win over Providence come on the ground. "Friedman's usual exhibition of overhead pyrotechnics was conspicuously absent for the simple reason that Providence backs hung leachlike to Giant receivers," the *New York Times* reported. The count: 5.

■ **Game 6, November 3**—Friedman gets back on track with a 35-yarder to Flaherty in the third quarter of a 26–14 victory over the Bears at Wrigley Field. His passing is largely responsible for the Giants scoring three TDs in a 10-minute span. At one point he completes six straight throws. The count: 6.

■ **Game 7, November 5**—Friedman picks up two more TDs—both to Flaherty—in little more than a quarter's work against the Buffalo Bisons. The Giants breeze, 45–6. The count: 8.

■ **Game 8, November 10**—The Giants run their victory streak to seven with a 22–0 win over Orange.

Friedman accounts for the team's second TD with a 21-yard pass to favorite-target Flaherty in the first quarter. The count: 9.

■ **Game 9, November 17**—In an amazing performance, Friedman riddles the Bears for four TD passes in a 34–0 victory at the Polo Grounds. The barrage starts with a 37-yarder to Glenn Campbell in the second quarter. It continues in the third with Moran catching two (from 6 and 15 yards out) and Snyder one (20 yards). Friedman also throws for gains of 35, 35 and 40 yards. The count: 13.

■ **Game 10, November 24**—The Packers overwhelm the Giants' offensive line and harass Friedman into his worst performance of the season in a game that ultimately decides the NFL title. Friedman manages to throw for one TD—for six yards to Tony Plansky—but has two key interceptions in a 20–6 defeat. The first, by Hall-of-Fame tackle Cal Hubbard, came at the Green Bay one in the second quarter (following a 65-yard completion to Flaherty). The second came deep in Giants territory late in the game and set up the Packers' final touchdown. The Pack will finish the season 12–0–1, the Giants 13–1–1. The count: 14.

■ **Game 11, November 28**—Friedman throws for two as the Giants get back in the win column, 21–7, over Staten Island at the Polo Grounds. The first is a 40-yarder to Sedbrook, the second a 20-yarder to Flaherty off a fake field-goal attempt. The count: 16.

■ **Game 12, December 1**—In one of the decade's best games, the Giants beat the Cardinals, 24–21, at the Polo Grounds. The ambidextrous Plansky wins it with a 40-yard, left-footed drop kick from a bad angle on the final play. Friedman has TD passes of 12 yards to Sedbrook and 21 to Flaherty early in the game but throws an interception to Ernie Nevers that nearly costs the Giants the game. The count: 18.

■ **Game 13, December 7**—Friedman's streak of consecutive games with a touchdown pass ends at seven in a 12–0 Giants victory on a sloppy field at Frankford. He does, however, contribute a 23-yard interception return for a TD. The count: 18.

■ **Game 14, December 8**—The Giants throw for three TDs in a 31–0 victory over Frankford (this time at the Polo Grounds), but Friedman has just one of them—a 15-yarder to Flaherty. Plansky has the other two. The count: 19.

■ **Game 15, December 15**—Friedman's final TD pass of the season proves to be the game winner in a 14–9 win over the Bears at Wrigley Field. With the Giants trailing 9–7 in the fourth quarter, he rolls right, pump-fakes and then throws back across the field to a wide-open Sedbrook for a 27-yard score. The count: 20.

■ ■ ■

THREE JOHNNY BLOOD STORIES WE HADN'T HEARD

Hall-of-Fame running back Johnny Blood was the playboy of the pro football world in the '20s and '30s. He retired in 1939—from the NFL, that is—but his legend lives on.

■ Blood once checked into the Packers huddle with a pass play from coach Curly Lambeau. He made the call, then turned to quarterback Arnie Herber and said: "Arnie, throw it in the direction of Mother Pierre's whorehouse."

Herber, no stranger to the Green Bay nightlife, knew Blood was heading for the goal post at the northeast end of the stadium. The pass was there, and so was Blood.

■ When Blood first joined the Packers in 1929, he asked for a salary of $100 a game. Lambeau came back with an offer of $110 with the stipulation that he not drink past Tuesday of each week. "I countered with an offer to take the $100 I had proposed and drink through Wednesday," Blood said. "Curly agreed."

■ The Packers won their first title in '29, and the city held a banquet for the players. Each was presented a $220 check, a wallet and a pocket watch.

Blood was the last to address the gathering of over 400 and, after thanking the fans and Packer ownership, said: "I am especially grateful for the check."

■ ■ ■

WHO WAS SAND?

The story of how John McNally became Johnny Blood is well known. He and a college friend were trying to come up with pseudonyms on their way to a pro tryout when they passed a theater showing Rudolph Valentino's *Blood and Sand*.

"I'll be Blood and you be Sand," McNally said in a moment of inspiration.

But who *was* Sand?

Blood identified him as Ralph Hanson, a former classmate at St. John's University in Minnesota. School records indicate Hanson was from Minneapolis and attended St. John's the same years Blood did—1921 to '23.

What's puzzling is that he doesn't show up in any of the football team pictures with Blood. According to the yearbook, Hanson's extracurriculars included glee club.

■ ■ ■

LET THERE BE LIGHTS

The Providence Steam Roller usually played its games at the Cycledrome, a stadium built for bicycle races. The game on November 6, 1929, against the Chicago Cardinals, however, was moved to Kinsley Park, a soccer field. The reason? It had lights.

A crowd of 6,000 watched the first night game in NFL history. The Steam Roller, playing for the second day in a row, lost to the Cardinals, 16–0. The lighting was "terrible," says Pearce Johnson, the Roller's assistant general manager. "We painted the ball white, and I supposed that helped some." A photo in the *Providence Journal* came out surprisingly clearly.

Ernie Nevers scored all the Cards points, running and passing for touchdowns and kicking a field goal and an extra point. He finished with 102 yards rushing and 144 passing (on 10 completions in 14 attempts).

Major league baseball's first night game was still nearly six years away.

THE FIRST NIGHT GAME

CARDS (16)   **ROLLER (0)**

Dowling	LE	Harvey
Tinsley	LT	Hanny
Kiesling	LG	Fleischman
Rooney	C	Rehnquist
Williams	RG	Golembeski
Slater	RT	McGuirk
Kassel	RE	Spellman
McDonnell	QB	Welch
Rooney	LH	Wilson
Rose	RH	Williams
Nevers	FB	McBride

Chicago	0	10	0	6	—	16
Providence	0	0	0	0	—	0

CHI—Kassel 46 pass from Nevers (Nevers kick)
CHI—FG Nevers 23
CHI—Nevers 2 run (kick failed)

Substitutes—Cardinals: Method, HB; Butts, HB; Underwood, C; Hogue, E; Larsen, FB. Steam Roller: Cronin, E; Conzelman, QB; Wilson, G; Cronin, HB; Garvey, G.

. . .

WHO'S GOT THE BALL?

Three years before Providence staged its night game, the Hartford Blues and Canton Bulldogs played under the lights at the Hartford Velodrome. Not by design, mind you. Nothing as wacky as what happened November 7, 1926, could ever have been planned.

The Blues and Bulldogs played an afternoon game that turned into a night game. The starting time was supposed to be 2:45 P.M., later than usual because of an Armistice Day parade in the city. But the actual kickoff wasn't until after 3:00. It seems the Bulldogs' bus got stuck in parade traffic.

By the time the fourth quarter rolled around, it was almost completely dark. Desperate stadium officials did what they could. They turned on the low-hanging floodlights used for bicycle races. The resulting glare made visibility even worse for the players, and that's when things started getting crazy.

With about eight minutes to play, the Bulldogs finally punched over their first score, cutting the Blues' lead to 16–7. At that point, referee Bill Halloran wanted to call the game because conditions were so bad. But the Bulldogs, convinced they could come back, argued him out of it. So on it went.

For some reason (accounts are not clear why) Canton received the kickoff following its own touchdown. The deep men were Harry Robb and Dutch Vick, standing side by side. The kick came to Robb, who circled toward the sidelines. Meanwhile, Vick tucked a leather helmet under his arm to simulate the ball and charged straight upfield. The ruse worked. Robb made it all the way to the Hartford 20 before being hauled down.

But the fun was just beginning. Hartford fans who had come up close to the sideline to see better noticed a Canton player standing near them just inside the field of play. Presumably he was going to run out for a pass as soon as the ball was snapped,

Coming
1918--Howard Cosell (Howard Cohen), Winston-Salem, N.C.
1920--Marion Motley, Leesburg, Ga.
       Steve Van Buren, La Ceiba, Honduras
1921--Bill Willis, Columbus, Ohio
       Otto Graham, Waukegan, Ill
1922--George Allen, Detroit
1923--Crazylegs Hirsch, Wausau, Wis
1924--Lou Groza, Martins Ferry, Ohio
       Leo Nomellini, Lucca, Italy
       Tom Landry, Mission, Texas
1925--Chuck Bednarik, Bethlehem, Pa.
       Art Donovan, Bronx, N.Y.
1926--Buddy Young, Chicago
       Pete Rozelle, South Gate, Calif.
       Norm Van Brocklin, Eagle Butte, S.D.
       Bobby Layne, Santa Ana, Texas
1927--Gino Marchetti, Smithers, W.Va.
       Joe Perry, Stevens, Ark.
       George Blanda, Youngwood, Pa.
1928--Night Train Lane, Austin, Texas
       Hugh McElhenny, Los Angeles
1929--Al Davis, Brockton, Mass.
       Dan Jenkins, Ft. Worth, Texas

Going
1926--Lou Feist, 23, Buffalo end-fullback, meningitis
1928--Chuck Corgan, 25, Giants end, cancer

The female Frankford Yellow Jackets in the heat of battle in 1926. The perception is that pro football wasn't popular in the '20s, yet here is a *women's* team. (UPI/Bettmann Newsphotos)

catching the Blues unaware. The irate crowd chased the "sleeper" onto the field, where a riot nearly broke out.

Halloran, having seen enough, declared the game over.

■ ■ ■
SCORING MACHINE

Any student of the game knows that Ernie Nevers scored all his team's points, a record-setting 40, in the Chicago Cardinals' 40–7 victory over the Bears on Thanksgiving Day, 1929. Less well known is the fact that, four days earlier against Dayton, he had scored every point for the Cardinals in a 19–0 win.

That's 59 consecutive points. And the total could have been as high as 64 if Nevers had had a little more success kicking extra points. He missed two attempts in the two games, had another one blocked and a fourth botched by a bad snap. He had yet another miss—after the Cards' only score—in the game before the streaked started.

There's reason to believe Ernie was a little irked by these failures. After missing his first point-after against the Triangles, he tried to drop kick the next one. That was the one that was blocked.

EDITORIAL: NINE AREN'T ENOUGH

Only nine players who played mainly in the '20s are in the Pro Football Hall of Fame—not even enough for a team. That's probably all there's going to be, too.

The last '20s player elected to the Hall was Joe Guyon in 1966. Jim Thorpe, Ernie Nevers and Fats Henry were charter members in '63, George Trafton, Ed Healey and Link Lyman were inducted in '64 and Paddy Driscoll and Guy Chamberlin went in in '65. Nine pioneers. Period.

The main problem is documentation. The NFL didn't start keeping strict records until 1933, and pro football didn't get much newspaper space back then. It's hard enough building a case for skill-position players like Benny Friedman, Verne Lewellen and Lavie Dilweg, let alone interior linemen such as Duke Slater, Gus Sonnenberg and Swede Youngstrom.

There *is* a five-man old-timers subcommittee to the Hall's selection committee. Each year it puts one player on the ballot. But just two pre-'50s players have gotten in since 1978—Red Badgro ('81) and George Musso ('82), both '30s stars.

Here's the breakdown of Hall-of-Fame players by decade, excluding Steve Owen and Ray Flaherty, who made it as much for coaching as for playing (some players straddled two decades; thus the fractions):

'20s: 9	'50s: 36
'30s: 18	'60s: 34
'40s: 14½	'70s: 22½

As you can see, it isn't just the '20s players who have been slighted. There are nearly as many Hall-of-Famers from the '50s as from the '20s, '30s and '40s combined (41½).

In the Hall's defense, it did conduct a survey of enshrinees and coaches from the early years to find out what players it might be overlooking. All the most-mentioned names are now in Canton, according to librarian Joe Horrigan.

Still, *nine* players from the '20s? We have to do better than that. Maybe the electors should let the all-pro teams, like the ones selected by the *Green Bay Press-Gazette,* be their guide. If modern sportswriters can be entrusted to decide whom to allow into the Hall of Fame, then '20s sportswriters can, too.

THE 1930s

'30s CHALKBOARD

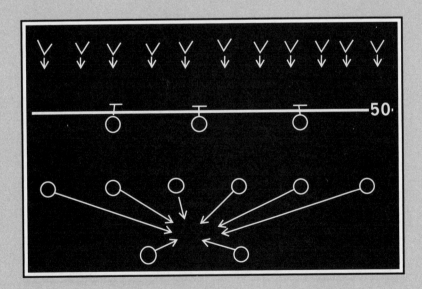

The Squirrel Cage (or Befuddle Huddle)

The Squirrel Cage (or Befuddle Huddle)

There's never been a return play quite like it: Eight men ran to where the kickoff landed, huddled momentarily and then broke in different directions, each hunched over as if he had the football. It was left to the coverage team to figure out who really did, and the resulting confusion was exactly what Washington Redskins coach Ray Flaherty had in mind when he popularized the Squirrel Cage in the late '30s. The Redskins would run it about once a year and usually give the ball to the player least likely to carry it. Once that happened to be 260-pound tackle Turk Edwards. "Turk had good speed for his size and had been after me for some time to let him run with the ball," Flaherty said. "So I decided to give it to him but warned him not to run too fast after he got out of the huddle because they'd know he had it. Well, he broke into the clear right away and probably would have scored if he hadn't gotten anxious. He started sprinting and they caught him from behind at about the 15 [yard line]." The play became obsolete when the NFL required the receiving team to keep five men 10 yards from the spot of the kickoff.

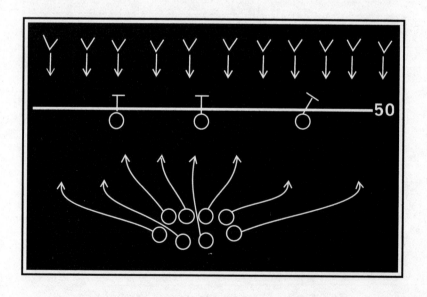

THE 1930s AT A GLANCE

Decade Standings

East	W	L	T	Pct.	West	W	L	T	Pct.
Giants (2)	80	39	8	.661	Bears (2)	85	28	11	.730
Redskins (1)	46	36	8	.556	Packers (4)	86	35	4	.704
Dodgers	40	67	9	.384	Lions (1)	73	39	9	.640
Steelers	22	55	3	.294	Cardinals	35	67	9	.356
Eagles	18	55	3	.257	Rams	10	22	1	.318

(Figures in parentheses are championships won.)

Best Regular–Season Record Chicago Bears, 1934, 13-0

Worst Regular–Season Record Philadelphia Eagles, 1936, 1-11

League Attendance 4,918,305 (1934-39)

In	Out
big-city teams	Ohio-city teams
streamlined ball for passing	fat ball for kicking
Chicago Bears	Canton Bulldogs
George Preston Marshall	C. C. Pyle
halftime shows	black players
laterals	drop-kicking
Sammy Baugh, Ace Parker	Benny Friedman, Paddy Driscoll
the draft	competition for talent
championship games	championship arguments
hash marks	0-0 games

Biggest Player Ted Isaacson, Chicago Cardinals tackle, went 6'4", 272. The wide-body award goes to 5'8", 250-pound Boston Braves lineman Marne Intrieri.

Smallest Player Butch Meeker, a tailback with the Providence Steam Roller, was 5'3", 143. The smallest lineman was 5'3", 180-pound John Law, who played for the Newark Tornados in 1930. The aptly named Law went on to coach football at Sing Sing Prison.

Best Athlete Ace Parker

Fastest Player Don Hutson

Slowest Player Maybe Mose Kelsch, the bald, beefy (5'10", 225), Pittsburgh kicker. The guy was so slow he didn't get to the NFL until he was 37.

Most Intimidating Player Bronko Nagurski

Failed Franchises Minneapolis Redjackets, 1930
Newark Tornadoes, 1930
Cleveland Indians, 1931
Frankford Yellow Jackets, 1931
Providence Steam Roller, 1931
Staten Island Stapletons, 1932
Cincinnati Reds/St. Louis Gunners, 1934

Failed League The second AFL, 1937

Smartest Franchise Shift	George Preston Marshall moving the Redskins from Boston to Washington in 1937. The team drew more people for its first three games in the nation's capital than it did for the entire '36 season (56,530).
Sports Medicine Update	Dr. Frederic Besley, president of the American College of Surgeons, recommended in 1938 that injured players not be moved until a doctor can examine them. Injuries were being compounded by players being dragged off the field.
►Famous Firsts	College All-Star Game, 1934 Nationally broadcast game, 1934 (Bears-Lions, Nov. 29, CBS) Football cards, 1935 College draft, 1936 West Coast team, 1937 (the L.A. Bulldogs of the second AFL) Pro Bowl, 1939 League highlight film, 1939 Televised game, 1939 (Eagles-Dodgers, Oct. 22)
Famous Lasts	Player who didn't wear a helmet *or* shoulder pads (Al Nesser) Team owned by players, 1933 (Chris Cagle and Shipwreck Kelly bought the Brooklyn Dodgers) Last drop-kicked field goal in NFL, 1937 (Dutch Clark)
Best Race	1935 Western Division This was the only time in NFL history that every team in a division had a winning record. Detroit (7-3-2) finished first, followed by Green Bay (8-4) and the Chicago Bears (6-4-2) and Cardinals (6-4-2). Today the Lions and Packers would have had the same winning percentage (.667). Ties didn't count in '35.
Best Title Game	The Bears' 23-21 victory over the Giants in 1933 had six lead changes, over 600 yards of offense and two trick plays that produced touchdowns.
Upset of the Decade	Bronko Nagurski was pinned by Jim Londos in 47 minutes, 11 seconds, to lose his world wrestling championship in 1938.
►Owner vs. Owner	Dan Topping vs. Bert Bell, 1938-39
►Trials of the Decade	Willard Bent vs. Green Bay Packers, 1933 Bill Fleckenstein vs. Benny Friedman, 1937
Major Rules Changes	1933--hashmarks added (10 yards from sideline), passing legalized from anywhere behind line, goal posts moved back to goal lines 1934--player entering game can immediately talk to teammates 1935--hashmarks moved farther in from sidelines (15 yards) 1938--roughing the passer becomes a penalty
►New Equipment	slimmer ball cantilevered shoulder pads slip-on, square kicking toe
Fashion Trend	knit fabrics

Best Uniforms	The 1933 Boston Redskins. Marshall outfitted them in gold satin pants (all the other teams wore khaki) and scarlet jerseys with an Indian head on the front and gold numbers on the back.
New Statistics	The NFL began keeping team and individual statistics in most of the major categories: touchdowns (rushing/passing), field goals, rushing (attempts/yards), passing (attempts/completions/yards) and punting (average). Team interceptions, fumbles and penalty yards also were recorded.
▶**Best Play**	The Befuddle Huddle (see L.A. Bulldogs item)
▶**Hit of the Decade**	Clarke Hinkle et al. vs. Bronko Nagurski
▶**Fight of the Decade**	Redskins-Bears, 1937 championship game
Highest–Paid Player	Byron "Whizzer" White made $15,800 as a Pittsburgh Pirates rookie in 1938. It could have been more, but the future Supreme Court Justice waived a clause calling for $200 an exhibition game because the team was losing money. There were rumors his envious teammates didn't block hard for him. When three players were released early in the season, owner Art Rooney publicly denied it was because of team dissension.
Least Appreciated Players	Detroit guard Ox Emerson Brooklyn back-kicker Ralph Kercheval
Best Trade	Another George Halas heist. The Bears boss sent end Eggs Manske to the Steelers in 1938 for their No. 1 pick in the next draft. It turned out to be Hall-of-Fame quarterback Sid Luckman.
Best Football Book	*Pro Football: Its Ups and Downs*, by Dr. Harry March, 1934
Worst Idea	The "gentlemen's" agreement to ban black players, 1933
▶**Individual Record That Has Never Been Equaled**	Johnny Blood's 10 touchdown catches by a running back, 1931

HOW THE BIG NAMES BROKE IN

■ **Bronko Nagurski**—Possibly the greatest fullback of all time made his pro debut at left tackle in a 0–0 tie against Brooklyn in 1930. The Bears' starting fullback that day was another rookie, Joe Lintzenich. Nagurski had received All-American consideration at both positions at Minnesota. At some point in the game he moved to the backfield. There's no mention of him carrying the ball until late. In the final minutes the Bears drove 92 yards to the Brooklyn one, where they had two shots to get it over and win. Bill Senn took one and so did Nagurski. Both failed. The Bronk was stuffed on his first one-yard plunge! The following week he was at fullback, pretty much for good.

■ **Sammy Baugh**—Slingin' Sam's first NFL game in 1937 was the Redskins' first in Washington. He'd been with the team only a week because of a contract dispute and probably wouldn't have started against the Giants if tailback Cliff Battles hadn't been hospitalized with an infected knee. On the Redskins' first play he brought the crowd to its feet by zipping a five-yard flat pass to blocking back Erny Pinckert. Riley Smith wound up scoring all the Redskins'

1930s football manhood: bronzed, barechested Bears Hall-of-Famers Bill Hewitt (left) and Bronko Nagurski. (Pro Football Hall of Fame/NFL Photos)

points in a 13–3 victory, but Baugh (11 of 16 for 116 yards) was the star of the evening.

■ **Byron "Whizzer" White**—The Pittsburgh Pirates' $15,000 man played about half the 1938 opener, rushing for 41 yards, catching a 35-yard pass and throwing a seven-yard completion in a 16–7 loss at Detroit. His only notable mistake was misplaying a fourth-quarter punt. He let it go through his fingers at the Pittsburgh 20 and scrambled to recover at the 3. The visibility in Detroit must have been poor, because the day before at practice he'd also misjudged a punt. That time it hit him in the eye and left him with a shiner for his debut.

■ ■ ■

HOW THE BIG NAMES BOWED OUT

■ **Jim Thorpe**—Pro football's first great running back signed on as an end with the Chicago Cardinals for their 1928 season finale against the Bears. He was 40. "Chris [O'Brien, the Cards owner] thinks Thorpe will be of value in stopping the Bears' end runs," the *Chicago Daily Tribune* said. "Thorpe still possesses the phenomenal kicking ability that was his a decade ago." The Bears blocked two punts, scored 28 second-quarter points and won the Thanksgiving Day game, 34–0, the biggest victory in the history of the series. Thorpe, in his last NFL game, backed up Ed Allen on the left side.

■ **Ernie Nevers**—The legendary iron man broke his wrist returning a kickoff on his final play. It happened in a charity game in January 1932 at San Francisco's Kezar Stadium. Years later, Nevers said it was Hall-of-Famer Clarke Hinkle who put the hit on him, but it ain't so. Hinkle and the Packers had been the opposition in a benefit game earlier that month. In his farewell appearance, Nevers scored all his team's points in a 26–14 win over a group of former Notre Dame and St. Mary's players led by ex–Irish quarterback Frankie Carideo.

■ **Red Grange**—The month after the Giants upset the Bears in the 1934 title game—the celebrated "Sneakers Game"—the teams played an exhibition rematch at Los Angeles' Gilmore Stadium. This was Grange's swan song. Near the end, with the Bears leading, 21–0, he broke away for a 41-yard gain. He always suspected the Giants let him do it.

"I started running as fast as I could," he said sometime later, "only it seemed like the doggone goal posts kept getting farther and farther away. At any rate, I could hear one of the Giants—a huge tackle named Cecil [Tex] Irvin, who was so slow you could have timed him with a calendar—sneaking up on me. Finally . . . he caught up with me. I know he didn't want to tackle me, but he had to."

■ ■ ■

GEORGE TRAFTON VS. PRIMO CARNERA

The boxing bug bit George Trafton, Hall-of-Fame center and legendary tough guy, rather late in life. The baddest Chicago Bear was 32 when he fought Art "the Great" Shires, the White Sox first baseman, in Chicago in December 1929. Trafton spotted Shires 10 years; Shires spotted Trafton 40 pounds. The old man scored a knockdown in the opening minute and won a five-round decision.

"I didn't know the difference between a left hook and a right tackle," Trafton said later. "I threw everything but George Halas at him."

After beating several more stiffs, he managed to get a match with future heavyweight champ Primo Carnera in Kansas City in the spring of 1930. The Ambling Alp was on his first tour of the U.S., punching out one bum after another. One opponent had shown up drunk.

"The consensus of those who know him," the *Kansas City Star* said of Trafton, "is that he possesses a wealth of real physical courage, that his boxing skill is confined to wild but vicious swings and that he absolutely believes he has a chance to defeat Carnera."

And Trafton, a champion talker, apparently convinced a lot of other people, too. Said New York Giants coach Roy Andrews: "He looks fat, but he always has been that way, so far as I can remember. I don't know what chance he has with Carnera, but

I believe he won't deliberately quit. The big Italian will have to knock him out. But even that won't stop George from talking."

The largest fight crowd of the year, 8,000, turned out for the bout March 26 at Convention Hall. It lasted 54 seconds, during which Trafton went down three times and was counted out. The Associated Press account said Carnera "pushed, rather than jabbed his opponent to the canvas. The Chicagoan was still flat on his back when Primo left the ring."

The *Star* charged: "Trafton not only went into the tank, but he was so eager he must have bumped his head on the bottom. The last blow, the only blow delivered for that matter, could not possibly have knocked out a lightweight. . . . But George, inexperienced in the sort of thing he was doing last night, took no chances. He wasn't sure if he would be hit again, and he hopped avidly on the opportunity this wallop afforded.

"Down he went, hands stretched out in the orthodox fashion. Perfectly still. His handlers rushed in to douse water in his face. George finally opened his eyes, put on that 'Where am I?' expression and gasped."

Carnera took his $4,725 and moved on to Denver, where he knocked out another punching bag in the first round two days later. Trafton—"the toughest, meanest, most ornery critter alive," in the estimation of his manager, one Red Grange—earned $2,500 and an indefinite suspension by the Missouri boxing commission for, as AP put it, "failing to offer any semblance of a fight in his 54-second swooning session in the ring here last night with Primo Carnera, immense Italian."

■ ■ ■

JOHNNY BLOOD'S 1931

Pre-1933 offensive statistics look pretty puny next to the numbers being put up today. But the season Johnny Blood had in '31—like Benny Friedman's 1929—is an exception. Blood had 10 touchdown catches for Green Bay that year. No running back has had that many since.

The NFL doesn't list receiving records by position (wide receiver, tight end, back). If it did,

Blood's would probably be the oldest offensive mark in the books. Lenny Moore came close in 1960 but finished with nine TDs. So did Billy Cannon in '61, Bill Brown in '64 and Chuck Foreman in '75. Not bad company for "The Vagabond Halfback."

Some consider Blood's Hall-of-Fame credentials suspect, but you can't take 1931 away from him. He was a wonder that season, leading the league with 78 points, intercepting six passes (one of which he took back all the way), running for two touchdowns and throwing for another. He was also the middleman on a lateral play that ended in a score. That's 14 TDs he had a hand in. *And* he punted.

Blood was simply too fast for most defensive backs of his era. Coach Curly Lambeau often put him at flanker on passing downs, and when Blood got the ball in the open field—watch out. He even had soft hands. Just a superior athlete.

The league-champion Packers played 14 games in 1931. Blood didn't catch his first touchdown pass, however, until Week 4. Counting to 10:

■ **(1) October 4 vs. New York Giants at Green Bay**—25-yard TD pass from Red Dunn in fourth quarter of 27–7 victory. The *Green Bay Press-Gazette* said, "It was a great catch by Blood and he took the ball out of the hands of a Giant back."

■ **(2, 3) October 11 vs. Chicago Cardinals at Green Bay**—Scoring passes of 40 and 15 yards, both from Dunn, in 26–7 win. On the first he leaped high in the air, took the ball away from Ernie Nevers and ran the remaining 30 yards. On the second he "raced to the far right-hand corner of the field . . . took the ball out of the air with a seemingly impossible catch, stumbled three yards and fell over the goal," the *Press-Gazette* reported.

■ **(4) October 18 vs. Frankford Yellow Jackets at Green Bay**—7-yard pass from Roger Grove for first touchdown in 15–0 victory. *Press-Gazette:* "Grove . . . shot a flat, wide pass to Blood who fell on his face catching the ball, rolled over and lunged across the goal line."

■ **(5) November 8 vs. Staten Island Stapletons at Green Bay**—40-yard TD pass from Dunn in second quarter of 26–0 romp. "There wasn't a man near him" when he caught the ball at the 20, the *Press-Gazette* said.

■ **(6) November 22 vs. Giants at New York**—Scoring pass of at least 53 yards from Dunn in first quarter of 14–10 win. *P-G:* "Blood made a leaping catch on the 35-yard line and raced to the right and down the field."

■ **(7, 8, 9) November 26 vs. Providence Steam Roller at Providence**—22-yard touchdown pass from Paul Fitzgibbon and 45- and 17-yarders from Bo Molenda in 38–7 blowout. The first came on a ball deflected by the Steam Roller's Herb Titmas.

■ **(10) December 6 vs. Bears at Chicago**—32-yard TD pass from Molenda in season-ending 7–6 loss. The second-quarter score would have tied the game, but Dunn's extra-point try missed. *P-G:* "Blood caught the ball on the five yard line, evaded Red Grange who slipped on the icy turf and dashed for a touchdown."

■ ■ ■

THE WORST SEAT IN GREEN BAY

The September 20, 1931, game between the Packers and Dodgers was only a few minutes old when Willard Bent fell from the bleachers at Green Bay's City Stadium and broke two vertebrae in his back. No one knew it at the time, but the minor commotion in the northwest stands would nearly cause the franchise's downfall two years later.

Bent, a 51-year-old alcoholic who worked part-time in his brother's sporting goods store, sued the Packers in September 1932. He claimed to be "permanently crippled" and blamed his fall on the unsafe condition of the bleachers. He wanted $20,000.

The case went to trial in February 1933 and lasted three and a half days. The Packers were represented by the law firm of starting end Lavie Dilweg. They couldn't have been too concerned. Coach Curly Lambeau attended an owners meeting in Pittsburgh and signed a couple of players in Chicago while the trial was in progress.

Both sides agreed on the circumstances of Bent's fall: He and those around him stood to watch a play. Somehow the plank serving as his seat came loose.

When Bent sat back down, there was nothing under him. He fell about 12 feet.

The real issue was whether his injuries had caused permanent damage to his spine. The Packers' attorney insisted Bent's health problems (a bad back and heart) were his own doing—he'd twice been hospitalized for delirium tremens and had an advanced case of syphilis.

Bent's attorney did what he could to paint his client in the best light. It wasn't easy.

ATTORNEY: Now . . . did you marry in December [1930]?
BENT: Yes.
ATTORNEY: Now what have been your habits in the way you drink since your marriage?
BENT: I quit.
ATTORNEY: And have you taken any drinks since?
BENT: Yes.

DECADE LEADERS

PASSING
Yards: Arnie Herber, 6,464*; Ed Danowski, 3,688; Bernie Masterson, 3,182.
Completion percentage (350 attempts): Sammy Baugh, 49.9; Danowski, 48.1; Ace Parker, 44.5.
Touchdowns: Herber, 62; Danowski, 37; Masterson, 33.
Interceptions: Herber, 78; Danowski, 42; Masterson, 35.

RUSHING
Yards: Cliff Battles, 3,613; Ace Gutowsky, 3,381*; Bronko Nagurski, 3,346*.
Yards per carry (400 attempts): Ernie Caddel, 5.0; Dutch Clark, 4.63; Nagurski, 4.59*.
TDs: Clark, 36; Clarke Hinkle, 28; Nagurski, 23.

RECEIVING
Receptions: Don Hutson, 159; Johnny Blood, 119*; Charley Malone, 114.
Yards: Hutson, 2,902; Blood, 2,232*; Malone, 1,641.
TDs: Hutson, 36; Blood, 31; Bill Hewitt, 23.

OTHER CATEGORIES
Scoring: Clark, 370; Jack Manders, 340; Ken Strong, 307.
Field goals: Manders, 38; Ralph Kercheval, 27; Armand Niccolai, 24.

*Career statistics are incomplete.

Bent must have been a pathetic figure. All his teeth had been pulled because of "rotten gums." He had only a sixth-grade education. And the effects of alcohol and syphilis were evident in his mumbled and sometimes inappropriate answers to questions.

But the trial had its lighter moments. A man named Ringer and his son had been next to Bent in the bleachers. Ringer dropped, too, but was able to break his fall by grabbing the loose plank. His son was called to testify in the hope that he could provide details of the accident.

ATTORNEY: How close was your father to you?
BOY: Right next to me.
ATTORNEY: How does it happen that your father fell without your seeing him fall?
BOY: I don't know exactly.
ATTORNEY: What were you doing?
BOY: Watching the game.

The jury found the Packers negligent but didn't consider Bent's injuries completely disabling. They awarded him $5,203.82, most of which covered lost wages.

The decision itself wasn't a problem for the Packers. It was the sudden failure of their insurance company, a victim of the Depression, that made the situation serious. The team had lost money in '31 and '32 and didn't have the funds to pay Bent *and* field a squad in '33.

On August 15, the Packers were placed in receivership by president Lee Joannes to protect the club from creditors (in particular Bent). The team's debts reportedly totaled $12,300. Joannes also made a plea for public support. Not much was forthcoming. Times were tough even in football-mad Green Bay. The Packers struggled financially throughout the season.

Eleven years earlier, the team had been saved from bankruptcy by the sale of public stock. Following the '33 season, the community got involved again. The city's leading businessmen set up a fund for the team and helped raise an estimated $15,000. Also, more stock was sold and management was reorganized to include a board of directors. Only then did the Packers put the Bent lawsuit behind them.

■ ■ ■

HIT(S) OF THE DECADE

Clarke Hinkle et al. vs. Bronko Nagurski

Clarke Hinkle made himself a reputation on September 24, 1933, by smashing head-on into Bronko Nagurski and getting up first.

"The collision knocked me back 10 yards," the Packers' Hall-of-Fame fullback told Myron Cope in *The Game That Was*. "And I sat there for a few seconds to see if I was all right. I was shook up pretty good. Then I looked over at Bronk. His nose was over on the side of his face. It was bleeding and broken in two places, I think. His hip was cracked, they say. Whether it was or not, I don't know. But he was out cold. They took him off the field, and that's the first time he'd ever been jolted."

Nagurski's hip wasn't broken, nor was it the first time the big Bears fullback had ever been *jolted*. But collisions that shook the mighty Bronk were rare. So rare they achieved a special notoriety around the league.

Hinkle's was the most famous, and one of the few that can actually be documented. He was Nagurski's counterpart on the Packers—a punishing runner and aggressive linebacker—but much smaller at 5'11", 205. (Nagurski was 6'2", 230.)

The hit occurred at Green Bay's City Stadium in the first of three games between the teams in 1933. Newspaper accounts differ on the details. Sometime in the first half, Hinkle carried around left end or over right tackle (choose one) and came together with Nagurski.

Hinkle told Cope the play was a fake punt on third down. He said he ran to his right.

"I got through a hole," he said. "I started upfield, and out of the corner of my eye I could see Nagurski coming over to really nail me to the cross. He was edging me to the sideline . . . and what he would do instead of tackling you was run right through you. . . .

"So just before I got to the sideline I cut abruptly, right back into him. I thought I might as well get it now as any other time. I caught him wide open and met him head-on."

The *Green Bay Press-Gazette* used the word "thud" to describe the sound of impact. Hinkle, the paper said, gained one yard.

Nagurski's nose was indeed broken, and he had to be assisted from the field. In various histories of the Packers, he also suffered everything from bruised ribs to a broken hip and sat out much of the season healing. In fact he played the following week, though Chicago newspapers hint that he may have worn a special mask to protect his nose.

Hinkle and Nagurski had another memorable collision November 1, 1936, in Chicago. Once again Hinkle got the better of it. The two met in a hole off left tackle in the second quarter. The impact drove Hinkle back "two or three yards," according to the *Press-Gazette*. But "as he bounced," the paper reported, "Hinkle pivoted to his right and got going again, breezing past Nagurski before the big fellow could raise a hand." The Packers fullback went 59 yards for what proved to be the game-winning touchdown.

"That's the only time in my career that the ball carrier went by me three times on the same play," Bears tackle George Musso supposedly said.

Erny Pinckert, a bruising blocking back and linebacker for Boston/Washington from 1932 to '40, is given credit for laying Nagurski low, too. His claim is a lot more difficult to prove, though.

The story is this: In a 1933 game in Boston, Redskins coach Lone Star Dietz set up a defensive play he hoped would give Pinckert a clear, running shot at Nagurski when the Bears fullback had the ball. Nothing fancy. Dietz simply told guard Jack Riley to get out of the way when he saw Bronko coming. Sure enough, Riley did and Pinckert hit Nagurski a wicked shot and put him on the bench for the rest of the first half. The Redskins used the play again in the second half, and Nagurski was put out of the game for good.

It's another of those neat anecdotes, but we couldn't find a single word to back it up in the Boston or Chicago newspapers. The Redskins upset the Bears 10–0, and you'd think something as significant as Nagurski missing most of the game would have been mentioned. Nothing.

Pinckert was a colorful and entertaining guy (as well as the brother of psychic Jeanne Dixon). Maybe he goosed the story a bit in later years.

We came across one other instance where Nagurski took his lumps. On November 1, 1931, Packers end Lavie Dilweg sliced through the Bears interference on an end sweep and leveled him. The *Press-Gazette* reported Nagurski was knocked out.

■ ■ ■

FOOTNOTE

Father Lumpkin, a bruising blocking back in the '30s, didn't wear socks. It seems Portsmouth Spartans players were responsible for supplying their own pants, shoulder pads, shoes and whites (T-shirt, supporter and socks). Tape was free. So to save a few bucks, Lumpkin would wrap his feet and ankles in adhesive, wear it for a few days and then get fresh tape.

Bears back Beattie Feathers, who in 1934 became the league's first 1,000-yard rusher, did the same thing but for a different reason. He just hated socks. It wasn't until '45 that the league made them mandatory.

■ ■ ■

FLECKENSTEIN VS. FRIEDMAN

A 1933 court case involving two NFL players helped shape the modern definition of libel. The plaintiff was Bill Fleckenstein, a lineman who spent most of his seven-year career with the Bears; the defendant was Benny Friedman, the celebrated quarterback of the Giants.

Fleckenstein sued Friedman for an article he wrote in the October 15, 1932, issue of *Collier's*. In it Friedman characterized him as a thug. The "Fleckenstein Formula," Friedman said, was "loser take all—on the chin." A sample:

"The Cleveland Bulldogs [Friedman's first team] were about unanimous after one meeting with Mr. Fleckenstein that he was a specialist at infighting during scrimmages. As a committee of one I warned him about this before our next match. But Fleckenstein went on impartially pasting when inspiration seized him. It just isn't part of the code to call the attention of officials to a rough gent who's discreet enough to slug under cover. We told Fleckenstein to his face. His reply was instant—sock upon sock."

The suit was filed in July 1933. Fleckenstein, who was retired and operating a liquor store in California, sought $12,500 in damages. Friedman was in the final full season of his career.

Pretrial maneuverings lasted four years. The trial itself started in December 1937 and lasted five days. If the depositions taken of ex-players and a game official are any gauge, it must have been entertaining.

Fleckenstein was indeed a *rough gent*. From the deposition of Robert Howard, guard for the Detroit Wolverines in 1928:

Q: Did anything unusual that you now recall, happen in that game played between the Chicago Bears and the Detroit Wolverines?

A: Yes, sir. That was the game I got my nose broken in.

Q: Well, tell us what happened.

A: [Fleckenstein] was playing left guard and I was playing right guard, and we were on offense. The Chicago Bears, of which Mr. Fleckenstein was a member were on the defense. Mr. Fleckenstein punched me in the face with his closed hand and broke my nose.

Q: Where were you when he did this?

A: I was in a half kneeling position and had one hand on the ground [he was down in his stance]. . . . I was taken from the game. Blood was streaming down both nostrils in my nose; I was temporarily blinded, I just could not see, everything went white. . . . I went to the dressing room where the trainer put absorbent cotton up my nostril and tried to stop the bleeding. . . . This occurred Sunday afternoon; it was Wednesday before my nose completely stopped bleeding.

Hall-of-Fame end Ray Flaherty testified that Fleckenstein punched him in the face during the opening kickoff of a Giants–Bears game in 1929. Later that same game, Fleckenstein was thrown out for punching someone else.

"I walked over near him and laughed at him for being put out of the game," Flaherty testified. "As I turned and started to walk away, Mr. Fleckenstein took a vicious right swing at my chin."

Several weeks later the two teams met again. After the game Giants guard Clifford Ashburn was walking off the field when Fleckenstein ran up to him and punched him in the face, breaking his nose.

"Ashburn was too startled to retaliate," the *Chicago Tribune* reported. "Had he cared to he would have to imitate a paddock [sic] to catch Fleckenstein, who ran full speed to the Bears' dugout. Others of the New York team were in pursuit but Fleck won the footrace by yards and dived head foremost for the safety of the tunnel leading to the dressing rooms."

Ashburn testified that he quit pro football because of the incident. "I was through playing football with Mr. Fleckenstein or against him," he said.

Fleckenstein's lawyers argued that the lengthy list of incidents did not prove their client had punched anyone with "contempt" or "when the officials' backs were turned," which was what Friedman had implied in his article.

The jury agreed. It found Friedman guilty of libel per se. It then turned around and awarded Fleckenstein *6 cents*. He wasn't even allowed to collect trial costs from Friedman.

Fleckenstein vs. *Friedman* established that if what was written created no worse effect in the mind of the reader than the truth, there was no damage. In other words, being close to right is OK. (The jury obviously thought Fleckenstein was a thug, too.)

The decision has been cited frequently in libel cases through the years, most notably in Israeli defense minister Ariel Sharon's 1984 suit against *Time* magazine.

THE STREAK THAT TIME FORGOT

One of the more remarkable—and least-remembered—NFL records is the Detroit Lions' seven straight shutouts in 1934. During the streak, the Lions didn't allow an opponent inside the 20-yard line. Heck, they weren't scored on until November. The shutouts came in their first seven games.

Granted, pro football was different then. But maybe not as much as you might think. By 1934 the game had emerged from the dark ages. The passing revolution, brought on by the slimmed-down ball, was underway. There were hashmarks on the field. Offenses were using men in motion.

This is a record that deserves respect. After all,

No one could score on the 1934 Lions, and now no one remembers them. They shut out
a record seven straight opponents. (Pro Football Hall of Fame/NFL Photos)

no other team since 1932 has managed more than three shutouts in a row. Take a look at some of the statistics from the Lions' streak and see if it doesn't rank with the great defensive performances of any period:

- 835 total yards allowed, or 119 per game.
- Opponents' pass completion percentage under 33.
- At least 19 interceptions (statistics are incomplete).

Who were these guys? Outside of Dutch Clark, Glenn Presnell and Ace Gutowsky, they were the original no-name defense: Father Lumpkin, Ox Emerson, Cowboy Jack Johnson, George Christensen, Chuck Bernard, Maurice Bodenger, Harry Ebding and Frank Christensen. Not exactly the Steel Curtain or Purple People Eaters.

They weren't unusually big, either. The average NFL player weighed 204 pounds in '34, and the Lions came in at about that. They had some size at tackle—George Christensen was 6'2", 240 and Johnson 6'4", 220—but Emerson played guard at 5'11", 190.

And they apparently didn't do anything fancy. Their basic defense was the 6-2-2-1, which just about everyone used at the time. Their one distinguishing characteristic seems to be that, for a while anyway, no one played it better.

The shutout streak started on September 23 against the defending Eastern Division champion New York Giants and ended November 3, when the Pittsburgh Pirates faked a punt in the first quarter and passed 62 yards for a touchdown. The Lions won the game anyway, 40–7.

They won their first 10, in fact, and were hailed in one wire story as "the perfect football team" and possibly "the greatest eleven ever assembled." But they dropped their last three—one to Green Bay, two to the Chicago Bears—by a total of nine points. The Bears finished 13–0 and took the Western Division title. The Lions settled for second place and faded into history.

Still, the shutout streak was not in vain. As much as anything, it probably helped sell pro football in Detroit. The NFL had failed three times trying to get a franchise going in the Motor City. In 1934 eccentric radio station owner George Richards took another shot when he bought and moved the Portsmouth (Ohio) Spartans.

The streak generated a lot of interest at a time when the city was going bananas over the baseball Tigers, who took the pennant for the first time in 25 years. The following season the Lions won their first NFL championship, and the franchise was over the hump.

GAME BY GAME

Game 1, September 23—Lions 9, New York Giants 0, at Detroit: The streak nearly ends before it begins when the Giants' Harry Newman breaks a kickoff return in the third quarter. Clark's open-field tackle prevents the score.

Game 2, September 30—Lions 6, Chicago Cardinals 0, at Detroit: The *Detroit Free Press* noted that center-linebacker Chuck Bernard "wore the same pair of pants as last week and consequently tackled most of the evening with one hand. He used the other to hold up a pair of trousers that were too big for him around the waist."

Game 3, October 7—Lions 3, Packers 0, at Green Bay: The Packers cross midfield only once and miss a 29-yard field-goal attempt. Presnell's NFL-record 54-yard field goal in the second quarter wins it.

Game 4, October 14—Lions 10, Philadelphia Eagles 0, at Philadelphia: The Eagles manage only eight first downs and five completions in 26 pass attempts.

Game 5, October 17—Lions 24, Boston Redskins 0, at Detroit: "If we get by these Redskins tonight, we're liable to keep on going for some time and set a record for scoreless games that no team ever will approach," says Lions coach Potsy Clark. The Lions hold the Redskins to 112 total yards and intercept four passes.

Game 6, October 21—Lions 28, Brooklyn Dodgers 0, at Detroit: The Dodgers are the first team to reach the Lions' 20 when they recover a fumble. They run three plays, lose three yards and then miss a field-goal try. The Lions limit them to 56 yards rushing, five passing and again intercept four passes.

Game 7, October 28—Lions 38, Cincinnati Reds 0, at Portsmouth, Ohio: A gimme. The Reds, in their second year in the league, scored only 10 points in eight games before the team folded. The Lions don't let them get past midfield.

Game 8, November 4—Lions 40, Pittsburgh Pirates 7, at Detroit: Pittsburgh owner Art Rooney predicts his team will be the first to score on the Lions and even names the player who will do it—tailback Warren Heller. Rooney offers Heller a cash bonus for a touchdown.

The Pirates score, but Heller's not involved. Harp Vaughan passes to Muggsy Skladany from punt formation, and Skladany goes 62 yards for the TD. Clark is right with Skladany when the pass is thrown but tries for the interception and misses. Otherwise, the Pirates don't enter Detroit territory. The Lions, meanwhile, gain an NFL-record 426 rushing yards.

AN ODE TO THE GIANTS

No team in all my memory
E'er battled on to victory
With greater vim or showed more fight,—
    (No wonder I'm inspired to write!)
Yes, all these lads, it seems to me,
Outgame their foes consistently,
Refusing to admit defeat,—
Keeping cool 'mid gridiron heat.

Fall furnishes each year, you see,
On Sundays opportunity
Of watching stars with names renowned
Try all their tricks in gaining ground.
Believe me, these boys know their stuff,
A Pro League player *must* be tough,—
Learning, even after college,
Lots of further football knowledge.

Give me a team which shows real class
In kicking and the forward pass,—
A team with such defensive skill
No foe can ever gain at will.
These football traits, I must confess,
Spell out the GIANT team's success!

—Tom McCarthy, *1934*

The Giants initiate Harry Newman in 1933. (UPI/Bettmann Newsphotos)

WEDDING BELLS

The increased stability and popularity of professional football is best illustrated by the increasing numbers of married players in the National football league. There are 74 married players in active roles with the 10 clubs, or 30 per cent of the total competing this season. The greatest number of married men can be found on the Chicago Bears. Ten of the 25 men on that squad are married.

—*Green Bay Press-Gazette, 1934*

■ ■ ■

POINT OF TOE DROP KICK

1. Accuracy rather than distance is acquired as follows: Stand with both feet parallel the right foot slightly in advance of the left. Grasp ball with palm of right hand directly underneath steadied by palm of left hand resting on top of the ball. Hold ball vertically—the lower end about two feet from the ground.

2. Preparatory to taking one step ahead with left foot which will leave the right foot in position to swing forward in kicking arc. Crouch and sight ball to make certain it is still vertical.

3. As step with left foot is taken, a slight hop off right foot is natural to some kickers. At the same time the hands are opened so as to allow the ball to slide vertically towards the ground. Keep eyes on ball.

4. Body straightens—right leg is bent at right angle at knee. Right foot is locked at right angle to leg. Ball is dropping vertically about a foot ahead of toe of left foot. Eyes are on the ball!

5. Right foot still locked at right angle to leg—swings sharply in forward arc contacting ball with toe in center of area indicated by dotted line as it rebounds from ground. Time kick to contact ball immediately after rebound. Head down, eyes on ball!

6. Leg is snapped out straight at knee as it follows through—ankle is still locked—eyes are still on the ball.

NOTE: Always crouch well when drop-kicking drop ball from lowest height that is comfortable.

DROP KICKING WITH INSTEP

1. Preparatory to this style of drop kick, stand with both feet parallel, right foot slightly in advance of the left, body bent at waist, ball held either with the palms of the hands on opposite sides or with the palm of the right hand underneath the ball and the palm of the left hand on top. The ball is held directly in front of the body, pointing down at a little less than 45 degrees.

2. Preparatory to taking the forward step with the left foot, note body lean with ball still held at an angle of a little less than 45 degrees. Be sure and keep eyes on ball.

3. Forward step with left foot has been taken leaving right or kicking foot back in position

to begin swing of kicking arc. The right leg is bent at the knee. Hands have released the ball so it is dropping at a little less than 45 degrees with the forward point down. Ball is met by instep instead of toe. Eyes remain on the ball.

4. Right leg is bent at the knee at an approximate 45 degree angle and forward swing is starting. Ball has not yet hit the ground.

5. Right foot contacts ball just as same hits the ground. The angle of the ball as it strikes the ground allows same to land lengthwise on the instep of the arched foot.

6. The right leg swings through with a snap at the knee as the leg straightens out with the follow through. Eyes still remain on the ball.

From *The Lost Art of Kicking* © 1939. (Pro Football Hall of Fame)

DROP-KICKING

The most famous kickers in pro football's beginnings—Paddy Driscoll and Fats Henry—were drop-kickers. Both are said to have drop-kicked field goals of 50 yards.

Drop-kicking's biggest advantage was that it involved only the snapper and kicker and eliminated the holder. That meant there was one person fewer to screw up and one more to block.

The drawbacks were that a drop kick usually didn't get as much distance as a place kick and wasn't as effective under bad conditions. The drop could be disrupted by a gust of wind and the whole kick thrown off if the tip of the ball got stuck in the mud. The best kickers were proficient at both methods.

When the ball was made slimmer in the '30s to open up the passing game, the drop kick's days were numbered. Kickers now had to be much more precise on their drops, otherwise the ball wouldn't be straight at the moment of impact.

A New York Giant practices the lost art of drop-kicking. (UPI/Bettmann Newsphotos)

"The longer I played, the less accurate I became," said Lions Hall-of-Famer Dutch Clark, "because the ball was getting trimmer all the time. . . . In my last year I place-kicked instead of drop-kicking, because the ball had gotten so narrow."

According to the 1938 *Spalding Guide,* Clark had the only drop-kicked field goal in '37, a 17-yarder. That's the last mention of any field goal being drop-kicked in the NFL.

In 1951 Gene Simmons, a 135-pound rookie drop-kicker from West Virginia, reportedly was in the Bears camp, but he didn't make the club. A story in the *Pittsburgh Press* said Simmons could kick accurately with either foot and "has developed the knack of holding the ball himself and place-kicking it. This he can do because he does not step forward into the kick, but merely swings his leg from a stationary position."

Said Simmons: "In case the center's snap is bad, or I fumble, or have to kick from a particularly wet spot on the field, the place-kicking comes in handy."

Arena Football in the late '80s awarded four points for a drop-kicked field goal and two for a conversion.

■ ■ ■

ALABAMA PITTS

Sing Sing Prison made its one and only contribution to the NFL in September 1935 when Edwin "Alabama" Pitts signed with the Philadelphia Eagles.

Pitts' pro football career lasted just four games. He lacked both the size and all-around ability to compete at that level. But no one went away from the league's first work-release experiment unhappy. Pitts made money. The Eagles made money. And the league got some much-needed attention.

Alabama Pitts was a hot story in the summer of '35. At age 19 he'd been arrested on a robbery charge and sentenced to about eight years in prison. By the time he was paroled in June 1935, he'd served five and a half of those years and become a three-sport legend in and around the upstate New York prison.

Pitts' baseball ability prompted the Triple-A Albany Senators to offer him a contract. But league president W. G. Bramham ruled that ex-cons weren't welcome in baseball. This touched off a debate in the local press.

"It seems to me that if a man is able to do any

legitimate work, he should be allowed to do it," said Sing Sing warden Lewis Lawes, one of Pitts' many champions.

The story went national, and Bramham eventually was overruled by the minor league's executive committee. Pitts got his crack at pro baseball that summer and was a dud. Nonetheless, when the International League season ended, Eagles owner Bert Bell was waiting with another offer: $1,500 for four regular-season NFL games and three exhibitions.

At a time when some players were still making $50 a game, that might seem an outrageous sum for an untested athlete. But there's no underestimating the NFL's need for attention in the '30s. Never mind the larger colleges in the Philadelphia area, Bell was battling the likes of Swarthmore for space in the city's newspapers. Pitts had a name, and sometimes that counted more than ability.

The Eagles certainly weren't alone in their interest. Two other NFL teams—Brooklyn and Pittsburgh—made a pitch for him. He also had a standing offer for a vaudeville tour.

But on September 10, Pitts arrived in Philadelphia. He was met at the train station and driven to the Eagles' suburban training site, where the press was waiting. Photographers clicked away as he pulled on his uniform (number 50) and answered questions. He told reporters his poor showing in the International League was due in part to night games.

"You see, where I was we didn't get out much at nights," Pitts said. "If any did, it wasn't to play ball."

Philadelphia Evening Bulletin columnist Cy Peterman remarked that Pitts "isn't physically impressive" compared to other Eagles. And he wasn't. He was 5'10", maybe 185 pounds and didn't have exceptional speed.

"If 'Bama doesn't become another Red Grange, let us not condemn," Peterman wrote prophetically. "Give him time. He's most determined."

The Eagles had been in camp three weeks, and Pitts was far behind the other players. He didn't play in the opener against the Pittsburgh Pirates September 13 but still had a dramatic effect on the game. About 20,000 fans showed up at Temple University Stadium in downtown Philly, some of whom chanted, "We want Pitts." (In 1935, 20,000 fans at an NFL game was a big crowd. The break-even figure for most owners was 10,000 to 12,000.)

Pitts didn't play in the Eagles' second game either, a 35–0 loss to the Lions in Detroit. His debut came September 26 in an exhibition against the Orange Tornadoes. He apparently carried the ball once or twice for no appreciable gain but was described by one writer as "brilliant" as a defensive back.

Two weeks later, Pitts appeared in his first NFL game. In a rematch against the Pirates in Pittsburgh, he had two interceptions in a 17–6 loss. The Eagles returned to Philly for their fourth game, against the Chicago Bears, and once again a big crowd (22,000) turned out and chanted for Pitts. He got some playing time late in the game and caught a 20-yard pass for the Eagles' longest gain in a 39–0 defeat. But that was it for Alabama. His contract was up. The following day, Bell offered him a new deal at $50 a game.

"Pitts has a bright future," Bell said. "And we appreciate that he tries all the time and eventually should be a top-flight player. But he lacks experience and needs a lot of work."

Pitts turned down the offer. He tried his hand at professional basketball. The following summer he gave baseball another try and washed out again. He eventually settled in Valdese, North Carolina, where he found work in a mill and married a coworker.

On June 6, 1941, Pitts was fatally stabbed at a local dance. It was the sixth anniversary of his release from Sing Sing.

■ ■ ■

ANOTHER ELECTION JERRY FORD LOST

The 1935 Chicago All-Star game was almost over when a player wearing a clean, gold number 23 jersey ran onto rain-drenched Soldier Field. University of Michigan center Jerry Ford had finally gotten a chance to play.

The future U.S. president went in on defense for Pittsburgh's George Shotwell, but there wasn't much he could do. The Chicago Bears quickly ran out the clock to wrap up a 5–0 victory.

Ford was probably lucky to get into the game at all. He'd been only the fourth-leading vote-getter at center in the nationwide balloting of fans. His 80,356 votes placed him behind Notre Dame's Jack Robinson (124,854), Shotwell (117,738) and Princeton's Elwood Kalbaugh (102,618).

But Robinson, the designated starter, was recovering from an appendectomy and couldn't play. Had Robinson been healthy, Ford might well have stayed on the sideline.

How good was he? Well, Wisconsin coach Clarence Spears called him "a fine defensive center" in an analysis of the collegiate team for the *Chicago Tribune*. And Michigan State coach Charles Bachman, an All-Stars assistant, said Ford played a better game against the Spartans in 1934 than Chuck Bernard had the year before. Bernard was a consensus All-American for the Wolverines.

The NFL draft wasn't instituted until '36, so we can only guess how high Ford would have gone. But at 6'1", 202, he had the size—and certainly the smarts—to play the pro game.

Footnote: One of Ford's opponents on the Bears, tackle George Musso, enjoys a unique distinction. He's the only person to play football against two U.S. presidents-to-be. At Millikin University in 1929, Musso faced Eureka College guard Ronald Reagan.

■ ■ ■

FOOTBALL CARDS

Pro football trading cards first appeared in 1935. The National Chicle Company in Cambridge, Massachusetts, published a set of 36 cards and sold them with gum. The Bronko Nagurski card is now worth $3,000, making it the most valuable football card in existence.

Paintings of the players are colorfully reproduced on the front. The pose is sometimes instructional. Boston's Cliff Battles demonstrates the stiff arm, Green Bay's Clarke Hinkle the place kick, the New York Giants' John Dell Isola the center snap and so on.

On the back is basic information about each player and tips by Redskins coach Eddie Casey. The latter give you a real feel for '30s football.

The recommended stance for a defensive lineman, for instance, is standing up, slightly crouched, with arms and hands outstretched "to ward off the charge of opposing linemen." Quarterbacks are given this advice:

"Don't wait until fourth down to punt, as a general rule, punt on third down. Then if the kick is

A facsimile of the most valuable football card in existence. (National Chickle Company, Cambridge, MA, 1935)

blocked and recovered you will have another chance, instead of losing the ball on downs inside your territory."

For halfbacks there's an analysis of the "sewing machine" running style of Brooklyn's Shipwreck Kelly. Kelly had a high knee action.

There are also references to pulling guards, the forearm shiver and a "roving centre on defense . . . stationed three or more yards behind the line"— the precursor of the middle linebacker. Pro football in those days wasn't nearly as Neanderthal as we've been led to believe.

Why National Chicle chose the players it did remains a mystery. Some were far from famous as pros. Homer Griffith (Chicago Cardinals), and Cliff Montgomery and Stan Kostka (both Dodgers) played only one NFL season.

The company also misidentified Detroit Lions star Dutch Clark as a Philadelphia Eagle. And the only coach it included was Knute Rockne of Notre Dame. But for a first attempt it was an amazingly good job.

Pro football cards weren't seen again until 1948, when two other gum companies, Bowman and Leaf, each published a set. Leaf dropped out of the business after another year. Bowman was bought in 1956 by Topps Chewing Gum, the country's biggest baseball card supplier. Topps is now number one in the pro football card field.

Little-known facts:

■ The first black player featured on a pro football card was Los Angeles' Kenny Washington in 1948 (number 8 in Bowman's series and number 17 in Leaf's). Bob Mann of Detroit also had cards that year.

■ It took three tries to spell quarterback Ralph Guglielmi's name right. He was Gugliemi in the 1959 and '60 Topps sets.

■ Johnny Unitas was the number-one card from 1959 to '63.

■ Sam Huff, Mr. Middle Linebacker, is listed as a defensive tackle in 1960. (He *did* have a defensive tackle's number—70.)

■ Ernie Davis, the 1961 Heisman Trophy winner who died of leukemia and never played in the NFL, is in the '62 set.

■ Cornerback Erich Barnes is still pictured in a Chicago Bears jersey in 1963. That was his third season with the Giants.

■ The first father and son to appear on cards were Ted Fritsch Sr. (1948) and Jr. (1973).

■ Topps put out two George Blanda cards in 1975 because his record was too long to fit on one.

■ The 1979 set is the only one that includes Earl Campbell. He's on four cards.

In 1989 NFL Properties branched out into football cards. The early returns were encouraging. Still, pro football cards have less than 5 percent of the $300-million-a-year trading card market in the United States.

■ ■ ■

KILL THE OFFICIAL!

Officiating could be a hazardous occupation in pro football's early years. Consider what happened to field judge Doc Mooney in a 1936 game between the Chicago Cardinals and Boston Redskins at Fenway Park.

The Cards, trailing 13–10, had the ball at midfield with about a minute to go when Pug Vaughn completed a desperation pass to Hal Pangle at the Boston 10. Mooney, however, ruled Pangle was out of bounds when he caught the ball, killing their comeback hopes.

Cardinals came running from every direction to protest. They were joined by a "wild-eyed, gesticulating mob" from the stands. Mooney was surrounded and pinballed from player to player. No one punched him, but that's the best that can be said for the situation. When order was finally restored, Mooney's shirt hung in tatters from his belt.

Asked about it afterward, he said, "What, my shirt? Oh, that's nothing. I've had it torn off me lots of times." The Cardinals weren't even penalized on the play.

Officials in the '30s expected such abuse. There were only three and later four of them to keep the game under control. And the penalties they had to enforce were much stiffer than today's.

Some were so ridiculous officials hesitated to call them. The result was terrible inconsistency. Clipping, for instance, was a 25-yard offense, and any penalty could be stepped off to within an inch of the goal line. Until 1941, an illegal shift cost a team 15 yards. Such losses were hard to overcome in an era of hit-and-miss passing attacks.

The granddaddy of them all was the disqualifiable offense. Before '41, fighting, punching a referee or anything that called for automatic ejection could result in a half-the-distance-to-the-goal-line penalty *from anywhere on the field.* (There was one instance of a 40-yard markoff.)

But the officiating was more than inconsistent; it was downright bad. Part of the problem was that officials generally worked college games Saturdays and pro games Sundays. The rules were similar but not the same. In the pros, for instance, the ball carrier could get up after he was knocked down as long as he wasn't in the grasp of an opponent. Referees were often accused of having a quick (translation: college) whistle.

During a 1932 game, the Packers' Cal Hubbard held up play protesting (as only a 6'2", 250-pound tackle can) the enforcement of a defensive holding penalty against the Bears. The referee, one K. Harris of Duluth, had stepped off the yardage but hadn't awarded the Pack a first down. He finally agreed to look it up in the rule book. First down, Green Bay. (Hubbard, the off-season baseball umpire, knew his rules.)

The year before, the Providence Steam Roller protested a 13–6 loss to the Cleveland Indians,

Was it good or not? This photo of Bo Russell's controversial last-minute kick to decide the 1939 Eastern Division title is inconclusive. Referee Bill Halloran called it wide, and the Redskins, 9–7 losers to New York, chased him off the field. (UPI/Bettmann Newsphotos)

claiming umpire Larry Spellman had shortened the third and fourth quarters to 10 and 11 minutes. The Steam Roller was at the Cleveland seven when Spellman ended the game.

The protest was denied, even though Providence was right. Spellman's stopwatch had broken during the game, and he'd had to use his own watch. He was only guessing at the time in the second half.

Another minus was that there were no set officiating crews or positions. This hurt coordination and made it more difficult for an official to specialize at a particular spot. And the men who were hired were not always most able—or objective. Some were recently retired players who still had strong allegiances to (and grudges against) teams. Paddy Driscoll is just one example. He retired from the Bears in 1929 and officiated the next year.

The more powerful owners, such as the Bears'

George Halas and the Giants' Tim Mara, could influence the selection of game officials and didn't hesitate to do so. They had their favorites.

In a 1938 game in Chicago, Redskins owner George Preston Marshall became incensed at the Bears' unchecked aggressiveness and at halftime demanded that referee Bobby Cahn start penalizing them. "I'm no disciplinarian," replied Cahn, a regular at Bears games. This was probably wise, since he was also 5'1½", 150 pounds.

In the late '30s, rules committee chairman Halas even arranged to have three Chicago sportswriters—Wilfrid Smith and Irv Kupcinet of the *Tribune* and Ed Cochrane of the *American*—work NFL games. At least Kupcinet had played a season with the Eagles. As for Cochrane, he "was a referee, and was changed to an umpire, then released, couldn't officiate," longtime head linesman Dan Tehan told

Hall of Fame librarian Jim Campbell in a 1975 letter. (Smith, Kupcinet and Cochrane weren't the first sportswriters to moonlight as officials, by the way. Paul Menton of the *Baltimore Evening Sun* did pro games as early as 1925, and there were probably others before him. League president Joe Carr, remember, was a former sportswriter.)

Unfortunately, the league was too busy trying to survive to make officiating a priority. To cut down on travel expenses, president Joe Carr often used local officials. Doc Mooney swung between the colleges and pros in the Boston area. Minutes before the Cardinals attacked him, they'd had a touchdown negated by another judgment call. The officiating couldn't have seemed impartial to *them*.

It wasn't until 1938 that the league hired a technical adviser—the unsung Hugh "Shorty" Ray—to do something about the situation. It's a wonder there weren't more incidents of official bashing, really.

Packers coach Curly Lambeau summed it up after a particularly brutal game against the Giants in 1937: "You can talk about great players starring and doing sensational things on the field, but poor officials can also make football history."

■ ■ ■

ROUGHING UP THE REF

■ **October 25, 1936, Polo Grounds, New York—** Field judge George Vergara needed a police escort to escape an angry group of Philadelphia Eagles after their 21–17 loss to the Giants. Vergara's controversial pass interference call late in the game led to the winning touchdown and infuriated the Philadelphia players. Their protest began immediately after the penalty when center Hank Reese kicked the ball off the field. It continued in earnest when the game ended. Reserves George Mulligan and Joe Pivarnick led an Eagle charge that caught up to Vergara at midfield. Vince Zizak reportedly threw a punch at Vergara, and police had to come to the rescue. Vergara emerged from the melee with "his tie pulled, his shirt torn and his hair mussed," according to the *New York Times*.

■ **December 4, 1939, Polo Grounds—**Referee Bill Halloran was one of the few people at the crucial Redskins–Giants game who thought Bo Russell's last-minute 15-yard field-goal attempt was no good. His decision preserved a 9–7 Giants victory and gave New York the Eastern Division title over Washington. No sooner had Halloran made his call than the Redskins rushed him, coach Ray Flaherty leading the way. As the argument raged, back Ed Justice had to be restrained. About 45 seconds remained in the game, and an uneasy truce was struck so the Giants could run out the clock. At the gun Halloran made a sprint for the locker room, but Redskins Turk Edwards, Boyd Morgan, Bob Masterson, Flaherty and Justice overtook him. According to some press accounts, Justice punched Halloran. League president Carl Storck investigated the charge but determined that the excitable Redskin had hit several fans, not the referee. "If that fellow has any conscience," Flaherty said of Halloran, "he'll never have another good night's sleep as long as he lives."

■ **September 27, 1941, Shibe Park, Philadelphia—** Red Friesell never doubted the broken leg he suffered was an accident. NFL commissioner Elmer Layden was satisfied it was, too. We only bring up the incident because the feeling wasn't unanimous. Friesell was injured in the first quarter of an Eagles–Dodgers game when he was caught in the flow of a play. The circumstances were suspicious because the Eagles had been hit with three consecutive 15-yard penalties before Friesell went down—one for clipping, one because Eagles coach Greasy Neale rushed onto the field to protest and one for fighting on the first snap after the commotion. Brooklyn owner Dan Topping and coach Jock Sutherland made it clear they thought Philadelphia had been out to get the referee. Topping put the blame on Neale. "You can quote me as saying that Greasy Neale will never be allowed to bring a team into Ebbets Field to play the Dodgers," he said. "He should never be permitted to make a burlesque of the game as he did tonight. I will have him fined if I have to go all the way to Chicago to see Layden. In my opinion, Neale incited the whole thing." Neale not only denied the charge, he protested the game, a 24–13 loss. "In all my career as a coach, I have never had as poorly officiated a game," he said after mailing 10 pages of complaints to Layden. The commissioner looked into the matter and decided Friesell had been hit by Brooklyn end Perry Schwartz, who'd been blocked into him by Eagles center Pete Bausch. (Bausch called Friesell in the hospital to see how he was doing.) In the end, Layden fined Neale and Topping $100 each for their public statements.

■ ■ ■
AN OFFICIATING CHRONOLOGY

The well-dressed NFL official in the early '30s wore "white trousers, white shirt, black [bow] tie and preferably black stockings." Those, at least, were the league's instructions in 1933. Officials that year also were told to buy "reduced rate weekend" train tickets. They were hired and paid by the home team, receiving $25 apiece.

Crews consisted of three or sometimes four men—the referee, umpire, head linesman and field judge. Each official could be identified by the initials on his arm band (R, U, HL and FJ). The field judge, stationed 20 or more yards behind the defense, had been added in 1929 as the passing game began to develop.

Either the field judge or the umpire would time the game. The timer was permitted to state approximately how much time was left when asked by the team captain, "provided he does not comply with such request more than three times during the last five minutes of either half," the 1939 rule book stated.

Only the referee had a whistle. There were no penalty flags. When an official spotted a foul, he blew a small horn worn around his wrist. Hand signals, invented by college referee Ellwood Geiges in the late '20s, were used to inform the fans (and press box) of infractions. Most were the same as they are today. One exception was the signal for unnecessary roughness. Until 1955, it was a military salute.

An official's name—"Thorp"—was on the ball. That was Tom Thorp, a head linesman from New York. His sporting goods company made the balls for a while before Spalding (and later Wilson) took over.

Officials were put in black-and-white striped shirts in 1935. Their white shirts had caused too

much confusion for teams that had the same color in their jerseys. Three years later the league finally began to get serious about officiating. A chronology of major developments:

■ **1938**—Control of the officials was taken away from the clubs and given to the league. Carr organized permanent crews (giving each member a specific job), paid them out of league funds and handled game assignments.

■ **1941**—Under new commissioner Elmer Layden, officials were given season instead of single-game contracts. Also, it wasn't announced until just before the kickoff time which crew was working the game. Numbers were put on officials' shirts this year, too. Another of Layden's ideas was to have each official wear a different-colored shirt—black and white for the referee, red and white for the umpire, orange and white for the head linesman and green and white for the field judge. This was to help spectators distinguish between them. A "circus on parade" was how veteran head linesman Dan Tehan described it. Everybody went back to black and white when Bert Bell became commissioner in '46.

$$$$

50 cents	Children's admission to Packers games in 1930
$9.73	Cost of Spalding football jersey (numbered, with pads sewn in) in 1930
$20	First prize won by Giants' Leonard "Feets" Barnum in halftime punting contest in 1938
$110	Approximate average player salary (per game) in 1934
$210.34	Winning share in the first NFL title game, 1933
$300	Rookie salary of Packers' Don Hutson in 1935 (the team paid him with two $150 checks from different banks so the veterans wouldn't find out what he made)
$1,500	What Lloyd's of London had to pay Eagles for every game QB Davey O'Brien missed due to injury in 1939
$2,000	Value of Bronko Nagurski's championship wrestling belt
$4,000	Average guarantee for visiting team in 1936
$5,203	Damages awarded Packers fan who fell out of grandstand in 1931
$50,000	Fee paid by General Mills for league radio rights, 1938
$100,000	Purchase price of Cleveland Rams in 1941
$200,000	Profit made by NFL champion Giants in 1938
$560,000	Total payroll for NFL's 10 teams in 1938

■ **1945**—The following directive appeared in the official rules for the first time: "The offending player [the one who commits the penalty] is to be designated by Referee when known."

■ **1947**—The back judge was added. He was initially called the "assistant head linesman," according to the *New York Times*. His primary job was to watch the man in motion and keep an eye out for illegal shifts. The All-America Football Conference had introduced the fifth official the previous year. For the first time, pro football had more officials than the college game. Long content to follow the colleges, the pros had begun to take a leadership role in the sport. The back judge didn't come to college ball until '55.

■ **1948**—A watershed year, right up there with 1938 and '41.

■ Crews were required to meet in their dressing room at least an hour and 15 minutes before the game for a conference on rules and mechanics led by the referee.

■ The dressing room was made off limits to coaches and owners before and after the game. Violators would be dealt with harshly. In other words, no intimidation allowed.

■ Officials started recording all penalties and submitting them to the league.

■ White penalty flags replaced horns. The latter had proved too impractical. For one thing, the sound of them sometimes caused players to ease up, knowing a penalty was coming. For another, fans were bringing similar-sounding horns to games.

■ All officials were given whistles and white caps with visors. Veteran referee Ron Gibbs, who worked 15 NFL title games, continued to make his own fashion statement. Instead of the league-issued baseball-style cap, he sported an Ivy League model.

■ **1965**—The line judge was added. Call him the Fran Tarkenton Official. Crews had been having a hard time keeping up with the scrambling Tarkenton and other quarterbacks of his type. The sixth official lightened everyone's load. He essentially assumed the responsibilities of the back judge, who moved farther downfield and became more involved with policing the passing game. Also, bright gold penalty flags replaced the white ones. They were easier to see.

■ **1970**—The scoreboard clock became the official time. It had been that way in the AFL since '62.

■ **1975**—Referees were equipped with wireless microphones. Now the whole world knew who the penalty was on.

■ **1978**—The side judge was added. His major function was to help enforce the new one-bump rule in the secondary and make the world safe for receivers.

■ **1981**—Fashion note: This was the year the referee and the referee alone began wearing a black cap with white piping.

■ **1986**—The final frontier: instant replay. The USFL had tried it on a limited basis the year before. Coaches could challenge up to three calls a game and were assessed a timeout when they were wrong. The NFL had experimented with instant replay in the '85 preseason but fell five votes short of the three-fourths majority needed to use it in the regular season. In '86, commissioner Pete Rozelle and Cowboys president Tex Schramm were able to push the measure through. It was renewed annually, though not without resistance, for the next three years.

■ **1990**—Top pay for officials is $2,100 a game.

■ ■ ■

NICE GUYS FINISH SECOND

It took Pittsburgh 42 years to get to the NFL championship game. It might have taken only four if owner Art Rooney hadn't (a) done a friend a favor, and (b) tried to make himself and his players a few extra bucks by scheduling an exhibition game late in the 1936 season.

The friend was league commissioner Joe Carr, who came to Rooney before the season with a problem. Giants owner Tim Mara had backed out of a scheduled date with the Bears in Chicago. Would Rooney consider taking the game?

Of course. Rooney never tired of being a nice guy, even if it meant letting Mara off the hook and playing the Bears twice.

The result was two lopsided losses. Ordinarily, that wouldn't mean much to the Pirates; they'd won just nine games in their first three seasons. But in '36 they surprised everyone by taking four of their first five and contending for the division crown. The extra game with the Bears hurt.

Still, the Pirates had a chance to win the East by beating the Redskins in Boston in the final game. But once again Rooney had unwittingly stacked the odds against his club. He'd filled the off weekend before the Redskins game with an exhibition against the Los Angeles Bulldogs *in Los Angeles.* The Pirates spent much of the two weeks before the Redskins game on trains and were pooped when they pulled into Boston.

This didn't make the club any less confident. Earlier in the season, the Pirates had beaten the Redskins, 10–0, and on the eve of the rematch the *Pittsburgh Press* noted the players had collected a pool of "several hundred dollars" and put a bet down on themselves. It was money foolishly spent. The Redskins won, 30–0. The Pirates had minus 2 yards rushing and 35 passing and made two first downs.

HAVE CHAMPIONSHIP GAME, WILL TRAVEL

The 1936 NFL championship game was played in New York, which wouldn't have been a big deal if the two teams involved hadn't been the Green Bay Packers and Boston Redskins. It was the only time in the pre–Super Bowl era the title game was played at a neutral site.

Boston was supposed to host it, but Redskins' owner George Preston Marshall asked for and received permission from the league to move to New York. The reason? Marshall couldn't have given away tickets in Boston.

In December 1936 the worst-kept secret in the league was Marshall's plan to move the Redskins. Rumors had him going to Washington, Buffalo or Los Angeles or merging with the financially shaky

Redskins owner George Preston Marshall made his players pose for ridiculous publicity photos like this. (UPI/Bettmann Newsphotos)

Philadelphia Eagles. In five years in Boston, he'd lost approximately $90,000 and was fed up. Which was fine, because Bostonians were fed up with him.

"About all the Boston football followers lose by the transfer of the Redskins-Packers championship game . . . is the right to stay away," *Boston Herald* columnist Bob Dunbar wrote. "While they have been exercising that privilege enthusiastically all fall, chances are they will not miss it much Sunday."

Marshall put the gun to the city's head before the season started. For four years, he'd given Boston mediocre teams and been rewarded with lousy support. But in '36 he made a determined effort to improve the Redskins' talent and hired former Giants assistant Ray Flaherty as coach. Then he nearly doubled ticket prices.

The city responded with a yawn. The Redskins won four of their first seven games but averaged less than 9,000 fans. When only 11,220 showed up for the November 8 game with the Packers, Marshall went off at the mouth.

"The nice thing about owning a pro football team is that all you have to do to move is pack your trunks," he said. "I can understand why no one came to see us play Philadelphia or the Cardinals, but when they aren't even interested in seeing a team like the Packers, it is time to consider moving. Why, the Packers would draw more people in Paterson, New Jersey, than they did here today."

Marshall also assailed the newspapers for their lack of coverage. "A little college from Whoopsis with a student body of 100 gets streamers and banners [headlines]," he said, "while we get a paragraph on the sixth page of the fourth section."

Then came the ultimatum: Turn out for the Bears game next week or else.

Only 11,200 heeded Marshall's call. It was the smallest crowd Chicago had played to all season. NFL president Joe Carr was in attendance, and as the two teams trotted onto the field to near silence, he turned to Marshall and said: "OK, George, you're right."

Clearly, the decision to dump Boston had been made. Marshall said nothing publicly because he had two more home games. (He drew less than 5,000 for each even though the Redskins were in the running for their first championship.) The Eastern Division title came down to the final game of the season between the Redskins and Giants in New York.

Though nothing had been announced, the Boston press was onto the possibility the league championship might be moved if the Redskins won. For one thing, the football bleachers at Fenway Park had been taken down. For another, the Redskins players left for New York with all their belongings. When backs Cliff Battles and Pug Rentner were stopped for speeding on their way to New York, one columnist cracked: "The sentiment shown by Battles and Rentner as they turned on the heat in their haste to leave this state is apparently shared by George P. Marshall."

The Redskins beat the Giants, 14–0, and sure enough Marshall announced afterward that he would ask the league to move the championship site. He received rubber-stamp approval two days later.

"We did it for the players' sake," Marshall explained. "They get 60 percent of the playoff gate with 20 percent going to the league and 10 percent to each club. We'll get a much bigger gate here than we would in Boston. And besides, there's the weather to consider. You know how it is in Boston this time of year."

Boston Globe writer Paul Craigue wasn't buying any of it. "I'll admit Boston is no tropical paradise at this time of year, George, but the only palms I noticed in New York over the weekend were those extended by ticket-takers," he wrote. "You noticed them, too, I guess."

On a cold and drizzly December 13, 29,545 non-aligned fans turned out at the Polo Grounds to see the Packers beat the Redskins, 21–6. The crowd was the second largest in the four-year history of the title game. Three days later, Marshall announced he was moving his team to Washington.

■ ■ ■

LET'S LET 'EM HAVE IT GOOD

Excitement gripped the nation's capital on the night of September 15, 1937. The Redskins were making their Washington debut, and Sammy Baugh was making his pro debut. To top the evening off, the opponents were the archrival New York Giants. Washington Post *columnist Shirley Povich was in the Redskins locker room before the game and recorded fiery coach Ray Flaherty's address to the team.* Reprinted with permission of the Washington Post

"Awright, you guys. You've got a football game out there in 10 minutes, whaddya gonna do about it? You're gonna lick hell out of the Giants, that's what. You gotta. You've moved into a new town [from Boston]—you and me and all of us—and the future of pro football in Washington depends on this game tonight, hear?

"You've got pretty good jobs, all of you, and me, too. And we want to keep those jobs. And that means we gotta win this ball game. Not only that, there's a helluva crowd out there tonight. They've come out to see what pro football is like. Well, show 'em. You gotta give 'em a show, too. But first, we've gotta win this football game.

"Now listen. You're damn well paid, all of you. And all we're asking from you is 60 minutes of time, once a week. But I want 60 minutes of the best that's in you. I won't take anything less. Sixty minutes of 100 percent effort. Don't worry about giving. When you get tired in there, I'll pull you out and give you a rest. We'll have plenty of substitutes. But the guys on that field have gotta produce for me and [owner George Preston] Marshall.

"Those Giants are gonna be tough tonight. You know how they hate us. And I'll tell you something. I've found out that they're out to get [blocking back] Erny Pinckert. They're still sore at him for what happened last year. Well, I want you guys to give Erny plenty of protection. I don't want anybody standing around when they start to give Erny the works. You've got hands, use 'em. You're as big as they are, and I think you're tougher. Understand?

"For three years now you guys who've been with the Redskins have been complaining that you haven't had a passer. Well, we've gone out and got you one. And I want plenty of protection for Sammy Baugh. You know damn well those Giants will be out to cut Sammy down the first chance they get and try to get him out of there. Well, what are you going to do about that? You know damn well what I want you to do. I don't want to see a Giant get to Sammy. There will be 10 guys out on the field with him. Don't let 'em get to Sammy, understand?

"There will be a lot of new men in that Giant lineup playing their first pro game. Well, you know what to do about that. You gotta scare hell out of those new guys in the first five minutes of this ballgame. You gotta hit 'em and hit 'em hard. Take all the fight out of 'em. Then it'll be easier for us. If you don't, it'll be tough. Remember that—bang into those new guys.

"This game tonight means a helluva lot to us. If the Giants take us, we might just as well forget about winning the Eastern Division championship. So, we gotta win this one. If we can get away with it, I don't see who's gonna stop us from winning in the East, and that means we'll be in the playoff against the Western champion. And after that, well, there's that easy money to be picked up in California [barnstorming]. But we gotta get this one tonight, you hear?

"I only wish [running back] Cliff Battles was in that lineup tonight. He'd have something to say about winning this ballgame. But Cliff's laid up in the hospital with that bad leg, and it's up to you guys not to let him down. It'll be tougher, but you can win without him if you go out there and play 60 minutes of football. Not 58 minutes, or 59. You can't afford to loaf a single minute or those Giants will murder you, you hear?

"Awright now, they want us out there. Come on, guys, let's let 'em have it good."

The Redskins won, 13–3.

■ ■ ■

'30s MYTHOLOGY: ART ROONEY'S BETTING BONANZA

Art Rooney bought the Pittsburgh franchise with winnings from his big killing at New York's Empire City and Saratoga race tracks.

This myth found its way into many of Rooney's obituaries in September 1988. The Steelers owner himself is at least partly responsible. He rarely spoke of the big parlay and was deliberately vague when reporters brought it up. He seemed to enjoy and appreciate the mystery that surrounded it.

"Dad had a little bit of that in him," says club president Dan Rooney. "I don't even know how much he won or many of the details."

What we *were* able to determine is that Art Rooney's legendary parlay—which supposedly netted him anywhere from $250,000 (the consensus figure) to $380,000—occurred in late July and early August 1937. He became an NFL owner in '33.

Too bad. It's a wonderful story. According to

SARATOGA CHART

Monday, July 26, 1937. First day. Weather cloudy for first three races, showery thereafter; track muddy. The horses Rooney bet on are marked with asterisks.

FIRST RACE—Purse $1,000; maiden 2-year-old colts and geldings; five furlongs and a half. Start good; won driving; place easily.

STARTERS	WT.	P.P.	ST.	1/4	1/2	STR.	FIN.	JOCKEYS	ODDS
Taken*	119	1	1	2^{hd}	$2^{1/2}$	2^3	1^{hd}	Gilbert	8-1
Dan Cupid	119	2	6	6^8	3^2	1^{hd}	2^3	Arcaro	11-5
Tedium	119	7	4	5^1	5^1	$3^{1/2}$	$3^{1/2}$	Knapp	4-1
Maefleet	114	4	5	4^{hd}	6^5	5^2	4^5	Sarno	10-1
Carbeck	119	5	2	3^{hd}	$4^{1/2}$	$4^{1/2}$	5^2	H.Richards	4-1
Easter Holiday	119	6	3	1^2	$1^{1/2}$	6^8	6^5	Pollard	4-1
Foliage	119	3	7	7	7	7	7	Bepshak	30-1

SECOND RACE—Purse $1,000; steeplechase; selling; 4-year-olds and upward; about two miles. Start good; won easily; place driving.

STARTERS	WT.	P.P.	ST.	1/2	M.	1 1/2	STR.	FIN.	JOCKEY	ODDS
Little Marty	154	6	5	3^4	3^3	3^{10}	$1^{1/2}$	1^3	Mr. Jones	9-5
Fly. Feathers	140	5	6	1^4	1^4	1^3	2^1	2no	Penrod	12-1
Garryvogne	142	7	7	6^4	6^{10}	4^5	3^{20}	3^{20}	Scott	5-1
Cireno	147	2	1	5^{10}	$5^{1/2}$	6^{20}	5^{10}	4no	Clements	10-1
Bonnie Lad	146	4	4	2^5	2^2	2^{hd}	4^{hd}	5^6	Morris	18-5
The Scaup	140	3	2	7	7	7	7	6^4	Leonard	15-1
Budget Boy	142	1	3	4^1	4^6	5^{hd}	6^4	7	Baldwin	2-1

THIRD RACE—The Columbia; purse $1,000; fillies and mares; 3-year-olds and upward; six furlongs. Start bad; won driving; place same.

STARTERS	WT.	P.P.	ST.	1/4	1/2	STR.	FIN.	JOCKEYS	ODDS
Dressy	104	6	2	1^1	1^{hd}	1^{hd}	1^{hd}	DeCamillis	10-1
Jewell Dorsett	106	2	3	3^{hd}	3^4	$2^{1/2}$	$2^{1/2}$	L.Dubois	5-1
Evening Tide	100½	7	1	$3^{1/2}$	$2^{1/2}$	3^4	3^2	Eccard	4-1
Little Miracle	115	5	4	4^5	4^5	4^5	4^6	Pollard	7-5
Whichprint	100	1	7	7	5^3	5^3	5^5	F.Jones	15-1
Janeen	107	4	6	6^{hd}	6^2	6^1	6^1	Longden	10-1
Coequel	106	3	5	5^{hd}	7	7	7	Sarno	4-1

FOURTH RACE—The Flash; $4,000 guaranteed; 2-year-olds; five and a half furlongs. Start poor; won easily; place driving.

STARTERS	WT.	P.P.	ST.	1/4	1/2	STR.	FIN.	JOCKEYS	ODDS
Maetall*	117	2	1	1^5	1^5	1^4	1^3	Longden	5-2
Now Then	117	7	5	4^4	$2^{1/2}$	2^1	$2^{1/2}$	Gilbert	4-1
aSpillway	112	1	2	2^{hd}	3^4	3^2	$3^{1/2}$	Westrope	12-1
Dauber	110	6	10	9^2	$6^{1/2}$	4^3	4^5	I.Hanford	5-1
Bucking	110	3	4	$5^{1/2}$	$7^{1/2}$	$6^{1/2}$	$5^{1/2}$	Wright	12-1
Wood Song	114	4	9	8^5	8^5	$8^{1/2}$	$6^{11/2}$	Arcaro	20-1
Pasteurized	117	8	8	7^{hd}	$4^{1/2}$	$5^{1/2}$	7^3	H.Richards	5-1
aStephen Jay	110	10	11	10^4	10^8	$9^{1/2}$	8^4	D.Dubois	12-1
Encore	110	11	7	6^{hd}	$5^{1/2}$	$7^{1/2}$	9^3	H.LeBlanc	12-1
Regal Sun	110	5	3	3^{hd}	9^2	10^{10}	10^{15}	Kurtsinger	8-1
Floragina	112½	9	6	11	11	11	11	Pollard	40-1

FIFTH RACE—The American Legion Handicap; purse $2,000 added; 3-year-olds and upward; seven furlongs. Start good; won easily; place same.

legend, Rooney was looking for an investment after winning this huge sum of money and decided to buy into the young league. Commissioner Joe Carr told him the going rate for a franchise was $2,500, and Rooney pulled a thick wad of bills from his pocket, peeled off a few, and Pittsburgh had its team.

The truth about Rooney's hot streak at the horse tracks also has been tampered with. For instance, the spree lasted longer than two days. Rooney was at Empire City for several days in late July, moved on to Saratoga for two more days and returned twice during the month-long meet.

Though he won big at Empire City, he arrived at Saratoga a virtual unknown in racing circles. He wasn't unknown long. He picked five winners on opening day and shocked the bookies by winning $100,800, according to Frank Ortell, who covered the meet for the *New York World-Telegram*.

Rooney picked a 5–1 shot in the first race, passed on the second, then won with a 13–5 horse in the fourth, a 7–5 in the fifth, a 7–1 longshot in the sixth and a 13–5 in the finale. Ortell reported that Rooney wanted to bet $2,000 on a horse called Dressy in the third race but switched to Little Miracle when he couldn't get 10–1 odds. Dressy won.

"He likes to bet fancies, hunches, on a whim, and the man is not afraid to bet," Ortell wrote. "He sends it along in a fashion that recalls the days when the old plungers used to go into action."

Suddenly people wanted to know who Rooney was. Ortell identified him as "the pudgy owner of the Pittsburgh professional football team" and a friend of Giants owner Tim Mara, who was a legal bookie and one of the Saratoga commissioners. *New York Journal American* columnist Bill Corum picked up the story at this point and supplied more details.

"We always wanted to know what a fellow who had won a hundred grand on the races would do with his evening," Corum wrote. "Rooney met Jack Mara [Tim's son] at a picture show in Lake Lucerne, and when the show was over said: 'Let's go some place and have a dish of ice cream.'

"That's what ruins those fast-gaited guys. Nibbling at ice cream at 9:30 at night, when sober, hard-working folk are in the shucks."

Corum furnished more information about the streak, too. He said Rooney had won $19,000 on his last day at Empire City despite dropping $20,000 on one race (he'd put it all on an 8–1 shot called Erickson). On the second day at Saratoga, Corum reported that Rooney picked winners in the first four races to go up $23,000. But at this point the Artful Plunger cooled. He put $10,000 on each of the next three races and lost.

"When I saw him a few minutes ago," Corum wrote, "he was peering into the gloaming toward the west. In that direction lies Pittsburgh."

But Rooney was far from finished. The following week, Ortell reported: "That man is back again. Art Rooney, the turf's most daring plunger around today, who clipped the bookies for more than a hundred grand last week, returned yesterday to belt the layers for another $50,000."

This time Rooney made it all on one play, a 6–1 longshot called Time Signal in the first race. When he placed his bets, the bookies cut the odds on the horse to 2–1, according to Ortell. Word was out.

By then the legend had taken on a life of its own. One story making the rounds at Saratoga was that Rooney tried to lay $2,000 on a horse called Count Stone when he was at Empire City. The bookmaker refused to take it because he thought Rooney "knew something."

"I'll tell you what I'll do to prove I have no ace in the hole on the race," Rooney told the bookie. "I'll toss a coin to determine whether I shall play Count Stone or Jimmy Cabaniss [another horse]."

Rooney flipped the coin and wound up putting his money on Jimmy Cabaniss. Count Stone won. It was said that Rooney "didn't bat an eyelash." The great plungers never do.

Assuming Ortell's and Corum's figures are accurate, Rooney won $162,800 in just four days. That leaves a number of other days unaccounted for. Rooney's actual winnings could be considerably higher or lower. We'll probably never know.

We do know Rooney loved to gamble, on just about anything. In 1938 Brooklyn Dodgers owner Dan Topping acquired fullback Scrapper Farrell from him in a straight cash deal. The final price was determined by a coin flip between Rooney and former Dodgers back-owner Shipwreck Kelly. Rooney won, and Topping had to pay an additional $500.

■ ■ ■

FIFTH RACE—The American Legion Handicap; purse $2,000 added; 3-year-olds and upward; seven furlongs. Start good; won easily; place same.

STARTERS	WT.	P.P.	ST.	1/4	1/2	3/4	STR.	FIN.	JOCKEYS	ODDS
Jay Jay*	117	8	1	7^4	$6^{1\frac{1}{2}}$	$4^{1\frac{1}{2}}$	$1^{1\frac{1}{2}}$	1^5	H.Richards	8-5
Sgt. Byrne	118	6	2	3^{hd}	4^1	3^{hd}	$2^{1\frac{1}{2}}$	2^4	Gilbert	5-1
Advocator	106	5	7	8	8	7^2	7^4	$3^{1\frac{1}{2}}$	Longden	15-1
Rebellion	109	2	3	$1^{1\frac{1}{2}}$	1^1	1^1	3^2	4^2	B.James	10-1
Orientalist	110	3	6	$6^{1\frac{1}{2}}$	$5^{1\frac{1}{2}}$	6^2	$5^{1\frac{1}{2}}$	5^{hd}	Kurtsinger	5-1
Ferryboat	109	4	4	$4^{1\frac{1}{2}}$	$3^{1\frac{1}{2}}$	5^2	6^1	$6^{1\frac{1}{2}}$	Sarno	30-1
Crossbow II	116	1	5	$2^{1\frac{1}{2}}$	2^{hd}	2^{hd}	$4^{1\frac{1}{2}}$	$7^{1\frac{1}{2}}$	Arcaro	4-1
Mower	113	7	8	5^{hd}	7^3	8	8	8	Wall	6-1

SIXTH RACE—Purse $1,000; maiden 2-year-old colts and geldings; five furlongs and a half. Start bad; won driving; place same.

STARTERS	WT.	P.P.	ST.	1/4	1/2	STR.	FIN.	JOCKEYS	ODDS
Quick Devil*	119	5	4	4^2	2^2	$1^{1\frac{1}{2}}$	1no	Longden	6-1
Spring Melody	119	6	7	6^1	3^3	$2^{1\frac{1}{2}}$	2^2	Gilbert	5-1
Censor	119	4	5	3^{hd}	$4^{1\frac{1}{2}}$	4^1	3^1	Wright	15-1
Pernie	119	12	3	1^1	$1^{1\frac{1}{2}}$	3^1	4^2	Pollard	9-5
At Play	119	2	2	$5^{1\frac{1}{2}}$	6^1	$5^{1\frac{1}{2}}$	5^{hd}	Wall	20-1
Play Gold	119	3	1	2^3	5^1	$6^{1\frac{1}{2}}$	6^{hd}	Coucci	15-1
Spring Meadow	119	8	9	8^4	$8^{1\frac{1}{2}}$	8^1	7^4	Peters	4-1
Prince Cloud	119	9	6	$7^{1\frac{1}{2}}$	7^1	7^2	8^8	Westrope	15-1
Big Victory	119	7	10	10^5	10^3	9^1	$9^{1\frac{1}{2}}$	Shultz	30-1
Jubal Junior	119	11	8	9^5	9^2	10^4	10^6	H.LeBlanc	30-1
Maebeau	119	10	11	11^{15}	11^{15}	11^{15}	11^{15}	Arcaro	12-1
Lone Gallant	119	1	12	12	12	12	12	H.Richards	15-1

SEVENTH RACE—Purse $1,000; claiming; 3-year-olds and upward; Wilson Mile. Start good; won easily; place same.

STARTERS	WT.	P.P.	ST.	1/4	1/2	3/4	STR.	FIN.	JOCKEYS	ODDS
Quel Jeu*	114	4	3	3^2	2^4	1^1	1^3	1^5	H.Richards	5-2
Twice	114	5	7	8	6^1	$4^{1\frac{1}{2}}$	2^2	2^3	Arcaro	5-1
P'pey's Squaw	109	3	6	$1^{1\frac{1}{2}}$	1^3	2^3	3^1	3^{hd}	Merritt	6-1
Stocks	106	2	5	$4^{1\frac{1}{2}}$	3^{hd}	3^1	4^5	4^4	F.Jones	10-1
Buttermilk	104½	1	1	$2^{1\frac{1}{2}}$	4^3	5^2	5^3	5^1	Seabo	15-1
Sunanair	114	7	8	6^1	$7^{1\frac{1}{2}}$	7^5	6^2	6^6	B.James	5-2
Bootmaker	111	3	4	$7^{1\frac{1}{2}}$	5^{hd}	$6^{1\frac{1}{2}}$	7^5	7^2	Kurtsinger	5-1
Bulwark	106	6	2	5^{hd}	8	8	8	8	Schraud'ch	6-1

A TEAM AHEAD OF ITS TIME: THE 1937 L.A. BULLDOGS

Pro football wasn't ready for the 1937 Los Angeles Bulldogs. It *still* might not be ready. Undefeated champions of the American Football League and L.A.'s first major league team, the razzle-dazzle Bulldogs would make the Run-and-Shoot look like Three Yards and a Cloud of Dust.

Lateral plays, *double* lateral plays, reverses, spinner plays—they had 'em all. Their basic offensive set was the Henderson spread, in which the ends were split out so far, they "almost climb into the lower stands," a New York newspaper said. They also had a kickoff return play known as the "befuddle huddle." The *Los Angeles Times* described it:

"Howard caught the ball on his 3 and ambled to the 15, where all of the Bulldogs converged. . . . With each player bent over as if he had the ball, the Bulldogs broke out of the huddle and went flying down the field. The Tigers were just as startled as were the fans. Nobody knew he had the ball until finally everybody saw Moore streaking along at midfield. He was finally downed on the Rochester 38, from where the Bulldogs marched to a touchdown."

To football fans in 1937, accustomed to tight formations and a grind-it-out game, the wide-open Bulldogs must have seemed like players from another planet. But they were earthlings, every one of them. Unfortunately, not many people caught their act. The AFL—the second AFL—went under at the end of the season, and the Bulldogs went back to the Pacific Coast Football League.

Their AFL affiliation shouldn't be held against them, though. The Bulldogs were an NFL-caliber club. The previous season they had gone 3-2-1 against NFL teams that had come to the West Coast. In 1937 they were even better. They added half a dozen NFL veterans—halfback Al Nichelini, center Bernie Hughes, guard Pete Mehringer and tackle Harry Field from the Chicago Cardinals and tackles Steve Sitko and Gail O'Brien from the Boston Redskins.

The '37 roster included 12 players with NFL experience and six more who would later play in the league. The Bulldogs tried to get into the NFL but were turned down because L.A. was too far away. They outclassed their AFL competition, winning all eight games by an average score of 27-9.

The brains behind this breathtaking bunch was a man called "Gloomy Gus." Elmer Henderson, inventor of the Henderson spread, had been a successful coach at Southern Cal and Tulsa before taking over the Bulldogs in 1936. He ran them like a college team, as the *Rochester Democrat and Chronicle* reported:

"The daily routine of the Bulldogs is based on college principles. There is a set time for arising in the morning. Only special foods are allowed at the training table—at home and on the road. The players always travel in one group and never are allowed to separate without special permission from Coach Henderson.

"Their uniforms are closely similar to those of the Golden Bears of California [blue and gold]. Practice sessions begin with a series of calisthenics and a short talk by the coach.

"Each workout . . . is marked by the pep and enthusiasm often displayed by freshmen in their first engagement of the season with the varsity. There is no 'let down.' Each man does his job and does it well—or else."

Said business manager Harry Meyers: "When 10 o'clock rolls around each night those sheets feel good to the boys. They're up at 7:30 and at the field an hour later."

It was a unique group of guys. Bob (Poi) Miller punted barefooted. Tackle Jerry Donnell played bareheaded. Ed Stark, a 5'11", 165-pound "hula-hipped" halfback, had the nickname "Crazylegs" before Elroy Hirsch did. Henderson would often let a player who scored a touchdown attempt the extra point, just for the heck of it. In one game, five different players gave it a whack.

"Football for the Fans" was the Bulldogs' advertising approach—and they delivered. Take their game against the Boston Shamrocks at L.A.'s Gilmore Stadium, the one the *Times* called "the most fantastic football game you'll ever hope to see." That statement may still be true.

In the first quarter at the Boston 44, the Bulldogs' Bill Howard passed to Nichelini, who lateraled to Sinko, who lateraled to Donnell. Touchdown.

In the second quarter the Shamrocks tried a lateral play themselves, but they botched it and the Bulldogs' Cal Clemens scooped up the ball at the L.A. 44. Clemens lateraled to Gordon Gore. Gore chugged to the Boston 12 and fumbled. Davie Davis recovered and ran the rest of the way for another TD.

In the fourth quarter at the L.A. 21, Howard handed to Nichelini on a reverse. Nichelini lateraled to Bill Moore, who ran the last 67 yards.

Final score: Los Angeles 45, Boston 26.

"I think we can score on anybody," Henderson said.

(He created a monster. Two scoreless plays into the Bulldogs' last game, some jokester in the stands shouted, "We want a touchdown!")

Gloomy Gus got a shot in the NFL with the Detroit Lions in 1939. He even brought four of his L.A. players with him. Though not nearly as adventurous as the Bulldogs had been, the Lions surprised the league by winning six of their first seven games. But they lost their last four, and Henderson was fired in the off-season because of a draft day foul-up.

Oh, well, it was fun while it lasted.

■ ■ ■
GAYNELL TINSLEY

Gaynell "Gus" Tinsley didn't play long enough to be much remembered today. His NFL career lasted only two and a half seasons, and you'd never know from his lifetime totals (93 receptions, 1,356 yards, 14.6-yard average, 7 touchdowns) that he was considered in a class with Don Hutson.

He didn't have quite as much speed as Hutson. Who did in the 1930s? But he ran like a halfback after the catch. In his rookie season with the Chicago Cardinals he scored a 97-yard touchdown. The next year he had a 98-yarder. Those were the two longest TD receptions in league history up to then.

A sturdy 6'1", 195 pounds, Tinsley was a genuine phenom. In the 1937 College All-Star Game, fresh off the Louisiana State campus, he caught a 47-yard touchdown pass from Sammy Baugh to give the collegians a 6-0 victory over the defending champion Packers. He also reportedly put Arnie Herber, Green Bay's Hall-of-Fame quarterback, out of the game in the second half.

"Tinsley . . . is everything they have so long said about him," Packers coach Curly Lambeau said. "His coordination, his sidestepping and his speed in the [touchdown] run . . . was one of the finest pieces of individual play I have ever seen."

In his third pro game, Tinsley became the third NFL player to catch three TD passes in a game. He did it against the team that would win the title, the Redskins.

"We knew he was good," Washington coach Ray Flaherty said, "but we hadn't prepared for anything like he turned out to be."

Tinsley finished the season with 675 yards receiving, a league record (and 123 more than Hutson). The following year he tied Hutson's record of 41 catches. And he did it for a team with little else in

the way of offensive weapons. The '38 Cardinals were shut out four times.

But in 1939 Tinsley began having problems with management. Early in training camp he threatened to take a coaching job if he wasn't paid more. (The lucrative deal signed by back Marshall Goldberg, the team's top draft pick, might have had something to do with it.) The Cards capitulated.

Shortly afterward, new coach Ernie Nevers accused Tinsley of not putting out in practice. Tinsley walked out. He spent the season coaching the high school team in his hometown of Haynesville, Louisiana. Without him, the Cardinals went 1–10.

The Cards had yet another coach in 1940, Jimmy Conzelman, and he helped coax Tinsley into returning. But Gus didn't report until a few days before the opener. After sitting out a year, he really needed more work than that.

His subsequent play made that plain. He had just 16 receptions for a 10.3-yard average and one touch-

NICKNAMES

Alphonse "Tuffy" Leemans	Eddie "King Kong" Kahn
Arthur "Tarzan" White	Mort "Devil May" Kaer
John "Popeye" Wager	George "Sunny" Munday
Paul "Socko" Szakash	George "Automatic" Karamatic
Bill "Knuckles" Boyle	Edgar "Eggs" Manske
Charles "Pug" Vaughn	Charles "Buckets" Goldenberg
Clarence "Ace" Parker	Byron "Pills" Gentry
Byron "Whizzer" White	Max "Bananas" Krause
Arnie "Flash" Herber	Glenn "Wackie" Frey
Clyde "Cannonball" Crabtree	James "Goofy" Bowdoin
Elvin Hutchinson, "The Red Oak Express"	Dave "Nubbin" Ward
	Joe "Midnight Express" Lillard
Henry "Honolulu" Hughes	Carl "Moon Eyes" Littlefield
Jim "Sweet" Musick	Roy "Father" Lumpkin
Clarence "Dimp" Halloran	Bill "Sidecar" O'Neill
Taldon "Tillie" Manton	Elvin "Kink" Richards
Frank "Toadie" Greene	Howard "Screeno" Bailey
Ken "One Round" Hauser	Cliff "Gyp" Battles
Al "Big Un" Rose	Ben "Scaggie" Ciccone
"Iron" Mike Mikulak	Lyle "Hoot" Drury
Glen "Turk" Edwards	Joe "Muggsy" Skladany
Ross "Timber Beast" Carter	Joe "Mink" Kresky
Maurice "Mule" Bray	**Not Nicknames:**
Grover "Ox" Emerson	Seaman Squyres
Albert "Man 'O War" Johnson	Marger Apsit

down. In the eighth game he tore ligaments in his left knee tackling Cleveland Rams star Parker Hall. The next day he turned in his uniform—forever. He was 25.

"The loss of Gaynell Tinsley . . . is not a crushing blow to the Cardinals," the *Chicago Tribune* said. "Tinsley was not able to get in shape after a year's layoff and had been of little value to the club. After reporting late, Tinsley discovered a season of inactivity had left him susceptible to muscle strains in his legs."

Ah, what might have been. . . .

• • •

THE ONE AND ONLY HUGO BEZDEK

Only one man has ever been an NFL head coach *and* a major league manager: Hugo Bezdek.

Bezdek, Czechoslovakian-born, held the baseball job first. Pittsburgh Pirates owner Barney Dreyfuss hired him in mid-1917 to replace Nixey Callahan. It caused quite a stir. Bezdek was head football coach at the University of Oregon at the time and had never played pro baseball. But he had impressed Dreyfuss with his work as a West Coast scout, the Pirates were deep in last place and, well, things were different then.

Pittsburgh played better than .500 ball under Bezdek the next two seasons, but he left the major leagues to become head football coach and later athletic director at Penn State. Football was his true

calling. He learned the game from Amos Alonzo Stagg at the University of Chicago and had five undefeated and two Rose Bowl teams at Arkansas, Oregon and Penn State.

He's even credited with inventing—accidentally—that single-wing staple, the spinner play. It reportedly happened one day when his tailback turned to hand the ball off, found no one there, spun around and ran the other way for a touchdown.

After being ousted as Penn State AD, Bezdek, 53, signed a three-year contract in 1937 at the age of 53 to coach the Cleveland Rams of the NFL. The Rams were an expansion team, and it figured to take that long to build a winner. But he lasted just 14 games, a victim of bad players, meddlesome management and perhaps his own conservatism.

When the Rams went 1–10 in his first season, the owners tried to get Bezdek to resign. He wouldn't, so they punished him. They forced an assistant coach—their man—on Bezdek. They interfered with personnel decisions and told one player to sit next to Bezdek on the bench and suggest plays and substitutions. During another game, the team president sat at Bezdek's side, sending in subs.

The owners wanted Bezdek to open up the offense to attract more fans. He told them the team had to run the ball better first, otherwise it wouldn't be able to throw effectively. Finally, after an 0–3 start in 1938, he was fired. The players, many of whom had come out in support of him, bought him a watch as a going-away present.

• • •

FIGHT OF THE DECADE
Redskins vs. Bears, 1937 Championship Game

It all started when Bears end Dick Plasman threw a left hook at the Redskins' Sammy Baugh midway through the last quarter. Baugh, playing defense, had ridden Plasman out of bounds near midfield after a 35-yard gain and "seemed to be very active" doing it, a Chicago paper said. But then, Baugh already had a swollen knee, sore hip and bloody hand thanks to the *very active* Bears.

BEZDEK AS A MANAGER
Pittsburgh Pirates

YEAR	W	L	PCT.	PLACE
1917	30	59	.337	8th*
1918	65	60	.520	4th
1919	71	68	.511	4th
Totals	**166**	**187**	**.470**	

BEZDEK AS A HEAD COACH
Cleveland Rams

YEAR	W	L	PCT.	PLACE
1937	1	10	.091	5th*
1938	0	3	.000	—
Totals	**1**	**13**	**.071**	

*last place

The mistake Plasman made was throwing the punch in front of the Redskins bench. The bench responded like a bees' nest under attack. Plasman was swarmed under, pummeled and kicked. His teammates rushed to his aid. Redskins guard Ed "King Kong" Kahn soon found himself "prying somebody's foot out of my eye."

Fans spilled onto the field, encircled the area and threatened a riot. It was about three minutes—the length of one boxing round—before police and Wrigley Field ushers got things under control. When the last of the bodies was unpiled, there was Redskins trainer Roy Baker on top of massive Bears tackle Joe Stydahar, banging away at his face and reportedly trying to bite him.

Plasman came away from the fracas with a bloody nose, a gashed lip and puffy eye. Baugh suffered no additional damage. He won the game, too, completing 18 of 33 passes for a record 354 yards and three touchdowns as the Redskins pulled a 28–21 upset.

HONORABLE MENTION

Packers vs. Cardinals at Wrigley Field, November 5, 1933—Enraged by a fumble ruling, Packers tackle Cal Hubbard took a swing at referee George Lawrie. He missed and hit a Cardinals player, starting a brawl.

"In two minutes Hubbard and [Cards guard Phil] Handler started to shadow box, in three minutes some of the crowd broke out on the field, in four referee George Lawrie reversed his decision, and in five the town coppers finally arrived all out of breath," the *Milwaukee Journal* reported.

■ ■ ■

HIGH-TECH TOES

In 1938 Lions player-coach Dutch Clark introduced a square-toed "over shoe" for place-kicking. Players could slip it on and off as needed.

The square-toe was nothing new—Pottsville's Charlie Berry had made it famous in the '20s. But convenience was. With Clark's little device, you didn't have to change shoes to kick.

Typical of the times, the stodgy college coaching fraternity reacted negatively to Clark's innovation.

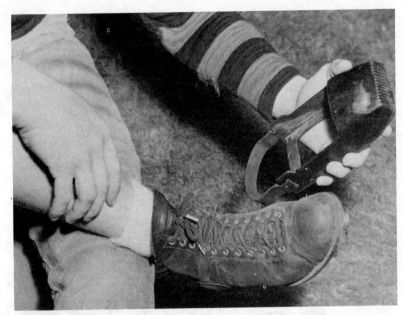

The square-toed "overshoe" for place-kicking developed in the 1920s. (UPI/Bettmann Newsphotos)

Gus Dorias of the University of Detroit saw it as the beginning of the "mechanization" of football.

"If such boots are given a place in football, we will eventually have mechanical aids for every phase of the game," Dorias said, presumably with a straight face. "Why, one can even visualize slingshots for forward passes!"

■ ■ ■

WOE IS WHIZZER

Byron "Whizzer" White on the burden of being the NFL's highest-paid player as a rookie in 1938:

"You know, I've been exhibited like a freak since I signed up with the [Pittsburgh] Pirates. Not that I'm complaining. If I paid a player $15,000, I would exploit him to the hilt, too. But it's tough to play your best game when you feel that nothing short of a 50-yard run or a 75-yard pass will satisfy the customers.

"I find myself pressing all the time in an effort to live up to my reputation. I try not to, but I can't help it. You know as well as I do that no player ever was as good as my publicity made me out to be. Well, maybe Dutch Clark is. But I'm no Dutch Clark."

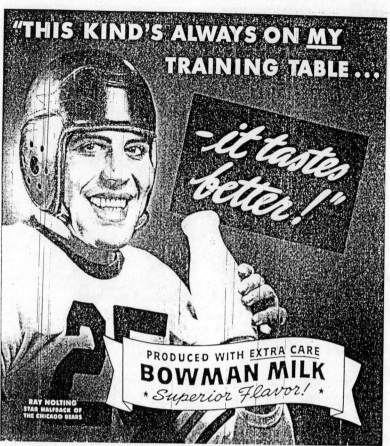

"THIS KIND'S ALWAYS ON MY TRAINING TABLE...

it tastes better!"

PRODUCED WITH EXTRA CARE
BOWMAN MILK
★ *Superior Flavor!* ★

RAY NOLTING
STAR HALFBACK OF
THE CHICAGO BEARS

(Dean Foods Corporation)

I DON'T TOUCH THE STUFF

Bears back Ray Nolting was allergic to milk, but that didn't deter Bowman's Dairy from using him as a pitchman in 1938. He made $35 every time the ad appeared in one of the Chicago dailies, which was big money then.

The original ad pictured him with pinky extended, but the company didn't think the image was right and had it redone. Note the fine dental work in that upper bridge.

● ● ●

HAIR TODAY, GONE TOMORROW

If there was a hall of fame for facial hair, Ace Parker would be in that, too.

Parker was the first NFL player in the modern era to appear in a game with a mustache. We think. A wire story in the *Brooklyn Eagle* on October 12, 1938, heralded the growth under the headline "Shades of 1898!" It stated that the Dodgers' all-around star "will officially become the first mustached big league football player" in Sunday's game against the Green Bay Packers.

He apparently had started the 'stache the previous week "just for fun." But when he gained 103 yards rushing and threw a 54-yard TD pass to lead the Dodgers past the Pittsburgh Pirates . . . well, you remember what happened to Samson.

The trouble is there's no mention of a mustache in the Dodgers–Packers game stories. For all we know, league president Joe Carr ordered Ace to shave before taking the field.

One thing seems certain: The hair on his upper lip didn't last long. Green Bay gave Brooklyn a 35–7 going-over. Parker was the superstitious type.

Only a handful of players in the '20s wore mustaches. Hartford's Dutch Webber, the Giants' John Alexander and Kansas City's Horace Randels were three we came across. In the days before facemasks, it was just one more thing for an opponent to grab and pull.

● ● ●

GREAT WORK IF YOU CAN GET IT

An IRS agent caught two people in the Giants ticket office scalping tickets to the 1938 championship game. One was Helen Mara, niece of owner Tim Mara; the other was a college student named Charles Chaplin.

The agent, who had posed as a ticket broker, testified that Chaplin added a $10 service charge. An *untaxed* $10 service charge. Tim Mara claimed it was "nothing worse than perhaps a mathematical error on the part of a 21-year-old boy whose honesty I do not question."

The day after the arrests were reported, the *New York Times* ran four letters complaining about the team's ticket policy and the unavailability of decent seats.

The Giants were fined $800. Helen Mara and Charles Chaplin were placed on probation for a day and had their sentences suspended. The judge said the embarrassment they had suffered was enough punishment.

The following year Chaplin became part owner of the Detroit Lions.

■ ■ ■
PLAYING HURT

Remember the fuss raised during the 1988 playoffs when Seattle nose tackles Joe Nash and Ken Clarke took turns faking injuries to slow down Cincinnati's no-huddle offense? Well, that was amateur hour compared to what George Halas and the Chicago Bears pulled in 1938.

During the final two minutes of three consecutive games, the Bears faked a total of 27 injuries to stop the clock. The combined six minutes of playing time took nearly an hour to complete, according to the *Chicago Daily News. An hour.* And this was in the days before television dragged the game out.

"If all the Bears who had been helped, dizzy and staggering from the field in those six minutes had actually been hurt," the *Daily News* said, "Coach George Halas wouldn't have enough able-bodied men left to start a tiddle-de-winks match."

The flow of traffic to and from the Bears bench was so great that Halas had a system in place to make the scam work smoothly. As the newspaper described it: "The end of each play in these time crises finds a player sprawled on the sod and a sub warmed up on the sidelines ready to rush in."

Halas outfoxed himself against the Packers. Two Bears went down on a play, and one of them—guard Danny Fortmann—was really hurt. But by the time

Players actually blocked like this in the '30s. It's a wonder there wasn't an outbreak of hoof-and-mouth disease. This style of blocking was called the Indian Block. (Rae Crowther/Eve Morgenstein)

anyone discovered it, Halas' warmed-up sub had already checked into the game for the other Bear. Fortmann had to hang in there.

Halas' tactics might have created more of a problem had the Bears been able to win any of the games (Cleveland beat them 23–21, Detroit 13–7 and Green Bay 24–17). As it was, the owners legislated against such tactics at the '39 league meeting.

The "Halas rule" is in effect today and allows a team one extra timeout for injury during the final two minutes of either half. Each subsequent injury timeout results in a five-yard penalty.

■ ■ ■

This is the face of early pro football. Pictured is Cal Hubbard, Hall-of-Fame tackle, in his last season with the Giants in 1936. Hubbard played 45 minutes that day, earning $150, in a rainy, muddy 25–7 loss to the Chicago Bears at the Polo Grounds. (Peter Stackpole/*Life* magazine © 1936 Time Inc.)

SID LUCKMAN, MINOR LEAGUER

George Halas' preoccupation with victories and profits sometimes clouded his judgment. Like the time he loaned Hall-of-Fame quarterback Sid Luckman to the Bears' minor league farm club for a playoff game.

This was in 1939, Luckman's rookie year. Chicago had just concluded a second-place season. The Newark (New Jersey) Bears, however, had a game coming up against the Wilmington (Delaware) Clippers for the division title. The two teams had finished tied for first.

The Newark club, which Halas had bought 60 percent of that year, was running in the red. The added attraction of Luckman would boost ticket sales. A win, moreover, would give Newark another home game—against the Paterson (New Jersey) Panthers for the American Pro Football Association title. That meant even more money.

So Halas sent Luckman, his starting QB, to the minors. Wilmington was the Washington Redskins' farm team, and Halas always enjoyed tweaking George Preston Marshall. Newark coach Gene Ronzani even tried unsuccessfully to talk Chicago fullback Joe Maniaci into playing.

Wilmington played the game under protest. According to league rules, a player had to be a member of a team for at least two weeks to be eligible for a championship playoff. But the APFA commissioner ruled for Newark. It wasn't a championship game, he said, only a game to determine a division winner.

Luckman did his job. The biggest crowd of the season came out—14,000. Late in the game, he threw a 15-yard touchdown pass to "Cowboy Dick" Schweidler to give Newark a 13–6 victory.

But from the sound of things, Luckman was lucky to get out alive. Newspaper accounts say he got off only eight passes because the Clippers were coming so hard. When the final gun sounded, there was a free-for-all involving several players and several hundred fans. The mounted police finally broke it up.

In the Newark locker room, end Charlie Heileman displayed an opponent's teeth marks in his side. Luckman called it "the roughest" game he had ever played in.

THE RAIN IN PHILLY

In the 1930s, even into the '40s, NFL games were postponed because of bad weather. The badness of the weather was usually determined by the number of people sitting in the stands. This, after all, was in the days before television. The gate was everything.

Eagles owner Bert Bell, struggling to make a go of it in Philadelphia, postponed his 1939 opener against the Steelers for the flimsiest of reasons: *threatening* weather. The *Evening Bulletin* cracked: "a dark cloud passed over the sky somewhere north of Manayunk."

The same day at Shibe Park, the Athletics played a doubleheader against the Red Sox and held an old-timers game in-between—21 precipitation-free innings. The attendance was 23,235. That may have been what Bell found threatening.

Three weeks later, he wanted to postpone a game against Brooklyn at Municipal Stadium. It was pouring out, and he figured to lose money. But Dodgers owner Dan Topping, who had come down to the game with several friends, refused.

"[Coach Potsy] Clark said he felt it would have been unwise to postpone the game because people might get in the habit of having games called off at the last moment and stay away for that reason," the *Brooklyn Eagle* reported.

So they played the game and nobody scored. The Dodgers got only one first down. A crowd of 1,880 suffered through the sloppy exhibition. Bell took an $11,600 mudbath.

(In Washington, the Redskins and Giants played under similar conditions with the same result—a 0–0 tie. But no thought was given to rescheduling that game, not with 26,341 tickets sold.)

Bell's and Topping's difference of opinion "engendered one of the strongest owner feuds that the National League has ever known," the *Bulletin* said. The next time the teams played, Bell was rumored to have threatened his players with fines or suspensions if they didn't beat Brooklyn. They lost anyway, 23–14.

But Bell got even the next year. He used rainy weather as an excuse to postpone his last home game, against the Steelers, and move it to Thanksgiving Day, four days later.

There was only one problem. The Eagles had to play in Washington the Sunday after Thanksgiving. With only two days' rest, they would be in no shape to upset the Redskins. And who would this hurt most? The Dodgers, who were a game behind the fading Redskins in the Eastern Division standings.

When Topping heard the Eagles weren't playing, he immediately phoned NFL president Carl Storck to lodge a protest. (The rain didn't stop the Dodgers that day. They defeated the Cardinals, 14–9, at Ebbets Field.) Topping told Storck the Eagles–Redskins game should be played before the Eagles–Steelers game because of its importance in the race. Storck agreed and postponed the Eagles–Steelers game indefinitely.

The next day he changed his mind—or had it changed for him. It's hard to believe Redskins owner George Preston Marshall didn't play a part in Storck's about-face. There was nothing, however, in the rules to prevent a team from playing two games in four days.

The Eagles drew only 4,200, their smallest crowd of the season, for the Thanksgiving Day game. They shut out the Steelers, 7–0, for their first victory. Then they went to Washington and put up a surprisingly good fight before losing, 13–6.

The Redskins were in the championship game. In 1945 Topping was out of the NFL. He decided to join the All-America Football Conference.

■ ■ ■

THE ALL–TIME ALL–NAME TEAM

Player	Pos.	Hgt.	Wgt.	Team(s), Year(s)
Ben Bangs	DB	5'10"	180	L.A. Buccaneers, 1926
Frank Blocker	C	NA	NA	Hammond Pros, 1920
Ronnie Bull	FB	6'0"	200	Bears, 1967-70, Eagles, '71
Derrick Hatchett	CB	5'11"	183	Colts, 1980-83; Oilers, '83
John Jett	OE	6'7"	225	Lions, 1941
Dennis Lick	OT	6'3"	267	Bears, 1978-82
Tuffy Maul	LB	5'11"	200	L.A. Buccaneers, 1926
Les (Goal) Post	K	NA	NA	AFL, 1937
Jerry Rush	DT	6'4"	264	Lions, 1965-71
Glen Spears	DE	5'10"	185	Kansas City Cowboys, 1926
Willie Thrower	QB	5'11"	182	Bears, 1953
Tom Wham	DE	6'2"	217	Cardinals, 1949-51
Coach -- Chuck Knox (Rams, 1973-77; Bills, '78-83, Seahawks, '83-)				
Honorary member -- DT-LB Steve Smear, CFL, 1970-75				
Injured Reserve -- DB Eric Hurt, Cowboys, 1980				
Biggest Regret -- That Jim Kiick didn't				

LET'S PLAY TWO

The Green Bay Packers and Pittsburgh Pirates played a doubleheader on August 25, 1939, the only one in NFL history. We're not talking about 80-man training camp rosters, either. The Packers had 42 players, the Pirates 30.

The games were played on a Friday night at Green Bay's City Stadium in front of a larger-than-expected crowd of 9,416. The opener ended in a 7–7 tie. The nightcap went to the deeper, fresher Packers, 17–0. Neither was an artistic masterpiece.

"Both coaches were trying out their men with almost reckless abandon, never once attempting to field a team that had experience as a unit," wrote Stoney McGlynn of the *Milwaukee Sentinel*.

That was the logic behind the doubleheader. Green Bay coach Curly Lambeau and Pittsburgh's Johnny Blood each wanted a long look at their prospects before having to make cuts. With the Pirates training at nearby Two Rivers, Wisconsin, it was easy and cheap to get together. So why not play two?

A couple of concessions were made. Free substitution was permitted, and quarters were only 10 minutes long. But it still boiled down to a lot of football (80 minutes instead of the usual 60) for a relatively small number of players.

The Pirates were most affected. They scored on their first possession and should have won the opener. The Packers went 80 yards in the closing minutes to tie. Arnie Herber hit Moose Mulleneaux with a 22-yard pass on fourth down for the TD.

But Blood's boys were described as "worn to a frazzle" in the second game. They gained only five yards on offense. Lambeau, meanwhile, put in a fresh team at the start of each quarter and finally broke the Pittsburgh defense. Cecil Isbell passed 13 yards to Don Hutson for one Green Bay touchdown. Clarke Hinkle ran four yards for another and kicked a 29-yard field goal.

The *Green Bay Press-Gazette* raved about the doubleheader, calling it "an ante season grid show on a scale never before attempted." But in Pittsburgh it wasn't nearly as big a story as the possible return of Pirates back Whizzer White, in England on a Rhodes Scholarship.

From 1962 to '71, Cleveland owner Art Modell staged preseason doubleheaders involving four teams. He's thought to have dreamed up the idea. But the Packers and Pirates did it first. And they did it the hard way.

SUMMARIES

First Game

PIRATES		PACKERS
Boyd	LE	Becker
Karp	LT	Schultz
Gentry	LG	Biolo
Tosi	C	L.Mulleneaux
Kase	RG	Miketinac
Niccolai	RT	Zoll
Scherer	RE	Moore
Bond	QB	Lock
McCullough	LH	Wilson
Nardi	RH	Laws
Francis	FB	McGroarty

Pittsburgh	7	0	0	0	-- 7
Green Bay	0	0	0	7	-- 7

First Quarter
Pitt -- Francis 2 run (Francis kick)
Fourth Quarter
GB -- M. Mulleneaux 22 pass from Herber (Engebretsen kick)

Second Game

PIRATES		PACKERS
Boyd	LE	Hutson
Karp	LT	Schultz
Gentry	LG	Letlow
Grabinski	C	Greenfield
Kase	RG	Tinsley
Niccolai	RT	Kilbourne
Sortet	RE	Steen
Bond	QB	Craig
Bartlett	LH	Wilson
Tommerson	RH	Herber
Francis	FB	Jankowski

Pittsburgh	0	0	0	0	-- 0
Green Bay	0	10	0	7	-- 17

Second Quarter
GB -- Hutson 13 pass from Isbell (Smith kick)
GB -- FG Hinkle 29
Fourth Quarter
GB -- Hinkle 4 run (Engebretsen kick)
Attendance -- 9,416.

THEY COULD HAVE BEEN COMMISSIONER

The last four NFL commissioners—Elmer Layden, Bert Bell, Pete Rozelle and Paul Tagliabue—have been compromise or alternative choices. The league has never seemed able to handle these transitions neatly.

It didn't have to worry about the position for its first two decades. Jim Thorpe was elected president in 1920 (the title of commissioner didn't come until later) as a publicity stunt. The capable Joe Carr took over the next year and reigned until his death in 1939. Only then did the owners have to conduct their first serious search for a leader. Carr's assistant, Carl Storck, ran things while they did.

Finding people wasn't easy then and hasn't been since. But it's interesting to think how different the league might have been had any of the leading candidates gotten the job. Here are two of the men who might have been commissioner (the others appear elsewhere in the book).

J. EDGAR HOOVER

Yes, J. Edgar Hoover. In December 1939 owners George Preston Marshall of Washington and Dick Richards of Detroit approached the FBI director about the job. In fact, there appeared to be a full-scale draft-Hoover movement afoot in the league, led by Marshall, Richards and Brooklyn's Dan Topping. It died only after the head G-man himself squelched it.

"Sorry," Hoover said in a telegram from Florida, "but I cannot consider the proposition at this time."

Details of the story are sketchy. As soon as word leaked to the press, the owners closed ranks.

"Whoever offered Mr. Hoover the presidency of the league is talking out of turn and unnecessarily embarrassing him," said the Bears' George Halas. "No action can be taken on a new president except in the league meeting."

Sure, George. Hoover would have had the job in 48 hours if he'd expressed an interest. In December 1939 the NFL was looking for a star to lead it into the big time. Carr had died in May, and Storck was watching the shop on an interim basis.

Storck was a capable man and one of the league's pioneers, but he didn't project the image the NFL wanted heading into its third decade. During his playing days his nickname was "Scummy."

The owners wanted a headliner, someone whose name would bring prestige, credibility and—not least of all—attention to the still-struggling league. That's why they went after Hoover.

"Dan Topping is attempting to line up the club owners in the movement to elect Mr. Hoover to the presidency, and I have also talked to Mr. Hoover about it," Marshall admitted. "So has Dick Richards. Mr. Hoover is a man of outstanding character and integrity and would be a fine league president [the title was changed to commissioner in 1941]."

It's unclear how seriously Hoover considered the offer. The league wound up reelecting Storck for another year and continuing its search.

DECADE ALL–STAR TEAM

For skill position players, figures under "Data" are their best seasons.

Pos. Player	Years*	Data
E Bill Hewitt	8	15 catches, 358 yds., 6 TDs; 4 all-NFL
T Cal Hubbard	5	3 all-NFL
G Mike Michalske	7	3 all-NFL
G Ox Emerson	8	1 all-NFL; played on best rushing team ever
C Mel Hein	9	7 all-NFL
T George Christensen	8	2 all-NFL
E Don Hutson	5	34 catches, 846 yds., 6 TDs; 3 all-NFL
B Dutch Clark	7	763 rushing yds., 6.3 avg., 8 TDs; 6 all-NFL
B Bronko Nagurski	8	586 rushing yds., 4.8 avg., 7 TDs; 3 all-NFL
B Cliff Battles	6	874 rushing yds., 4.0 avg., 5 TDs; 3 all-NFL
B Johnny Blood	9	22 catches, 490 yds., 10 TDs; 1 all-NFL

OTHER SELECTIONS

Kick Returner -- Whizzer White **Wild Card Selection** -- Ace Parker
Kicker -- Jack Manders **Enforcer** -- Father Lumpkin
Punter -- Ralph Kercheval **Coach** -- Curly Lambeau

*Number of years he played in the decade.

Coming
1930--Don Shula, Painesville, Ohio
      Doug Atkins, Humboldt, Tenn.
      Frank Gifford, Santa Monica, Calif.
1931--Big Daddy Lipscomb, Detroit
      Bill Walsh, Los Angeles
1932--Roosevelt Brown, Charlottesville, Va.
1933--Raymond Berry, Corpus Christi, Texas
      Johnny Unitas, Pittsburgh
      Lenny Moore, Reading, Pa.
1934--Bart Starr, Montgomery, Ala.
      Jim Parker, Macon, Ga.
      Sonny Jurgensen, Wilmington, N.C.
      Sam Huff, Edna Gas, W.Va.
1935--Jack Kemp, Los Angeles
      Alex Karras, Gary, Ind.
      Paul Hornung, Louisville, Ky.
1936--Jimmy Brown, St. Simons Island, Ga.
      John Madden, Daly City, Calif.
1937--Billy Cannon, Philadelphia, Miss.
1938--Jim Otto, Wausau, Wis.
      Deacon Jones, Eatonville, Fla.
1939--Herb Adderley, Philadelphia
      Mike Ditka, Carnegie, Pa.

Going
1939--Joe Carr, 58

ARCH WARD

The influential sports editor of the *Chicago Tribune* turned down the job twice.

In December 1939—the same time Hoover was approached—Ward was offered a 10-year, $250,000 deal by Halas (so much for electing presidents at league meetings). He turned it down saying he "could not overlook the splendid opportunities in my position with the *Chicago Tribune.*" One year later, the NFL made another pitch offering more power and authority.

Ward said he turned down the second offer on the advice of his critically ill 17-year-old daughter. But he was far from being done with the league. It was his recommendation that the league go after Notre Dame athletic director Elmer Layden. Layden signed his contract at the Tribune offices.

Ward probably would have been a great commissioner. He was a promotional genius who made ideas such as baseball's All-Star Game, football's College All-Star Game and the national Golden Gloves tournament reality. The All-America Football Conference, which was a bitter rival to the NFL from '46 to '49, was his creation, too.

■ ■ ■

GEORGE PRESTON MEGALOMANIAC

Time has been kind to George Preston Marshall—a lot kinder than he was. As the years go by, NFL fans remember him only for his contributions to the game and not for the many unadmirable aspects of his personality. The same sort of positive erosion is at work on George Halas' memory.

Marshall was a loud and obnoxious bully. He was cheap and often ruthless. He had a hairtrigger brain when it came to coaches. He didn't sign a black player until 1962, 16 years after the color barrier was broken, and then only under pressure from the league and the federal government.

As owner of the Redskins and a power in league politics, he pushed for changes—the creation of divisions and rules opening up the offense, to name only two—that made the game a better product; he also correctly foresaw the potential of television.

But there are just as many reasons to dislike Marshall. Here's the first (in a continuing series):

THE BO RUSSELL AFFAIR

The game to decide the 1939 Eastern Conference title came down to a controversial 15-yard field-goal attempt by Washington's Bo Russell. There were 45 seconds remaining, and the Giants led the Redskins 9–7.

Russell's kick appeared to hook just inside the left upright, but referee Bill Halloran, standing behind the offense, called it no good, giving the Giants the victory and the title. The Redskins were furious, and Marshall appealed to NFL president Carl Storck to overturn the decision. Storck refused, and it probably cost him his job.

Four months later, *New York Post* columnist Jack Miley wrote that Marshall was presurring Postmaster General Jim Farley to fire Halloran from his post office job in Providence, Rhode Island. The accusation wasn't true (Giants owner Tim Mara was accused of planting the story), but Halloran didn't work a Redskins game during the '40 season and had his overall schedule reduced.

Storck was the main target, though. His contract was up for renewal in April 1940, and Marshall set about finding a replacement. When that didn't work, the Redskins owner saw to it that Storck was re-elected to a one-year term only. He also stripped Storck of an important duty—the assignment of referees to games. It fell to a committee of owners headed by Marshall. The following year, Storck was gone, replaced by Notre Dame athletic director Elmer Layden.

It's typical of Marshall that his indignation over the Russell affair also led to a positive rule change. Beginning in 1940, an official was stationed behind the goal posts for all field-goal and extra-point attempts to help the referee determine whether the kick was good.

THE 1940s

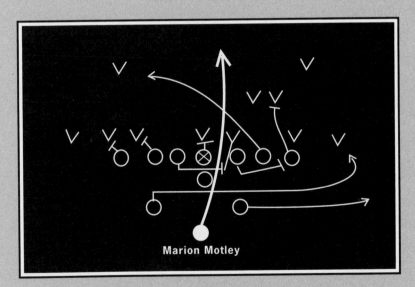

Marion Motley

The Motley Trap

The Motley Trap

Along with Otto Graham's passing, this play was the cornerstone of the great Cleveland Browns offenses that dominated the All-America Football Conference from 1946 to '49. Marion Motley was a 6'1", 230-pound fullback with tremendous acceleration. The idea was to spring him into the secondary untouched, where his instructions from coach Paul Brown were: "If there is someone in front of you, just run in one end of him and out the other." It had to be every defensive back's worst nightmare. Motley averaged 6.2 yards per carry in the AAFC and made it nearly impossible for teams to concentrate solely on stopping Graham.

THE 1940s AT A GLANCE

Decade Standings

NFL

East	W	L	T	Pct.	West	W	L	T	Pct.
Redskins (1)	65	41	4	.609	Bears (4)	81	26	3	.750
Eagles (2)	58	47	5	.550	Packers (1)	62	44	4	.582
Giants	55	47	8	.536	Rams (1)	50	45	5	.525
Steelers	40	64	6	.391	Cardinals (1)	41	65	4	.391
Dodgers	20	33	0	.377	Lions	35	71	4	.336
Yanks	14	38	3	.282					

ALL-AMERICA FOOTBALL CONFERENCE

East	W	L	T	Pct.	West	W	L	T	Pct.
New York	35	17	2	.667	Cleveland (4)	47	4	3	.898
Buffalo	23	26	5	.472	San Francisco	38	14	2	.722
Baltimore	10	29	1	.263	Los Angeles	25	27	2	.481
Brooklyn	8	32	2	.214	Chicago	11	40	3	.231

(Figures in parentheses are championships won.)

Best Regular–Season Record

Cleveland Browns, 1948, 14-0
Chicago Bears, 1940, 11-0

Worst Regular–Season Record

Detroit Lions, 1942, 0-11

Attendance Figures

Total (NFL only): 12,805,288
Biggest Crowd: 82,769, 49ers at Browns, Nov. 14, 1948

In	Out
World War II	The Depression
black players	color line
Commissioner Elmer Layden	President Carl Storck
gambling scandals	Frank Filchock, Merle Hapes
split T-formation	single wing
Greasy Neale	"Stout" Steve Owen
All-America Conference	The third AFL
red ink	black ink
Steve Van Buren	Bronko Nagurski
passing on third down	punting on third down
Bob Waterfield-Jane Russell	Dan Topping-Sonja Henie

Biggest Player

Chubby Grigg, Browns tackle, at 6'2", 300-plus. He used to starve himself to get down to his reporting weight of 275 and earn a $500 bonus. Then he'd start putting the pounds back on. Tallest: John "Tree" Adams, 6'7" Redskins tackle.

Smallest Player

Rudy Mobley, a halfback with the Colts in 1947, went 5'7", 155. Teammate Buddy Young was even shorter -- 5'4".

Best Athlete

Sammy Baugh

Fastest Player

Buddy Young. In college he tied the world record in the 60-yard dash (6.1).

Slowest Player

Chubby Grigg (after the weigh-in)

Most Intimidating Player

Bears end Ed Sprinkle

Best Career–Ending Game

Philadelphia's Davey O'Brien completed 33 of 60 passes for 316 yards -- all records -- with no interceptions in the 1940 season finale at Washington. The Eagles still lost, 13-6. O'Brien retired at 23 to become an FBI agent.

Failed Franchises

Brooklyn Dodgers, 1944
New York Bulldogs, 1949

Failed Leagues

The third AFL, 1941
AAFC, 1949

Failed Romance

L.A. Ram-to-be Glenn Davis was engaged to Elizabeth Taylor in 1948, but *she* broke it off.

►Famous Firsts

NFL record manual, 1941
Undefeated-untied team (all games), 1948 (Browns, 15-0)
Sunbelt team, 1946 (Miami Seahawks, AAFC)

►Famous Lasts

Player without a helmet, 1941 (Bears end Dick Plasman)
Scoreless tie, 1943 (Giants-Lions)
Player to outscore a team in a season, 1945 (Steve Van Buren had 110 points to the Steelers' 79 and the Cardinals' 98)
Drop-kicked extra point, 1948 (49er Joe Vetrano)

Best Division Race

There were so many. The NFL had playoffs in the West in 1941 and the East in '43 and '47. The '44 Eagles went 7-1-2 and wound up second. In '47 and again in '48, the Bears and Cardinals played for the West title on the last day. The '49 season saw the Bears win their last *six* and finish behind the Rams.

All that said, the best race may have been in the AAFC between the Browns and 49ers in 1948. Both teams had a shot at a perfect season. (The Niners started out 10-0.) When they met for the first time in Cleveland, they drew the biggest crowd of the decade.

Best Title Game

In their 28-21 win over the Eagles in 1947, the Cardinals scored on a punt return of 75 yards and runs of 70, 70 and 44.

►Owner vs. Owner

Dick Richards vs. George Halas and Tim Mara

►Player vs. League

Bill Radovich vs. the NFL, 1949

Major Rules Changes

1940 -- clipping penalty reduced from 25 to 15 yards
1941 -- sudden death overtime adopted for division playoffs and championship games
1943 -- free substitution; helmets made mandatory
1944 -- coaching from bench legalized
1945 -- hashmarks now 20 instead of 15 yards from the sidelines
1946 -- substitution limited to three players at a time
1948 -- artificial tee allowed on kickoffs
1949 -- free substitution restored for one year

New Equipment   plastic helmets and facemasks
                           low-cut shoes

Fashion Trends   team socks required for league games, 1945

New Statistics   interceptions, 1940
                           punt returns, 1941
                           kickoff returns, 1941

Best Play   Sid Luckman's bootleg for the winning touchdown in the 1946 championship game against the Giants
                           The Bears quarterback almost never ran (four rushing touchdowns in eight seasons up to then). That's why "Bingo keep it" was the perfect call. It came with the score tied 14-14 early in the fourth quarter. Luckman faked to halfback George McAfee going left, took off the other way and went 19 yards for a TD.
                           Even veteran referee Ron Gibbs was fooled. "I realized my mistake," he recalled later, "about the time the Giants tackled McAfee. Boy, was I glad I didn't blow that whistle!"

►Hit of the Decade   Crazylegs Hirsch fractures his skull, 1948

Fight of the Decade   World War II

Highest–Paid Player   Glenn Dobbs reportedly made $25,000 quarterbacking the AAFC's L.A. Dons. The best contract, however, may have been the one Bill Dudley signed with Detroit in 1947. It was a *six*-year guaranteed deal -- the first three as a player (at $20,000 annually), the next three as backfield coach (at $6,500 to $8,500). Total package: $79,500-85,500. If an injury prevented him from coaching, the team had to pay him, anyway. He also got the money if there was a coaching change and the new man preferred another backfield coach. The coaching half of the contract was voided when he decided to continue his playing career with the Redskins in 1950.

Least Appreciated Players   Rams receiver Jim Benton
                                Eagles tackle Al Wistert
                                New York Yankees back Spec Sanders

Best Trade   The Giants dealt end Howie Livingston to the Redskins in 1948 for the draft rights to Charley Conerly. Livingston had three more undistinguished seasons; Conerly went on to throw 173 TD passes.

►Worst Idea   Letting the Colts into the NFL and keeping the Buffalo Bills out after the AAFC folded in 1949.

Individual Records That   Sammy Baugh's 51.4-yard punting average, 1940
Have Never Been Equaled   Don Currivan's 32.6-yard receiving average, 1947 (24 catches)

THE LIVING DEAD

The NFL fined Lions owner Dick Richards $5,000 in 1940 for tampering with Bulldog Turner, the Bears' first-round draft pick. Richards, who sold the team that year, never forgot.

When he found out the Bears' top pick in '41, Tom Harmon, was interested in a broadcasting career, he offered him a job with his Detroit radio station. Of course, he told Harmon, your assignments will keep you from playing pro football.

But when the New York Americans of the rival AFL began talking to Harmon, Richards' attitude changed. He had no problem with Harmon playing for the Americans as long as he continued to do his radio show. Harmon signed with the one-year-old league.

Then there's this story from Brooklyn Dodgers owner Dan Topping: "I was visiting Richards at his home in Palm Springs, California, and after cocktails he took me out to see his back yard, and there a very strange and horrifying sight met my eyes. A row of tombstones in a plot of ground that has all the macabre appearances of a small cemetery. Names of people were chiseled in the marble. I peered closer and read. One was erected to the memory of George Halas, another to Tim Mara, a third to Potsy Clark [who had quit as Lions coach after the 1936 season and gone to the Dodgers]. I don't recall the others."

All were very much alive.

■ ■ ■

BEGINNER'S LUCK

On October 27, 1940, at the Polo Grounds, Bears backup tackle Lee Artoe booted a 52-yard field goal against the Giants. One observer said, "The ball carried at least 10 yards over the center of the crossbar."

It was the second-longest field goal in NFL history. It would be 10 more years before someone else kicked one as long. And it came on the first field-goal attempt of Artoe's pro career, his only attempt of the season, in fact.

A strong-legged rookie out of the University of

California, Artoe did some kicking off for the Bears. But coach George Halas let him try a couple of place kicks against the Giants after the Bears had built a 27–0 first-half lead. Artoe missed the first, an extra-point attempt, then nailed the 52-yarder.

He reportedly was so nearsighted that he didn't even follow the flight of the ball. Only when he heard Halas screaming on the bench did he know the kick was good.

Artoe booted just one other field goal in seven pro seasons.

■ ■ ■

REVENGE IS MINE SAYETH THE LANDLORD

While the Bears were pouring it on the Redskins in the 1940 championship game, a Washington fan heckled owner George Preston Marshall relentlessly, letting him have it with all manner of vulgarities. Losing 73–0 can have that effect on people.

Marshall finally got fed up. He jumped from his seat and confronted the loudmouth. Ushers stepped between the two, but Marshall noted the rowdy's seat number. When it was discovered the man was a season-ticket holder, Marshall refused his request to renew for 1941.

But wait, it gets better. The fan turned out to own a building that housed one of Marshall's Palace Laundry stores. He refused to renew Marshall's lease and kicked him out.

■ ■ ■

THE BALLBAG WAS EMPTY

The Redskins and Bears were using an old practice ball at the end of the 73–0 championship game in 1940. All the good ones had been kicked into the Griffith Stadium stands on extra-point attempts.

As the supply of balls dwindled in the second half, Redskins business manager Jack Espey went into the crowd to get fans to give them back. One of the people he approached turned out to be a high school classmate.

"I explained the predicament we were in and asked him if he would let me have the ball if we needed it in exchange for a brand new one autographed by every Redskin player and the Bears, too," Espey said. "He was sort of reluctant but finally agreed."

Several minutes later, the Bears scored again and booted the last good ball into the seats. Espey ran onto the field in front of the section where his classmate was sitting.

"OK, let's have it," he yelled.

"Go peddle your papers," his classmate yelled back.

Into the game went the old practice ball. At the behest of the Redskins, the Bears attempted their final two extra points on plays from scrimmage instead of kicks. They converted one on a pass from Joe Maniaci to Solly Sherman.

■ ■ ■
'40s MYTHOLOGY

During a 1941 exhibition game against Brooklyn at Ebbets Field, Chicago Bears assistant Luke Johnsos sat in the stands and helped with the play calling, a then-unusual practice. When Johnsos thought a play would work, he drew a diagram, balled it up, let out a high-pitched whistle and tossed the wad of paper down to the field.

The first time he did this, George McAfee ran 47 yards to set up a touchdown. The Flatbush faithful made the connection. The next time Johnsos whistled and dropped a play from the upper deck, the surrounding crowd filled the air with crumpled scorecards.

The Bears never got his second message. The clean-up crew found it the next day.

Some stories you just *want* to be true—like this one. It seems to have gotten its start in a 1946 profile of Johnsos in the *Saturday Evening Post* titled "Press-Box Quarterback."

The *Post* described the process in great detail. Johnsos, the magazine said, wrapped the diagram around a "worn-out football cleat" to give it more

weight and flipped it to "a youngster waiting in the grandstand shadows" who "made a one-hand catch and took off for the Bears' bench." It's a wonder the fans could keep their eyes on the game.

The episode appeared in print again in a 1960 column by Arthur Daley of the *New York Times*. What's suspicious is that Daley didn't write about it in '41 when he *covered the game.* He probably just had a subscription to the *Saturday Evening Post.*

McAfee and quarterback Sid Luckman laughed when they heard the tale. Johnsos sent down plays, according to Luckman, but they weren't passed on to the quarterback right away. This, remember, was the single-platoon era. Coaching from the sideline was illegal. A substitute could be used to relay information, but the player he replaced had to sit out the rest of the half.

"We'd find out about them [Johnsos' plays] during timeouts," says Luckman.

As for McAfee's 47-yard run, the one called by Johnsos, well, he didn't have one. He did score both Chicago TDs, but they came on a fumble and a punt return.

Johnsos was indeed one of the pioneers of press-box coaching, but he didn't invent it. It was being done in the NFL at least as far back as 1934. During the Bears–Giants title game that year, Columbia coach Lou Little was "sitting up in the stands and phoning to the [New York] bench," the *Times* reported.

*   *   *

George Halas distributed saltpeter disguised as vitamins to keep his great Bears teams of the early '40s in line. (For the uninformed, saltpeter is an age-old cure for passion. It allegedly does for male sexual ability what 1929 did for the stock market.)

We looked into the legend—for the sake of historical accuracy, of course—and found absolutely no hard evidence to support it. In fact we found a player who claims to be its source: McAfee.

"It's a joke," he says. "I made it up. It makes a good story, so I tell it as the truth."

The story is that Halas had a no-sex policy the night before games (it deadens the legs, remember?). When the Bears developed an annoying pattern of letting up on teams after building big leads, he suspected some players of breaking the rule. So he instituted a "vitamin" program. Each Bear was given his own jar of mysterious white pills. The plot was uncovered when someone had the pills analyzed at a drug store.

The truth is this: Halas did indeed distribute vitamins to the team. But they didn't contain saltpeter.

"We got that in the eggs at training camp," says back Ray Nolting.

THE RADOVICH CASE

It took a big man to stand up to the NFL in the days before players associations and agents. Bill Radovich was certainly that. He was a 5'9", 260-pound guard, an all-pro with the Detroit Lions in 1945 after returning from a three-year Navy hitch. "Rado" was the kind of lineman opponents worked around, not through.

In '46 he jumped to the Los Angeles Dons of the All-America Football Conference. His father, who owned a butcher shop in L.A., had developed cancer, and Radovich wanted to be closer to home to keep an eye on him and the family business. He'd asked the Lions to trade him to the Rams, but they'd refused.

"I had to do it," Radovich says. "My father didn't have any insurance. I couldn't live back there [in Detroit] and keep expenses going here for my family."

The NFL got even with him two years later. He'd already agreed to take a player-coaching job with San Francisco of the Pacific Coast Football League when the Clippers were told they couldn't hire him. The minor league had a working agreement with the NFL that prohibited it from signing, for five years, former NFL players who'd run out on their contracts. Radovich had been blacklisted.

He sued for $35,000, charging the NFL with violating the Sherman Antitrust Act. Thus began a lengthy legal process that wasn't resolved until 1958, when a settlement was reached. The case went all the way to the Supreme Court, a first for the NFL. Two lower courts had refused to hear it because they considered pro football the same as major league baseball, which the Court had exempted from antitrust laws in 1922.

After the Court upheld baseball's exemption in a 1953 antitrust suit, Radovich's original attorney, Joseph Alioto, dropped the case. He told Radovich he didn't think it could be won. But Radovich got another San Francisco lawyer, Maxwell Keith, and pressed on.

By the late '50s the climate was changing. In 1955 the Court had refused to extend baseball's antitrust umbrella to cover boxing and the theater. The 1922 decision was coming to be seen as "an historic accident." Those were the words used by Philip Elman, assistant to the solicitor general, who joined Radovich's side on behalf of the government.

In 1957 the Court voted 6–3 that the NFL was indeed subject to antitrust laws and threw the Radovich case back to the lower courts. In the majority opinion, Justice Thomas C. Clark wrote: "If this ruling is unrealistic, inconsistent or illogical, it is sufficient to answer, aside from the distinctions between the businesses, that were we considering the question of baseball for the first time upon a clean slate we would have no doubts." Translation: We're not going to make the same mistake twice.

Keith hailed the ruling as "the athlete's charter of freedom" and "the most important decision in the history of sport." The final result, he said, could be "the end to the draft system under which athletes are not even permitted to select the teams they play for." A congressional investigation of pro sports and its relationship to antitrust laws soon followed.

Back in California, Radovich said he simply wanted to prove "that a player shouldn't be treated like a piece of furniture. I'm not out to wreck football or sports. I wouldn't want to do anything like that. I put 22 years in the game. But I didn't like to have a man tell me I could play for one club and nobody else."

John O'Dea, a member of the NFL's legal team, claims the Court's ruling wasn't nearly as catastrophic for pro football as Keith made it out to be. "If Radovich prevailed," he says, "it would have been on that narrow issue [blacklisting], not whether we employed a draft or a uniform contract or anything like that."

Still, it's difficult to predict how trials will turn out. *L.A. Times* sports columnist Paul Zimmerman blamed commissioner Bert Bell for the whole mess. It never would have gotten this far, he wrote, "had Bell not placed so much emphasis at the time on the then-insignificant case of an NFL jumper trying to get a comparatively negligible coaching job in a little league that was already destined to die."

The trial was finally set for March 14, 1958, in

San Francisco but was postponed when Bell's doctors said he had hypertension. Keith got permission from U.S. District Judge George B. Harris to have a heart specialist examine Bell and determine whether he was really too sick to travel.

"[I] don't understand how a doctor can come in there and examine me once and pass an opinion on a case that is five years old," Bell said. ". . . I think it's silly to send a doctor all the way from California when we have plenty [of] fine, competent doctors other than mine in Philadelphia, which is a world-renowned medical center."

In early March, Keith, Radovich and Dr. Lawrence Feigenbaum flew east. Feigenbaum's examination revealed Bell had a heart problem, Radovich says, the result of a mild heart attack. According to the newspapers, Keith then took a deposition from Bell, but Radovich tells a different story. He says NFL attorney Marshall Leahy questioned the commissioner first, then they stopped for lunch.

During the break, Radovich says, Keith told him he had the name of a New York City gambler who took Bert Bell's bets on the NFL games each week. Keith planned to ask Bell if he knew the gambler. " 'If he says, no, I've got him lying under oath,' " Radovich quotes Keith as saying. " 'And if he says yes, I've got him admitting knowing a gambler.' "

"We came back," Radovich says, "and Marshall Leahy was sitting in Bert Bell's chair behind his desk. And he said, 'Gentlemen, I'm sorry to inform you that Mr. Bert Bell is incommunicado. He's ill in the hospital.' They threw him in the hospital to stop the deposition."

Radovich says Keith took depositions from Bell's doctors "and caught 'em lying about why they put him in the hospital. This is evidence for the trial, that he clearly avoided his deposition by going in the hospital."

After they returned to San Francisco another trial date was set. About this time the NFL started looking to settle. One day, Radovich says, Keith called and said he'd agreed to a figure of $42,500. Radovich thought it was a rotten deal. Had he won in court, he would have collected triple damages— $105,000. He went to San Francisco and told Keith there was no way he'd accept it. He also accused Leahy of buying Keith off and said Keith was no longer representing him. (Keith refused to be interviewed on the subject.)

Radovich reconsidered, however. "I'm thinking: If I go ahead and kick his ass out because he didn't

follow my orders," he says, "he'll sue me. [Then] I've gotta get another attorney to handle the case against the league, and I'm just proving what they've said all these years, that I'm a troublemaker.

"So I finally said [to Keith], 'OK, I'll settle. But there's one thing I insist on.' I went back up to

---

DECADE LEADERS

PASSING

Yards: Sammy Baugh, 17,002; Sid Luckman, 13,867; Tommy Thompson, 8,792. AAFC*: Otto Graham, 10,085.

Completion percentage (800 attempts): Baugh, 58.7; Thompson, 52.7; Luckman, 52.4. AAFC: Graham, 55.8.

Touchdowns: Baugh, 149; Luckman, 131; Thompson, 79. AAFC: Frankie Albert, 88.

Interceptions: Baugh, 140; Luckman, 125; Bob Waterfield, 93. AAFC: Albert and George Ratterman, 53.

RUSHING

Yards: Steve Van Buren, 4,904; Tony Canadeo, 3,628; Bill Dudley, 2,305. AAFC: Marion Motley, 3,024.

Yards per carry (500 attempts): Van Buren, 4.8; Canadeo, 4.5; Dudley, 3.8. AAFC: Motley, 6.2.

TDs: Van Buren, 59; Pug Manders, 34; Ted Fritsch, 31. AAFC: Spec Sanders, 33.

RECEIVING

Receptions: Don Hutson, 329; Jim Benton, 240; Bill Dewell, 178. AAFC: Mac Speedie, 211.

Yards: Hutson, 5,089; Benton, 3,995; Kavanaugh, 3,291. AAFC: Speedie, 3,554.

Yards per catch (100 receptions): Kavanaugh, 22.7; Scooter McLean, 21.6; Mal Kutner, 21.2.

TDs: Hutson, 63; Kavanaugh, 48; Benton, 33. AAFC: Alyn Beals, 46.

OTHER CATEGORIES

Scoring: Hutson, 589; Van Buren, 404; Pat Harder, 349. AAFC: Beals, 278.

Interceptions: Irv Comp, 33; Frank Reagan, 27; Howie Livingston, 24. AAFC: Cliff Lewis, 24.

Punt return average (50 returns): Ernie Steele, 16.0; George McAfee, 14.5; Charley Trippi and Bill Dudley, 13.7

Punt return TDs: Scooter McLean and Em Tunnell, 2; AAFC: Rex Bumgardner, 2.

Kickoff return average (50 returns): Van Buren, 27.0; Frank Seno, 24.0; Eddie Saenz, 23.6.

Kickoff return TDs: Van Buren, 3. AAFC: Sanders and Buddy Young, 2.

Field goals: Fritsch, 33; Ward Cuff, 29; Waterfield, 29. AAFC: Groza, 30.

Punting average (150 punts): Baugh, 45.5; Joe Muha, 43.2; Waterfield, 43.0. AAFC: Dobbs, 46.4.

*All-America Football Conference leader, 1946-49.

Marshall Leahy's office and said, 'I want Bert Bell to write this check out and sign it himself.'

" 'What do you mean? This is a certified check.'

"I said, 'I don't want it.' And I reached for it and tore it in half. I said, 'If you want this case settled, you tell Bert Bell to send me his own check,' and about three days later I got it. He [Leahy] said, 'What's the reason behind that? It's going to hold everything up for three days.' I said, 'Bert Bell will know when he writes that check out what the hell I mean.' "

Radovich says he saw $30,000 of the $42,500. Keith got $10,000, and the rest went toward legal expenses. The lawyer was supposed to receive a third of the settlement, but Radovich says he told Keith he could sue him for the rest.

"Nobody knows what I got [until now]," says Radovich. "I was embarrassed to tell anybody. Bill Howard [the former Southern Cal teammate who'd offered him the player-coach job] thought for years I'd gotten $100,000."

Keith phoned him six months later, he says, and tried to sell him on the idea of their becoming agents and representing athletes. Keith thought Radovich had credibility with the players. Radovich hung up on him.

■ ■ ■

IF IT'S THREE O'CLOCK, THIS MUST BE DUQUESNE

In 1941 Buff Donelli became the first and last man to serve as a college and pro head coach *at the same time.*

The crazy experiment took place in Pittsburgh but abruptly ended after five weeks when NFL commissioner Elmer Layden made Donelli choose between a West Coast trip with undefeated Duquesne and a cross-stater to Philadelphia with the winless Steelers.

Donelli, smart man, chose Duquesne.

It was an interesting juggling act while it lasted. For weeks Donelli's daily schedule went like this:

8:00 A.M.—Meet with Steelers' assistant coaches.

9:00 A.M.—Team meeting.

9:30 A.M.–Noon—Practice.

After lunch—Drive 35 miles from Steelers' suburban practice site to Duquesne's downtown campus.

1:30–3:00 P.M.—Attend to athletic director duties (he was that, too).

3:00 P.M.—Team meeting with Duquesne players.

3:30–6:00 P.M.—Practice.

After dinner—Drive back to Steelers' practice site.

8:00 P.M.—Team meeting.

10:00 P.M. (or so)—Sleep in a nearby motel.

"How'd I do it? By losing a lot of weight," he says.

Donelli was already established at Duquesne when Steelers owner Art Rooney approached him about the job in early October. Only 34, he was one of coaching's rising stars. He'd lost only one game in two-plus years at the school, and his pioneering of the Wing-T had given him a reputation as an innovator. He and Rooney had been friends for a while. They'd already agreed that Donelli would coach the Steelers beginning in 1942 with a three-year, $30,000 contract.

But Rooney found himself in a fix. The Steelers had lost all their exhibitions and their first two regular-season games. After the second regular-season loss, co-owner Bert Bell resigned as coach. Rooney appealed to Donelli.

On September 24 came the startling announcement. Donelli had accepted the Steelers job but would stay on as coach and athletic director at Duquesne. Initial reports had Donelli coaching the Steelers "in his spare time."

No sooner had the announcement been made than Layden intervened. He'd coached at Duquesne from 1927 to '34. Donelli was captain of the undefeated '28 team and later joined Layden's coaching staff.

None of which kept the commissioner from putting his foot down. "It is impossible, physically and mentally, to direct two major football teams at the same time," he said. "If Donelli is not in a position to sever connections completely at Duquesne, or if he is unwilling to make such a change, the Steelers will have to secure another coach."

Donelli could have made a case that he *had* only one major football team. In their hardscrabble eight years, the Steelers had won 24 (games) and lost six (head coaches).

Instead, he, Steelers owner Art Rooney and the Duquesne administration worked out a dubious compromise. Duquesne "released" Donelli to coach the Steelers full-time. He stayed on as athletic director and was given the title "advisory" football coach. His assistant, Steve Sinko, became "acting coach," but Donelli had license to attend practice and an agreement with Rooney to be on the bench for every Duquesne game. No one in Pittsburgh doubted he was still calling the shots.

With Layden temporarily appeased, Donelli set to work making over the Steelers. He installed his own offense, changed the starting backfield assignments and signed his kid brother Alan, a 5'7", 165-pound ex-Duquesne star.

Donelli's pro coaching debut against the Giants at Forbes Field was a rude awakening. The overmatched Steelers gave up three touchdowns in the first 10 minutes of the fourth quarter and were embarrassed, 37–10. During the game Donelli was shocked that players asked to come out when they were winded. He accused some of faking injuries when the Giants started to roll. In the locker room afterward, he was incensed.

"He seethed and raged up and down the benches, turning loose a flood on every player," the *Pittsburgh Press* reported. "It was the worst licking any Donelli-coached team ever took, and 'The Buffer' breathed fire as he emphasized the way in which it was taken."

The Steelers improved in subsequent weeks but not enough to win (a brutal schedule didn't help). They lost to the Redskins (24–20), Giants (28–7), Bears (34–7) and Redskins again (23–3).

Meanwhile, Duquesne won its first six. Donelli made all the games, home and away. The only away game that presented a logistics problem was Marquette, and the Steelers happened to be playing in Chicago that weekend. Donelli missed only a light Saturday workout.

In early November the schedule caught up to him. Duquesne played St. Mary's in San Francisco while the Steelers had a date with the Eagles. Layden told him: Be in Philadelphia or resign.

"My agreement with Art Rooney was that I would go with the team that had the better record," Donelli says. "There was no question where I had to go. I'd promised the boys [at Duquesne] when I took the job I'd be there, and Art understood that."

Layden's ultimatum ended his friendship with Donelli and brought a rare criticism from Rooney. "He could have helped us and helped the league, too," Rooney said.

Rooney and Bell named assistant coach Walt Kiesling to take over, and he brought the Steelers in at 1–9–1. Donelli's Duquesne team finished 8–0 and ranked first in the East. His deal with Rooney to coach in '42 fell through. In '44 he coached the Cleveland Rams and then entered the service. He later coached at Columbia and Boston College.

■ ■ ■
VISIONARY

The 1941 Philadelphia Eagles had a jersey-numbering system similar to the one adopted 32 years later by the NFL. It was the brainchild of owner Alexis Thompson.

The first number on a player's jersey indicated offensive position (remember, this is the single-platoon era). For quarterbacks it was 1, right halfbacks 2, fullbacks 3, tailbacks 4, centers 5, guards 6, tack-

$$$$$

$1	Dollar figure that appeared on Sammy Baugh's 1940 Redskins contract (he also had personal-services contract with owner George Preston Marshall)
$100	Signing bonus Browns gave Marion Motley in 1946
$156	Price Eagles coach Greasy Neale paid film company for copy of Bears' 73-0 victory over Redskins in 1940 title game (Neale used film to learn T-formation)
$200	Fine assessed Steelers' Al Wukits for slugging umpire Harry Robb in 1945
$300	Monthly pay Lou Groza received from Browns while in the service in 1945
$430	Winning share in 1941 championship game
$1,250	Salary of umpire Red Friesell for 11 games in 1940
$5,400	What Bears' six-game TV contract was worth in 1946
$50,000	Loss suffered by NFL champion Cleveland Rams, 1945
$105,000	Reported value of five-year contract Dan Topping offered Charley Trippi to play football *and* baseball for the New York Yankees, 1947
$250,000	Purchase price of Philadelphia Eagles in 1949
$680,384	Amount raised by NFL for War Relief charities in 1942

les 7 and ends 8. The second number identified the individual player (names weren't required on jerseys until 1970). So if you saw number 55 on the field, you'd be able to determine that it was Eagles center Tony Cemore.

For some reason, the other owners weren't impressed. Thompson's idea didn't catch on.

• • •
THEY COULD HAVE BEEN COMMISSIONER

JOHN B. KELLY.
Aka Jack. Aka Grace Kelly's father.

Kelly, a wealthy Philadelphia contractor and Democratic leader, made his mark in athletics as a rowing champion. But he was one of the top three candidates when the NFL was looking for a commissioner in 1941. He and Notre Dame athletic director–coach Elmer Layden were interviewed in Pittsburgh in January by the Bears' George Halas and Philadelphia's Bert Bell.

Bell then left for Florida, thinking a decision wouldn't be made until they had talked to the third finalist, Minnesota AD Frank McCormick. But while he was en route, Halas pulled a power play. He hastily conferred in Chicago with Detroit's Fred Mandel, the Cardinals' Charles Bidwill and Eagles co-owner Art Rooney, lobbied New York's Tim Mara, Washington's George Preston Marshall, Green Bay's Curly Lambeau and Cleveland's Edward P. Bruch over the telephone and got all of them to agree to hire Layden. Bell learned the league had a new leader when he read about it in the newspaper.

"It was necessary to sign Layden in a hurry or we would have lost him," Mandel told the press.

Bell, Pittsburgh's Alexis Thompson and Brooklyn's Dan Topping accused the other owners of railroading Layden into office. But they couldn't do anything about it. Halas had a majority. When Layden's appointment was made official at the April league meeting, the vote was unanimous.

The creation of the commissioner's post made Carl Storck, acting president since 1939, obsolete. He didn't take the news at all well. He spent seven weeks in bed with nervous exhaustion and attended the league meeting against the advice of his doctor. His right side was partially paralyzed. But he vowed to fight to keep his job—and created a scene doing so.

"How would you feel if you had given 20 years to something and then been treated this way?" asked Storck, who was one of the league's founders and became secretary-treasurer in 1921. "I haven't had a letter in my files criticizing my work as president for two years. They made the rules, and I simply enforced them. For 15 years I worked for nothing. Two years ago when I became president I didn't quit my job at General Motors because I was afraid something like this would happen."

When he saw he had no support, however, he resigned and left with his family to recuperate in Miami Beach. Layden assumed the title of president, too, and was given powers that made him, according to one account, "the most powerful executive in sports."

SWEDE LARSON

Rumors were rampant in 1945 that Elmer Layden, commissioner since 1941, planned to step down when his contract ran out the next year. Larson, a former coach and star athlete at Navy, was approached about taking the job and "at least two clubs in the NFL were strong supporters" of him, the *Washington Post* reported.

He was an inspirational leader who was 6–0 against Army as a player and coach. His success against the Cadets became known around Annapolis as "Larson luck." A big man with a voice to match, he was a Marine colonel—the first Marine Corps officer, in fact, to coach the Midshipmen.

While on assignment in Atlanta during World War II, however, he suffered a heart attack at a football game and died two weeks later. He was 47. When Layden did indeed leave, the league looked within and named Bell, half-owner of the Pittsburgh Steelers, to replace him.

• • •

DON HUTSON'S DUBIOUS RECORD

Almost everything you read about Green Bay Hall-of-Famer Don Hutson mentions his 95-game receiving streak from 1937 to '45. It was the NFL record for nearly a quarter century. But there's reason to believe his streak was only about half that long—50 games at the time of his retirement.

We came across a league release, dated January 28, 1943, announcing that Hutson had won the Joe F. Carr Trophy as the NFL's most valuable player for the second straight season. The release contained this revelation:

"In all except two of the 91 National league games in which he has participated, including three championship playoffs, he has caught at least one pass. Cleveland stopped him for the first time in a league game on Sept. 21, 1941. In the 1938 championship playoff against the Giants in New York, he got off crutches to participate in the last three plays of the game while the Packers were attempting to rally and, hobbling along on one leg, acted as a decoy for three desperate, but futile attempts."

Cleveland stopped him for the first time in a league game on Sept. 21, 1941. If that's the case, then it would have broken his 95-game streak virtually in two. That was the 45th of the 95 games.

Newspaper accounts support the claim. We checked six papers—three in Milwaukee, one in Green Bay and two in Cleveland. None mentions Hutson catching a pass against the Rams.

The Packers completed only four all day. Two went for touchdowns, to Joe Laws (from Tony Canadeo) and Clarke Hinkle (from Cecil Isbell). And the other two?

Well, the *Milwaukee Sentinel* credits Laws with another reception, after which "Joe was downed by [Jack] Hamann after an eight yard gain as the half closed." The Cleveland *Plain Dealer* gives the last to Ray Riddick, saying he caught a nine-yard pass from Hal Van Every in the third quarter.

The *Green Bay Press-Gazette* provides even better proof. It ran individual game statistics, unusual for the time. The Packers' receiving stats were as follows: Laws 2-30, Riddick 1-9, Hinkle 1-7, Hutson zip.

"Last Sunday's game at Milwaukee is believed to be the first in Packer history in which Don Hutson, ace Green Bay end, didn't receive a forward pass," the paper reported three days later. "None of the 12 tosses—an unusually low number—landed in his mitts."

If there was ever a game in which Hutson *wasn't* going to catch a pass, this was it. George Halas and the Chicago Bears were sitting in the stands scouting for their big game the next week against Green Bay, and the Packers wisely kept their passing game under wraps.

Staying mostly on the ground, they pounded out a 24–7 victory at State Fair Park. Commissioner Elmer Layden was among the crowd of 18,463. Hutson did catch a pass, but it was a Cleveland pass. His third-quarter interception set up the third Green Bay TD.

How Hutson's 95-game streak got into the record book is anyone's guess. The first time it appears is 1963. Maybe a recordkeeper, years later, simply misread the interception as a reception. It's also possible

NICKNAMES

Al "The Human Howitzer" Blozis

Tony Canadeo, "The Gray Ghost of Gonzaga"

Merlyn "The Magician" Condit

Edward "Ty" Coon

Jim "Casey" Jones

"Long" John Wilson

Larry "Superman" Craig

John "Tree" Adams

Gil "Cactus Face" Duggan

"Bullet" Bill Dudley

Nello "Flash" Falaschi

"Squirmin'" Herman Wedemeyer

Foster "Flippin' " Watkins

"Pitchin' " Paul Governali

"Indian" Jack Jacobs

Wilbur "Little Indian" Moore

Marshall "Biggie" Goldberg

Leonard "Bear Tracks" Barnum

Lamar "Racehorse" Davis

Clyde "Bulldog" Turner

Frank "Bruiser" Kinard

Fred "Chopper" Vanzo

Kenneth "Kayo" Lunday

George "Bad News" Cafego

Earl "Greasy" Neale

Walter "Piggy" Barnes

Hugh "Bones" Taylor

Wilbur "Wee Willie" Wilkin

"Baby Jack" Torrance

Harry "Jiggs" Kline

Charles "Cotton" Price

Abisha "Bosh" Pritchard

"Old Stoneface" (Bob Waterfield)

Bob "Twenty Grand" Davis

Johnny "Mr. Zero" Clement

Hodges "Burr" West

Bill "Bubbles" Young

Ezzret "Sugarfoot" Anderson

John "Blondy" Black

Special mention: "Carpets" for the merged Cardinals-Steelers team that went winless in 1944.

Not Nicknames:

Sloko Gill

Army Tomaini

Prince Scott

Noble Doss

the Packers' statistician "accidentally" recorded it that way to keep the streak going.

Whatever the explanation, Hutson's "record" lasted 24 years. When it was finally broken by San Diego's Lance Alworth in 1969, Hutson was there to congratulate him.

The real record belonged to St. Louis' Bobby Joe Conrad, who had a 94-game streak from 1961 to '68. Before him, Tommy McDonald caught a pass in 93 straight games for Philadelphia and Dallas from 1957 to '64. They owned the record and didn't even know it.

▪▪▪
BANG-BANG PLAY

Then there was the time umpire C. W. "Chick" Rupp shot himself in the hand with his timer's gun. It happened October 19, 1941, during a Giants–Steelers game at the Polo Grounds.

At the end of the first quarter, Rupp fired the gun, checked to make sure the blank had discharged, then started toward the other end of the field, the gun in his left hand. Bang! The gun went off again.

The webbing between two of his fingers was blown away, and he sustained deep powder burns on his hand. He recuperated for a few days in St. Elizabeth's Hospital before returning home to Akron, Ohio.

The mishap apparently ended his NFL officiating career. He isn't on the list of officials for 1942 or any year after that. He did, however, work in All-America Football Conference for a couple of seasons without doing himself in.

▪▪▪
A STAR IS BORN

In 1941 Republic Studios featured Redskins quarterback Sammy Baugh in the rip-roaring serial *King of the Texas Rangers*.

Baugh played Slinging Tom King, quarterback of the Texas All-Stars, whose lawman father is killed by bad guys. King trades in his football for a six-shooter to avenge his pa's death and keep the Southwest safe for decent folk. His most memorable line is: "C'mon gal, we've gotta git goin'."

Director Jack English had never heard of Baugh and didn't like working with athletes. "Why oh why don't they send me an actor?" he complained. "Even a seal. At least I could train one of them."

Baugh wasn't thrilled, either. He was afraid his celebrity status might come back to haunt him on the field.

"I can see it coming already," he said. "Some big guy is going to knock me down and then give me his hand and say, 'Mister Barrymore, can I assist you to your feet?' "

▪▪▪
THE LAST BARE HEAD

The last NFL player to go helmetless was about what you'd expect. On the field, Chicago Bears end Dick Plasman was ferocious, tough and mean. Away from it, he was a loner who could do crazy things "with booze, with girls and so forth. Not the kinds of things you'd want to put in your book," a teammate says.

Plasman's bareheaded career lasted from 1937 to '41. He then went into the service for two years, and during that time the NFL made the headgear mandatory (beginning in 1943). He wore a helmet in his last three seasons—one with the Bears, two with the Cardinals.

Plasman said he simply wasn't comfortable in a helmet. He hadn't used one in high school or college (Vanderbilt) and didn't see any reason to change once he got to the pros. He was 6'3", about 225 and could more than take care of himself. He grew his hair long and thick to provide some padding against blows, but teammates say he probably didn't need it.

"About the only way you could have taken advantage of it was with a baseball bat," says back Hugh Gallarneau. "I mean, he had a piece of cement for a head."

"We called him Eric the Red," says back Ray Nolting. "Not because he had red hair but because of his temper. He was something."

But at least once—on November 6, 1938—Plasman paid the price for playing without a helmet. In the first quarter of a game against the Packers at Wrigley Field, he dove for a pass from Ray Buivid and crashed into the brick wall at the south end of

The Bears' Bill Hewitt, one of the last bareheaded players, catches one in a crowd. (UPI/Bettmann Newsphotos)

the field. He suffered a nasty cut that ran almost completely across the top of his head and was carried from the field semiconscious.

According to one account, when he came to in the locker room, his first words were: "Did we score?"

Plasman died December 6, 1981, at 67. In his later years, he had a number of health problems, including blindness. Some believe his helmetless days were a contributing factor.

■ ■ ■
DECEMBER 7, 1941

December 7, 1941, was Tuffy Leemans Day at the Polo Grounds. Before the game against the Dodg-

ers, Postmaster General James Farley presented the Giants' star back with $1,500 in defense bonds. Leemans also came away with a gold watch and a silver tray.

Two other games were scheduled on the last day of the regular season. The Bears were playing the Cardinals at Comiskey Park, and the Eagles were on the road against the Redskins. The Bears–Cards game was the only one that mattered. The Bears (9–1) were half a game behind the Packers (10–1) in the Western Division and needed a win to force a playoff. The NFL had never had a divisional playoff before.

The Bears had crushed the Cardinals (3–6–1), 53–7, two months earlier and weren't expected to encounter much resistance. Four Bears made the 11-man all-league team that season and two more

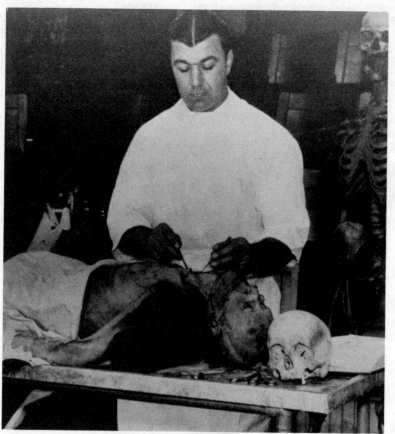

Our editor was dead-set against using this photo, but it was two against one. Granted it's gruesome, but it's also the most unusual picture on file at the Pro Football Hall of Fame (and probably any other Hall of Fame, for that matter). That's Bears lineman Joe "Doc" Kopcha working on the cadaver. (Pro Football Hall of Fame/NFL Photos)

made the second team. George Halas' club averaged 36 points a game, a record. This was a powerhouse.

But the Cardinals jumped out to a 14–0 lead and were still ahead, 24–21, early in the fourth quarter. Halas got so riled up at one point he charged onto the field, earning himself a $100 fine. The Bears' Ray (Muscles) Bray was ejected for "slugging." Afterward Cards coach Jimmy Conzelman told Halas he "never wanted to win a game like this one."

Several Packers were sitting in the stands watching the goings-on and taking notes. Coach Curly Lambeau was there, along with Don Hutson, Cecil Isbell, Clarke Hinkle, Andy Uram, Ed Frutig and Buford Ray. But maybe there wasn't going to be any playoff.

Then again, maybe there was. The Bears were at the Cardinals 41, and line coach Luke Johnsos called down a play to Halas from his second-deck perch. It was a pass over the middle to halfback George McAfee. McAfee was wide open. He grabbed Sid Luckman's throw at the 17 and went in standing up to put the Bears in front, 28–24.

A short time later McAfee broke away for a 70-yard TD—the longest run in the NFL in '41—to seal the 34–24 victory. It also gave him 12 touchdowns for the season, tying Hutson's league mark.

In New York, the Dodgers were as determined as the Cardinals. The Giants (8–2) had already wrapped up the Eastern Division title, but second-place Brooklyn (6–4) wanted to sweep the season series and prove it was the better team.

The Dodgers dominated. Before the biggest NFL crowd of the season, 55,051, they shut out the Giants until late in the game and won, 21–7. Pug Manders scored all three of their touchdowns, one on a 65-yard interception return.

Mel Hein, the Giants' seemingly indestructible center, was taken to St. Elizabeth's Hospital with a broken nose and a concussion. It was the first time in his 11-year pro career he had been knocked permanently out of a game because of an injury.

Near the end, the Giants' Lou DeFilippo and the Dodgers' Happy Sivell got into a fight. DeFilippo knocked Sivell down. Both were fined $50 by the league.

During the game, the *New York Times* reported, "An ominous buzzing was heard around Coogan's Bluff after an announcement over the public-address system informed Colonel William J. Donovan that he was being paged by Washington."

But it wasn't until the crowd was filing out that suspicions were confirmed. This is what came over the PA: "All Navy men in the audience are ordered to report to their posts immediately. All Army men are to report to their posts tomorrow morning. This is important."

The game in Washington had a thrilling finish. Sammy Baugh rallied the Redskins to two fourth-quarter touchdowns to pull out a 20–14 victory over the Eagles. But as Baugh was directing the winning drive, most of the 27,102 in attendance had either already left or were heading for the exits. Rumors of war were rampant, and people wanted to know what was going on.

They weren't going to find out much at Griffith Stadium. Redskins owner George Preston Marshall wouldn't allow any announcements about Pearl Harbor "because it is against the policy of the Redskin management to broadcast non-sports news over the stadium's public-address system," the *Washington Star* reported.

Radio broadcasters gave fans listening to the game regular war bulletins. But at Griffith Stadium there was a virtual news blackout. At halftime, however, the crowd began to get an inkling. Usually only doctors get paged during football games, but on this day calls started going out for prominent newspapermen and high-ranking military officials.

"Report to your office at once," they were told.

By the time Baugh flipped a four-yard pass to rookie end Joe Aguirre for the deciding score, the place had pretty well emptied out. There were a few things more important than football, and war was one of them.

WORLD WAR II'S TOLL

World War II claimed the lives of 20 NFL men—18 active or former players, an ex–head coach and a front office worker.

Probably the best active player killed was New York Giants tackle Al Blozis. Blozis was 6'6", 250 pounds and an all-league choice in 1943, his second season. He was killed by machine-gun fire in France six weeks after playing in the 1944 NFL championship game.

Blozis insisted on joining the Army even though he could have been exempted because of his size. He'd been a world-class shot-putter at Georgetown and reportedly set a U.S. Army record in the hand-grenade throw during basic training.

In all, 638 NFL people (players, coaches, management) served during the war, 355 as commissioned officers. Sixty-nine were decorated. Two—Giants end Jack Lummus and Lions end Maurice Britt—were awarded the Congressional Medal of Honor.

Lummus received his posthumously. He played one year, 1941, with the Giants and caught one pass for five yards. He died after stepping on a land mine on Iowa Jima. He'd led his platoon against the Japanese during two straight days and nights of fighting.

Britt, too, played only the 1941 season and caught one pass—a 45-yarder for a touchdown. He was the NFL's most-decorated soldier. In addition to the Medal of Honor, he received the Silver Star, Bronze Star, Distinguished Service Cross, Purple Heart with Oak Leaf cluster and the British Military Cross. He had his arm amputated after being wounded in Italy.

Those killed during the war:

- **Cpl. Mike Basca** (HB, Philadelphia, 1941)—Killed in France in '44.
- **Lt. Charlie Behan** (E, Detroit, 1942)—Killed on Okinawa in '45.
- **Maj. Keith Birlem** (E, Cards–Washington, 1939)—Killed trying to land combat-damaged bomber in England in '43.
- **Lt. Al Blozis** (T, Giants, 1942–44)—Killed in France in '45.
- **Lt. Chuck Braidwood** (E, Portsmouth–Cleveland–Cards–Cincinnati, 1930–33)—Member of Red Cross. Killed in South Pacific, winter 1944–45.
- **Lt. Young Bussey** (QB, Bears, 1940–41)—Killed during Philippines landing assault in '44.
- **Lt. Jack Chevigny** (Coach, Cards, 1932)—Killed on Iowa Jima in '44.
- **Capt. Ed Doyle** (E, Frankford–Pottsville, 1924–25)—Killed during North Africa invasion in '42.
- **Lt. Col. Grassy Hinton** (B, Staten Island, 1932)—Killed in plane crash in East Indies in '44.
- **Capt. Smiley Johnson** (G, Green Bay, 1940–41)—Killed on Iowa Jima in '44.
- **Lt. Eddie Kahn** (G, Boston/Washington, 1935–37)—Died from wounds suffered during Leyte invasion in '45.
- **Sgt. Alex Ketzko** (T, Detroit, 1943)—Killed in France in '44.
- **Capt. Lee Kizzire** (FB, Detroit, 1937)—Shot down near New Guinea in '43.
- **Lt. Jack Lummus** (E, Giants, 1941)—Killed on Iwo Jima in '44.
- **Pvt. Jim Mooney** (E-G-FB, Newark–Brooklyn–Cincinnati–St. Louis–Cards, 1930–37)—Killed by sniper in France in '44.
- **Lt. John O'Keefe** (Front office, Philadelphia)—Killed flying a patrol mission in Panama Canal Zone.
- **Lt. Len Supulski** (E, Philadelphia, 1942)—Killed in plane crash in Nebraska in '44.
- **Lt. Don Wemple** (E, Brooklyn, 1941)—Killed in plane crash in India in '44.

■ **Lt. Chet Wetterlund** (HB, Cards–Detroit, 1942)—Killed in plane crash off New Jersey coast in '44.

■ **Capt. Waddy Young** (E, Brooklyn, 1939–40)—Killed in plane crash following first B-29 raid on Tokyo in '45.

■ **Note:** Chief Spec. Gus Sonnenberg (Buffalo–Columbus–Detroit–Providence, 1923–28, '30) is often listed among the killed. He died of leukemia at Bethesda (Maryland) Naval Hospital in '44.

■ ■ ■

FOOTBALL: AMERICA'S LAST BEST HOPE

Football coaches have always been apologists for their profession. For years we've been on the defensive against attacks from reformers who regard us as muscle-bound mentalities exploiting kids for an easy living. Football has been under fire because it involves body contact and it teaches violence. It was considered useless, even dangerous.

But that's all over now. The bleeding hearts haven't the courtesy to apologize to us, but they're coming around and asking our help in the national emergency. Why?

Why, because the college commencement classes this month find the customary challenge of life a pale prelude to the demands of a world at war. Instead of job seekers, or home makers, the graduates suddenly have become defenders of a familiar way of life, of an ideology, a religion and of a nation. They have been taught to build. Now they must learn to destroy.

It may seem reprehensible to inculcate a will to destroy in these amiable young men; but war is reprehensible—and its basic motive is to destroy. The transition will not be an easy one. Democracy makes us a pacific people. The young man must be toughened not only physically, but mentally. He must become accustomed to violence. Football is the No. 1 medium for attuning a man to body-contact and physical shock. It teaches us that after all there isn't anything so terrifying about a punch in the puss.

—*Cardinals coach* JIMMY CONZELMAN, *May 1942*

■ ■ ■

DAY OF DAYS

There's something to be said for honoring a guy with a day when he can still play.

Sid Luckman threw an NFL-record seven touchdown passes against the Giants on Sid Luckman Day at the Polo Grounds in 1943. He also established another mark with 433 yards passing.

Sammy Baugh fired six TD passes against the eventual league champion Cardinals on Sammy Baugh Day at Griffith Stadium in 1947.

Luckman, by the way, received two $1,000 war bonds. Baugh got a $3,000 station wagon—Redskins maroon.

■ ■ ■

THE PUZZLING 1941-43 PACKERS

If football really is—as coaches are forever telling us—a game of mistakes, then how do you explain the 1941–43 Green Bay Packers?

Each of those Packers teams ranks among the 10 best of all time in turnover differential (turnovers caused minus turnovers committed). Not one of them, however, won a division title, let alone a league title.

The '43 Packers had a per-game turnover edge of plus 2.6, the second-highest ever. But the Bears, who had a *negative* turnover differential, beat them out in the Western Division.

BEST TURNOVER DIFFERENTIAL		
Year Team (W–L)	Edge	Avg.
1983 Redskins (14-2)	+43	+2.68
1943 Packers (7-2-1)	+26	+2.60
1958 Colts (9-3)*	+30	+2.50
1960 Browns (8-3-1)	+28	+2.33
1939 Giants (9-1-1)	+25	+2.27
1941 Packers (10-1)	+24	+2.18
1959 Colts (9-3)*	+26	+2.17
1944 Giants (8-1-1)	+21	+2.10
1963 Bears (11-1-2)*	+29	+2.07
1950 Giants (10-2)	+24	+2.00
1942 Packers (8-2-1)	+22	+2.00

*won title

MAKING WEIGHT

Bulldog Turner's surefire tips for beating the weekly weigh-in:

■ Always wear a T-shirt and underwear. Just before getting on the scale, take off the T-shirt and nonchalantly place it at the left end of the balance arm. This will act as a counterweight and buy you several pounds. If that isn't enough, use the underwear, too. "I can still put a jock strap in exactly the right place to knock off five pounds," Bulldog says.

■ Be sure a friend follows you in line. When you step on the scale, have him put a finger under each of your buttocks and lift ever so gently. Be sure he's a *good* friend.

■ Place your feet on the scale so that your big toes extend over the edge. Curl them over and push up. You'll be surprised at how many pounds you can take off.

Note: Turner was fined ($50 a pound) only once in his 13 years with the Bears. He claims to have been over his 230-pound playing weight quite a bit more than that.

■ ■ ■

ZEROING IN

The last 0–0 tie in the NFL was played between the New York Giants and the Detroit Lions at Briggs Stadium on November 7, 1943. Neither team got inside the 15-yard line in the rainy and muddy conditions. The Lions' Augie Lio missed three field-goal attempts and the Giants' Ward Cuff one. The next week, the Giants gave up 56 points and a league-record 682 yards against the Chicago Bears.

■ ■ ■

DOUBLE TAKE

On the NFL officiating rolls in 1943 and '44 was a fellow by the name of Fay Vincent, an umpire who went to Yale. Sorry to report it's not the baseball commissioner, only his father. Fay Vincent, Sr., also called 'em as he saw 'em in the All-America Football Conference from 1946 to '49.

THE TOUGHEST TRAINING CAMP OF ALL TIME

"We're starting from scratch. . . . All positions are wide open."

With those words, Jock Sutherland opened the most torturous training camp of all time. The year was 1946. Sutherland, the famous college coach, had just signed a lucrative contract ($12,500 a year, 25 percent of the profits *plus* a stock option) to whip the bedraggled Steelers into a winner.

To his assistants, he said: "Let's get rid of the loafers first. Work them hard. The ones we don't want will quit early, and we won't have to waste time with them."

To his players, he said: "We must have the will to win, the determination to see the game through. Without it we have nothing."

Reveille was at 7:30. By 8:45, the players had breakfasted and dressed for practice. The morning workout ran about two hours, the afternoon session three. The team scrimmaged on the second day and kept right on hitting until the final cut.

Sometimes there were two scrimmages a day. To Sutherland, there was "only one way to find out who's who and what's what."

Meetings were held every night at 8:00. Lights had to be out by 10:00—not that there was much to do at that hour in Hershey, Pennsylvania. But it must have made a lot of men wonder if they should have stayed in the service.

Sutherland was merciless. He had oatmeal put in the water so it wouldn't taste as good and the players wouldn't drink as much during practice. He cut one player for smoking a cigarette at dinner. (Guard Mike Rodak, who liked to chew tobacco during workouts, *wasn't* cut, however. At least not right away.) A lot of the players simply cut themselves. Who needed it?

Bob Drum of the *Pittsburgh Press,* a former Alabama player, practiced with the team one day. "There will be only two kinds of men on the Pittsburgh Steeler roster this fall," he wrote, "—those who are in shape and those who are dead."

Tackle Joe Coomer's waistline was whittled from 44 to 40 inches. The Steelers were easily the lightest team in the league that season. Only five players topped 210 pounds. Tackle Art McCaffray weighed 190, guard Ray Bucek 186.

"We must strive for perfection," Sutherland told them. "One mistake is enough to cost us a ballgame, and we must have a club which refuses to make that mistake."

He also issued this threat, as the final cut approached: "Unless some of the big-name and highly touted performers do a rapid changeover, they'll go out on the waiver list Monday morning."

(One Saturday night, Sutherland ate at the local steakhouse with general manager John Halloran and University of Tennessee coach Bob Neyland. Not long after they left, the place burned to the ground. You can imagine how disappointed the players were that he didn't have a later reservation.)

The Steelers went undefeated in the preseason, beating four minor league teams by lopsided scores. After the last exhibition game, a 55–0 pummeling of the Paterson Panthers, Sutherland actually cracked a smile.

Only 9 of the 33 players who suited up for the opener against the Chicago Cardinals at Forbes Field had been with the Steelers before. Sutherland used just 22 men in the game—to 31 for the Cards—until the last two plays.

Pittsburgh won, 17–7, and stayed in contention for the division title until the next-to-last week.

■ ■ ■

BAD BREAK

Rookie halfback Bill McArthur was on his way to winning a starting job with the 1946 Chicago Rockets when he fractured his leg in an intrasquad game. The injury was so severe doctors had to amputate above the knee.

Dick Hanley, coach of the AAFC club, called McArthur a "second Dutch Clark." That may have been a slight exaggeration, but McArthur *was* a tremendous athlete. He ran the 100-yard dash in 9.5 seconds in high school and might have competed in the decathlon in the 1940 Olympics if they'd been held.

He could even drop-kick. Four years of rugby at Santa Barbara State College had helped him develop that talent. His range was 50 yards. There wasn't much he couldn't do on a football field.

He made honorable mention All-America, but at 5′9″, 165 pounds wasn't built for pro ball. So he went to Oregon College of Education and got his master's degree in physical education.

In 1942 he enlisted, and in '45 he starred on the Air Transport Command team in Nashville, Tennessee. By then he'd filled out to 188 pounds. George Halas of the Chicago Bears offered him a contract at $300 a game, but McArthur got a better deal from the first-year Rockets.

"I thought I was right on the verge of popping into the big time," he says.

He was hurt running back an interception. As he was about to cut across the field, he was hit high from the back and low from the front. His left leg simply snapped. He had planted his left foot the moment before impact, and the long cleats players wore in those days locked it in the ground.

"What a hell of a short career that was!" he reportedly cracked as teammates carried him off.

Doctors couldn't restore circulation in his foot. The shattered bones had severed an artery. Gangrene developed. Amputation was the only alternative.

"One of the things that upset me was that I thought I was every bit as good as Elroy [Hirsch, one of the team's other halfbacks]," he says. "I wasn't quite as big, but I was faster. I never had an opportunity to show people how good I was."

McArthur scouted for the Rockets while he was recovering but lost the job when owner John Keeshin sold the club after the season. The following September he returned to Oregon College of Education (now Western Oregon State) as head football and track coach. He stayed 37 years, later becoming athletic director. The school's sports complex is named for him. He's also in the NAIA coaches' Hall of Fame.

■ ■ ■

REASON NUMBER TWO TO HATE GEORGE PRESTON MARSHALL

No one fought the rival All-America Football Conference with more fervor than George Preston Marshall. His goal wasn't capitulation but annihilation, and his hard-headedness nearly broke several NFL franchises. Marshall squashed a merger effort in 1948, almost did it again the following year and took every opportunity to cheapen the opposition publicly.

In '47, AAFC commissioner (and retired Admiral) Jonas Ingram proposed a championship game between the leagues, the proceeds to go to charity. "Why doesn't Ingram play Navy for charity if he has to have another game?" Marshall replied snootily.

Several months later, Redskins quarterback Sammy Baugh was quoted as saying the championship game wasn't a bad idea. Halas read the remarks in a Chicago paper and called Marshall. After some *checking*, Marshall reported back to Halas that Baugh either had been misquoted or hadn't made the statements. Halas called the Chicago paper, relayed Marshall's information and reminded the editor of "the penalties of perjury."

Marshall and Halas could afford a hard-line approach. The Redskins and Bears were the only teams in either league to make money in each year of the war. Most clubs lost big. The war cost the NFL its Boston franchise (relocated to New York in '49), while those in Detroit, Green Bay and Los Angeles teetered. AAFC teams, meanwhile, lost an estimated $6.48 million.

A merger appeared imminent late in the '48 season. But needing a unanimous vote for approval, the NFL came up nine owners for, one against. Guess who the one was. (Hint: It wasn't Halas.)

Marshall's stated objection was Baltimore. He wanted $250,000 from the struggling AAFC franchise because the Colts would be playing within his 75-mile territorial border. So the war continued. In December 1949 the two leagues came together

Redskins owner George Preston Marshall strikes a Gatsbyesque pose. (Pro Football Hall of Fame/NFL Photos)

again. As the final details were being worked out, Marshall pulled one more stunt. He insisted the Cleveland Browns (the AAFC's best and strongest franchise) be the "swing" team in the new 13-team, two-division alignment. That meant the Browns would have to play every club once.

"We threatened to dissolve the agreement unless

we got a square deal," ex–Browns coach Paul Brown said. "I knew that being a swing team was a no-win situation; no such team has ever had success in the NFL."

Marshall finally relented. The swing-team role fell instead to Baltimore, by far the weakest of the three AAFC teams absorbed by the NFL. The Redskins were the only NFL club that got to play the Colts twice in '50. They beat them both times—and went 1–9 in their other games.

The Colts also wound up paying Marshall a "nominal" fee of $50,000 for territorial rights. They folded after one season.

...

PRO FOOTBALL'S FORGOTTEN SCANDAL

Books have been written and a movie made about the 1919 World Series fix. Why the same fascination hasn't been aroused by the attempt to rig the 1946 NFL championship game, it's hard to say.

Maybe it's because the plot was uncovered beforehand. Or because the Giants' Merle Hapes and Frank Filchock never agreed to throw the game. Or because neither player was nicknamed Shoeless Joe.

Still, it's a terrific story, the only such scandal in NFL history. During the two trials that followed— one for Alvin Paris, the 28-year-old gambler who tried to set it up, the other for the three New Jersey bookmakers he was fronting for—the public got a titillating glimpse of the off-field activities of pro football players.

Boozing. Womanizing. Late-night carousing. It's all there. A Hollywood actress was even subpoenaed. Bit-part player Ida McGuire, a friend of Paris, never testified, but she did tell the press she had had several dates with Hapes. Both players were married and had children. Filchock was divorced shortly afterward.

One of the gamblers convicted, Harvey Stemmer,

Alvin Paris, the would-be fixer. (UPI/Bettmann Newsphotos)

was already in Rikers Island prison for bribing Brooklyn College basketball players to throw games in 1945. In the second trial, Paris revealed that Stemmer called him "four or five times a day" while in prison, that he had occasionally visited Stemmer at Bellevue Hospital, where Stemmer worked as a trusty, and that Stemmer even visited him. The city's commissioner of corrections lost his job over this.

Paris' attorney was Caesar Barra, who had once defended mobster Lucky Luciano. Paris was found guilty, but he received a reduced one-year sentence (and served nine months and one day) after agreeing to turn state's evidence.

Some legal history was made, too. The convictions of Paris, Stemmer (5 to 10 years), David (Pete) Krakauer (5 to 10) and Jerome Zarowitz (up to 3) were the first under the state's new law against bribing or attempting to bribe athletes.

Stemmer and Krakauer appealed the case all the way to the Supreme Court. Their lawyer argued that evidence was obtained by wiretapping in violation of the Federal Communications Act. The court was divided 4–4 (one justice didn't participate), however, so the convictions stood. No written opinion was issued.

"The case was considered a landmark in wiretapping cases," the *New York Times* said, "which would tend to increase the use of wiretapping by state law enforcement officers."

It would be interesting to see what would happen if the case were tried today. Another thing that came out in the trials was that the wiretapped phone conversations weren't tape-recorded but written down in longhand by a policeman. The officer admitted it was sometimes difficult to keep up, but "I write down everything I can. . . . The errors I make are as far as spelling words."

Another effect of the fix attempt was to increase the power of NFL commissioner Bert Bell. In January, league owners gave the commissioner the authority to suspend for life anyone involved in the rigging or attempted rigging of a game. But because the old rules applied to Hapes and Filchock, all Bell could do was suspend them indefinitely for failing to report the bribe offers.

Ida McGuire, a minor film actress who got caught up in the attempt to fix the 1946 NFL championship game. What a tomato. (UPI/Bettmann Newsphotos)

The testimony indicates Hapes was the more involved of the two. Through him, Paris met Filchock and several other Giants players. Paris could have tried to recruit tackle Vic Carroll, back Howie Livingston and perhaps even end Jim Poole if he had wanted to. Filchock was the key, though, because he was the quarterback. Hapes was only the fullback (though he figured to play a more important role with Bill Paschal injured). And Filchock turned Paris down twice.

Bears quarterback Sid Luckman called the title game "the most vicious football game I'd ever played in my life." The Giants, and especially Filchock, who was allowed to play, felt they had something to prove.

The home team took most of the lumps, however. Filchock broke his nose in the first quarter, fullback Frank Reagan fractured his later in the first half and had to go to the hospital, and wingback George Franck separated his shoulder.

The *Times* said Filchock played "furiously," rallying the Giants from a 14–0 deficit with two touchdown passes. But he also threw six interceptions, still a playoff record, and one was returned for the Bears' second score. Had the fix attempt come to light *after* rather than before the game, we wonder if Filchock's efforts would have been viewed quite so kindly.

The indefinite suspensions didn't turn out to be for life, by the way. Filchock was reinstated in July 1950 and Hapes in December 1954. Both played in Canada in the interim. Filchock was the first American pro star to play in the Canadian leagues. The two-year package he signed with the Montreal Alouettes in 1949 was worth $25,200.

His goal, however, was to return to the NFL, and he grew impatient waiting. At one point he groused: "They needed a goat in the whole business and I was it. They dealt me one off the bottom of the deck. They took the easy way out.

"Twice since my suspension I wrote to Bell and asked him for the chance to talk this over. He answered me, all right, but just wrote that if I had any new evidence to put it into writing. . . . He's just got me hanging. Paris is out [of prison], isn't he? What about me?"

Years later he said: "If I had a lawyer, the whole thing probably wouldn't even have happened. Some lawyer advised me to sue them after I was reinstated, but I didn't. Why be bitter about anything?"

When Bell finally cleared Filchock to play, praising the quarterback for making "a real contribution to the promotion and development of clean sports in Canada," no team would touch him. So Filchock played for Montreal again.

But after the Canadian season ended, the last-place Baltimore Colts—a desperate, dying club—added him to the roster for the last couple of games. Filchock got into one of them, his last in the NFL, and completed one of three passes for one yard.

THE CHRONOLOGY OF THE FIX ATTEMPT

November 1946—At an Elks Lodge gathering in New York City, Giants fullback Merle Hapes meets Sidney Paris. Unknown to Hapes, Paris is a convicted felon who served four years for mail fraud in Atlanta. Paris invites Hapes to a cocktail party November 30 at his son Alvin's apartment on West 56th Street.

Saturday, November 30—Hapes finds a lively party at Alvin Paris' place—and good-looking women. He asks Paris if it would be all right to call Giants quarterback Frank Filchock and tell him to come over. Sure, Paris says. The players wind up making dates for the following Wednesday with two of the women. At one point, Paris asks Hapes how he thinks the team will do the next day against the Rams. Hapes says he doesn't think the Giants should be seven-point favorites. Paris and gambling partner Harvey Stemmer subsequently bet on the Rams and win $200.

Sunday, December 1—After the game, Hapes, Giants tackle Vic Carroll and back Howie Livingston and their wives have drinks at Paris' apartment. Paris talks to the players about becoming salesmen in his giftware and novelty business. You can make as much as $15,000 a year, he tells them, which is more than they make in football. The Livingstons leave shortly afterward. Paris takes the other two couples to the Copacabana and picks up the tab. The evening ends at 4:00 A.M.

Tuesday, December 3—Paris sounds out Hapes and Filchock about the upcoming game against second-place Washington, considered a virtual toss-up. The players tell him the Giants are determined to beat the Redskins and play the Bears for the title. Playoff shares could mean a couple of thousand dollars to each man.

Wednesday, December 4—Stemmer asks Paris if Hapes and Filchock could be talked into throwing the Redskins game. Paris says he doesn't think so and cites his conversation with the players the day before. The gamblers then put down $2,500 on the Giants, including a $500 bet for each of the players.

That night, Paris, the players and their dates go to a club in Mount Vernon. Paris again pays the bill.

Thursday, December 5—Hapes and Filchock go to Paris' place to discuss the sales jobs, which they're very interested in. The three then adjourn to a nearby restaurant.

Sunday, December 8—After the Giants rout the Redskins, 31–0, Hapes, his wife and brother go to dinner with Paris. Later, Hapes and Paris go out on the town, ending up at the Copacabana at about 3:00 A.M. As they sit at the bar, Paris makes his move. He offers to pay Hapes and Filchock $2,500 apiece—plus make a $1,000 bet for each of them—if they see to it that the Bears win the championship game by 10 points. Paris wants Hapes to feel Filchock out about the idea, but Hapes refuses. He does agree, though, to tell Filchock to call Paris. Paris, as usual, pays for everything.

(The same night, Paris claimed, he gave Hapes the $500 he bet for him on the Redskins game. Hapes, who knew nothing about the wager, took the money, according to Paris.)

Tuesday, December 10—Paris makes the same $3,500 proposition to Filchock. The quarterback says he isn't interested. Paris, not easily discouraged, asks him to think it over. Later at dinner, he introduces Filchock to a car salesman. Filchock had been talking about buying a Chevrolet, and the salesman tells Filchock he might be able to get him the car he wants.

Afterward, Paris tells his fellow gamblers he thinks he can buy off the players. The syndicate bets $15,000 to $20,000 on the Bears.

(That evening, Paris claimed, he gave Filchock the $500 he bet for him on the Giants–Rams game. Filchock at first wouldn't accept the money, "but I insisted, and he finally took it," Paris said.)

Wednesday, December 11—Paris makes his last pitch to Filchock at a luncheonette on 110th Street and Broadway. The Giants are leaving later in the day to finish training at their Bear Mountain camp. Paris may have upped his offer to Filchock to $5,000 at this time. Filchock still declines. Paris advises his associates to start hedging their bets.

Thursday, December 12—Paris phones Hapes at Bear Mountain. Hapes tells him that the fix is no go.

Friday, December 13—Paris drives Hapes' wife and daughter, end Jim Poole's wife and daughter and Mrs. Poole's sister up to Bear Mountain for the afternoon. The group has lunch and watches practice before returning to the city. Paris is introduced to some of the Giants players.

Saturday, December 14—Paris again calls Hapes at Bear Mountain. Hapes tells him the Giants are primed, and Paris says he's going to try to get some money down on them. "Tell Francis I'll be rooting there," he adds. "He better show some [expletive deleted] good passing." Paris reminds Hapes of their plans to get together for dinner after the Bears game—Paris, the two players and their wives. (Filchock's wife is coming up from their home in Washington for the game.)

That night, Mayor William O'Dwyer summons Hapes and Filchock to Gracie Mansion and confronts them with evidence, gathered by police, of the fix attempt. Hapes admits having been offered a bribe to throw the championship game; Filchock doesn't (yet).

Sunday, December 15—Just after 2:00 A.M., Paris is arrested and brought to the West 54th Street station. Filchock goes there with O'Dwyer, NFL commissioner Bert Bell, Giants and police officials and doesn't leave until almost 3:00. Bell lets him play against the Bears. Hapes, however, is suspended for failing to report the bribe offer. Filchock breaks his nose in the first quarter but remains in the game. The Bears, 10-point favorites, win by exactly that margin, 24–14.

■ ■ ■

ON THE WITNESS STAND

MERLE HAPES

Q: When did you next see Alvin [Paris]?

A: On Sunday [December 7, after the Giants-Redskins game] about 7 P.M. at his apartment. He invited me and my wife and brother, Ray, a lieutenant in the Army.

(Hapes said they went to a restaurant and stayed for three hours, drinking. Paris picked up the check. Then Hapes and his wife put his brother on a train to Baltimore.)

Q: Where else, then, did you go?

A: Alvin, my wife and myself went to the Carnival [a nightclub].

Q: Who paid the bill there?

A: Alvin.

Q: What next did you do?

A: I took my wife home to our apartment.

Q: Then where did you go?

A: Alvin and I went to the Martinique [another night spot].

Q: Did you have any drinks there?

A: Yes.

Q: Who paid the bill?

A: Alvin.

Q: Did you go anywhere else?

A: Yes, to the Copacabana.

Q: How long did you stay there?

A: Two-and-a-half hours.

Q: Did you have any conversation with the defendant about football?

A: Yes. He asked me to see if the Bears would win by 10 points.

Q: What did you say?

A: I said: "What do you mean?" And Alvin then said: "I want you to throw the football game." I said: "What do you mean?"

(Hapes is asked to tell everything about the conversation he can remember.)

A: Well, he told me that there would be money in it for him if the Bears would win by 10 points. He told me that there would be $2,500 in it for me and that he would put a $1,000 bet down on the game for me and Filchock. I told him to speak to Frank Filchock himself.

Q: What did you say then to him?

A: I told him I could only fumble the ball, and that was no go. I told him Frankie Filchock would be the man if anything like that could be done. I told him he should speak to Filchock himself, and he went to the phone.

ALVIN PARIS*

Q: What happened after that?

A: Filchock called me on Tuesday [December 10] and came down to the apartment around 3:30.

Q: Tell us the full conversation.

A: I asked him if he thought the game could be thrown, and he said he had heard that people did help to throw games. I asked him if he could do it. He said he didn't know what to do or how to do it. I told him it would be worth $2,500 if he threw the game.

Q: Go ahead.

A: He said he would think about it and let me know.

Q: After you spoke with Filchock on Tuesday, what did you do?

A: I called the bookmaking office in Elizabeth, N.J. . . . I told him [associate Jerry Zarowitz] what had happened and that I thought something might be done. . . . I told him I thought I was going to be able to buy these two players off and get them to throw the game.

Q: What was the result of your conversation?

A: They bet about 15 to 20 thousand dollars on the Chicago Bears. . . .

* * *

Q: Did you know that Hapes and Filchock were married family men?

A: Yes.

Q: Did it not occur to you that these parties with young women would break up their homes?

A: No.

Q: Yet you supplied girls for them?

A: I never supplied a girl for anybody. I merely arranged the dates out of the goodness of my heart. . . .

* * *

*The first part is excerpted from his signed confession.

(Phone conversation between Paris and accomplice Harvey Stemmer on December 13, as recorded by police.)

STEMMER: Did you hear from Jerry?

PARIS: I was talking to Jerry and Pete [Krakauer, another of the gamblers] and we're all of the same opinion—to drop it [the bet] off as long as F.F. can't be induced to go along.

STEMMER: Okay. Tell him it is both of them or out.

FRANK FILCHOCK

Q: When was this party?

A: November 30. It was on a Saturday. About 5 P.M. At Paris' apartment, 56 West 56th St.

Q: Who did you find there that you knew?

A: The place was filled with people. I didn't know anybody but Hapes.

Q: Was it a stag or a mixed party?

A: A mixed party.

Q: Did you meet some very nice girls?

A: Yes, sir, I did.

Q: When did you next see Paris?

A: Next Wednesday. That was December 4.

Q: What was the occasion?

A: I had dinner with him.

Q: Who was present at the dinner?

A: Hapes, the defendant Paris, two girls and myself.

Q: You had made a date?

A: Yes, that's correct. We had made a date at the party. . . .

* * *

Q: [After December 10,] did you hear from the defendant again?

A: Yes, the next day. We met in the Liberty Lunch at 110th Street and Broadway.

Q: What did Paris say at that meeting?

A: He said: "Have you thought over what we were talking about?" I said: "Al, damn it, I just won't do it. I won't have anything to do with a thing like that. The boys depend upon me too much. I have my family to think of." He said: "Aren't we still friends?" I said: "I don't give a damn if we are friends or not."

Q: You never reported this to anybody?

A: No.

Q: You were in Mayor [William] O'Dwyer's home at Gracie Mansion, weren't you?

A: Yes, I was.

Q: Did you talk to the mayor?

A: Yes.

Q: Did you conceal anything from the mayor?

A: Yes, the money part.

Q: Isn't it a fact that you told the mayor you never were offered a bribe?

A: Yes. That is right.

· · ·

THE GAMBLING SCANDAL THAT WASN'T

On December 8, 1943, the nation's capital woke to the news that several Redskins players might be part of an NFL gambling investigation. No names were mentioned in the copyrighted story in the *Washington Times-Herald,* but it was evident quarterback Sammy Baugh was one.

The league office reacted with rancor, claiming reporters Vince Flaherty and Dick O'Brien had "misrepresented" their information and misquoted commissioner Elmer Layden. Redskins owner George Preston Marshall gathered 24 of his players and stormed into the *Times-Herald* offices to demand proof of the accusations. He received none.

The basis for the story turned out to be streetcorner rumors arising from the team's performance in a series of four games. On November 7, the then-undefeated Redskins were tied by the "Steagles" (the World War II–inspired merger of Pittsburgh and Philadelphia) after being 12-point favorites. Two weeks later, they beat the Chicago Bears 21–7 as heavy underdogs. On November 28 they lost to the Steagles as 4–1 favorites. And, finally, on December 5, they lost to the New York Giants as 3–1 favorites.

The *Times-Herald* reported that "all betting on National Professional League football games now has been curtailed and under no circumstances will book-makers accept a bet." The story also claimed Marshall had asked D.C. police to look into the possibility that players were involved in gambling.

Layden emphatically denied an investigation was underway. In his usual understated way, Marshall went on the radio and offered $5,000 to anyone who could prove players were in cahoots with gamblers.

But behind the scenes Marshall was concerned enough to have Baugh's hotel room bugged and his conversations secretly recorded. The quarterback was a logical subject for the rumors because of his position. Plus, he was known to associate on occasion with a local gambler named Pete Gianaris.

The *Times-Herald* story touched off a frantic catch-up effort by Washington's other dailies. But no news was forthcoming, and the story died a quick death.

"I investigated [it] thoroughly and found nothing," says *Washington Post* columnist Shirley Povich. "I knew Baugh well—I was his ghostwriter for a number of projects—and there was no way I could see him doing that [tanking games]. No one found anything."

On December 11, just three days after the story broke, the *Times-Herald* ran a picture of Flaherty standing between Baugh and teammate Ray Hare in Baugh's room. Sammy was holding a copy of the paper. Everyone was smiling.

"I'm doggoned glad the *Times-Herald* printed that story," the Redskins QB said in an accompanying column. "It was the best way to stop the rumors from going around."

Ironically, Baugh played one of the worst games of his career the next day. In a 31–7 loss to the Giants, he had a punt blocked for a touchdown, threw an interception and missed a number of wide-open receivers.

The defeat forced a playoff between the two teams for the Eastern Division title. The Redskins, 8–5 underdogs, stomped the Giants, 28–0.

For his 1989 book *Interference: How Organized Crime Influences Professional Football*, investigative reporter Dan Moldea obtained Marshall's secret recordings of Baugh's conversations. Moldea wrote that while "Baugh and other players" were heard discussing "point spreads, player injuries, inside information, bets and their bookmaker friends," there was nothing to indicate the Redskins were fixing games.

■ ■ ■

PAUL GOVERNALI, SCHOLAR-QUARTERBACK

Buried in the library stacks at Columbia University is a doctoral dissertation about pro football by former NFL quarterback Paul Governali. It's one of the best sources we have on the game in the late '40s.

Governali, who played for the Boston Yanks and New York Giants from 1947 to '49, got 393 players to respond to a questionnaire and interviewed 25 in depth. The result was "The Professional Football Player: His Vocational Status," which he submitted in 1951 for his doctorate in education.

His study is filled with nuggets large and small. For instance:

■ 32 percent of the players in 1949 were first-generation Americans.

■ 67 percent either rented housing or lived with relatives.

■ 64 percent worked in the off-season.

■ 68 percent had gotten their college diplomas (whereas 13 percent of their fathers had gone to college).

■ 47 percent had played service ball.

■ 63 percent played both offense and defense (23 percent played only offense and 13 percent only defense).

■ 94 percent would play pro football again (but 19 percent wouldn't recommend it to their sons).

■ Median age: 25.9. Height: "a little better than 6 feet." Weight: 207.

■ States that produced the most players: Pennsylvania 45, California 43, Texas 41, Ohio 32 and Illinois 28. (Some things never change.)

■ Colleges that produced the most players: Notre Dame 25, Ohio State 15, Southern Cal 14, Indiana 13, California 11. (Go Hoosiers!)

Governali also conducted what was probably pro football's first salary survey. He found 85 percent of the players had game-to-game contracts, which meant they could be released at any time and their teams wouldn't owe them a dime.

This was the salary structure in '49, according to Governali's figures:

Position	Range	Median
Ends	$5,000–13,000	$6,393
Tackles	5,000–10,000	5,844
Guards	4,000–10,000	5,611
Centers	4,000–10,000	6,550
Backs	4,000–20,000	7,568
Offense only	4,000–20,000	6,750
Defense only	4,000–9,000	5,789
Both ways	4,000–20,000	6,555

Guards, as you can see, were the lowest-paid players. Isn't it interesting, though, that not a single interior lineman (center, guard, tackle) made more than $10,000? Anybody smell a conspiracy?

Note, too, that the highest-paid defensive specialist earned just $9,000. Offensive specialists, on the other hand, got better contracts than players who went both ways. At the top of the scale were starting quarterbacks and single-wing tailbacks, who pulled down between $15,000 and $20,000.

What's more, "Figures show the number of years a professional competes in the league bears no relation to his earning powers," Governali wrote. "It is a well accepted reality among professionals that a player's over-all earnings during his professional career will depend greatly on his salary immediately after endorsing his first contract. The time the player should assure himself of a good income is immediately after he leaves college, for in many instances a good performance is left unrewarded because of a bad financial year by the owner."

Governali considered '49 salaries high because the NFL and AAFC were still at war. He expected them to drop about 25 percent in the next three to five years as a result of the merger. (Competition from the Canadian Football League, however, caused them to hold steady.)

The dissertation's weakness is that it doesn't name names. Players are quoted throughout, but neither they nor the people they refer to are identified. Governali, who died in 1978, likely did this to encourage candor.

Still, the comments reveal much about the players and their concerns. For a sampling, see the box, "Governali's Guys."

■ ■ ■

GOVERNALI'S GUYS

"I'm still playing because I haven't achieved my ambition. I've been playing with a losing team. I keep coming back year after year hoping we'll have a winner, but we never do. I've been making $10,000 a year in the off season as a car salesman but still come back every year for football just to get on a winner. I lost the sales managership of the agency because I left every year. I was recommended for it first and they wouldn't give it to me."

"I didn't want to come back this year. I wanted to play semi-pro ball and continue with my government job. While they [management] didn't come out and say they wouldn't let me go, they referred to the option on my contract and the understanding I got from my talk was that if I didn't play for them, I wouldn't play for anybody."

"Everybody reads about the $20,000 a year football player and they think everybody makes that kind of money. They expect more of you because you play pro ball and we really can't afford it. If we buy a gift for less than $10 around Christmas, people are insulted."

"This is my last year, boy. I'm gone 4½ months a year. She's [his daughter's] getting to the age where she knows who I am and she wants me around. I want to build a companionship between us and everything, and every year I have to leave for football just when we're getting used to each other and then when I come back we have to start all over again. I was lucky this year. We played an exhibition game in Texas and I was lucky. I got to see my wife and daughter for a day."

Continued on p. 114.

"Governali's Guys" *continued from p. 113.*

"You remember that exhibition game in Dallas against the ——— [name of team], the one that I came out of with a cut under the eye? The trainer had to take stitches because there was no doctor there. Everybody had left, coaches, players, hangers-on. There was just me and the trainer in an empty and lonesome old locker room 2,000 miles from home. I was on my back nude, with a towel between my legs, staring at the ceiling as ——— [the trainer] stitched me up. I realized then that nobody much cared or worried and I asked myself, 'Was it worth it?'"

BLACKS IN PRO FOOTBALL

Question put to Bears owner-coach George Halas in the early '60s: Why were there no black players in the NFL from 1934 to '45?

Halas' answer: "I don't know! Probably it was due to the fact that no great players were in the colleges then. That could be the reason. But I've never given this a thought until you mentioned it. At no time has it ever been brought up. Isn't that strange?"

Yes. What's even stranger is that Halas had considered signing a black player, UCLA's Kenny Washington, in 1940—*six years* before Washington reintegrated pro football with the Los Angeles Rams. The Bruins tailback had just starred in the College All-Star Game, and "Halas kept me around for a month trying to figure out how to get me in the league," he later recalled.

While he waited, Washington got married and played (the next day) with an all-black team in an exhibition game against the Waukegan (Illinois) Collegians. He finally went home, he said, "before he [Halas] suggested I go to Poland first."

Closing the door to black players caused no cataclysms. Only 13 had played in the league since its inception in 1920. Six were active in 1923 and '25, but there were never more than two after that.

The last were Chicago Cardinals back Joe Lillard and Pittsburgh Pirates tackle Ray Kemp. Lillard led the Cards in scoring in his final season; Kemp was a starter. They played minor league ball for several more years.

The NFL's attitude toward blacks in those days was "bad, very bad," says Pearce Johnson, then assistant GM of the Providence Steam Roller. "It was always 'Get that nigger!' No matter where you went on away games, it was the same thing: 'Get that nigger! Get that nigger!' Pollard [Fritz, a black who played with Providence] got drilled badly. . . . He was a marked man, no question."

Pollard learned to reduce the abuse by rolling on his back when he was tackled and raising his feet to expose his cleats. This helped him protect himself against would-be pilers-on.

When he played with the Akron Pros, Pollard used to dress for games in owner Frank Neid's cigar factory. "[T]hey'd send a car over for me before the game," he said in 1978. "The fans booed and called me all kinds of names, because they had a lot of southerners up there working. You couldn't eat in the restaurants or stay in the hotels. Hammond and Milwaukee were bad then, too, but never as bad as Akron was."

In 1924 Rock Island tackle Duke Slater had to sit out a game at Kansas City because the home team refused to play against a black. The Independents suffered an upset loss, and it helped keep them from winning the title.

The ability of these black pioneers was obvious, which makes the 1934–45 period all the more puzzling. Pollard made all-pro in 1920 and Hammond end Inky Williams did so in '23. The *Philadelphia Inquirer* heaped this praise on Pollard in '26: "Fritz Pollard was the only man on the field who could make any real impression, and Pollard, colored wizard, just tore around. He did not bother about headgear nor shinguards. . . . [H]e was the Akron attack."

Colored wizard. Newspapers never failed to make note of a player's blackness. Lillard was "the midnight express," "the ebony-hued tornado." Slater was the "colored colossus." It was no different—just a little less heavy-handed—in the late '40s and '50s.

Slater had the longest career of the early blacks—

10 seasons. He was probably also the best player. He made second-team all-pro six times.

NFL commissioner Elmer Layden called him "the greatest tackle I ever saw." In its account of Ernie Nevers' record-setting 40-point game for the Cardinals in 1931, the *Chicago Herald and Examiner* said: "Duke Slater, the veteran colored tackle, seemed the dominant figure in that forward wall which had the Bear front wobbly. It was Slater who opened the holes for Nevers when a touchdown was in the making."

How great was Slater? Put it this way: He was an interior lineman, and he was *well-known.*

Then came 1934. Halas and others have always claimed the disappearance of black players was something that *just happened,* that there was no written or unwritten agreement among the owners. No one with an ounce of intelligence has ever believed them.

So what brought it about? One possible explanation is the strong influence major league baseball had on pro football in the '30s. Most NFL clubs played in stadiums owned by baseball teams. Some even had the same name as those teams (New York Giants, Brooklyn Dodgers, Pittsburgh Pirates, Cincinnati Reds).

In 1933 the NFL split into two divisions, the winners of which would play for the championship (à la baseball). That was also the year a slimmer, easier-to-pass ball was introduced and the rules changed to make it a more offensive game (the beginning of football's "lively ball" era).

Baseball was booming—without black players. It's not hard to imagine NFL owners deciding to go the same route.

Five years after pro football went all-white, Halas' Bears played a black all-star team—a first—in a charity game at Soldier Field. A hundred black papers conducted a poll to pick the all-stars. The *Herald and Examiner* said it was "probably . . . the strongest Negro football team ever assembled."

Ray Kemp was the player-coach, assisted by Duke Slater and Inky Williams. Joe Lillard was one of the backs. The all-stars practiced for two weeks.

"Our boys have rhythm," Kemp said. "We can make that Notre Dame system work. We got some heft on this squad, too. We will match the Bears in size at the tackles and center and may have an advantage in speed in the backfield.

"We have a number of players who would be outstanding players in the leading colleges in the country. In fact some have been. Joe Kendall of Kentucky State, for example, is as good a passer as you will find anywhere in football, barring Sammy Baugh. We have excellent receivers in Dwight Reed and Doc Kelker of Western Reserve. Our passing may bother the Bears."

The *Chicago Tribune*'s George Strickler, however, didn't think much of the black opposition. "Graduates of ability are so few," he wrote, "that it has been necessary to include on the squad several men of established ability who have not been on a campus for a number of years." Then he added this backhanded compliment: "The All-Stars have sufficient dynamite to score once or twice before they wilt under the pace late in the game."

A crowd of 30,000 was expected; 6,000 showed up. The all-stars' performance did nothing to help the black cause. The Bears routed them 51–0 as 12 different players scored.

Strickler was no easier on the all-stars after the game than he was before. "The outstanding colored football players in the United States, selected in a nationwide poll, held the Chicago Bears to seven touchdowns, a field goal and six extra points in Soldiers' Field last night," his story began. He later became the NFL's publicist.

Reintegration in the '40s came slowly. In 1949, three years after Washington broke the color line, the NFL still had only five black players. The All-America Football Conference had 11—with three fewer clubs. (Note: Branch Rickey, the man who integrated baseball in 1947 with Jackie Robinson, owned the AAFC's Brooklyn Dodgers for a season in '48 and didn't have a black on the roster. Five of the eight teams in the league did.)

The impact of the black players was immediate. Fullback Marion Motley and guard Bill Willis helped Cleveland dominate the AAFC and then the NFL. Washington had the second-longest run in NFL history in 1947, 92 yards for a touchdown. In 1949 Bob Mann of Detroit became only the third receiver to gain 1,000 yards.

The Rams' Dick "Night Train" Lane had 14 interceptions as a rookie in 1952, a record that still stands (and he didn't make the Pro Bowl). Wally Triplett of the Lions set two kickoff-return marks in '50 that haven't been topped. The Browns' Horace Gillom led the league in punting in 1951 and '52. In 1954 the top *five* rushers were black.

By the end of the '50s, the number of black players had increased to 52—almost 12 percent of the league. Scouts were even beginning to stop at black colleges. Progress might have come more quickly, though, if the NFL, during its bidding war with the AAFC in 1949, hadn't cut rosters from 35 to 32 to save money. It wasn't until 1957 that rosters returned to 35.

The teams that met for the NFL title in 1950 and '51, the Browns and Rams, were the teams with the most black players in the league. Such coincidences continued for the rest of the decade. In four of the next eight years, the club that had the most blacks (or in the case of a tie, *one* of the teams) won either a league or conference title.

Only the Lions managed to win championships without significant numbers of black players. For some reason the franchise went backward in this area. In 1949 Detroit had as many blacks as any team in pro football—three (Mann, Triplett and halfback Melvin Groomes). The following year only Triplett remained. In five of the next six seasons, the club had zero blacks. The '53 Lions were the last all-white NFL champs.

Halas, who could have taken a leadership role in 1940, also dragged his feet. He didn't have a black on the team until 1952. Then he had four in '53 and just one in '54. Some have blamed the Bears' decline on this. The Redskins, too, refrained from signing blacks and went downhill. They were the last team to integrate, in 1962. The year before they'd had the worst record in the league.

Some clubs were suspected of having quotas. Defensive tackle Rosey Grier said of the '58 Giants: "We knew only six black guys would make the team no matter how good they were." Actually, only four black guys made the team that season.

There was also economic discrimination. In a 1951 doctoral thesis on pro football by former NFL quarterback Paul Governali, an unnamed player makes this comment:

"I believe this [black] fellow is without a doubt the best defensive back in the league. He tackles, returns punts, pass defends. There's nobody like him. They [teams] take advantage of every situation when they pay you. They feel that he can't get a job anyplace else on account of his color, so they give him chicken feed."

There's little question he's talking about Emlen Tunnell, the Giants' Hall-of-Fame safety.

What made integration even more difficult was that pro football was moving into cities in the South and Southwest—Miami, Baltimore, Dallas, Houston, Atlanta, New Orleans—where there was still separation of the races. There were some incidents over segregated seating policies. Many black players had problems finding housing.

The 1965 AFL All-Star Game was moved from New Orleans to Houston after the black players walked out, charging discrimination by the locals. They said they were being barred from Bourbon Street night spots and couldn't get cabs to stop for them.

Some whites weren't very understanding. One influential owner reportedly wanted to fine the players and suspend them for a year. And New Orleans Mayor Victor H. Schiro said, "If these men would play football only in cities where everybody loved them, they would all be out of a job today."

Most of the barriers to blacks have fallen. There was a black quarterback in 1953 (the Bears' Willie Thrower), a black assistant coach in '63 (Tunnell, with the Giants), a black official in '65 (field judge Burl Toler), a black referee in '88 (Johnny Grier) and a black head coach in '89 (the L.A. Raiders' Art Shell).

Equality, however, is still a ways away. The week of Super Bowl XXIV, a Washington television station presented evidence suggesting the NFL's drug-testing policy was biased against blacks.

■ ■ ■

THE FOUR WHO BROKE THE COLOR LINE

Pro football had four Jackie Robinsons—Kenny Washington, Woody Strode, Bill Willis and Marion Motley. In 1946, the year before Robinson ran the basepaths for the Brooklyn Dodgers, Washington and Strode played for the Los Angeles Rams and Willis and Motley for the Cleveland Browns, then in the All-America Football Conference.

Today Washington, the first to sign, is all but forgotten, and Strode is known only as a Hollywood character actor. Willis and Motley would have suffered the same fate if they hadn't been Hall-of-Famers.

Washington was Hall-of-Fame material himself, possibly the greatest player in college football when he came out of UCLA in 1940. A single-wing tailback, he had size (6'1", 195) and speed, and could pass and kick. He and Strode, a Bruins end, formed a famous passing combination. (Also in the backfield was a fellow named Jackie Robinson.)

But by 1946 Washington was 28 and his knees were shot. He'd ruined them playing in the Pacific Coast Football League. Both had been injured the previous season, and in the spring they were operated on. He wore a brace on his left knee.

After Washington joined the defending champion Rams March 21, *Los Angeles Times* columnist Dick Hyland described him as "a beaten-up ballplayer who is neither so strong nor so quick in his reactions as he was before the war. He has a trick leg which kept him out of games on many occasions last season, and he has lost just enough of his speed to enable tackles who would have missed him or run into his murderous straight arm when he was at his best, to nail him with punishing tackles."

The only reason the Rams gave him a chance was to placate the L.A. Coliseum Commission. They'd just moved from Cleveland, and the commission wouldn't give them a lease unless they let Washington try out. Strode, even older at 31, was added to the club May 7.

Rams coach Adam Walsh wasn't sure Washington's knees would hold up—they had to be drained constantly that season—so he started him out at quarterback. Washington saw his first action near the end of the College All-Star Game. He immediately scrambled for a 10-yard gain, but then he threw an interception and on his next play was tackled for a safety, the final ignominious points in a 16–0 defeat.

In the season opener against Philadelphia, Washington got to play in the second half when Bob Waterfield tore a rib muscle. He completed his only pass of the season in the fourth quarter, hitting end Jim Benton for a 19-yard gain to move the ball into Eagles territory. But then Waterfield went back in. The Rams failed to score and wound up losing, 25–14.

After two weeks of inactivity, Washington was shifted to fullback. The team could make better use of him there. Waterfield, the league's MVP the year

TIME IS MONEY

A look at the payrolls of the 1948 and '88 NFL champions shows how far the game has come financially. The average NFL salary in 1988 was approximately $230,000. In '48 it was probably about $6,000.

Keep in mind the Eagles were a well-paid team. They'd won the Eastern Division the year before. Their salaries reflect not only their ability but the ongoing price war with the All-America Football Conference.

The 49ers numbers, on the other hand, are simply base salaries. Additional payments such as roster bonuses, signing bonuses, incentive clauses, insurance payments and other features of modern contracts aren't included. Wide receiver Jerry Rice, for instance, received a $200,000 roster bonus which would put his income over $1 million. So the real value of most of the '88 contracts is significantly higher than shown.

1988 SAN FRANCISCO 49ERS		1948 PHILADELPHIA EAGLES	
Coach Bill Walsh	$1,300,000	Coach Greasy Neale	$12,000
QB Joe Montana	1,100,000	B Steve Van Buren	13,000
DB Ronnie Lott	825,000	B Joe Muha	12,500
WR Jerry Rice	750,000	QB Tommy Thompson	11,000
LB Keena Turner	730,000	E Pete Pihos	10,000
QB Steve Young	700,000	L Al Wistert	10,000
RB Roger Craig	600,000	B Bosh Pritchard	9,000
DL Michael Carter	450,000	E Dick Humbert	8,500
C Randy Cross	450,000	E Neill Armstrong	7,500
CB Eric Wright	425,000	L Fred Hartman	7,500
LB Riki Ellison	400,000	C Vic Lindskog	7,500
TE John Frank	325,000	B Pat McHugh	7,500
DB Don Griffin	325,000	L John Magee	7,500
OT Bubba Paris	325,000	L George Savitsky	7,500
DB Tim McKyer	300,000	B Ernest Steele	7,500
LB Jim Fahnhorst	290,000	C Frank Szymanski	7,500
DL Pete Kugler	290,000	B Russell Craft	7,000
LB Mike Walter	275,000	B Ben Kish	7,000
OL Guy McIntyre	236,500	B Jack Myers	7,000
WR Mike Wilson	236,500	L Vic Sears	7,000
DB Jeff Fuller	225,000	C Alex Wojciechowicz	7,000
DB Tory Nixon	225,000	B Noble Doss	6,650
OL Harris Barton	200,000	E Jack Ferrante	6,250
OL Bruce Collie	200,000	B Leslie Palmer	6,250
OL Jessie Sapolu	200,000	L Frank Kilroy	6,000
WR Terry Greer	175,000	B James Parmer	6,000
RB Terrence Flagler	175,000	L Walter Barnes	5,500
RB Tom Rathman	175,000	L Mario Giannelli	5,500
DL Larry Roberts	175,000	L John Patton	5,500
DB Tom Holmoe	170,000	E Jay MacDowell	5,400
DL Dan Stubbs	155,000	L Otis Douglas	5,200
DL Pierce Holt	150,000	L Duke Maronic	5,000
WR John Taylor	140,000	B Bill Mackrides	5,000
LB Bill Romanowski	115,000	E John Green	4,800
DL Kevin Fagan	100,000	E Harold Prescott	4,500
LB Charles Haley	100,000		
OL Steve Wallace	100,000		
LB Ron Hadley	95,000		
TE Brent Jones	90,000		
C Chuck Thomas	82,500		
P Barry Helton	80,000		
K Mike Cofer	75,000		
DB Darryl Pollard	75,000		
RB Harry Sydney	75,000		
TE Ron Heller	70,000		
DB Greg Cox	65,000		
LB Sam Kennedy	62,500		
RB Del Rodgers	N/A		

before, was entrenched at QB. The second time Washington played the position, against the Cardinals in Chicago, he "brought the crowd up with some brilliant runs after receiving four passes for gains of 11, 13, 8 and 13 yards," the *Times* reported.

But he injured his knee again and played little the rest of the season. The *Times* said his "trick knee will only hold together for so long in a game. One hard tackle at a certain spot . . . and the former Bruin is generally through for the day."

Washington finished with 114 yards rushing, six receptions and a touchdown. He came back the next year, however, to lead the team with 444 yards rushing and the league with a 7.4 average.

He played one more season (301 yards rushing, 5.3 average, two interceptions at defensive back) before retiring. He died at age 52 in 1971 of polyarteritis (inflammation of the arteries) and heart and respiratory problems.

As for Strode, he caught just four passes in 1946. It was his only year in the NFL. He went to Canada in 1948 and played two more seasons, helping the Calgary Stampeders win the '48 Grey Cup.

Willis and Motley slipped quietly into pro football. They didn't join the Browns until after training camp opened. Coach Paul Brown says in his autobiography *PB: The Paul Brown Story* that he planned it that way because he thought it would put less pressure on them. But Brown's story doesn't appear to be the whole story, certainly not in Motley's case.

As Brown tells it: "Motley had returned to his Canton home following his Navy discharge with no interest in returning to the University of Nevada and resuming his college career. He was twenty-seven years old and, with a family to support, had taken a mill job. I called Oscar Barkey, a friend from Canton, and asked him to drive Marion to our training camp and have him ask for a tryout. I felt that was the best way to handle the situation, again in light of the potential publicity, because there was nothing unusual in a player's coming to his former coach and asking him for a chance to play." (Brown had coached Willis at Ohio State and Motley at Great Lakes Naval Base.)

Motley remembers it a little differently. In *Iron Men,* he says he wrote Brown after he got out of the service and asked for a job, but that Brown "turned me down and wrote back that he had enough backs."

He did indeed intend to go back to Nevada. In fact, he called the school in early August and said he'd be there "as soon as living quarters were found for his wife and three youngsters," the *Nevada State Journal* reported. Then the Browns contacted him.

They desperately needed a fullback. They'd signed Green Bay Packers star Ted Fritsch, but Fritsch, a Wisconsin boy, was having second thoughts and wanted the Browns to release him. (Another fullback, Gene Fekete, had suffered a rib injury in a scrimmage.) They eventually granted Fritsch's request, and he went back to the Packers and made all-pro.

The day he left the Cleveland camp (August 9), Motley arrived. Had Fritsch stayed, it stands to reason there would have been no Motley—at least not that season.

The Browns almost didn't have Willis either. He, too, had tried and failed to get a tryout with the team. He was all ready to play for the Montreal Alouettes when Brown got back in touch. Willis agreed to stop at the Browns' camp on the way to Canada (August 5), and he never left.

As with Motley, there seems to be more involved than mere altruism. Four days after Willis reported, the *Cleveland Press* said: "The Browns are woefully weak at the guards [Willis' position], having not a single man who ever played professional ball."

So the question becomes: Did Willis and Motley arrive late because Brown wanted to make it easier on them or because he wanted to see if he *needed* them first?

Unlike Washington and Strode, Motley and Willis weren't past their prime when they got to the pros. They helped make the Browns practically unbeatable that season and for years to come. And such a contrast of styles! Motley was known for running through people, Willis for leapfrogging over them from his middle guard position.

But they were also blacks, and they had many reminders of that. They stayed home when the team traveled to Miami for the last game of their rookie season. Florida law prohibited mixed sporting events.

■ ■ ■

PEPPER MARTIN GETS HIS KICKS

The Brooklyn Dodgers had an unlikely place-kicking candidate in their 1948 training camp. The name on his birth certificate was Johnny Leonard Roosevelt Martin, but he was known to baseball fans as Pepper Martin, "The Wild Hoss of the Osage."

The Gashouse Gangster was 44 and had been out of the major leagues for four years. One day at the baseball Dodgers' Vero Beach, Florida, complex he started fooling around with a football and kicked so accurately that Branch Rickey, owner of the football Dodgers as well as the baseball team, signed him up.

It was a crazy quest. Martin's only previous football experience had been with a semipro team in Hominy, Oklahoma. Most of the players were Osage Indians.

"Maybe I should be back in Oklahoma pulling corn," he said. "Maybe I'm too old."

Not too old to go four for four on extra points in one exhibition game. He also helped keep the Dodgers loose. One day in practice he attempted a point-after wearing a ski boot. Another time there was a bad snap and he tried to drop-kick the ball over the crossbar. Nearly did, too.

One night Martin was discussing kicking with some of the coaches. One of them offered the opinion that Ben Agajanian of the Los Angeles Dons might have an advantage because he didn't have any toes on his foot.

"Do you really think so?" asked Martin, sounding interested.

"I spoke up in a hurry," head coach Carl Voyles said. "I said that I thought Agajanian was a good placement kicker in spite of, not because of his accident. I don't want Pepper cutting off his toes just to help him make the team, and I wouldn't put anything past a fellow with as much enthusiasm as he has."

Martin didn't make the club. But newspaper reports indicate he was kept around for a while as a kind of spirit coach.

■ ■ ■

FOOTBALL FATALITIES

After the 1948 Cardinals–Eagles season opener at Comiskey Park, Chicago's Stan Mauldin helped Philadelphia's Alex Wojciechowicz off the field. It had been a long, hot night. Wojie had thrown out his back; Mauldin had a splitting headache.

When they got to the dugout, Mauldin suddenly dropped him and ran off—probably to throw up, Wojie figured. But soon a rescue squad was hooking the big Cardinals tackle up to a synthetic lung.

He died in the locker room at 1:00 A.M. on September 25, two hours after the defending champion Cards, in a rematch of the previous year's title game, had defeated the Eagles, 21–14. Early reports said his death was due to a "hemorrhage at the base of the brain," but the autopsy showed it was a heart attack.

Defensive back Marshall Goldberg testified at the

DECADE ALL–STAR TEAM

For skill position players, figures under "Data" are average season totals; for specialists, they're decade totals.

Pos. Player	Years*	Data
E Don Hutson	6	55 catches, 848 yds, 11 TDs; 6 all-NFL
T Bruiser Kinard	7	4 all-NFL, 1 all-AAFC
G Bill Willis	4	3 all-AAFC
C Bulldog Turner	10	7 all-NFL
G Dan Fortmann	4	4 all-NFL
T Al Wistert	7	5 all-NFL
E Jim Benton	7	34 catches, 571 yds., 5 TDs; 2 all-NFL
QB Sammy Baugh	10	58.7%, 1,700 yds., 15 TDs; 5 all-NFL
FB Marion Motley	4	756 yds., 6.2 avg., 7 TDs; 3 all-AAFC
HB Steve Van Buren	6	817 yds., 4.8 avg., 10 TDs; 5 all-NFL
HB Bill Dudley	6	384 yds., 3 TDs, 4 interceptions, 2 all-NFL

OTHER SELECTIONS		
Pos. Selection	Years	Data
KR Steve Van Buren	6	27.0 avg., 3 TDs; led NFL in 1947
PR George McAfee	7	14.5 avg., 2 TDs; led NFL in 1948
K Bob Waterfield	5	29 FGs, 53.7% made; led NFL in 1947 & '49
P Sammy Baugh	10	45.5 avg., led NFL, 1940–43
Enforcer -- Ed Sprinkle		Wild Card Selection -- Spec Sanders
Wife -- Jane Russell		Coach -- George Halas

*Number of years he played in the decade.

Zany former baseball star Pepper Martin gave place-kicking a try with the All-America Conference's Brooklyn Dodgers in 1948. He's shown here practicing at the baseball Dodgers' training camp. (UPI/Bettmann Newsphotos)

inquest that Mauldin complained of the headache before the game and asked him to rub the back of his neck. Headaches, Goldberg said, were common before games, when players were apt to be nervous. The coroner found no evidence of an injury.

"The National Football League has just lost its greatest tackle," Eagles coach Greasy Neale said.

That may have been overstating it a bit. Mauldin hadn't even, as the *Chicago Tribune* claimed, been all-NFL the year before. And despite his loss, the Cardinals posted an 11–1 record in '48, the best in the league, before losing the championship game in a Philadelphia blizzard. But Mauldin was 27, in only his third pro season, and his best football figured to be ahead of him.

Mauldin is one of five players who have died after playing in NFL or AFL games. Only two deaths were caused by injuries. The others were mysteries like Mauldin's. The roll:

■ **Dave Sparks, 26, Washington tackle**—Suffered a heart attack less than three hours after a 34–14 home loss to Cleveland, December 5, 1954. That afternoon, Sparks had recovered a fumble to stop a Browns drive at the Washington 18. There was a pileup, but he emerged complaining of nothing more than a bruised hip. The coroner said Sparks had suffered a minor heart seizure less than 24 hours before the game. If Sparks had gone to a doctor then, "He'd be alive today."

■ **Howard Glenn, 24, New York Titans offensive guard**—Died of a broken neck after a 27–21 loss at Houston, October 9, 1960. He left the game under his own power early in the second half and was thought to be merely shaken up. But he collapsed in the locker room afterward, was taken to the hospital and never regained consciousness. The medical examiner said Glenn's injury might have occurred the week before at Dallas, but probably happened against the Oilers.

■ **Stone Johnson, 23, Kansas City wide receiver**—Died September 8, 1963, in Wichita, Kansas, eight days after suffering spinal cord damage in a preseason game against Houston. He dove headfirst to make a block on a kickoff return and was left partially paralyzed. Don Klosterman, the Chiefs' director of player personnel, called him "probably the fastest man in professional football." Johnson once shared the world record in the 200 meters and competed in the 1960 Olympics. At Grambling, he averaged better than 40 yards a punt and kicked a 50-yard field goal. Kansas City traded two players to Oakland to obtain his rights. Former Chiefs coach Hank Stram claims running back Abner Haynes "lost it . . . he just wasn't the same," after Johnson's death.

■ **Chuck Hughes, 28, Detroit wide receiver**—Collapsed going back to the huddle near the end of a 28–23 home loss to Chicago, October 24, 1971. He was taken to the hospital, where he was pronounced dead of a heart attack about an hour later. "His heart stopped on the field," a Lions team doctor said. Moments earlier, Hughes had been crunched by two Bears defenders while catching a 32-yard pass, but seemed all right. It was his only reception of the season. Buddy Alex Karras said Hughes had severe abdominal pains and difficulty breathing after a collision in a preseason game against Buffalo and "never did feel good after that." Doctors attributed the death to a degenerative disease of the arteries.

■ ■ ■

Crazylegs Hirsch shoes himself for practice. (Department of Special Collections, University Research Library, UCLA)

HIT OF THE DECADE
Crazylegs Hirsch Fractures His Skull, 1948

Elroy "Crazylegs" Hirsch still doesn't know what happened to him September 26, 1948. He was carrying the ball on a simple off-tackle play late in the first quarter, and then . . .

"Maybe I was too low going through the hole or had my head down or what, but I took a blow to the back of my neck," he says. "I don't remember feeling it. I don't remember anything about it."

Hirsch suffered a fractured skull. The injury

nearly ended his career before he'd ever set foot in the National Football League.

This was during his All-America Football Conference days. Hirsch's Chicago Rockets were playing the champion Browns in Cleveland. The game was described as "rough" by the Cleveland *Plain Dealer.* Browns tackle Lou Rymkus was kicked out for fighting, and end Mac Speedie was sidelined temporarily when a Rockets player threw dirt in his eyes.

But there was nothing out of line about the shot Hirsch took. There were no penalties on the play. Hirsch's teammates watched the game films and couldn't tell exactly who hit him or how. The best guess is he was inadvertently kicked on the ground.

The extent of the injury wasn't clear at first. There was no blood. Hirsch never lost consciousness. He was dazed badly enough to leave the game. On the sideline he couldn't remember the score or even who the Rockets were playing.

The following day he was yawning constantly—a symptom of a concussion—but X-rays showed nothing. When the yawning persisted, Hirsch was X-rayed again. That evening, he was listening to the radio in his Chicago apartment when Rockets physician Sylvam Solarz called.

"Stop whatever it is you're doing," Solarz told him, "and get to bed. We've just discovered you have a fractured skull."

The two-centimeter crack was behind the right ear in an area protected by his helmet. Doctors told Hirsch he'd probably taken the blow on the neck and the shock had carried up the spine to the point of the fracture.

Hirsch's season was over. He spent several weeks in the hospital and was ordered to take it easy after he got out. When he resumed workouts in the spring, he found his coordination off.

In the 1953 movie about his life, *Crazylegs, All American,* Hirsch's coach (played by Lloyd Nolan) asks the doctor: "Will he be able to play again?"

The doctor's response sets up Hirsch's stirring return to football: "It's highly dubious. The motor nerves controlling his reflexes, you see, appear to have been damaged."

Hirsch says it was never as dramatic as Hollywood portrayed it. He had problems getting his hands up for high passes, but not much more than that. The problem corrected itself over time, he says. Still, he seriously considered retirement.

"When you get an injury like that you think about it," he says. "My wife wanted me to. I had this food distribution business back in Wisconsin to fall back on. But when the season rolled around I got the bug again."

Hirsch had an option year left on his contract with the Rockets. But the team was losing money and had some doubts about his ability to come back. It didn't put up a fight when he jumped to the NFL's Los Angeles Rams. The Rams had the Riddell Company design a special helmet for him with extra padding over the area of the fracture.

The rest of the story reads like a B-movie plot (come to think of it, it was). Hirsch was a backup halfback with the Rams in 1949, moved to wide receiver in '50 and is now in the Pro Football Hall of Fame.

· · ·

THE PERFECT '48 BROWNS: EIGHT DAYS IN NOVEMBER

Nothing against the 1972 Miami Dolphins, but they never had to go through what the 1948 Cleveland Browns did to achieve perfection. Sure, 17–0 is better than 15–0, which is what the Browns were, but were the Dolphins required to play three road games and travel 6,000 miles in eight days—*in the closing weeks of the season?*

The Browns left on their long journey with a 10–0 record, having just stopped unbeaten San Francisco, 14–7, and been pretty banged up in the process. The worst of the injuries was end Mac Speedie's partially separated shoulder, which would keep him on the sideline for the first two games of the trip.

Any one of the Browns' next three opponents were quite capable of knocking them off. The first would be the New York Yankees, who had played Cleveland in the AAFC title game the previous two years. The Yankees had won their last three by impressive margins. Then the Browns would fly to the West Coast for a Thanksgiving Day meeting with the 7–5 Los Angeles Dons. Finally, three days later, they would have to play their biggest game of the season against the better-rested 49ers in San Francisco.

Three road games on two coasts in eight days. With the pressure of a perfect season closing in. With four months of football beginning to take its toll on the Browns' bodies. In front of large (average: 57,445) and hostile crowds. *I'd turn back if I were you.*

None of the games was a snap. Cleveland blew a 14–0 lead at Yankee Stadium before pulling away to a 34–21 win. The Browns beat the Dons, 31–14, but it was 14–14 at the half. And in the fourth quarter Otto Graham suffered a twisted knee courtesy of L.A. tackle Clyde Johnson.

When the Browns arrived at their retreat that night in Boyes Hot Springs, after two hours on a plane and two more on a bus, "Members of the squad took a plunge in the mineral water, hoping to ease some of the bumps and bruises," the Cleveland *Plain Dealer* reported.

But Graham was limping the next day. "I felt it snap," he said, "and I was afraid it was broken." Cleveland had never gone into a game without him. His backup, Cliff Lewis, was primarily a defensive back who attempted a grand total of 69 passes in his career.

Graham hobbled out on the field to face the 49ers. But despite their leader's presence, the Browns fell behind 21–10 in the third quarter.

Then Graham got hot. He connected with Marion Motley, Dub Jones and Special Delivery Jones for three touchdowns in an eight-minute span, and Cleveland hung on for a 31–28 victory.

"Under the circumstances," coach Paul Brown said, "it was Otto's greatest performance."

Before getting off the plane back home, Brown said something else. "I wish you fellows would continue to bear down for two more weeks," he told his players. "I'd like to finish without a defeat. That hasn't happened very often in professional football."

The Browns obliged. They took care of last-place Brooklyn, 31–21, to wrap up the regular season and then blew away Buffalo, 49–7, for the championship.

■ ■ ■

THE DROP KICK'S LAST HURRAH(S)

Pro football's last (we think) successful drop kick didn't start out to be one. The man who made it, San Francisco's Joe "The Little Toe" Vetrano, was a conventional kicker—and a good one. He scored in all 56 of the team's games from 1946 to '49, at the time a record.

But in the November 28, 1948, game against Cleveland at Kezar Stadium, Vetrano had to do a little improvising on an extra point attempt in the third quarter. The snap was bad, and holder Frankie Albert couldn't handle it. Thinking quickly, Vetrano picked up the ball and drop-kicked it through.

It could have been the key play in the biggest game of the year. The conversion increased San Francisco's lead to 21–10, which meant a touchdown and field goal wouldn't be enough for Cleveland. But the Browns came back to win, anyway.

Seven years earlier, Scooter McLean of the Chicago Bears was the last to make a drop kick in the NFL (again, probably). It happened in the '41 championship game against the Giants. After scoring their last touchdown in a 37–9 runaway, the Bears were looking to rub it in. So McLean, who hadn't tried a single point-after all season, booted a drop kick between the uprights.

■ ■ ■

GENE ROBERTS' HIDDEN RECORD

There have been just two 200-yard receiving days by a running back in NFL history. Gene "Choo Choo" Roberts of the Giants had them both in 1949—three weeks apart.

Against the Bears October 23, he caught four passes for 201 yards and three touchdowns in a 35–28 victory at the Polo Grounds. The TDs measured 31, 62 and 85 yards. The last, in the fourth quarter, came on a screen pass and won the game.

On November 13 in Green Bay, Roberts topped himself. He had seven receptions for 212 yards and

The problem with having the goal posts on the goal line was that they sometimes got in the way. The Browns' Tony Adamle gets "posted up" by Walt Clay of the Los Angeles Dons in a 1948 game. (UPI/Bettmann News-photos)

three more touchdowns to lead his team to a 30–10 win. The lengths of the scores were 45, 44 and 10 yards. He also had catches of 40 and 51 yards, according to the *Green Bay Press-Gazette.*

Roberts had a remarkable season. He finished fourth in the league in rushing yards (634) *and* receiving yards (711). His 17 touchdowns were one short of the NFL record. All for a .500 (6–6) team.

In 1950 he broke Hall-of-Famer Cliff Battles' 17-year-old league mark by rushing for 218 yards against the Cardinals. Only one other NFL player has had a 200-yard rushing game and a 200-yard receiving game (Bobby Mitchell, another Hall-of-Famer).

So why haven't you heard much about Roberts? One reason is that the record book doesn't list receiving marks for running backs. Another is that he

was a "jumper." He went to Canada in 1951 and played his last four seasons with the Montreal Alouettes and Ottawa Rough Riders. For a couple of years, though, he was a statistical phenomenon.

Note: A back *did* have a 200-yard receiving game in the premerger AFL. In 1965 the Chiefs' Curtis McClinton gained 213 yards on five catches in a 45–35 victory over the Broncos. The game was played five days after Chiefs fullback Mack Lee Hill died on the operating table after knee surgery. McClinton, the starting halfback and Hill's roommate on road trips, moved over to Hill's spot against Denver.

...

THE SCREWING OF BUFFALO

Buffalo got the shaft when the NFL and All-America Football Conference merged in December 1949. Pittsburgh Steelers owner Art Rooney said excluding the AAFC's Bills was "a sad mistake." And Grantland Rice wrote, "If any city belongs in pro football, it is Buffalo." But it was 11 years before the city got back in.

The Bills were one of the top clubs in the league. In 1948 they played in the title game against Cleveland. In '49 they tied the mighty Browns twice in the regular season. In a game that year between the Browns and an AAFC all-star team, the Bills' Chet Mutryn and Al Baldwin scored both the all-stars' touchdowns in a 12–7 victory.

Average home attendance in Buffalo that season was 26,600—despite a 1–4–1 start. In the NFL it was 23,196. And unlike most teams, the Bills didn't have stadium conflicts. No baseball or college team used Civic Stadium.

Buffalo had everything you'd look for in a franchise. But the NFL took in only three AAFC clubs—the Browns, the San Francisco 49ers and the last-place Baltimore Colts, who were admitted on a one-year trial basis. The indignity of it all.

Bills fans didn't realize it, but their fate was sealed a month before the merger deal was struck. That was when owner Jim Breuil announced at a secret AAFC meeting in Cleveland that he was pulling out at the end of the season. He'd lost $700,000 in four years and couldn't afford any more. His attempts to find local backing had failed. A week earlier, quarterback George Ratterman had signed to play the next season for the NFL's New York Bulldogs. Breuil had given up on Buffalo.

Cleveland owner Mickey McBride offered him 25 percent of the Browns; Breuil accepted. The cost was three of his team's best players—offensive guard Abe Gibron, halfback Rex Bumgardner and defensive tackle John Kissell.

Bills supporters were stunned when the two leagues agreed in December to merge and Buffalo was left out, but they quickly regrouped. Four days later, a "Keep the Bills in Buffalo" drive was launched. The Buffalo Bills Football Club, Inc., was formed, and 100,000 shares of stock were offered at $5 a share. A rally at Memorial Auditorium drew 20,000. In the first 24 hours, over $200,000 was pledged.

"If public enthusiasm can do it," said citizens committee spokesman Arthur Rich, "we will have our franchise."

NFL commissioner Bert Bell was encouraging. But he told the group it needed to do more than raise working capital. If it could sell enough season tickets to guarantee a gate of at least $60,000 a game, its application would be looked upon more favorably.

In five days the committee reached its goal of 10,000 season-ticket pledges, double the 1949 figure. Breuil himself was down for 150. Later he would say: "It never occurred to me there would be such a tremendous public reaction for pro football in Buffalo. Had I known that, I would have taken a Buffalo franchise in the new league myself."

Bell informed the committee he had drafted a 14-team schedule that included Buffalo, but it needed more work. "I am convinced I must do everything I can for people who have acted the way Buffalo people have," he said.

The Buffalo delegation that attended the NFL meeting in Philadelphia in January, however, came away wondering whether Bell had done much of anything. Despite having more than 15,000 season-ticket pledges and $175,000 in the bank, the Bills were turned down.

Los Angeles Rams owner Dan Reeves said he voted no because Bell never produced a 14-team schedule and "it was silly to vote in a new city without first having a good idea where my team would be playing and when." In the days before television, playing dates were everything.

Bell's explanation: "Before the vote was taken, I told the owners I *would* make a schedule somehow, *if* they voted to increase the league to 14 teams." That, of course, wasn't what he'd told the Buffalo people. Asked afterward whether he'd been for or against Buffalo's admission, he refused to answer.

But all the blame can't be laid on Bell. After all, Breuil's agreement to give Cleveland three players— one the Browns expected him to honor—weakened the Bills. So did the defection of Ratterman and coach Clem Crowe, who was hired by Baltimore. It's also possible Buffalo's rejection was merely a parting

Coming
1940--Fran Tarkenton, Richmond, Va.
       Lance Alworth, Houston
       Merlin Olsen, Logan, Utah
1941--John Mackey, New York
       Dave Meggyesy, Cleveland
1942--Roger Staubach, Silverton, Ohio
       Pete Gogolak, Budapest, Hungary
       Dave Kopay, Chicago
       Paul Warfield, Warren, Ohio
       Dick Butkus, Chicago
1943--Gale Sayers, Wichita, Kan.
       Joe Namath, Beaver Falls, Pa.
       Joe Don Looney, San Angelo, Texas
1944--Ken Houston, Lufkin, Texas
1945--Bubba Smith, Beaumont, Texas
       Alan Page, Canton, Ohio
       Gene Upshaw, Robstown, Texas
1946--Joe Greene, Temple, Texas
       Art Shell, Charleston, S.C.
1947--O.J. Simpson, San Francisco
       Ted Hendricks, Guatemala City, Guatemala
1948--Terry Bradshaw, Shreveport, La.
       Jack Tatum, Cherryville, N.C.
1949--Lyle Alzado, Brooklyn, N.C.
       John Riggins, Centralia, Kan.

Going
1943--Milt Simington, 24, Steelers guard, heart attack
1947--Bill Hewitt, 55, car accident
       Charles Bidwill, 51
       Jeff Burkett, 26, Cardinals end-DB, plane crash
1948--Jock Sutherland, 59, brain tumor
       Stan Mauldin, 27, Cardinals tackle, heart attack

shot at the AAFC. The NFL had lost $3 million in its war with the upstart league.

If so, the owners paid for their pettiness. The Colts were a catastrophe; they lasted only one more season. The Bills were broken up in an allocation draft. Nineteen of them found jobs in the NFL in 1950, and five more played in Canada.

Ratterman led the league in touchdown passes. Baldwin was the Packers' number-one receiver. Joe Sutton had a team-high eight interceptions with the Eagles. Bumgardner started for the champion Browns. And Mutryn was one of the few bright spots for Baltimore.

All this from a team the NFL didn't want.

THE 1950s

'50s CHALKBOARD

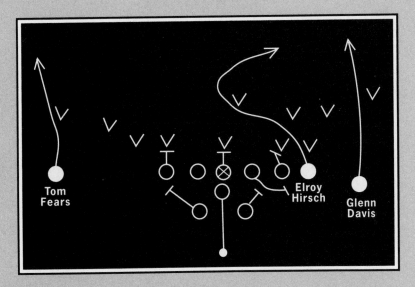

Pass from the Rams' 3-receiver spread formation

Pass from the Rams' three-receiver spread formation

The Los Angeles Rams broke nearly every scoring record in the book with their three-receiver spread formation in 1950. It wasn't the first time anyone had split two ends wide, but what the Rams did was add a "flanker" to the equation. They took a fast halfback out of the backfield—usually Elroy Hirsch or Glenn Davis—and lined him up 10 to 12 yards wide and a yard off the ball to one side. Inside the flanker was a "tight" end close to the formation. The third receiver was split wide on the opposite side, giving quarterbacks Bob Waterfield and Norm Van Brocklin three primary targets. Defenses, which used basic man-to-man coverages, couldn't cope. L.A. averaged 38.8 points per game. Fears caught a record 84 passes, Hirsch and Davis 42 apiece. The formation's creator was Rams assistant coach Hamp Pool, one of the game's forgotten innovators. Pool also came up with a defensive antidote when other teams began copying the Rams—zone pass defense.

THE 1950s AT A GLANCE

Decade Standings

East	W	L	T	Pct.	West	W	L	T	Pct.
Browns (3)	88	33	2	.742	Bears	70	48	2	.592
Giants (1)	76	41	3	.646	Lions (3)	68	48	4	.583
Steelers	54	63	3	.463	Rams (1)	68	49	3	.579
Eagles	51	64	5	.446	49ers	63	54	3	.538
Redskins	47	70	3	.404	Colts (2)	41	42	1	.494
Cardinals	33	84	3	.288	Packers	39	79	2	.333

(Figures in parentheses are championships won.)

Best Regular–Season Record

Cleveland Browns, 1951 and '53, 11-1
  The '51 Browns won their last 11, the '53 Browns their first 11. Neither team won the title.

Worst Regular–Season Record

Baltimore Colts, 1950, and Dallas Texans, 1952, 1-11.

Attendance Figures

Total: 24,353,595 (up 90.2 percent)
Highest: Los Angeles Rams, 1958, 502,084 (83,681 average)
Lowest: Dallas, 1952, 56,499 (14,125 average -- estimated)
Biggest Crowd: 102,368, 49ers at Rams, Nov. 10, 1957

In	Out
passing	running
scouting systems	Street and Smith
Otto Graham, Johnny Unitas	Sammy Baugh, Sid Luckman
Paul Brown	George Halas
Vitalis	Jeris Hair Tonic
CBS	DuMont
quarterback	tailback
fullback	blocking back
black ink	red ink
The Alley Oop	jump pass
4-3-4 defense	5-2-4 defense

▶**Biggest Player**

Les Bingaman, the Lions middle guard, who packed 349½ pounds on his 6'3'' frame in his last season in 1954. Bingaman was once described as "the only player in the National Football League who specializes in not moving." He measured 55 inches at the chest and 50 at the equator. 49ers tackle Bob St. Clair was the tallest at 6'9''.

Smallest Player

Tad Weed, a kicker with the Steelers in 1955, was 5'5'', 140.

Smallest Real Player

Billy Cross, Cardinals halfback from 1951 to '53, was listed at 5'6'', 151. Shortest (still): 5'4'' Buddy Young.

Best Athlete

Jimmy Brown

Fastest Player

Bob Boyd. The Rams receiver was an NCAA 100-yard dash champ.

Slowest Player

Les Bingaman. Among non-linemen, it was probably Norm Van Brocklin ("moves with all the speed and elusiveness of a pregnant hippopotamus," according to one report).

▶**Most Intimidating Player**

49ers linebacker Hardy Brown

New Stadiums	1950--Memorial Stadium, Baltimore 1953--County Stadium, Milwaukee 1957--City Stadium, Green Bay (the second one)
Failed Franchises	Baltimore Colts, 1950 New York Yanks, 1951 Dallas Texans, 1952 The league relocated the Yanks in Dallas under new owners, but the result was the same.
Integration Update	1950: 18 black players (4 percent) 1959: 52 blacks (11.5)
Time Magazine Cover Boys	Bobby Layne (Nov. 29, 1954) Sam Huff (Nov. 30, 1959)
Famous Firsts	NFL encyclopedia, 1952 National television contract, 1956 Chants of "De-fense! De-fense!" 1956 Meeting of NFL Players Association, 1956 Minimum salary ($5,000), 1957
Famous Lasts	Single-wing team, 1951 (Steelers) Player to make all-pro on offense and defense in his career (Ollie Matson) Running back to average 8 yards a carry (at least 50 attempts), 1954 (Hugh McElhenny)
Best Conference Race	1951 American Conference Going into the last day, *four* of the six teams had a chance to win the conference outright or get into a playoff. The standings looked like this: Detroit (7-3-1), Chicago Bears (7-4), Los Angeles (7-4), San Francisco (6-4-1). The Rams beat Green Bay and snuck into the title game when the Lions lost to the 49ers and the Bears were upset at home by the last-place Cardinals.
Best Title Game	1950, Browns over Rams, 30-28
▶**Owner vs. Owner**	George Halas vs. George Preston Marshall, 1951
▶**Trial of the Decade**	Philadelphia Eagles Wayne Robinson and Bucko Kilroy vs. Life magazine, 1958
Best Running Quarterback	Tobin Rote
Special Citation for Ballhandling Wizardry	Eddie LeBaron
Best Place to Watch a Game	Wrigley Field, in the folding chairs Halas sold as seats in and around the opponents' bench. "The game would be in progress," Tex Schramm said, "and this hot dog vendor would be walking out there in front of our bench, leaning over players to make a sale to the fans."
New Positions	middle linebacker flanker
Major Rules Changes	1950--free substitution permanently adopted

1955--ball carrier can no longer get up and run after being knocked down

1956--grabbing the facemask (except the ball carrier's) made illegal

New Equipment

tubular, single-bar face masks

brown ball with white stripes replaced white ball with black stripes for night games

Fashion Trends

painted helmets

synthetic fabrics

Best Play

The gadget play the New York Giants used to beat Cleveland in the 1958 Eastern Conference playoff. The ball went from fullback Alex Webster to halfback Frank Gifford (reverse) to quarterback Charley Conerly (lateral) and resulted in an 18-yard touchdown, the only one in a 10-0 Giants victory. Without that play, there might have been no sudden death game.

►Hit of the Decade

The Bears' Ed Meadows vs. Bobby Layne, 1956

►Fight of the Decade

Eagles vs. 49ers, 1953

Highest–Paid Player

Doak Walker made close to $30,000 his last few seasons. Besides drawing a top salary, the former SMU star got a percentage of the gate from the Lions' annual exhibition game in Dallas. That was worth $9,000 or $10,000.

Least Appreciated Players

Packers receiver Billy Howton

Steelers linebacker Dale Dodrill

49ers receiver Billy Wilson

Most black players who were any good

Best Trade

The Lions got Bobby Layne from the New York Bulldogs in 1950 for fullback Camp Wilson. Wilson never played in another NFL game.

Best Football Book

1952--*The Official National Football League Encyclopedia*, by Roger Treat

Best Football Movies

1951--*Jim Thorpe: All-American*

1953--*Crazylegs, All-American*

Worst Idea

One of the owners of the ill-fated 1952 Dallas Texans suggested having substitutes run on the field carrying the Texas state flag. The sub would give the flag to the player he was replacing, who would carry it back to the sideline. Fortunately, it never became more than a suggestion.

Second–Worst Idea (Tie)

Two more from that memorable Dallas management group: gun holsters embroidered on game pants and pregame introductions with players mounted on horseback. These, too, wound up in the circular file.

Worst Punishment

Coaches used to deal with players they thought were drinking too much by making them do a "roll drill." Offending players had to lie down and roll the length of the field until they threw up.

►Individual Records That Have Never Been Equaled

Tom Fears' 18 receptions vs. Green Bay, 1950

Norm Van Brocklin's 554 yards passing vs. the N.Y. Yanks, 1951

Night Train Lane's 14 interceptions, 1952

Johnny Unitas' streak of 47 games throwing a TD pass, 1956-60

DINER: OUT TO LUNCH

In the 1982 movie *Diner,* Baltimore Colts fanatic Eddie Simmons makes his fiancée, Elise, pass a test on pro football trivia before he'll marry her. The scene is a classic. But writer-director Barry Levinson, a Baltimore boy, messed up one of the questions and 1½ of the answers. No wonder the club left town.

The questionable question: Name the Heisman Trophy winner who went to Canada first but now plays for the Colts.

Answer: Billy Vessels.

The key word is "now." Vessels did indeed put in a year with the Edmonton Eskimos before coming to Baltimore. But the only season he was on the Colts was 1956. The movie is set in 1959.

Wrong answer number one: The colors of the original (1950) Colts team were green and gray.

According to the media guide, they were green and *silver.*

Wrong answer (sort of) number two: The defunct club that ex–Colts star Buddy Young used to play for was the New York Yankees.

Young had played for *two* clubs that no longer existed. The other was the Dallas Texans.

This last item might seem picky, but we're only playing by Eddie's rules. After all, he marked Elise wrong when she answered "True" to the question: "Was George Shaw a first-round draft choice?"

Shaw was the first player taken in 1955. But technically he was the *bonus pick.* The bonus pick was a special selection made before the start of the draft from 1947 to '58. A different team had it each year. Tripping her up on a trick question like that was the height of cruelty (unless it was refusing to let her go to the bathroom during the test).

• • •
NO JUSTICE

What happened to the Pittsburgh Steelers on October 7, 1951, shouldn't happen to anybody.

Early in the second quarter, the Steelers trailed the Green Bay Packers in Milwaukee, 28–0. Sud-denly, however, they got hot. Lynn Chandnois scored two quick touchdowns, Charlie Mehelich tackled the Packers' Jack Cloud for a safety and fullback Fran Rogel ran for another TD.

In the first minute of the second half the Steelers took the lead, 30–28, on an interception return by Jim Finks. Joe Geri's field goal a short time later made it 33–28.

It was the greatest comeback in NFL history. Today, nearly four decades later, only one team has ever made up 28 points in a game and won (San Francisco in 1980 against New Orleans).

Unfortunately, the Steelers lost. With four and a half minutes left, Bob Mann caught a 16-yard touchdown pass from Tobin Rote to give the Pack a 35–33 victory.

• • •
GOING LIKE 70

What would happen if the best offense in NFL history went up against the worst defense? How many points would it score?

Seventy.

Seventy.

Seventy.

We didn't get that figure from a computer. We didn't have to. You see, the best offense and the worst defense actually played each other. They're the 1950 Los Angeles Rams, who scored 38.8 points per game, and the 1950 Baltimore Colts, who in their one miserable year of existence allowed 38.5 points per game.

The irresistible force met the movable object October 22 before a record-low crowd of 16,026 at Los Angeles Coliseum. The Rams didn't waste any time, scoring on the first scrimmage play on a 58-yard halfback pass from Glenn Davis to Elroy Hirsch. The next time an L.A. player touched the ball, Vitamin Smith ran a kickoff back 95 yards for a touchdown.

The Rams were merciless. Leading 49–20 in the fourth quarter, they ran a reverse to set up another touchdown. They reached 70 just before the final gun on a 37-yard TD pass from Bob Waterfield to Bob Boyd.

"It's strictly mental," Baltimore coach Clem Crowe tried to explain. "We don't do too badly against other teams, even though we lose. But against the Rams it's a different story. It just seems we can't stop 'em."

Postscript: The Rams and Colts also played in the preseason that year in San Antonio. Final score: Los Angeles 70, Baltimore 21. Waterfield went for 77 and threw a touchdown pass to Fred Gehrke with a second to go, but a penalty nullified the play.

"Sure, we poured it on," L.A. coach Joe Stydahar said after that one. "I wish we could have beaten them by a hundred points."

■ ■ ■

'50s MYTHOLOGY

After the Browns beat the defending-champion Eagles 35–10 in their NFL debut in 1950, Philadelphia coach Greasy Neale said all Cleveland could do was throw the ball. When the teams met later in the season, the Browns won 13–7 without attempting a single pass.

First of all, they *did* throw a pass. Otto Graham completed it to Dante Lavelli. But a penalty nullified the play.

Cleveland coach Paul Brown wasn't trying to prove anything to Neale. The game was too important to the Browns' title hopes for that. They needed a victory to remain tied with the Giants for first with a game to play. The real reason for his ultraconservatism was the weather. Conditions that day were terrible—rain and mud—and passing was a gamble.

The Eagles illustrated that on the third play when Tommy Thompson tried to hit Steve Van Buren in the right flat. His throw was short and wobbly, and the Browns' Warren Lahr picked it off and ran 31 yards for a touchdown.

The Browns sat on the lead. They even punted five times on third down. No sense in taking any unnecessary chances. Two more Eagles mistakes led to Browns field goals, and that was enough.

"We got that quick one and then held on like a bulldog," Brown said afterward. "It was close-to-the-vest strategy."

* * *

Sammy Baugh came off the bench to start the last two games of his career in 1952 and led the Redskins to a pair of victories.

This would be a great story if it really happened. The Redskins had lost six straight going into those final two games. And by upsetting the Giants and Eagles, they kept both teams from tying the Browns for first place.

In fact, Eddie LeBaron was the Redskins' quarterback of record in the games. He threw four touchdown passes in the 27–17 win over the Giants and rallied the team past the Eagles, 27–21.

In his last game, the 38-year-old Baugh played the first three plays, didn't throw a pass and spent the rest of the day on the sideline (except when he held for kicks). Management had planned to put him back in for at least one play at the end, but that was scrapped when the team started staging a comeback.

* * *

John Henry Johnson competed in the 1952 Olympic decathlon trials.

We looked it up, wondering how John Henry compared to the great Bob Mathias. He wasn't listed in the final results. That's because he wasn't there.

Johnson told us he was a decathlete in high school and was better in some events than Mathias but didn't compete in college.

"My last year in high school I was going to compete against Mathias but couldn't because of a football knee injury," he said. "I was being looked at as a potential decathlon champ, but didn't want to wait around for the Olympics."

* * *

Another story we sought to debunk was that Bob St. Clair, the 6'9" 49ers tackle, blocked 10 field-goal attempts in 1956.

Ten blocks in 12 games seemed a little much, especially since San Francisco opponents missed only 11 field-goal tries that season. But research revealed he might have had that many if you count exhibition games and extra-point attempts. That would still be quite a feat.

Based on newspaper accounts and what's left of the 49ers' game films from that year, St. Clair got his hands on at least seven kicks—six field-goal tries and a point-after attempt. One of the field-goal blocks was wiped out by a penalty.

Because the NFL didn't keep track of such things

in the '50s—there's still no official record for blocked kicks—there's no way to account for all the missed extra-point tries. And newspapers didn't mention the misses unless they were important. But it doesn't seem farfetched that St. Clair could have gotten his mitts on a few more.

He certainly was a master of the art. The 49ers lined him up over the ball, and he perfected a number of moves designed to get quick penetration. One of his favorites was hurdling the center.

■ ■ ■

WORST-EVER PERFORMANCE BY A PLAYER

In a 45–7 season-opening loss to Philadelphia in 1950, Jim Hardy of the Chicago Cardinals threw a league-record eight interceptions and lost two fumbles. Both fumbles set up Eagles touchdowns. His last interception was returned for a TD. And it all happened, naturally, in front of the home fans at Comiskey Park.

Under normal circumstances, Hardy never would have played long enough to commit 10 turnovers. But his backup, Frank Tripucka, hurt his knee in the game, so Hardy had to go all the way. The next day, newspapers in both Chicago and Philadelphia erroneously reported that Hardy's interception total was "one below the league record." Yeah, the record for a *team*. But, hey, the guy deserved one break, right?

Also worth noting:

■ At the time, Hardy held the league record for most consecutive passes *without* an interception—114, set in 1948 with the Los Angeles Rams.

■ Three different players had three or more interceptions in the game. The Eagles' Russ Craft had four, tying the NFL mark, and teammate Joe Sutton and the Cardinals' Jerry Davis each had three. It's unlikely that that has ever happened before or since.

■ In his next game, Hardy threw six touchdown passes against Baltimore, one shy of the league record.

■ ■ ■

TELL US WHAT YOU REALLY THINK

Pro football began to pose a serious threat to the college game in the '50s. The first indication was a 1950 Collier's *article in which Army coach Red Blaik roundly criticized pro ball. Blaik caused quite a fuss, and you'll understand why after you read his comments.*

BLAIK

■ "It's a show. The pros are in the entertainment business."

■ "If [a] pro team were put in a league with good college teams . . . it would have to learn to play football the way the colleges do or it wouldn't stand a chance."

■ "The colleges have the boys in their best years. Few of them ever play as well after they become professionals. As they grow older they acquire responsibilities and perspective, also caution. They lose the reckless abandon that marked their play in college."

■ "All the pro teams are full of big fat men, some of them playing 40 pounds over their most efficient playing weight."

■ "I do not concede that an uninterrupted succession of passes is football. . . . The truth is, the pros won't pay the price to develop a running attack. After their preseason training they don't scrimmage."

■ "Pursuit. . . . The pros don't have it."

■ "Downfield blocking? The pros don't have that either."

THE PROS REPLY

■ Telegram from Colts owner Abe Watner to Blaik: "Read your article in *Collier's*. Would you care to test your theory by playing your Army team against the Baltimore Colts at Baltimore any date after December 3?"

■ Rams coach Joe Stydahar: "Were we able to drop the Philadelphia Eagles and the Chicago Bears from our schedule when we found them too tough, as Blaik dropped Notre Dame, we might run up a 23-game unbeaten streak, too."

■ Eagles coach Greasy Neale: "Where does he get off calling pro football a showman's game? Why, I helped install the 'T' formation [in 1942] at West Point. I asked for about $500, but Blaik cried that West Point couldn't afford that kind of money for such a thing. So I went up for nothing.

"I showed them pictures of the Philadelphia–Brooklyn game, featuring my favorite 'stutter play' with which we ran over great NFL players like Perry Schwartz and Bruiser Kinard. Blaik was amazed. He told me he wouldn't have believed it if he hadn't seen it with his own eyes."

■ ■ ■

THE RECORD THAT LASTS AND LASTS

Passing records tend to have short lifespans in the NFL. That's what makes Norm Van Brocklin's 554-yard game on September 28, 1951, so special. Despite all the rules changes favoring passing, despite the institution of overtime, his record hasn't been topped in 38 years.

He did it against a terrible team, of course. Most single-game marks that enjoy any longevity were accomplished against terrible teams. Van Brocklin's patsies were the 1951 New York Yanks, who folded after a 1–9–2 season and were reborn the next year as the Dallas Texans.

It was a Friday night game at Los Angeles Coliseum, the season opener. Van Brocklin was playing the whole way because his alternate, Bob Waterfield, was out with a knee injury. Another of the Rams' offensive weapons, Glenn Davis, also was sidelined.

No matter. Yanks coach Jimmy Phelan made the mistake of trying to single-cover L.A. receivers Elroy Hirsch and Tom Fears with Bob Celeri and Paul Crowe. Hirsch and Fears caught 16 passes between them, good for 335 yards and four touchdowns. The Yanks couldn't do anything with Vitamin Smith, either. His only two receptions went for TDs of 36 and 67 yards.

But despite the competition, or lack thereof, Van Brocklin's is a remarkable record. He broke the existing mark, held by the Chicago Bears' Johnny Lujack, by 86 yards. No one has come within 32 yards of him since. Heck, this record might survive the century.

Van Brocklin himself never had another *400-*

yard game in his career. And to think that the morning after throwing for 554, he occupied a secondary place on the sports page. Allie Reynolds of baseball's New York Yanks had pitched his second no-hitter of the season to help his team sweep a doubleheader from Boston and clinch another pennant.

■ ■ ■

HALAS VS. MARSHALL

An 0–3 start in 1951 sent Redskins owner George Preston Marshall searching for a new head coach. His number-one candidate was 53-year-old Hunk Anderson, one of the game's great line coaches, who had recently left pro football to take a sales job with a Detroit steel company.

Marshall offered him a three-year contract. Anderson preferred one that covered only the rest of the season. He arranged for a leave of absence and flew to Washington, where he held a news conference and talked about some of the changes he planned to make.

Unfortunately for Marshall, Anderson was still under contract to the Chicago Bears until the end of the season. He had taken a leave of absence from the *Bears* to see how he liked it in the business world.

George Halas demanded compensation. Marshall offered him the Redskins' number-two draft pick the next year. Halas at first accepted, then changed his mind and asked for Pro Bowl defensive tackle Paul Lipscomb.

Even if Marshall had wanted to make the deal, which he didn't, he would have needed unanimous league approval. It was past the trading deadline.

He appealed to commissioner Bert Bell but got no help. Halas told Bell he'd been trying to get Anderson to coach part-time and still wanted him.

The stalemate forced Marshall to give the head job to backfield coach Dick Todd, a former Redskin. Anderson returned to Detroit. But there was speculation Marshall and Halas would eventually make some kind of arrangement.

"It would come as no surprise," the *Washington Star* said, "if Anderson turns up as head coach of the Redskins on November 4. On that date, the Redskins play the Bears here."

Anderson did indeed turn up at Griffith Stadium on November 4, but it was as a Bears assistant.

Halas had talked him into coming back, reportedly at the same salary the Redskins offered him. At the end of the season Anderson got out of pro ball for good, never having been a head coach.

(Fifteen years later, Halas blocked a similar move by George Allen to the Rams. But at least Allen was an active member of the Bears staff. Halas won the court case, then let Allen go to Los Angeles, saying he had made his point.)

■ ■ ■

THE BINGAMAN DIET

Les Bingaman received a note from Lions coach Buddy Parker in the summer of 1951 ordering him not to report to training camp weighing more than 290. Parker figured his massive nose guard would be quicker if he took off 40 pounds or so.

Bingaman went along with it. His description of the experience:

"During the off-season I went to work driving one of those asphalt-finishing machines on a road construction project. Where I sat on that machine—about six feet above the hot asphalt—the temperature was around 360.

"I steamed eight hours every day for about two months, and those pounds really melted off. I also skipped breakfast, drank only a can of stewed tomatoes for lunch and ate nothing but lean steak and green vegetables for supper.

"I finally reported to camp weighing about 300, but people started shoving me all over the place in intrasquad scrimmages. So I put those pounds back on in a hurry at the training table. Actually, I ate my way onto the team that year."

* * *

Bob St. Clair, the 49ers' monstrous Hall-of-Fame tackle, ate his meat raw (and still does). One of his favorite stunts in training camp every year was to sit with the rookies when liver was being served. St. Clair would take his seat at the table with a napkin over his plate. He'd then remove the napkin to reveal a bloody piece of raw liver and dig in.

Oh, yeah, his second toe was longer than his wife's little finger.

■ ■ ■

TOUGH TO TOP

When Cleveland's Dub Jones tied the NFL record in 1951 by scoring six touchdowns against the Bears, he scored the last five times he touched the ball. The TDs came, in order, on a 34-yard pass, runs of 12, 27 and 43 yards and a 43-yard pass.

■ ■ ■

VERY FUNNY

From 1949 to '51 Tex Schramm and Tex Maule worked side by side in the Los Angeles Rams' front office, Schramm as assistant to owner Dan Reeves, Maule as team publicist. Frank Finch of the *L.A. Times* thought the situation so unusual that he made a point of telling people the Rams were the only team in the NFL with co-Texes.

■ ■ ■

MR. SMITH DOESN'T COME TO WASHINGTON

Redskins owner George Preston Marshall let a Washington sportswriter draft a player for him in 1952. The writer was Mo Siegel, who was covering the team for the *Washington Post*. The player was Flavious Smith, an end from Tennessee Tech.

You won't find Smith on the team's list of draftees from '52. Or the league's, for that matter. He somehow disappeared between the time commissioner Bert Bell announced his selection and the end of the draft. Therein lies the mystery of an otherwise hilarious story.

Siegel, now a columnist for the *Washington Times*, says he pestered Marshall into letting him make the pick on the train ride to New York, where the draft was taking place.

"Marshall's theory was writers didn't always know as much football as they should," Siegel says. "I told him, 'Give me a pick in a later round, and

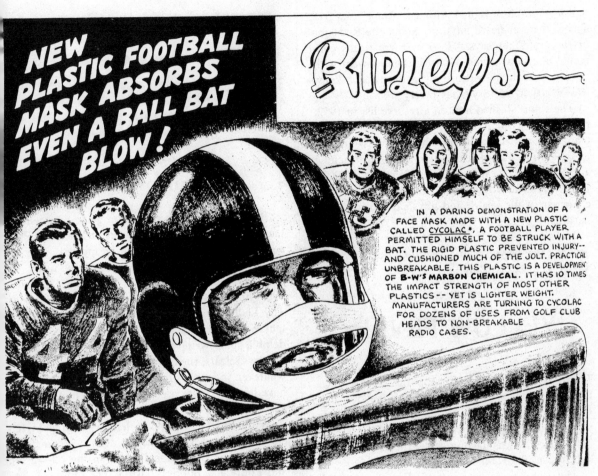

NEW PLASTIC FOOTBALL MASK ABSORBS EVEN A BALL BAT BLOW!

RIPLEY'S—

IN A DARING DEMONSTRATION OF A FACE MASK MADE WITH A NEW PLASTIC CALLED CYCOLAC*, A FOOTBALL PLAYER PERMITTED HIMSELF TO BE STRUCK WITH A BAT. THE RIGID PLASTIC PREVENTED INJURY-- AND CUSHIONED MUCH OF THE JOLT. PRACTICAL UNBREAKABLE, THIS PLASTIC IS A DEVELOPMENT OF B-W's MARBON CHEMICAL. IT HAS 10 TIMES THE IMPACT STRENGTH OF MOST OTHER PLASTICS -- YET IS LIGHTER WEIGHT. MANUFACTURERS ARE TURNING TO CYCOLAC FOR DOZENS OF USES FROM GOLF CLUB HEADS TO NON-BREAKABLE RADIO CASES.

(Borg/Warner Corporation)

we'll see what I can do.' He didn't have anything to lose, anyway. It was very rare that a player drafted in the later rounds ever made a team in those days."

Sure enough, Marshall approached Siegel after the early rounds were done and told him to come up with the name of a player. Siegel did, and as he recalls the Redskins selected that player—Flavious Smith—somewhere between the 15th and 20th rounds.

"Congratulations," Siegel remembers Marshall saying, "you've just become the first sportswriter to draft a player."

"Congratulations, George," Siegel replied, "you've just integrated the Redskins."

What a stunt. Marshall had a strict whites-only policy on the Redskins. Siegel hadn't known whom to draft and had turned to the *Chicago Tribune*'s Ed Prell for help. It was Prell who'd given him Smith's name and the information that he was black.

"I'm quite sure he [Marshall] thought I was kidding," Siegel says. "I'd been kibitzing with him a lot. But then he tells me the next day that he'd traded Smith, and I'm pretty sure he said to Green Bay."

It's unclear what Marshall did with Smith, but he didn't trade him. The transaction doesn't show up in the Redskins' records or in press accounts of the draft. According to the Associated Press' team-by-team and round-by-round selections, no player named Flavious Smith was drafted in 1952. Yet Siegel was present when Bell announced the pick for the Redskins. What gives?

We're not certain, but it isn't hard to imagine Marshall and Bell "fixing" the situation behind the scenes. The Redskins could easily have relinquished their rights to Smith and been given another pick later in the draft. No one was paying much attention then, anyway.

Smith, an all–Ohio Valley Conference end as a

senior, eventually signed with the Rams as a free agent. "I never heard anything about the Redskins or the draft," he says. "Two or three teams contacted me about trying out with them. I went with the Rams as much because my college coach knew [Rams coach] Joe Stydahar pretty well."

The Rams stashed him on a reserve list in 1952, paying him a small amount to play for a semipro team. He was traded to Pittsburgh in '53 and released during training camp. He went into teaching and coaching and eventually completed his Ph.D. In 1962 he returned to Tennessee Tech, where he's now chairman of the health and physical education department.

He chuckles at the suggestion he might have become the player who integrated the Redskins. Smith, you see, is white.

■ ■ ■

YELLOW FEVER

Teams tried everything to stop the Los Angeles Rams' high-powered passing attack in the '50s. In a 1952 game in L.A., the Green Bay Packers wore yellow jerseys almost identical to the Rams'. The only difference was the numbers—the Packers' were light green, the Rams' deep blue.

The Rams were not amused. But there wasn't anything they could do about it. The Packers claimed they didn't have a change of jerseys (a violation of league rules). The green jerseys they usually wore at the Coliseum had been left at the practice field they'd used during the week.

That, at least, is the story coach Gene Ronzani gave. It wasn't hard to see through, though. The Packers had dropped eight straight to the Rams, most by lopsided scores. Ronzani was just looking for an edge. One more loss and the Pack was out of the conference race.

The Rams called commissioner Bert Bell to complain—he later fined Ronzani—and announced they were playing the game under protest. They needn't have worried. The Packers were more perplexed by all the yellow jerseys than they were. Green Bay quarterbacks Babe Parilli and Tobin Rote threw five interceptions, L.A.'s Norm Van Brocklin only one. The Rams won, 45–27.

Even so, fullback Tank Younger said, "It was

mighty confusing. We were blocking the wrong guys all afternoon."

■ ■ ■

FIGHT OF THE DECADE
Eagles vs. 49ers, Opening Day 1953

Background: In an exhibition game between the teams in San Antonio three weeks earlier, three Philadelphia players were seriously injured. The rematch at Kezar Stadium promised to be nasty.

Blow-by-blow account: In the second quarter, 49ers linebacker Hardy Brown broke running back Toy Ledbetter's cheek with his notorious shoulder tackle. The game degenerated from there. A Philadelphia sportswriter said the Eagles were victims of "elbows, cleats, the closed fist, the plastic helmet or whatever their honorable antagonists happened to have handy. It was a good thing that miners' pickaxes had to be checked at the door."

With about six minutes left, a shoving match started between San Francisco defensive end Charley Powell, a professional boxer in the off-season, and Philly end Bobby Walston. The same two had squared off in San Antonio. This time, the 49ers' Joe Perry sprinted off the bench and threw a punch at Walston. Both benches emptied.

As many as a dozen fights broke out from the Eagles 30 to the 49ers end zone, where stars Hugh McElhenny and Pete Pihos "fought their way across the field and pelted each other with helmets and fists."

Back judge Norm Duncan tried to come between some of the players and had to be helped off the field. Fists flew in the stands. About 150 fans spilled onto the field. It was several minutes before police could restore order.

The next day, commissioner Bert Bell declared that fighting simply wouldn't be tolerated. No one paid any attention.

Final score: 49ers 31, Eagles 21.

■ ■ ■

TAKE MY CHIN STRAP—PLEASE!

When Elroy "Crazylegs" Hirsch retired for the first time in 1954, he left behind more than pass receiving records. He left his jersey, uniform pants, helmet, shoulder pads, shoes and socks.

The popular Rams end was "practically denuded," in the words of the *Los Angeles Times,* by a gang of kids as he came off the field following what was supposed to be his last game. After 20 minutes of pandemonium, he reached the Rams' locker room wearing only girdle pads and ankle tape.

"If I'd had the regular wrap-around hip pads, I'd have been down to my jock strap," Hirsch says.

And there's no telling how far those kids were willing to go.

Hirsch had signed off like a true champ, catching five passes for 119 yards in a 28–20 victory over the Packers at the L.A. Coliseum. He'd announced his plans to retire during the season, and at halftime he'd been honored in a ceremony along with linebacker Don Paul. Each was given a '54 Oldsmobile.

When the final gun sounded, swarms of kids ran onto the field looking for souvenirs, as was their custom. Usually, a chin strap sufficed. This time, though, they were after the greatest prize of all—Hirsch's yellow and blue number 40 jersey.

"A big group surrounded me, and what really bothered me was they got me off my feet," Hirsch says. "They actually started to trample me. They were tugging at my jersey trying to get a piece, but you know those things didn't tear away like they do now. I yelled, 'Hey, back off and I'll give it to you.' So I took off my jersey and threw it one way. And a pack of them went off after it. I took off something else and threw it another way and got a few more out of the way. Little by little I bartered my way off the field."

Several police finally arrived on the scene and escorted Hirsch—bare-headed, bare-chested, bare-legged and bare-footed—to the safety of the locker room.

As it turned out, that wasn't the end of Crazylegs. He returned in 1955 when injuries depleted the Rams' receiver corps. He wound up playing three more seasons and left the game fully clothed.

ILLEGAL PROCEDURE

Browns coach Paul Brown had what he called the "Tuesday Rule." He thought sex in the days before a game took away from a player's performance, so he advised the married men to abstain after Tuesday.

Wednesday through Saturday? That's a lot of abstinence. We got out the calculator and figured out exactly how much.

DECADE LEADERS

PASSING
Yards: Norm Van Brocklin, 20,539; Bobby Layne, 20,035; Y.A. Tittle, 17,206.
Completion percentage (1,000 attempts): Otto Graham, 55.7; Tittle, 55.3; Johnny Unitas, 54.1.
Touchdowns: Layne, 151; Van Brocklin, 143; Charley Conerly and Tobin Rote, 119.
Interceptions: Layne, 173; Van Brocklin, 159; Rote 158.

RUSHING
Yards: Joe Perry, 7,151; Ollie Matson, 4,194; Hugh McElhenny, 3,941.
Yards per carry (500 attempts): Dan Towler, 5.2; Jimmy Brown, 5.07; Perry, 5.05.
TDs: Perry, 49; Towler, 43; Brown, 40.

RECEIVING
Receptions: Billy Wilson, 404; Billy Howton, 342; Elroy Hirsch, 321.
Yards: Howton, 6,091; Hirsch, 5,973; Wilson, 5,851.
Yards per catch (150 receptions): Ray Renfro, 20.55; Bob Boyd, 20.52; Harlon Hill, 20.49.
TDs: Hirsch, 49; Wilson, 48; Howton, 44.

OTHER CATEGORIES
Scoring: Lou Groza, 742; Gordie Soltau 644; Bobby Walston, 631.
Interceptions: Emlen Tunnell, 59; Jack Butler and Bobby Dillon, 52.
Punt return average (50 returns): Billy Grimes, 13.2; Ray Mathews, 12.77; Jack Christiansen, 12.75.
Punt return TDs: Christiansen, 8.
Kickoff return average (75 returns): Lynn Chandnois, 29.6; Buddy Young, 27.9; Matson, 27.7.
Kickoff return TDs: Matson, 6.
Field goals: Groza, 131; George Blanda, 81; Pat Summerall, 73.
Field goal percentage (75 attempts): Fred Cone, 59.6, Groza, 58.5; Doak Walker, 56.3.
Punting average (200 punts): Pat Brady, 44.5; Don Chandler, 44.8; Sam Baker and Horace Gillom, 43.8.

Brown coached the Browns for 17 seasons and had, let's say, 35 players on the team each year. Add it all up and you get 118 years, 20 days, 11 hours, 56 minutes and 53 seconds of not fooling around. Roughly.

"We kid him about it today that he would only talk to the married guys, not the ones who were single," Otto Graham says. "I think only .0000001 percent of the players—if that—ever observed the rule."

• • •

TREPTITUDE AND TERESHINSKI

If Tereshinski doesn't get involved in moral treptitude [sic], get drunk and break club rules, and behaves himself in a fairly decent way he will be given $250.00 at the end of the season—provided, of course, the club doesn't win the championship.

Redskins end Joe Tereshinski's last two contracts contained this addendum, which would lead you to believe he had his fun in family-sized portions. Actually, Tereshinski was almost a teetotaler and a notorious good boy. This was owner George Preston Marshall's way of slipping him an extra $250.

• • •

THE DARK SIDE OF THE DUTCHMAN

A teammate once described Norm Van Brocklin as the man "most likely to be babied by an airline hostess." But Van Brocklin also could be a Hall-of-Fame jerk. Before they called him "The Dutchman," they called him "The Brat."

Van Brocklin was known to rifle a football off the head of anyone not paying attention at practice. He once threw a cup of water in tackle Tom Dahm's face after Dahm allowed him to be sacked. Rams coach Hamp Pool predicted Van Brocklin would break every passing record in the book "if somebody doesn't break his neck first."

It's a wonder they didn't. Some other not-so-golden moments:

▪ Van Brocklin was one of the founders of the NFL Players Association. Conciliation wasn't his style. Of antiunion Redskins owner George Preston Marshall, he said: "The best thing that could happen to Marshall's players and the National Football League would be for him to step in front of a moving cab."

▪ Van Brocklin's disagreements with L.A. coach Sid Gillman eventually led to the Dutchman being traded to Philadelphia in 1958. One time when the Rams were struggling, Van Brocklin made a request to an accordionist at a restaurant where the team was eating. The tune, dedicated for all to hear to Gillman, was "So Long, It's Been Good to Know You."

▪ As coach of the Minnesota Vikings, Van Brocklin had this to say about former Rams teammate Les Richter: "Richter is an overrated oaf. If he could just go as hard while the ball is in play as he does after the whistle, he'd be one helluva boy. But he doesn't and isn't."

▪ ▪ ▪

THE GOSPEL ACCORDING TO SAINT PAUL

Every year for 17 years, Paul Brown opened the Cleveland Browns' training camp with The Speech. The words barely changed, former players say. The content never did.

In 1959, Gordon Cobbledick, a sportswriter for the Cleveland Plain Dealer, *sat in on The Speech and took notes. Here it is.*

"I'm talking to the veterans as well as the rookies today. If you're an older player and have reached the point where you can't concentrate on what I have to say, maybe you've reached the point where you ought to be looking for other work.

"If you think about football only when you step on the field, we'll try to peddle you. You've got 4½ months of this ahead of you, and for 4½ months I expect football to be the biggest thing in your life, as it is mine. In this game, more men fail mentally than physically.

"Maybe you've read or heard there are four or five jobs open on this team. I want to tell you right now that that isn't true. There are 35 jobs open. They're going to be won by the men who convince me and the other coaches that they're the best qualified to fill them.

"I like to think that the Cleveland Browns are somewhat different from the average professional football team. I want to see some exuberance in your play, some sign that you play for the sheer joy of licking somebody.

"We've been in business 13 years. In 11 of them we've won division championships. In several others we've taken the whole pot. We're the Ben Hogans, the Joe Louises, the New York Yankees of our game, and that's the way we aim to keep it.

"At home and on the road we stay together. On the nights before home games we go to a downtown hotel in Cleveland, we eat together, go to a movie as a group. It gives us a feeling of one-ness that helps to make us a team and not just a collection of 35 football players.

"I expect you to watch your language, your dress, your deportment and especially I expect you to be careful of the company you keep. That pleasant guy who invites you to dinner may be a gambler. Probably he doesn't intend to offer you a bribe. Maybe he isn't even after information. But he wants to be seen with you in public. I'm telling you to avoid him.

"Here's a rule: In your rooms at 10, lights out at 10:30. Occasionally, the coaches make a bed check. For the player who sneaks out after the bed check there's an automatic fine of $500. And it sticks. I have had to levy many fines for violations of many rules, and I have never rescinded one for good subsequent behavior or meritorious performance.

"Here in Hiram [Ohio] we eat three meals a day together. Sport shirts are approved, but I don't want to see any player in the dining room in a T-shirt. I expect civilized table manners and table talk. There have been people who failed to make this team simply because they were obnoxious to eat with.

"We're determined to have a team of men who are willing to pay the price of success in football, and the price is high. If you approach this as just another job, another means to a payday, we don't want you.

"I want you to keep your wives out of football. Ask them not to talk football with other wives. I've seen it cause trouble.

"Before the season opens I'm going to have to tell some of you—many of you—that you won't make it. It's the part of my job that I like least, but when the time comes my good wishes will go with you. Now let's go to work."

···
REASON NUMBER THREE TO HATE GEORGE PRESTON MARSHALL

Head coaches who worked for George Preston Marshall were wise to rent rather than buy. The Redskins owner made 12 coaching changes in 32 years—an average of less than one three-year adjustable mortgage. But none was more sensational than his firing of Curly Lambeau in August 1954. This was Marshall at his tyrannical best.

The drama took place at the Senator Hotel in Sacramento at about 1:00 A.M., following a 30–7 exhibition loss to the San Francisco 49ers. Marshall and his wife, actress Corinne Griffith, had gone out for a bite to eat after the game and returned to the hotel shortly after midnight. On the way to their suite, they ran into end Hugh "Bones" Taylor and defensive back Don Paul. The players were headed into their room with a six-pack of beer. Both were "sober and well-behaved," according to accounts.

Alcohol was one of Marshall's pet peeves. He didn't want his players drinking in public or while in training. He was one of the few owners who banned beer from the locker room. So when he saw Taylor and Paul, he snapped. He berated the two and confiscated their beer. Then he stormed off in search of general manager Dick McCann or Lambeau.

The head coach was in the hotel bar just off the lobby, and he wasn't delivering a temperance lecture. He was old school. He expected his players to put out on the field but didn't see anything wrong with a beer or two after a game, even a loss. Marshall found Lambeau, and the fireworks began immediately.

There was shouting back and forth, and the two grabbed and pushed each other. Then Lambeau drew back to throw a punch. McCann latched on to his arm and prevented what would have been a massacre. Curly was about 5′11″ and a still-solid 195 pounds. Marshall was 6′2″, but all his muscle was in his mouth. (One report claimed he struck a fighting pose reminiscent of John L. Sullivan's.)

The two men took their shouting match outside to the sidewalk, where Marshall reportedly told Lambeau: "You're all washed up with this team." Marshall then summoned McCann and startled assistant coach Joe Kuharich to his room. A few minutes later, Kuharich was head coach. His instructions were to tighten team discipline.

The suddenness with which Lambeau was fired surprised even veteran Marshall watchers. The two men had been friends since the '30s, when Lambeau was in his glory running the Green Bay Packers. In 1952 Marshall hired his buddy even though many in the league felt the game had passed Curly by. For two seasons they'd coexisted well. Now, all of a sudden, it was over.

"I'm no quitter," Lambeau said. "When a coach loses his self-respect, he ceases to be a coach."

Coaches had a way of losing their self-respect working for Marshall. When the Redskins were in Boston (1932–36), he'd sit on the bench and give players instructions as they were sent into the game. In Washington, he stayed in the stands but had a phone in his box with a direct line to the bench.

He often decided who was to be cut, who was to be drafted and even who was to start. As many of his coaches resigned as were fired.

"It was a choice between being a man or a mouse," Lambeau's predecessor, Dick Todd, said as he gave up the job.

The only Redskins coach able to keep Marshall at bay was Ray Flaherty (1936–42). It was said he had a clause in his contract that assured his independence. Flaherty says that isn't true; his agreement with Marshall was understood. Either way, it's probably no coincidence that he was Marshall's most successful coach.

■ ■ ■

AN ADVANCED CASE OF THE YIPS

Before a big game at Pittsburgh in November 1956, Chicago Cardinals quarterback Lamar McHan asked coach Ray Richards not to start him because he was *too nervous.* The Cards, who lost that day, hit their 24-year-old QB with a $3,000 fine, the second-largest in NFL history at the time.

It must have been some scene. Richards had suffered a gallstone attack the morning of the game and probably shouldn't have gone to the stadium. (After a postgame attack, he was taken to the hospital, where he spent the night.) Probably the last thing he needed to hear was his starting QB complaining of stage fright.

BANG! ZOOM!

McHan started, all right. But he played so badly at the outset that Richards replaced him with Jim Root in the second quarter. McHan went back in in the second half, though, and threw a 45-yard touchdown pass to Ollie Matson with 2:19 left for the Cardinals' only score in a 14–7 defeat.

When McHan went to practice Monday and was told he wouldn't receive his paycheck, he left. The team then decided to suspend him. Managing director Walter Wolfner went as far as to say McHan would never play for the Cards again.

"I gave him a big salary boost this year," Wolfner said, "but he's a badly confused and mixed-up guy. McHan has never learned to be a team man. He has a persecution complex. I'm sure the team will be better off without him."

Later in the day, though, McHan returned and apologized to Wolfner. He was allowed to practice with the team that week and was reinstated for the next game, a 38–27 victory over the Steelers in Chicago. He played in the second half and scored on a one-yard run. That was the extent of his probation. The Cardinals, after all, still had a chance to win the division and needed McHan in there.

Teammates said the whole thing may have come about because McHan was worried the club would draft another quarterback later in the month. Either the Cardinals or the Packers were going to have the first pick that year, and the Heisman Trophy–winner-to-be, Notre Dame's Paul Hornung, was a QB.

Here's the explanation McHan gave: "I was just trying to be honest about the situation with the best interests of the team at heart. I felt if I could sit on the bench for the first five minutes or so, I'd get myself under control.

"Mr. Richards has been mighty nice, too, and that makes me especially sorry to see this happen. . . . Mr. Richards was sick before the game and he took my remarks the wrong way."

Now what was that you were saying about temperamental modern players?

(P.S.: The team later gave him the money back.)

■ ■ ■

A DECADE OF VIOLENCE

The game was never rougher than in the '50s. Modern players may be bigger, faster and stronger than those of four decades ago, but they're no tougher or meaner. Ever-quotable Art Donovan said pro football in the '50s was populated by "oversized coal miners and West Texas psychopaths."

He may have something there.

How *do* you explain the violence of the '50s? One popular theory is that the players had been hardened by their experiences in World War II and Korea. Sounds plausible enough, and it may even be true. What we know for sure is that the game was rougher because it *could* be. Here's why:

■ Quarterbacks weren't the coddled creatures they are today. Late hits—even late, late hits—were routine. "You'd see guys chasing the quarterback when the play went the other way," says ex–Bears defensive end Ed Sprinkle. The bigger the quarterback's reputation, the bigger the bull's-eye on his chest, particularly early in the decade.

■ Facemasks didn't gain wide acceptance until the late '50s. Before then, the head was more a target than a weapon. There was a lot of high tackling and not much complaining about it. "My nose was broken 11 times," Pat Summerall said. "Tony Trabert and I do tennis together on CBS, and after I got to know him he said, 'Pat, you're in the television business. Don't you think you ought to have something done about your nose?' I said, 'I already have.' "

■ The game was policed more by the players than by the officials or the league office. And the law on the field was pure Old Testament—an eye for an eye, a tooth for a tooth. Literally.

■ The rules left more room for rough play. Until 1955, for instance, ball carriers could get up and continue running after being knocked down (as long as they weren't in the grasp of an opponent). This made piling on legal in some circumstances. "Everybody waited around for the son of a bitch to so much as raise his head," says ex–Lions linebacker Joe Schmidt.

■ Television used only a couple of cameras, and the instant replay hadn't been invented yet. Thus, on-field behavior wasn't monitored nearly as closely as it is today.

What was the NFL *really* like back then? Imagine an entire league of Oakland Raiders. But maybe that's not such an apt analogy. To the players of the '50s, the Raiders would probably be wimps.

■ ■ ■

BREAKING EVEN

Two of the decade's headline-making hits involved Cardinals Hall-of-Famer Charley Trippi. In 1951 Trippi knocked out the Bears' Ed "The Claw" Sprinkle with one punch, and in '55 he had his face caved in by the 49ers' John Henry Johnson.

Sprinkle was one of the league's tough guys, a small (6'1", 210) but exceptionally vicious defensive end who in the words of one writer had a "Midas-like" talent—"Everything he touches turns to broken noses."

Trippi had put up with Sprinkle's abuse for years, and in the closing seconds of a 24–14 Cardinals upset he decided it was time to settle the score. After handing the ball off on a clock-killing running play, he whirled as Sprinkle barreled in and knocked him cold with a right.

Trippi was ejected. Asked later about the automatic fine he'd have to pay, he said: "It was worth it."

"Sprinkle's job was to intimidate," he says today. "I knew that. It was no secret. But it was my job to perform the best that I could under the circumstances. Then, when the opportune time came, to get even."

The Johnson episode occurred in the first quarter

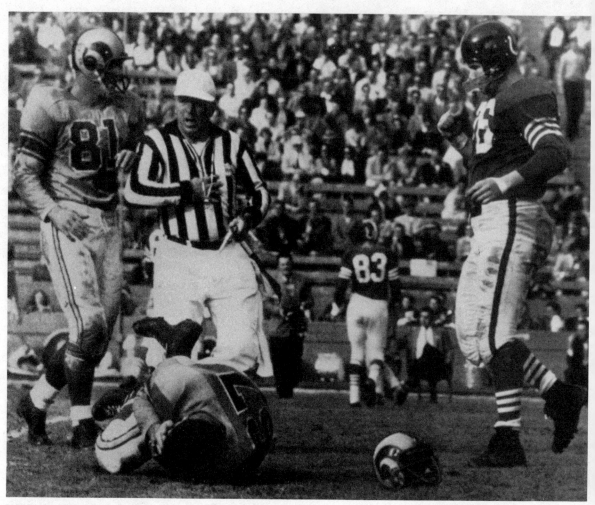

Justice in the '50s was dispensed by the players as much by the officials. Here's the Rams' Les Richter writhing in pain in 1954 after the Colts' Don Joyce (right), taking exception to a block, ripped Richter's helmet off and bashed him in the face with it. (UPI/Bettmann Newsphotos)

of an exhibition game. Trippi, in his last season, had moved to safety. CBS broadcaster Pat Summerall, the Cardinals' defensive captain that day, describes what happened:

"John Henry, as I recall, was split out on the opposite side of the field. The play [a short run] was almost down, but not quite down. There was a lesson they told us when you came into the league that if you were going to make a tackle, either get into the pile or get away from the pile, because that's where accidents happen. Charley was standing there watching; somebody else had made the tackle. He was just standing there, and John Henry came from the other side of the field and hit him with an elbow upside the head."

The blow came over Trippi's single-bar facemask and broke bones above and below the eye as well as the nose in two places. His teammates swore revenge.

In the second half, the game deteriorated into a cheap-shot contest. When 49ers defensive back Rex Berry was tackled near the sideline after an interception, Cards center Jack Simmons dove on top of him with knees and elbows flying. It got so bad that referee Harry Brubaker called the game late in the fourth quarter.

Trippi needed plastic surgery but postponed it until after the season. Two months later, he returned to the lineup for the final five games. Doctors used rib cartilage to rebuild his nose.

The matter didn't end there. The following year, the two teams met in another exhibition. On the next-to-last play, Johnson was knocked out of bounds and jumped by three Cardinals—one of whom was Summerall. Justice in the '50s was ever vigilant.

■ ■ ■

FIGHTIN' WORDS

It's not what you do, but what they see you do.
—DON PAUL

The pileup is where most players are injured. It's intentional and can be avoided. That's vicious football. Officials don't call this as often as they call clipping. And it's a much more dangerous practice.
—GREASY NEALE, *1954*

I don't feel it was ever justified, me having a reputation as a dirty football player. I was very aggressive. I never missed an opportunity to try to put a little hurt on somebody, but everything legal. To me, it wasn't a game of pitty-pat.
—ED SPRINKLE

More and more players are wearing faceguards every year. . . . They're chiefly interested in protecting themselves against dirty football.
—DOAK WALKER, *1955*

If one of our guys got another guy, he'd get a punch from me. . . . I saved Jimmy Brown . . . Johnny Unitas . . . Ollie Matson.
—ROSEY GRIER

I remember hitting a guy on the running track at Kezar Stadium. That's 15 yards out of bounds.
—PAT SUMMERALL

I hit a lot of guys hard, but on the other hand they didn't have any problem hitting me. I can't tell you all the teeth I lost. I had my nose broken three or four times, stitches over the eyes four or five times.

Somebody was hitting me, you understand? I wasn't doing all the "getting." I was doing a lot of taking.
—JOHN HENRY JOHNSON

We try to hurt everybody. We hit each other as hard as we can. This is a man's game.
—SAM HUFF, 1959

■ ■ ■

HARDY BROWN

I saw my first Hardy Brown hit while watching films of the 1951 Browns-49ers game at the Pro Football Hall of Fame. A San Francisco defensive back intercepted a pass by Otto Graham and was weaving his way upfield when a sudden movement at the bottom of the screen caught my eye. It was like the flash a fisherman might see in a stream before his line grows taut. I reversed the film and watched again.

As a Browns receiver turned to pursue the play, he was struck so violently in the face that his helmet popped up on his head and his back hit the ground before his feet. Standing over him was Hardy Brown. You could almost hear him chuckling.
—BOB O'DONNELL

There isn't much left of Hardy Brown. He's been institutionalized in northern California with dementia, the result of years of hard drinking. He also has emphysema, and the arthritis in his right shoulder is so bad he can't lift his arm to scratch his head.

Let's start with The Shoulder. That's where the legend begins. Hardy Brown played linebacker in the NFL at 6', 190 pounds, and hit harder than any player before or since. His right shoulder was his weapon. He usually aimed it at an opponent's head, and the results often were concussions and facial fractures—noses, cheeks, jaws . . . you name it, Brown broke it.

"It was early in the game," former Eagles running back Toy Ledbetter recalls of his 1953 run-in with Brown, "and I was carrying on a sweep to the right. I knew about Brown because I'd been at Oklahoma State when he was at Tulsa. I usually kept my eye on him, but this time I cut inside a block and never saw him. He caught me with the shoulder and the next thing I knew I was on the ground looking for my head."

The hit broke Ledbetter's cheek. Dr. Tom Dow,

Eagles team physician, said it was the worst facial fracture he'd seen. Brown played 10 pro seasons in four different leagues, and he laid low dozens. Backs, ends, linemen, it didn't matter. Brown was an indiscriminate maimer.

And what a mystery. No one could figure out how he hit with the force he did. In 1951, Bears coach George Halas had officials check Brown's shoulder pads before a game. They found nothing. Nor could anyone figure Brown's fury. He lived for the big hits. Relished them. They were his one marketable skill. Away from the game, he was reserved but friendly. On the field, he was a killer.

"I came out of the huddle at the beginning of the game and figured I'd say hello," says ex–Giants lineman Tex Coulter, who grew up with Brown in a Fort Worth, Texas, orphanage. "I came up to the line and looked across at his linebacker spot and his eyes looked like they belonged to some cave animal. They were fiery, unfocused. You don't know if he could see anything or everything. I kept my mouth shut."

Y. A. Tittle claims in his book *I Pass* that Brown knocked out 21 opponents as a 49er in 1951, including the Washington Redskins' entire starting backfield. That's an exaggeration (for starters, the 49ers didn't play the Redskins that year). But Brown inspired exaggeration. Ex-players speak of him the way fight people speak of Sonny Liston.

"To me, Hardy Brown was the most unique player ever," Coulter says. "Think of it this way:

What Hardy Brown was all about in football wasn't physical. Hardy was a psychic occurrence."

Coulter knows Brown as well as anyone. They are about the same age and arrived at the Masonic Home orphanage at about the same time in 1929. Coulter is working on a book about their lives. To understand Hardy Brown, he says, you have to understand his past. That isn't easy.

Hardy Brown's father was murdered. Shot dead in a neighbor's home in rural Kirkland, Texas, November 7, 1928. Two men pumped four bullets into him. Hardy was in the room when it happened. He was four. Four months later, Brown was present again when a family friend murdered one of his father's killers at point-blank range.

After the second incident, Brown's mother sent her four youngest children to the Masonic Home in Fort Worth. Hardy was five. He claimed it was 12 years before he heard from his mother again, and then only to get her permission to enlist in the Marines.

The Masonic Home orphanage sits on over 200 acres of land southeast of downtown Fort Worth. It has its own dairy farm and school, with grades one through 12. In the '30s, there was a matron for every 12 to 15 children. Discipline was rigid. Those who didn't do their chores or got caught slipping off to Sycamore Creek after hours could expect to be cuffed.

Football was the great escape. It was rough, wild and (almost) without rules. Unless you were a sissy boy, you played. That was the last thing Hardy Brown was.

"Football gave us self-worth," Coulter says. "We were orphans, but you couldn't call us orphans. When the newspapers came out and wrote stories, they'd refer to us as rag-tag kids and that made us angry. That was pity from above, and we hated it. Football was a way to alleviate that."

The Shoulder was born at the Masonic Home. It was the brainchild of his older brother Jeff. Jeff Brown reasoned correctly that human beings, like fenceposts, were easier to knock down if you hit them high. So when an opponent approached, he'd crouch slightly and then spring into his chin with his shoulder. In no time, everyone at the home was using "the humper," as it came to be called.

"The city boys were frightened as hell of us," Coulter says. "I don't blame 'em, the way Hardy Brown was and I was, too, to some extent. The

---

$$$$$

$10	Typical training camp pay, per week
$1,113	Winning share in 1950 championship game
$3,000	Fine assessed Cardinals quarterback Lamar McHan in 1956 for insubordination
$5,090	Bonus earned by 49ers' Joe Perry for gaining 1,018 yards in 1953 ($5 a yard)
$7,884	Average Redskins salary in 1957
$25,000	Salary for which Giants all-pro tackle Arnie Weinmeister jumped to CFL in 1954
$35,000	Scouting costs, highest in league, for Rams in 1959
$75,000	Fee paid by DuMont network in 1956 to televise NFL title game coast-to-coast for first time
$80,000+	What Buddy Parker made as coach of Steelers
$272,365	Financial loss suffered by 1953 Cards
$600,000	Purchase price of Cleveland Browns in 1953
$1,000,000	Rejected offer for New York Giants in 1955

goddamn guys would be bleeding all over the place. You know, in high school ball, you just aren't used to that. We speared, we leg-whipped, we used the humper, and I'm almost positive the man who invented the crack-back block was our coach, Rusty Russell. We did all them things and didn't think anything of it. We thought we were good, clean, rough boys."

Brown got out of the Masonic Home in 1941, enrolled at SMU and then went into the Marines, where he became the problem of the Japanese. Brown saw action in the Pacific as a paratrooper and, according to his sister Cathlyn, was on his way to Iwo Jima when a call came from West Point, of all places. It seems Army had pulled Coulter out of the enlisted ranks to play on its football team, and Coulter had put the coaches on to his Masonic Home teammate.

But Brown washed out of the Academy's prep school after failing the math requirement (though a night of drunken revelry at a nearby girl's school didn't help). None too disappointed, he landed at Tulsa University in the fall of 1945. For the next three years, he terrorized the Missouri Valley Conference as a blocking back and linebacker.

New Orleans Saints president Jim Finks was Brown's roommate at Tulsa and says he may have been at his destructive peak during those years.

"We'd put Brown at fullback if we wanted him to block one defensive end and put him at halfback if we wanted him to block the other," Finks says. "There were many games when he literally knocked out both defensive ends. I think it was a game against Baylor that he put out the two ends on consecutive plays.

"He broke *my* nose and gave me four stitches at a goddamned practice!"

Brown got poor Toy Ledbetter in *college*, too. It came on a kickoff return, and Finks says it's the hardest hit he's ever seen. "Ledbetter lay there quivering," he says. "Snot came out of his nose. He was bloody. He was down five minutes before they finally carried him off."

Off the field, Brown occasionally got wild when he was drinking. He and his future wife, Betty, woke up Finks one night and shot up the dorm room with a .22 rifle. But for the most part, Finks says, Brown was "intelligent, warm and shy," nothing like his on-field persona.

It took Brown a while to find permanent employ-ment in pro ball. He broke in with the All-America Football Conference's Brooklyn Dodgers in '48 and went to the Chicago Rockets the next year. When the AAFC folded, he wound up with the Washington Redskins, who waived him eight games into the '50 season. Small, slow linebackers weren't in demand.

But the word on Brown was getting around. He'd begun to leave a trail of bodies. Harry Buffington, head of National scouting combine, was a guard for Brooklyn in '48 and says one AAFC team assigned a player to shadow Brown on the field and act as a "protector" for the other players. Tittle was with the Colts in '50 and says running back Rip Collins told him before a game with Washington that he didn't want to run pass patterns in Brown's area.

It was the Colts who signed Brown after the Redskins waived him, and in his first game with them he broke Giants running back Joe Scott's nose with The Shoulder. The hit infuriated the Giants, and they tried to take their revenge.

Teams went after Brown as a matter of routine. He was a menace and could influence a game if he put a star player out. In a notorious incident in 1954, Lions defensive tackle Gil Mains jumped feet first into Brown on a kickoff return and opened a 20-stitch cut on his thigh. Brown was sewn up and returned to the game.

"I remember Hardy came up to me before a kickoff once and said, 'How about an onsides kick?' " says CBS broadcaster Pat Summerall, a teammate of Brown's in '56. "It was a close game with the Giants, and I told him I couldn't do that on my own without hearing from the coaches. He said he thought it would be a good idea. . . . Anyway, I kicked off as far as I could kick it, and here comes the whole Giant team after Hardy. They never even looked at the ball."

The Colts folded after the 1950 season, and Brown found a home in San Francisco. He was the 49ers' starting left linebacker for five seasons. It's difficult even to estimate how many players Brown KO'd with The Shoulder. One a game? That's probably too many. But you just don't know, because newspapers didn't devote much space to defensive play.

Game stories on a 49ers–Cardinals exhibition in '51, for instance, state that as many as six Chicago players were put out of the game, three with broken noses. The *San Francisco Chronicle* added the line:

Hardy Brown, the most dangerous man in pro football history. (Pro Football Hall of Fame/Nate Fine Collection)

"Against the Cards, Hardy Brown . . . played as vicious a line backing game as the 49ers ever had." How many of those broken noses were Hardy's doing is anyone's guess.

Brown may have been most dangerous on special teams, where it was easier to freelance and there was a field full of targets. Lions linebacker Carl Brettschneider said one of Brown's favorite tactics on punts was to line up behind an official so the opposing center couldn't see him, then catch him with The Shoulder as soon as he raised his head after the snap.

"He broke more jaws than any guy going," Brettschneider said.

Brown loved to talk about those bone-rattling blows. He apparently didn't lose any sleep over the injuries he caused, either. He also missed a lot of tackles because he aimed for the head.

"I don't think he ever went out to hurt anyone," Coulter says. "I think Hardy was shaped a certain way. One thing about a hard hitter is that you don't realize what it feels like to be hit. When you're doing the hitting, when you stick someone with that shoulder, it's a beautiful feeling. By God, it gives you a sense of power that reaches right to the back of your head. I think Hardy enjoyed that feeling."

Age and size caught up to Brown in '56. The 49ers waived him in training camp. He played briefly with Hamilton in the CFL and then signed with the Cardinals. At the end of the '56 season, the Cards released him.

In 1960, Toy Ledbetter had stopped by the locker room of the newly formed Denver Broncos to visit two former Eagles teammates when he heard a high-pitched cackle behind him. Ledbetter turned to see, of all people, his old nemesis Hardy Brown sitting in front of a locker.

"How's the cheekbone, Toy Boy?" Brown said.

Ledbetter laughed and shook hands with Brown. "No hard feelings," Ledbetter told him.

"You asshole."

After being released by the Broncos, Brown fell on hard times. He and his wife, Betty, broke up for a while. He held a number of construction jobs in the Southwest. And he continued to drink heavily. In 1986 he had to be institutionalized.

Family members say Brown never lost his desire to play football. At some point after he retired, he became involved with a semipro team.

The story is some young punk was giving him lip one day, and Brown decked him. Put him in the hospital.

■ ■ ■

HIT OF THE DECADE
Ed Meadows Lays Out Bobby Layne, 1956

The game film of the infamous 1956 Lions–Bears showdown for the Western Conference title is in the archives of the Pro Football Hall of Fame. The only thing missing is the infamous part. A nice, neat splicing job marks the point in the game where Bears defensive end Ed Meadows slammed Lions quarterback Bobby Layne to the turf and touched off one of the decade's biggest controversies.

What happened to the footage is anyone's guess. It may have been clipped and sent to commissioner Bert Bell for review. Then again, someone might have wanted to make the Meadows–Layne incident disappear. It wasn't, after all, one of the NFL's finest moments. In the weeks that followed, violence in pro football became a national issue.

The play in question occurred early in the second quarter. Layne handed off to Gene Gedman and, while he watched the ball, Meadows knocked him cold with a blindside hit. The Lions' leader left the game with a concussion. The Bears went on to a 38–21 home victory, which gave them the division title by a half game.

The losers were livid. Lions coach Buddy Parker threatened to resign in protest. Team president Edwin Anderson accused Meadows—wrongly, it turned out—of punching Layne and wanted him banned from the league for life. Who could blame them?

Just two weeks earlier, Detroit had routed Chicago, 42–10. Also, this was hardly the first time George Halas' team had knocked an opposing quar-

Bears defensive end Ed Meadows denied he deliberately went after Lions quarterback Bobby Layne in the 1956 showdown for the Western Conference championship. These four photos, however, suggest otherwise. The ball carrier is seven yards upfield when Meadows blindsides Layne, and Referee Ron Gibbs, who later said the hit was legal, is obviously in no position to judge. He's following the play, like the other 10 members of the Chicago defense. (UPI/Bettmann Newsphotos)

terback out of a big game. The previous Sunday, their manhandling of Cardinals QB Lamar McHan had caused a near-riot. And Meadows, when he was with the Steelers, had put Layne out of a game the year before.

Around the league, players and ex-players came forth with other sordid stories. They told of putting $5 or $10 apiece into a pot before games, with the money going to whoever incapacitated a particular opponent. They also said the cryin' Lions were no less dirty than any other team.

It was a public relations nightmare for the NFL. Much attention had already been focused on violence during the 1955 season, and now this.

Meadows, of course, denied he was out to get Layne. He said he wasn't sure if Layne had faked to Gedman or not. "What was I supposed to do?" he said. "Ask somebody if Layne still had the ball?"

But even the edited version of the game film indicates the hit was extremely late. Still photos taken from the film show Gedman was seven yards upfield from Layne and nearly *down* when Meadows unloaded. A Detroit reporter who saw the actual footage said Meadows took six steps after Layne handed off. Even in an era when quarterbacks were fair game—with or without the ball—this hit stands out.

"I don't know whether he hit me on purpose or not, but he knew I didn't have the ball," Layne said.

After a brief investigation, Bell pronounced Meadows and Halas innocent of any conspiracy to get Layne. The whitewash wasn't surprising. The commissioner was suspected by many of being in Papa Bear's back pocket.

What tends to be overlooked is how well the Bears played that day. They controlled the line of scrimmage, as evidenced by Rick Casares' career-high 190 yards rushing in 17 carries. Whether Layne could have done anything about the outcome is debatable.

Meadows eventually got thrown out of the game, by the way. He punched Lions tackle Lou Creekmur, allegedly in response to a kick in the stomach.

The hit on Layne turned out to be the high point—or low point, depending on your point of view—of Meadows' career. He spent six years in the league with four different teams and retired after the 1959 season. In 1974 he shot himself to death.

■ ■ ■

BELL DUCKS THE ISSUE

After the Ed Meadows incident, Sports Illustrated interviewed commissioner Bert Bell about dirty play in the NFL. His responses have to be read to be believed. (So do our responses to his responses.)

Q: Do you think that pro football is dirty and getting dirtier?

A: No. I don't believe there is dirty football. I never have. Sure, there are flare-ups. But I have never seen a maliciously dirty football player in my life, and I don't believe there are any maliciously dirty players in the National Football League.

[See the story on Hardy Brown.]

Q: How do you explain the protests from coaches, owners and fans?

A: I believe this. If you go back seven or eight years, three or four teams dominated the league. So games and individual plays weren't always as vital as they are now. Now any team can beat any other team in the league, and every game is important. The players get more excited, and officials have maybe 50 or 60 judgment calls to make in every game. They don't come equipped with radar or a zoomar lens, either. Now you got to remember every team uses movies, too. They can look for things and find things the officials may miss. But the situation is this—the movies aren't always right, either. . . .

Q: How about the protest the Chicago Cardinals made against the Chicago Bears on their Dec. 9 game in which the Cards claimed their movies showed over 20 fouls by the Bears which were not called by the officials? Did you see those movies?

A: Wolfner [Walter, the Cards' managing director] sent the thing to me. I agree some mistakes were made. Nothing malicious.

Q: Then why did you refuse to let the Cardinals give a public showing of their game film?

A: I didn't say they couldn't show the film. What I said was that they couldn't show the thing and stop it whenever they wanted so they could point out the mistakes of the officials. I will never condone anyone holding the officials up to public ridicule.

[*This reminds us of a postgame comment made that season by 49ers owner Tony Morabito: "The officials were no more competent than the commissioner who appoints them—and that's very incompetent. The officials were the quintessence of nothing."*]

Q: Has any owner or coach ever complained to you about "hatchet men"?

A: No. I never heard of a "hatchet man" in pro football, if you mean by that a player who is sent into a game deliberately to injure an opponent. A hatchet man wouldn't live a year in pro football.

[*Allow us to introduce Lions defensive back Jim David. Nickname: "The Hatchet." (They called Hardy Brown that, too.)*]

Q: Do you mean by that the opposing teams would take care of him?

A: I go back to Davey O'Brien, the little TCU back who played for the Eagles. Somebody fouled Davey once. That guy got straightened out a little bit—in language—and every time he got hit. It was a little harder every time he got hit.

Q: Have you heard of a play called "dead dog" in which the quarterback simply keeps the ball and the rest of the team goes to work on a dirty player on the other team?

A: Dead dog? No, I never heard of that. Sure, if a guy is looking for trouble, he gets it. That's true. He'll take a pretty fair thumping from the players, but legally. You figure, too, if a guy gets in too much trouble, he's no good to his team and the coach will get rid of him. That's another reason no dirty player can last in the pros.

[*The "dead dog" also was called the "bootsie" play. As Sammy Baugh described it: "Everybody'd hit one man and just try to tear him to pieces. If they cripple you, fine." Pat Summerall provides a little more detail: "I remember my first year with the Giants after I'd been traded, and John Henry (Johnson) was with Detroit. He'd hit Ed Hughes a shot and—I won't say who the coach was—but . . . the coach said, 'I want everyone to get after him, and I want you to know I mean everybody. I don't want to see anyone standing. I want everyone after John Henry.' Well, John Henry saw what was coming and ran out of bounds after the snap, and they never put him*

back in the game because they knew what was going on."]

Q. Twice this season, Bear opponents have lost their quarterback early. George Shaw of the Baltimore Colts was hurt and, of course, Layne of the Lions. Do you think any team ever deliberately tries to knock out a quarterback?

A: Well, the quarterback is a natural target, but how long have these quarterbacks played? Take Otto Graham. He played 10 years and never missed a game. Most quarterbacks don't get hurt. No team ever deliberately tries to get a quarterback.

[*Real clever, Bert. The quarterback the commissioner used as an example probably spoke out more against the violence than any other player. Graham had a facemask made especially for him. Then there's this from the Lions' Joe Schmidt on the Meadows episode: "You can't tell me it wasn't planned. There ain't a man in the world that can tell me it wasn't planned. George Halas did a lot for football, but there's a hell of a lot of things that go unsaid because of who he was."*]

Q. One of your rules on TV coverage prevents cameras from staying on a fight on the field. Why?

A: I don't believe for the best interests of football or the best interests of women and children who watch football it should be shown. We're selling a product just like, say, Atlantic Refining is selling one. You don't see them putting out a story about a bad situation or a bad month, do you? The people who want to watch fights, let them tune in on Wednesday night.

■ ■ ■

"SAVAGERY ON SUNDAY"

The only thing they called me outside of Buck or Bucko was "the choir boy." When I was young I was a member of St. Ann's choir.

—FRANK "BUCKO" KILROY

I myself acted as a Big Brother for a ten-year-old boy.

—WAYNE ROBINSON

The October 24, 1955, issue of *Life* caused palpitations throughout pro football. In an exposé entitled "Savagery on Sunday," the magazine said dirty play was epidemic in the NFL—and ran pictures to prove it.

Two of the players singled out, middle guard Bucko Kilroy and linebacker Wayne Robinson of the Eagles, brought $250,000 libel suits against the magazine's publisher, Time, Inc. The article called Kilroy the "toughest" of the league's "bad men" and accused him of using his knee on Giants quarterback Arnie Galiffa in 1953, injuring Galiffa's spine; Robinson was shown making a two-fisted tackle in one photo and kicking a blocker in the groin in another.

It was two and a half years before the cases were tried in U.S. District Court in Philadelphia, in April 1958. Kilroy and Robinson had retired by then. The trial took eight days. Among the score of players, ex-players and officials who testified were Bert Bell, Otto Graham, Doak Walker and Em Tunnell.

Kilroy and Robinson were hardly angels. They'd earned five Pro Bowl berths between them, but also had been ejected from two games apiece in their careers. Graham described Kilroy as "one of the bad boys in the league." Former Lions end Elbie Nickel said Bucko liked to use his elbow, while Robinson preferred the clothesline.

Life stringer Bob Lowry, who interviewed Kilroy for the article, said Bucko told him, "They all wear thick helmets and facemasks today. It's silly to punch them. My argument is to kick their head off. My advice to the guys who play beside me is to use your feet not your hands—you'll only bust your hands."

The celebrated Ray Bray case also was brought up. (In 1948 Kilroy had been thrown out of an exhibition game for kicking the Bears guard in the groin.) And former Giants quarterback Marion Pugh testified that in '45 Kilroy chased and finally tackled him "8 to 10 seconds" after a play was over. Pugh suffered a dislocated ankle.

But it turned out to be a case of mistaken identity, one which no doubt damaged the defense. Former Eagles lineman Jack Sanders said in court that *he* did it. Sanders wore number 67, Kilroy number 76.

"I remember the incident very well," Sanders said, "because he screamed for about, I don't know, five or six times and I felt very bad about that."

Robinson was reminded of a similar chase scene in 1952, when he pursued an opponent for some 30 yards before throwing a punch. "I didn't hit him, though," he said.

That was only the second-best line of the trial. The best was delivered by Lions end Cloyce Box. "Savagery on Sunday" had referred to the Eagles as "ornery critters," and Box, a Texan, was asked to define the term. "A domesticated animal which at periods of time acts without the scope of that domestication," he said.

Graham, it came out in the trial, had been a consultant on the article and had been paid $500. He was the "pro quarterback" quoted as saying, "The game is getting rougher every year. It's war rather than sport." He also told the magazine which games and players to watch and helped select pictures. The names he named: Ed Sprinkle, John Kreamcheck and Doug Atkins of the Bears; Jerry Groom, Fred Wallner and Charley Trippi of the Cardinals; Paul Lipscomb ("just about the dirtiest player in the game") and John Martinovic of the Packers; and Hardy Brown of the 49ers.

Graham was perhaps the most vocal opponent of roughhouse tactics. The year before, he had written a piece for *Sports Illustrated* that claimed "Football Is Getting Too Vicious." During the trial he spoke of the "moral obligation" he thought football players had, as heroes and role models, to play cleanly.

Still, Graham was seen in some quarters as a

NICKNAMES

Casimir "Slug" Witucki	"Bullet" Bill Dudley
Clyde "Smackover" Scott	Charley "Choo Choo" Justice
Bob "The Geek" St. Clair	"The King" (Hugh McElhenny)
Hardy "The Hatchet" Brown	Tom "Emperor" Jones
Ed "The Claw" Sprinkle	Don "Dopey" Phelps
Paul "Tank" Younger	Floyd "Breezy" Reid
Tom "The Bomb" Tracy	"Deacon" Dan Towler
Frank "Gunner" Gatski	Hugh "Bones" Taylor
Elroy "Crazy Legs" Hirsch	Volney "Skeets" Quinlan
Howard "Hopalong" Cassady	"Touchdown" Tommy Wilson
Eugene "Big Daddy" Lipscomb	Earl "Jug" Girard
Dick "Night Train" Lane	Frank "Bucko" Kilroy
Alan "The Horse" Ameche	"The Dutchman" (Norm Van Brocklin)
Gil "Wild Horse" Mains	Lou "The Toe" Groza
Norm "Wild Man" Willey	"The Toeless Wonder" (Ben Agajanian)
Leo "The Lion" Nomellini	**Not Nicknames:**
"Spats" (Lenny Moore)	Toy Ledbetter
Ed "Bibbles" Bawel	Zollie Toth ("Tug Boat")
Jack "Flying" Cloud	Proverb Jacobs
Bob "Seabiscuit" Boyd	
L.G. "Long Gone" Dupre	

turncoat. John Steadman, one of the country's leading pro football writers, gave him this going-over in the *Baltimore News Post:*

"He played 10 years with the Cleveland club and there were afternoons when he should have paid his way in the park. People going through the turnstiles got rougher treatment than 'Touch Me Not' Otto.

"Not bad. A $25,000 salary for 12 games, the best protection humanly possible and sometimes he didn't have to think for himself. The 'Brains Department' was directed by Paul Brown."

When "Savagery on Sunday" was still in the planning stages, *Life* reporter Jack McDermott wrote Graham: "We don't want to go off half-cocked on a story of this size and importance." But that's exactly what the magazine did. The photographic "evidence" often was inconclusive if not misleading. Browns end Pete Brewster testified that Robinson didn't punch him, as one picture suggested.

Also, the article simply didn't have its facts straight. It said the Giants got even with Kilroy for the Galiffa incident, putting him out for most of the '55 season with a knee injury. According to testimony, however, the injury was caused when a teammate was pushed into Kilroy's leg.

Lowry sent *Life* a telegram saying there was "not the slightest suspicion here that Kilroy's football injury . . . was the Giant's [sic] ganging up on him," but the magazine ignored the information. It also used the photo of Robinson kicking an opposing lineman even though Graham had cautioned, "It could be construed either way."

The NFL's laissez-faire policy toward dirty play didn't help *Life*'s case any. Kilroy, for instance, was fined $150 for kicking Bray, but Bell refunded the money to Kilroy's wife after the season when Bucko didn't get into any more trouble. Dorothy Kilroy had complained to the commissioner that the fine had cost her a new coat. If the league was that casual about it, how serious—or unusual—could such behavior be?

The jury found for Kilroy and Robinson. Each was awarded $11,600—much less than they had sought but more than they had ever earned in a season. No publication since has taken such an aggressive approach to the problem of dirty play.

Eight years later Kilroy was director of player personnel for the Redskins when they hired a new head coach. It was Graham. Kilroy "resigned" to become the Cowboys' chief scout.

TRIAL TALK

BERT BELL

Q: In 1955, Mr. Bell, the penalty for unnecessary roughness was what?

A: I don't know. I am not a rules man but I believe it was 15 yards. . . . I don't read the rules too thoroughly. . . . I couldn't study those rules in a hundred years. They are technical in every way else.

CHARLEY CONERLY (As Quoted by *Life* Reporter John McDermott)

I think the Philadelphia Eagles are the dirtiest team in the league.

WAYNE ROBINSON

The sportsmanship code is no different in the pros. Men are bigger and have more abilities, over-all, but they certainly have a code of ethics. We don't try to go out and act like uncivilized human beings and try to maim people.

BUCKO KILROY

I have always been on the defense no matter where I go. This is always brought up to me. *Life* magazine said that you were a dirty football player and that you are a coward.

MIKE JARMOLUK, Eagles Defensive Tackle

I never heard anyone condemn him [Kilroy] as yet, outside of a few people we term as cry-babies in the League. You have got to understand those things.

MARSHALL SMITH, *Life* Sports Editor

Q: Going back to the first page, you refer to Mr. Kilroy as the toughest of the "bad men." Will you tell us what you intended to convey to the readers by the use of that language concerning Mr. Kilroy?

A: Well, I don't consider bad men or bad man a

derogatory name. It is more of a—it is a good way to get a raise at the end of the year.

OTTO GRAHAM

Q: Do you consider the players on the Cleveland Browns as rough, tough football players?

A: . . . It is a rough and tough game, it is a contact sport. We are all rough and tough, except quarterbacks.

Q: What is the difference between quarterbacks?

A: Well, quarterbacks, we just hand the ball off to somebody else and let them do the work and get the credit for it.

DR. THOMAS F. DOWD, Eagles Team Doctor

Q: Dr. Dowd, in your experience in endeavoring to prevent injuries, do you recommend a partial clenching of the hands in football?

A: Yes, sir.

Q: Why?

A: Well, one of the most vulnerable parts of the body to injure in professional football is the fingers.

EDDIE BELL, Eagles Cornerback

I have never seen anyone intentionally try to hurt another football player . . . all the time that I have been in [the NFL].

■ ■ ■

IRONMEN

No one can say for sure who the first pro to pump iron was, but three players from the '50s can accurately be called the pioneers of NFL weightlifting: Jack Stroud, Stan Jones and Duane Putnam.

All three were guards, which is no surprise. Offensive linemen are generally smarter than other players. What's puzzling is that so few people paid attention to what these guys were doing. Combined, the big three appeared in 14 Pro Bowls and were recognized around the league for their strength.

Stroud, for example, went from 218 pounds as a

Giants rookie in 1953 to 260 by his fourth year. Jones would do pushups with Bears teammates on his back. He could military press—that is, lift over his head—a full-sized man. You'd think a coach or two would have noticed.

But Stroud, Jones and Putnam lifted in relative solitude. Conventional thinking well into the '60s was that weights made you "musclebound." The AFL's Chargers probably were the first team to adopt a full-time weight program. They hired Alvin Roy as a strength coach in 1962. But the vast majority of clubs didn't come around until the early '70s.

Stroud remembers working out with two young Giants players in 1961 when an assistant coach happened by. The coach told the youngsters to knock off the lifting.

"But what about Stroud?" they asked.

"That's different," the coach said. "He's eccentric."

A brief look at the three eccentrics who helped change the game:

■ **Stroud** (1953–64, Giants)—Began to see the light on the first play of the '51 College All-Star Game when he fired out on 300-pound Browns tackle Chubby Grigg. "I put my helmet right under his chin and planted my forearm right into what I thought was his big, fat stomach," Stroud says. "He didn't budge. It was like an inch of rubber around a concrete piling. What an eye opener." . . . Started lifting during the '56 off-season when a gym opened near his home in Chattanooga. Reported to training camp 30 pounds heavier, and in the first one-on-one blocking drill put 300-pound Rosey Grier on his back. . . . Made the Pro Bowl in '56, '58 and '61. . . . Became a much-feared enforcer.

■ **Putnam** (1952–62, Rams, Cowboys and Browns)—Weighed 210 as a rookie, or 20 pounds less than Rams running backs Deacon Dan Towler and Tank Younger. Only played special teams. . . . Became friends with a shot-putter while doing graduate work at UCLA during the off-season and was talked into lifting. "One of the first things I told him was that I was afraid it would tie me up," Putnam says. "He said, 'C'mon, I'll sprint you.' So we went out and he outsprinted me. He could also high jump 5'6" and had a [vertical leap] of 39 inches. He said, 'Do you think [weight training] is bothering me?'" . . . Reported to camp 20 pounds heavier in '53 and became a starter. . . . Pro Bowl selection in '55, '56, '58, '59.

■ **Jones** (1954–66, Bears and Redskins)—Grew up near Iron City—York, Pennsylvania—and began lifting early. Gained 20 pounds a year for eight straight years beginning as a high school freshman. Was a 260-pound monster when he reached the Bears. . . . May have been the first NFL player to lift during the season. Hooked up with Clyde Emrich, former world record holder in the clean and snatch, who convinced him to keep pumping year-round. Wound up doing just that with Emrich for the next eight years. . . . Pro Bowler from 1956 to '62. . . . After retiring, became one of the early strength coaches while an assistant at Denver.

● ● ●

K. C. JONES' ROLE IN NFL HISTORY

The bump-and-run style of pass defense didn't get its start in the early days of the AFL, as is generally thought. It was first used in the Los Angeles Rams' 1955 training camp by future Boston Celtic K. C. Jones.

Jones had a brief tryout with the Rams. They'd taken a flyer on him in the last round of the draft—it was then 30 rounds—even though he'd played only basketball at the University of San Francisco.

Completely on his own, Jones would line up in front of the Rams receivers during one-on-one drills and hand-check them all over the field. Drove them nuts with the technique, as a matter of fact.

"The receivers started complaining that what he was doing was against the rules," says Jack Faulkner, then the team's secondary coach. "So I went through the rule book, and I'll be damned if I could find anything that said it was illegal. That's where I learned it. I was so impressed I took it with me when I went to the AFL [as defensive coach of the L.A. Chargers]."

Jones could have been a great defensive back in the NFL, Faulkner says. He had the size (6'1", 200), quickness, toughness and intelligence. Unfortunately, basketball was his first love.

Faulkner talked him out of leaving camp once, but Jones quit the team to return to USF for his final year of eligibility. Ultimately, he wound up in the National Basketball Association and the Basketball

> *The weightlifting gave you an edge, everything else being equal. But it's not going to make a football player out of a non–football player because that comes out of your head and your heart. The notion that because the guys in the '50s didn't lift weights and take steroids they weren't strong is a crock. A lot of those guys would have whipped the hell out of these guys today.*
>
> *Take Doug Atkins. He was 6'8" and 265 and was solid muscle and bones. And he high-jumped six feet. And he never touched a weight in his life. With the frame he had, he could have weighed 300 pounds no problem. His arms were 18 inches around as it was. We measured them once in Knoxville [they were teammates at the University of Tennessee]. I took him over to the gym to try to get him to work out. He allowed that that was a lot of extra work he didn't need.*
>
> —JACK STROUD

Hall of Fame. He made his reputation, naturally, as a defensive specialist.

● ● ●

YOU CAN CALL ME JOHNNY

From the *Pittsburgh Press,* September 6, 1955: "Burrell Shields, who played half the season last year, failed in his bid for a left-halfback job and led the parade out of [Steelers training] camp today.

"Others leaving with him are halfbacks Bill Staudenmaier of Chattanooga and Ed Smith of Southwest Texas, quarterback Jack Unitas of Louisville, guard Vince Werl of Dayton and tackle Joe Cimini of Mississippi State."

The following spring the Baltimore Colts saw enough in "Jack" Unitas to sign him to a contract.

DECADE ALL-STAR TEAM

For skill position players and defensive backs, figures under "Data" are average season totals; for specialists, they're decade totals.

OFFENSE

Pos. Player	Years*	Data
WR Elroy Hirsch	8	40 catches, 747 yds., 6 TDs; 3 Pro Bowls
TE Pete Pihos	6	45 catches, 665 yds, 7 TDs; 6 Pro Bowls
T Rosey Brown	7	5 Pro Bowls
G Jim Parker	3	2 Pro Bowls
C Frank Gatski	8	1 Pro Bowl
G Dick Stanfel	7	5 Pro Bowls
T Lou Creekmur	10	8 Pro Bowls
QB Otto Graham	6	55.8%, 2,250 yds., 15 TDs; 5 Pro Bowls
FB Jimmy Brown	3	1,266 yds., 5.1 avg., 13 TDs; 3 Pro Bowls
HB Hugh McElhenny	8	493 yds., 5.0 avg., 4 TDs; 5 Pro Bowls
WR Lenny Moore	4	37 catches, 643 yds, 5 TDs; 3 Pro Bowls

DEFENSE

Pos. Player	Years	Data
E Gino Marchetti	8	5 Pro Bowls
T Leo Nomellini	10	8 Pro Bowls
T Art Donovan	10	5 Pro Bowls
E Len Ford	9	4 Pro Bowls
LB Chuck Bednarik	10	7 Pro Bowls
LB Bill George	8	6 Pro Bowls
LB Joe Schmidt	7	6 Pro Bowls
CB Night Train Lane	8	6 interceptions; 4 Pro Bowls
CB Jack Butler	9	6 interceptions; 4 Pro Bowls
S Em Tunnell	10	6 interceptions; 9 Pro Bowls
S Jack Christiansen	8	6 interceptions; 5 Pro Bowls

SPECIALISTS AND OTHER SELECTIONS

Pos. Selection	Years	Data
KR Ollie Matson	7	27.7 avg., 6 TDs; 5 Pro Bowls
PR Jack Christiansen	8	12.8 avg., 8 TDs
K Lou Groza	10	131 FGs, 742 pts.; 9 Pro Bowls
P Horace Gillom	7	43.8 avg.; led NFL in 1951–52; 1 Pro Bowl
Special Teams -- Hardy Brown		Wild Card Selection -- Doak Walker
Kick Blocker -- Bob St. Clair		Coach -- Paul Brown
Enforcer -- Tex Coulter		PR Man -- Pete Rozelle

*Number of years he played in the decade.

Ever wonder why the Steelers cut Unitas?

Reason number one was his lack of versatility. He was competing for the third-string quarterback job behind starter Jim Finks and backup Ted Marchibroda. In the days of the 35-man roster, extra skills were a must. Unitas was beaten out by another rookie QB, Vic Eaton, who punted for the team in '55, returned punts and could play defensive back in a pinch.

Reason number two was that Steelers coaches didn't think Unitas was smart enough for pro ball. They didn't let him play a single down in a preseason game. Head coach Walt Kiesling told owner Art Rooney the rookie couldn't remember the plays. Unitas had flunked the freshman entrance exam at Louisville before being admitted but never had much trouble with grades.

■ ■ ■

MOORE I

Halfway through his rookie season in 1956, the Colts' Lenny Moore was averaging 10.1 yards a carry (45 attempts, 453 yards).

He finished the year with a 7.5-yard rushing average. In two games, however, he had negative yardage. In the other 10, he had 70 attempts for 673 yards—9.6 yards per rush.

■ ■ ■

MOORE II

Moore's statistics had a supernatural quality. Check out his 1957 kickoff-return totals: 1 return, 108 yards, 1 touchdown.

What's this? The record book says that the longest kickoff runback in NFL history is 106 yards. Does this mean . . . ?

No. Moore actually had one return for 16 yards. He scored the touchdown when he received a lateral on another kickoff and ran 92 yards. Under the rules, he's credited with the yards but not a return. Thus his 1–108–1 line.

■ ■ ■

HARDTOP

A steel flagpole—18 inches around—once hit Rams end Leon Clarke on the head when he was driving with the top down in Los Angeles. The pole wrecked his car and left a 32-stitch cut. Miraculously, Clarke lived to play another day.

"When I was little," he explained, "my uncle used to hit me on the head with boards to toughen me up. Honest he did. He used to call me egghead and hit me with these boards. The doc said the only reason I wasn't killed was because my head was so tough."

THE STADIUM GAME, 1950s STYLE

Louisville had a couple of pro football teams in the 1920s. The first was named the Brecks (1921–23), the second the Colonels (1926). They played a total of 12 games, were shut out in 11 and won the other.

In November 1956 the city decided it wanted to get back in the NFL. So it put together a package Washington owner George Preston Marshall called "the most fantastic offer ever made by a community to acquire a professional sports team." The specifics:

■ Expansion of the 22,000-seat Fairgrounds Stadium to 47,000—all under cover, with no end-zone seating.

■ A guaranteed season-ticket sale of 25,000 annually for the first three years.

■ Stadium rental at 6 percent of the gross.

■ Team gets 100 percent of concessions income and 20 percent of parking revenue. Parking facilities for 27,000 cars.

Marshall, alas, was locked into a lease at Griffith Stadium that still had four years to run. So Louisville turned its attentions to Pittsburgh and Philadelphia. The Steelers had the highest overhead in the league, according to owner Art Rooney, and their lease at Forbes Field expired at the end of the season. The Eagles had a year-to-year lease at Connie Mack Stadium. They also had played a preseason game in Louisville that year and drawn more than 22,000.

But after listening to Louisville's proposal, both clubs stayed put. In 1958, the Eagles moved to the University of Pennsylvania's much-bigger Franklin Field and almost doubled their attendance in two years. The same year, the Steelers began playing home games at 57,000-seat Pitt Stadium.

In 1961, D.C. (now RFK) Stadium became the Redskins' new playground. Everybody got what he wanted except Louisville.

Maybe the timing was wrong. The city's Triple-A baseball team was bankrupt and in danger of being moved. Then again, maybe the NFL, in the grand tradition, was just jerking Louisville around. For some reason, though, this city that wanted pro football so badly in 1956 didn't join the AFL in '60, the WFL in '74 or the USFL in '83.

RUNNING LISTS

Ollie Matson's five qualifications for an NFL halfback:
1. Speed.
2. Maneuverability.
3. Power.
4. Intelligence.
5. Desire.

Jim Brown's composite greatest running back:
1. Earl Campbell's power.
2. Walter Payton's heart.
3. O. J. Simpson's speed.
4. Gale Sayers' moves.

UNSOLVED MYSTERY

The Resignation of Lions Coach Buddy Parker

Date: August 12, 1957.

Place: A "Meet the Lions" dinner at a Detroit hotel.

Story line: When it was Parker's turn to speak, he went to the podium and told 600 fans he was quitting. Someone in the audience laughed, thinking it was a joke. No one had a clue the coach was even considering it. In seven years in Detroit Parker had won two NFL championships and three division titles and finished second twice. The Lions were loaded again. He also had a new, two-year $60,000 contract with incentives.

Possible explanations:

1. Front-office interference—Parker insisted on complete control of the team. He told several

A million-dollar backfield if there ever was one: Frank Gifford (left) and Bonzo of *Bonzo Goes to College* fame. (UPI/Bettmann Newsphotos)

players he was sick of part-owner D. Lyle Fife's meddling.

2. Inability to control his players—The Lions had a reputation as a party team around the league. A bedcheck several nights before had turned up 25 AWOL players. An hour or so before he resigned, Parker discovered several Lions at a cocktail party in the owners' suites. "I've got a situation here I can't handle anymore," he told the audience. "These ballplayers have gotten too big for me or something. I'm getting out."

3. Alcohol—Booze, even a moderate amount, had a drastic effect on Parker. His postgame behavior was notorious. He'd have a few drinks and start haranguing players. He once cut two of them in midair following a West Coast loss. He sometimes threatened to quit, too. He'd had a few drinks before announcing his resignation.

Hypothesis: Parker was a complex, temperamental man. The best guess is that all of the above were contributing factors.

Footnote: Two weeks after his resignation, Parker signed a five-year contract with the Pittsburgh Steelers and coached them through 1964. Two weeks before the 1965 season, he resigned suddenly, citing front-office interference.

■ ■ ■

REASON NUMBER FOUR TO HATE GEORGE PRESTON MARSHALL

Redskins quarterback Eddie LeBaron wouldn't have his picture taken with the other team reps at the first NFL Players Association meeting in 1956 because he was afraid George Preston Marshall might see it. What does that say about the Big Chief's position on organized labor?

"I am not antiunion," the Redskins owner said. "I simply do not think there is a place for a players' union in professional football."

Marse George's act might play better today. It's hard to sympathize with players walking picket lines and driving Mercedeses. But in the mid-'50s there was a legitimate need for a union. The league was setting attendance records. Television revenues were going up and so were profits. The only ones not benefiting were the players.

Most weren't even paid for exhibition games. Some owners made enough money on those to break even for the year. In 1956 it was estimated the 12 NFL teams grossed nearly $8 million from exhibition games.

In December of the same year, representatives of 10 teams met in New York and organized the NFLPA. (The two teams not represented were the Bears and Steelers. George Halas paid his players not to join. The Steelers' Lynn Chandnois simply couldn't make the meeting.) Their list of demands was modest and reasonable:

■ Formal recognition of the union.
■ $50 pay for exhibition games.
■ Minimum training camp expenses.
■ An injury clause in the standard contract assuring a player with a football-related injury that he'd be paid.
■ A $5,000 minimum salary.

Most owners were amenable. Marshall wasn't.

"One of our league's great virtues has been the fact that the 12 teams have been given the freedom to run their own business," he said. "Now [the union] wants to come in and tell us how to run it."

As usual, Marshall's opposition was both entertaining and ruthless. Rams quarterback Norm Van Brocklin, a union leader, became a regular target for his barbs, and vice versa. Before a Rams-Redskins game, Marshall ridiculed Van Brocklin's efforts "to sign up" players with the line: "If he keeps his pencil in his back pocket against us, he's going to get lead poisoning."

Van Brocklin's response was that he wasn't worried about signing Redskins because Marshall was so cheap the job would be easy. The average Washington salary in 1957 was $7,884.

But Marshall's best work came behind the scenes. He shot down recognition of the union at owners' meetings in 1956 and early '57. The '57 setback was particularly galling to the players. Days before the owners' meeting, union leaders met with commissioner Bert Bell to go over their demands. Bell told them he'd push hard to get the union recognized and thought it would happen. In return, union leaders released a statement saying the college draft was in the best interest of football.

This was an important concession to the owners because Congress was growing more and more suspicious of the legality of some NFL practices, specifically the draft. But the players' good faith got them nowhere. The owners adjourned without officially recognizing the union. Marshall was credited with stonewalling the debate.

At a congressional hearing in August, Bell made the stunning announcement that *he* recognized the NFLPA. Marshall wouldn't let him get away with it, saying, "He doesn't have the power to recognize them. Bell works for us."

Finally, in December, the players threatened a $4 million antitrust suit. Then and only then did the league—and Marshall—give in.

■ ■ ■

SUDDEN DEATH

No drive in pro football history is more famous than the one the Colts made to win the 1958 sudden-death overtime classic against the New York Giants. Here's the play-by-play, interspersed with quotations from Baltimore's Johnny Unitas and our own comments. (The figures in the second column are down, distance and yard line.) After a punt, the Colts take over on their 20.

1. **1-10-C20**   **Halfback L. G. Dupre sweeps right. Gain 11.** ("I didn't give a damn about the clock. It was our pace to set.")

2. **1-10-C31**   **Unitas' long pass to Lenny Moore is deflected by Lindon Crow.** (If Crow doesn't get a finger on the ball, Moore scores.)

3. **2-10-C31**   **Unitas fakes to fullback Alan Ameche, then gives on a draw to Dupre. Gain 2.** (The play is designed to take advantage of middle linebacker Sam Huff keying on Ameche. It just misses going for big yardage.)

4. **3-8-C33**   **Unitas sees Raymond Berry is covered and dumps off to Ameche in the left flat. Gain 8.** (Ameche barely makes the first down.)

5. **1-10-C41**   **Dupre sweeps right again. Gain 3.**

6. **2-7-C44**   **Unitas is sacked by tackle Dick Modzelewski. Loss of 8.**

7. **3-15-C36**   **Unitas hits Berry behind Carl Karilivacz, who had slipped. Gain 20.** (The key play. The primary receiver is Moore, running out of a slot-right formation. But he's double-teamed. So, after avoiding a rusher, Unitas finds Berry free and calmly waves him farther downfield before throwing. "This was a new formation for this game. Our steady slamming into the line had helped set things up, and when Ray shook loose, I unloaded.")

8. **1-10-G44**   **Ameche carries on a trap up the middle. Gain 23.** (Unitas changes the play from a pass at the line of scrimmage when he sees Huff cheating back. "We'd run this once or twice in the game. It's not a long gainer. Usually we

As far as we know, this Bears fan wasn't paid by penurious owner George Halas to help save the team money on lost footballs in 1956. (*Sun-Times*/Pro Football Hall of Fame)

figure it [for] four or five yards. But Huff had been playing to his left and back. This made an easy blocking assignment for our tackle. Huff was playing for a pass, and the way Mo [Modzelewski] had been crashing I figured they were right for a trap.")

9. 1-10-G21   **Dupre off right tackle. Gain 1.**
10. 2-9-G20   **Unitas to Berry on a quick slant. Gain 12.**
11. 1-8-G8   **Ameche off right guard. Gain 1.** (The same trap that worked for 23 yards three plays earlier.)
12. 2-7-G7   **Unitas lofts a pass to Jim Mutscheller in the right flat. Gain 6.** (A surprising call, because everyone assumed the Colts would play for the field goal. "They were playing the run, [and were] one-on-one with Moore, the linebacker head up on

Mutscheller. I told Jimmy to get out there real quick.")

13. 3-1-G1   **Ameche off right tackle. Gain 1. Touchdown.** ("Our only call, a power play. We got the halfback blocking ahead of Ameche with a double team on the tackle. When I slapped the ball in Al's belly and saw him take off, I knew nobody was going to stop him with one yard. They couldn't have done it if we'd needed 10 yards.")

■ ■ ■

WHEN ROZELLE RAN THE RAMS

As general managers go, Pete Rozelle was a great commissioner. The same man who helped build the

NFL into a corporate giant in his three decades as boss all but wrecked the Los Angeles Rams in three years as GM (1957–59).

To be fair, it was a less-than-ideal situation. Disharmony among the owners—Dan Reeves on one side, Fred Levy, Jr., and Edwin Pauley on the other—left the once-model franchise paralyzed at the top. But by almost every measure of a general manager, Rozelle fell short:

- The team didn't draft well under him.
- His major trades—especially the whopper for Ollie Matson in 1959—didn't work out.
- The Rams had one winning season during his tenure and none in the six that followed it.

It's a good thing the commissionership came along when it did in 1960 or Rozelle's place in league history might have been alongside Vic Schwenk. Remember him? Precisely the point.

"Rozelle," said Tex Schramm, his friend and predecessor as Rams GM, "managed to destroy a great football team and lead it into the cellar."

That's not entirely true. Led into the cellar, yes. Great team, no.

The Rams Rozelle inherited were once great. But after winning their third and final Western Conference title of the decade in 1955, they slipped to 4–8 in '56. By 1957 it was time to rebuild.

In his biography, Schramm also accused Rozelle of trading away such top talent as quarterbacks Norm Van Brocklin, Billy Wade and Frank Ryan, receivers Del Shofner and Red Phillips, and running back Jon Arnett. In fact, the only one Rozelle traded was Van Brocklin. And the Dutchman, determined to get out from under coach Sid Gillman, forced him into it by announcing his retirement.

Any analysis of Rozelle's GMship has to begin with the Matson deal. It remains one of the biggest body swaps on record and is virtually all that's remembered of his stint with the Rams. What exactly did he give the Cardinals?

- Three starting linemen: offensive tackle Ken Panfil, defensive tackle Frank Fuller and defensive end Glenn Holtzman, plus defensive tackle Art Hauser, a regular in '57.
- Three 1959 draftees: running backs Don Brown (second round) and Larry Hickman (third) and end John Tracey (fourth).
- A player to be named later, who turned out to be 1960 fourth-round pick Silas Woods, another end.

- His 1960 number-two choice, which the Cards used to take guard Mike McGee.

Panfil was the prize in the package. He was considered one of the league's best tackles. Holtzman and Fuller were expendable; the Rams felt they had young players ready to replace them. Hauser was coming off a knee injury that had sidelined him in '58.

As for the others, Brown, Hickman and Tracey were high picks, but the Rams had plenty of those—seven in rounds two through four that year. It's not as if Rozelle gutted his draft. Woods never played a down in the NFL. McGee had a promising career cut short by a neck injury.

Of the nine players, the only one still active when Matson finished his career in 1966 was Tracey, and he was in the AFL with Buffalo.

Coming

1950--Franco Harris, Fort Dix, N.J.
1951--John Hannah, Canton, Ga.
     Dan Fouts, San Francisco
1952--Billy "White Shoes" Johnson, Bouthwyn, Pa.
     Jack Lambert, Mantua, Ohio
1953--Randy White, Pittsburgh
     Hollywood Henderson, Austin, Texas
     Harry Carson, Florence, S.C.
1954--Tony Dorsett, Rochester, Pa.
     Walter Payton, Columbia, Miss.
     Steve Largent, Tulsa, Okla.
1955--Lester Hayes, Houston
     Earl Campbell, Tyler, Texas
1956--Ozzie Newsome, Muscle Schoals, Ala.
     Joe Montana, Monongahela, Pa.
     Mark Gastineau, Ardmore, Okla.
1957--Kellen Winslow, East St. Louis, Ill.
1958--Anthony Munoz, Ontario, Calif.
     Mike Singletary, Houston
1959--Lawrence Taylor, Williamsburg, Va.
     Ronnie Lott, Albuquerque, N.M.
     Jim McMahon, Jersey City, N.J.

Going

1952--Fats Henry, 54
1953--Jim Thorpe, 64
1954--Dave Sparks, 25, Redskins tackle, heart attack
1956--Hugh "Shorty" Ray, 71
1957--Roy Barni, 30, Redskins DB, shot in barroom brawl
     Tony Morabito, 49, at Bears-49ers game (October 27)
     Red Dunn, 55, '20s great
1959--Galen Laack, 26, Eagles guard, car accident
     Tim Mara, 71
     Bert Bell, 65, at Steelers-Eagles game (October 12)

The '50s were not only the greatest decade for pro football but also the greatest for pro football photography. Players would pose doing just about anything. We rest our case with this shot of Johnny Unitas and the Colts offensive line. You gotta believe that as soon as those guys heard the shutter, they were out of there. (*Baltimore News Post*/Pro Football Hall of Fame)

Gillman approved of and helped with the trade, but it was Rozelle's baby. He had been an admirer of Matson's since their days at the University of San Francisco, when Matson was the school's outstanding athlete and Rozelle the athletic department's publicist.

On paper, the deal looked great for the Rams, who were coming off an 8–4 season in '58. Matson was to be teamed with Arnett in an offense that already had Shofner, Phillips, "Touchdown" Tommy Wilson and Wade. Sportswriters across the country saw the new, improved Rams challenging the Colts in the Western Conference.

But injuries decimated the team, and it limped in at 2–10. Gillman was caught short on reserves because ownership did away with the taxi squad (and because Rozelle had given up so much for Matson). After the last game of the season, he resigned.

Thus, the trade has been viewed as a gigantic gaffe. Matson rushed for 863 yards in his first season, third in the league, but gained only 351 in his next three. And the deal, so disruptive to the team, caused dissension.

Rozelle made another disastrous personnel move in 1959. He gambled that 33-year-old defensive end Gene Brito had something left and acquired him from the Redskins for linebacker Larry Morris, a first-round choice in '55. Brito broke his leg in the second game of the season and played one more year. Morris wound up in Chicago, where he had half a dozen good seasons and starred in the Bears' 1963 championship game victory.

Still, the Rams could have survived had Rozelle's drafts been more productive. Though the team he took over in '57 needed repair, he had the tools for the job. From 1957 to '59, he had 21 picks—nine extra—in the first four rounds. This at a time when a fourth-round choice still got you a top-50 player.

But only nine of those players lasted three years with the team. Rozelle also continued the Rams' tradition of drafting heavily for offense in the early rounds. Six of his seven number-one picks were offensive players. Four were running backs. The defense, not surprisingly, regressed from average in 1957 to bad in '60.

Losing Billy Cannon, the number-one pick in the 1960 draft, to the AFL's Houston Oilers was Rozelle's final folly. The Rams went to court, but were defeated there, too.

The bottom line on the Rozelle years? Team records of 6–6 in 1957, 8–4 in '58 and 2–10 in '59—to be followed by 4–7–1, 4–10 and 1–12–1 marks. It wasn't until George Allen came in as coach in 1966 that the franchise got its head back above .500. By then only four Rozelle players remained on the roster.

THE 1960s

'60s CHALKBOARD

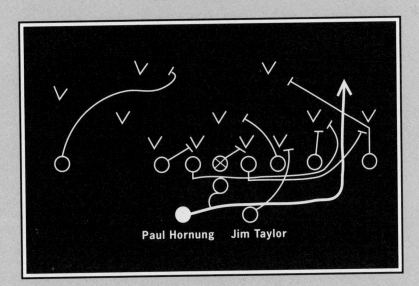

Paul Hornung   Jim Taylor

The Packer Sweep

The Packer Sweep

Green Bay coach Vince Lombardi liked his football basic and hard-nosed, and that's exactly what his sweep was. It was an updated version of the old single-wing power plays. In fact he used the same pulling guard techniques Jock Sutherland taught at Pitt in the '20s and '30s. Lombardi demanded that his backs block as well as run, and you'll notice that the fullback's assignment on the play was a one-on-one with the defensive end ("Greater love hath no man . . ."). That's why Paul Hornung and Jim Taylor were perfect for the play—and the Packer system. Neither had great speed, but both were big and tough and didn't mind sacrificing their bodies for the other. Hornung also could throw the option pass.

THE 1960s AT A GLANCE

Decade Standings

NFL

East	W	L	T	Pct.	West	W	L	T	Pct.
Browns (1)	92	41	5	.685	Packers (5)	96	37	5	.714
Giants	69	63	6	.522	Colts (1)	92	42	4	.681
Cardinals	67	63	8	.514	Lions	66	61	11	.518
Cowboys	67	65	6	.507	Bears (1)	67	65	6	.507
Eagles (1)	57	76	5	.431	Rams	63	68	7	.482
Redskins	46	82	10	.370	Vikings (1)	52	67	7	.440
Steelers	46	85	7	.359	49ers	57	74	7	.438
Saints	12	29	1	.298	Falcons	12	43	1	.223

AFL

East	W	L	T	Pct.	West	W	L	T	Pct.
Oilers (2)	70	66	4	.514	Chiefs (3)	87	48	5	.639
Jets (1)	69	65	6	.514	Chargers (1)	86	48	6	.636
Bills (2)	65	69	6	.486	Raiders (1)	77	58	5	.568
Patriots	63	68	9	.482	Broncos	39	97	4	.293
Dolphins	15	39	2	.286	Bengals	7	20	1	.268

(Figures in parentheses are championships won.)

Best Regular–Season Record   1962 Packers, '67 Raiders and '68 Colts, all 13-1

Worst Regular–Season Record   Dallas Cowboys, 1960, 0-11-1

Attendance Figures

Total (AFL and NFL): 65,182,511 (NFL up 96 percent)
Highest: Cleveland Browns, 1969, 578,360 (82,623 average)
Lowest: New York Titans, 1962, 36,161 (5,166 average)
Biggest Crowd: 84,850, Cowboys at Browns, Nov. 2, 1969

In	Out
Pete Rozelle	Bert Bell
merger	signing war
Vince Lombardi	Paul Brown
Packers' power sweep	Colts' trap play
low-cut shoes	hightops
sideburns	flattops
Dexedrine	adrenaline
Joe Namath, Dick Butkus	Bobby Layne, Sam Huff
Gatorade	H_2O
zone pass defense	man-to-man
color TV	black-and-white
Rams' Fearsome Foursome	Giants' Front Four

►Biggest Player   Ernie Ladd, who played defensive tackle for three teams, went 6'9", 315 pounds. Richard Sligh, a Raiders defensive tackle in 1967, was the tallest player in pro football history at 7 feet.

Smallest Player   Noland Smith, the Chiefs' 5'6", 155-pound returner

Best Athlete   Jim Brown (again)

Fastest Player   Bob Hayes

Slowest Player	Sherman Plunkett. The Jets' 6'4'' offensive tackle had ballooned to 337 by the end of his career and was more an obstruction than a blocker.
Most Intimidating Player	Dick Butkus

New Stadiums	1961--D.C. (RFK) Stadium
	    Metropolitan Stadium
	1964--Shea Stadium
	1965--Astrodome (Oilers didn't move in until 1968)
	    Atlanta-Fulton County Stadium
	1966--Busch Stadium
	    Oakland-Alameda County Coliseum
	1967--San Diego (Jack Murphy) Stadium
	  The American Seating Co. did a study for D.C. Stadium that showed the average American's rump was four inches wider than a century earlier. Thus seats were made 20 to 22 inches across instead of 17 to 19, the old standard.

Failed Franchises	The first decade there weren't any
Franchise Shifts	1960--Cardinals from Chicago to St. Louis 1963--Texans from Dallas to Kansas City (became Chiefs)
▸**Famous Firsts**	Million-dollar gate, 1961 (Giants-Packers title game) Soccer-style kicker, 1964 (Pete Gogolak) Nationally televised Monday night game, 1966 (CBS) Second-place team to win a championship, 1969 (Chiefs) Purely defensive player elected to the Hall of Fame, 1967 (Emlen Tunnell)
▸**Famous Lasts**	Two-way player, 1960 (Chuck Bednarik) NFL champ to lose to the College All-Stars, 1963 (Packers) Lineman without a facemask, 1964 (Jess Richardson) Two-point conversion, 1969 (Boston's Kim Hammond ran for it against Houston, Dec. 7)
Best Division Race	1967 NFL Coastal Division Baltimore was 11-0-2 and Los Angeles 10-1-1 going into their final-week showdown. The Rams won the game and the division's only playoff berth.
▸**Best Title Game**	1967, NFL (The Ice Bowl)
Owner vs. Owner	Clint Murchison vs. George Preston Marshall, 1960 Marshall was the biggest opponent of a Dallas franchise, but Murchison found his weakness. One of Murchison's buddies bought the rights to ''Hail to the Redskins,'' the team's fight song, and refused to let Marshall use it until he knuckled under. In January 1960 the Cowboys were born.
▸**Player vs. Team**	Cookie Gilchrist vs. the Bills
Coach Most Likely to Have A Service Area on the New Jersey Turnpike Named After Him	Vince Lombardi
Best Running Quarterback	Fran Tarkenton

New Positions	tight end strong/free safety
Major Rules Changes	1962--face-mask rule broadened to protect ball carrier 1969--modified kicking shoes outlawed
Fashion Trends	names on the backs of jerseys home teams wearing white The decade's most dramatic fashion moment was when the Cowboys unveiled their new uniforms in 1964. The key color had to be invented first. General manager Tex Schramm described it as "a sort of blue-hued silver sort of."
New Statistics	team sacks lengths of field goals made/missed
Best Play	the first safety blitz, 1961
▸Hit of the Decade	Chuck Bednarik vs. Frank Gifford, 1960
▸Fight of the Decade	The Eagles' Ben Scotti vs. teammate John Mellekas, 1963
Highest–Paid Player	John Brodie, quarterback-golfer with the 49ers, had a 4-year, $827,000 deal from 1967 to '70.
Least Appreciated Players	Eagles receiver Tommy McDonald Eagles offensive tackle Bob Brown Cowboys linebacker Chuck Howley
Least Likely to Forget the Snap Count	Frank Ryan, Browns quarterback Ryan had a Ph.D. in mathematics and an IQ of 155. His thesis was titled "A Characterization of Asymptotic Values of a Function Holomorphic in the Unit Disc."
Best Trade	The Giants obtained Y. A. Tittle from the 49ers for guard Lou Cordileone in 1961. Tittle took the team to three straight division titles; the Niners unloaded Cordileone, a former No. 1 pick, the next year.
Best Football Books	1963--*Run to Daylight* by Vince Lombardi with W. C. Heinz 1964--*Paper Lion* by George Plimpton *The Fireside Book of Football*, edited by Jack Newcombe 1968--*Instant Replay* by Jerry Kramer with Dick Schaap
Best Football Movies	1968--*Paper Lion* 1969--*Number One*
Worst Idea	San Diego general manager Sid Gillman tried to get injured starting quarterback Jack Kemp through waivers and onto the injured list in 1962. The Bills claimed Kemp, and he quarterbacked them to two AFL title game victories over the Chargers.
▸Individual Records That Have Never Been Equaled	Paul Hornung's 176 points, 1960 Don Hultz's 9 fumble recoveries, 1963 George Halas coaching an NFL champ at age 68, 1963 Bart Starr's 294 passes without an interception, 1964-65 Jim Brown's 126 career touchdowns, 1957-1965 Travis Williams' 41.1-yard kickoff-return average, 1967 Steve O'Neal's 98-yard punt, 1968

THEY COULD HAVE BEEN COMMISSIONER

Austin Gunsel and Marshall Leahy were the two leading candidates going into the January 1960 meeting to elect Bert Bell's successor.

Gunsel was acting commissioner. He was a former FBI man who'd been the league treasurer (and first security man) under Bell. But he killed his chances on the first night of what turned out to be a week of haggling when he declared: "I'm tired. I don't think I want to continue on with this meeting tonight."

Leahy actually was the odds-on favorite to be the next commissioner. He was a prominent San Francisco attorney who had represented the league on a number of occasions, including the merger with the All-America Football Conference and the Bill Radovich case. There was just one problem. He wanted the league office moved to San Francisco, his hometown.

This didn't go over well with most of the Eastern teams. From the start, Leahy had seven of the eight votes needed for election but couldn't get one of the five others to budge. The seven clubs for him were Los Angeles, San Francisco, Cleveland, Green Bay, Detroit, New York and the Chicago Cardinals. Opposed were Washington, Pittsburgh, Baltimore and Philadelphia. The Chicago Bears abstained.

At one point the Redskins' George Preston Marshall said he'd throw his vote to Leahy so long as league headquarters was anywhere but the West Coast.

"We're voting for a man," Rams owner Dan Reeves cracked. "George must be voting for a city."

Leahy refused to budge and it cost him the commissionership. After nearly a week at deadlock, the owners went in search of compromise candidates. Paul Brown turned them down. L.A. general manager Pete Rozelle didn't. Leahy faded from the scene.

"I think he would have been an excellent commissioner," Brown says. "He was an impressive man and had the support to be elected. But he wouldn't move from San Francisco. I think if you really want something, you don't give too much thought to where you're living."

THE GOLF SHOT THAT AFFECTED NFL HISTORY

When he was a quarterback-in-training with the San Francisco 49ers, John Brodie had a chance to win a tournament on the PGA Tour. Good thing he didn't pull it off, or pro football might have lost one of its finest QBs.

The event was the 1960 Yorba Linda (California) Open, then one of the Tour's January stops. Brodie had the low second round, a five-under-par 67, and

1960 YORBA LINDA (CALIF.) OPEN RESULTS	
Jerry Barber, $2,800	67-70-69-72=278
Billy Maxwell, 1,900	71-71-68-69=279
Harry Weetman, 1,300	68-71-70-72=281
Tom Nieporte, 1,300	71-73-69-68=281
Bob Goalby, 1,100	71-72-69-71=283
Julius Boros, 860	71-72-69-72=284
Mike Souchak, 860	72-71-72-69=284
Lionel Hebert, 860	68-72-74-70=284
Billy Casper, 860	70-72-71-71=284
Doug Sanders, 860	68-73-72-71=284
Joe Campbell, 710	69-74-70-72=285
Dave Ragan, 610	69-72-75-70=286
Dave Marr, 610	68-73-74-71=286
Arnold Palmer, 610	72-71-70-73=286
Howie Johnson, 610	74-72-67-73=287
Mason Rudolph, 361.12	70-76-72-69=287
Bill Johnston, 361.12	72-73-71-71=287
John McMullin, 361.12	70-73-73-71=287
John Barnum, 361.12	69-72-74-72=287
Bo Wininger, 361.12	68-72-75-72=287
Paul Harney, 361.12	68-74-72-73=287
Jack Fleck, 361.12	72-73-70-72=287
Bob Harris, 361.12	73-71-69-74=287
John Brodie, 112.50	**74-67-72-75=288**
Dow Finsterwald, 112.50	71-69-72-76=288
Art Wall, 112.50	70-73-70-75=288
Tommy Jacobs, 112.50	70-75-71-72=288
Tony Lema, 112.50	66-75-74-73=288
Charlie Sifford, 112.50	73-70-72-73=288
Jack Burke, 112.50	70-68-75-75=288
Tommy Bolt, 112.50	69-73-71-75=288

Out of the money:
289 -- J.C. Goosie, Johnny Pott, Alex Sutton, Bob Goetz, Chick Harbert. 290 -- Babe Lichardus, Don Fairfield, George Bayer, Ernie Vossler, Bill Blanton. 291 -- Doug Ford, Al Feminelli, Dick Stranahan, Lloyd Mangrum. 292 -- Jimmy Clark, Gay Brewer, Jim Ferrier, Henry Williams. 293 -- Bob Dudan. 294 -- Al Balding. 296 -- Jim Ferree, Chuck Malchaski, Fred Hawkins. 297 -- Walker Inman, Eric Monti. 298 -- Walter Burkemo. 300 -- Gene Coghill, Frank Wharton, Jim King. 301 -- Bob Brue, Ray Hane, Jerry Magee. 306 -- Ron Drimak.

trailed leader and eventual champion Jerry Barber by only four strokes. The field was formidable. Brodie's halfway total of 141 put him a shot ahead of Billy Casper and two in front of a fellow named Arnold Palmer.

If the idea of Brodie giving up football seems farfetched, remember that in 1960 he hardly had a lock on the 49ers' quarterback job. Y. A. Tittle was still around, and the following year the team would draft Billy Kilmer in the first round. Then, too, coach Red Hickey had begun to dicker with a shotgun offense, which Brodie detested because the QB was more like a tailback and generally took a beating.

"Billy Kilmer used to check the ambulance before we'd run out on the field," Brodie says. "He'd say, 'Well, which one of us is gonna get it today?'"

So golf might have looked pretty good to Brodie if he'd won at Yorba Linda, or even come close. It was, after all, just his 10th pro tournament. He was still in contention, he recalls, when he came to the par-five 15th hole on the last day. But he gambled and tried to reach the green in two from about 240 yards away with a three-wood. He reached a pond instead and took a double-bogey.

"I always wondered what would have happened if I had knocked that ball on the green and holed it and won the tournament," he says.

What did happen was that Brodie finished tied for 24th at even-par 288 (two strokes behind Arnie), took home $112.50 and went on to throw 214 touchdown passes.

• • •

12 MEN ON THE FIELD

To further international relations—and make a tidy $28,000 in the process—the Pittsburgh Steelers traveled to Toronto in August 1960 to play the CFL's Argonauts. There had been previous games between American and Canadian pro teams, but this was the first one played entirely under Canadian rules.

Well, *almost* entirely. The Steelers were granted concessions on blocking, timeouts and the time required to put the ball in play, but that was it. They still had to adjust to the 12 players, the three downs, the much bigger field and all the rest.

"We won't learn very much about our club," coach Buddy Parker said, "and I don't expect they will find out much about theirs. But financially, that's another question."

Parker hired Peahead Walker, former coach of the CFL's Montreal Alouettes, to help his team prepare. Probably the best advice Walker gave the Pittsburgh players was this: "All the officials are homers. That's why the home team frequently wins."

So the Steelers didn't fool around. After spotting

DECADE LEADERS (NFL)

PASSING

Yards: Johnny Unitas, 26,548; Sonny Jurgensen, 26,222; Fran Tarkenton, 23,140.
Completion percentage (1,500 attempts): Bart Starr, 58.9; Jurgensen, 56.4; Unitas, 55.3.
Touchdowns: Jurgensen, 207; Tarkenton, 186; Unitas, 182.
Interceptions: Norm Snead, 175; Unitas, 165; Jurgensen, 154.

RUSHING

Yards: Jim Brown, 8,514; Jim Taylor, 7,898; Don Perkins, 6,217.
Yards per carry (750 attempts): Brown, 5.3; Gale Sayers, 5.1; Leroy Kelly, 4.9.
TDs: Taylor, 76; Brown, 66; Kelly, 51.

RECEIVING

Receptions: Bobby Mitchell, 470; Boyd Dowler, 416; Raymond Berry, 412.
Yards: Mitchell, 7,472; Tommy McDonald, 6,733; Carroll Dale, 6,356.
Yards per catch (200 receptions): Homer Jones, 22.6; Buddy Dial, 20.4; Paul Warfield, 20.2.
TDs: Sonny Randle, 64; Gary Collins, 63; McDonald, 62.

OTHER CATEGORIES

Scoring: Lou Michaels, 870; Sam Baker, 712; Tommy Davis, 671.
Interceptions: Bobby Boyd, 57; Dick LeBeau, 47; Dave Whitsell, 45.
Punt return average (75 returns): Bob Hayes, 11.9; Kelly, 11.4; Tommy Watkins, 10.1.
Punt return TDs: Rickie Harris, Hayes, Kelly and Watkins, 3.
Kickoff return average (75 returns): Sayers, 30.6; Abe Woodson, 29.1; Travis Williams, 27.7.
Kickoff return TDs: Sayers, 6.
Field goals: Michaels, 171; Fred Cox, 136; Jim Bakken, 134.
Field goal percentage (100 attempts): Bakken, 61.5; Cox, 60.7; Don Chandler, 58.8.
Punting average (200 punts): Yale Lary, 46.4; Tommy Davis, 44.7; Jerry Norton, 44.2.

Try as he might, Coach Marty Feldman couldn't get the Raiders over the hump in the early '60s. (UPI/Bettmann Newsphotos)

What hump? (UPI/Bettmann Newsphotos)

the Argonauts an early field goal, they rolled to a 43–16 victory before 23,570 at Exhibition Stadium. It was 36–3 at the half. Bobby Layne threw three long touchdown passes to Preston Carpenter and Buddy Dial in a little more than two quarters' work.

The Argos caught the Americans off guard a couple of times with onside punts, but one backfired and resulted in a Steelers TD. The Canadian team did produce the most exciting play of the day, though: Johnny Wardlaw's 102-yard interception return for the final score.

The game was billed as a duel between Layne and Toronto quarterback Tobin Rote. The two had been teammates and rivals on the Detroit Lions. But Rote suffered a bruised knee late in the first half and sat out the rest of the game.

The Argonauts had a pretty good club. Besides Rote, who had just joined them, they had future AFL star Cookie Gilchrist and ex–Chicago Cardinals back Dave Mann. You'd have to say, on the

STEELERS 43, ARGONAUTS 16

Pittsburgh	20	16	0	7	—	43
Toronto	3	0	6	7	—	16

TOR—FG Bill Mitchell 17
PIT—Preston Carpenter 59 pass from Bobby Layne (Layne kick)
PIT—Tom Tracy 41 run (kick blocked)
PIT—Buddy Dial 40 pass from Layne (Layne kick)
PIT—Larry Krutko 5 run (Layne kick)
PIT—Junior Wren 5 punt return (kick failed)
PIT—FG Bert Rechichar 41
TOR—Cookie Gilchrist 1 run (kick failed)
PIT—Dial 61 pass from Layne (Layne kick)
TOR—Johnny Wardlaw 102 interception return (Mitchell kick)

basis of this game, that the Steelers would have been a real threat to win the Grey Cup.

What they mostly felt afterward, however, was relief. Said defensive back Dean Derby: "I'm sure glad I don't have to defend in any of those 25-yard end zones again."

This, by the way, was believed to be the first pro football game viewed on pay TV. Thousands of fans in the Toronto suburb of Etobicoke paid two dollars a set.

• • •
"THE VIOLENT WORLD OF SAM HUFF"

Watch "The Violent World of Sam Huff" today and you wonder what the fuss was about. CBS's celebrated show, aired in 1960, isn't very violent—or sophisticated. Narrator Walter Cronkite tells you things like the job of offensive linemen is to block, not tackle.

"That privilege belongs to the defense," he says authoritatively.

The best sequence in the 30-minute program probably takes place off the field. During a quiet moment at the New York Giants training camp, Huff and several teammates accompany tackle Dick Modzelewski in a Polish folk song—in Polish. It's priceless.

But what the show purported to do—take the viewer closer to pro football than he or she had ever been—it did. This, remember, was in the days before instant replays, isolated cameras or extensive media coverage of pro football. It must have been quite a revelation.

A CBS News camera crew followed Huff through several weeks of training camp and an exhibition game with the Chicago Bears in August 1960. CBS also wired him for sound, which had never been done. He wore a microphone in the front of his pads, a battery pack in the back and an antenna down his leg. The whole rig weighed a pound.

"A pound doesn't sound like much, but let me tell you," Huff says, "by the fourth quarter or late in a practice, you feel it."

The effect was terrific. America got to hear pro football for the first time, the grunting and groaning, the impact of pads and bodies colliding, everything but the cussing. Huff insisted that CBS edit the profanity. The roughest the language gets is when he threatens to break the nose of a Bears receiver. ("You do that one more time, 88, and I'm going to sock you one!")

"Violent World" was broadcast at 6:30 P.M., October 30, 1960—a Sunday—on the CBS News program The Twentieth Century. It received a modest 26 share, meaning one of every four television sets in use was tuned in. The critical reaction to the show was tremendous. The popular reaction has probably been exaggerated a bit.

Don Smith, the Giants PR man at the time, claims that just after the broadcast the team was in Los Angeles for a game with the Rams. On a whim, he dropped a postcard into a mailbox "at the corner of Wilshire and Crenshaw Boulevard." The only thing written on the card was "Number 70." There was no address, no name, nothing but "Number 70."

"Seven days later that card showed up in Huff's locker at Yankee Stadium," Smith says.

It's a good story. Unfortunately, the Giants didn't play in Los Angeles after the show aired. They were there in the preseason only. The week after the show, they were in Cleveland to play the Browns.

"Violent World" is credited with creating an identity for defensive players that didn't exist up to then. It's probably more accurate to say it helped. The zanies at Yankee Stadium had been chanting "Dee-fense!" and "Huff-Huff-Huff!" for years. Time magazine, not exactly a trendsetter in sports coverage, had put the Giants middle linebacker on its cover in 1959.

Huff has bittersweet feelings about the show. On the one hand it made him the most visible defensive player in America. On the other . . .

"In 1959, I was named defensive MVP of the NFL," he said in his autobiography, Tough Stuff. "In 1960, after 'The Violent World of Sam Huff,' I didn't even make all-pro, and I had a better year in 1960 than I'd had in 1959. There's just no question that there was a lot of resentment for all the attention I was getting, and in later years it really hurt me."

By that, Huff means the Hall-of-Fame voting. He wasn't elected until 1982, 13 years after his career ended and eight after he became eligible for induction. The charges that he was overrated as a player

AN EXCERPT FROM THE SCRIPT

WHAT YOU SAW

1. Split screen with narrator Walter Cronkite on the right, a Giants scrimmage in progress on the left.

2. Sound of offensive and defensive signals being called. Focus on Huff at middle linebacker during scrimmaging. He drops into the middle on a pass play and gets in on the tackle. The contact is audible.

3. Huff, jersey off, is having a transistorized radio transmitter inserted into the back of his pads and a microphone attached to front.

3a. Back to the scrimmage. Huff's voice can be heard clearly as he makes the tackle on a running play. Big pileup. "Attaway, defense!"

4. Back to a split screen with Cronkite.

COMMERCIAL BREAK

5. Huff sitting on a couch.

6. Cut to scrimmage action. Huff is heard shouting, "Here we go. Play for pass! Play for pass!" as signals are called. "The Violent World of Sam Huff" appears on the screen. The ball is snapped. Huff blitzes up the middle and runs over a running back.

6a. More scrimmage shots. You can hear Huff huffing and puffing. Signals are called, the ball is snapped. Huff moves right to avoid blocker. He's really breathing hard. Cronkite comes in at this point—

WHAT YOU HEARD

1. Cronkite: I'm Walter Cronkite. If you were a professional football player—the middle linebacker of the New York Football Giants—and your name was Sam Huff—this is what it would be like.

2. Cronkite: Huff is number 70.

3. Cronkite: Today you will play pro football, riding on Sam Huff's broad back. . . .

3a. Cronkite: . . . We've wired him for sound with a tiny, transistorized radio transmitter. It's not allowed in regular league play and it's the first time it has been done on television. The transmitter is embedded in his pads. The microphone goes in front. You're on the receiving end, and you're going to be closer to pro football than you have ever been before.

4. Cronkite: This is our story—"The Violent World of Sam Huff"—as The Prudential Insurance Company of America presents "The Twentieth Century."

5. Huff: Anytime that you play football on the field there is no place for nice guys. I mean you have to be tough. You have to go all out. I always feel real good whenever I hit someone. You just hear that leather thud in there, you know, and you feel that you've accomplished something. You've made a beautiful tackle. When we're out on the field, we have to shake them up. It's either . . . an expression . . . kill or be killed.

6. Cronkite: That was Sam Huff doing what he's paid to do—knock the other guy down!

6a. Cronkite: The running, passing, kicking halfback used to be Saturday's football hero. . . .

6b. Huff blitzes and is upended by a blocker.

7. Huff comes off the field, tired, limping a little.

7a. Cut to a shot of Huff on the bench, helmet off, an ice pack on the back of his neck.

7b. Quick shot of more scrimmage action.

7c. Cut back to the bench. Huff drinks out of a dipper, an ice pack atop his head.

6b. Cronkite: Today, a triple threat is three men, and the man whose job is not to score, but to stop the score is now Sunday's idol.

7. Cronkite: Sam never plays when the Giants have the ball, yet the middle linebacker is a key man in pro football, the flexible man on a team of rigid specialists. He must be big. And Sam, who is 26, is 6 feet 1, 230 pounds. He must be strong enough to shed a 260-pound blocker then to meet a 230-pound ball carrier under a full head of steam and with a five-yard start. . . .

7a. Cronkite: Above all, he must be as rough and mean as the rules allow, . . .

7b. Cronkite: . . . and Sam is respected for his toughness in a league which includes crack linebackers like Schmidt, George, Michaels and others.

7c. Cronkite: A good middle linebacker may make 10–12,000 dollars a season—less than a star back, who may earn 20.

---

and largely a creation of the New York media still rankle him.

"Look at my stats," he says. "I played in six championship games in eight years. I was the only rookie middle linebacker to ever start in a championship game. I had 30 interceptions, more than any linebacker in the Hall of Fame when I was elected. I probably blocked more kicks than anyone in the history of the game, but they don't keep track of things like that. I made sacks. . . .

"It ['Violent World' and the attendant notoriety] is the only thing I can think of that kept me out of the Hall of Fame in five years. All the guys I was compared to and who were compared to me—Joe Schmidt, Bill George—made it in five."

One of the rumors surrounding the show was that Giants defensive end Andy Robustelli, not Huff, was CBS' first choice. The network turned to Huff, the story goes, because Robustelli asked for too much money.

Robustelli says there's nothing to it. So do the people at CBS. In the first place, there wasn't a lot of money involved. Huff received $500 and the use of a rental car during the filming.

"The car was very important," Huff said in his book. "Nowadays, you look in a professional football team's parking lot and you see brand-new Mercedes, Jaguars, Cadillacs, and Oldsmobiles. Back then, none of us drove to camp because we had only one car, and the wife and kids needed it. I was about

the only guy in camp with a car that year, and I was a very popular man."

There are two versions of how Huff came to be the subject of the documentary. The late Burton Benjamin, who came up with the idea and produced the show, wrote in a 1982 story in the *New York Times* that he decided on Huff because so many people on the commuter train he rode to work were talking about him. But Don Smith says *he* convinced Benjamin that Huff was the right choice. Smith's version also might explain the rumors about Robustelli.

"Burton Benjamin and I went to lunch at Al and Dick's Steak House on 57th Street, and he laid it all out for me about how he wanted to wire a pro player and bring the sounds of football to the viewer," Smith says. "He mentioned a couple names, one of which was Robustelli. Huff wasn't one. He [Benjamin] already had the title, 'The Violent World of . . .'

"I said, 'For chrissakes, "The Violent World of Andy Robustelli"? It doesn't have a ring to it. What about Sam Huff?" And I explained how in the Giants defense everything was funneled to him at middle linebacker, and how he'd be in on a lot of plays. So he [Benjamin] thought that was great."

The Giants trained in Winooski, Vermont. Everyone involved said the filming was a difficult time. Huff broke six microphones. The camera crew ran its cables (this was well before the minicam) into meeting rooms and dormitories and was often a distraction. This, of course, gave coach Jim Lee Howell another excuse to be grouchy.

The grand experiment culminated with the game against the Bears in Toronto August 15. The Chicago players knew what CBS was up to and joked beforehand about making Huff a target. This led to one of the best anecdotes about the show.

At one point in the game, Bears wide receiver Harlon Hill knocked down Huff with a late hit.

"Harlon, for godsake you never hit anyone in your life," Huff said, "what the hell did you do that for?"

"Aw, Sam," Hill replied, "I was just trying to get on TV."

It's a good thing CBS was focusing on Huff and not the game. It was a dull and poorly played affair, won by the Bears, 16–7. There actually was some historical significance to it aside from its role as the backdrop for "Violent World." It was the first game between two NFL teams in Canada. It's a wonder there was ever another.

Only 5,401 people showed up at seedy old Varsity Stadium, and the promoters, one of whom was a waiter at a Toronto hotel, stiffed the Bears and Giants for half of their $25,000 guarantees. (The teams might not have gotten anything if they hadn't been paid $12,500 in advance.)

"I'll always remember that game as we drove away for the airport," says Giants owner Wellington Mara. "The last thing I saw was one of the promoters backed up against a wall, and George Halas was the backer-upper. I've always had a suspicion that one way or the other George got paid and we didn't."

∎ ∎ ∎

HIT OF THE DECADE
Chuck Bednarik Flattens Frank Gifford, 1960

With one blindside hit, Eagles linebacker Chuck Bednarik put Frank Gifford out of pro football for a year and turned him from a halfback into a wide receiver. It's probably the most famous tackle in pro football history, and understandably so. It involved two Hall-of-Famers and happened in a big game in the Big Apple.

The date was November 20, 1960. Philadelphia was at New York for the first of back-to-back games that figured to decide the Eastern Conference championship. More than 20,000 people were turned away at Yankee Stadium.

The collision occurred late in the game at the Philadelphia 35. The Eagles were leading 17–10, but the Giants were driving. On third and 10, Gifford cut across the middle from the left, grabbed George Shaw's pass and was trying to get out of bounds to stop the clock when he was hit low by defensive back Don Burrough and high by Bednarik. He landed hard on the back of his head and was knocked unconscious. He also fumbled, Philly's Chuck Weber recovering to clinch the victory.

As Gifford lay motionless, Bednarik stood over him shaking his fist and dancing a jig. Some in the stands booed, but most had been stunned into silence.

"Someday they're going to kill somebody," Dr. Francis Sweeny, the Giants' team physician, said afterward. For a few tense minutes, it looked as if Bednarik had.

Gifford was still out cold when he was taken by stretcher to the locker room. He was being treated for a severe concussion when a special policeman, who had had a heart attack as the game ended, was carried in.

The policeman died. As the Giants' Lee Grosscup recalled in his book, *Fourth and One:* "Outside, Maxine Gifford, Frank's wife, heard something about a death in the Giant locker room and thought it was her husband. Father Benedict Dudley, Giant chaplain, informed Maxine that it was a cop who had died and that Frank was coming along fine."

Suspicions that Bednarik had cheap-shotted Gifford were unfounded, as the game film showed. Giants coach Jim Lee Howell said: "He hit Frank the way a football player is supposed to hit people."

Bednarik likened the tackle to "a truck hitting a sports car. He was going full speed and I was going full speed, and when I hit him I knew one of us wasn't going to get up." The reason he exulted after the hit, he explained, was that the Eagles had recovered the fumble and were about to win the game, not that Gifford was hurt.

Bednarik even sent him a basket of fruit at St. Elizabeth's. The card read: "Sorry you're in the hospital and I hope you get out soon enough to play your usual great game on Sunday." But the Giants put Gifford on the injured list, then went to Philadel-

The Eagles' Chuck Bednarik celebrates his game-saving hit against the Giants' Frank Gifford in November 1960. Gifford suffered a serious concussion and didn't play football again until 1962. (AP/Wide World Photos)

phia and lost again, 31–23, to fall out of contention. The Eagles went on to take the league title.

The hit almost never happened. Two plays earlier, Shaw had just missed a touchdown pass to end Bob Schnelker. The *New York Herald Tribune* reported that the ball "slid off his fingertips—and Schnelker was left standing and pounding a goalpost upright in frustration."

Another irony: Bednarik had been put in on defense only a few minutes before. He had started the game at left linebacker, but with the Eagles behind 10–0 at the half, coach Buck Shaw had moved him to center in hopes of getting the offense going. When Philadelphia pulled even with 4:24 left, Bednarik went back to linebacker.

The hit almost never happened, but it did. The next day Gifford couldn't even remember the game. "We should all be so lucky," teammate Kyle Rote said.

■ ■ ■

SOME INCENTIVE

The Philadelphia Eagles by Vincent A. McNally, General Manager, will give Charles P. Bednarik a bonus of Two Hundred Fifty ($250.00) Dollars if, in the opinion of Coach Shaw, he has a good year in 1960 or if he plays both offense and defense.

As this clause in his 1960 contract shows, Chuck Bednarik didn't make much extra money for being the NFL's last (full-time) two-way player. The next season he received a $30 bonus for intercepting two passes, $10 for the first and $20 for the second.

■ ■ ■

ONE LAST REASON TO HATE GEORGE PRESTON MARSHALL

In March 1961 a messenger hand-delivered a letter to George Preston Marshall at the Redskins' downtown Washington headquarters. It was from the new Secretary of the Interior, Stewart Udall, and said, in effect: Sign a black player or forget about using brand-new D.C. Stadium in the fall.

Udall warned Marshall that he "was in for a moral argument with the President [Kennedy] and the Administration and even possible criminal prosecution if his all-white National Football League team practices discrimination."

Think Marshall was intimidated?

"I would consider it a great honor to meet and discuss this with the President of the United States," he said. "Yes, I'd like to debate that kid. I could handle him with words. I used to handle his old man in Boston."

George Preston Marshall's last great fight as owner of the Redskins was over his stubborn refusal to sign black players, and he went down with guns blazing. People who knew him well insist Marshall wasn't racist, that his Jim Crow policy was strictly business—at first, anyway. Until the Dallas Cowboys came into the league in 1960, the Redskins were the southernmost NFL franchise, and Marshall turned the distinction into profit. He pushed the Redskins television and radio network as far south as Florida. He drafted a lot of southern players. He even added a few stanzas of "Dixie" to "Hail to the Redskins." But as the pressure to integrate increased, Marshall's contrary and stubborn nature took over. Or so the argument goes.

"I think he had the attitude that nobody is going to run me off my front porch; nobody is going to tell me how to run the Redskins," said Lew Atchison, long-time Redskins beat writer.

That's tough to swallow whole. Bigotry by any other name is . . . well, what Marshall was practicing.

In 1960 the all-white Redskins were 1–9–2. The year before: 3–9. They'd had two winning seasons since 1948. How was that going to sell in the South?

There certainly wasn't any doubt about Marshall from the black perspective. The NAACP began picketing the team in the early '50s. As for black players in the league . . . "We try a little harder when we play Washington," said Ollie Matson.

Udall and the Kennedy administration finally forced the issue. Washington's new stadium was federally funded and fell under the jurisdiction of the Department of Interior. Udall directed the National Park Service to prohibit discrimination on public land, and Marshall had to act if he was to use the stadium.

"All the other teams have Negroes; does it matter which teams have Negroes?" he asked facetiously. "Are they going to demand that the National Symphony Orchestra have Negroes? The Army and Navy football teams don't have colored players. Will they be barred from the stadium?"

The controversy raged through the spring and summer. Marshall remained true to character throughout; he was outrageous. In June he told a Los Angeles columnist that he'd arranged for the Rams to sign Kenny Washington in 1946. Washington was one of the four black players who integrated pro football that year.

"I'm the Branch Rickey of the National Football League," Marshall said.

Udall kept up the pressure. Finally, in August, the two sides reached a compromise. Marshall agreed to draft black players in 1962, and the Redskins were allowed to use the new stadium in the fall.

The following year, the Redskins added four black players to their roster. They traded for running backs Bobby Mitchell and Leroy Jackson and guard John Nisby and drafted running back Ron Hatcher. Mitchell recalls his first meeting with Marshall:

"Bob," Marshall told him. "You're in a political town and I'd like you to stay away from politics. Secondly, be a good guy. And third, don't ask for too much money."

● ● ●
I LOVE L.A.

Kicker Ben Agajanian played with the Los Angeles Dons (1947–48), Rams (1953) and Chargers (1960). This is even harder than it sounds. The Dons lasted only four seasons, and the Chargers were in L.A. for just one.

••• THE FIRST SAFETY BLITZ

- **When**—September 17, 1961, in the second quarter of a game between the St. Louis Cardinals and New York Giants.
- **Where**—Yankee Stadium.
- **Who**—Cardinals safety Larry Wilson.
- **What**—Wilson blindsided Giants quarterback Charlie Conerly for an 11-yard sack. "It was a good shot, all right," Wilson says. "I earholed him."
- **Why**—The Cardinals were 12½ point underdogs and decided to gamble defensively with a variety of blitzes. They won, 21-10.
- **The brains behind the blitz**—Cardinals defensive coaches Chuck Drulis and Ray Willsey.
- **Minutiae**—Wilson blitzed several times during the game and finished with two sacks. . . . The Giants never did catch on. Says Wilson: "Chuck told me that if I got to the quarterback, get up real quick and hide your number and get back to the huddle so they don't know who you are." . . . Conerly was 40 when Wilson earholed him. He was playing only because Y. A. Tittle, acquired in an off-season trade with San Francisco, had injured a knee in training camp. . . . Willsey had used a safety blitz when he was an assistant at the University of Washington in 1956. The target that day was Stanford QB John Brodie.

••• WAITING FOR GERDA

The last time a pro football game was postponed because of the weather was on a day that turned out to be sunny and 60 degrees.

The date was October 20, 1961. The Buffalo Bills were in Boston to play a Friday night game against the Patriots, but Hurricane Gerda also was expected to hit town that evening.

IN-SEASON COACHING CHANGES

When the defending AFL champion Houston Oilers got off to a 1-3-1 start in 1961, owner Bud Adams got rid of coach Lou Rymkus and brought in Wally Lemm. The Oilers won their nine remaining regular-season games under Lemm, then beat San Diego for their second straight title.

The team that finished second to Houston in the Eastern Division that year did the same thing -- with almost the same results. The Boston Patriots fired Lou Saban after five games, replaced him with Mike Holovak and went 7-1-1 the rest of the way. Those are two of the three most successful in-season coaching changes in NFL/AFL history.

You always hear how destructive canning the coach is, but statistics show that most in-season coaching changes have been for the better. There have been 52 such changes (minimum: three games left). The new coach has had a better record than the old coach 39 times, a worse record 11 times and the same record (actually, winning percentage) twice.

THE BEST IN-SEASON COACHING CHANGES IN NFL/AFL HISTORY		
Year Team	First Coach (Record)	Successor (Record)
1961 Oilers [1]	Lou Rymkus (1-3-1)	Wally Lemm (9-0)
1986 Colts	Rod Dowhower (0-13)	Ron Meyer (3-0)
1961 Patriots	Lou Saban (2-3)	Mike Holovak (7-1-1)
1952 Rams [2]	Joe Stydahar (0-1)	Hamp Pool (9-2)
1969 Chargers	Sid Gillman (4-5)	Charlie Waller (4-1)
1931 Cardinals	Roy Andrews (0-2)	Ernie Nevers (5-2)
1978 Chargers	Tommy Prothro (1-3)	Don Coryell (8-4)
1971 Eagles	Jerry Williams (0-3)	Ed Khayat (6-4-1)
1982 Seahawks	Jack Patera (0-2)	Mike McCormack (4-3)
1951 Redskins	Herman Ball (0-3)	Dick Todd (5-4)

[1] won AFL title   [2] lost Western division playoff

It rained lightly in the morning. Around noon, Pats owner Billy Sullivan announced the game was being rescheduled to Sunday. Soon, however, the sky began to clear.

"I've seen girls softball games played in worse weather than this," the Bills' Archie Matsos groused.

Conditions were practically perfect when Matsos and his teammates worked out later in the day. Indeed, some 30 high school games were played in the Boston area that night.

Buffalo coach Buster Ramsey cried foul. His club was coming off two big victories over Houston and Dallas, and he thought Sullivan was trying to take away some of the Bills' momentum. He called the postponement "a deliberate attempt to upset my team. . . . A bush-league trick."

Sullivan also may have been afraid the game wouldn't draw because of the hurricane threat. The Patriots had money problems.

If he *was* trying to discombobulate the Bills, he succeeded. The players didn't have enough clothes to last three days and had to go out and buy more. They also lost their emotional edge. The Patriots pounded them, 52–21, setting a slew of team offensive records.

The weather on Sunday afternoon was far worse than on Friday night—35 degrees with 25- to 30-mph winds. The fans, just 9,398 of them, froze.

● ● ●
FOILED BY FATE

President John F. Kennedy and his family, whose *touch* football prowess was much photographed, once were interested in buying the Philadelphia Eagles. This was in October 1962, after Eagles owner Jim Clark died.

The three Kennedy boys—John, then–Attorney General Bobby and freshman Senator Ted—were sitting in the Oval Office one day when they read that the team was for sale. Jack and Bobby thought it would be a terrific investment. Jack pointed out that he would still be young (51) when his second term was completed. He then instructed Ted to go up to Philadelphia and meet with the club's management.

Alas, something came up: the Cuban Missile Crisis.

● ● ●
CONTEST OF WILLS

The death of St. Louis Cardinals owner Violet Bidwill Wolfner in January 1962 touched off a court fight for control of the team. It was one of two such battles in the NFL in the '60s. The other involved the Washington Redskins.

On opposite sides in the Cardinals case were Walter Wolfner, Violet's second husband, and Bill and Stormy (Charles) Bidwill, sons from her first marriage. The fight lasted four years and was plenty nasty.

In her will, Violet Wolfner left most of her $3 million to $5 million estate to her sons. This included 82 percent of the Cardinals' stock. Walter Wolfner was bequeathed the income from five Oklahoma oil wells. Monthly profit: a paltry $400.

The unequal distribution of wealth was based in part on a postnuptial agreement Violet and Walter signed in 1954. In it, each waived any claim to the other's property.

Sometime between 1954 and 1962, Walter had a change of heart. Soon after his wife's death, he moved to invalidate the will. His opening gambit was a shocker. But first, some background:

Walter and Violet were married in 1949, two years after the death of "Blueshirt" Charley Bidwill, the Chicago sportsman who had owned the Cardinals since 1933. From 1950 to '61 the two of them ran the club, Wolfner on a daily basis as the team's managing director.

The Bidwill boys had titles in the organization—Stormy was president, Bill vice-president—but these were largely ceremonial. There was never any love lost between Walter and the boys. He testified during court proceedings that the two "hated" him.

When the terms of the will were revealed, the Bidwills made it clear they were going to have a more active role in the Cardinals and that Wolfner was out. Bill was 30, Stormy 32. They immediately took over the search begun by their stepfather for a new coach and hired Wally Lemm.

In March 1962, Wolfner dragged them into court. The boys, he claimed, had misrepresented themselves at the proof of heirship hearings: Neither had told the probate judge he was adopted.

The reason the Bidwills hadn't was that they didn't know. They learned of their adoption from Wolfner's legal action. They weren't even biological brothers. Each had come from a different family. Stormy's given name at birth was Chester. Bill's was Robert. It was a cruel blow.

Wolfner also questioned the legality of their adoption. He asked the court to throw out the will and make him executor of Violet's estate.

It took probate judge Robert J. Dunne a month to accept an amended proof of heirship from the Bidwills and decide the adoptions were indeed legal. The case dragged on for three more years as Wolfner exhausted his appeals. At one point, a St. Louis court assumed custody of the Cardinals and appointed as trustee a local movie theater owner. In August 1965 Wolfner and the Bidwills settled out of court.

* * *

The fight for the Redskins involved two wills, both belonging to owner George Preston Marshall. The first, made out in 1963, left the team in control of stockholders Edward Bennett Williams, Leo DeOrsey and Milton King. The second, dated 1966,

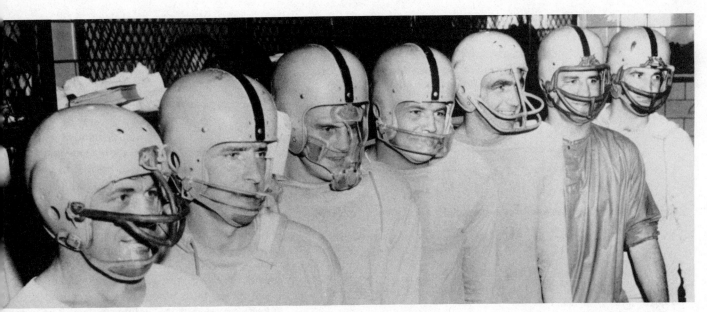

By 1954, facemasks had become fashionable. Uniformity, however, was still years away. Here the Steelers model some of the variations. That's Jim Finks, who nearly became NFL commissioner in 1989, second from left. (UPI/Bettmann Newsphotos)

left the team to Marshall's two children, George Jr. and Mrs. Catherine Price.

Marshall's deteriorating mental and physical health in the last decade of his life complicated matters. A court ruled he was incapable of handling his own affairs and appointed Williams, DeOrsey and King conservators in 1963. Marshall's children fought this, too, accusing the three of managing the team in their own best interests. At one point George Jr. spent three weeks in jail for contempt of court.

Marshall Sr. died in August 1969, but the court battle lasted for two and a half more years. In January 1972 the two sides finally agreed to a settlement. Marshall Jr. and Price each received $750,000 plus $10,000 a year for life. In return they threw out the second will.

■ ■ ■

ANOTHER IMELDA

When she died in 1962, Cardinals owner Violet Bidwill Wolfner owned:
- More than 1,000 dresses.
- 1,500 pairs of shoes.
- Several hundred hats, negligees, purses and pairs of gloves.

- Two full-length mink coats and dozens of other fur pieces.
- One full-length white ermine dressing gown.

Wolfner, oddly enough, was shy. She did little socializing. Some of the items she left behind dated back to the '20s. Many were in unopened boxes and had never been worn.

■ ■ ■

"THE MOST RIDICULOUS THINGS I EVER SAW"

One summer night at Bears Stadium in 1962, the Denver Broncos paraded one by one past a mock-up of the Olympic flame and dropped the team's *vertically* striped socks in the fire. It was a major victory for good taste, cheered on by a crowd of 8,377.

The ceremony was new coach Jack Faulkner's idea. He wanted everything associated with the Broncos' dismal first two seasons gone, especially those socks. There were two sets: alternating brown and mustard yellow stripes for home games, brown and white for the road.

"They were the most ridiculous things I ever saw

in my life," says defensive tackle Bud McFadin.

The man responsible for them was Dean Griffing, the club's first general manager. He was a legendary tightwad—"the kind of guy who took off his glasses when he wasn't looking at anything," says broadcaster Bob Martin—and outfitted the Broncos with used uniforms purchased from the Copper Bowl College All-Star Game in Tucson, Arizona. The bizarre socks, he insisted, made the players appear taller.

DECADE LEADERS (AFL)

PASSING
Yards: Jack Kemp, 21,130; George Blanda, 20,029; John Hadl, 19,026.
Completion percentage (1,500 attempts): Len Dawson, 56.8; Joe Namath, 50.2; Hadl, 49.3.
Touchdowns: Dawson, 182; Blanda, 176; Babe Parilli, 144.
Interceptions: Blanda, 195; Kemp, 181; Parilli, 152.

RUSHING
Yards: Clem Daniels, 5,101; Paul Lowe, 4,995; Abner Haynes, 4,630.
Yards per carry (750 attempts): Lowe, 4.9; Daniels, 4.5; Haynes, 4.47.
TDs: Haynes, 46; Kemp, 40; Lowe, 39.

RECEIVING
Receptions: Lionel Taylor, 567; Don Maynard, 546; Art Powell, 478.
Yards: Maynard, 10,289; Lance Alworth, 8,976; Powell, 8,015.
Yards per catch (200 receptions): Alworth, 19.6; Maynard, 18.8; Otis Taylor, 18.7.
TDs: Maynard, 84; Powell, 81; Alworth, 77.

OTHER CATEGORIES
Scoring: Gino Cappelletti, 1,100; Blanda, 936; Jim Turner, 612.
Interceptions: Dave Grayson, 47; Jim Norton, 45; Goose Gonsoulin and Johnny Robinson, 43.
Punt return average (75 returns): Hoot Gibson, 12.6; Speedy Duncan, 12.3; Rodger Bird, 11.3.
Punt return TDs: Dick Christy and Duncan, 4.
Kickoff return average (75 returns): Bobby Jancik, 26.5; Duncan, 25.9; Larry Garron, 25.8.
Kickoff return TDs: Charley Warner, 3.
Field goals: Cappelletti, 170; Blanda, 152; Jim Turner, 134.
Field goal percentage (100 attempts): Jan Stenerud, 70.3; Turner, 60.6; Mike Mercer, 58.0.
Punting average (200 punts): Jerrel Wilson, 43.9; Bob Scarpitto, 43.8; Mike Eischeid, 43.1.

"They made you look like a peg is what they did," says safety Goose Gonsoulin. "You had these real broad shoulders because of the pads, and then you had these up-and-down striped socks. . . . It was unique, put it that way."

The players were ridiculed on the road by fans and opponents. At one point several Broncos went to coach Frank Filchock and demanded new socks. Filchock refused. The team didn't have the money.

Owner Bob Howsam sold the club to Cal Kunz in 1961. Kunz got rid of Griffing and Filchock after the season and hired Faulkner, who launched a campaign that promised: "There's Lots New in '62." He started with the uniforms. The hated socks were torched before an intrasquad game.

A handful did escape the flames. One is on display at the Pro Football Hall of Fame. Faulkner has a set hidden in a drawer somewhere. And several players are said to be holding a few. The cursed things are now worth $500.

■ ■ ■

THE UGLIEST UNIFORMS EVER?

Our vote goes to the 1960–61 Denver Broncos.
■ **Helmet**—brown with a white logo of a scraggly cowpoke, toothpick in mouth, riding a bucking horse.
■ **Jersey**—mustard yellow.
■ **Pants**—brown (some had a satin sheen, some didn't).
■ **Socks**—alternating brown and yellow *vertical* stripes.

■ ■ ■

HONDO'S TRYOUT

K. C. Jones wasn't the only Boston Celtic to get the once-over from the NFL. In 1962 John Havlicek went to training camp with the Cleveland Browns as a split end. He lasted until August 22, when it became clear he wasn't going to make the team. Coach Paul Brown cut him loose early so he could concentrate on a pro basketball career.

Havlicek's problem was lack of experience, not ability. He'd been an all-star quarterback in high school. The Browns thought enough of his potential to gamble a seventh-round draft pick on him, even though he'd played only basketball at Ohio State. As a matter of fact, they selected him before Clifton McNeil (11th round) and Paul Flatley (20th), both of whom had good NFL careers.

Havlicek appeared in one exhibition game, against the Steelers August 18. He didn't catch a pass but did throw a key block that sprang Jim Brown for a 45-yard run. Four days later, the Browns decided to release him. He signed with the Celtics.

In 1966 Browns owner Art Modell offered Havlicek a $40,000 contract to try again. Three other NFL teams, including the Redskins, made overtures, too. This time, Celtics coach Red Auerbach blew his stack. (Guard Larry Siegfried also had been approached, by two AFL teams.)

Auerbach's rage prompted National Basketball Association commissioner Walter Kennedy to complain to NFL counterpart Pete Rozelle about tampering. The NFL then backed off.

■ ■ ■

A LONG WAY FOR NOTHING

Touchdowns are called back because of penalties all the time, but what happened to the Dallas Cowboys on September 23, 1962, is thought to be unique in NFL history. The Cowboys had a 99-yard TD pass against the Pittsburgh Steelers nullified by a holding penalty.

In the end zone.

Which resulted in a safety.

Which turned out to be the Steelers' winning margin in a 30–28 victory.

The Cowboys thought they had tied the game at 21 on the Eddie-LeBaron-to-Frank-Clarke bomb. But as Clarke was crossing the goal line, referee Emil Heintz was waving his arms at the other end of the field and calling for the ball. After a brief discussion with his colleagues, he made the signal for a safety—two points for Pittsburgh.

The Cotton Bowl crowd of 19,478 went crazy. Dallas coach Tom Landry rushed onto the field to

question the call. Afterward he said: "I didn't think there was a rule . . . that could give points."

It was news to Steelers coach Buddy Parker, too. And he'd been in the league as a player and coach since 1935. "I just don't know about it," he said later, "but the guy gave it to us."

When Pittsburgh got the ball again after the free kick, Cowboys fans raised so much of a racket that the Steelers couldn't hear Bobby Layne's signals. Landry appealed unsuccessfully for quiet. Layne finally tried to run a couple of plays, but both lost yardage.

At this point Heintz called time, walked to a sideline telephone and told the public-address announcer:

"Will you please tell the folks this foul was on Dallas' number 62 [guard Andy Cverko], who held in the end zone, and by the rules a violation committed in the end zone makes it a safety.

"Furthermore, it was said by another official that the man going downfield stepped out of bounds and came back to catch the pass, and so we didn't take a touchdown away from Dallas. Now will you please explain this to 'em and let us play the game?"

■ ■ ■

DEATH OF BIG DADDY

Big Daddy Lipscomb was so big his feet stuck out over the end of the autopsy table. Twenty-five years later, many still refuse to believe this 6′6″, 303-pound man mountain killed himself with an overdose of heroin. These include respected people who knew Eugene Alan Lipscomb, good points and bad.

"I talked to everybody involved, and to this day I believe that somebody did that to him," says Steelers president Dan Rooney. "We never had any sign of that [heroin use] and we would have had a sign. He drank, no question about that. But there was never a sign of anything else. What I believe happened is he was drinking, probably fooling around with some girls or whomever. They shot him up figuring he'd be a great guy to get hooked, and he died of an overdose."

Dr. Rudiger Breitenecker has heard the theory off and on since Big Daddy's death May 10, 1963, in Baltimore. Lipscomb's story periodically resurfaces—it's as close to a murder mystery as the NFL gets—and when it does Breitenecker gets a call.

He performed the autopsy. It was his conclusion that the big defensive tackle died of an accidental overdose and that he knew what was going on. Breitenecker hasn't changed his mind, and it doesn't bother him that the other side hasn't either.

"You see, heroes can't die of drug overdoses," he says.

Many of the details of Big Daddy's death are known. On Thursday evening, May 9, 1963, he pitched a doubleheader for a Baltimore softball team and then went to a bar with teammates. Softball and drinking were two of his passions. He was good enough at the first to have played semipro as a high schooler in Detroit. His capacity for the second—usually V.O. straight—was said to be extraordinary.

"He'd pour himself a water glass full and drink it down like most people drink soda pop," said teammate Johnny Sample.

Big Daddy planned to drive his yellow Cadillac convertible to Pittsburgh in a few days and talk contract with the Steelers. He was optimistic about a sizable raise (he'd been selected outstanding lineman in the Pro Bowl). So on this night, he had every reason to be in a good mood.

Big Daddy left his teammates at the bar at about 11:00 P.M. Shortly afterward, he picked up Tim

"Hap" Black outside another bar. Black was a heroin user and later told police he'd purchased the drug for the player on occasion. He and Lipscomb picked up two women and a six-pack of malt liquor and went to Black's apartment on North Brice Street, in a seedy section of the city.

Black told police they took the women home at about 3:00 A.M. and then drove to the Block, a notorious strip of bars and topless joints in downtown Baltimore, to buy heroin. Black purchased about four grams of the drug with $12 Lipscomb provided and they returned to Black's apartment. Black said they cooked the heroin in a wine bottlecap.

Big Daddy, using Black's belt to tie off his arm, then injected the drug (or had it injected) with a makeshift syringe—an eyedropper with needle attached. It was about 5:00 A.M. Almost immediately, he began to convulse. His lips quivered and saliva appeared at the corners of his mouth.

Black recognized what was happening and applied ice to the top of Big Daddy's head and under his testicles, hoping to bring him around. He tried slapping him and Big Daddy sagged out of the chair and onto the floor of Black's dingy little kitchen.

Black said he called for a friend, who injected Lipscomb at least once with a salt water solution (a common street remedy), but there was no response. Finally, at about 7:15 A.M., an ambulance was summoned.

Big Daddy was dead on arrival at Lutheran Hospital.

Suspicion arose almost as soon as news got out that he had overdosed. Steelers physician Raymond Sweeney said he'd never detected evidence of drug use in Lipscomb. He said Big Daddy hated needles and had once turned down a pain-killing injection during a game for that reason.

Friends and teammates concurred. Ex–Colts running back Buddy Young, a close friend, championed Big Daddy's cause. He said Big Daddy never would have taken heroin willingly. Young and others questioned Black's motives and account of what happened. Thus was born the "unwilling participant" theory.

None of this concerned Breitenecker, a 33-year-old Austrian-born pathologist in his second year as assistant medical examiner in Baltimore. He didn't know who Big Daddy Lipscomb was, had never even seen a professional football game. His focus was the large body in front of him.

$$$$$

20 cents	Cost of Gino's (Marchetti) hamburger in 1967
$1.25	Paperback price of Jerry Kramer's *Instant Replay*, 1968
$12	Amount Big Daddy Lipscomb paid for fatal dose of heroin in 1963
$24	Value of Jack Kemp's Topps football card (mint), 1961
$40	Price of Vikings season ticket in 1961
$175	Charge for cleaning Joe Namath's llama-skin rug
$270.62	Charley Hennigan's monthly salary as biology teacher before trying out for Oilers in 1960
$2,000	Fine assessed Paul Hornung and Alex Karras (along with one-year suspension) for gambling in 1963
$2,600	What Packers' first Super Bowl rings were worth, 1967
$15,000	Ernie Davis' signing bonus with Browns in 1962
$40,000	Guarantee for visiting NFL team in 1960
$72,000	Cost of one-minute commercial during NFL game, 1964
$326,000	Annual per-team revenue from NFL TV contract, 1962
$7,100,000	Dan Reeves' winning bid for Rams in 1963
$18,000,000	Indemnities AFL teams paid to merge with NFL

His examination turned up:

- Four needle marks on Lipscomb's right arm and one on his left.
- 10 milligrams of morphine in the bile.
- A blood-alcohol level of .09.
- An alcoholic liver.
- No bruises or cuts.

Big Daddy's liver condition indicated he'd been a heavy drinker for some time. A .09 blood-alcohol level meant he was under the influence but not blind drunk. So there was no way, Breitenecker reasoned, that Big Daddy was passed out or incapacitated when the drug was administered.

The lack of bruises and cuts on the body indicated no violence involved in the death. Big Daddy hadn't been knocked out or held down before the heroin was administered. (Black was small and slight; it's difficult to imagine him forcing Big Daddy to do anything under any circumstances.)

The morphine level was high—roughly five times the therapeutic dose—but not an uncommon level for the street. The conclusion was inescapable. No one had forced Big Daddy to do anything. Black was arrested but charged only with possession of narcotics paraphernalia.

"We never considered making it a homicide," Breitenecker says. The question that's never been answered conclusively is whether Big Daddy had used heroin before the morning he died.

Black told police he first bought heroin for Lipscomb about six months before his death. He said Big Daddy had begun injecting or "mainlining" the drug after his return from the Pro Bowl in San Diego.

Again, Big Daddy's friends and teammates denied the possibility. Indeed, Breitenecker found no evidence of addiction or chronic drug use. The needle mark on the left arm was described in the autopsy report as "recent" and there was evidence it was the site of the injection that killed Lipscomb. Three of the needle marks on his right arm were "very recent." If Black's story about the salt-water injections is true, that could account for them.

The fourth needle mark on the right arm was older, however, and contained cotton fiber, Breitenecker says. Cotton is used to filter heroin as it's being drawn into the syringe. Fibers often show up at the injection site. It's evidence but not proof of previous drug use.

"There's no way to tell what was injected, but we

know that something was," Breitenecker says. "It wasn't just this single incident. There was something earlier also and in a sense one doesn't know how long it's been going on. But you don't know for sure that it was a narcotic that was injected. All you see is the leftover evidence that there was an injection."

What's overlooked in most analyses of Lipscomb's death is the condition of his liver. It was just a matter of time before he was incapacitated. If heroin hadn't killed Big Daddy, alcohol almost certainly would have.

···
HOW GOOD WAS BIG DADDY LIPSCOMB?

SCOUTING REPORT

Height: 6′6″.
Weight: 285–305.
Speed: Excellent. (He once ran down the Lions' Hopalong Cassady after a 57-yard gain and could beat many backs to the corner.)
Notes: Not much of a pass rusher. Didn't come off the ball well. Colts coach Weeb Ewbank tried for years to get him to drive off his back foot. Big Daddy often just stood up. . . . Outstanding tackler. When he got you, you stayed got. Led the Colts in tackles one year, unusual for a defensive tackle. . . . Known to pile on. Broke teammate Gino Marchetti's leg in the '58 championship game that way. . . . Had a reputation as a cheap-shot artist when he was with the Rams (1953–55) but played it pretty straight later in his career. Sometimes used rough stuff to intimidate opponents—especially rookies. Liked to drop in on piles knees first. . . . Great headslap. Wadded his hands and forearms with tape and used them as weapons. Hit Browns guard Jim Ray Smith once, and Smith's knees buckled. The Browns ran the film of the play over and over again for laughs.

Signed as a free agent in '53 out of the Marines. Three teams wanted him. Went with the Rams when PR director Pete Rozelle flew to San Francisco, where Big Daddy was playing in a basketball game. . . . Didn't do much in L.A. Fell asleep in meetings, had money and women troubles. Showed inconsistent effort. The team finally waived him. . . . Picked up by the Colts in '56, and Ewbank made him a project. The coach talked him up to the press and is responsible for much of the Big Daddy mystique. . . . Made two Pro Bowls and two all-league teams in five seasons with Colts but consistently graded lower than other linemen. Wasn't even Baltimore's best tackle: Art Donovan was. . . . Wore out his welcome with his Colts teammates with his style of laying back and making tackles. . . . Crashed white teammate L. G. Dupre's party and a fight broke out. . . . The Colts traded him and OG Buzz Nutter to Pittsburgh in '61 for WR Jimmy Orr, DT Joe Lewis and Dick Campbell. . . . Played well for the Steelers. Was unstoppable in the '63 Pro Bowl: 11 tackles, two forced fumbles, one pass batted down.

Summary: Good player. Great on occasion. Let him make a play early and you'd have your hands full all day. Stick him hard on the first series of each half and you'd probably be OK. Instead of charging hard, Big Daddy usually just floated until he diagnosed the play and then ran it down, so you had to stay with your block on him.

WHAT OTHERS SAY

Art Donovan, Colts defensive tackle: "During the Cleveland game [1959], the Browns turned Big Daddy every which way but loose. I never saw a defensive lineman get blocked from as many directions as Big Daddy was blocked that afternoon. He was screaming and hollering in the defensive huddle, and naturally we're all asking him what the hell they were doing to him. 'They're triple-teaming me! They're quadruple-teaming me!' he cried, a statement that kind of took Ray Krouse and me by surprise. Because if they were triple-teaming Big Daddy, we were wondering where the hell the guys were coming from who were running over us. In truth, Big Daddy never had more than two Browns blocking him in that game. . . .

"On the defensive line he was nothing more than an overgrown kid, and men have a way of handling overgrown kids."

Weeb Ewbank, Colts coach: "He would accept blocks. But he was strong and wouldn't give an inch. He'd hold his ground and stay in his lane. A lot of guys would get irritated with him because they'd be in there flushing the guy out and Big Daddy would

make the tackle. I used to say that although we had a four-man front, we played one of the first three-man lines [because Big Daddy dogged it so much]."

Jack Stroud, Giants guard: "He did a good job on a couple of our rookies in an exhibition game and our regular left guard was hurt, so I went in. I butted him a few times and punched him a few times and he calmed down. But that lulled me to sleep. All of a sudden he swung that fist and hit me alongside the head and he was by me. I couldn't get back in front of him so I chopped his knees out from under him. He fell on me with his knees, one of his favorite tricks. He helped me up and said, 'Did I hurt ya?' I said, 'Big Daddy, you're not big enough to hurt me.' I was still hearing bells."

Harley Sewell, Lions guard: "The last game I played against him was the '63 Pro Bowl, and he whipped my hind end. He did whatever he wanted to. He really made me look bad. I got traded the next year. I always blamed that on Big Daddy. We played him and Pittsburgh the week before the Pro Bowl in that runner-up [Playoff] bowl. I played in front of him in that game, but he didn't play anywhere close to the way he did in the Pro Bowl. There were some other guys—Forrest Gregg and Jim Ringo—who went in for me in the game, and they came out in a few plays and told me I was the designated left guard and I should be in there. That was the first time in my life I was completely overcome and couldn't do anything about it."

■ ■ ■

BIG DADDY SPEAKS

I'm a B and B man—booze and broads.

I didn't mind losing the second wife as much as losing the '56 Mercury to her. I loved that car. It was the first decent car I ever owned.

Say, chum, I wonder if those cats up there on the moon have a football team. If they do, Big Daddy would have himself a ball. And when those scientists look at the planet at night and see somebody making tackles all over the surface, they'll be able to say, "There's the man in the moon, and it's Big Daddy Lipscomb."

When we're on the football field, man, I got a degree, too.

I don't believe in riling the grain. I like a nice, hard game where everybody keeps his blood cool.

New York, New York. So big they had to say it twice.

• • •
THE HORNUNG–KARRAS SUSPENSIONS

The '60s saw the NFL's second major gambling scandal. On April 17, 1963, commissioner Pete Rozelle announced he'd suspended indefinitely two of the game's biggest stars, Green Bay Packers running back Paul Hornung and Detroit Lions defensive tackle Alex Karras, for betting on games and associating with "undesirables."

Rozelle also fined Lions players Wayne Walker, Joe Schmidt, John Gordy, Gary Lowe and Sam Williams $2,000 apiece for betting on the 1962 Packers-Giants championship game. He docked Detroit management—principally coach George Wilson—$4,000 for allowing unauthorized people to sit on the bench during games and not acting on police information quickly enough. A number of unidentified players in the league were reprimanded for playing one-dollar betting cards and making small wagers with friends.

Rozelle's actions were the culmination of a three-and-a-half-month investigation in which players from eight different teams submitted to lie-detector tests. More than 50 were interviewed.

"There is no evidence that any NFL player has given less than his best in playing any game," Rozelle concluded. "There is no evidence that any player has ever bet against his own team. There is no evidence that any NFL player has sold information to gamblers."

That was the good news. The bad news was that Hornung and Karras were gone—for at least a year, anyway.

Hornung was The Golden Boy, a lovable rake who could run, throw, kick and catch. Only Johnny Unitas and Jim Brown enjoyed as much fame in 1963.

But from 1957 to '62, he had regularly discussed upcoming NFL games with a West Coast gambler. He started betting through the gambler—up to $500 on individual college and pro games—in 1959.

Karras didn't have Hornung's magnetism but was probably the better player. At the time of his suspension, he'd been all-pro three straight years and some considered him the best tackle in football.

Rozelle found him guilty of making six "significant" bets between 1958 and '62, one of which was on the Lions. "Significant" in those days meant $50 to $100. The average salary, remember, was about $12,000.

Detroit police also had observed Karras in the company of "known hoodlums" at a restaurant called the Grecian Gardens and a bar named Lindell's A.C. Cocktail Lounge. They notified the Lions, who in turn warned Karras to stay away. The headstrong tackle thumbed his nose at management. In fact he went ahead with plans to buy one-third ownership in the Lindell A.C.

The suspensions so shocked the sports world that the fines against the other Lions and the team were largely overlooked outside Detroit. Today they're all but forgotten.

Schmidt, Gordy, Walker, Lowe and Williams were guilty of a "single violation," according to Ro-

---

NICKNAMES

Jim "Cannonball" Butler	Hornung)
Leslie "Speedy" Duncan	"The Duke" (Gino Cappelletti)
Carlton "Cookie" Gilchrist	"The Catawba Claw" (Bucky
David "Deacon" Jones	Pope)
Ernie "Big Cat" Ladd	Fred "The Hammer"
Walter "Flea" Roberts	Williamson
Noland "Super Gnat" Smith	Julian "Sus" Spence
"Bambi" (Lance Alworth)	Stewart "Smokey" Stover
Austin "Goose" Gonsoulin	Fred "Fuzzy" Thurston
Ron "Dancing Bear" McDole	Edmund "Zeke" Bratkowski
Alex "The Mad Duck" Karras	**Not Nicknames:**
Daryle "The Mad Bomber"	Eagle Day
Lamonica	Fate Echols
Sherman "Tank" Plunkett	Marty Feldman
"Dandy" Don Meredith	Wahoo McDaniel
Len "Daddy Cool Breeze"	**Expedient Nicknames:**
Dawson	Junious "Buck" Buchanan
"The Boomer" (Bob Brown)	Christian "Sonny" Jurgensen
"The Golden Boy" (Paul	Ulmo "Sonny" Randle

zelle. While in Miami for the Playoff Bowl in December 1962, they'd been invited by Karras to watch the NFL title game at a friend's home. There they bet $50 apiece on the Packers. Karras bet $100.

The investigation determined "this was basically a group action, an action of extremely rash judgment but one abnormal for each." For this the players forfeited roughly one-sixth of their '63 salaries (the equivalent of about $50,000 for today's player).

The police information Lions management failed to act on dealt mostly with Karras. Wilson was first told of the tackle's various activities at the Grecian Gardens and Lindell A.C. in August 1962. Nothing was done about it for months.

Among the unauthorized persons allowed on the Detroit bench during games was Jimmy Butsicaris, one of Karras' partners in the Lindell A.C. and a suspected gambler.

The league's investigation began in late December 1962. It was triggered by an unusual number of rumors about players being involved with gamblers. NFL treasurer and ex–FBI man Austin Gunsel was the coordinator. He used the 16 "security" agents the league retained in cities around the country.

The probe was carried out in anything but secrecy. In early January the *Chicago Tribune* ran a story leaked by Bears owner-coach George Halas that the NFL was investigating a prominent player from a Midwestern team (which could have meant Karras *or* Hornung).

It's impossible to say what Halas' motives were, but the story set off a chain reaction around the league and took the heat off his own fullback, Rick Casares, who had already been the subject of gambling rumors. (Casares reportedly took and passed two lie-detector tests.)

Several days after the *Tribune* story appeared, the *Detroit News* revealed that Karras and Gordy had returned from an exhibition game in Cleveland the previous year on a "party bus" owned by friends. The players had Wilson's permission to do so. The trouble was several of their "friends" turned out to be under police surveillance. Two allegedly had ties to organized crime.

The paper also revealed that Walker, a linebacker, and defensive end Darris McCord had been interviewed by Rozelle when the team was in Miami. Rumors started to fly at this point. San Francisco offensive tackle Bob St. Clair was said to be under investigation for his choice of partners in a failed oil-well investment.

On January 16 Karras caused a furor when he admitted in an interview on NBC's *Huntley-Brinkley Report* that he had bet not only on NFL games but on games in which he had played. Rozelle was irate. He ordered Karras to New York for a meeting the next day.

"I got nothing to hide," Karras later told reporters. "The guy [NBC interviewer] asked me a question and I gave him a truthful answer. What did everybody expect me to do . . . lie about it?"

Over the next few weeks, his problems with Lions management over ownership of the Lindell A.C. and dinners at the Grecian Gardens spilled into the papers. General manager Edwin Anderson had warned Karras on several occasions to stay out of the restaurant and not to buy into the bar. Karras had refused.

"Trade me," he told Anderson at one point.

Hornung's name was never mentioned in the sometimes sensational coverage. But a week before Karras sat down with Rozelle, he, too, was called in by the commissioner.

"It was one of the few times I've ever come to New York that I wasn't looking for a date," Hornung wrote in his book *Football and the Single Man.*

Like Karras, Hornung was honest about his activities and admitted to Rozelle what he'd done. The commissioner's primary concern was whether Hornung or Karras had shaved points or fixed a game. Both passed lie-detector tests.

The investigation dragged on through March, and no one knew how Rozelle was going to respond. Hornung later said he felt suspension was a possibility. Karras expected only a fine.

The phone calls came on the morning of April 17. Hornung was at work. His mother answered at the family home in Louisville, Kentucky, and later said Rozelle sounded emotional. When Hornung got the news, he and a close friend decided a round of golf might help him deal with the shock. He was called in off the course to meet with reporters.

"It was a carefree, thoughtless thing I did," he admitted to the press.

Karras was in Detroit. He was furious at the commissioner and reportedly shouted at him during the conversation.

"This is guilt by association and innuendo," he told the media. "I'm not guilty, and I've done nothing to be ashamed of."

Lions management was upset, too. "The commissioner's ruling was slow in coming and rough when got here," owner William Clay Ford said. Ford fired off a telegram to Rozelle. In it he said:

"I consider your fines unduly harsh. You have not helped pro football and locally you have damaged it. It is hard to believe that in the entire National Football League only seven players are guilty of gambling and of these six [are] on the Lions team.

I have read the statements of other club presidents and I can understand why they are glad to be cleared of any allegations.

"Locally, Captain Joe Schmidt and others have suffered personally because they were honest. I only wish other teams and players could make the same statement."

But Rozelle's actions were almost universally praised. He'd acted decisively and forcefully. By suspending big-name stars, he'd made it clear no player would be allowed to compromise the league's integrity. It was tremendous PR, as well as the right thing to do.

The two players handled their suspensions in completely different ways. Hornung admitted his guilt and did everything he could to regain favor. He routinely called Rozelle's office to clear his activities. Was it OK to attend the Kentucky Derby? Could he put his byline on a national magazine piece about the NFL?

He kept busy, too. The suspension didn't affect his lucrative endorsement contract with Jantzen sportswear. He hit the lecture circuit, commanding anywhere from $250 to $750 per speaking engagement. He did radio and TV work for stations in Louisville.

And, of course, there were the evenings. "Women weren't running away from me because of my suspension," he said.

Karras was recalcitrant and remained that way for some time. He tended bar and steadfastly refused to sell his interest in the Lindell A.C., the one thing Rozelle made clear he wanted done.

A local promoter offered him a $40,000 wrestling contract, but he turned it down because of the travel. His one bout, with a wrestler named Dick the Bruiser, was the source of some bad publicity. Several nights before the match, he and the Bruiser were involved in a brawl at the Lindell A.C. Needless to say, the league office was not pleased.

Finally, in late January 1964, Karras relented. He would sell his interest in the bar. By then, he was nearly 20 pounds under his playing weight and genuinely concerned about being reinstated. The pressure was evident in an interview with *Detroit News* columnist Doc Greene:

"Everybody always wanted me to be sorry, I guess, and I am. And I'm tired of it. And I want to play football and well, if I can't I'll have to do something else. But right now I'm sick of that bar and everything, and I'm going back to Iowa [his wife's home] and wait. And hope a little."

In March, Rozelle met with each player and then reinstated them. Both showed the effects of their layoff.

The 1964 season was a nightmare for Hornung. His place-kicking ability deserted him (he made only 12 of 38 field-goal attempts). He also was fined twice by coach Vince Lombardi for rules violations.

He lasted two more seasons and was rarely the player he once was. He had a five-touchdown game against Baltimore in '65 and 105 yards rushing in the NFL championship game that year, but injuries slowed him down. He rushed for only 299 and 200 yards in his final two seasons.

Karras showed some rust in '64 but eventually returned to form. In 1966 he made his fourth and final trip to the Pro Bowl. He played through 1970 and was released during training camp in '71.

■ ■ ■

GOODNIGHT, ALEX

On January 16, 1963, millions of Americans watching NBC's *Huntley-Brinkley Report* heard Alex Karras, the Detroit Lions' all-pro defensive tackle, say he bet on NFL games. The admission brought national attention to a league-wide gambling investigation and no doubt contributed to Karras' one-year suspension from football.

Karras claimed he was quoted out of context. He said he had talked with NBC reporter David Burk for about 40 minutes at the Pro Bowl three days earlier, and only a small portion of the interview had been used. The *Detroit News* published this transcript:

BURK: You don't personally know of any case of point-shavings at all?
KARRAS: I know of none whatsoever in this league. I think the boys play too hard to be shaving points.
BURK: Would you conceive that it is possible to shave points?

KARRAS: I can't even conceive that idea, because it isn't a sport where it is an individual effort. There's 11 football players, both defense and offense, and sure, a quarterback has probably complete control of the ballgame. But so does the referee, so does your best receiver, so does your best defensive tackle. I think it works together more than an individual effort as perhaps boxing or even perhaps basketball.

BURK: Do you admit that some of the people you have been associating with in Detroit are in fact undesirable?

KARRAS: Yes, I do. I suppose that some of the people I have said hello to perhaps I shouldn't have associated with at one time. I say might. Because the way that I met these people is through myself going down to a restaurant [the Grecian Gardens in Detroit] which they hang out at or are supposed to own. I have gone there for five years or so. Naturally I have a bar in Detroit and naturally I can't check everyone's identity who comes into the bar.

BURK: I think you mentioned yesterday that coaches and managers and owners of ball teams and frequently players bet on games. Is that correct?

KARRAS: Well, I don't know if they do or not, but I assume that is going on. I enjoy betting. Naturally, I bet the dogs in Miami. I bet an occasional horse race. I don't bet big money. I don't know how big a lot of them do bet, but I would assume there is betting going on in the league.

(At this point Burk asks him if he has bet on pro football.)

KARRAS: Yes, I have bet on ballgames.

BURK: Have you ever bet on a ballgame in which you were playing?

KARRAS: Yes, I have.

■ ■ ■

NO MATCH FOR THE BRUISER

Two weeks after being suspended from football, Alex Karras appeared in a professional wrestling match against Dick the Bruiser. The Bruiser, a bad guy known for his crazy stunts, pinned him in 11 minutes, 21 seconds. Karras left the arena with teeth marks in his bicep. He should have seen it coming.

Five nights before the match, the Bruiser tore apart Karras' bar in downtown Detroit. It took eight cops to subdue him. They had to cuff his hands and feet.

The Bruiser's given name was Dick Afflis. Before he got serious about a career, he was an offensive lineman for the Green Bay Packers (1951–54). The day before his rampage, the *Detroit Free Press* ran an article in which Karras referred to him as a journeyman football player. The Bruiser didn't appreciate it, and showed up at Karras' bar, the Lindell A.C., to make that clear.

He no sooner walked in the door than the punches started flying. The first two policeman arrived in no time, but they weren't a match for the 6', 250-pounder. One suffered a broken wrist, the other a torn elbow ligament. (Neither knew how to counter a body slam.)

Six more cops arrived, and only then was the Bruiser subdued. Nearby, a television set and vending machine lay in ruins.

Friends kept Karras clear of most of the action. The last thing NFL commissioner Pete Rozelle needed to hear about was a bar fight.

■ ■ ■

NOVEMBER 24, 1963

Pete Rozelle regretted nothing in his 30-year commissionership as much as his decision to allow games to be played two days after the assassination of President Kennedy. He was never more widely criticized, that's for sure. Most big-city columnists came down hard against the move, accusing him and the league of everything from callousness to greed.

The NFL wasn't the only sports organization to carry on that weekend, though. While most events around the country were either canceled or postponed, the Southeastern Conference went ahead with its football schedule the day after Kennedy's death. Wake Forest and North Carolina State played the very night of the assassination.

Pimlico Race Course in Baltimore stayed open. The National Basketball Association and National

Hockey League cut back some but not all of their games. And Nebraska and Oklahoma staged their annual football showdown even though Sooners coach Bud Wilkinson was a personal friend of the president's and a special consultant on physical fitness.

But it was Rozelle who was roasted by the press. In a backhanded way, this was probably a compliment. The attention was further proof of the NFL's tremendous rise in popularity. But how much comfort could that have been as the negative newspaper clippings piled up on the commissioner's desk?

The decision to play was made late Friday afternoon, November 22, after Kennedy was pronounced dead in Dallas. Rozelle seriously reconsidered Saturday night when several owners, among them Cleveland's Art Modell and Pittsburgh's Art Rooney, appealed to him by telephone. But they failed to change his mind.

His logic was that the president would have wanted it this way. It was a conclusion based largely on a phone conversation with White House Press Secretary Pierre Salinger. The rival AFL, on the other hand, put its games off a week.

"It has been traditional in sports for athletes to perform in times of great personal tragedy," Rozelle said. "Football was Mr. Kennedy's game. He thrived on competition."

The idea that greed was the motivating factor didn't make sense. If anything, attendance figured to be well below average for the games, and fans were given the option of turning in tickets for refunds. As for the television money ($320,000), it was guaranteed whether the games were postponed or not. CBS elected not to televise them (or any entertainment programming that day).

The only thing Rozelle was truly guilty of was poor judgment. He argued that it should be left to the individual to decide whether attending a game was disrespectful. But at a time of great national sorrow, he came off looking like an insensitive brute.

He did take care to set forth special guidelines for the games. There were to be no player introductions, halftime shows or music during stoppages in play. There would a silent tribute to the president before each game.

Owners around the league added their own touches. In several cities "Taps" was played during the pregame tribute. In Minnesota, the Vikings distributed 20,000 copies of the "Star Spangled Banner" and played "Auld Lang Syne" at halftime. In Cleveland, Modell instructed his PA announcer to refer to the Browns' opponents only as the "Cowboys." He thought using the word "Dallas" might remind the crowd of the tragedy.

In Los Angeles, there was a rumor that fans would stage a sit-down protest on the 50-yard line, but it failed to materialize. A high school band from Clovis, New Mexico, however, performed at halftime against league policy. Rams owner Dan Reeves gave it the go-ahead after hearing the kids had been practicing over a year and spent two days on a bus to get to L.A.

The majority of the players didn't want to play. Cowboys coach Tom Landry said his team reacted to the assassination "like a big drain plug had been pulled out" of it. At a team meeting Saturday night, the Philadelphia Eagles discussed the possibility of approaching their opponents, the Washington Redskins, about defying the commissioner's order. Sunday morning, New York Giants defensive end Andy Robustelli made an emotional appeal to owner Wellington Mara but was told Rozelle's decision was final.

"I remember having a very hollow feeling," says former Eagle Pete Retzlaff. "By game time, everyone was emotionally drained. Then we lined up and they played 'Taps,' which isn't exactly a fight song. It left you limp. We had no emotion at all, and you don't play the game of football without emotion."

But play they did.

"I feel as bad about it as anybody," said Giants linebacker Sam Huff. "But staying home and moping around wouldn't do any good. Last year, [safety] Jimmy Patton's father died the day before the Dallas game. Nobody can say he didn't grieve, but he played the game. That is our life. The people who don't like it, that's their right. Maybe that's what the president died for."

Rozelle was at least partially vindicated by the turnout. A total of 336,892 attended the seven games, a big weekend in 1963 regardless of the circumstances. There were three sellouts: in New York for the Eastern Conference battle between the first-place Giants and second-place St. Louis Cardinals; in Pittsburgh for the big interconference game between the Steelers and Chicago Bears; and—of all places—in Philadelphia, where the Redskins were playing the Eagles for last place in the East.

What kind of football did the people get for their

HOW MANY SHOWED UP?

NFL ATTENDANCE ON NOV. 24, 1963

New York (Cardinals-Giants)	62,992*
Philadelphia (Redskins-Eagles)	60,671*
Milwaukee (49ers-Packers)	45,905
Pittsburgh (Bears-Steelers)	36,465*
Cleveland (Cowboys-Browns)	55,096
Bloomington (Lions-Vikings)	28,763
Los Angeles (Colts-Rams)	48,555
Total	**336,892**

*sellout

money? It depended on the game. Once the action started, many players were able to put the weekend's events aside for a few hours.

"When all those guys pile on you, you don't have time to think about anything else," Giants quarterback Y. A. Tittle said.

Tittle's team turned the ball over four times in a 24–17 loss to the Cardinals. The Giants had to deal with another emotional jolt when assistant coach Ed Kolman suffered a mild heart attack at halftime.

The Steelers and Bears played to a tough and tense 17–17 tie. Across the state, the Redskins ended a seven-game losing streak by edging the spiritless Eagles, 13–10, and sent the game ball to the White House. Philly owner Frank McNamee skipped the game—the first he'd missed in 15 years—to attend a memorial service for Kennedy at Independence Hall.

In Milwaukee, Bart Starr returned to the lineup after missing five weeks with a broken hand and directed the Green Bay Packers to a 28–10 victory over the San Francisco 49ers. Elsewhere, the Browns beat the Cowboys, 27–17, to create a three-way tie for first in the East; a Danny Villanueva field goal pushed the Rams past the Baltimore Colts, 17–16; and, in the most exciting game, the Vikings rallied in the fourth quarter to down the Detroit Lions, 34–31.

Rozelle attended the Giants–Cardinals game. Well after it ended, he sat at a table in the press room of darkened Yankee Stadium and talked with reporters about the day's events.

He allowed that had either Washington or Dallas

been scheduled to play at home his decision might have been different. But they hadn't, and he stood by his judgment.

"Everyone has a different way of paying respects," he said. "I went to church, and I imagine many of the people at the games did, too. I cannot feel that playing the game was disrespectful."

In time he thought differently.

■ ■ ■

POLLING THE PRESS

In times of national bereavement I think our toys should be put aside.

—JIMMY CANNON

The commissioner's sense of decency, respectability and reverence will measure up to that of any of his detractors.

He easily could have postponed the games, and nothing would have been made of the incident. But he chose to leave it up to the conscience of the public. The people, not Rozelle, made the choice.

—MO SIEGEL, *Washington Star*

A football game at that particular time had the general flavor of a sick joke and it tended to symbolize the frightening trend toward self-indulgence in our culture.

—MELVIN DURSLAG, *Los Angeles Herald Examiner*

For the first time since I began writing about games and the people who play them, I am ashamed of this fatuous dreamland.

—SANDY GRADY, *Philadelphia Inquirer*

Maybe it's important to determine whether the St. Louis Cardinals can upset the Giants in Yankee Stadium Sunday, whether the Bears can push on against the Steelers in Pittsburgh. There's a race to be finished and there's money to be invested. Money.

—RED SMITH, *New York Herald Tribune*

Today, most of the 62,000 who hold tickets for Yankee Stadium will be there, and they will rise and say

heir silent prayer, each man in his own way. Then
he football game will start; there will be a mighty
roar, and the world will go on.

—DICK YOUNG, *New York Daily News*

Sunday's game seemed silly and frivolous and was
very poorly played. . . . Football players are aware
of events, too. Playing a game while the nation is in
mourning did not seem to them of the highest importance, either.

—BUD SHRAKE, *Dallas Morning News*

FIGHT OF THE DECADE

Even after all these years, members of the 1963 Philadelphia Eagles are reluctant to talk about the Ben
Scotti–John Mellekas incident. It was that ugly.

On November 23—one day after President John
Kennedy's assassination and the night before a game
with the Washington Redskins—Scotti punched
Mellekas senseless after a team meeting at the Shera-
ton Motor Inn in Philadelphia. Both men had to be
hospitalized for several days, Mellekas for facial injuries, Scotti for severely cut hands (a tendon in his
right hand had to be surgically repaired). "It was a
bloody mess," one eyewitness said of the scene.

Eagles management investigated the matter and
wound up waiving Scotti, a starting cornerback.
Mellekas, a defensive tackle, was fined $500 but
played the following week. He finished the season
with the Eagles and retired.

Exactly what happened remains unclear. The '63
Eagles weren't a happy lot to begin with. The team
had talent but had been hit by injuries and was
struggling through a 2–10–2 season. Dissension was
a problem.

Scotti's version came out shortly after the incident in a prize-winning story by the *New York Post*'s
Milton Gross. It painted him in a noble light as a
man who objected to an ethnic slur and wouldn't
back down from a bigger teammate.

Mellekas refused comment. Today, he still won't
go into much detail other than to refute key parts of
Scotti's story. "It makes me sick to think about," he
says. "I was with two other teams and never had any

trouble. I played seven years and that [the fight] is
what I'm remembered for."

Teammates aren't much help. Some say they
don't remember details, others come right out and
say they'd prefer not to talk about it. Certainly it was
an odd match. Scotti had a reputation for being a
tough, hot-tempered player, but Mellekas was low-
key and fairly popular. Though not close friends, the
two had socialized on occasion.

According to Gross' story, the main topic of discussion at the players-only meeting was the Kennedy assassination. Most of the players were upset
about having to play a game the following day.

At one point, defensive end Bill Quinlan referred
to commissioner Pete Rozelle as "that guinea bas-
tard" for his decision to go ahead with the schedule.
Scotti, of Italian descent, objected to the slur. Mellekas jumped in on Quinlan's side, and the two had
a heated exchange.

"You're not so tough," Mellekas reportedly said
at one point. "I've had about as much of you as I'm
going to take."

"I'll fight you right here in front of the team,"
Scotti responded.

The two were separated and after the meeting
broke up went to another room, closed the door and
had it out. According to Gross, the 250-pound Mellekas was left with a broken nose, black eyes and
many of his teeth "strewn in his blood." The 185-
pound Scotti's hands were sliced up as he punched
out those teeth.

"I just don't go for that guinea, kike, black stuff,"
Scotti told Gross. "People are people. I let all my
anger of the whole year and everything else out on
him. I knocked him down, and I stood over him and
worked him over."

Mellekas denies calling Scotti a guinea and says
the fight was not over the Kennedy assasination or
Rozelle. "It was just a misunderstanding, let's leave
it at that," Mellekas says. "I was called a dumb
Greek all the time. That's just locker room stuff. The
guy [Scotti] is a wacko."

Mellekas says the fight took place in a hallway,
not a room, and that Scotti sucker-punched him
when he was putting money into a vending machine
(a detail supported by accounts in the Philadelphia
papers and several teammates).

"He must have caught me in the temple because
the next thing I knew I woke up in the hospital,"
Mellekas said.

The damage wasn't nearly as great as reported by Gross, either. Mellekas said he needed "about eight stitches" to close several cuts and suffered one broken tooth. He says Scotti came into his hospital room and apologized.

"I was out cold, but my wife was there and she said he saw me and started crying and apologizing," Mellekas said.

FEAST OR FAMINE

The 1963 Kansas City Chiefs finished 5–7–2 but outscored their opponents by 84 points, a record for a losing team. They did this by winning their games by 52, 21, 31, 32 and 48 points. Average margin: 36.8.

KEITH LINCOLN'S GAME OF GAMES

We don't usually go gaga over feats from the AFL's early years, but the performance San Diego's Keith Lincoln put on in the 1963 title game is an exception. Lincoln gained 328 yards from scrimmage against Boston—205 rushing, 123 receiving—and completed a pass for 20 more.

Only one pro running back has ever gained more yards from scrimmage in a game. That would be Houston's Billy Cannon, who totaled 330 (216 rushing, 114 receiving) against the New York Titans in 1961.

But that was hardly a championship game. The Titans were terrible defensively (so terrible they changed their name to the Jets the next year). Also, Cannon had 30 rushes and receptions; Lincoln had 20.

Heck, Lincoln had 242 yards *in the first half.* The second time he touched the ball he ran 56 yards, the next time he went 67. The Chargers exploded along with him, running up a 51–10 score against a Patriots defense that had held them to 24 points in two previous games.

The day wasn't perfect in every way for Lincoln.

Early in the game he became ill on the bench. After which he said, "They won't catch me now."

They didn't.

How he did it (the figures on the left are down distance and yard line):

FIRST QUARTER

1-10-SD28	12 yards, pass
1-10-SD40	56 yards, run
2-18-SD33	67 yards, run (TD)
3-6-SD31	11 yards, run
1-10-SD20	Long completion to Lance Alworth nullified by penalty
1-15-SD15	Loss of 5 yards, run
2-20-SD10	8 yards, pass
3-12-SD18	3 yards, run

SECOND QUARTER

2-2-SD34	44 yards, run
1-10-B22	11 yards, pass
2-7-SD32	11 yards, pass
2-9-SD44	24 yards, pass

Halftime totals: Rushing, 6-176; receiving, 5-66; total, 11-242.

THIRD QUARTER

3-7-SD23	32 yards, pass
1-10-B45	Loss of 3 yards, run
1-10-SD30	No gain, run
2-10-SD30	10 yards*, run
1-10-SD40	8 yards, run
3-10-B49	3 yards, run

FOURTH QUARTER

1-10-SD30	3 yards, run
4-2-B25	25 yards, pass (TD)
1-10-SD20	8 yards, run
2-2-SD28	Pass to Jacque MacKinnon, 20 yards

Game totals: Rushing, 13-205; receiving, 7-123; passing, 1-1-20. Yards from scrimmage: 328. Total offense: 348.

*The record book gives Lincoln 206 yards rushing and 329 from scrimmage, but it's a yard off. The mistake was made on this play. It was originally recorded as an 11-yard gain, then crossed out and changed to 10. The line of scrimmage on the next play is the 40, so the corrected figure must be right.

'60s MYTHOLOGY

In the spring of 1964 Jim Ringo, Green Bay's great center, brought an agent along when he went to negotiate a new contract with Vince Lombardi. Lombardi, who hated agents, excused himself from the room and was gone for a few minutes. When he returned, he told Ringo's agent: "I'm afraid you're negotiating with the wrong man. Jim Ringo has just been traded to the Philadelphia Eagles."

This classic story first appeared in *Instant Replay,* the book by Ringo's Packers teammate, Jerry Kramer. Ringo suspects Lombardi might have told it to the players to discourage them from getting agents.

Ringo claims he had no agent. He also says he didn't deal with Lombardi. As he tells it, he went to assistant general manager Pat Peppler, told him how much money he was looking for and said he wanted to be traded if he didn't get it. Later, Peppler called and told him he'd been traded to Philadelphia.

"I didn't see Vince in person for another five years after that happened," Ringo says in *Iron Men.* "We ran into each other when I was coaching for the Bears and he was with Washington. It was a very emotional moment. We embraced, and he told me, 'You're where you belong Ringo . . . but remember, this is a tough business.' "

It *is* a little hard to believe that Lombardi could have made the trade so quickly. True, Joe Kuharich, the Eagles' new coach, was in a wheeling-and-dealing mode, but trades of this magnitude usually take a little time.

Green Bay also sent fullback Earl Gros, its first-round draft choice in 1962, to Philadelphia. The Eagles gave up an outstanding young linebacker, Lee Roy Caffey, and their number-one pick in 1965, which the Packers used to select halfback Donny Anderson.

* * *

Ben Davidson broke Joe Namath's jaw in the 1967 Oakland–New York Jets game.

Almost everything you hear about the Raiders' archvillain is true, but not this. It was the team's other defensive end, Ike Lassiter, who was responsible. And he broke Namath's *cheek,* not his jaw.

The game was played December 17 at the Oakland Coliseum. Late in the fourth quarter, Davidson made a spectacular hit that sent Namath one direction and his helmet another. Photos of it were published in newspapers across the country.

When postgame X-rays showed Namath's cheek to be broken, most people simply assumed Davidson had done it. Overlooked was the even harder shot Lassiter landed in the third quarter. He whacked Namath with a wicked forearm upside the head that put the Jets quarterback flat on his back.

"You could hear that hit all over the stadium," Lassiter says.

There's never been any doubt in the Raiders camp who did the damage. Davidson caught Namath with two fists under the jaw, which accounts for the helmet flying off but not the fracture. Lassiter's blow landed on the right side of the head, just over Joe's two-bar facemask and the area of the break.

"I've never denied that it was him," Davidson says, "and I think Ike resents the fact that I got the publicity."

There's a bit of that in Lassiter. "I never made a big deal of it because I didn't care," he says. "I think sometimes Ben feels guilty because he gets all the credit and didn't do all the work."

Namath, by the way, didn't leave the game after either hit. He played the next week with a new half-cage facemask.

■ ■ ■

THE FIRST SOCCER-STYLIST

Hungarian-born Pete Gogolak was perfect for the role of pro football's first soccer-style kicker—accurate, strong-legged and a little weird.

He had this thing about his hair. He even combed it before he put his helmet on.

He began his career in Buffalo in 1964, and the Bills had a tradition called "branding," where veterans barbered rookies' heads in odd ways. Gogolak refused to let anyone touch him and nearly came to blows with 250-pound Cookie Gilchrist. Coach Lou Saban intervened and prevented a massacre.

The Bills drafted Gogolak in the 12th round.

There's a story—probably just that—about personnel director Harvey Johnson's trip to Cornell to scout him.

"I stood off to the side and told him go ahead and kick a few," Johnson said. "He said, 'Excuse me.' I was standing right where he starts his approach."

The new style actually caused very little fuss. The *Buffalo Evening News* ran a series of photos illustrating it during training camp. But people just seemed happy that Gogolak could get the ball through the uprights. The team had gone through six kickers in its first four seasons with terrible results.

Gogolak made his professional debut August 8 in an exhibition game against the Jets. His first field-goal attempt—from 31 yards—was good. On the last play of the game, he hit from 57 yards, one better than the existing pro record. The kicking revolution was underway.

Gogolak was terrific in his first two seasons in Buffalo: 102 points as a rookie, 115 in 1965. But had it not been for the merger in June 1966, he might have been remembered for a lot more than his kicking.

In May 1966 he jumped leagues, signing a three-year contract worth about $100,000 with the New York Giants. It made him the highest-paid kicking specialist in NFL history. It also touched off a brief but fierce bidding war. The AFL retaliated by signing big-name NFL stars such as Roman Gabriel and John Brodie. Things were starting to heat up when the merger was announced.

■ ■ ■

FACEMASK-FREE IN 1964

Jesse Richardson played defensive tackle without a facemask for 12 pro seasons and didn't lose a single tooth. Seems like that should be some kind of record.

Richardson wasn't the last pro player to disdain the mask—that was probably wide receiver Tommy McDonald—but he certainly was the last lineman. He played for the Philadelphia Eagles from 1953 to '61 and the AFL's Boston Patriots for three seasons after that, a span of years in which the cage-style mask became the norm for linemen.

All except Jesse. He got special permission from commissioner Bert Bell to continue playing *au naturel* after facemasks were made mandatory and stuck it out to the end. Somehow, he kept all his teeth in his head.

"Every one of them was his own, and yes, it is remarkable," says Dorothy Richardson, his wife. "It was his nose that took the beating. He must have broken it at least 10 times. It got to the point where he used to set it himself. He'd put a little Vaseline on his finger, stick it up his nose and just put it back in place again."

Richardson, who died in 1974, was an underrated player. You don't hear much about him, but he was 6'2", 270, and had good quickness. He spent most of his career at left tackle and was a Pro Bowl selection in 1960, the Eagles' championship season.

But he was known primarily for his maskless helmet. He refused to change because he had deepset, narrow eyes and was afraid his peripheral vision would be affected.

"You know and I know that probably isn't true, but it was the way he wanted to play," Dorothy Richardson says. "It's like these people who do free falls with parachutes. They're nuts as far as I'm concerned, but it's what they do. I looked at it as an occupational hazard. Jesse just didn't want to feel hampered. He didn't wear thigh pads either."

McDonald played through 1966 and was maskless most of the time. There's a photo of him catching a pass with the Eagles in '62 wearing a helmet with a single bar. His explanation:

"Sometimes I'd crack mine [helmet], and the Eagles didn't have a replacement for me. So I had to borrow one from a teammate. I had a very small head, 6¾. I'd take a towel, or half a towel, and stuff it in there to make it fit. That's the only time I'd have a facemask."

■ ■ ■

COACH-FOR-LIFE

Coaching contracts got crazy in the '60s and early '70s. Six head men—Tom Landry of Dallas, Joe Kuharich of Philadelphia, Allie Sherman of the New York Giants, Lou Saban of Denver, Bill Peterson of Houston and Hank Stram of Kansas City—were given deals of 10 years or longer.

Only Landry lasted even five seasons. Three of

the coaches never had a winning year during the contract. One won just one game.

The owners learned their lesson. Such long-term agreements are rare today. The only coach so blessed is the Cowboys' Jimmy Johnson, and he's buddies with the boss. A rundown of the six 10-year-or-more pacts:

■ **Landry, 10-year extension (February 5, 1964)—** He still had a year left on the five-year contract he signed when the team was founded in '60. What was amusing was there were rumors Pittsburgh's Buddy Parker was going to replace him. Dallas was coming off a 4–10 season, down from 5–8–1 in '62, and Landry was catching some flak. Owner Clint Murchison put an end to that. "We've been trying to get Tom to sign this contract for a couple of years," he said. "He didn't know whether he liked us. I guess we finally wore him down."

Reported value of contract: None (estimated: $500,000). Regular-season record during contract: 98–40–2 (10 years).

■ **Kuharich, 15 years (December 9, 1964)—**This was actually a contract to be the Eagles' general manager. He already had a four-year coaching deal that had three years to run. But obviously he could continue to coach as long as he was the GM. Owner Jerry Wolman was wild about him. In Kuharich's first season, the team improved from 2–10–2 to 6–8. "This must be the way Sutter felt when he found all that gold in 1849," Kuharich said when the agreement was announced. Philly went 9–5 in 1966, but two years later the fans were organizing a "Joe Must Go" campaign. He was fired after Leonard Tose bought the club in '69. Tose still had to pay him 11 years' salary.

Reported value of contract: $900,000. Record: 22–34–1 (four years).

■ **Sherman, 10 years (July 26, 1965)—**After three straight Eastern Conference titles, the Giants slumped to 2–10–2 in 1964. Sherman was rewarded with a 10-year contract by acting president Wellington Mara. (He was already working on a five-year deal signed in '63.) The team never finished above .500 again under Sherman, and Yankee Stadium crowds soon were serenading him with choruses of "Goodbye, Allie." He was canned during training camp in '69.

Reported value of contract: $400,000. Record: 22–33–1 (four years).

■ **Saban, 10 years (December 19, 1966)—**Travelin' Lou left Buffalo in 1965 after two straight AFL championships to become coach at Maryland. But Denver owner Gerry Phipps brought him back to the AFL by offering him "a contract that knocked my eyes out," Saban said. It was a combination coach-GM job. Saban was unable, however, to work

DECADE ALL-STAR TEAM

For skill position players and defensive backs, figures under "Data" are average season totals; for specialists, they're decade totals (except where indicated).

OFFENSE		
Pos. Player	**Years***	**Data**
WR Lance Alworth	8	57 catches, 1,122 yds, 10 TDs; 7-time all-star
TE Mike Ditka	9	41 catches, 573 yds., 5 TDs; 5 Pro Bowls
T Forrest Gregg	10	8 Pro Bowls
G Jim Parker	8	6 Pro Bowls
C Jim Ringo	8	7 Pro Bowls
G Gene Hickerson	9	5 Pro Bowls
T Bob Brown	6	4 Pro Bowls
QB Johnny Unitas	10	55.3%, 2,655 yds, 18 TDs; 7 Pro Bowls
FB Jim Brown	6	1,419 yds., 5.3 avg., 11 TDs; 6 Pro Bowls
HB Gale Sayers	5	973 yds., 5.1 avg., 8 TDs; 4 Pro Bowls
WR Otis Taylor	5	41 catches, 763 yds, 7 TDs; 1 all-star game

DEFENSE		
Pos. Player	**Years**	**Data**
E Deacon Jones	9	6 Pro Bowls
T Merlin Olsen	8	8 Pro Bowls
T Bob Lilly	9	7 Pro Bowls
E Willie Davis	10	5 Pro Bowls
LB Dick Butkus	5	5 Pro Bowls
LB Bobby Bell	7	6-time all-star
LB Chuck Howley	9	5 Pro Bowls
CB Herb Adderley	9	4 interceptions; 5 Pro Bowls
CB Willie Brown	7	4 interceptions; 5-time all-star
S Larry Wilson	10	4 interceptions; 7 Pro Bowls
S Willie Wood	10	4 interceptions; 7 Pro Bowls

SPECIALISTS AND OTHER SELECTIONS		
Pos. Selection	**Years**	**Data**
KR Travis Williams	3	27.7 avg., 5 TDs
PR Leroy Kelly	6	16.8 avg., 3 TDs before becoming regular HB
K Jan Stenerud	3	78 FGs in 3 seasons, 70.3% made
P Yale Lary	5	Averaged 48.4 in 1961, 48.9 in '63
S.T. -- Dave Meggyesy	**Wild Card Selection** -- Bobby Mitchell	
Enforcer -- Ben Davidson	**Coach** -- Vince Lombardi	

*Number of years he played in the decade.   S.T. = Special Teams

the wonders he had with the Bills. The best he could do was 5–8–1 in '69 and '70. Nine games into the '71 season, he quit.

Reported value of contract: $500,000. Record: 20–42–3 (four-plus years).

■ **Peterson, 10 years plus a 5-year option (December 23, 1971)**—Previously a successful coach at Florida State, he'd just completed a 3–8 season in his first year at Rice when Houston owner Bud Adams came calling. The Oilers were bad, but Peterson was worse. Nineteen games games later, he was gone.

Reported value of contract: $1.25 million (including option). Record: 1–18 (one-plus years).

■ **Stram, 10 years (January 28, 1972)**—He was the only coach the club had ever had, and Kansas City had just completed a 10–3–1 season. "From an age evaluation standpoint [Stram was 48] it seemed logical to go to a longer contract," owner Lamar Hunt said. Stram also was given the title of vice-president for team operations. But while he was still young, the Chiefs were getting old. Their victory total dropped to eight in 1972, seven in '73 and five in '74, after which Stram was sent packing.

Reported value of contract: $1 million (at least). Record: 20–20–2 (three years).

■ ■ ■

BUCKY POPE

Frank Buckley Pope III—otherwise known as Bucky—had just one healthy season in the NFL, but it was a season to remember. As a rookie with the Rams in 1964, he averaged an astonishing 31.4 yards on 25 receptions, the second-best receiving average in league history (minimum: 24 catches).

He also tied for the NFL lead with 10 touchdown receptions. Nobody else on the 5–7–2 club had more than two. His longest measured 95, 70, 68, 65, 55 and 48 yards. (He also had nonscoring gains of 67, 50 and 48.)

All this was accomplished in nine games. He didn't catch a pass in the other five. Who knows what he could have done if Bill Munson and Roman Gabriel, the Rams' young quarterbacks, had done a better job of getting him the ball.

Pope was a 6′5″ former basketball player from

Pittsburgh who didn't even go out for football in high school. He agreed to play the sport at Catawba (North Carolina) College only after the coach assured him that, as a split end, he wouldn't have to block or tackle.

The Rams drafted him in the seventh round. "The Catawba Claw" quickly became a local hero. Against the Lions in the second game, he bent over backward to pull in an underthrown pass from Munson, landed flat on his back, got up and ran the rest of the way for a score, a 65-yard play.

L.A. Times columnist Sid Ziff called it "one of the most phenomenal catches of all time."

Rams coach Harland Svare said, "We may never see another like it."

That was just the beginning. Season highlights:

■ **49ers**—Scored three touchdowns in second quarter to turn 7–7 game into 28–7 rout.

■ **Packers**—Started winning rally with 55-yard TD grab late in first half.

■ **Eagles**—Acrobatic 31-yard reception and another of 48 yards led to 10 points.

■ **Bears**—TDs of 12 and 14 yards, the first set up by his own 50-yard catch.

■ **Colts**—21-yard TD for team's only points.

■ **Packers II**—Gave Rams 7–0 lead with 95-yard score and set up second TD with 17-yard run on end-around.

Ziff said Pope "could wind up the biggest favorite the Rams have had since Elroy Hirsch." For some reason, however, Bucky didn't make the Pro Bowl. His peers preferred another rookie, the 49ers' Dave Parks, who scored fewer touchdowns (eight) and gained fewer yards (703 to 786). Go figure.

Alas, that was the best of Bucky Pope. He suffered a knee injury the next year, missed the whole season and caught only eight passes the rest of his career. Three went for touchdowns.

■ ■ ■

YOU'RE FIRED!

Cookie Gilchrist was leading the AFL in rushing 10 weeks into the 1964 season when the Buffalo Bills fired him. For a day, anyway.

Oakland's Al Davis considered Gilchrist "the best all-around back in football." In the AFL, maybe. The 6′3″, 250-pound fullback was the league's first 1,000-yard rusher in 1962 and fell just short of that figure in '63.

But he was as temperamental as he was talented. He'd asked to be traded the previous spring because he didn't think the Bills gave him the ball enough. He then reported to training camp late and skipped several more practices. His blocking for quarterback Jack Kemp was suspect, too.

He ran out of chances in a November loss to Boston. Upset that he'd carried only five times in the first half, he told backup Willie Ross to take his place late in the second quarter.

Gilchrist and coach Lou Saban had words at half-time. Two days later Saban put him on waivers. Any team could claim him for $100, and three did—the Raiders, Patriots and New York Jets.

Before the waiver period expired, however, Kemp talked some sense into Gilchrist. He got Cookie to apologize to the team—personally and then on television (the latter took three takes).

"I acted impulsively," Gilchrist admitted.

His teammates asked Saban to recall him, and the coach agreed. Gilchrist wound up taking the rushing title again with 981 yards. He also had a game-high 122 yards as Buffalo beat San Diego for the championship.

It was his last game as a Bill. In the off-season Saban dealt him to Denver for fullback Billy Joe.

■ ■ ■

THE DANGER OF TRYING TO RUN UP THE SCORE

Pro Bowls tend to be passive affairs, but that wasn't the case in 1965. Cleveland quarterback Frank Ryan came out of the game with a dislocated shoulder courtesy of Baltimore defensive end Gino Marchetti, who'd been quoted saying a few days before that he wanted "one more shot" at Ryan.

Marchetti thought Ryan had tried to make the Colts look bad at the end of the NFL championship game two weeks earlier. What happened was this:

The Browns were leading 27–0 and had the ball at the Baltimore 16 with 26 seconds left when their fans stormed the field and tore down the goal posts.

The officials decided to call the game right there, and the Colts were amenable. But Ryan protested. He wanted to score another touchdown.

In the third quarter of the Pro Bowl, Marchetti got even. He, Merlin Olsen and Roger Brown broke through the line and buried Ryan, who had to be helped from the field.

Marchetti's comment afterward was: "Yes, sir, I was in on the tackle. And I'd say it was a pretty good tackle."

Lions linebacker Wayne Walker, who played on Marchetti's West team, wrote all about it in the *Detroit News.* The Colts, his column read, "got satisfaction in the Pro Bowl, and Marchetti was the man who was in on it, although he didn't want things to turn out quite the way they did.

"It was a clean, hard shot, nothing dirty. Gino just wanted to let Ryan know he was around. I guess Frank will remember, all right."

Ryan, who also got a pretty good bump on the head, was a little fuzzy following the game. "I don't remember a thing," he said. Back home in Houston, however, he was more talkative.

"I don't think the Colts had any reason to get upset," he said. "After all, they didn't hold back in their 52–0 rout of the Chicago Bears earlier in the season. But no one heard the Bears complaining.

"Sure I wanted to call one [more] play. The object of the game is to score points. We've got a slot end named Johnny Brewer. He's a fine player, but he hasn't gotten much acclaim. I wanted to give him the opportunity to score in the championship game, but I guess the Colts interpreted it as an attempt to belittle or embarrass them.

"There were three quotes in three different Los Angeles papers. In each one Marchetti said he wanted one more shot at me. He's supposed to be a good ballplayer. He didn't get within breathing distance of me in the championship game. Maybe that had something to do with the way he felt."

Unfortunately for Ryan, he never got *his* revenge because Marchetti retired after the Pro Bowl. He came back to play for the Colts in 1966, but the Browns weren't on their schedule that year.

■ ■ ■

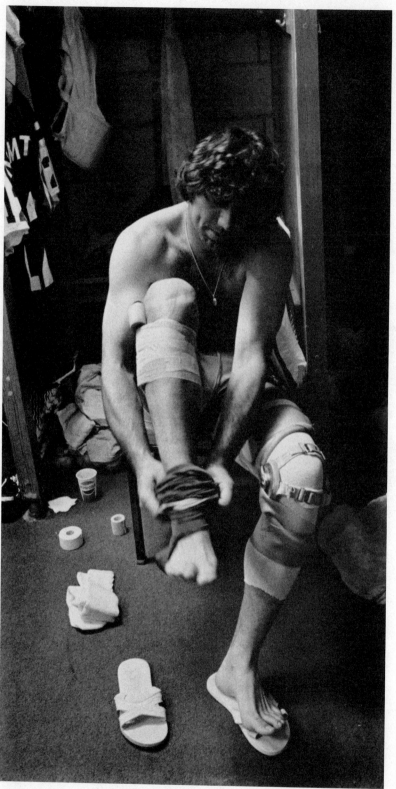

Namath's knees—as famous as his right arm. (Herb Weitman/St. Louis)

JOE NAMATH'S KNEE SURGERIES

1. **Date:** January 25, 1965, three weeks after signing with the Jets.
   Age: 21.
   Knee: Right.
   Procedure: Major surgery. Torn medial cartilage was removed; damaged medial collateral ligament was tightened (shortened).
   Notes: Namath originally hurt the knee during his senior year at Alabama. Some critics have accused coach Bear Bryant of ruining it by playing him in the Orange Bowl. That's unfair. Namath appeared in the Senior Bowl one week later and threw 38 passes. There was no hurry to operate.

2. **Date:** December 28, 1966.
   Age: 23.
   Knee: Right.
   Procedure: Major surgery. Torn lateral cartilage was removed; tendon attached to the kneecap was rerouted to strengthen the inside of the knee.
   Notes: Reinjured the joint in an exhibition game but played the entire season. There was already evidence of arthritis.

3. **Date:** March 20, 1968.
   Age: 24.
   Knee: Left.
   Procedure: Major surgery. Torn tendon below the kneecap was repaired.
   Notes: Namath now had two bad knees.

4. **Date:** August 8, 1971.
   Age: 28.
   Knee: Left.
   Procedure: Major surgery/complete reconstruction. Torn medial collateral and anterior cruciate ligaments were rebuilt; torn medial cartilage was removed.
   Notes: Namath blew out the knee trying to tackle Detroit Lions linebacker Mike Lucci in an exhibition game. Knee injuries don't get much worse than this.

5. **Date:** November 9, 1976.
   Age: 33.
   Knee: Right.
   Procedure: Arthroscopic examination. Nam-

ath's mobility was so limited at this point he'd lost his starting job to Richard Todd. He walked with a constant limp. The exam confirmed what everyone suspected: The knee was badly arthritic. Retirement was just over a year away.

• • •
. . . AND A SIDE ORDER OF BACON

Ernie Ladd had an appetite to match his 6′9″, 315-pound frame. Or to put it another way, his portions were in proportion.

The legendary defensive tackle rewrote the caloric record book during his eight-year AFL career with San Diego, Houston and Kansas City. His crowning achievement came in 1965 when he was invited to a charity pancake-eating contest.

He ate 124.

What's even more remarkable is that he didn't win. It was a two-man team competition—except for Ladd. He was a team unto himself.

"If I hadn't been late, I think I still could have won," he says. "They had already started when I got there, and I was only four or five behind at the end. And they [the other contestants] were going to the bathroom and throwing up, too."

Ladd spent the rest of the day trying to come down from the sugar buzz induced by six containers of syrup. "Worst drunk I've ever had," he says.

• • •
PAYDAY

The Atlanta Mustangs were taken over by the Southern Professional Football League just one game into their existence in 1965. Owner William Westcott, a local investment banker, wasn't meeting his financial obligations.

In their second game, the Mustangs pulled a 15–7 upset at Jacksonville. For this they received an unexpected reward. Westcott showed up afterward and told the coaches and players he wanted to pay them.

The gesture "overwhelmed us," coach Jerry Wilcoxon said.

When Wilcoxon went to take care of the team's hotel bill, however, the clerk noticed something funny about the money. All the serial numbers were the same.

Westcott was arrested by the Secret Service for distributing about $2,500 in counterfeit $20 bills.

• • •
CONSIDER IT DON'S

Fumble recoveries is an obscure category, so it's only fitting that a lesser light should hold the NFL record for opponents' fumbles recovered in a season.

Joe Schmidt had eight recoveries one year (1955), and Alan Page (1970) and Jack Lambert (1976) both had seven, but Don Hultz beat 'em all. Hultz had *nine* for the Vikings in 1963.

He was a rookie that season, a free agent defensive end out of Southern Mississippi. (His brother George, a defensive tackle, played for the Cardinals in 1962.) In his second game, Hultz fell on a fumble by the Bears' Willie Galimore. The loose balls kept on bouncing his way.

Soon his teammates were calling him "The Magnet." The newspapers began to notice, too. After he got number six, the *Minneapolis Tribune* reported: "His fumble recovery play is now an integral part of the Viking offense."

Indeed, six of Hultz's recoveries set up scores (two touchdowns, four field goals). Three got the Vikings on the board first, while another, with four and a half minutes to go against Detroit, led to the game-winning TD.

That was his eighth recovery, tying Schmidt's mark. The record became his when he pounced on a fumble by Philadelphia's Sonny Jurgensen in the season finale.

"I just happen to be there when another one of our guys is shaking somebody up," said Hultz, who considered his feat an accident. "I don't go hunting for the ball. I try to be alert, but you can say the same thing about anybody else on our defensive line.

"I don't have much of a history for this sort of thing. I played on defense and offense at Southern Mississipi, and if I do say so, I caught a couple of touchdown passes. But fumbles? Not much."

Hultz was traded to the Eagles the next season—the Vikings had drafted Carl Eller—and played 11 more years, finishing with the Bears in 1974. He recovered only three more fumbles.

· · ·

GROUNDED

Only once in NFL history have both teams finished with negative passing yardage in a game. Amazingly, the weather wasn't much of a factor. Even more amazingly, the teams were Vince Lombardi's Green Bay Packers and Tom Landry's Dallas Cowboys.

It happened on October 24, 1965, in Milwaukee—before a record County Stadium crowd of 48,311, no less. The sun was out, and temperatures were in the low 40s. The *Milwaukee Sentinel* described the conditions as "cool," the *Dallas Morning News* as "chilled." Guess it depended on where you were from.

The Packers' Bart Starr completed just 4 of 19 passes for 42 yards and was sacked 5 times for 52 yards in losses, leaving him with minus 10 passing yards. The Cowboys' Craig Morton hit 10 of 20 passes for 61 yards but was sacked 10 times for 62 yards in losses—a net of minus one.

These were two good teams. The Pack won the first of three straight NFL championships that year, and the Cowboys placed second in the Eastern Conference. But their passing attacks went poof on this day.

"I can't remember when Bart Starr has had a worse day moving the team," said Lombardi, whose club wound up winning, 13–3.

· · ·

WAR AND PEACE

For several weeks before the 1966 merger, the NFL and AFL appeared on the verge of all-out war. The NFL started it when the New York Giants signed Buffalo kicker Pete Gogolak. The AFL retaliated by signing as many as 25 NFL players to contracts for the next season, including Roman Gabriel, John Brodie, Mike Ditka, John David Crow, Dave Parks, Jim Ninowski, Rudy Bukich and possibly Paul Hornung.

Had the hostilities not ceased, Pete Rozelle might have been gone as NFL commissioner. That was the rumor, anyway.

The trouble started April 7, 1966, when Oakland Raiders head coach and general manager Al Davis succeeded Joe Foss as AFL commissioner. This signaled a distinct change in the already less-than-cordial relationship between the leagues.

Davis was a hawk. He took the job on the condition that he have dictatorial powers and a mandate to get rough with the NFL. He set an unmistakable tone for his administration by leaking the league's intention to expand first into Los Angeles and then Chicago—two of the NFL's top three markets.

"I want a confrontation in Los Angeles," he declared. It was the NFL's turn next. On May 17, Giants owner Wellington Mara announced he had signed Gogolak, who had played out his option with the Bills.

Gogolak was technically a free agent. But since the birth of the AFL in 1959 the two leagues had abided by a gentleman's agreement not to sign each other's players. Draft picks were fair game, veterans weren't. (Only one—end Willard Dewveall—had jumped leagues in six years, going from the Bears to the Oilers in 1961.)

Within 24 hours of Mara's announcement, the Associated Press reported that four Giants players had been contacted by AFL teams: back Steve Thurlow, end Bobby Crespino and center Greg Larson by the Chargers and back Tucker Frederickson by the Oilers. A Detroit radio station said the Miami Dolphins had talked to Lions stars Alex Karras, Wayne Walker and Gail Cogdill. Stories seemed to spring up everywhere in the next few days.

New York Daily News columnist Dick Young wrote that Bills owner Ralph Wilson had flashed two $500,000 checks in front of an NFL counterpart. One was made out to Dick Butkus, the other to Gale Sayers. "If you raid Gogolak," Wilson supposedly said, "I will have these checks certified and go shopping. I can write 100 checks like these."

Wilson denied the story ("It's nice to find out I can write checks like that"), but few papers around the country bothered with that detail. War was in the air.

"If that's what the National League wants, we'll give it to them," Oilers owner Bud Adams said.

Davis was hard at work behind the scenes, coordinating the plan of retaliation. On May 27, he let go his first big bomb. The Raiders announced they had signed Rams quarterback Roman Gabriel to a four-year, $300,000-plus contract to begin in 1967. Just hours later, the Rams called their own press conference to announce that Gabriel had signed a new three-year deal with them. Confusion reigned.

Gabriel, while not denying having signed with Oakland, said the Rams "were his team." No way, Raiders GM Scotty Stirling replied. He insisted Gabriel belonged to Oakland and vowed to fight the NFL in court. Davis backed him 100 percent.

Four days later came word that 49ers quarterback John Brodie was in Houston talking contract with Oilers general manager Don Klosterman. The figure being thrown around was astronomical for the time—$750,000.

"[The NFL] struck the first blow," Klosterman said. "We'll battle them with any ounce gloves they want."

Players from both leagues recognized a bargaining chip when they saw it and started leaking stories to the press about phantom contacts. According to Adams, about 100 NFL veterans made inquiries to the AFL.

Davis' actual plan was much more selective. He targeted between 7 and 25 NFL players. He used Klosterman and Stirling as his point men.

Ditka and Brodie were headed for Houston. Ninowski, a capable backup quarterback with the Cleveland Browns, was going to Oakland. Gabriel, while Raiders property, was destined to be the flagship of the AFL's new LA franchise. Hornung reportedly was on his way to the Jets.

All activity stopped in early June when rumors began circulating that the two leagues were at work on a peace agreement. On June 8 the merger was announced.

It was assumed the signing war had forced the agreement. On the contrary, it had almost wrecked it.

Secret peace talks had begun April 6, the day before Davis was named AFL commissioner. Only a handful of people in either league knew what was going on. The Cowboys' Tex Schramm represented the NFL, the Chiefs' Lamar Hunt the AFL. Rozelle was in on it, Davis wasn't.

All of which makes the Gogolak signing harder to understand. By mid-May Mara, too, knew serious negotiations were taking place. Yet he signed the kicker, anyway.

"At a time when we wanted the owners in as harmonious a mood as possible, it created division

and anger," Schramm wrote in *Sports Illustrated*.

Rozelle could have minimized the damage by voiding Gogolak's contract. By not doing so, he upset a number of NFL owners. Key figures such as the Bears' George Halas and Packers' Vince Lombardi were said to be furious with him.

"Legally, there is no question the New York Giants had the right to sign Gogolak," Halas said. "But I think it was a mistake in judgment because of what it is leading to."

In several papers, unnamed NFL owners were quoted as saying Rozelle's job was on the line. The *Dallas Times Herald* went so far as to say he would have been replaced by Schramm had the merger fallen through. (Schramm vehemently denied it.)

It was left to the NFL to make good on the contracts the AFL was holding. The 49ers had to pay Brodie the salary figures he'd accepted from the

UPS & DOWNS

Parity has supposedly made it more difficult to win year after year. So how do you explain the Dallas Cowboys and Oakland/Los Angeles Raiders? The Cowboys had 20 consecutive winning seasons from 1966 to '85 and the Raiders 16 straight from '65 to '80 -- the two longest streaks in NFL history. Every other team that has strung together 10 winning seasons did it before 1970.

The bottom can fall out quickly, however, as the accompanying charts show. The Washington Redskins had 10 consecutive winning seasons from 1936 to '45 and nine losing seasons in a row from '57 to '65. The New York Giants had 10 straight winners from 1954 to '63 and eight straight losers from '73 to '80.

MOST CONSECUTIVE WINNING SEASONS BY AN NFL TEAM

No.	Team, Years	W	L	T	Pct.	Titles
20	Cowboys, 1966-85	208	79	2	.723	2
16	Raiders, 1965-80	164	57	9	.733	2
15	Bears, 1930-44	128	36	13	.760	5
14	Packers, 1934-47	106	45	5	.696	3
13	Browns, 1957-69	117	51	6	.690	1
12	Packers, 1921-32	93	33	15	.713	3
10	Giants, 1954-63	86	35	5	.702	1
10	Browns, 1946-55*	105	17	4	.849	7
10	Redskins, 1936-45	74	29	5	.708	2

*Played in All-America Football Conference, 1946-49.

MOST CONSECUTIVE LOSING SEASONS BY AN NFL TEAM

No.	Team, Years	W	L	T	Pct.	Coaches
12	Saints, 1967-78	46	119	5	.285	6
10	Broncos, 1963-72	38	98	1	.281	6
10	Eagles, 1933-42	23	82	4	.229	3
9	Colts, 1978-86	38	98	1	.281	6
9	Redskins, 1957-65	34	77	7	.318	3
8	Giants, 1973-80	33	84	1	.284	4
8	Steelers, 1964-71	30	79	3	.281	4
8	Cardinals, 1938-45*	12	70	3	.159	4

*Combined with Pittsburgh in 1944.

Oilers—$75,000 in '66, '67 and '68 and $90,000 in '69—while the league picked up $512,000 in deferred payments.

Ninowski revealed in 1972 that he had to threaten an antitrust suit to get his money. The league finally agreed to increase his salary to $100,000 for four years if he would forget the deal with the Raiders. (At one point, he said, he received a $100,000 check from then–league president Art Modell).

Davis might have been the real loser. He was convinced the AFL could defeat the NFL under his direction. "You sold me down the river," he told Patriots owner Billy Sullivan.

Davis was offered the job of president of the AFL under the new alignment of the leagues but turned it down. On April 25 he resigned as commissioner.

"Generals win wars," he said. "Politicians negotiate peace."

■ ■ ■

FRANKS 2, BURGERS 1

Lyndon Johnson was the first president to attend an NFL game while in office. He arrived unannounced at a Redskins–Colts exhibition August 3, 1966, at D.C. Stadium and watched from Redskins president Edward Bennett Williams' executive box. During the game LBJ put away two hot dogs, one hamburger, ice cream and a container of milk. Baltimore led 35–0 at the half, so what else was there to do?

In the visiting owner's box, the Colts' Carroll Rosenbloom pitched a fit because he couldn't get even one hot dog delivered for him and his guests, Robert and Teddy Kennedy. Rank has its privileges.

■ ■ ■

MONDAY NIGHT FOOTBALL

Monday night football actually was born October 31, 1966, while Dandy Don Meredith was still quarterbacking the Cowboys and Howard Cosell was just an obnoxiously entertaining boxing commentator.

It was CBS, not ABC, that gave the country the first nationally televised prime-time game. The St Louis Cardinals beat the Chicago Bears, 24–17, at brand-new Busch Stadium in what must have been a pretty entertaining show. The Cards' Larry Wilson intercepted three passes, returning one for a touchdown. And Gale Sayers of the Bears turned a routine flat pass into an 80-yard score.

But viewer response was lukewarm. The telecast started at 9:30 P.M. EST, and the overnight ratings were no higher than 19.8. *Family Affair*, one of the two shows preempted by the game, had an average rating of 22.6 that season, which made CBS a loser for the night. (Hard to believe America would prefer Buffy, Jody, and that wimp Mr. French to Gale Sayers, isn't it?)

CBS televised one Monday night game the next season, two in 1968 and another in '69. But the network was never very hot for the idea. It wasn't until 1970 that ABC gambled on it, and we all know how that turned out.

Prime-time NFL football was Pete Rozelle's doing. He'd been pushing it for years, and it was at his insistence that CBS finally gave it a try. A few years earlier, he and ABC had discussed a Friday night package of games but decided against going head-to-head with high school football. Monday was the ideal night in the commissioner's mind.

CBS didn't make a big deal of its presentation. The game was advertised as a Halloween special, but none of the newspapers in Chicago or St. Louis seemed to think playing on Monday night was unusual.

The network chose as its announcers Lindsey Nelson and—get ready—Frank Gifford. Gifford, of course, joined the ABC Monday night team in 1971 and became a fixture.

■ ■ ■

DON'T TOUCH THAT DIAL

What you could have watched instead of the first nationally televised Monday night football game October 31, 1966:

■ *Peyton Place* (9:30–10:00, ABC)—Fowler refuses Rodney's plea unless Rossi intervenes; Rachel becomes enraged in the hospital and Rossi sends for Rita to help; for Lee, a strong conflict with his brother Chris becomes evident.

- *The Big Valley* (10:00–11:00 ABC)—The Barkleys are accused of acquiring their fortune in an unscrupulous way by an ambitious politician.
- *Run for Your Life* (10:00–11:00, NBC)—Paul (Ben Gazzara) helps a famous novelist discover his true feeling about a revolution the writer witnessed in South America.

• • •

72–41

It's hard to believe a single field goal could stand out in the highest-scoring game in NFL history, but it did.

On November 27, 1966, the Washington Redskins defeated the New York Giants, 72–41, at D.C. Stadium. The two teams set nine league records, including most points by one team in a regular-season game.

The Redskins achieved that distinction with seven seconds remaining when, with a four-touchdown lead, they had Charlie Gogolak kick a 29-yard field goal. It was a bloodthirsty act, even for such age-old rivals as the Redskins and Giants. Redskins coach Otto Graham was roundly criticized for record-chasing, though he claimed he didn't know what the old record was (70, by the 1950 L.A. Rams).

As it turned out, sending in Gogolak wasn't his idea. It was defensive captain Sam Huff's. Two years earlier the Giants had traded Huff to Washington after eight memorable seasons in New York, and he was still burning over it. When the Giants failed to convert a fourth-down pass deep in their territory in the closing seconds, he saw an opportunity to humiliate coach Allie Sherman.

"I called for the field goal," Huff says. "Otto was puttering around with his clipboard, talking to [quarterback Sonny] Jurgensen or something, and I hollered for the field-goal team. They were out on the field before Otto knew what was going on. Blood, that's what I was after."

Huff wasn't alone. A number of Redskins veterans felt the Giants had run up big scores on them in the past. They especially remembered a 53–0 defeat in 1961. There wasn't any remorse in the Washington locker room on this day.

The game produced some bizarre statistics. Even with 113 points scored, it took only 2 hours, 50 minutes to play. The Giants outgained the Redskins, 389–341. They also had more first downs (25–16) and ran 29 more plays.

Washington led 34–14 at the half despite having minus-2 net passing yards (Jurgensen was 4 for 9 for 5 yards). The two Gogolak brothers (Pete played for the Giants) kicked 14 extra points. And 13 of the 14 game balls the Redskins had on hand were lost in the stands (cost: $315).

Turnovers were what did it. The Redskins intercepted five passes. One they returned for a touchdown. Three others set up short TD drives. They also ran a fumble back for a score (DB Brig Owens had both defensive touchdowns).

The game got so out of hand in the fourth quarter that Graham moved flanker Bobby Mitchell—against his wishes—to running back. Mitchell, then 31, hadn't played the position since being traded from Cleveland after the '61 season. On his first carry, he gained 9 yards. On his second, he swept to the left, cut back off tackle and went 45 yards for the Redskins' final touchdown.

"Otto had sent the play in, and I didn't want to run it," Mitchell says. "I knew the plays from that position and everything, but I was too old to go back there. I think once you get past a certain age, playing running back is just asking for a serious injury.

"Sonny made me do it. He said, 'Get up there and run it,' and the next thing I knew I was lining up at halfback."

• • •

TWIN TOWERS

The '60s gave us pro football's only seven-foot player. His name was Richard Sligh, and Oakland drafted him as a 10th-round project in 1967.

Sligh had played more basketball than football at North Carolina College. He weighed 300 pounds—thus his nickname, "300"—but was all legs and easy for offensive linemen to get under. The Raiders tried him at defensive tackle for a year, then let him go to Cincinnati in the '68 expansion draft. The Bengals cut him in training camp.

Owner Al Davis had hoped Sligh would become another Buck Buchanan. Oakland quarterbacks always had trouble throwing over the 6'7" Kansas

City tackle. Raiders tackle Tom Keating remembers asking Davis what the team was doing with Sligh, who wasn't much of an athlete.

"You can't buy seven feet!" Davis replied.

One day basketball star Rick Barry came to practice and ran pass patterns. He showed excellent hands and decent speed. Davis watched in wonderment.

"God," he said, "if I could just have a guy like that! A 6'7" receiver!"

Chiefs coach Hank Stram's passion for big people rivaled Davis'. He once tried to talk Wilt Chamberlain into playing football. In the third round in 1969 he drafted the second-tallest player in NFL history, 6'10" tight end Morris Stroud.

Stroud had a background similar to Sligh's. He, too, had gone to a small school (Clark College in Georgia) and played basketball. Stram got him to bulk up from 218 to 255 pounds by the end of his career. Unfortunately, the guy had bad hands.

Stroud did manage to catch 54 passes for seven touchdowns in five seasons. Wonder what Wilt would have done.

■■■
TWIN SEASONS

Consistency is one thing, but this is ridiculous. Look at Hall-of-Famer Bobby Mitchell's receiving statistics for the Redskins in 1965 and '67:

	NO.	YDS.	AVG.	TD
1965	60	867	14.45	6
1967	60	866	14.43	6

A difference of one yard. (Mitchell also caught 60 passes in 1964.)

■■■
THE SNEAK REVISITED

If one play has come to symbolize Vince Lombardi's great Green Bay Packers teams, it's Bart Starr's quarterback sneak that won the 1967 Ice Bowl. Remember?

Sixteen seconds left. Dallas ahead 17–14. Temperature: minus 19. Guard Jerry Kramer drives the Cowboys' Jethro Pugh out of the hole, and Starr falls behind him into the end zone for the winning score. It's one of pro football's golden moments.

What you don't hear about Starr's sneak is that (1) it was a lousy call, (2) Kramer was offside and (3) Packers center Ken Bowman should have shared the credit for the famous block.

Let's start with the play itself. It was an outrageous gamble, really. Cowboys assistant coach Ermal Allen muttered afterward: "I just wish it had failed. You think there wouldn't have been a few million words written about that? Then we'd see how smart he [Lombardi] felt."

Allen was right, if a little bitter. The Packers had the ball two feet from the Dallas goal line, third down. They were out of timeouts. Had the sneak been stopped, the Packers wouldn't have had time to attempt the tying field goal or any way to stop the clock. The Cowboys would have been 1967 NFL champions, and the legendary Lombardi would have been second-guessed for centuries.

"We thought they would throw," then–Dallas coach Tom Landry says. "We thought they probably would go on an option, a rollout run or pass so they could stop the clock [with an incompletion] if it didn't work."

So did most people. It was the percentage move.

The sneak was Starr's idea. On the two plays preceding it, halfback Donny Anderson slipped taking the handoff and was stopped for almost no gain. The south end of Green Bay's Lambeau Field lay in the shadow of a large scoreboard and was frozen solid. When Anderson slipped the second time, Starr decided the Packers' best shot was for him to keep the ball.

He called the team's final timeout. Before coming to the sidelines to meet with Lombardi, he asked Kramer and Bowman if they could get enough footing to run 31 Wedge. They said they could. The play was a simple dive right. The guard and center double-teamed the defensive tackle, and the quarterback handed off to a back running straight ahead.

"I told Coach Lombardi there was nothing wrong with the plays we had run, it's just that the backs couldn't get their footing," Starr says. "I said, 'Why don't I just keep it?' All he said was run it and let's get the hell out of here. That's all he said."

There was no discussion of a fourth-down play or possible field-goal try. That's testimony either to

Lombardi's supreme confidence or the effect the cold was having on his brain. What made the call even more unusual was that Starr rarely ran the sneak. He could recall doing it on only one other occasion, a few years earlier against the 49ers. Sleet had turned the field to ice and the footing was terrible that day, too. Nonetheless, he had scored.

"I still don't think it was a smart play," says Cowboys halfback Dan Reeves, now the Denver Broncos' coach. "But maybe that's the reason Lombardi won all those championships and I haven't won any."

Packers fullback Chuck Mercein looks at it this way: "Bad is only bad if it doesn't work. To me, success justifies a lot of questionable calls."

Of course it always helps if your right guard can beat the snap count. A fraction of a second before Bowman hiked the ball to Starr, Kramer picked up his hand and started out of his three-point stance. You can't imagine what a comfort that knowledge is to Pugh.

In December 1967, he was in his third year in the NFL. He played 11 more and never shed the label as The Guy Who Got Blocked On Starr's Sneak. For years after the Ice Bowl, he carried inside him this image of Kramer moving before the snap. The Cowboys never bothered to watch the game films, so he kept it to himself. It sounded like the cheapest kind of excuse.

"In a goal-line situation like that you key the football," Pugh says. "And I could visualize Kramer's hand moving an instant before the ball did. My first thought [after the play] was, 'We got 'em. He's offsides, and that'll cost 'em five yards.' I was shocked when I didn't see a flag. I kept looking around for one."

Four times in the '70s Pugh's Cowboys went to the Super Bowl. Reporters never failed to bring up the play. He answered their questions but kept the little picture of Kramer moving a split second early to himself. Years later, he finally had an opportunity to see the game films and watched with a combination of curiosity and anxiety.

"I saw it, and I said, 'My goodness. I was right,'" Pugh says.

Even Kramer doesn't deny it. In his 1968 best seller *Instant Replay* he says: "I wouldn't swear that I didn't beat the center's snap by a fraction of a second. I wouldn't swear that I wasn't actually offside on the play."

The block made him famous. The networks showed the play over and over in the days after the game, and Kramer didn't hesitate to take credit. He became America's Guard. Every football fan knew him and his block—and soon, his book.

Largely overlooked was Bowman's contribution. Pugh lined up on Kramer's inside shoulder on the play, and his instructions were to stay low and clog the middle so linebacker Lee Roy Jordan could make the tackle. It was Kramer's job to raise Pugh up so Bowman could get a clean shot at him. Together, the two could then drive the Cowboys tackle out of the hole. That was precisely what happened on the play, and it still rankles Bowman that Kramer got almost all the glory.

"The older I get, the more it bothers me," he says. "I was young [a fourth-year pro] and stupid, and he patted me on the shoulder as he went up to the [television] podium after the game and said, 'Let an old man have his moment in the spotlight. You've got 10, 12 more years.'

"What I didn't realize was that blocks like that come along once in . . . hell, it's been two decades now."

Says Kramer: "My feeling is that I don't know how much he contributed. I did say to him, 'You tell them about what you did because you've got a few more years. I'm talking about what I did.'"

Pugh sides with Bowman. "Kramer had good position, but Bowman did more of the blocking," he says.

All this was lost in the strange beauty and confusion of the moment. As the Packers broke the huddle and came to the line of scrimmage, the 50,000 frigid fans started to cheer. There hadn't been much opportunity for that since early in the game.

The Cowboys had dominated the second half and appeared on their way to winning until the Packers put together their final, improbable drive. Now a third straight NFL title for Green Bay was 24 inches away.

The sun was sinking. The wind chill factor was minus 50. Many of the fans were dressed in brightly colored hunting gear, and Green Bay assistant coach Phil Bengston said the effect was that of a red halo around the field. Breath poured from them like smoke from chimneys.

Pugh tried to dig himself a foothold in the frozen turf, but his toes were numb. He gave up and took his position. So did the Packers. The crowd hushed. Bowman snapped the ball, and before Pugh could get out of his stance, Kramer was on him. Then

Bowman was, too, and Pugh slid helplessly out of the way. Starr took a step to his right, then slipped into the fast-closing opening. Touchdown.

■ ■ ■

LUCKY SHOT

The famous instant replay from the '67 Ice Bowl was a fluke. Instead of the shot of Bart Starr's one-yard sneak from behind the Cowboys defense, the world almost had Packers wide receiver Boyd Dowler doing nothing.

With time out and 16 seconds left in the game, CBS director Tony Verna asked commentator Pat Summerall what play he thought Green Bay would run. Rollout pass, Summerall said.

That made sense. The Packers were out of time-outs. They trailed 17–14. If Starr couldn't find an open receiver or score himself, he could throw the ball away and stop the clock. The Pack then would have a chance at a tying field goal.

"We had a camera in each end zone, and so what we wanted to do was isolate one on each [Packers] wide receiver," Summerall says. "Tony said to the cameraman behind the Cowboys, 'You get Dowler.' But at that point the cables behind the camera were frozen and the cameraman couldn't turn it. So he had to leave it behind the Cowboys defense."

Talk about a lucky break. It proved to be the best angle to see the winning play. From behind the Cowboys you could dissect all the components of Starr's dramatic plunge: the double-team block on Cowboys tackle Jethro Pugh, Starr going over with head down and fullback Chuck Mercein coming over the top with hands raised.

"If it hadn't been for those cables freezing, we wouldn't have had the shot," Summerall says.

■ ■ ■

FROZEN IN TIME

All I have to say is, there was trouble on every corner and it just didn't seem like Christmas out there.

—*Cowboys quarterback* DON MEREDITH

Good morning, Mr. Rentzel. It's 8 A.M. It's 15 below zero, and there's a 20 mile-per-hour wind coming out of the northwest. Have a nice day.

—*Wake-up call to Cowboys receiver* LANCE RENTZEL

I don't know why they scheduled this game here—I guess because the top of Mt. Everest was booked.

—*L.A. Times columnist* JIM MURRAY

If I owned Green Bay, I'd dome the whole town.

—*Cowboys owner* CLINT MURCHISON

I think I'll have another bite of my coffee.

—*Announcer* FRANK GIFFORD

This game was our mark of distinction.

—*Packers offensive tackle* BOB SKORONSKI

You hear that stuff about the Packers being able to deal with [the weather] better than we did, and that's a lot of bull. I think we handled it as well as they did. It's just that they made the play at the end.

—*Cowboys running back* DAN REEVES

It was so cold that winning wasn't uppermost in my mind. Getting out of the weather was.

—*Packers defensive end* LIONEL ALDRIDGE

Falling on that ground was like falling on the side of a stucco wall. It made Astroturf feel like a pillow.

—*Packers running back* CHUCK MERCEIN

It was kind of an eerie feeling. I was standing there on the sidelines, and I'd look around and there'd be nobody. Everyone would be back at the heaters trying to stay warm. I was all by myself, just like I was up at the North Pole. It was the kind of feeling where you wonder what you're doing here and why this thing wasn't called off.

—*Cowboys coach* TOM LANDRY

■ ■ ■

THE GREAT EXTRA-POINT EXPERIMENT

People have been trying to get rid of the extra point since 1933. Giants owner Tim Mara was the first to propose it, and Bert Bell took up the fight during his commissionership from 1946 to '59. Like Mara, Bell considered the play a waste of time and supported a sudden-death period to break ties.

Finally, in 1968, NFL and AFL owners decided to experiment with the extra point. In the 23 interleague preseason games that year, teams had the choice of running or passing for the point from the two-yard line. Kicks weren't allowed.

Mark Duncan, the NFL's supervisor of officials, suggested the idea. According to his figures, 82 plays had been run from the two the previous season, and the offense had scored on 48.9 percent of them.

Oakland coach John Rauch was intrigued by the possibilities. The rule, he said, "would force a coach to develop a two-yard offense. You might go to a single wing, or use a quarterback rollout, or a tall tight end. It definitely would add something to the game."

The first game affected was the one between Washington and Houston at the Astrodome August 1. The Oilers scored the only touchdown. On the extra-point attempt, Pete Beathard's pass to halfback Woody Campbell was broken up by safety Frank Liberatore, but the Redskins were offside. Campbell then tried to run the ball in from the one but was stopped short.

There were 98 extra-point tries in the 23 games. Fifty-five—56.1 percent—were successful. This made for goofy scores like 39–16 and 22–12. Teams passed almost twice as much as they ran (62 to 36), but the run got better results (58.3 percent conversion rate to 54.8).

The Houston–New Orleans game was decided by an extra point in the last minute. Beathard ran six yards for a TD with 56 seconds left to tie the score at 23. Here's how the *Houston Post* described the point-after attempt:

"The wildly cheering crowd came to its feet as, for the first time in the game, Beathard lined up his backs in the I formation.

"Pete faked to Hoyle Granger, the fullback, who slammed adroitly into the middle to set in motion the old option play. When he drew the defense across the line, Beathard then pitched back to [Sid] Blanks, who was trailing him.

"For a nervous second, Blanks fought to control the pitch, finally grabbed it on the dead run and raced into the end zone for the point that decided the game. Wildly cheering partisans rattled the Dome. . . ."

Gives you goose bumps, doesn't it?

Not surprisingly, the Saints didn't have much good to say about the new extra-point rule. Coach Tom Fears said: "I think it holds a big advantage for the real strong defensive teams. I'd sure hate to have to run for one point every time against teams like the Rams, the Colts or Green Bay."

And quarterback Billy Kilmer said: "I guess I'm old-fashioned. . . . I think the AFL has a good rule on it. If you want to run or pass for two points, then OK, but not just one."

At the next league meeting, the Great Extra-Point Experiment died a quiet death. It needed a unanimous vote to become permanent. Six years later the World Football League adopted the same rule but marked the ball at the 2½-yard line. It renamed the point-after the "action point."

■ ■ ■

LOMBARDI THE GENERAL MANAGER

Vince Lombardi was as good a general manager as he was a coach. Well, almost. He was aggressive—just like his teams—and for 10 years he made virtually all the right moves.

In 1962 he began accumulating huge stockpiles of draft picks, the draft picks that would secure the Packers' future into the '70s. Green Bay players had market value—often inflated market value—and he took full advantage of it. Teams paid dearly for veterans Lombardi was phasing out and for rookies who couldn't make his roster.

Bill Quinlan, Tom Bettis, John Symank, Jim Ringo, Hank Gremminger—all were traded for draft choices. Ringo brought a first-round pick. Lombardi got two other number ones when Ron Kramer and Jim Taylor played out their options and

Packers fans thought Vince Lombardi could walk on water. We don't know anything about *that,* but we did come across photographic evidence from Lombardi's playing days at Fordham that he could indeed fly. Here he is, arriving for practice. (Pro Football Hall of Fame/NFL Photos)

signed with the Lions and Saints. His finest moment, though, may have been when he swapped defensive end Lloyd Voss and rookie tight end Tony Jeter for the Steelers' 1967 first-round choice.

"There are two ways of looking at trades," Lombardi said after the Ringo deal in 1964. "Some teams wait until they are run down and then turn toward trading to rebuild. Others keep turning over personnel while they are contenders. I'm a believer of the latter. We . . . want to keep our team comparatively young."

From 1963 to '69, when Lombardi left to rebuild the Redskins, the Packers had 11 number-one picks, more than any other team in pro football. They also had *20* extra choices in the third through eighth rounds. And let's not forget, an eighth-rounder for most of the '60s was like a fourth-rounder today because there were half as many teams then.

Even without Lombardi, the Packers dynasty could easily have continued. Believe it or not, Green Bay had two more number-one picks in 1970 and again in '72. This team should have been set for years. There was only one problem.

The Packers hardly drafted any good players.

90-YARD PUNTS

Man's pursuit of the perfect punt officially ended September 21, 1969. It was on that date—on national television, no less—that New York Jets rookie Steve O'Neal blasted one 98 yards against the Denver Broncos in the second quarter at Mile High Stadium.

The line of scrimmage was the New York one. The ball rolled dead at the Denver one. A 99-yard kick is still possible, of course, but that would involve a touchback. No, there'll never be a better boot than O'Neal's.

Things were so tight in the Jets end zone that he had to move up-back Matt Snell to get the ball off. The punt soared over the head of returner Billy Thompson and hit at about the 30—77 yards away.

The light air in Denver has always been kind to punters, but O'Neal didn't think it made any difference. He claimed to have kicked "farther than that a lot of times before, other places in the country."

At least the boot was legitimate. Five other punts in pro football history have been said to measure at least 90 yards, and only two seem to be the genuine article. Our findings:

Joe Guyon, Canton Bulldogs, 95 yards (November 14, 1920, vs. Chicago Tigers at Canton)—The ball might have traveled 95 yards, but it wasn't a 95-yard punt. This distinction wasn't made in the early years. The kick in question came in the third quarter. The *Canton Evening Repository* says "Guyon punted mightily for 95 yards and over the Tiger goal line," but the play-by-play indicates the line of scrimmage was probably the 22. That would make it a 78-yard kick.

Fats Henry, Canton, 94 yards (October 28, 1923, vs. Akron Pros at Canton)—This one was listed in the NFL record book as late as 1973. Obviously nobody had checked it out. The headline in the *Repository* reads: "Punt Of 85 Yards By Henry Turns Tide In 7–3 Victory Of Bulldogs." The accompanying story calls it "a wonderful punt of between 80 and 85 yards." The play-by-play puts it at 83 yards (approximately)—from his own 15 to the Akron 2. It was a huge play, though, shifting the field position in Canton's favor midway through the fourth quarter and setting up the winning touchdown.

Joe Lintzenich, Chicago Bears, 94 yards (November 15, 1931 vs. Giants at New York)—The NFL might want to look more closely at Lintzenich's punt, too. It's currently number two on the all-time list, but it wasn't added to the record book until 1976. Strange. What piece of pre-1933 evidence could have convinced the league? Record-

THE JOY OF SECOND-GUESSING

Hindsight is always 20-20, but Green Bay really did make big drafting mistakes in the 1960s and '70s. Here are some of the players they picked in the first round -- and some of the players they could have had.

SOME FIRST-ROUND PICKS THE PACKERS MIGHT LIKE TO HAVE BACK

Year	Pick	Selection	Who Was Available (Pick)
1964	13th	DT Lloyd Voss	CB Mel Renfro (17th), S Paul Krause (18th)
1965	7th	RB Donny Anderson,	QB Joe Namath (12th)
	10th	WR Lawrence Elkins	LB Mike Curtis (14th)
1966	10th	FB Jim Grabowski	TE Milt Morin (15th), RB Mike Garrett (18th)
1967	9th	C Bob Hyland,	DT Alan Page (15th)
	25th	QB Don Horn	CB Lem Barney (34th)
1968	26th	OG Bill Lueck	DT Curly Culp (31st)
1969	12th	DT Rich Moore	DE Fred Dryer (13th), WR Gene Washington (16th), CB Roger Wehrli (19th), RB Ron Johnson (20th)
1970	2nd	DT Mike McCoy	DT Mike Reid (7th)
	16th	TE Rich McGeorge	TE Raymond Chester (24th)
1972	11th	QB Jerry Tagge	RB Franco Harris (13th)

PICKS APLENTY

Thanks to the wheeling and dealing of Vince Lombardi, Green Bay had more first-round draft picks than any other team in pro football from 1963 to '72 -- 16. Only one other club had more than 12. The Packers also stockpiled dozens of other high picks. One year they had seven extra selections in the first eight rounds. So why didn't their success continue into the '70s? Good question.

A YEAR-BY-YEAR BREAKDOWN OF PACKERS DRAFT PICKS, 1963-72

Year	1st	2nd	3rd	4th	5th	6th	7th	8th	Total Picks*	Extra Picks
1963	1	1	2	2	2	2	3	2	15	7
1964	1	1	3	2	2	0	1	1	11	3
1965	2	1	1	1	2	2	3	1	13	5
1966	2	1	2	1	0	0	1	1	8	0
1967	2	2	1	1	3	1	2	1	13	5
1968	2	0	2	2	2	1	1	1	11	3
1969	1	0	1	1	1	2	1	1	8	0
1970	2	1	1	2	1	1	1	1	10	2
1971	1	1	1	0	2	1	2	1	9	1
1972	2	1	0	1	0	3	1	1	9	1
Totals	16	9	14	13	15	13	16	11	107	27

*In first eight rounds.

Coming

1960--Howie Long, Somerville, Mass.
 Marcus Allen, San Diego
 Art Schlichter, Washington Court House, Ohio
 John Elway, Port Angeles, Wash.
 Roger Craig, Davenport, Iowa
 Eric Dickerson, Sealy, Texas
1961--Dan Marino, Pittsburgh
 Reggie White, Chattanooga, Tenn.
1962--Herschel Walker, Wrightsville, Ga.
 Don Rogers, Texarkana, Ark.
 Bo Jackson, Bessemer, Ala.
1963--Randall Cunningham, Santa Barbara, Calif.
1965--Brian Bosworth, Oklahoma City
1966--Tony Mandarich, Oakville, Canada
1967--Deion Sanders, Fort Myers, Fla.
1968--Barry Sanders, Wichita, Kan.

Going

1960--Howard Glenn, 24, N.Y. Titans guard, broken neck
1962--Walt Kiesling, 58
1963--Big Daddy Lipscomb, 31, drug overdose
 Stone Johnson, 23, Chiefs receiver, spinal injury
1964--Steve Owen, 66
 Willie Galimore, 29, Bears halfback, and Bo Farrington, 28, receiver, car accident
1965--Curly Lambeau, 67
 Mack Lee Hill, 23, Chiefs fullback, hypothermia (post-op)
1966--Dick Barwegan, 44, heart attack
1967--Guy Chamberlin, 73
1968--Paddy Driscoll, 73
1969--George Preston Marshall, 72
 Frank Buncom, 29, Bengals linebacker, heart attack
 Arnie Herber, 59

keeping was rudimentary in the early years. We looked at five newspapers and none mentions the kick. The *New York Herald Tribune* refers to the Giants receiving "one of Lintzenich's long punts"

but doesn't offer any specifics. That doesn't mean it didn't happen, but you have to wonder. All the other 90-yarders were written about.

Don Chandler, Green Bay, 90 yards (October 10, 1965, vs. San Francisco at Green Bay)—Chandler's fourth-quarter boot got up in the wind and rolled dead either 111 or 113 yards away, depending on the source. The ball went 75 yards on the fly—from the Green Bay goal line, over the head of return man Kermit Alexander, to the San Francisco 25—and bounced through the end zone. Five years earlier, when he was with the Giants, Chandler had had an almost identical kick against the Packers on the same field in a preseason game. That one also sailed from the goal line to the 25-yard line and came to a stop in the end zone. Total distance: 105 yards. Length of punt: 87.

Randall Cunningham, Philadelphia, 91 yards (December 3, 1989, vs. Giants at the Meadowlands)—The Eagles quarterback was an All-American punter in college, but he'd punted only six times in his five-year pro career before getting off this monster. He did it in the fourth quarter of a 17–17 game. Philly was backed up to its two. Max Runager, the regular punter, wasn't having much of a day, so Cunningham stayed in to kick. With the help of a 25 mph wind, he boomed one that landed at the New York 38, 67 yards away. Returner Dave Meggett let the ball roll to the 7 before picking it up and running it back to the 16. The Giants fumbled on the next play, all but handing the Eagles the winning TD.

None of the above, however, ever kicked the ball as far as Brooklyn's Ralph Kercheval did October 20, 1935, against the Bears at Wrigley Field. Kercheval's punt reportedly carried from his four-yard line to the Chicago five—91 yards in the air—and bounded into the end zone. It went in the books, though, as an 86-yarder.

THE
1970s

'70s CHALKBOARD

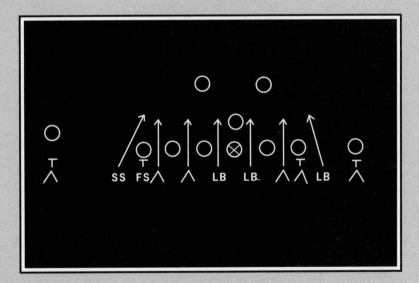

The Grits Blitz

The Grits Blitz

The '70s were a defensive decade, and no team played defense with greater abandon than the 1977 Atlanta Falcons. Hardly the league's most talented team, the Falcons blitzed opponents into oblivion under rookie coach Leeman Bennett. The Grits Blitz was so successful that Atlanta allowed just 129 points, the fewest (on a points-per-game basis) in the last 45 years. The diagram is of the "sticky blitz," in which the Falcons sent everybody but the defensive coordinator. Unfortunately, they scored only 179 points themselves and finished 7–7.

THE 1970s AT A GLANCE

Decade Standings

NFC	W	L	T	Pct.	AFC	W	L	T	Pct.
Cowboys (2)	105	39	0	.729	Dolphins (2)	104	39	1	.726
Vikings	99	43	2	.694	Raiders (1)	100	38	6	.715
Rams	98	42	4	.694	Steelers (4)	99	44	1	.691
Redskins	91	52	1	.635	Broncos	75	64	5	.538
Cardinals	69	71	4	.493	Bengals	74	70	0	.514
Lions	66	75	3	.469	Colts (1)	73	70	1	.510
Falcons	60	81	3	.427	Browns	72	70	2	.507
49ers	60	82	2	.424	Patriots	66	78	0	.458
Bears	60	83	1	.420	Chiefs	60	79	5	.434
Packers	57	82	5	.413	Oilers	60	82	2	.424
Eagles	56	84	4	.403	Chargers	58	81	5	.420
Giants	50	93	1	.351	Seahawks	25	35	0	.417
Saints	42	98	4	.306	Jets	53	91	0	.368
Buccaneers	17	43	0	.283	Bills	51	91	2	.361

(Figures in parentheses are championships won.)

Best Regular–Season Record Miami Dolphins, 1972, 14-0

Worst Regular–Season Record Tampa Bay Buccaneers, 1976, 0-14

League Attendance 109,278,657 (up 67.7 percent)

In	Out
field goals	touchdowns
home games on TV	home games on radio
John Facenda	Ray Scott
turf toe	deviated septum
end-zone dances	handshakes
Tom Landry, Roger Staubach	Vince Lombardi, Bart Starr
3-4	4-3
Monday Night Football	Monday night marital relations
George Plimpton	Hunter Thompson
off-season training	pot bellies
Steel Curtain	Doomsday defense

Biggest Player Milton Hardaway, a one-year wonder at offensive tackle for the Chargers, was 6'9'' and at least 310 pounds. He wore a size 8¼ helmet. Cowboys defensive end Ed "Too Tall" Jones also went 6'9''.

Smallest Player Howard Stevens and Mack Herron, two running backs, stood 5'5''. Stevens, who played for the Saints and Colts, was seven pounds lighter (167 to 174). The drug-troubled Herron set an NFL record for combined yardage with the Patriots in 1974 (2,440).

Best Athlete Walter Payton

Fastest Player Cliff Branch. At the University of Colorado he tied the world indoor record in the 60-yard dash (5.9).

Slowest Player Sonny Jurgensen

Most Intimidating Player Joe Greene

As a rookie he once ran on the field when things were getting rough and spit in Dick Butkus' face. (And unlike Dexter Manley years later, he didn't claim it was a sneeze.) Butkus walked away from the challenge.

Player Most Likely to Propose To His Wife on National TV

Ahmad Rashad

New Stadiums

1970--Riverfront Stadium
  Three Rivers Stadium
1971--Sullivan (Schaefer) Stadium
  Texas Stadium
  Veterans Stadium
1972--Arrowhead Stadium
1973--Rich Stadium
1975--Louisiana Superdome
  Pontiac Silverdome
1976--Giants Stadium
  Kingdome

During a tour of Texas Stadium with Cowboys general manager Tex Schramm, one of the players' wives mentioned how hard the artificial surface was. "It only feels that way when you walk on it," Tex supposedly said.

Failed League

WFL, 1975

▶Famous Firsts

Tight end to lead a conference in receptions, 1971 (Bob Tucker)
Defensive player named conference player of the year, 1971 (Alan Page)
Regular-season overtime game, 1974 (Steelers-Broncos)
Quarterback to wear glasses in an NFL game, 1977 (Bob Griese)
AFL player elected to the Hall of Fame, 1978 (Lance Alworth)
Season of parity scheduling, 1978
Reference to the Cowboys as "America's Team," 1979

Famous Lasts

Player to play pro basketball, 1972 (Lonnie Wright)
College All-Star Game, 1976
Player to score a touchdown three different ways in a game, 1976 (Freddie Solomon)
Winless team, 1976 (Buccaneers)

Best Division Race

1979 NFC East
Philadelphia, Dallas and Washington were all 10-5 going into the last week. The Eagles won in Houston, and the Redskins led the Cowboys, 34-21, with less than seven minutes left. But Roger Staubach threw two touchdown passes, the last with 39 seconds remaining, to give Dallas the division title. The Redskins were beaten out by the Bears for the final playoff berth on the basis of net points in conference games. They had the Cardinals to thank. St. Louis had rolled over for Chicago, 42-6, earlier in the day.

Best Super Bowl

1979, Steelers over Cowboys, 35-31

Owner vs. Owner

Paul Brown vs. Art Modell, 1979
Modell had fired Brown as Cleveland's coach after the 1962 season. Brown struck back in his autobiography, criticizing his ex-boss' handling of the club in the early '60s. Theirs was "a basic conflict between two different philosophies of operating," he wrote, "-- one from knowledge and experience; the other from a complete lack of either." The league fined him $10,000 for badmouthing an opponent.

Player vs. Team	Duane Thomas vs. the Cowboys
►**Trial of the Decade**	George Atkinson vs. Chuck Noll, 1977
Best Running Quarterback	Bobby Douglass
New Positions	inside linebacker nickel and dime defensive backs

Major Rules Changes

1972--hashmarks now width of goal posts apart; ties counted in standings (half win, half loss)

1974--regular-season overtime games; goal posts moved to back of end zone; kickoffs from 35-yard line; ball spotted at line of scrimmage after missed field goals; crackback blocks outlawed

1977--defenders can bump receiver just once; head slap banned

1978--pass blockers allowed to extend arms and open hands; defenders can bump receiver only in first 5 yards

1979--blocking below waist on kicks made illegal; play ends when quarterback is in grasp of defender; spearing penalized

New Equipment

turf shoes
air-cushioned helmet and shoulder pads
gloves for linemen
flak jacket

Fashion Trends

cage facemasks (at every position)
personalized towels
scantily clad cheerleaders

New Statistics

passer rating, 1973
no-shows, 1973
net punting average (individual), 1976

Best Play

The Forward Fumble, 1978
   Oakland trailed San Diego 20-14 with 10 seconds left when Ken Stabler dropped back to pass from the Chargers 14. He was hit by defensive end Fred Dean but intentionally flipped the ball forward as he was going down. Raiders tight end Dave Casper batted the bouncing ball into the end zone, where he recovered it for the winning touchdown. The next year a rule was passed to prevent such a play from happening again.

►**Hit of the Decade**	Jack Tatum vs. Darryl Stingley, 1978
►**Fight of the Decade**	Chiefs vs. Raiders, 1970
►**Highest–Paid Player**	O.J. Simpson made $806,668 with the 49ers in 1979.
Least Appreciated Players	Falcons defensive end Claude Humphrey Redskins quarterback Billy Kilmer Rams receiver Harold Jackson

Best Trade

Rams for Colts, 1972
   The first of Bob Irsay's many bonehead deals. Honorable mention: Don Shula for Don McCauley. The Dolphins had to give the Colts a first-round draft pick as compensation for signing Shula away in '70. It turned out to be McCauley.

Best Football Books

1970--*The Game That Was* by Myron Cope
    A Thinking Man's Guide to Pro Football by Paul Zimmerman
1972--*Semi-Tough* by Dan Jenkins
1973--*North Dallas Forty* by Pete Gent
1974--*About Three Bricks Shy of a Load* by Roy Blount Jr.

Best Football Movies

1970--*M*A*S*H* (the football game near the end)
1978--*Heaven Can Wait*
1979--*North Dallas Forty*

Worst Idea

In 1975 the World Football League wanted players to wear pants color-coded by position -- blue for defensive linemen, red for linebackers, yellow for defensive backs, *purple* for offensive linemen, green for running backs, orange with black vertical stripes for wide receivers and white with stars down the sides for quarterbacks. The players wisely refused. Said Paul Warfield, who jumped to the league from the NFL: "I've spent 11 years trying to build a serious image. I'm too far along in my career to begin playing Emmett Kelly."

What Might Have Been

The Raiders' Warren Wells averaged 48 receptions, 23.3 yards per catch and 12 touchdowns from 1968 to '70. In '71, however, the emotionally disturbed receiver was jailed for parole violations. He came to training camp in '72 but quit in early September. He was only 29.

▶Individual Records That Have Never Been Equaled

Tom Dempsey's 63-yard field goal vs. the Lions, 1970
Walter Payton's 275 yards rushing vs. the Vikings, 1977
Jim Marshall's 282 consecutive games, 1961-1979
Paul Krause's 81 career interceptions, 1964-79

THE LONGEST FIELD GOAL

Dempsey didn't kick that football. God did.
—WAYNE WALKER, *Detroit Lions linebacker*

It was a [expletive] miracle.
—JOE SCHMIDT, *Lions coach*

As the years pass, Tom Dempsey's record 63-yard field goal in 1970 seems more and more mystical. The closest anyone has come since is Steve Cox's 60-yarder in '84, even though indoor stadiums and artificial surfaces have made kicking easier.

The miracle began with Dempsey himself. He was born with only a nub for a right hand and a short, toeless right foot, his kicking foot. In 1969, his rookie year with the Saints, the *New Orleans Times-Picayune* ran a photo of him booting a game-winning field goal with a whole foot. A deskman at the paper figured there had to be something wrong with the picture and had airbrushed the rest in.

Handicaps aside, Dempsey was a good—not great—kicker. He had a powerful leg, but there was no telling where his long kicks might end up. As a rookie, he made 21 of 30 field-goal attempts inside the 49, 1 of 11 from 50 and beyond. Nothing he'd done in his second season foreshadowed a record, either. He'd been nagged by a pulled hip muscle and made only 5 of 15 tries going into the fateful game against Detroit at Tulane Stadium.

The events leading up to the kick were unusual, too. With 6:42 left, the Lions had the ball at their own 14-yard line, trailing 16–14. Greg Landry drove the team to the New Orleans 10, where Errol Mann kicked the go-ahead field goal. Eleven seconds remained.

It came out afterward that the Lions' drive had been kept alive by an official's oversight. They got an extra down while still deep in their territory and should have had to punt with about four minutes to go. That would have changed everything.

Also, on the play before Mann's field goal, Landry called a timeout immediately after running back Mel Farr was downed. He could have used up most of the clock before stopping it and prevented New Orleans from getting the ball back.

Finally, there was the Saints' one play before the kick. Billy Kilmer hit Al Dodd on a sideline pattern for 17 yards. Game films showed Dodd didn't get both feet in bounds. The pass should have been incomplete. Had instant replay been around in '70, Dempsey probably would have been on the sidelines watching a desperation heave downfield. Clearly, something more powerful than Pete Rozelle was at work here.

The clock read :02 when Dempsey trotted onto the field. He'd hit from 29, 27 and 8 yards earlier in the game, but 63? The NFL record was 56, set by Baltimore's Bert Rechichar 17 years before. Who could blame the thousands of people streaming for the exits?

The line of scrimmage was the New Orleans 45. In the huddle Dempsey told holder Joe Scarpati to line up eight yards deep instead of the usual seven. He asked his linemen to hold their blocks a little longer. He wanted more time to stride into the ball.

"I tried to do it like I do on a kickoff," he said. "I started my left foot six inches back of where it is on a regular kick to get more leg swing."

The snap from Jackie Burkett and the hold by Scarpati were perfect. The Lions mounted only a token rush (they didn't want to be offsides and like everybody else were having a hard time taking the kick seriously). Dempsey caught the ball dead solid perfect.

"When he hit it, I could tell it was a helluva impact," Lions assistant coach Bill McPeak said. "I said to myself, 'Oh, my God.'"

The ball seemed to stay in the air forever. Mann, who watched with a trained eye, said it probably got some help from a breeze blowing above the stadium, but not much.

"He could stand there and kick it 200 times and not hit it that sweet again," he said. "Boy, did he ever hit it sweet."

It floated through the uprights to the right of center and hit the ground about three yards behind the crossbar. Back judge Bill Kestermeier said, "It cleared by a short foot. There was no doubt about it."

The stadium erupted. Dempsey's teammates mobbed him, and fans tumbled onto the field. It took the kicker 15 minutes to reach the locker room.

"I knew I could do it," he said. "There's so much involved in kicking one that long, but I knew I could do it. The only question was if this was going to be the time and if it would be straight enough."

The Lions, nine-point favorites, were understandably stunned. "You'll never see it again," Schmidt said in the tomblike locker room. "It's like winning the Masters with a 390-yard hole-in-one on the last shot."

The national reaction was tremendous. Dempsey was deluged with speaking requests. A New England ski resort renamed its longest slope for him. The NFL made him co–player of the week with

DECADE LEADERS

PASSING

Yards: Fran Tarkenton, 23,863; Jim Hart, 23,026; Roger Staubach, 22,279.
Completion percentage (1,500 attempts): Ken Stabler, 59.9; Tarkenton, 59.7; Bob Griese, 58.2.
Touchdowns: Tarkenton, 156; Staubach, 152; Stabler, 150.
Interceptions: Terry Bradshaw, 163; Hart, 145; Stabler, 143.

RUSHING

Yards: O.J. Simpson, 10,539; Franco Harris, 8,563; Larry Csonka, 6,975.
Yards per carry (750 attempts): Mercury Morris, 5.2; Greg Pruitt, 4.8; Simpson, 4.7.
TDs: Harris, 72; Walter Payton and Simpson, 59.

RECEIVING

Receptions: Harold Jackson, 432; Harold Carmichael and Bob Tucker, 407.
Yards: Jackson, 7,724; Ken Burrough, 6,343; Gene Washington (49ers), 6,145.
Yards per catch (200 receptions): Mel Gray, 20.0; Paul Warfield, 19.9; John Gilliam, 19.4.
TDs: Jackson, 61; Carmichael and Washington, 57.

OTHER CATEGORIES

Scoring: Jan Stenerud, 875; Garo Yepremian, 865; Jim Turner, 827.
Interceptions: Jake Scott, 49; Mel Blount, 42; Paul Krause and Emmitt Thomas, 41.
Punt return average (75 returns): Billy Johnson, 13.2; Rick Upchurch, 12.6; Mack Herron, 11.7.
Punt return TDs: Upchurch, 6.
Kickoff return average (75 returns): Clarence Davis, 27.1; Terry Metcalf, 26.5; Vic Washington, 25.9.
Kickoff return TDs: Cecil Turner, 4.
Field goals: Stenerud, 201; Yepremian, 177; Don Cockroft and Turner, 170.
Field goal percentage (100 attempts): Efren Herrera, 69.7; Yepremian, 68.6; Toni Fritsch, 66.9.
Punting average (200 punts): Dave Lewis, 43.7; Ray Guy, 43.1; Ron Widby, 42.0.

Raiders kicker George Blanda, whose chip-shot 52-yarder had beaten the Browns.

The buzz had barely subsided when Dallas Cowboys president Tex Schramm did the unthinkable—he challenged the validity of the new record. Out loud.

Schramm accused Dempsey of having an unfair advantage because his specially designed kicking shoe was like "the head of a golf club with a sledgehammer surface." He argued that while most kickers met the ball with a squared-off sole, Dempsey used the entire front of his shoe.

"I have great admiration for Dempsey in overcoming his physical disability," Schramm said. "But I believe he should use the same surface to meet the ball that other kickers use."

It was not one of Schramm's better moments. He'd questioned Dempsey's shoe before, but he hadn't come off looking *this* bad.

Modified kicking shoes had been outlawed the year before. Things had been getting out of hand, with players adding metal ribbing and tying the toes in the air to increase lift on the ball. The new guidelines specified that you couldn't wear in an NFL game what you couldn't buy off the shelf of a store. In Dempsey's case that was a problem. His shoe ended just past the ankle with a flat surface. It cost $200. (He'd begun his kicking career barefooted, with just a piece of tape protecting his stub.)

In August 1969 Mark Duncan, the NFL's supervisor of officials, examined the shoe at the Saints' request and called it legal. For some reason that wasn't good enough for Schramm.

"I told the chairman of the competition committee I didn't feel they had the authority to approve Dempsey's shoe," he said.

Dempsey held his tongue, referring reporters to general manager Vic Schwenk. Columnists in New Orleans ripped into Schramm. One printed the address of the Cowboys offices, and Schramm was bombarded with hate mail. He finally retracted his statement.

"It was a mistake and bad timing on my part," he said. "That 63-yarder was a heck of an accomplishment and a tremendous tribute to him. I don't give a damn what you've got on your foot, I say that if you can kick that darn thing 63 yards through the goal posts, it is one heck of an accomplishment."

Dempsey's season turned around after the kick.

He made 10 of his last 15 field-goal attempts. The Saints, however, didn't win another game. They finished 2–11–1.

The next summer, Dempsey was cut. He and coach J. D. Roberts couldn't agree on the proper weight for a place-kicker. Dempsey saw nothing wrong with being 275 pounds. Roberts did. Dempsey lost the debate.

He signed with the Eagles and spent four seasons (1971–74) with them. Over the final five years of his career, he kicked for the Rams, Oilers and Bills. He never booted another field goal longer than 54 yards.

...
WHAT IF?

College coaching legends Joe Paterno, Frank Leahy and Bear Bryant came close to taking NFL jobs. Paterno almost made the move twice. The scenarios:

Joe Paterno—Steelers owner Art Rooney offered the Penn State coach a reported $50,000 a year for more than five years in 1969. Paterno was sorely tempted. "I'd never dreamed about making that kind of money," he said. "Then I decided to sleep on it. I started to think of what I wanted to do. I had put some things out of whack."

Two years later he turned down a coach–general manager position with the Packers. Then came the last temptation of Saint Joe. In 1973 the Patriots' Billy Sullivan put a six-year, $1.3 million deal—with plenty of perks—on the table. Paterno called it "the best offer I ever had," and told Sullivan he was going to take it. But again he slept on it, and again he changed his mind.

The three spurned clubs made good second choices. Pittsburgh became the team of the '70s under Chuck Noll. Green Bay turned to Dan Devine and won the NFC Central title—their last—two years later. And New England went with Chuck Fairbanks and made the playoffs in 1976 and '78.

Frank Leahy—When he was at Boston College in 1941, he interviewed for the Lions job. Hall-of-Famer Alex Wojciechowicz, the Detroit center, claims he set the whole thing up. Leahy had been his line coach at Fordham.

"They had worked out salary figures and everything," Wojie said in *What a Game They Played.*

But then Notre Dame came calling. That was the year coach–athletic director Elmer Layden left to

GIANT STEP

Joe Paterno, Frank Leahy and Bear Bryant were probably wise to stay in the college ranks. Here are the five winningest college coaches (minimum: 10 seasons) who tried the pros. As you can see, only one won more games than he lost.

HOW FIVE COLLEGE COACHING GREATS FARED IN THE NFL

Coach, College*	Record	NFL Team, Yrs.	Record
Bud Wilkinson, Oklahoma	145–29–4	Cards, '78–79	9–20–0
Jock Sutherland, Pittsburgh	144–28–14	2 teams, '40–47	30–17–1
Frank Kush, Arizona State	176–54–1	Colts, '82–84	11–28–1
John McKay, Southern Cal	127–40–8	Bucs, '76–84	45–91–1
Dan Devine, Missouri	172–57–9	Packers, '71–74	25–28–4

*college he was at longest

become NFL commissioner. It was an opportunity Leahy couldn't pass up. The Lions wound up hiring Bill Edwards, who lasted 14 games.

Bear Bryant—Joe Robbie came "within an ace" of getting Alabama's Bryant to coach the Dolphins in 1970, according to one report. He had to settle for Don Shula, poor fellow.

...
FIGHT OF THE DECADE
Chiefs vs. Raiders, 1970

The bitter Chiefs–Raiders rivalry reached a peak November 1, 1970. All hell broke loose on the field that day at Kansas City's Municipal Stadium.

With 1:08 to go, the Chiefs had a 17–14 lead and the ball at the Oakland 48. It was third and 10. A first down meant victory. On a sensational call, quarterback Len Dawson bootlegged around right end and gained 19 yards. He'd assumed the fetal position at the Oakland 29 when defensive end Ben Davidson caught up to the play.

Not-so-gentle Ben went helmet first into Dawson's back. The force of impact flipped him up and over the fallen quarterback.

"To be perfectly honest," Davidson says, "what went through my mind was that if I can spear him and break a couple of ribs, maybe he won't be able to play next week and they'll lose. I knew they had the first down and the game."

The first irate Chief on the scene was wide receiver Otis Taylor. He and Davidson tumbled to the ground, fists flying. Both benches cleared, and a huge pile of bodies formed.

"I was at the bottom of the pile, and nobody could really get at me," Davidson says. "Only one small part of me was exposed, and one of the Chiefs, I think it was Frank Pitts, was kicking it over and over."

Raiders linebacker Dan Conners wasn't as lucky. "They got me down and took my helmet off and started beating me," he said. "There must have been 35 of them."

It took referee Bob Finley about five minutes to halt the free-for-all. He immediately stepped off 15 yards against Oakland for Davidson's late hit. The Raiders protested, insisting the Chiefs had to be penalized, too, because Taylor had been ejected.

Finley and his crew held a conference. They emerged moments later with a new ruling: offsetting penalties, replay the down. Confusion reigned.

To find the original line of scrimmage, Finley had to watch NBC replays. He wound up spotting the ball at the Oakland *49,* a yard off. That set up the frenzied final minute.

The Chiefs failed to get the first down and punted. The Raiders quickly drove to the Kansas City 41, where, with eight seconds remaining, George Blanda kicked a field goal. The game ended in a 17–17 tie.

Remarkably, Dawson wasn't hurt by Davidson's hit. In fact, the two remain good friends to this day. In 1989 they filmed a commercial together. Davidson's final line was: "It's always fun to drop in on you, Len."

...
A WOMAN'S TOUCH

The alignment of the NFC was determined by commissioner Pete Rozelle's secretary, Thelma Elkjer.

The old NFL had to be reduced to three divisions after the merger with the AFL, but the owners couldn't agree on how. When they were still stalemated eight months later, Rozelle had his secretary reach into a cut-glass vase and pick one of five plans.

She pulled out plan number three. It was the only one that kept the black-and-blue division (Chicago, Green Bay, Detroit, Minnesota) intact. If she'd selected any of the other four, the Vikings would have been in the Eastern Division.

Earlier there had been *nine* plans. The possibilities were positively frightening. Two broke up the Bears-Packers rivalry. Another put Philadelphia and Detroit in the West.

The current setup isn't perfect, but it could have been a lot worse. Thanks, Thelma.

...
OLD QUARTERBACKS NEVER DIE

There's never been an unlikelier MVP than George Blanda in 1970. He was the oldest player in the league, a 43-year-old kicker and backup quarterback. But during one sensational five-week stretch he became a national story as he kicked and passed the Oakland Raiders to four victories and a tie.

Without his heroics, the team wouldn't have finished first in the AFC West. How George did it:

October 25 vs. Pittsburgh—Replaced injured Daryle Lamonica in the first quarter and threw three touchdown passes (44, 19 and 43 yards) to lead the Raiders to a 31–14 win.

November 1 at Kansas City—Booted a 48-yard field goal with three seconds left to salvage a 17–17 tie. The Chiefs had 6'10" Morris Stroud stand by the goal post and try to bat the ball down, but it just cleared his fingertips—and the crossbar.

November 8 vs. Cleveland—Came in at QB in the fourth quarter after Lamonica got hurt again. Hit Warren Wells with a 14-yard TD pass to tie the game at 20 with 1:14 remaining, then kicked a 52-yard field goal, his longest as a Raider, with three seconds to go for the victory. Blanda: "I didn't kick it any different than last week. Well, maybe I put a little more rear end into it." *San Francisco Chronicle* headline: "It's Blanda Again!"

November 15 at Denver—Took over for Lamonica with 4:01 to play and the Broncos leading, 19–17. Drove the team 80 yards on four completions, the last a 20-yarder to Fred Biletnikoff for the winning score. Headline: "Routine Raider Win—Blanda Again."

November 22 vs. San Diego—Booted a 16-yard field

goal with four seconds left for a 20–17 victory. Had missed earlier tries from 42 and 41 yards. Blanda: "Hell, I was just setting up those last few seconds." Headline: "Ho-Hum, Blanda Again."

Blanda's run finally ended on Thanksgiving Day against the Lions in Detroit. He was put in in the fourth quarter but couldn't produce any points as the Raiders lost, 28–14.

■ ■ ■

GEORGE PLIMPTON'S FOUR PLAYS

Author George Plimpton lived every pro football fan's fantasy on August 22, 1971. He quarterbacked the Baltimore Colts for four plays against the Detroit Lions during a preseason game.

Eight years earlier, Plimpton had trained with the Lions and run five plays in an intrasquad scrimmage, the basis for his bestselling book, *Paper Lion.* This time, however, it was the real thing.

Practically. Plimpton's four plays were staged just after the first half ended, so they didn't count in the game. But the Lions had their first-string defense in, and the players were in a particularly foul mood.

It was 88 degrees that day in Ann Arbor, Michigan, and much hotter on the field. The last thing the Lions wanted was extra work. And what if one of them got hurt? Or worse, if Plimpton completed a pass? They'd never live *that* down.

They considered not going through with it until ABC, which was filming a special on Plimpton, agreed to pay them. When the network asked them to play it straight—that is, no blitzing—they refused. If it was football Plimpton wanted, it was football he was going to get.

The referee put the ball on the 50, and Plimpton's name was announced on the PA system. He had a Super Bowl–sized audience. The crowd at Michigan Stadium was 91,745. He called the first play, then stepped up to the line, wearing jersey number 1. How his series went:

1. Fullback up the middle: In *Mad Ducks and Bears,* the sequel to *Paper Lion,* Plimpton identifies the play as Ride 38 Sucker, but that can't be right.

Ride 38 was a sweep right by the halfback. The fullback, Don Nottingham, carried the ball on this play. Plimpton had trouble with center Bill Curry's snap and handed the ball off nose down. Nottingham was lucky to get back to the line of scrimmage. After the whistle, defensive end Jim Mitchell belted Plimpton in the helmet and drew a 15-yard penalty. First down at the Detroit 35.

Nottingham: "We probably ran a P-12. [On that play] I'd be running right for the center's left cheek. I was really not too crazy about being in there with George. I was the last guy picked in the draft that year and was more concerned with getting into the [real] game for a couple of plays. I felt like I was a guinea pig being in there to get slammed."

2. Halfback over the right side: In Colts terminology, 34 Wham. The hole is between the guard and tackle. The fullback helps out on the defensive tackle. Just before the snap, Lions tackle Alex Karras shifted into the designated hole. Halfback Jack Maitland had no chance. No gain.

Maitland: "There should have been an audible called. He never checked off, and I got crunched."

Audible? Heck, Plimpton only *knew* half a dozen plays.

3. Quick slant to the split end: Otherwise known as 68 CI. Rookie Gordon Bowdell, the intended receiver, was lined up wide left. Plimpton took a three-step drop and let 'er fly, but the pass was bat-

---

$$$$$

$.15	First cash dividend paid by Patriots, 1972
$1.50	What Falcons raised ticket prices in September 1971, in violation of Nixon's wage-price freeze (the Justice Department brought suit)
$5	NFLPA "No Freedom, No Football" T-shirt in 1974
$9	Dinner allowance for players on road in 1973
$1,000	Steelers coach Chuck Noll's fine for calling the Raiders' George Atkinson a dirty player in 1976
$1,500	George Atkinson's fine for being a dirty player in 1976
$10,000	Bonus Colts owner Bob Irsay gave kicker Toni Linhart after he missed three field-goal tries in a game, 1979 (Linhart was cut the next day)
$13,000	Minimum salary, 1970-73
$41,403	Average defensive back's pay in 1977 ($103 less than for *kickers*)
$295,000	Damages awarded ex-defensive lineman Houston Ridge in malpractice suit against Chargers, 1973
$2,135,000	Projected budget for a WFL team in 1974
$3,300,000	Value of contracts Dolphins' Larry Csonka, Paul Warfield and Jim Kiick signed with WFL in 1974
$175,000,000	Construction cost of Louisiana Superdome in 1975

ted down by tackle Jerry Rush. In George's defense, he had hurt his thumb in training camp and wasn't 100 percent (whatever that was). Third and 10.

Bowdell: "Actually, he was pretty accomplished at it in practice. He could throw it out there. [But] that's an awful tough way to write a book. What's he doing now, anyway? He kinda reminds me a little bit of Pat Paulsen. You're not sure what he ever did, but you sure liked him."

4. Quarterback draw: When in doubt, as Dandy Don Meredith used to say, go to your power runner. This one was called Quarterback 52 Trap Draw. Plimpton took a step back, watched blitzing middle linebacker Mike Lucci shoot by, then ran for about a six-yard gain before Karras tackled him. "Mitchell came up and sat on me to make sure," he wrote.

Totals: Four plays, 21 yards.

■ ■ ■

DOUBLE DEALING

In his zeal to rebuild the Redskins in 1971, coach-GM George Allen traded not one, not two but three future draft choices twice. The league didn't catch on for almost a year.

The picks were Washington's second-, third- and fourth-rounders in 1973. Allen originally sent the number two to the New York Jets as compensation for signing free-agent defensive end Verlon Biggs. He later used the same pick to acquire strong safety Richie Petitbon from the Los Angeles Rams.

The number three and number four first went to Buffalo in a deal for defensive end Ron McDole. Then they were shipped to San Diego for cornerback–kick returner Speedy Duncan.

"There was no intent to deceive," Allen said. "It was just a matter of a million and one things to do with a team we had just taken over and trying to do them all at the same time. If we finished in last place, this probably wouldn't even have been an issue."

But the Redskins had made the playoffs, and Petitbon and Duncan—players they'd obtained in bogus trades—had helped them get there. Duncan had led the NFL in punt returns and run back an interception for a touchdown to knock the Rams out of the NFC West race. Petitbon had started and picked off five passes, three in a victory over St. Louis.

Commissioner Pete Rozelle said the trades weren't stopped when they were made because the league office was going through a personnel change. He added, however, that another shady Allen deal—with the New York Giants for wide receiver Clifton McNeil—*was* blocked. The Redskins wound up giving the Giants other draft picks.

"It also happened a couple of times when Allen was coach at Los Angeles," Rozelle said, "but there were no fines because the opposing clubs worked out an immediate settlement with him."

He fined the Redskins $5,000, the maximum amount. And, in an almost unprecedented move, he hauled Allen in before the club owners during a special session in New York and lectured him for five minutes.

Allen also had to settle with the Rams and Chargers. Petitbon ended up costing a number one and number six and Duncan a number three, number four and number five.

■ ■ ■

GEORGE ALLEN'S FAVORITE TRADES

1. **SS Ken Houston and TE Alvin Reed from the Oilers for TE Mack Alston, OT Jim Snowden, S Jeff Severson, WR Clifton McNeil and DE Mike Fanucci (1973).** "The Oilers originally gave me Houston and a sixth[-round draft pick]. But two weeks later, I sent the pick back for Reed. It had been prearranged. The Oilers wanted to make the Houston trade look as good as possible." Only Alston lasted more than two seasons with the Oilers. Houston, of course, made the Hall of Fame the first year he was eligible.

2. **QB Billy Kilmer from the Saints for LB Tom Roussel and a number four (C Richard Winther) and number eight (DB James Elders) (1971).** Allen might be sentimental about this one because it was the first trade he made as Redskins coach, but he says it's "because of the way he [Kilmer] produced. When I made the trade he was on the operating table. He was having a separated shoulder mended. . . . Roussel was from Louisiana. I figured they'd like that."

3. DT Dave Butz and three draft picks from the Cardinals for a number one in 1977 (QB Steve Pisarkiewicz), number one in '78 (DB Ken Greene) and number two in '79 (traded to the Raiders for picks that brought LB Calvin Favron and WR Mark Bell) (1975). Butz was a starter on a Super Bowl winner 13 seasons later. "You can't block him."

■ ■ ■

A NEW STAT

Hall-of-Famer Alan Page was the inspiration for the pass-rushing statistic known as the "hurry." Bud Grant, his coach with the Vikings, came up with the term to better measure Page's effect on opposing quarterbacks. Sacks didn't tell the whole story.

Grant defined a hurry as making the quarterback throw the ball before he wanted to. Every team uses it now.

In 1971 Page had 42 hurries, in addition to 10 sacks. It may have been the finest season ever by a defensive lineman and earned him NFC Player-of-the-Year honors from UPI. He had 109 tackles, 35 assists and three safeties, astonishing figures for a tackle.

■ ■ ■

DUANE THOMAS SPEAKS

No one who saw Duane Thomas' interview with CBS's Tom Brookshier after Super Bowl VI is likely to forget it. Brookshier certainly hasn't.

"I still have nightmares about that interview," he said. "I think of it and break into a cold sweat. I keep a blown-up photo of it next to my desk—so I'll never forget."

Thomas, Dallas' sensational second-year running back, had maintained virtual silence during the 1971 season. He not only didn't talk to the media, he hardly said anything to his teammates and coaches. It was his way of protesting the club's refusal to tear up his original contract and pay him what he thought he was worth.

Thomas was the near-unanimous MVP choice of the writers that day, rushing for 95 yards and a

We wouldn't hit a guy with glasses, but the Colts' Mike Curtis would—and did in 1971. This unfortunate fan ran on the field between plays and took the ball, so Curtis, like a true middle linebacker, let him have it. (UPI/Bettmann Newsphotos)

touchdown in a 24–3 victory over Miami. But *Sport* magazine, which has the final say, opted to award its car to the Cowboys' Roger Staubach, who threw for a mere 119 yards. The magazine was simply playing it safe. Who knew what Thomas might say—or not say—at the presentation in New York? That is, if he showed up.

Brookshier was working the winners' locker room when Thomas suddenly appeared behind him on the TV platform. With him was his friend and advisor, Jim Brown. The sphinx was going to speak! The following conversation was seen and heard coast to coast:

BROOKSHIER: Duane, how are you?
THOMAS: All right, how are you?

BROOKSHIER: My name is Tom Brookshier, and it's nice to talk to you. Behind you is a fellow that used to run over me for a living, the great Jimmy Brown. How are you, Jim?

BROWN: Hi, Tom, how are you?

BROOKSHIER: Duane, uh, you do things with speed but never hurry, a lot like the great Jim Brown. Uh, you never hurry into a hole. You take your time, make a spin, yet you still outrun people. Are you that fast, are you that quick, would you say?

THOMAS: Evidently.

(The room explodes with laughter.)

BROOKSHIER: Really, I saw a couple of times, I know one time John Niland was pulling leading the sweep and he didn't get a good block on it and the fellow was in good position and you simply stepped around him and turned it up the sidelines. Jimmy, maybe you can answer for us. He does have better speed than it appears, don't you think a little bit?

BROWN: Well, actually, Duane Thomas is probably the most gifted runner in football today. He's big and he has great speed, it's very obvious, but he has fantastic moves. And I think that he's probably as smart as any football player playing today. So that combination is, you know, fantastic.

BROOKSHIER: It is great. Duane, uh, uh, people don't know you, and I know this is sort of a tight situation . . .

BROWN: Are you nervous, Tom?

BROOKSHIER: I'm nervous, I'm anxious to get the interview, I'm nervous. But what I . . . you like football, you must like this game, because they tell me in practice you run further than anybody else with the ball and all. You must like the game of football.

THOMAS: Yeah, I do. I do. That's why I went off in pro football, you know, that's why I am a football player. So that's what I have to live with.

BROOKSHIER: I'll tell you one thing, you're some kind of football player. Pat Summerall commented in the game that he thought you might be bigger than 205. Is 205 accurate, or are you going about 215?

THOMAS: Uh, it all depends on what I need.

BROOKSHIER: You mean you weigh in at different weights for different games?

THOMAS: Yeah.

BROWN: Can I say one thing before we go on?

BROOKSHIER: Surely.

BROWN: Duane consented [to talk]. He feels good today. I think he wanted to win the Super Bowl, he wanted to play football, he wanted to come back and show the American public that he is a good football player. I think that has been accomplished. I think his silence has enabled him to do this, I think because there was no controversy involved. There was no conflict with his teammates or his coaches. And I think he should be, uh, commended for this. But I don't think he wants to say any more at this particular time. But I think he did want the American public to know that he is a football player and that he did want to win the Super Bowl.

BROOKSHIER: Very good, Jimmy. I'll tell you something else: Dan Reeves says that you make adjustments on your own that are fantastic. You're a good, smart football player, too. Duane, uh, thank you very much and I appreciate it, you hear?

THOMAS: Thank you.

BROOKSHIER: Good luck to you. Duane Thomas, one of the great running backs, and we're glad it was done here, he broke the silence.

• • •

THE WILLY WONKA GAME

NBC got a rare second chance on November 23, 1975. Its 4:00 P.M. national game between the Raiders and Redskins was headed for overtime. Meanwhile, millions of kids in the Eastern time zone were gearing up for the television debut of *Willy Wonka and the Chocolate Factory*, scheduled to begin at 7:00. What to do?

Seven years earlier, the network had found itself in a similar mess. A big game between the Jets and Raiders was running long. The movie *Heidi* was supposed to air at 7:00.

With the Jets leading 32–29 and only 50 seconds remaining, the decision was made to cut to the movie. The NBC switchboard lit up like the New York skyline. Thousands of irate football fans demanded an explanation. The load of calls was so great the switchboard broke down.

The backlash got even worse at about 8:20 when the network ran a line at the bottom of the screen announcing the Raiders had rallied for two touchdowns to win 43–32 ("Details at 11"). With that, the "Heidi game" became part of pro football lore.

NBC was determined not to make the same mistake with Willy Wonka. So when the Raiders and Redskins went into overtime, the network went with them. Oakland's George Blanda finally ended the game with a 27-yard field goal at 42 minutes, 20 seconds past 7:00.

Willy Wonka was then joined *in progress*. Again the NBC switchboard went bonkers. The number of calls was estimated at 1,000. Irate parents couldn't believe the network had chopped off the first half of the movie. A beleaguered network spokesman explained that the film in its entirety would have ended "a little late for children to be up."

Moral:

If you're at a loss to choose what is right,
Schedule the movie for Saturday night.

WHAT YOU MISSED IF YOU WERE A . . .

■ . . . **football fan stuck with *Heidi*:** Forty-two seconds remained when Daryle Lamonica threw a 43-yard touchdown pass to running back Charlie Smith to give the Raiders a 36–32 lead. The Jets' Earl Christy fumbled the kickoff, and Raider Preston Ridlehuber recovered in the end zone for another score. Final: Raiders, 43–32.

■ . . . ***Willy Wonka* fan stuck with football:** Poor, hard-working young Charlie Bucket finds the last of the five gold tickets inside a Wonka Bar. He wins a lifetime supply of chocolate and a tour of Willy's mysterious candy factory.

■ ■ ■

PLAYS FROM THE PRESIDENT

What Richard Nixon really wanted to be was an offensive coordinator. While in the White House in 1971, the former Whittier College benchwarmer suggested plays to the Washington Redskins and Miami Dolphins.

Redskins coach George Allen made the mistake of listening to the president. Before Washington's playoff game against San Francisco, Nixon told him

GALLUPING AWAY

Football officially replaced baseball as Americans' favorite spectator sport in 1972. The Gallup Poll that year gave football an edge of 36 to 21 percent. In 1948 the results had been virtually the reverse. A 1981 Gallup survey found that 69 percent of the male respondents had watched a pro football game that season.

GALLUP POLL RESULTS

	FOOTBALL	BASEBALL
1937	26%	36%
1948	17	39
1960	21	34
1972	36	21
1981	38	16
1985	26	21

he thought an end-around play to Roy Jefferson might work.

Near the end of the first half, Allen called the play. The Redskins, leading 10–3, had a second and six at the San Francisco eight. It was a disaster. Jefferson was dragged down for a 13-yard loss, and then the 49ers blocked the field-goal attempt.

The Redskins lost, 24–20.

A week later, at 1:30 A.M., the phone rang in Miami coach Don Shula's house. Shula, up watching a tape of his team's 21–0 victory over Baltimore in the AFC championship game earlier that day, said afterward he thought it might be "some nut." It was Nixon.

He recommended that the Dolphins use the down-and-in pattern to Paul Warfield against Dallas in the Super Bowl. The next day it was national news.

The Cowboys were ready for the down and in. They kept strong safety Cornell Green back to close off the area and shut down Warfield and the Dolphins, 24–3.

"They made sure under any circumstances we wouldn't be able to catch that pass," Warfield said.

The following year Nixon sent Shula a telegram on the occasion of his 100th NFL victory and promised not to call any plays if Miami made it to the Super Bowl again. Shula publicly thanked him.

The president actually got to be a bit of a nuisance, according to Redskins quarterback Billy Kilmer.

"He's something else," he said. "He calls all the time. He even called the coach on election night to talk about the game. But he's really hurting us. He told some guy from Cleveland he met in New York that Cleveland had a good team but they had quarterback problems. Then Cleveland gets all psyched up and they're much harder to beat. I think I'm going to ask George Allen to tell the president not to talk about a game until after we've played it."

PLAYBOOK FOR SALE

Just before training camp opened in 1972, New Orleans Saints coach J. D. Roberts received a call from a "Miss Ramsey" in Dallas. Would Roberts, she asked, be interested in buying a Los Angeles Rams playbook?

Roberts informed NFL officials of the offer. Play along, they told him, and let's see if we can find out who's behind this. He wasn't too crazy about the idea, but he agreed. The league then called in the FBI.

"Miss Ramsey" probably thought she had a pigeon. The Saints were league laughingstocks. A victory over the Rams in the first game might help Roberts keep his job a little longer. She originally quoted a figure of $500 but later told him it would be more. A meeting was arranged for the next night at a New Orleans hotel.

The FBI wired Roberts for sound. As instructed by "Miss Ramsey," he carried an envelope full of cash. Shortly after midnight, a man named Wayne Boswell approached him and resumed negotiations for the playbook.

Periodically, Boswell left to confer with "others." A price of $2,500 was finally agreed on. They were about to make the exchange when FBI agents stepped in and arrested Boswell and his accomplice. It was former Rams and Saints quarterback Karl Sweetan.

Sweetan spent nearly two days in jail before posting $25,000 bond. He and Boswell, his cousin, were charged with interstate transportation of stolen property.

He told the judge at his arraignment he was broke and unemployed. He'd recently washed out with the CFL's Edmonton Eskimos. The offensive playbook he'd tried to sell was a photocopy. He'd turned in the original when the Rams cut him in training camp in 1971.

The U.S. attorney decided not to prosecute. He wasn't able to establish conclusively that the playbook was worth more than $5,000, which was necessary in the first of the two charges. Some experts had put the value above $5,000, others below.

OUT OF BOUNDS

Bubba Smith's pro football career was wrecked by a sideline marker. Or so he claimed. The huge defensive end sued the NFL, game official Ed Marion and Tampa businessman Robert Lastra for $2.5 million over it.

Lastra was the unfortunate soul hired to hold the marker for the Colts–Steelers preseason game August 26, 1972. He was paid $15, and there's no way it could have been worth it.

Late in the game at Tampa Stadium, Baltimore safety Rick Volk intercepted a pass. Smith tried to block for him but missed his target. He hurdled fallen Steeler running back Franco Harris and

NICKNAMES

"Broadway" Joe Namath	Joe "Big Bird" Lavender
Thomas "Hollywood" Henderson	Carl "Spider" Lockhart
"Mean" Joe Greene	Ken "Snake" Stabler
"Dr. Death" (Skip Thomas)	Willie "Sugar Bear" Young
"Juice" (O.J. Simpson)	Charles "King Kong" Philyaw
Charles "Bubba" Smith	Bill "Earthquake" Enyart
Billy "White Shoes" Johnson	John "Frenchy" Fuqua
Eugene "Mercury" Morris	Bob "Harpo" Gladieux
Roger "The Dodger" Staubach	Ernie "Fats" Holmes
Dick "Bam Bam" Ambrose	Billy "Furnace Face" Kilmer
Sam "Bam" Cunningham	Frank "Fudgehammer" Nunley
Charles "Boobie" Clark	Jack "Hacksaw" Reynolds
Danny "Lightning" Buggs	**Not Nicknames:**
Mike "The Animal" Curtis	Jubilee Dunbar
Ted "The Mad Stork" Hendricks	Fair Hooker
Joe "Turkey" Jones	Golden Richards
	Honor Jackson
	Cotton Fest

crashed into the sidelines near the Colts bench where Lastra was standing. He suffered a severe knee injury and was lost for the season.

There were two versions of how the injury occurred: Smith either caught his foot in the chain used to measure first downs or struck the aluminum down marker Lastra was holding.

Most of the Colts players blamed the marker. And Lastra. They were furious. The 6'7", 280-pound Smith was Baltimore's best pass rusher. Inconsistent, yes, but impossible to stop when motivated. He'd be hard to replace.

The Colts argued that if Lastra had simply dropped the pole, Smith wouldn't have been hurt. Lastra said he held on to it because he'd been told to. Marion had cautioned him before the game not to let go when the action got close because the spike used to sink the pole in the ground was dangerous when exposed.

After sitting out all of '72, Smith was traded to Oakland in '73. He lasted four more years (two with the Raiders, two with the Oilers) but wasn't the same player.

In 1974 he filed suit, claiming the equipment the NFL used in Tampa was dangerous and mishandled. The case went to trial in February 1978 and caused quite a stir. Smith's lawyers brought in broadcasters Howard Cosell and Don Meredith along with players Bill Curry, Larry Little and Curly Culp to testify. It ended with a hung jury. Five jurors sided with the NFL, one with Smith.

The case was retried in '79, and the jury voted 6–0 for the NFL. They determined that Smith was injured on the field, not when he hit the marker.

■ ■ ■

COAST TO COAST (ALMOST)

There aren't many records that can't be broken, but Ahmad Rashad owns one of them. In 1972, when he was a rookie with St. Louis, he had a 98-yard *nonscoring* reception, the only one in NFL history.

It happened December 10 at Busch Stadium. The Cardinals had just stopped the Los Angeles Rams on the goal line and taken over the ball at their one midway through the second quarter. On first down

Jim Hart went long to Rashad, who made a leaping catch at the St. Louis 40, eluded defensive backs Gene Howard and Dave Elmendorf and headed for the end zone.

DB Al Clark finally caught him at the 10 and pulled him down a yard short of the goal line. Ninety-eight yards and no touchdown. Running back Donny Anderson got that on the next play.

"If I scored, it wouldn't have been a record," said Rashad, who went by the name of Bobby Moore then. "Lew [Carpenter, the Cards' receivers coach] told me not to score. He wanted that record."

■ ■ ■

WRONG-WAY HAMPTON

Only one NFL back has ever had a 1,000-yard season and then lost it. Atlanta's Dave Hampton pulled the unusual U-turn in the last game of the 1972 season.

The Falcons were hosting Kansas City. On the second play of the fourth quarter, Hampton picked up a yard off left tackle to give him an even 1,000. He was the first back in franchise history to reach the mark, and play was stopped as he was presented the ball.

On the Falcons' next possession they had a first and 10 at the Kansas City 11 when quarterback Bob Berry pitched to Hampton running left. He bobbled the ball, and Kansas City end Marvin Upshaw knocked him down for a six-yard loss. There were about 10 minutes left in the game, so it didn't appear to be a problem. That was plenty of time to make up the difference.

But after Atlanta went ahead 14–10, the Chiefs launched an 81-yard drive that took over seven minutes. When the Falcons got the ball back there was only 2:14 left, and they trailed 17–14. They had to pass. Hampton got one more carry. He picked up one yard and finished the season with 995.

"I just wish I could describe how I feel right now," he said afterward. "It's just such a great feeling to get it [1,000] and then . . ."

It got worse.

The next season Hampton was 87 yards shy of 1,000 going into the final game against New Orleans.

At the start of the fourth quarter, he still needed 61. He carried the ball 16 times in the next 15 minutes and gained 58. He finished the season with 997 yards.

In 1974 he missed five games with a hip injury and didn't have a shot at 1,000. But in '75 he had 941 yards after 13 weeks. The Falcons' season finale was against Green Bay, and the Packers took a 22–6 lead into the fourth quarter.

Once again, Atlanta had to pass to get back in the game. With 2:35 remaining, Hampton still needed 28 yards, and the Falcons still trailed. Coach Marion Campbell instructed quarterback Pat Sullivan to "get it for him."

Hampton carried the ball three consecutive times. He gained four up the middle, 22 off right tackle and four more off the right side to go over 1,000. Haskel Stanback immediately replaced him in the lineup. Hampton finished the year on the sideline, his 1,002 yards safely in the record books.

It was the only 1,000-yard season of his career. The next year the Falcons waived him, and by '77 he was out of the league.

■ ■ ■
MORE WEIRDNESS

1972 was a strange year for rushing statistics. Dave Hampton was just one of several stories.

Ten backs gained 1,000 or more yards. That was four more than ever before. The increase was attributed to the hashmarks being moved closer to the middle of the field.

The Dolphins' Mercury Morris reached 1,000 three days *after* the season ended. NFL statisticians discovered he'd been incorrectly charged with a nine-yard loss in a game against Buffalo October 22. The extra nine gave Morris exactly 1,000 yards.

Bobby Douglass of the Bears nearly became the first quarterback to gain 1,000. He finished with 968 yards rushing and only 1,246 passing.

■ ■ ■
GETTING BURNED

Dozens of Rams and Cardinals players suffered second-degree burns in a December 1972 game when the Busch Stadium grounds crew mistakenly applied calcium chloride to the field. Calcium chloride is used to melt ice and snow from road surfaces.

"You couldn't even kneel on the field without feeling the heat from the acid," Rams trainer George Menefee said.

The crew thought it was putting down Urea, a harmless chemical that prevents synthetic surfaces from freezing. Someone got the bags mixed up.

In the three days following the game, the Cardinals used 48 tubes of hydrocortisone to fight infection from the burns.

■ ■ ■
'70s MYTHOLOGY

Let's clear up two myths about *North Dallas Forty,* Pete Gent's best-selling 1973 novel.

First, Gent did not have help writing it. It's been rumored for years that he did, from one of three Texas writers—Gary Cartwright, Mickey Herskowitz or Bud Shrake.

"Gary did give me some advice," Gent says with a laugh. "I remember him telling me one time, 'First, you put the paper in the typewriter, then you put the page number on it.' And the other thing he told me was don't let the facts get in the way of the story."

Cartwright read the manuscript before publication. So did playwright Larry King. But neither put a pencil to it or made suggestions, according to Gent.

"The only person I ever took any editing advice from was my agent," he says. "And that was after I'd finished the book. He went through it and gave me two pages of changes, the majority of which I did."

Second, Art Hartman, the squeaky-clean, second-string quarterback in the book, is not Roger Staubach. Staubach seemed to think so and was critical of Gent.

Gent insists all of the characters are composites of his former Dallas Cowboy teammates and bosses. Only a few are who they seem to be. (Quarterback Seth Maxwell is definitely based on Don Meredith, for instance.)

"But everybody thinks they're somebody," Gent says.

The Hartman character actually is based on a

defensive player, he says. Gent didn't know Staubach well at all. His career with the Cowboys ended in 1968, while Staubach's began in '69. They only crossed paths in training camps when Staubach worked out with the team while on leave from the Navy.

The novel, which covers eight days in the life of iconoclast-receiver Phil Elliott, has aged well. It's still in print, and Gent estimates total sales at around 1 million.

■ ■ ■
BYE-BYE BLACKOUTS

1973 was a historic year for pro football fans. In September, just before the season started, Congress passed a law banning television blackouts of pro sports events sold out 72 hours in advance. For the first time ever in most NFL cities, fans could watch home games on TV.

It was a long and bitter battle. The league had always maintained that televised home games would kill the live gate, the clubs' lifeblood, and stunt, if not reverse, its growth. And in the beginning, in the '50s, that was certainly true.

The Los Angeles Rams provided a dramatic example. When they put their home games on local TV in 1950—until '62 teams sold their television rights separately—their average gate receipts plummeted from $75,000 to $42,000. That same year, Chicago Cardinals coach Curly Lambeau lamented, "Our stadiums may have turned into studios." The next season, with home games blacked out, the Rams' average take was $105,000.

The NFL's television policy at the time was extremely protectionist. The 75-mile blackout radius was already in effect. Telecasts of games other than the local team's were limited.

For instance, if the Giants were playing at the Polo Grounds or had a road game that was on TV *or radio* back home, the Eagles couldn't televise their game in the New York area—unless it didn't conflict with the Giants'. In some cities on some Sundays, there was no pro football on television.

In 1951 the U.S. government filed suit against the NFL, charging its TV policy violated antitrust laws. The league claimed the case came about not because fans were unhappy with the rule restricting telecasts but because some radio and television networks weren't getting a piece of the pie and had complained to the Justice Department.

"We cannot divulge complainants to the department and they know it," said W. Perry Epes, chief government counsel. "But I can say that the public did complain and that we initiated this case from many complaints, not one or two."

U.S. District Judge Allan K. Grim heard the case in Philadelphia in 1953. He ruled the NFL was within its rights to black out home games but could no longer prevent clubs from televising or broadcasting their games in another club's area. The league considered appealing but decided against it.

"Throughout the trial we expressed continuously our desire to learn to live with television," commissoner Bert Bell said. "That's what we will try to do in this situation."

To learn to live with television. It was indeed a different era.

Blackouts became an issue again in 1957 when the Browns and Lions were getting ready to play for the championship in Detroit. The stadium was sold out, and Michigan Governor G. Mennen Williams appealed to Bell to allow the game to be shown on local TV. Bell wouldn't budge. It was a scene that would be repeated several times in the coming years.

"I don't think it's honest to sell tickets to thousands of people, then afterward, when all the tickets are gone, to give the game to television," he said.

By the late '50s the NFL was waging war against bars and restaurants that were showing home games with the help of special antennas. Motels beyond the 75-mile limit were beginning to do a big business because of the blackouts.

In 1963 the league experimented with closed-circuit TV for the first time. The '63 title game between the Giants and Bears was shown in three Chicago arenas. The next year the Giants tried closed circuit but gave up after just two games. Only 25 percent of the seats were being sold. The timing was terrible. The team fell from first to last place that season.

The NFL modified its blackout policy in 1966 at the height of its war with the AFL. Its new contract with CBS permitted another game to be shown in a city where a game was being played. (This was something Judge Grim's decision had allowed in 1953. But the NFL had gone back to its old restrictive ways when it signed its first league television contract in '62. It was able to get away with it because Congress had granted it an antitrust exemption.)

The NFL made the change because it wanted to give AFL telecasts competition. Which begs the question: Did the NFL's blackout policy help the AFL in its early years by giving the young league more exposure in major cities than it might otherwise have gotten?

In the '70s public sentiment against blackouts simply became too strong. With so many games sellouts, the policy had begun to seem punitive. It helped that the president, Richard Nixon, was a

football fan. He was able to put pressure on the NFL. The rebirth of the Redskins was another factor. Tickets were hard to come by, and politicians who couldn't get them were none too pleased when they couldn't see the games.

Then there was Ellis Rubin. A Miami Beach lawyer, he may have done as much to bring an end to blackouts as anybody. In 1970, when the Super Bowl was played at the Orange Bowl, he filed two suits against the league in an attempt to have the blackout lifted. He failed, but afterward Wisconsin Senator William Proxmire introduced a bill to eliminate blackouts if all the tickets had been sold.

"I think there is an economic basis for a blackout," said Ellis, who reportedly spent $15,000 of his own money carrying on the fight. "But when that economic basis has been satisfied, when all the tickets are sold, then I think the blackout should be lifted. I would put a cutoff date on it, Wednesday for example."

That's pretty close to the policy that exists today.

Rubin also represented a Redskins fan in a similar suit in 1972. Commissioner Pete Rozelle promised Nixon that year that he'd lift the Super Bowl blackout if the game sold out 10 days in advance. It didn't quite make it, but he lifted it, anyway. (Actually, Attorney General Richard Kleindienst, on behalf of the president, had asked Rozelle to lift the blackouts for *all* playoff games if they were sold out *48* hours ahead of time. Rozelle refused; Kleindienst threatened to have Congress re-examine the NFL's antitrust exemption.)

The league fought to keep its blackout power until the end. The day the Senate voted overwhelmingly to ban blackouts for three years in September 1973, Rozelle tried to impress upon a House subcommittee how fragile an enterprise pro football was.

"The business of professional football is in fact a very small business indeed," he said. "The entire football industry, in an economic sense, ranks with the American rope-and-twine manufacturing industry." (When he said that, they should have bound and gagged him.)

After the bill breezed through the House, Rozelle didn't even wait for Nixon to sign it. The blackout was lifted for 10 of the 13 opening-week games. There were 49,551 no-shows the first Sunday, more than half in Kansas City (16,031), where it rained until just before game time, and Miami (11,775), where it was 105 degrees. The Chiefs lost an estimated $28,000 in concessions and parking.

DECADE ALL-STAR TEAM

For all players except specialists, figures under "Data" are average season totals (except where indicated).

OFFENSE

Pos.	Player	Years*	Data
WR	Paul Warfield	7	30 catches, 603 yds, 6 TDs; 5 Pro Bowls
TE	Dave Casper	6	38 catches, 499 yds., 5 TDs; 4 Pro Bowls
T	Dan Dierdorf	9	5 Pro Bowls
G	John Hannah	7	3 Pro Bowls
C	Jim Langer	10	6 Pro Bowls
G	Larry Little	10	4 Pro Bowls
T	Art Shell	10	7 Pro Bowls
QB	Roger Staubach	10	57.1%, 2,228 yds., 15 TDs; 6 Pro Bowls
FB	Earl Campbell	2	1,574 yds., 4.7 avg., 16 TDs, 2 Pro Bowls
HB	O.J. Simpson	10	1,054 yds., 4.7 avg., 6 TDs; 5 Pro Bowls
WR	Drew Pearson	7	48 catches, 816 yds., 4 TDs; 3 Pro Bowls

DEFENSE

Pos.	Player	Years	Data
E	Jack Youngblood	9	7 Pro Bowls
T	Joe Greene	10	9 Pro Bowls
T	Alan Page	10	7 Pro Bowls
E	Claude Humphrey	10	6 Pro Bowls
LB	Jack Ham	9	7 Pro Bowls
LB	Jack Lambert	6	5 Pro Bowls
LB	Ted Hendricks	10	4 Pro Bowls
CB	Mike Haynes	4	6 interceptions; 4 Pro Bowls
CB	Mel Blount	10	4 interceptions; 4 Pro Bowls
SS	Ken Houston	10	4 interceptions; 10 Pro Bowls
FS	Jake Scott	9	5 interceptions; 5 Pro Bowls

SPECIALISTS AND OTHER SELECTIONS

Pos.	Selection	Years	Data
KR	Terry Metcalf	5	26.5 avg., 2 TDs
PR	Billy Johnson	6	13.2 avg., 5 TDs
K	Garo Yepremian	10	Averaged 18 FGs, 68.6% made
P	Ray Guy	7	43.1 avg.; 6 Pro Bowls
Special Teams -- Rusty Tillman		Wild Card Selection -- Chuck Foreman	
Kick Blocker -- Ted Hendricks		Coach -- Chuck Noll	
Enforcer -- Jack Tatum		PR Man -- Ernie Accorsi	

*Number of years he played in the decade.

Regular-season no-shows increased by 63 percent n 1973, according to NFL figures. Interestingly, though, the number of no-shows for sold-out games (5,808 average) wasn't much more than for nonsell-outs (5,221). In other words, being able to watch at home wasn't the main reason fans stayed away. Paid attendance actually went up 2.7 percent (though it dropped each of the next two seasons).

In October 1975, when the antiblackout law was about to expire, Rozelle told a House subcommittee it was causing the NFL "significant harm." It had cost teams $9 million in two years. (This figures out to about $175,000 a year per team. "Significant harm," you say?) The league, he said, might have to reconsider televising every game.

"This is one of the most arrogant things I've ever seen," said Michigan Representative William Brodhead. "Millions of senior citizens, jobless and others would be denied a chance to see games at home so millionaire owners can increase their profits."

The following spring, the House and Senate reached a compromise on a permanent antiblackout law. As the '90s began, the NFL was doing just fine.

• • •

THE ROLE OF THE NFL IN AMERICAN HISTORY

The National Football League got into the Bicentennial spirit in 1976 by sponsoring an essay contest for high school students. The theme: "The Role of the NFL in American History." Anna Jane Leider, a 16-year-old junior at T. C. Williams High in Alexandria, Virginia, received a $10,000 scholarship grant and an all-expense trip to the Super Bowl with her parents for this winning entry:

Henry Steele Commager, the noted historian, recently told the *Wall Street Journal* that in his view there was no connection whatsoever between the National Football League and the history of the United States.

Professor Commager is wrong. He should know that sports have always played a role in history. One cannot understand Sparta, for example, without considering that city's emphasis on gymnastics. One cannot study Athens without examining the Olympics. And one cannot explain England's greatness without hearing, over and over again, that the empire won its battles on "the playing fields of Eton."

What has been true for other nations is equally true for the United States. Sports are an expression of people, and people make history.

The most American of sports is football, of which the National Football League is the symbol, the pinnacle. Football is played only here and in Canada, a nation much like ours. No other country has taken to the game. Certainly, a historian cannot overlook this fact. He must ask, "What is it about football that makes it so attractive to Americans?"

The answer may be that our people's characteristics, self-view as a nation, and ideals closely resemble football.

We think of ourselves as a people who work together for the greatest good, but each member of society, whether he or she be a baker, a seamstress, a doctor, or a lawyer must contribute his personal skill to that objective. Combined, these talents form a great, unified nation. It is the same in football. Each member of the team is a skilled specialist. The efforts of these specialists, working together, create great teams.

We think of ourselves as people who overcame huge odds in our early history. The westward expansion was physically demanding. One had to closely note the weather and the timing of the seasons. A great amount of personal bravery was needed in these times. It is the same in football. We see these qualities with which we identify—stamina, planning, taking advantage of weather and time, courage—reflected in a game.

We think of ourselves as an orderly society that obeys the law, with punishments for those who break it. It is the same in football. There are the rules of the game and the rules set by the coaches. Break them, and there are penalties and fines.

We think of ourselves as a nation free of prejudices, where the best will get ahead. It is the same in football. One's ability as a football player counts, not one's race or religion. Influential friends or family cannot win a player a position on the team, nor can he buy one. Only skill and talent count. This total impartiality is a motivator and inspiration to youth. It has helped thousands gain an education that, otherwise, might have been beyond their reach.

We think of ourselves as a nation of many distinct

regions. We are Americans; but we are also Virginians, Texans, or New Yorkers. It is the same in football. The sport is American, but the major teams are associated with cities, states, and regions and thus help promote our sense of regional unity and pride. At the same time, teams help develop community spirit. Good high school and college teams develop a sense of unity in both their school and their community. A great National Football League team will accomplish the same for a major city, a state or even an entire region.

Thus, football is a mirror of ourselves. It reflects our desire for unity among people; our belief in courage, fitness, and good planning to reach our final goals; our respect for laws and rules; and our trust that skill and talent are what count in getting ahead. However, football protects our desire for regional unity and pride. We adopt these things into our lives, and are better off for it. That is what is American about football, and what Professor Commager needs to understand.

■ ■ ■

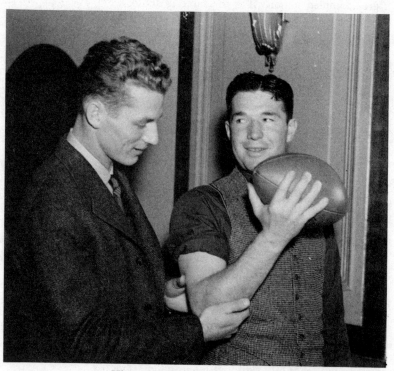

His stubby fingers didn't allow Packers Hall-of-Famer Arnie Herber to grip the football conventionally. Instead he just rested it in his palm and launched his passes. (UPI/Bettmann Newsphotos)

CHEAP, CHEAP

In the 1974 season finale against the Jets, the Colts' Bert Jones set an NFL record by completing 17 straight passes. The last was to halfback Lydell Mitchell for a six-yard loss.

■ ■ ■

THERE'S MORE THAN ONE WAY TO THROW A SPIRAL

Any grade-schooler can tell you the proper grip for throwing a football is fingers on the laces, thumb on a seam. But some of the great quarterbacks had their own way of doing things.

Sammy Baugh used only the seams, with the laces toward his palm. He felt he could make the ball "behave a little better that way."

The Packers' Arnie Herber did the same but had such short, stubby fingers that he couldn't actually hold the ball. He just rested it in his palm and heaved it the way a catapult would a stone. (Try it sometime and you'll be amazed that he could hit the broad side of a barn, let alone Don Hutson at 50 yards.)

Y. A. Tittle used the laces but held the ball with his fingertips only. The rest of the hand just went along for the ride.

Terry Bradshaw put only three fingers on the laces—middle, ring and pinky. His index finger was on the back point of the ball.

Finally there was the Lions' Dutch Clark. As far as we know, he did everything by the book. Except when it got cold. Then he wore wool gloves. (This was the '30s. Neoprene was a few years off.) Small wonder his teams were known for running the ball. "I couldn't pass worth a damn," he said.

■ ■ ■

Sammy Baugh's unusual passing grip, laces on the palm. (*Sun-Times*/Pro Football Hall of Fame)

THE BEATS GO ON

Pittsburgh Post-Gazette sportswriter Jack Sell gave up the Steelers beat in 1974 after 41 years. He started covering the team in its first season. Primo Carnera was the heavyweight champion. John Dillinger was Public Enemy Number One.

Sell hung in there through 26 losing seasons and 18 head coaches. He saw only one playoff victory, in 1972.

Six months after he stepped down, the Steelers won the first of four Super Bowls.

The '70s saw the end of what had to be the second-longest on-the-beat streak, too. Bob Oates of the *L.A. Times* turned over the Rams after the '77 season. He'd covered them for various papers since 1946, when the franchise moved west from Cleveland. He still writes about pro football for the *Times*.

■ ■ ■

THE CLOTHES MAKE THE SUB

Steelers running back Frenchy Fuqua dressed with the philosophy that "if you didn't gain 1,000 yards, you'd better get your name in the paper twice a week if you want to stay around." His was the never-ending quest for the perfect ostrich plume. He even gave his outfits names.

■ "The Count"—Skin-tight lavender jumpsuit accentuated by a pink, silver-studded cowbelt, white knee-high musketeer boots, white gloves and white musketeer hat with pink, white *and* purple plumes. A floor-length pink cape and glass cane completed the ensemble.

■ "The Superstar"—Blood-red knickers and open-front shirt set off by a black velour jacket with red stars. For those dramatic entrances, red gloves and a Bogart hat.

■ "The Caveman"—Leather jumpsuit with one shoulder strap running across the chest, no shirt and a groin-to-navel rhinestone-studded belt with a huge rhinestone "S" on the buckle. A club-shaped cane and a leather sombrero with a live cactus in it provided just the right flourish.

But nothing attracted more attention than Fuqua's platform shoes with water-filled heels and live goldfish. They were a gift from a New Jersey shoemaker and made him the best-known part-time back in the league in 1973.

"I had only two problems with those shoes," he says. "One, they were 10½ and I wear a size 11½ to 12. I have a corn on my right baby toe to this day from wearing them.

"Second, the goldfish always died. I'd fill them [the heels] with water and put the fish in, and 20 minutes later they'd be floating. I started getting all this hate mail from people saying how cruel I was to animals."

• • •

NOT SO DANDY

When Don Meredith first quit Monday Night Football in 1974, ABC Sports president Roone Arledge wanted to replace him with Joe Namath. The problem was that Namath was still an active player.

Commissioner Pete Rozelle apparently didn't object to Namath both playing and broadcasting. It was Jets management that shot down the idea.

Arledge settled for Fred "The Hammer" Williamson, for reasons few could fathom. Williamson had been a cocky defensive back in the old AFL.

The Evolution of the Monday Night Team
1970 -- Keith Jackson, Howard Cosell, Don Meredith
1971 -- Frank Gifford, Cosell, Meredith
1974 -- Gifford, Cosell, Alex Karras
1977 -- Gifford, Cosell, Meredith
1979 -- Gifford, Cosell, Meredith, Fran Tarkenton*
1983 -- Gifford, Cosell, Meredith, O.J. Simpson**
1984 -- Gifford, Meredith, Simpson
1985 -- Gifford, Simpson, Joe Namath
1986 -- Al Michaels, Gifford
1987 -- Michaels, Gifford, Dan Dierdorf
*Rotated with Meredith, 1979-82.
**Rotated with Meredith, 1983.

He'd gone on to become a star in black exploitation films such as *The Legend of Nigger Charley, Black Caesar* and our own personal favorite, *Boss Nigger.*

According to the book *Monday Night Mayhem,* he showed up for his first meeting with Arledge wearing two pendants around his neck. One was a clenched fist (the black power salute). The other was a penis. He lasted three preseason telecasts and was replaced by Alex Karras.

• • •

HONEY, I FORGOT TO DUCK

A snowball in Buffalo on the last weekend of the 1975 regular season kept Minnesota's Chuck Foreman from winning the 1975 NFC rushing title. It also prevented him from (1) becoming the only player in NFL history to lead his conference in rushing *and* receptions, and (2) sharing the league record for touchdowns in a season.

Well, sort of. This is what happened:

The Vikings were playing the Bills at Rich Stadium on Saturday, December 21. Foreman was having a fantastic game despite the conditions. He would finish with 85 yards rushing, 10 receptions and four TDs in less than three quarters.

After Foreman's third score—which gave him 21 for the year, one shy of the NFL mark—Fran Tarkenton joked in the huddle, "Anybody who gets to the one-yard line, go out of bounds. We want some touchdowns for Chuck."

The crowd was getting ornery. Not only were the Bills being clobbered, 28–6, but it was looking like Foreman and not hometown hero O. J. Simpson might walk away with the TD record. Simpson had gotten his 22nd of the season in the first half, equaling Gale Sayers' 1965 total, but Foreman and the Vikes were really on a roll.

Late in the quarter Foreman was chasing a pass thrown out of the end zone when he was hit in the eye by a snowball. He went out of the game for a couple of plays, then returned with blurred vision and caught a six-yard touchdown pass to tie Sayers and Simpson. That was it, though. He spent the last quarter on the bench.

Less than a minute later, Simpson scored on a 54-yard reception to surpass Sayers. The next day,

EXPENSIVE O.J.

There were two pay scales in the late '70s: O.J. Simpson's and everyone else's. A huge gulf existed between Simpson at No. 1 and Walter Payton at No. 2, as this 1979 list of highest-paid players shows. It's hard to image such a discrepancy today with salary information so freely shared.

Also note the absence of defensive players. The top 11 was made up of six running backs and five quarterbacks. The best-paid defender that year was Steelers linebacker Jack Ham at $230,000.

TOP NFL SALARIES, 1979

O.J. Simpson, RB		$806,668
Walter Payton, RB		450,000
Bob Griese, QB		400,025
Archie Manning, QB		379,000
Dan Pastorini, QB		358,333
Chuck Foreman, RB		300,000
John Riggins, RB		300,000
Ken Stabler, QB		282,000
Bert Jones, QB		275,000
Franco Harris, RB		275,000
Delvin Williams, RB		275,000

St. Louis' Jim Otis, playing only the first half, gained 69 yards in 14 carries to edge Foreman for conference rushing honors, 1,076 to 1,070.

Foreman did top the NFC, indeed the entire league, with 73 receptions. But it could have been much more.

Footnote: Strange things seem to happen whenever the touchdown record is in jeopardy. In 1965, the year Sayers scored 22, Jim Brown had 21.

Brown might have had more, too. But after getting his 21st in the second quarter of the last game, he got into a scuffle with St. Louis defensive end Joe Robb and was ejected by umpire Lou Palazzi. Robb reportedly started it by clotheslining Brown as he went out for a pass.

"I apologize for the entire league," Cleveland owner Art Modell told Brown. "To rob you of the chance to win the scoring title on such an incident is ridiculous."

FREE AT LAST

The NFL had a brief fling with free agency in the spring of 1976. A federal court overturned the Rozelle Rule, making players who had played out their options the previous season unrestricted free agents.

John Riggins, John Gilliam, Ahmad Rashad and Jean Fugett took advantage of their special status and reaped the rewards. Three others who had jumped to the World Football League after playing out their options—Larry Csonka, Paul Warfield and Calvin Hill—returned as unrestricted free agents and benefited similarly.

The deals they struck (all figures are reported):

- **Riggins**—The most he ever made with the Jets was $75,000. The Redskins gave the running back a four-year, $1.5 million contract ($100,000 annually for 15 years).
- **Fugett**—Signed a multiyear contract with the Redskins at $75,000 per. The Cowboys had tried to keep the tight end by offering him a two-year deal with salaries of $35,000 and $50,000.
- **Gilliam**—His Vikings pay had been $75,000. With the Falcons the 30-year-old receiver got as much as $275,000 over three years.
- **Rashad**—No numbers were announced. But the receiver did get a three-year deal—coming off major knee surgery—for jumping from the Bills to the expansion Seahawks.
- **Csonka**—Spurned Dolphins owner Joe Robbie said Csonka asked for a four-year contract at $250,000 per, plus a $50,000 signing bonus, a $15,000 annual reporting bonus and a 20-year loan of

THE ROZELLE RULE

Beginning in 1963, an NFL team that signed a free agent had to compensate the player's previous team. Until '77, when the league concocted a compensation formula, the compensation was usually worked out between the teams themselves. But when an agreement couldn't be reached, Commissioner Pete Rozelle stepped in. This happened five times, with the following results:

FREE-AGENT IMPASSES SETTLED BY THE COMMISSIONER

Year	Pos., Player	From	To	Compensation
1968	CB Pat Fischer	Cards	Redskins	1969 No. 2, '70 No. 3
1968	WR Dave Parks	49ers	Saints	DT Kevin Hardy, 1969 No. 1
1972	DT Phil Olsen	Patriots	Rams	1972 No. 1, '72 No. 3 + $35,000
1972	WR Dick Gordon	Bears	Rams	1974 No. 1
1975	WR Ron Jessie	Lions	Rams	1976 No. 1*

*Detroit was originally awarded FB Cullen Bryant, but the compensation was changed to a draft pick after Bryant brought suit.

$125,000 at minimum legal interest. The Giants won the bidding for the running back with a package that was "somewhat comparable," agent Ed Keating said. Csonka's top Miami salary: $50,000.

■ **Warfield**—Even though he was 33, the Browns were willing to give the receiver a three-year contract. No figures were announced, but he certainly improved on the $65,000 salary he'd earned with the Dolphins.

■ **Hill**—Like Rashad, he'd torn up a knee the season before. But that didn't keep the Redskins from coming up with a multiyear deal worth $135,-000 a season, nearly three times what the running back had pulled down with the Cowboys.

■ ■ ■

FORD IN '76

Eugene McCarthy's original choice for running mate in the 1976 presidential campaign was Detroit Lions owner William Clay Ford. Heading the Republican ticket, of course, was the old Michigan lineman himself, *Gerald* Ford.

"If you were a voter in Michigan, which candidate would get your attention," *New York Times* columnist Red Smith wrote, "one who could promise you seats between the 40-yard lines in . . . Pontiac or the guy who played center in that 34–0 humiliation by Minnesota in 1934?"

Voters never got the chance to decide. William Ford's candidacy lasted less than a week. He was technically a stand-in to help McCarthy's independent campaign get started and stepped aside when it did. But he continued to be a major contributor to McCarthy's longshot bid for the presidency, which ultimately received 1 percent of the popular vote.

McCarthy, a poet and former U.S. senator, had another unusual tie to pro football. He graduated from tiny St. John's University in Minnesota. So did the inimitable Johnny Blood.

■ ■ ■

LOOK OUT BELOW

Low-flying aircraft posed a serious threat to pro football fans in the '70s.

Minutes after the 1976 Colts–Raiders playoff game ended at Memorial Stadium, a plane piloted by a Baltimore-area man, Donald Kroner, crashed into the upper deck.

A stadium employee said the plane looked like it was going to land, but there were 40 or 50 people still on the field. When Kroner tried to take the plane back up, the engine faltered.

Fortunately, the section where the plane crashed was empty. Kroner and three policemen suffered minor injuries. No one else was hurt.

Kroner apparently had buzzed the field in another plane during the fourth quarter. He also was suspected of flying low over Colts practices twice that week.

Rescuers found this note to Bert Jones in the cockpit: "To Bert Jones, QB, from Blue Max. Good luck, you B-More Colts."

Kroner's lawyer offered the defense "that Kroner had engine trouble and was forced to land at the lighted stadium because his glasses were broken," the *Baltimore Sun* reported. The judge gave Kroner two years.

Three years later, during a halftime show at Shea Stadium, a remote-control model plane nosedived into the stands and injured two New Englanders in town for the Jets–Patriots game. One of them, 20-year-old John Bowen of Nashua, New Hampshire, died a week later.

■ ■ ■

THE STEEL CURTAIN SLAMS SHUT

No team ever played better defense than the Steelers did in the final nine games of the 1976 season. They had five shutouts, allowed only two touchdowns and gave up 26 points *total.* The statistics seem to jump off the page at you:

They had 35 sacks, 28 turnovers and held five teams under 200 total yards. They limited opponents to just three yards per rush and a completion percentage of 40.8.

What fueled the remarkable stretch was desperation. The two-time defending Super Bowl champions had started the season 1–4. Also, quarterback Terry Bradshaw missed most of the nine games with neck and wrist injuries. Rookie Mike Kruczek took his place and did a lot of handing off to Franco Harris and Rocky Bleier.

It was up to the defense to see the Steelers through, and did it ever. They won all nine during the streak to take their third straight AFC Central Division title. Postseason injuries to Harris and Bleier probably prevented them from three-peating.

"Part of [coach] Chuck Noll's philosophy was when one department was foundering another had to pick up the slack," says defensive end Dwight White. "Chuck did a great psych job on us. We were playing terrific defense but it was never good enough. We'd hold a team to 125 total yards and you'd get this attitude like, hell, they were only supposed to get 75. It made you want to turn it up a bit more."

The lineup included four future Hall-of-Famers: tackle Joe Greene, middle linebacker Jack Lambert, outside linebacker Jack Ham and cornerback Mel Blount. Ironically, it wasn't considered as good as the '74 and '75 units.

Greene was in his eighth season and starting to slip a bit. Outside linebacker Andy Russell was 34 and playing his last season. Strong safety Glen Edwards was showing some age. A transition was definitely underway. The Steeler teams that would win Super Bowls in '78 and '79 would be known more for their offense. But not in '76.

■ ■ ■

THE STEELERS' STREAK, 1976

Week 6, October 17—Steelers 23, Bengals 6 at Pittsburgh: Jack Lambert intercepted a pass and forced a fumble to set up 10 quick Steeler points. But his best play may have been forearming Bengals linebacker Bo Harris on the sideline after Harris had hit Steelers quarterback Mike Kruczek out of bounds. "It's pretty simple," Lambert explained. "Some of our guys have been getting banged around lately and nothing's been done." Notice had been served.

Week 7, October 24—Steelers 27, Giants 0 at the Meadowlands: The Giants were 0–6 going into the game. The Steelers held them scoreless despite being penalized 15 times.

Week 8, October 31—Steelers 23, Chargers 0 at Pittsburgh: San Diego had only seven first downs and 124 total yards. Quarterback Dan Fouts was 10 for 28. The Steelers had five sacks for the third straight week.

Week 9, November 7—Steelers 45, Chiefs 0 at Kansas City: The AFC's number-two-ranked offense was limited to 34 yards rushing and 223 passing. "They have the best total defense I've ever seen," said K.C. quarterback Mike Livingston, who threw four interceptions.

Week 10, November 14—Steelers 14, Dolphins 3 at Pittsburgh: Miami ended the string of scoreless quarters at 15 with a third-period field goal but couldn't get in the end zone. For the first time in five games, the Steelers allowed more than 100 yards rushing (116).

Week 11, November 21—Steelers 32, Oilers 16 at Pittsburgh: Lambert recovered his fifth and sixth fumbles of the year to set a team record. The string of consecutive quarters without a touchdown ended at 23 when John Hadl hit Ken Burrough with a 69-yard pass.

Week 12, November 28—Steelers 7, Bengals 3 at Cincinnati: In a game crucial to Pittsburgh's slim playoff chances, the defense held the Bengals to eight first downs. QB Ken Anderson, a 60.2 percent passer on the year, connected on just 10 of 26. He threw incomplete four times inside the Steeler 30 in the final 90 seconds. Cornerback J. T. Thomas knocked down one of them, a sure touchdown to wide receiver Chip Myers.

Week 13, December 5—Steelers 42, Buccaneers 0 at Pittsburgh: The first-year Bucs were on their way to 0–14. They found the Steel Curtain nigh impenetrable (105 total yards, 11 passing). "I'd like to think we could beat them if we gave them the playbook," defensive end Dwight White said.

Week 14, December 12—Steelers 21, Oilers 0 at Houston: Shutout number five. The Oilers had only nine first downs, 93 yards rushing and 64 passing.

■ ■ ■

THE NFL'S CRIMINAL ELEMENT

Raiders–Steelers games in the '70s explored the boundaries of brutality. In July 1977 the teams' intense rivalry spilled into U.S. District Court in San Francisco. Oakland defensive back George Atkinson claimed he'd been slandered by Pittsburgh coach Chuck Noll and wanted $2 million to repair his good name.

Atkinson's lawsuit stemmed from remarks Noll had made the day after the 1976 season opener between the teams. The Steelers coach was steamed over a cheap shot that had put wide receiver Lynn Swann out of the game with a concussion.

"There is a criminal element in every aspect of society," he told reporters. "Apparently we have it in the NFL, too."

He meant Atkinson, of course, and everyone knew it. A national television audience had seen the Raiders defensive back lay Swann low with a forearm to the back of the head 15 yards away from the action.

"People like that should be kicked out of football," Noll continued. "It's a criminal act."

Atkinson was fined $1,500 for the incident and received an unusually harsh letter from Pete Rozelle. "In sixteen years in this office I do not recall a more flagrant foul," the commissioner wrote.

As if the teams didn't have enough bad blood between them. They were the bullies of the AFC, having decided the last three conference championships between themselves. Both were physical. Both used intimidation as a tactic. Both wore black.

The trial began July 11 and lasted two weeks. It was such a big deal Raiders owner Al Davis wore a suit and tie to testify. (He preferred turtlenecks and leather.) Players from both teams took the stand, as did NFL supervisor of officials Art McNally. Atkinson was represented by flamboyant California state legislator Willie Brown and Raiders attorney James Cox. Noll and the Steelers were defended by James MacInnes, whose client list included Patty Hearst.

On the first day the six-member jury was treated to a highlight film of Steelers cheap shots: cornerback Mel Blount forearming Raider Cliff Branch in the back of the head; safety Glen Edwards clothes-lining Bengals quarterback Ken Anderson out of bounds; tackle Ernie Holmes clubbing Raider Pete Banaszak on the ground, and so on.

Observers sensed Davis' unmistakable influence in the strategy. Anything to disrupt the competition. The controversial Raiders owner attended every day of the trial. He sent a steady stream of notes to Atkinson's attorneys, using his son Mark as a courier.

Noll took the stand on the third day and made headlines when he was trapped into admitting that several of his players—Blount, Edwards and tackle Joe Greene among them—had to be included in his definition of "criminal element." Blount reacted by filing a $5 million lawsuit against his coach and announced there was "no chance at all" he'd return to the Steelers.

It's hard to tell how serious the Hall-of-Fame cornerback was about it. He sat out all of training camp, but that had more to do with a contract problem than anything Noll had said. Blount dropped the suit in September when he reached an agreement.

Back at the trial, meanwhile, Atkinson was having a difficult time making his case. The jury not only watched him club Swann from a variety of angles but saw him forearm Patriots tight end Russ Francis in the face. The blow broke Francis' nose in four places. The film clip produced a groan from the spectators in the courtroom.

MacInnes also brought up Atkinson's past brushes with the law. He'd once pleaded guilty to a concealed weapons charge and on another occasion been acquitted of conspiracy to defraud a bank. The point was clear: How could Noll have damaged Atkinson's reputation?

On Day Eight Rozelle made a surprise appearance as a "neutral" witness. He wanted to clear up the accusations made by Atkinson's attorneys that the league office was biased against the Raiders. (The long-running feud between Davis and Rozelle was another of the trial's subplots. Just another example of Davis' influence.)

Cox, Davis' man on Atkinson's team, handled the cross-examination. He began by asking the always-tanned Rozelle if he'd flown in from New York or the Greek Islands. The commissioner kept his composure throughout the hostile questioning.

The case went to the jury the next day. It took the four women and two men four hours to find for Noll and the Steelers.

"It should never have gone to trial," Atkinson said. "All I ever wanted was a retraction from coach Noll."

There was no gloating at the Steelers' training camp in Latrobe, Pennsylvania. Noll and his players just seemed glad to put the distraction behind them.

"I knew it was nothing in the first place," said defensive tackle Dwight White. "George Atkinson meant so little to me before, and he probably means even less now. . . .

"Can I get sued for that?"

■ ■ ■
BALLSY

A 1978 survey of NFL players showed 73.7 percent didn't wear mouthpieces, 75.8 percent didn't wear hip pads and 85.8 didn't wear protective cups.

■ ■ ■
SWEET 17

The 1978 Giants scored exactly 17 points seven times in nine weeks.

■ ■ ■
HIT OF THE DECADE

Jack Tatum's Crunching Tackle Paralyzes Darryl Stingley, 1978

The hit that broke Darryl Stingley's neck and left him almost completely paralyzed in 1978 didn't even happen in a game that counted. It took place early in the preseason, a time when veterans like Stingley are subjected to only part-time duty.

In the second quarter against Oakland, the Patriots wide receiver ran an eight-yard slant pattern, jumped and missed a high pass from quarterback Steve Grogan. Raiders free safety Jack Tatum was waiting for him when he came down. It wasn't an exceptionally hard hit by NFL standards—certainly not by Tatum's—but its effect was devastating.

Stingley underwent two operations and nearly died when he contracted pneumonia and suffered a collapsed lung in the hospital. He regained only enough use of his body to operate a motorized wheelchair. His marriage eventually fell apart. He was 26 when it all started.

The game was played at the Oakland Coliseum on August 12, a Saturday night. The place was nearly full (53,339) for the two playoff-caliber clubs. With 1:26 left in the half, New England had a 14–7 lead and was deep in Raiders territory, second down. In the huddle Grogan called "94 Slant."

He had a choice of three receivers on the play: split end Stanley Morgan running a deep slant from the left, tight end Russ Francis running an out from the right or Stingley running a quick slant from Francis' side.

The quick slant was a dangerous pattern against the Raiders, who counted on their free safety to intimidate with big hits. If he read the play correctly, he'd have a clear shot at the receiver.

That was the last thing you wanted to give Tatum. He was only 5'10" and 205 pounds but hit as hard as anyone in the league. He was easily the most intimidating defensive back of the decade.

In his book *They Call Me Assassin* Tatum said he was looking for the slant pattern that night because the Patriots usually ran it about five times per game. His goal was "to put a halt to it."

Grogan compounded things by throwing the ball late and high. Stingley was already running toward the middle when the ball zipped past his outstretched arms. Tatum arrived a split second later.

Photographs indicate he hit Stingley directly in the facemask with his right shoulder. Stingley dropped as if he'd been knocked out. Most observers thought he had been. In fact he never lost consciousness.

"I wasn't in pain, or at least I couldn't feel any," Stingley said. "I just couldn't move. . . . I couldn't feel my feet. Or my arms. Or my body."

Patriots trainer Tom Healion was the first to arrive. He realized the severity of the injury almost immediately. He took Stingley's hand and asked him to squeeze. Nothing. He asked him to move his foot. Nothing.

"Am I going to be all right?" Stingley kept asking.

"No, you're not," Healion finally said.

It was 10 minutes before Stingley could be taken safely from the field on a stretcher. He was in surgery to repair two broken cervical vertebrae before the game was over.

Jack Tatum is about to deliver the hit that ended the career of the Patriots'
Darryl Stingley in 1978. It also left Stingley paralyzed. (UPI/Bettmann Newsphotos)

The hit was perfectly legal. There was no penalty. But some Patriots players questioned whether it was necessary. Stingley clearly had no chance to catch the ball, and it was after all a preseason game.

Tatum did nothing to help his own cause. He came across as remorseless afterward. "You don't like to see any player get hurt, but football is a contact sport," he said in what was described as an even voice. "And that's a dangerous pattern. We don't even run it in practice. But I had to do what I had to do. It was my job, and he was doing his job."

In his book Tatum said the incident "shattered" him. He said he didn't want to play in the Raiders' next game but forced himself to.

"For the first time in my career," he said, "I played a game with a passive attitude."

He also claimed to have been turned away from the hospital when he tried to see Stingley. Stingley doesn't believe it. Other Raiders players visited. Oakland coach John Madden was a regular. Tatum, he says, never even left a message.

The hit occurred at a time when pro football was under attack for excessive violence. Two days before the game *Sports Illustrated* had run an exposé on the increasing brutality in the NFL. A year earlier,

there'd been the "criminal element" slander trial. Tatum and teammate George Atkinson had been accused by Steelers coach Chuck Noll of malicious actions on the field. Atkinson sued and lost.

Stingley considered suing Tatum and the NFL but decided against it. In 1979 he reached a settlement with the Patriots and in return agreed not to take future legal action against the team or league.

■ ■ ■

WORST COACHING DECISION

The Patriots had clinched their first division title in 15 years and were getting ready to close out the 1978 regular season against the Dolphins when coach Chuck Fairbanks announced he was taking the University of Colorado job. The stunned New England players went out and got hammered by the Dolphins on ABC's *Monday Night Football*, then exited meekly from the playoffs two weeks later.

"The Jewish people have a word for [what Fairbanks did]. It's called chutzpah," Patriots owner Billy Sullivan said. "It means unmitigated gall."

Fairbanks broke the news at a team meeting about four hours before kickoff. A few minutes later, he informed Sullivan. He told the New England owner he planned to finish the season with the Patriots. All he asked was that he be allowed to fly to Colorado after the Dolphins game for a press conference and a few days of recruiting. He'd be back in time to prepare the Patriots for their first-round playoff game.

Sullivan couldn't believe his ears. He told Fairbanks to put off the announcement until after the Super Bowl. Fairbanks insisted he needed time to recruit. Sullivan finally suspended him.

That didn't stop Fairbanks from showing up in the Patriots' dressing room before the game, apparently ready to coach. It was a legal ploy meant to force Sullivan to fire him, but the players didn't know that.

Assistant general manager Jim Valek phoned Sullivan at the team hotel, and the Patriots owner rushed to the Orange Bowl. By then, the players were thoroughly confused.

"I had to get out of there," one said as he left the locker room. "This whole thing is unreal."

Sullivan wouldn't allow Fairbanks to take the field with the team. Assistants Ron Erhardt and Hank Bullough ran the show. The Patriots were routed, 23–3.

The situation got crazier in the next few days. Using the threat of legal action, Sullivan forced Fairbanks to remain with the Patriots. He even reinstated him for the playoff game, a 31–14 loss to Houston.

When the season ended, the Patriots owner still refused to let his coach go. It wasn't until April 1979, when a group of Colorado boosters agreed to buy out the remaining four years of Fairbanks' contract, that Sullivan did. The reported price was $500,000.

In December 1982 there was a similar situation involving Ray Perkins and the New York Giants. Perkins announced he was taking the head coaching job at the University of Alabama with three games left in the season and the team in the hunt for a playoff spot.

Perkins did so, however, with the blessing of the Giants organization—owner Wellington Mara and general manager George Young. He was an Alabama alum and had an opportunity to replace the retiring Bear Bryant.

The announcement was made before the NFL season ended because news of Bryant's impending retirement and successor had begun to get out. The Giants dropped two of the three remaining games and missed the playoffs.

■ ■ ■
PAINFUL PENALTY

In a 1979 game against the Vikings, Patriots tight end Don Hasselbeck was spotted holding. The official dutifully took the penalty flag from his pocket and threw it in Hasselbeck's direction. Unfortu-

Going

1970--Brian Piccolo, 26, cancer
      Jimmy Conzelman, 72, owner-coach
      Vince Lombardi, 57, cancer
      Bob Kalsu, 25, Bills guard, killed in Vietnam
1971--Dan Reeves, 58, brought Rams to Los Angeles
      Kenny Washington, 52
      George Trafton, 74
      Chuck Hughes, 28, Lions receiver, heart attack
      Joe Guyon, 79, car accident
1972--Len Ford, 46
      Jimmy Patton, 39, car accident
1973--Turk Edwards, 65
      Greasy Neale, 81
1974--Don McCafferty, 53, Colts coach
      Ed Meadows, 42, suicide
1975--Emlen Tunnell, 50
      Jacque McKinnon, 36, ex-Chargers tight end, fell off wall
1976--Henry McDonald, 85, early black player
      Paul Robeson, 77
      Ernie Nevers, 72
      Blenda Gay, 26, Eagles defensive end, knife wound
1977--Joe Stydahar, 65
      Cal Hubbard, 76
      Henry Jordan, 42, ex-Packers defensive tackle, heart attack
      Erny Pinckert, 69, '30s tough guy with Redskins
1978--Dutch Clark, 71
      Ed Healey, 83
1979--Tuffy Leemans, 66
      Ken Strong, 73
      Carroll Rosenbloom, 72, Rams owner, drowned
      J.V. Cain, 28, Cardinals tight end, cardiac arrest
      Troy Archer, 24, Giants defensive tackle, truck crash

Lyle Alzado gives Muhammad Ali a knuckle sandwich in their 1979 exhibition bout. (AP/Wide World Photos)

nately, he put a little too much on it. It went through Hasselbeck's facemask and inflicted a three-stitch cut on his lip.

The weighted flag "would have knocked out half my teeth if I hadn't been wearing a mouth guard," said Hasselbeck, who had to go to the locker room for repairs. "It's bad enough to get beat up, but to get beat up by a flag!"

■ ■ ■

TOO TALL AND THE MANLY ART

Ed Jones, the 6'9" defensive end, shocked the Dallas Cowboys in 1979 by retiring at 28 to pursue a heavyweight boxing career. He was three inches taller than Primo Carnera, 20 pounds heavier than George Foreman and had a longer reach than Muhammad Ali's. Too bad Too Tall couldn't fight a lick.

He beat six palookas in three months but looked so bad doing it that he decided football was where he belonged. He rejoined the Cowboys in 1980.

"He's the best defensive end in football," said ex-teammate Thomas Henderson, "but the worst fighter I ever saw."

Too Tall's ring record:

DATE	OPPONENT, SITE	RESULT
	1979	
Nov. 3	Yaqui Meneses, Las Cruces, N.M.	Dec. 6
Nov. 15	Abdullah Muhammad, Phoenix, Ariz.	TKO 6
Nov. 24	Fernando Montes, Washington, D.C.	TKO 1
Dec. 14	Jim Wallace, Dallas	TKO 2
	1980	
Jan. 22	Billy Joe Thomas, Indianapolis	KO 4
Jan. 26	Rocky Gonzalez, Jackson, Miss.	KO 1

Won 6, Lost 0.

Won by knockout: 5. Won by decision: 1.

THE 1980s

'80s CHALKBOARD

The Counter Trey

The Counter Trey

The Washington Redskins' hallowed Hogs brought recognition to offensive line play in the '80s. Some of the faces up front changed over the years, but the offense's philosophy remained the same: power football all the way. The "counter trey" or "counter gap," a run off right tackle out of the one-back set, was their trademark. Russ Grimm and Joe Jacoby, the Redskins' Pro Bowl left guard and tackle, pulled on the play and led the interference. That's a lot of beef to come bearing down on an outside linebacker or, worse, a defensive back. It was up to the center and off-side tight end, lined up as a wingback, to cut off the pursuit through the area Grimm and Jacoby vacated. The New York Giants' Lawrence Taylor slipped through a time or two and ran the ball carrier down from behind, but for the most part the counter trey worked against everybody.

THE 1980s AT A GLANCE

Decade Standings

NFC	W	L	T	Pct.	AFC	W	L	T	Pct.
49ers (4)	104	47	1	.688	Dolphins	94	57	1	.622
Redskins (2)	97	55	0	.638	Broncos	93	58	1	.615
Bears (1)	92	60	0	.605	Raiders (2)	89	63	0	.586
Rams	86	66	0	.566	Browns	83	68	1	.549
Giants (1)	81	70	1	.536	Bengals	81	71	0	.533
Cowboys	79	73	0	.520	Patriots	78	74	0	.513
Vikings	77	75	0	.507	Seahawks	78	74	0	.513
Eagles	76	74	2	.507	Steelers	77	75	0	.507
Saints	67	85	0	.441	Jets	73	77	2	.487
Packers	65	84	3	.438	Chargers	72	80	0	.474
Cardinals	62	88	2	.414	Bills	69	83	0	.454
Lions	61	90	1	.405	Chiefs	66	84	2	.441
Falcons	57	94	1	.378	Oilers	62	90	0	.408
Buccaneers	45	106	1	.299	Colts	54	97	1	.359

(Figures in parentheses are championships won.)

Best Regular–Season Record   San Francisco 49ers, 1984, and Chicago Bears, 1985, 15-1

Worst Regular–Season Record   New Orleans Saints, 1980, and Dallas Cowboys, 1989, 1-15

League Attendance   126,547,266 (up 15.8%)

In	Out
outside linebackers	middle linebackers
players vs. management	Steelers vs. Raiders
John Madden	Howard Cosell
instant replay	games under 3 hours
bigger linemen	big linemen
Bill Walsh, Joe Montana	Chuck Noll, Terry Bradshaw
46 defense	bend but don't break
third wide receiver	tight end
drug testing	trust
Broncos' Super Bowl opponent	Broncos
Paul Tagliabue	Pete Rozelle

►**Biggest Player**   William "The Refrigerator" Perry, for sheer density. The Bears' 6'2" defensive tackle was pushing 340 pounds in 1988, the year he visited a fat farm.
   Too Tall Jones, meanwhile, was *still* 6'9".

Smallest Player   Reggie Smith, Falcons receiver-returner, was 5'4". Lightest: Gerald "The Ice Cube" McNeil of the Browns at 140.

Best Athlete   Bo Jackson

►**Fastest Player**   Darrell Green

Slowest Player   Dave Butz. You wouldn't nickname a fast guy "Bruno."

Most Intimidating Player   Lawrence Taylor

New Stadiums   1984--Hoosier Dome
1987--Joe Robbie Stadium

Franchise Shifts	1982--Raiders from Oakland to Los Angeles 1984--Colts from Baltimore to Indianapolis 1988--Cardinals from St. Louis to Phoenix
Failed League	USFL, 1986
Famous Firsts	Coach to lead three different teams to the playoffs, 1983 (Chuck Knox) Games on cable television, 1987 (ESPN) Woman to do TV play-by-play, 1987 (Gayle Sierens, NBC) Black quarterback to start in the Super Bowl, 1988 (Doug Williams) Black referee, 1988 (Johnny Grier) Black head coach, 1989 (Art Shell)
▶**Famous Lasts (?)**	Combination punter/kicker (full-time), 1981 (Frank Corral) NFL game played in New York City, 1983 White 1,000-yard rusher, 1985 (Craig James) Straight-on kicker, 1987 (Steve Cox, Redskins)
Best Division Race	1983 NFC East 　When Washington and Dallas met in Week 15 at Texas Stadium, both had 12-2 records. The defending champion Redskins had suffered two one-point losses (one to the Cowboys). The Cowboys' defeats had been by a total of three points. The showdown, alas, was anticlimactic: Redskins 31, Cowboys 10.
Best Super Bowl	1983, Redskins over Dolphins, 27-17 　The 49ers and Bengals (1989) produced the best finish of any Super Bowl, but Washington-Miami was the best *game* of the '80s. The Dolphins scored on big plays by Jimmy Cefalo (76-yard pass) and Fulton Walker (98-yard kickoff return) before the Redskins wore them down with John Riggins running behind the Hogs.
Owner vs. Owner	Al Davis vs. Gene Klein, 1984 　Davis and Klein hated each other's guts. The Raiders boss had named Klein as a defendant in his 1980 suit against the league and tried to sue him again in '83, claiming he'd attempted to block a deal with the Patriots for Mike Haynes. The Chargers owner returned the favor in '84, blaming Davis for, among other things, a heart attack. A jury awarded Klein $10 million, though the figure was substantially reduced on appeal.
Player vs. Team	John Riggins vs. the Redskins, 1980 　After rushing for 1,000 yards two straight seasons, Riggins wanted more money than the team was willing to pay. So he sat out the year, one that saw Washington slump from 10-6 to 6-10 and coach Jack Pardee get fired. He returned in '81 with the famous words: "I'm bored, I'm broke and I'm back."
Trial of the Decade	Al Davis vs. the NFL, 1981-82
Best Running Quarterback	Randall Cunningham
New Position	H-back
Major Rules Changes	1981--stickum outlawed 1984--anti-celebration penalty (5 yards) 1988--more contact allowed between defenders and receivers

New Equipment	gloves for receivers (replaced stickum) knee braces (almost universal use for linemen and quarterbacks) plastic eye shields
Fashion Trends	skin-tight jerseys for linemen headbands
New Statistics	third-down efficiency, 1981 sacks, 1982
Best Play	the Bengals' no-huddle offense
►Hit of the Decade	The Giants break Joe Theismann's leg, 1985
►Fight of the Decade	Bills receivers coach Nick Niccolau vs. offensive line coach Tom Bresnahan, 1989
Highest–Paid Player	John Elway had a 6-year, $12.7-million package with the Broncos that averaged out to $2.117 million a season.
Least Appreciated Players	They're all overappreciated
Best Trade	The 49ers traded up in the first round of the 1985 draft to get receiver Jerry Rice. The picks they gave the Patriots were used to select center Trevor Matich and defensive lineman Ben Thomas. The Pats released Thomas in '86 and Matich in '89.
Best Football Books	1984--*Life Its Ownself* by Dan Jenkins 1986--*The League* by David Harris 1988--*Duane Thomas and the Fall of America's Team* by Paul Zimmerman 1989--*The Fireside Book of Pro Football*, edited by Richard Whittingham
Best Football Movie	1988--*Everybody's All-American*
Worst Idea	The NFL talent contest (1989). Honorable mention: Before the 1986 Super Bowl, NBC gave viewers a blank screen for one minute to enable them to go to the bathroom.
Individual Records That May Never Be Equaled	Mark Moseley's 161 kicking points, 1983 Dan Marino's 48 touchdown passes, 1984 Roger Craig's 1,000 yards rushing and 1,000 receiving, 1985 Jerry Rice's 22 TD catches (in 12 games!), 1987 Marino not being sacked in 759 pass attempts, 1988-89 Joe Montana's 112.4 passer rating, 1989

PLAYER-PRESS TIFFS

Members of the news media are at least entitled to freedom from physical interference, from threats of bodily harm and from openly challenging verbal abuse from players while they are . . . simply doing their jobs.

> —*Disciplinary letter from commissioner* PETE ROZELLE

I've taken enough crap from you.

> —*Oilers QB* DAN PASTORINI *to a Houston reporter*

Every so often the natural antagonism between NFL players and the press boils over into confrontation. In 1989 Chargers quarterback Jim McMahon found a novel way of expressing his displeasure with a San Diego beat writer—he blew his nose on him.

It's by no means a recent phenomenon. Steelers defensive tackle Joe Greene spit in a reporter's face back in 1970. In the early '50s, Rams quarterback Norm Van Brocklin spotted *Los Angeles Mirror* columnist Maxwell Stiles at a practice and ordered a power sweep in his direction. Stiles was knocked head over heels.

The following day, the columnist showed up wearing a Hugh McElhenny 49ers jersey. "The Rams have never hit anyone wearing this number yet and I don't think you'll start today," he explained to the players.

It does seem, though, that the '70s and '80s have had more than their share of these incidents. The best of the blowups:

1. **Will McDonough,** *Boston Globe,* **vs. Ray Clayborn, New England Patriots, September 9, 1979**

    Clayborn, a fine cornerback, had a reputation early in his career for being surly with the press. Following a 56–3 victory over the Jets, he elbowed and cursed his way through a pack of reporters interviewing wide receiver Harold Jackson. One of the reporters happened to be McDonough, the *Globe*'s veteran football writer.

    "You motherfucker, move or I'm going to bury you," Clayborn said.

"You're not going to bury me," McDonough responded.

Clayborn then grabbed McDonough by the shirt and poked a finger in his eye. McDonough countered with a punch that sent Clayborn sprawling into his dressing stall. The fracas continued briefly and Patriots owner Billy Sullivan was knocked into a nearby trashcan. Players and reporters finally broke it up.

McDonough emerged with his eye and face scratched, and he'd lost a button off his shirt. But he was unbowed, and for that he had the respect of pro football reporters everywhere (especially the small ones).

Clayborn had a long talk with coach Ron Erhardt the next day and apologized to the local media afterward. McDonough wasn't present and refused to accept it. The NFL eventually fined Clayborn $2,000.

2. **Bob Padecky,** *Sacramento Bee,* **vs. Ken Stabler, Oakland Raiders, January 22, 1979**

    Padecky was in Miami for Super Bowl XIII when he heard Stabler had called his paper looking for him. The Raiders quarterback, who'd struggled through a tough 9–7 season, wanted to "spill his guts" about Al Davis, coach John Madden, the team, everything.

    So the morning after the game, Padecky took a flight to Pensacola and rented a car for the 45-minute drive to Gulf Shores, Alabama, Stabler's hometown. They met at Lefty's, the quarterback's bar/restaurant.

    After a few minutes of small talk, Stabler asked Padecky to follow him to a nearby restaurant. The reporter did, and once there the small talk started again. Padecky remembered that Stabler sat with a view of the parking lot and repeatedly looked out over it as they spoke.

    Stabler excused himself to attend to some personal business and told Padecky to wait for him. About an hour later Padecky received a phone message to meet Stabler at yet another place, the Silver Dollar Lounge.

    This time Stabler harangued the reporter for a series of articles he'd written about him. Padecky had been in Gulf Shores a few weeks earlier and talked to residents for the stories.

    "You're the first reporter to come into my town trying to dig up dirt," Stabler said.

    Then the bizarre process repeated itself. Stabler left Padecky and later called with orders to meet him back at the second stop they'd made. No sooner had Padecky pulled out of the parking lot than three police cars surrounded him. One officer went to the front of the rental car and pulled a magnetic key case from under the bumper. It contained cocaine.

The stunned Padecky was arrested and jailed for several hours. The police released him when it was clear he'd been set up (they'd received two phone tips about a drug deal; Padecky's rental car was described in detail down to the magnetic key case under the bumper). He was driven under guard to the Pensacola airport that evening.

Padecky wrote a first-person account of the incident, and it became a national story. Stabler called a press conference the next day and denied he'd set up the reporter.

"Even to be associated with this is absurd," he said. "This is going to hurt me in my work with youth."

The Alabama attorney general's office conducted an investigation but did not find conclusive evidence to link Stabler to the incident.

3. Fran Blinebury, *Houston Chronicle*, vs. Ladd Herzeg, Houston Oilers, January 10, 1989

It was Houston radio personality Barry Warner's idea to bring Blinebury, an acerbic columnist, and Herzeg, the Oilers' unpredictable general manager, together for a peace lunch. Blinebury had been critical of the Oilers for years. Herzeg had taken some shots at Blinebury on Warner's radio show.

The three met at an exclusive Houston restaurant called Tony's, with the *Chronicle* agreeing to pick up the tab. Herzeg insisted on champagne for the table. Bottles of it. By the time the lunch ended—five hours later—he'd ordered five (at over $100 apiece). Only three were ever opened, according to Blinebury.

The bill for the afternoon came to over $1,000 (Herzeg also had ordered four ounces of beluga caviar at $85 an ounce). But the lunch seemed to have served its purpose. When Warner left at about three to do his show, the atmosphere was chummy. Herzeg and Blinebury had hashed things out, and while they weren't bosom buddies they had at least agreed to talk more often.

Sometime around 4:30, the bubbly must have kicked in.

"The two of us are just sitting there talking," Blinebury says, "and all of a sudden he just reaches across with his fist and jabs me in the face, right above the lip. It wasn't a Buster Douglas–does–Mike Tyson shot but it stunned me. I felt this warm stuff running over my lip and realized it was blood.

"I said, 'Did you just do what I think you did?' And he popped me again."

Herzeg then got up and left the restaurant, Blinebury in hot pursuit demanding an explanation. Herzeg refused and drove off with his car door wide open. That night he phoned Blinebury to apologize.

"Was it something I said?" Blinebury asked.

"No, it was three years of frustration and anger built up, and I hit you," Herzeg explained.

In a statement to the media, Herzeg said: "I am confident in stating that Fran and I both have a better understanding between us. I believe . . . we were able to reconcile our differences and open lines of communication that will remain open."

Blinebury didn't buy it. He thought Herzeg had meant to take a shot at him all along. The *Chronicle* suspended his column for 30 days.

4. Steve Serby, *New York Post*, vs. Richard Todd, New York Jets, November 4, 1981

Serby was interviewing back Mike Augustyniak in the Jets' locker room before practice when Todd, the team's starting quarterback, yelled across the room: "You don't have to talk to that fucker. Don't you know he roots against us?"

Todd was still angry at Serby for a critical story written a month earlier. He'd been disturbing the reporter's interviews for several weeks.

When Serby finished with Augustyniak, he decided to talk to Todd about it. Wrong move. The exchange quickly grew heated.

Serby: "Do you think this a mature way to act?"

Todd: "Now you're telling me how to act."

Serby: "I don't tell you or anybody else how to act."

Todd: "Get out of my fucking face."

Serby: "I'm not in your fucking face."

Todd (6'2," 205 pounds) then grabbed Serby (5'8," 150) by the neck and drove him backward into wide receiver Bobby Jones' locker. Another reporter and offensive tackle Marvin Powell quickly got between the two.

Serby emerged from the stall dazed, with

blood streaming from a cut on his nose. He later complained of dizziness and blurred vision and went to a hospital for tests, which proved negative.

The *Post* was outraged and ran a huge picture of Serby—bandage across his nose—under the headline "Todd Assaults Our Man." The paper wanted criminal charges brought against the quarterback, but the district attorney's office said the case had no merit.

Serby took two weeks off and returned to the beat. He and Todd patched things up later in the season. They shook hands and have been on good terms since.

5. Dale Robertson, *Houston Post,* vs. Dan Pastorini, Houston Oilers, January 3, 1980

Robertson thought he was just doing his job when he took a Pastorini quotation from another reporter and used it in a story. The AFC championship game was three days away and the moody quarterback's physical condition was a big factor.

Pastorini didn't see it that way. He'd been feuding with Robertson for 10 weeks and wasn't about to let up. The two ran into each other in the team laundry room after practice and nearly came to blows.

"Don't ever quote me again unless I speak to you or I'll sue your ass," Pastorini said. "I don't even want to see my name in your paper."

Robertson admits he was in no mood to take it and was equally abusive. Moments later, Pastorini was about to do a group interview with members of the national media when Robertson sarcastically asked him if he could listen in.

That touched off another heated exchange, this time in front of a full locker room.

"I've taken enough crap from you," Pastorini said.

"Yeah, you've had it real rough, you asshole," Robertson shot back.

Pastorini grabbed the reporter by the shirt with both hands as if to shove him against a wall. But there was no wall, only a half-open door to the Oilers' practice field. The two tumbled outside, Robertson on his back, Pastorini on top of him. They landed at the feet of coach Bum Phillips, who couldn't believe his eyes. He was explaining to an interviewer how good the Oilers' relationship with the local media was.

The entire exchange was captured on film by a TV camera crew and was shown over and over again in the days leading up to the game. There was nothing funny about it as far as Robertson was concerned. He received death threats from irate fans. The night of the incident, he was given a police escort home from the *Post* building.

6. Robertson vs. Pastorini II, December 27, 1980

The rematch took place in Oakland about a year later, and like most sequels just wasn't up to the original. Pastorini had been traded to the Raiders, where he'd suffered a broken leg and missed most of the season. Robertson was in town to cover the Oilers–Raiders playoff game.

The two ran into each other in the lobby of the Oakland Hyatt House. Pastorini had just come from the hotel bar. Witnesses said he was loud, abusive and tipsy.

"Dale, you're still a little fucker," he said at one point.

Robertson wanted no part of Pastorini this time and tried to leave. But the quarterback grabbed him by the coat. It was starting to get ugly when several bystanders pulled the two apart.

As soon as he got free, Robertson left. About a half hour later, Pastorini drove his car off the road and hit a tree, injuring his ankle and cutting his face. He blamed it on the fog.

■ ■ ■

THE DOUBLE LIFE OF ROY GREEN

Pro football hadn't had a two-way player in 21 years when St. Louis defensive back Roy Green started pulling double duty at receiver in 1981. The Cardinals were short-handed at the position with Mel Gray injured, so before the second game of the season at Dallas, coach Jim Hanifan went to the speedy Green and told him, "We're going to throw you in [on offense] for one play, and all you have to do is run a fly [pattern]."

The play came in the second quarter. Green sprinted downfield and caught a 60-yard pass from Neil Lomax, outfighting Cowboys cornerback Everson Walls for the ball. The rest of the day he played nickel back and special teams and returned kickoffs. But the next week against Washington he was on the field for 99 plays. As a receiver he had four receptions for 115 yards, including a 58-yard touchdown and a 35-yard gain that set up a field goal. As a DB he intercepted one pass and broke up another. He was the first NFL player since the Redskins' Eddie Sutton in 1957 to have a TD catch and an interception in the same game.

As the year went on Green played more at receiver, where he clearly had star quality, and less in the secondary, where he couldn't break into the starting lineup. He scored winning touchdowns against Dallas and New England, the latter with 33 seconds left. Final offensive totals: 33 receptions, 708 yards, 21.5-yard average, four TDs. Defensive: three interceptions, 15 tackles, 11 passes defensed.

Green wasn't the 60-minute man that Philadelphia's Chuck Bednarik, the last to go both ways, had been in 1960. He also played positions that were less punishing. Bednarik was a center-linebacker.

"What he's doing is not as tough as playing in the pits," said Bednarik. "I don't want to downplay him, but defensive backs and wide receivers are just not involved in every play like linemen. I was being blocked or hit every down."

Still, it was an amazing display of athleticism and endurance. The following season Green became a full-time receiver. Through 1989 he was at 469 catches and counting.

∎ ∎ ∎

THE SILENT GAME

Pro football fans were complaining so much about TV announcers by 1980 that NBC decided to do a game without any (announcers, not fans). It never did another.

The "Silent Game" was executive producer Don Ohlmeyer's idea. He had a dog of a matchup on his hands on the last Saturday of the regular season—Jets at Dolphins, two nonplayoff teams—so why not?

At the very least the gimmick figured to boost the ratings. It wasn't Ohlmeyer's intention to reinvent television football. He knew how important announcers were and thought viewers could stand to be reminded.

PLAYBOYS

Six pro football figures have had the distinction of being interviewed in *Playboy.* Some talked about football, some about other things. Selected highlights:

SUBJECT/ISSUE: Jim Brown, February 1968
COMMENT: "The problems [between players of different races] arise off the field—and I'd say that the major problem area is related, in some way, to white women. It's a major factor why black and white players don't socialize, because sooner or later they are going to be in some situation involving women."
CENTERFOLD/JOB: Nancy Harwood, college student
COMMENT: "I'd rather dispense with books and just *think*—but if I were educating myself, I'd never get around to most academic subjects."

SUBJECT/ISSUE: Joe Namath, December 1969
COMMENT: "I don't expect to go to bed with every good-looking girl I meet. I'd like it, but I don't *expect* it. All I want to do is get to know them and *hope* to get sexually involved with them. I'm a great believer of sex. I spent the nights before the Jets' two biggest games last year—for the AFL championship and the Super Bowl—with girls."
CENTERFOLD/JOB: Gloria Root, college student
COMMENT: "Individuals who have used hallucinogens or pot can experience life in more subtle ways and accept each other more readily than people who haven't."

SUBJECT/ISSUE: Howard Cosell, May 1972
COMMENT: "I really believe *I'm* the best [sportscaster], for I have sought to bring to the American people a sense of the athlete as a human being and not as a piece of cereal-box mythology. My relationship with the men who play the games—*all* games—is probably unparalleled in this country."
CENTERFOLD/JOB: Deanna Baker, Bunny
COMMENT: "As a Pool Bunny, I have an opportunity to establish one-on-one relationships with Club guests on a basis other than 'Can I get you another cocktail, sir?' "

SUBJECT/ISSUE: Pete Rozelle, October 1973
COMMENT: "When football can't be a relatively pure outlet, a fun thing, then it hurts itself. People are interested in pro football because it provides them with an emotional oasis; they don't want football to get involved in the same types of court cases, racial problems and legislative issues they encounter in the rest of American life."
CENTERFOLD/JOB: Valerie Lane, men's hair stylist
COMMENT: "Let's face it, men are peacocks, and now that they've gotten used to the idea that their hair can be styled to really improve their looks, they're not about to get out the Butch Wax again."

SUBJECT/ISSUE: O.J. Simpson, December 1976
COMMENT: "I also know that the game goes on and that while you may be the greatest today, no one will know where you are tomorrow. When your playing days are over, the roar of the crowd just becomes a loud echo. Players today know *exactly* what football can do for them: put money in the bank."
CENTERFOLD/JOB: Karen Hafter, waitress
COMMENT: "A man's physical attractiveness used to be the most important thing, but now I'm more concerned with his emotional makeup."

SUBJECT/ISSUE: Terry Bradshaw, February 1980
COMMENT: "Pittsburgh. Are you kidding? Do you think I wanted to come to Pittsburgh all the way from Shreveport, Louisiana? I had never seen Pittsburgh, not even on TV. I'd read about its team in the history books. They won one game before I arrived. No, Pittsburgh was the last place I wanted to come."
CENTEROLD/JOB: Henriette Allais, dental assistant
COMMENT: "I'm totally uninhibited, and I love running around naked. Once, in the mountains, I just decided to take off all my clothes and run around in the nude. I love the way nature feels when it makes contact with my body."

When he announced his plans, he sent telegrams to all his sportscasters that read: "Don't panic. Your jobs are safe."

They certainly were. The "Silent Game" was a disaster. NBC tried to fill the void with graphics, taped interviews and extra sideline microphones. The network even cheated a little and cut to Bryant Gumbel in the stands a couple of times a quarter for a brief comment. The PA announcer also could be heard.

But it didn't work. The interviews kept running too long and overlapping the next play. The microphones were perhaps the biggest disappointment. The quarterback's signals could barely be made out, and "the crunch of bodies," as one NBC official put it, wasn't picked up at all. The acoustics at the Orange Bowl were abominable.

As the clock wound down in the close game, won by the Jets, 24–17, director Ted Nathanson muttered, "If this bleepin' game goes into overtime, I'm jumping out of the truck."

Calls to NBC actually ran 60–40 in favor of the no-announcer format. There must have been a full moon that night.

■ ■ ■
WHAT ARE FRIENDS FOR?

Eagles coach Dick Vermeil was recovering from hepatitis in the weeks before the 1982 draft. But he kept busy. He was in touch with the team's front office and with sources around the league, one of whom was Buffalo coach Chuck Knox, an old and good friend.

The Eagles had the 20th pick in the first round, the Bills the 21st. Vermeil saw no harm in telling Knox the player he wanted was Clemson wide receiver Perry Tuttle.

On draft day Vermeil was well enough to be in the team's war room at Veterans Stadium. He had to feel even better as the first round unfolded and it appeared more and more likely the Eagles would have a shot at Tuttle. When Denver's turn came at number 19, the Eagles were home free; the Broncos needed a running back.

But with about three of its 15 minutes left, Denver announced it had traded places with Buffalo in

return for a fourth-round pick. The Bills then selected Tuttle.

The Eagles, in particular Vermeil, were furious. "Old friend" Knox had really stuck it to them.

"This is not to take a direct shot at Chuck Knox, but it proves once again there are no friends in the NFL," Eagles personnel director Carl Peterson said. "Even though my head coach disagrees with me."

Said Knox: "I'm sure I know what Carl meant. You can be friends . . . but business is business."

He actually did Philadelphia a favor. Tuttle turned out to be a bust. The receiver the Eagles wound up taking, Mike Quick, was one of the best in the '80s.

■ ■ ■
UNION VS. MANAGEMENT

Scoring the Decades-Old Fight on the 10-Point Must System

ROUND 1: THE BILL RADOVICH DECISION, 1957

Key Issue: Is the NFL subject to the Sherman Anti-trust Act?

Summary: The U.S. Supreme Court rules it is, unlike professional baseball. The decision opens the door to formal recognition of the Players Association and, ultimately, collective bargaining. Radovich, a lineman with the Detroit Lions in the late '30s and '40s, sued the league because he'd been blackballed for signing with the rival All-America Football Conference.

Winner: The players come out swinging, 10–9.

ROUND 2: THE 1968 LOCKOUT

Key Issue: Players' pension plan and other benefits.

Summary: After three months of negotiations fail to produce a collective bargaining agreement, the NFLPA threatens a strike. The owners counter by locking veteran players out of camp. The stalemate is broken in a couple of days, and the two sides sign a two-year agreement. Owners increase pension payments significantly and agree to make the plan retroactive to 1959. Other benefits, such as hospitalization, are improved.

Winner: The players draw blood, 10–9.

ROUND 3: THE 1970 LOCKOUT

Key Issue: Pension and other benefits.

Summary: Same scenario as in '68 only this time the lockout lasts two weeks. The union surprises the owners by hanging tough—only 19 of the approximately 1,300 veteran players report to training camp. A new, four-year agreement is finally reached after 22 consecutive hours of negotiating. Neither side is happy.

Winner: Even, 10–10.

ROUND 4: THE FIRST STRIKE, 1974

Key Issues: Free agency and the powers of the commissioner.

Summary: Led by new executive director Ed Garvey, the players announce their strike shortly before the first training camp opens. They already have "No freedom, no football!" T-shirts (supplied by then–sporting goods entrepreneur Sam Wyche) and bumper stickers made up. The strike lasts until August 14, when a two-week truce is called. On August 28, the union decides to stay on the job even though there's no agreement. It will be three years before one is reached.

Winner: Management refuses to be intimidated, 10–9.

ROUND 5: THE JOHN MACKEY CASE, 1976

Key Issue: Is the Rozelle Rule illegal? (In 1963 the commissioner was given the power to settle free-agent compensation disputes when the two teams were unable to do so themselves.)

Summary: In October 1976, a federal appeals court upholds a lower court decision and says it is. The players have won unrestricted free agency. The ruling also calls into question the legality of the college draft. The NFLPA filed the lawsuit after the aborted strike in '74 (Mackey was the union president).

Winner: The players score a knockdown, 10–8.

ROUND 6: THE 1977 COLLECTIVE BARGAINING AGREEMENT

Key Issue: Free agency.

Summary: The union sells management back the Rozelle Rule. In return for payroll deduction of dues, a healthy increase in benefits and a $13.65 million payment to settle damages from the Mackey suit, the NFLPA gives up free agency. It

also agrees to extend the draft through 1986. What a deal for the owners.

Winner: Management rallies decisively, 10–8.

ROUND 7: THE 1982 STRIKE

Key Issue: The players demand 55 percent of the league's gross revenues.

Summary: The owners refuse, calling the demand socialistic. A strike is called after the second week of the regular season and lasts 57 days. The union finally bails out and accepts a one-time, lump-sum payment of $60 million to go back to work.

DECADE LEADERS

PASSING

Yards: Joe Montana, 30,958; Dan Fouts, 28,301; Dan Marino, 27,853.

Completion percentage (1,500 attempts): Ken Anderson, 64.6; Montana, 63.9; Fouts, 59.9.

Touchdowns: Marino, 220; Montana, 215; Fouts, 172.

Interceptions: Fouts, 131; Steve DeBerg and Tommy Kramer, 128.

RUSHING

Yards: Eric Dickerson, 11,226; Walter Payton, 9,800; Tony Dorsett, 9,300.

Yards per carry (750 attempts): James Brooks, 4.8; Stump Mitchell, 4.72; Wendell Tyler, 4.67.

TDs: Dickerson, 82; Marcus Allen, 63; John Riggins, 62.

RECEIVING

Receptions: Art Monk, 662; Steve Largent, 595; Ozzie Newsome, 546.

Yards: James Lofton, 9,465; Largent, 9,336; Monk, 9,165.

Yards per catch (200 receptions): Willie Gault, 20.8; Stanley Morgan, 18.6; Lofton, 18.5.

TDs: Largent, 69; Jerry Rice, 66; Mark Clayton, 63.

OTHER CATEGORIES

Scoring: Nick Lowery, 1,006; Eddie Murray, 943; Pat Leahy, 904.

Interceptions: Ronnie Lott, 48; Dave Brown, 46; John Harris and Everson Walls, 44.

Sacks: Lawrence Taylor, 104; Dexter Manley, 91; Richard Dent and Reggie White, 81.

Punt return average (75 returns): John Taylor, 12.1; Vai Sikahema, 11.8; Henry Ellard, 11.4.

Punt return TDs: Ellard and LeRoy Irvin, 4.

Kickoff return average (75 returns): Rod Woodson, 24.7; Mel Gray, 24.0; Mike Nelms, 23.6.

Kickoff return TDs: Ron Brown, 4.

Field goals: Lowery, 225; Murray, 212; Gary Anderson, 186.

Field goal percentage (100 attempts): Lowery, 77.6; Morten Andersen, 77.0; Anderson, 76.9.

Punting average (200 punts): Rohn Stark, 44.2; Reggie Roby, 43.4; Sean Landeta, 43.3.

The owners hold on to the compensation system for free agents, the draft and control of the game. They also rid themselves of Garvey, who resigns under pressure.

Winner: Management has found the range, 10–9.

ROUND 8: THE 1987 STRIKE

Key Issue: Free agency.

Summary: The players walk out after the second week of the season, but this time the owners are ready. They cancel the third weekend's games but put together "scab" teams made up of free agents and resume play in Week 4. The strike falls apart after 24 days. The players return to work without an agreement. The union's only recourse is to file another antitrust lawsuit. It will be years before it's decided.

Winner: Management scores a knockdown, 10–8.

ROUND 9: THE UNION DECERTIFIES, 1989

Key Issue: Can the NFLPA win free agency by giving up its designation as sole bargaining agent for the players?

Summary: In progress.

Winner: ???

••• THE NFLPA GAMES

The highlight (if there was one) of the 1982 strike was the two AFC–NFC "all-star" games staged by the NFL Players Association. The first was held in Washington, the second the next day in Los Angeles.

A number of players appeared in both games. Pro players hadn't played back-to-back games since the '30s. One member of the group, Redskins running back John Riggins, said: "It was a great idea. It could kill somebody. I think this will be my last attempt at that. I guess I'll do anything for money."

Not *much* money, as it turned out. The winners of each game got $4,000 apiece, the losers $3,000. Almost all of it came from Turner Broadcasting, which paid $1 million to televise the games (and lost $800,000 on the deal).

Only 8,760 were in the stands at RFK Stadium. The L.A. Coliseum crowd was worse—5,331 announced, a reported 680 paid.

"I played at Cal Lutheran in front of 500 people," Chargers running back Hank Bauer said in L.A., "and that was if everybody brought their dog, so this wasn't that bad."

Because of shortages at certain positions, some players switched conferences. Eagles quarterback Dan Pastorini started for the AFC team in the second game. A few players who'd been cut in training camp also took part.

The officiating crews were made up of college and former pro officials. They asked the TV people not to mention their names.

The games were close—23–22 and 31–27—but heavy on passing (it was harder to get hurt) and not particularly well played. Two more were scheduled for the next week, but the league got a court order stopping them.

FIRST NFLPA GAME
At RFK Stadium

AFC East	0	12	10	0	—	22
NFC East	7	3	7	6	—	23

NFC—Spagnola 13 pass from Danielson (Moseley kick)

AFC—Moore 10 pass from Grogan (kick failed)

NFC—FG Moseley 27

AFC—Moore 21 pass from Grogan (kick failed)

AFC—FG Wood 23

NFC—M. Gray 48 pass from Danielson (Moseley kick)

AFC—Butler 61 pass from Strock (Wood kick)

NFC—FG Moseley 39

NFC—FG Moseley 45

INDIVIDUAL STATISTICS

RUSHING—AFC: Nathan 10-60, Barber 3-10, Tatupu 3-19. NFC: Riggins 8-30, Owens, 7-21, Middleton 3-7.

PASSING—AFC: Grogan 6-15-1, 112 yards; Strock 6-18-1, 137. NFC: Danielson 13-24-1, 198; Avellini 14-17-0, 131; Skladany 1-1-0, 14.

RECEIVING—AFC: Butler 3-98, Morgan 3-79, Moore 3-46. NFC: E. Gray 5-54, Middleton 4-42, Spagnola 3-45, Harmon 3-30, M. Gray 3-61, Riggins 3-8.

Attendance—8,760.

SECOND NFLPA GAME
At Los Angeles Coliseum

NFC West	7	10	7	3 —	27
AFC West	7	10	7	7 —	31

AFC—Delaney 26 pass from Pastorini (Lowery kick)

NFC—Hodge 12 pass from Evans (E. Murray kick)

AFC—FG Lowery 37

NFC—FG E. Murray 40

AFC—Carson 15 pass from Luther (Lowery kick)

NFC—Hodge 8 pass from Hipple (E. Murray kick)

AFC—Christensen 29 pass from Barnwell (Lowery kick)

NFC—Richardson 45 interception return (E. Murray kick)

AFC—T. Brown 54 pass from Luther (Lowery kick)

NFC—FG E. Murray 22

INDIVIDUAL STATISTICS

RUSHING—NFC: H. King 6-16, Hipple 1-14, Guman 4-10, Owens 3-0, Riggins 2-minus 6. AFC: Delaney 8-23, Cappelletti 5-18, Gaines 4-10, T. Brown 2-3, Bauer 4-1, Gagliano 3-minus 8.

PASSING—NFC: Evans 9-22-1, 112 yards; Hipple 15-29-1, 197; Hodge 0-1-0, 0. AFC: Pastorini 2-6-1, 39; Luther 10-18-1, 180; Gagliano 4-7-0, 35; Barnwell 1-1-0, 29.

RECEIVING—NFC: Nichols 5-95, L. Thompson 3-44, H. King 3-33, Riggins 3-23, Spagnola 2-47, Hodge 2-20, Guman 2-14. AFC: Christensen 4-80, Barnwell 3-24, T. Brown 2-59, Gaines 2-35, Carson 2-27, Walker 2-24.

Attendance—5,331.

■ ■ ■

A LESTER HAYES SAMPLER

In the world according to Lester Hayes, the Raiders were the "Silver and Black," dollars were "deceased presidents," reporters were "scoopmen" and the best movie ever made was The Empire Strikes Back. *He said he'd seen it 300 times.*

The Raiders produced their share of characters through the years but no one quite like Hayes. He was one of the top cornerbacks in the league from the late '70s to the mid-'80s, but the press knew him and loved him for his unique way of expressing himself.

He once accused Broncos wide receiver Steve Watson of "asinine-ing." He claimed to be the "27th leading minority land owner in Texas." And he liked to end his pronouncements with "so be it."

Some of his more memorable statements:

■ "I am the only true Jedi in the National Football League."

■ "There are some individuals in Silver and Blackdom who would rather run through a gauntlet of pit bulls wearing pork chop underwear than see me break the record for interceptions by a Raider."

■ "My forte is to observe and absorb everything I've seen for a decade. I haven't forgotten a thing in a decade. I have the memory of the National Archives."

■ "I study fish psychology, fish schooling patterns. I like to go into a fish's domain and sever his family ties."

■ "There comes a time when you have enough deceased presidents and you play for the ring."

■ "The past couple of years I've dubbed him 'John Goose Gooden Elway.' That name only applies at sea level. At 5,400 feet he turns into John Roger Clemens Elway.' He's throwing 98 mile-per-hour sliders."

■ "We had the opposing team so psyched that they hated going to Oakland. Without that intangible of mystique, we're a normal team. It distresses me. It causes mental malfunction. It bothers me to watch the mentality of the new Los Angeles Raiders. It's important to get the mentality back to our heritage, which is going out and biting, scratching and dusting eyebrows."

■ ■ ■

THE ELWAY AUCTION, 1983

How would quarterback John Elway have looked in the silver and black of the Raiders? How about Dan Marino and Jimbo Covert in the blue and white of the Colts? If a deal between the teams hadn't suddenly fallen through the night before the 1983 draft, we'd know.

Baltimore had agreed to send the number-one pick—which was to be Elway—to Los Angeles for three first-round and two second-round choices. The Colts wanted to draft a blue-chip offensive tackle—probably Covert—and were very high on Marino, who would have been available. Wouldn't *that* trade have changed the face of the AFC in the '80s?

It was so close to being done that both clubs had their official notices ready to send to the league office. The Bears pulled the plug on it. The Raiders needed one of their two first-round picks to complete the package for Baltimore. But at the last minute Chicago jacked up its price, and the trade fell apart. The Colts wound up selecting Elway, and the rest is history.

On May 2, six days after the draft, Baltimore owner Robert Irsay ignored the advice of general manager Ernie Accorsi and coach Frank Kush and traded Elway to Denver. He received offensive tackle Chris Hinton (the fourth player selected that year), a 1984 number-one pick, backup quarterback Mark Herrmann and $1 million. In Denver they still call it the Rocky Mountain Heist.

The Elway Pick dominated the '83 draft. If you believed all the hype, it was the opportunity of a lifetime for the Colts. They had a shot at one of the finest quarterback prospects ever.

But there was a problem. Elway refused to play in Baltimore and threatened to pursue a baseball career with the Yankees if the Colts drafted him. It wasn't the city that bothered him, it was the reputations of Irsay (a screwball) and coach Frank Kush (a martinet). Elway's father, Jack, then the coach at San Jose State, supposedly hated Kush.

The standoff produced a good bit of predraft drama. Would the Colts trade or take a chance on losing the top pick in the draft to baseball?

The situation was never quite as desperate as the media made it out to be. Accorsi and Kush knew from scouts that Elway was an average baseball prospect. Their philosophy from the beginning was to ask for the moon in a trade and make the pick if no team wanted to pay it.

The price was three number-one draft choices and two number twos. At least two of the ones had to be in '83, one of them within the top nine picks.

The Raiders were one of three teams that made a serious bid. The others were the San Diego Chargers and New England Patriots. San Diego wasn't willing to pay full price. New England was, but Accorsi refused to trade Elway to a team in the Colts' division.

There were plenty of lowball offers, and crazy rumors, too. The granddaddy of them all had the Raiders giving the Colts their entire '83 draft (11 picks). It wasn't true.

Some of the other rumored offers:

- From the Lions—running back Billy Sims plus draft picks.
- Seahawks—quarterback Jim Zorn, any running back on the roster plus draft picks.
- Chiefs—a choice of QBs Steve Fuller or Bill Kenney plus draft picks.
- Cowboys—QB Danny White, tackle Randy White plus a number one.
- Oilers—running back Earl Campbell, another player and draft picks.
- Falcons—QB Steve Bartkowski and draft picks.

The Chargers were the logical top contender. They had two number ones (the 5th and 20th picks) and two number twos in '83 plus their number one in '84 to work with. The trouble was they didn't want to give up three number ones.

KICKING KINGS

Expanded rosters spelled the end of all-purpose kickers -- players who punt as well as place kick. The last who was effective in both roles was the Rams' Frank Corral, who played in the NFL until 1981. Punter Steve Cox booted some long field goals for the Browns and Redskins later in the decade, but he was never a regular kicker.

The greatest combination kickers of the modern era were Sam Baker, Don Chandler and Tommy Davis. Baker led the league in scoring in 1957 (77 points) and in punting in '58 (45.4 average) while playing for the Redskins. Chandler led in punting in '57 (44.6) and in scoring in '63 (106) during his Giants days. And Davis led in field goals in '60 (19) and in punting in '62 (45.6) with the 49ers.

PRO FOOTBALL'S GREATEST ALL-PUROSE KICKERS (1933-)

Kicker	Career	Team*	Punts	Avg.	FG	%Made
Bill Dudley	1942-53	Redskins	191	38.2	33	50.0
Bob Waterfield	1945-52	Rams	315	42.4	60	54.5
Sam Baker	1953-69	Eagles	703	42.6	179	56.6
Don Chandler	1956-67	Giants	660	43.5	94	58.4
Tommy Davis	1959-69	49ers	511	44.7	130	47.1
Danny Villanueva	1960-67	Rams	488	42.7	85	53.1
Mike Mercer	1961-70	Raiders	307	40.6	102	52.8
Don Cockroft	1968-80	Browns	651	40.3	216	65.9
Dennis Partee	1968-75	Chargers	519	41.3	71	58.7
Frank Corral	1978-81	Rams	165	40.8	75	60.5

*team kicker played for longest

About five days before the draft, Chargers GM John Sanders tried a little gamesmanship. He quietly traded his two second-round picks to the 49ers for yet another number one. San Diego was now holding the 5th, 20th and 22nd picks in '83 plus their own in '84. Sanders then called Accorsi and "caved in." The Colts could have their number ones.

Had Accorsi pulled the trigger, San Diego would have come away from the deal with Elway and a first-round pick. The Colts would have been humiliated. But a source in the league office tipped Accorsi to the Chargers-49ers deal, and he had a counteroffer ready for Sanders: all four number ones. Negotiations broke down.

By this time talks with the Raiders had reached the serious stage. L.A. had first- and second-round picks in '83 and '84 to offer but needed the extra number one in '83. Enter the Bears, who had the 6th and 18th picks in the round. The Raiders went after the 6th. They offered Chicago cornerback Ted Watts (who'd been a number-one pick in '81), safety Kenny Hill plus draft picks. Chicago was receptive. Elway was as good as in Los Angeles.

But late in the afternoon on the day before the draft, Bears general manager Jim Finks asked for defensive tackle Howie Long, too. The Raiders were furious. They'd made it clear from the start that Long wasn't for sale, and now all of a sudden Chicago was making him a condition of the trade. It was too much to give up. The big three-team deal with the Colts was off.

Raiders managing general partner Al Davis accused the league office of conspiring to kill the trade. And for once he wasn't alone.

"You got to understand that this was right in the middle of Davis' lawsuit against the league," says an official from another team. "You know damn well they didn't want Elway to wind up a Raider. [Bears owner] George Halas is on his deathbed and Jim Finks is running the team, but I know Halas doesn't want the trade made. All of a sudden the Bears' end of the trade falls through. I think it came from Halas. From the league and Halas."

Accorsi and Kush showed up at Colts headquarters the morning of April 26 resolved they were going to select Elway. Of course there was always the Irsay factor.

Teams had begun bypassing Accorsi and calling the unpredictable Colts owner. Miami's Don Shula, Dallas' Tex Schramm, New England's Chuck Sullivan were doing all they could to steal the top pick.

Sullivan nearly did. Minutes before the draft started, Irsay was wavering over an offer of All-Pro guard John Hannah and a number-one pick. He was talked out of it.

The Raiders and Chargers also made last-minute bids, but didn't offer enough to change Irsay's mind. The Colts selected Elway.

Irsay continued to entertain bids after the draft and eventually made the deal with the Broncos on his own. Accorsi, meanwhile, talked to two teams.

The first was the Chargers. Sanders called with one more offer: nine players for Elway. Most were retreads and Accorsi turned him down.

The second was the 49ers. Accorsi called coach Bill Walsh to inquire about the availability of quarterback Joe Montana. Walsh wasn't interested.

■ ■ ■

$$$$$

$1	Jury award in USFL's antitrust suit in 1985
$1.75	Charge for two-minute call to Eagles coach Buddy Ryan's hotline (1-900-USA-RYAN) in 1989
$38.56	Cardinals' average ticket price, highest in NFL, in 1988
$65	Cost of hand-carved duck decoy by Redskins' Dave Butz in 1985
$200	Alleged bounty Eagles put on Cowboys kicker Luis Zendejas in 1989 (the equivalent of 3 hours, 48 minutes, 30 seconds on Ryan's hotline)
$1,000	Fine assessed Bears' William Perry for being over 320 pounds at his weekly weigh-ins, 1986
$4,000	Average game check for replacement players in 1987
$70,000	Severance pay for 5-year veteran in 1982
$200,000	What the 24-day strike cost Bills' Jim Kelly in 1987
$250,000	Fee Penthouse paid Bengals' Stanley Wilson for story of his pre-Super Bowl cocaine binge in 1989
$5,600,000	Amount Super Bowl visitors spent on alcohol in San Diego in 1988
$6,000,000	Value of 5-year contract free agent Wilber Marshall signed with Redskins in 1988

FRANCHISE QB

When Denver quarterback John Elway's current contract expires in 1992, he will have made $17.7 million in the first 11 years of his career. In 1976, Seattle and Tampa paid $16 million for their franchises.

• • •

AN EASY SIX

Lots of NFL teams have been accused of lying down, but the 1984 Tampa Bay Buccaneers were the first to admit it. They let the New York Jets score a meaningless touchdown late in their last game so running back James Wilder could have another shot at breaking a record.

The Buccaneers defense offered little or no resistance on the Jets' final 35-yard touchdown drive. The Tampa fans were in full support. They booed when Bucs safety Mark Cotney tackled Johnny Hector at the two with 56 seconds left. Hector scored on the next play without being touched.

"We tried to make it look inconspicuous," linebacker Scot Brantley said, "but I guess we didn't succeed."

NICKNAMES

"The Fridge" (William Perry)	Dennis "Dirt" Winston
"The Diesel" (John Riggins)	Elbert "Ickey" Woods
"Sweetness" (Walter Payton)	James "Tootie" Robbins
"The Ice Cube" (Gerald McNeil)	Fulton "Captain Crazy" Kuykendall
Lionel "Little Train" James	Dean "The Tasmanian Devil" Hamel
Gary "Big Hands" Johnson	George "Tiger" Greene
Ed "Too Tall" Jones	Don "Jaws" Hardeman
John "Jumbo" Elliot	Craig "Ironhead" Heyward
Alfred "Jitter" Fields	**Not Nicknames:**
Howard "Hokie" Gajan	Nuu Faaola
Walter "Bubby" Brister	Tunch Ilkin
Norman "Boomer" Esiason	**Expedient Nicknames:**
Roy "Jet Stream" Green	Tommories "Mossy" Cade
Tony "Thrill" Hill	Lyvonia "Stump" Mitchell
"Neon" Deion Sanders	

The irate Jets onside-kicked, but the Buccaneers recovered. That gave Wilder three more tries to top the league mark of 2,244 yards rushing and receiving, set just the day before by the Rams' Eric Dickerson. But the Jets keyed on him. He lost two yards on his first carry, gained them back on his second and was stopped at the line on his third.

The Jets blamed John McKay, who had announced his retirement and was coaching his last game for Tampa Bay. They shouted obscenities at him as he went off the field. Defensive lineman Barry Bennett called him "a dog." Coach Joe Walton said it was "a total embarrassment to the NFL. It set it back 20 years."

McKay's flimsy excuse: "If I hadn't done that I would have been lynched. I'm not too popular around here, anyway."

The league fined the Bucs.

• • •

FASTEST PLAYER

For the first time in the '80s you didn't have to guess who the fastest pro football player was. In 1986 Sprint Telephone Service (followed by Subaru) began holding the NFL's Fastest Man competition. Each year eight selected speed merchants—don't you wish they'd bring that term back?—went head-to-head.

Redskins cornerback Darrell Green surprised a lot of people by winning three of the first four competitions (he skipped the other). Along the way, he defeated U.S. Olympians Ron Brown, Sam Graddy and Willie Gault, plus world-class hurdler Rod Woodson. The guy who gave him the best race was Packers receiver Phillip Epps, whom he nosed out in a photo finish in '86.

"I am the fastest man in the NFL," Green said later. "I can outrun all the defensive linemen, I can outrun all the linebackers, I can outrun all the quarterbacks, I can outrun all the running backs, I can outrun all the coaches, I can outrun all the trainers, I can outrun all the ladies working upstairs in the offices, I can outrun all the general managers, I can outrun all the owners. . . . I've said it before, but no one believed me. Now I have the proof."

Green had run a 10.08 100 meters at Texas A&I. In his first NFL game he caught the Cowboys' Tony

. . . .

Dorsett from behind and started establishing a repuation. He probably could have become one of the greatest punt returners in league history, but the team only occasionally used him in that capacity because it was afraid he'd get hurt. He beat the Bears in the 1987 playoffs with a 52-yard runback for a touchdown.

■ ■ ■

HIT OF THE DECADE

The Giants Break Joe Theismann's Leg, 1985

Lawrence Taylor says he'll never forget the sound of Joe Theismann's leg breaking. "I heard it crack," the Giants linebacker said. "It went right through me." The moment and sensation were shared by millions watching *Monday Night Football* November 18, 1985.

Theismann suffered a compound fracture when he went down in a heap of Giants linebackers. ABC's instant-replay cameras captured with gruesome clarity the Redskins quarterback's lower right leg bending at nearly 90 degrees and giving way. It was a chilling sight.

"I have never seen anything like it before," said Harry Carson, Taylor's teammate.

The hit came less than a minute into the second quarter at RFK Stadium. The score was 7–7 in a game crucial to the playoff hopes of both teams.

With the ball on the Washington 46, Theismann handed to John Riggins running up the middle. Riggins stopped as he got to the line of scrimmage and pitched back to Theismann. It was the flea-flicker, a favorite trick play of the Redskins.

Theismann was supposed to pass, but the Giants swarmed him. Carson was first to arrive and spun him around. Taylor was next. He hit Theismann from behind and slid to one side, pulling Theismann with him. Gary Reasons then jumped on top and down they went.

Taylor was up instantly waving to the Washington bench. "Get the hell out here!" he yelled. Then he grabbed his head with both hands. Other Giants players were motioning to the Redskins.

"I was on top of the pile and Joe screamed and we got off as fast as we could," Giants nose tackle

FASTEST MAN RESULTS
(Figures in parentheses are seedings.)

1986
Heat 1 -- Willie Gault (1), 6.347; Dokie Williams, 6.590.
Heat 2 -- Vance Johnson (3) 6.402; Eddie Brown, 6.535.
Heat 3 -- Darrell Green (4), 6.097; Phillip Epps, 6.097. (Green won in photo finish.)
Heat 4 -- Ron Brown (2), 6.282; Anthony Carter, 6.782.
Semifinal 1 -- Gault, 6.180 (hand-timed, pistol malfunction); Johnson (unavailable).
Semifinal 2 -- Green, 6.117; Brown, 6.201.
Final — Green, 6.121; Gault, 6.195.

1987
Heat 1 -- Herschel Walker (1), 6.321; Darryl Turner, 6.757.
Heat 2 -- Ron Brown (4), 6.153; Vance Johnson, 6.314.
Heat 3 -- Phillip Epps (3), 6.310; Jerry Rice, 6.344.
Heat 4 -- Willie Gault (2), 6.259; Ernest Givins, 6.476.
Semifinal 1 -- Brown, 6.188; Walker, 6.272.
Semifinal 2 -- Epps, 6.149; Gault, 6.159.
Final — Brown, 6.095; Epps, 6.186.

1988
Heat 1 -- Darrell Green (1), 6.15; Mark Duper, 6.42.
Heat 2 -- Herschel Walker (3), 6.29; Vance Johnson, 6.42.
Heat 3 -- Rod Woodson (4), 6.35; Ricky Nattiel, 6.52.
Heat 4 -- Willie Gault (2), 6.36; Haywood Jeffires, 6.48.
Semifinal 1 -- Green, 6.12; Walker, 6.24.
Semifinal 2 -- Woodson, 6.28; Gault, 6.29.
Final — Green, 6.10; Woodson, 6.25.

1989
Heat 1 -- Darrell Green (1), 6.21; Clarence Verdin, 6.59.
Heat 2 -- Sam Graddy, 6.30; Phillip Epps (3), 6.45.
Heat 3 -- Anthony Miller, 6.22; Herschel Walker (4), 6.43.
Heat 4 -- Ron Brown (2), 6.38; Tim Brown, 6.43.
Semifinal 1 -- Green, 6.21; Graddy, 6.26.
Semifinal 2 -- Miller, 6.30; R. Brown, 6.32.
Final — Green, 6.14; Miller, 6.30.

Fastest Time in '80s: Ron Brown, 6.095, 1988.
Slowest Time: Anthony Carter, 6.782, 1986.

Jim Burt said. "It was just hanging there. He broke it all."

Theismann somehow managed to keep his composure. He joked with Carson as doctors and trainers worked on him. He wanted to know which Giant had gotten him. He said he'd be back to settle the score.

"Not tonight you won't," Carson said.

Not ever. It was the first and last serious injury of Theismann's 12-year NFL career. When the bones healed (he broke the tibia and fibula just above the ankle), his right leg was a quarter-inch shorter than his left and too weak to withstand the pounding of pro football.

After flunking the team physical in July 1986 he officially retired. He collected $1.4 million from a career-ending injury policy with Lloyd's of London.

■ ■ ■

JIM BROWN VS. FRANCO HARRIS

It galled Jim Brown to think Franco Harris might break his all-time rushing record in 1984. Brown didn't think Harris was in his class. Before the season, he criticized Harris' habit of running out of bounds and accused the Steelers back of prolonging his career just to pass Brown's hallowed mark.

He even talked about making a comeback. Why, he said, I could beat the guy in a race *right now.*

In January 1985, Harris took him up on it. He agreed to compete against Brown in four events over two days—racquetball, one-on-one basketball and football and the 40-yard dash.

"I Challenge You" was the ultimate in Trash-Sports. Some 140 stations televised the generational battle, which was held in Atlantic City. It fell a little short of being the "Duel of the Decade" promised by the promoters, but it *was* unique.

Beginning with the weigh-in. Brown tipped the scales at 229¾ pounds, a couple of pounds under his playing weight with the Browns. Not bad for 48. Harris, 14 years younger, was 228¼.

"I don't want to lose, and Jim doesn't want to

THE DRUG PROBLEM

The '80s were the drug decade in the NFL. Leaguewide drug testing was initiated in 1987 and steroid testing in 1989. Pro football's problem was of such scope that 13 players -- past, present and future -- were convicted of drug trafficking from 1976 to '89. Four had been Pro Bowlers. The roll:

13 NFL PLAYERS WHO WERE CONVICTED OF DRUG TRAFFICKING

Year	Player	Team,* Position	Career	Sentence
1976	Shelby Jordan	Patriots, OT	1975–86	2 years
1977	Randy Crowder	Dolphins, DL	1974–80	1 year
1977	Don Reese	Dolphins, DL	1974–81	1 year
1980	Bob Hayes	Cowboys, WR	1965–75	5 years
1982	Kirby Criswell	Cardinals, DE	1980–81	5 years
1982	Mike Strachan	Saints, RB	1975–80	3 years
1983	Mercury Morris	Dolphins, RB	1969–76	20 years
1983	John Williams	Rams, OT	1968–79	5 years
1983	Tony Peters	Redskins, SS	1975–84	4 years' probation
1986	Barry Word	Saints, FB	1987–	6 months
1986	Tony Robinson	Redskins, QB	1987	90 days
1988	Elvis Franks	Browns, DE	1980–86	3 years' probation
1989	Chuck Muncie	Chargers, RB	1976–84	2 1/2 years**

*team he played for longest **also convicted of perjury

lose," Harris said. "You'll be very surprised [at the intensity of the competition]."

They went at it pretty good the first day. Brown easily won in racquetball (11–4, 11–8), but the basketball games were brutal. The action was "so rough that at one point Brown and Franco almost got into a fight," wrote columnist Bob Dolgan of the Cleveland *Plain Dealer.* "They exchanged heated words after the first game."

Brown prevailed in that one, 22–12. But Harris took the next, 22–10, and was leading 20–14 in the rubber game when Brown called a timeout and sat down on the bench. Four kids who went to the elementary school where the event was being staged toweled him off.

Then he rose and proceeded to score the last eight points for a 22–20 victory. As his last shot, a hook, settled into the net, the crowd of a few hundred rejoiced so loudly "it made your hair hurt," Dolgan reported.

"It was real," Brown said afterward, "it was who was going to intimidate who. This is grueling. I've got a lot of respect for him. I didn't think he'd be that physical. His pride is on the line."

Admitted Harris: "I wanted to win bad."

The final two events were held in the ballroom of the Tropicana Hotel. There was a band, cheerleaders with F or J on their uniforms and comedy by Bill Cosby. Veteran NFL referee Jim Tunney officiated, as he had the day before.

The football competition was a ridiculous contrivance. Each man ran four pass patterns against the other on a carpet 12 yards wide. Whoever gained the most yards won. Phil Simms of the Giants did the throwing.

Brown started things off by catching a six-yard pass, but as he did he bent and grabbed his left leg. His injury was diagnosed as a slight tendon pull. The attending physician said Brown hadn't warmed up enough.

Brown, who never missed an NFL game, kept on. He caught one other pass for 30 yards and a "touchdown." But Harris gained 12 and 30 yards on his first two plays to beat him, 42–36.

During the hour break before the 40-yard dash, ointment was rubbed on Brown's leg. He decided to give it a go, even took the early lead in the race, but pulled up just as Harris passed him. Harris' time was 5.16 seconds.

"If I had been competitive, his time would have

been much faster," Brown said. ". . . I'll go back to my racquetball and basketball in the backyard. You won't be hearing from me again in this arena."

Brown took home a $15,000 men's mink coat and a vacation cruise to Hawaii, the prizes for winning the first two events. Harris got a Dodge Lancer and two gold watches worth $10,000. Each also received a reported $25,000.

It had been decided beforehand that the 40-yard dash would decide the overall winner, so Harris was the victor. But Brown got the last laugh. Harris never broke his record. The Bears' Walter Payton did.

THE FRIDGE PHENOMENON

No pro football player ever got more mileage out of 11 yards than William Perry. That was all the Refrigerator gained for the Chicago Bears in 1985, regular season *and* postseason. Yet he became the NFL's hottest commercial property, an American folk hero.

Perry was the phenomenon to end all phenomena. He was sort of a reverse Eddie Gaedel (the midget who batted for the St. Louis Browns in 1951). Twenty-five years from now, all that's going to be remembered of this 300-and-whatever-pound defensive tackle is his *ball carrying*, assuming his career keeps going the way it has.

The whole thing might never have happened if San Francisco coach Bill Walsh hadn't used guard Guy McIntyre as a blocking back for a few plays in the 1984 NFC title game against Chicago. It stuck in Bears coach Mike Ditka's craw and, as we all know, Ditka has a very large craw. So when the two teams played the next year, he had Perry, his pudgy number-one draft pick, ready. He had no idea the force he was about to unleash on the football world.

The Fridge carried the ball on the last two plays that day, both up the gut ("34 dive straight" were the calls). He picked up two yards each time. Those were his longest rushing gains of the season.

The following week he became a media sensation. The Bears played the Packers on Monday night, and Ditka put him at fullback for four goal-line plays.

Perry scored the go-ahead touchdown on a one-yard run and opened huge holes for Walter Payton to score two other TDs.

Green Bay linebacker George Cumby did, however, discover the only strategy that seemed to work against Perry. Cumby cut his legs out from under

DECADE ALL–STAR TEAM

For all players except specialists, figures under "Data" are average season totals (except where indicated).

OFFENSE		
Pos. Player	**Years***	**Data**
WR Jerry Rice	5	69 catches, 1,273 yds., 13 TDs; 4 Pro Bowls
TE Kellen Winslow	8	65 catches, 811 yds., 5 TDs; 5 Pro Bowls
T Anthony Munoz	10	8 Pro Bowls
G John Hannah	6	6 Pro Bowls
C Dwight Stephenson	8	5 Pro Bowls
G Russ Grimm	9	4 Pro Bowls
T Jackie Slater	10	6 Pro Bowls
QB Joe Montana	10	63.9%, 3,096 yds., 22 TDs; 6 Pro Bowls
RB Eric Dickerson	7	1,604 yds., 4.6 avg., 12 TDs; 6 Pro Bowls
RB Walter Payton	8	1,225 yds., 42 catches, 8 TDs; 5 Pro Bowls
WR Steve Largent	10	60 catches, 934 yds., 7 TDs; 5 Pro Bowls

DEFENSE		
Pos. Player	**Years**	**Data**
E Reggie White	4	20 sacks; 4 Pro Bowls
T Randy White	9	7 sacks; 6 Pro Bowls
T Doug English	5	6 sacks; 3 Pro Bowls
NT Michael Carter	6	4 sacks; 3 Pro Bowls
E Howie Long	9	8 sacks; 6 Pro Bowls
LB Lawrence Taylor	9	13 sacks; 9 Pro Bowls
LB Mike Singletary	9	7 Pro Bowls
LB Harry Carson	9	7 Pro Bowls
LB Andre Tippett	8	10 sacks; 5 Pro Bowls
CB Mike Haynes	10	2 interceptions; 4 Pro Bowls
CB Lester Hayes	7	4 interceptions; 5 Pro Bowls
SS Ken Easley	7	5 interceptions; 5 Pro Bowls
FS Ronnie Lott	9	5 interceptions; 8 Pro Bowls

SPECIALISTS AND OTHER SELECTIONS		
Pos. Selection	**Years**	**Data**
KR Mike Nelms	5	29.7 avg. in '81 without a TD
PR Darrell Green	7	11.1 avg.; used only on special occasions
K Nick Lowery	10	Averaged 23 FGs, 77.6% made
P Rohn Stark	8	44.2 avg.; 2 Pro Bowls
Special Teams -- Ron Wolfley	**Wild Card Selection** -- Roger Craig	
Kick Blocker -- Dan Hampton	**Coach** -- Bill Walsh	
Enforcer -- Lyle Alzado	**PR Man** -- Marty "Hunch" Hurney	

*Number of years he played in the decade, not in his career.

him the last time he led the interference, causing Payton to be stacked up. (The tactic had an unpleasant side effect, though: Perry fell on you.)

After Dallas tackled Perry the same way, a yard short of the end zone, he changed his running style. The next time he carried, against Atlanta, he went airborne for a one-yard touchdown.

In the rematch with the Packers, Ditka worked Perry into the passing game. The big guy went in motion and caught a four-yard TD flip from Jim McMahon. Cumby was supposed to cover him. Still, no one was prepared for what Perry did in the Super Bowl.

On second and goal at the New England three in a 3–3 game, he took a pitchout running right and *raised his arm to pass.* This may have been the single most exciting moment in the decade (to show you what we think of the '80s).

Unfortunately, tight end Emery Moorehead, the primary receiver, was covered, and Perry had to eat the ball. But in the third quarter he rumbled one yard for the final Chicago touchdown in a 46–10 victory.

The totals: six rushes for eight yards, one reception for four yards, one sack for a loss of one, four TDs.

And immortality.

PERRY'S 8 PLAYS

No. Opponent	Play	Gain
1. At 49ers	run	2
2. At 49ers	run	2
3. Vs. Packers	run	1*
4. At Packers	reception	4*
5. At Cowboys	run	1
6. Vs. Falcons	run	1*
7. Vs. Patriots	sacked	-1
8. Vs. Patriots	run	1*
Total yards		**11**

*touchdown

■ ■ ■

THE GAY QUESTION

Jerry Smith found in death the notoriety that often escaped him as a tight end with the Washington Redskins. He died in 1986 of complications from AIDS and was identified as the first professional athlete to do so.

Smith was a terrific player during his 13 seasons (1965–77). He still holds the NFL career record for touchdown catches by a tight end—60—though you don't hear a lot about him.

His bisexuality was a loosely kept secret in Washington for years. He was the "anonymous" athlete profiled in a 1975 series on gays in sports by the *Washington Star.* He was also "Bill Stiles" in ex-teammate Dave Kopay's confessional, *The David Kopay Story.*

"What's an All-American image today?" Smith told the *Star.* "Is it apple pie and gee whiz? Or is it honesty and integrity? If I enjoy being with somebody, male or female, and I'm not intruding on anyone else, I consider it normal."

And yet Smith never publicly acknowledged being gay, even after it was learned he had AIDS. Only one former NFL player has—Kopay, a reserve running back and special-teamer in the '60s and early '70s.

He came out of the closet in 1975 in the *Washington Star* series. It was the first time an athlete in any sport had, and it caused national shock waves.

Kopay had only been out of the NFL for three years at that point and supported the *Star's* claim that at least three starting quarterbacks in the league were homosexual or bisexual. He estimated that about 5 percent of all players were.

"It's so hidden [in the NFL]," he said. "You can pick up vibrations and things like that. You can interpret people's eyes. But going past a certain point is maybe just a matter of professional ethics."

Were the claims accurate? A number of players and coaches disputed them. The league itself steered clear of the issue. Always has.

■ ■ ■

JAMES DEAN, YOUR LIGHTS ARE ON

Houston coach Jerry Glanville got lots of laughs in 1988 when he started leaving tickets on the road for famous people—often *dead* famous people. Each was connected to the city or state where the Oilers were playing. His pass list:

August 13, Memphis—Elvis Presley. Glanville: "I hear Elvis is living now in Michigan or Minnesota. Well, we'd like him to come and be on our bench. We don't care how much he weighs."

September 4, Indianapolis—James Dean. "He's the biggest thing in Indiana that didn't play basketball."

September 18, New York—Phantom of the Opera. "It will be a sideline pass. I hear he wears black [Glanville's color]."

October 16, Pittsburgh—Charles Wikenhauser (Pittsburgh Zoo director). "We thought he could see some real animals at work."

October 23, Cincinnati—Loni Anderson. "I know the Bengals are real big there, and the Reds are too, but I'm leaving tickets for the biggest thing that ever hit Cincinnati."

November 13, Seattle—D. B. Cooper. "I figure it's about time he showed up."

November 24, Dallas—Buddy Holly. "We received letters from Oiler fans and Cowboy fans from West Texas, and both wanted Buddy Holly from Lubbock. Just goes to show you Oiler fans and Cowboy fans can agree on something."

Glanville didn't leave tickets in Philadelphia October 2 but had two candidates, W. C. Fields and Ed McMahon. "And I'm not so sure it's not the same person," he said.

■ ■ ■

HE COULD HAVE BEEN COMMISSIONER

Jim Finks

The favorite to succeed Pete Rozelle in 1989, Finks fell victim to a power struggle between old guard and new guard owners. He certainly had the credentials to be commissioner. He'd been a player for the Pittsburgh Steelers in the '50s. He'd done impressive jobs building teams and organizations in Minnesota, Chicago and most recently New Orleans. And he'd been a reasonable but firm presence in league matters.

His problems began July 6 at an owners meeting in Chicago when 11 teams formed a coalition and refused to vote for a new commissioner. At the time, Finks had 16 of the 19 votes necessary for election.

The band of 11 was led by the so-called new guard powers in the league, such as Minnesota's Mike Lynn, San Francisco's Eddie DeBartolo, Philadelphia's Norman Braman and Denver's Pat Bowlen. Their gripe wasn't with Finks, but with the old guard, in particular Cleveland's Art Modell and the New York Giants' Wellington Mara.

Modell and Mara had led the search committee for Rozelle's successor and nominated only one candidate—Finks—to the other owners. The new guard saw this as one more example of the older owners trying to determine the future of the league. A four-month power struggle ensued.

Paul Tagliabue, a Washington attorney who'd worked with the league for 20 years, became an unlikely symbol for the new guard. He was well liked by the old guard and would have been their second choice. He and Finks were good friends.

At an owners meeting October 12 in Dallas, the two candidates received 13 votes apiece (there were two abstentions). Two weeks later in Cleveland, it was 15–11–2 for Tagliabue. The process was at an impasse. Neither candidate could get the required votes.

Rozelle, who'd been forced to hang on as commissioner since March 22, put together a five-man committee to break the deadlock. It was composed of Mara, Modell, Bowlen, Lynn and Pittsburgh's Dan Rooney, who chaired it. Finally, Mara and Modell gave in. On October 26, Tagliabue was elected by a vote of 23–4–1.

■ ■ ■

FIGHT OF THE DECADE

Two Bills Coaches Battle, 1989

There's a bandage on the forehead of offensive line coach Tom Bresnahan in the 1989 Buffalo Bills team picture. It's protecting a cut suffered when receivers coach Nick Niccolau rammed his head through a wall.

The two went at it in a meeting room the morning

after a 34–3 victory over the New York Jets October 22. Niccolau reportedly decked the much bigger Bresnahan with an uppercut to the chin. Then he grabbed him in a headlock and ran him into the aforementioned wall, putting a hole in it the size of . . . well, Bresnahan's head.

The fight supposedly started when Bresnahan came into the coaches' meeting bragging about the offensive line play and blocking schemes against the Jets. Niccolau thought credit for the win should be more widely distributed, and Bresnahan confronted him. Niccolau apparently wasn't in the mood for it.

The other assistants hesitated to break up the fight at first, Bresnahan not being the most popular guy on the staff. They finally did, but not until the line coach needed stitches to close cuts on his chin and forehead.

"He looked like one of those Bay Area earth-

quake victims," a source told the *Buffalo Evening News*. "He looked like he'd been through a war."

Bills head coach Marv Levy originally denied any knowledge of the incident. A reporter asked him about the hole in the meeting-room wall.

"That room is a beaten-up room anyway," Levy said. "I didn't notice anything unusual about it."

Not even the bloodstains.

It wasn't until the next day that Levy and general manager Bill Polian acknowledged the fight. They released a joint statement saying the matter had been handled internally and that neither coach would be disciplined. The wall had already been repaired.

●●●
THE GREATEST TEAM OF ALL TIME?

In 1989 NFL Films and ESPN staged a computerized competition among 20 of the best pro football teams since World War II. The teams were divided into four divisions and played a six-game schedule, followed by the playoffs. *Dream Season*, it was called.

Appropriate footage from thousands of reels of film was pieced together—sometimes with the aid of an airbrush—to make it look like clubs from different decades were really playing each other. One game was featured each week, with highlights from other matchups shown at halftime.

Steve Sabol of NFL Films, who dreamed up the idea, says, "My opinion would have been that the ['66] Packers were the best team of all time." But the Pack didn't even win its division and advance to the semifinals. The Fantastic Four were the '78 Steelers (6–0), '84 49ers (5–1), '76 Raiders (6–0) and '72 Dolphins (6–0).

In the semis the Steelers beat the 49ers, 20–17, while the Dolphins maintained their undefeated mystique by downing the Raiders, 24–21. The Steelers prevailed in the Dream Bowl, though, 21–20, on the strength of some great goal-line defense and Franco Harris' three-yard touchdown run on the last play.

Interesting, isn't it, that three of the final four were from the '70s? Makes you wonder if pro football might have peaked in that period. The '89 49ers

Going
1980--Jim Tyrer, 41, ex-Chiefs tackle, suicide
  Verne Lewellen, 78, all-pro back with early Packers
  Don Floyd, 41, ex-Oilers defensive end, heart attack
  Harold McLinton, 33, ex-Redskins linebacker, hit and run
1981--Cliff Battles, 70
  Rusty Chambers, 27, Dolphins linebacker, car accident
1982--Bill George, 51, car accident
  Benny Friedman, 77, suicide
1983--George Halas, 88
  Bob Waterfield, 62
  Norm Van Brocklin, 57
  Mike Michalske, 80
  Joe Delaney, 24, Chiefs halfback, drowned
  Buddy Young, 57, car accident
  Larry Gordon, 28, Dolphins linebacker, heart attack
1984--Kirk Collins, 25, Rams safety, cancer
  David Overstreet, 25, Dolphins running back, car accident
1985--Johnny Blood, 81
  Bruiser Kinard, 70
1986--Fritz Pollard, 92
  Jack Christiansen, 57
  Bobby Layne, 59
  Don Rogers, 23, Browns safety, drug overdose
1988--Art Rooney, 87
  Joe Don Looney, 45
  David Croudip, 29, Falcons cornerback, drug overdose
1989--Clarke Hinkle, 87

would give anybody a game, but our money would be on the '78 Steelers.

While none of the '50s and '60s teams reached the playoffs, some individuals stood out. Jim Brown of the '64 Browns led the league in rushing with 717 yards and Herb Adderley of the '66 Packers in interceptions with five. The computer loved Lenny Moore of the '59 Colts. He gained a *Dream Season*–best 980 yards from scrimmage—163.3 per game against the greatest teams of all time.

THE DREAM BOWL
At Three Rivers Stadium

'72 Dolphins	7	3	7	3	—	20
'78 Steelers	0	14	0	7	—	21

MIA—Twilley 36 pass from Griese (Yepremian kick)
PIT—Swann 20 pass from Bradshaw (Gerela kick)
MIA—FG Yepremian 19
PIT—Stallworth 18 pass from Bradshaw (Gerela kick)
MIA—Csonka 8 pass from Griese (Yepremian kick)
MIA—FG Yepremian 24
PIT—Harris 3 run (Gerela kick)

	DOLPHINS	STEELERS
First downs	23	24
Run-Pass-Pen	13-9-1	9-14-1
3rd down conv	3-11	6-16

	DOLPHINS	STEELERS
Net yards	432	450
Plays-Avg.	67-6.4	60-7.5
Rushes-Yards	46-223	27-149
Passing yards	209	301
Return yards	121	134
Sacked-Yards lost	0-0	0-0
Passes	21-14-1	33-22-1
Punts	6-42.2	4-39
Fumbles-Lost	0-0	2-1
Penalties-Yards	3-26	4-45
Time of possession	27:00	33:00

INDIVIDUAL STATISTICS

RUSHING—Dolphins: Csonka 25-131, Morris 13-70, Kiick 7-21, Griese 1-1. Steelers: Harris 18-108, Bleier 5-24, Bradshaw 2-10, Thornton 2-7.

PASSING—Dolphins: Griese 21-14-1, 209 yards. Steelers: Bradshaw 33-22-1, 301.

RECEIVING—Dolphins: Warfield 4-85, Briscoe 2-42, Mandich 2-15, Fleming 2-14, Kiick 2-9, Twilley 1-36, Csonka 1-8. Steelers: Stallworth 8-101, Swann 7-90, Harris 4-33, Bell 2-73, Bleier 1-4.

KICKOFF RETURNS—Dolphins: Morris 4-104. Steelers: Anderson 3-92.

PUNT RETURNS—Dolphins: Leigh 1-7. Steelers: Bell 4-36.

INTERCEPTIONS—Dolphins: Mumphord 1-10. Steelers: Shell 1-6.

Attendance—61,875.

DREAM SEASON FINAL STANDINGS AND RESULTS

EAST DIVISION

'78 Steelers (6-0)
24	'83 Raiders	14
20	'68 Jets	7
31	'77 Cowboys	24
35	'55 Browns	17
27	'69 Chiefs	10
21	'66 Packers	17
158		**89**

'86 Giants (4-2)
21	'64 Browns	13
17	'77 Cowboys	28
31	'60 Eagles	20
34	'82 Redskins	31
17	'76 Raiders	21
31	'53 Lions	14
151		**127**

'59 Colts (3-3)
6	'72 Dolphins	24
13	'85 Bears	17
28	'51 Rams	14
17	'66 Packers	24
24	'82 Redskins	17
24	'68 Jets	19
112		**115**

'60 Eagles (2-4)
10	'66 Packers	38
17	'51 Rams	14
20	'86 Giants	31
27	'63 Chargers	21
21	'64 Browns	31
13	'77 Cowboys	24
108		**159**

'68 Jets (1-5)
27	'76 Raiders	28
7	'78 Steelers	20
31	'63 Chargers	24
20	'84 49ers	24
21	'72 Dolphins	24
19	'59 Colts	24
125		**144**

WEST DIVISION

'84 49ers (5-1)
21	'51 Rams	3
21	'66 Packers	28
26	'64 Browns	17
24	'68 Jets	20
28	'71 Cowboys	13
20	'83 Raiders	10
140		**91**

'77 Cowboys (3-3)
28	'85 Bears	34
28	'86 Giants	17
24	'78 Steelers	31
20	'69 Chiefs	10
20	'66 Packers	24
24	'60 Eagles	13
144		**129**

'83 Raiders (2-4)
14	'78 Steelers	24
27	'63 Chargers	17
17	'72 Dolphins	20
0	'85 Bears	12
20	'55 Browns	17
10	'84 49ers	20
88		**110**

'63 Chargers (1-5)
17	'53 Lions	27
17	'83 Raiders	27
24	'68 Jets	31
21	'60 Eagles	27
28	'51 Rams	21
24	'55 Browns	31
131		**164**

'51 Rams (1-5)
3	'84 49ers	21
14	'60 Eagles	17
14	'59 Colts	28
21	'53 Lions	28
21	'63 Chargers	28
30	'64 Browns	20
103		**142**

NORTH DIVISION

'76 Raiders (6-0)
28	'68 Jets	27
27	'82 Redskins	24
28	'69 Chiefs	24
24	'71 Cowboys	10
21	'86 Giants	17
28	'85 Bears	17
156		**119**

'85 Bears (5-1)
34	'77 Cowboys	28
17	'59 Colts	13
30	'66 Packers (OT)	24
12	'83 Raiders	0
33	'53 Lions	0
17	'76 Raiders	28
143		**93**

'66 Packers (4-2)
38	'60 Eagles	10
28	'84 49ers	21
24	'85 Bears (OT)	30
24	'59 Colts	17
24	'77 Packers	20
17	'78 Steelers	21
155		**119**

'53 Lions (2-4)
27	'63 Chargers	17
14	55 Browns	17
23	'82 Redskins	24
28	'51 Rams	21
0	'85 Bears	33
14	'86 Giants	31
106		**143**

'64 Browns (1-5)
13	'86 Giants	21
20	'69 Chiefs	28
17	'84 49ers	26
10	'72 Dolphins	31
31	'60 Eagles	21
20	'51 Rams	30
111		**157**

SOUTH DIVISION

'72 Dolphins (6-0)
24	'59 Colts	6
24	'71 Cowboys	9
20	'83 Raiders	17
31	'64 Browns	10
24	'68 Jets	21
24	'69 Chiefs	20
147		**83**

'82 Redskins (3-3)
31	'55 Browns	13
24	'76 Raiders	27
24	'53 Lions	23
31	'86 Giants	34
17	'59 Colts	24
27	'71 Cowboys	24
154		**145**

'55 Browns (3-3)
13	'82 Redskins	31
17	'53 Lions	14
31	'71 Cowboys	21
17	'78 Steelers	35
17	'83 Raiders	20
31	'63 Chargers	24
126		**145**

'69 Chiefs (2-4)
20	'71 Cowboys	17
28	'64 Browns	20
24	'76 Raiders	28
10	'77 Cowboys	20
10	'78 Steelers	27
20	'72 Dolphins	24
112		**136**

'71 Cowboys (0-6)
17	'69 Chiefs	20
9	'72 Dolphins	24
21	'55 Browns	31
10	'76 Raiders	24
13	'84 49ers	28
24	'82 Redskins	27
94		**154**

COMPLETE CAREER PROFILES OF 40 OF THE GREATEST OFFENSIVE PLAYERS

PROFILES OF THE OUSTANDING YEARS OF 39 OFFENSIVE PLAYERS

HOW TO READ THIS

Teams (W-L Record): Who the player played for and what his teams' overall records were.

Hall of Fame? Is he in or is he out? (How long did it take him to get in?)

Honors: The major ones. (The Bert Bell Trophy is an award given to the NFL's most valuable player by the Maxwell Club in Philadelphia.)

Records: Not just the records he holds, but the records he once *held*. Those that have been broken are marked with an asterisk. Significant records only.

Lifetime rankings: The first figure in the parentheses is where he ranked when he retired; the second is where he ranks now. It gives you a better idea not just of where he stood in his own time, but how he has held up against later generations. (In the second section, only the player's current ranking is given.) Also note that the totals listed for running backs are strictly rushing totals; for receivers, strictly receiving totals. For example, John Riggins scored 116 touchdowns, but he's listed with 104. Twelve of his TDs came on passes.

Everything else should be self-explanatory. In the game-by-game breakdowns, (P) = division or conference playoff; (SB) = Super Bowl; (C) = championship game (pre–Super Bowl period); and (PB) = Playoff Bowl (a postseason game for second-place NFL teams from 1960 to 1969).

22 BOBBY LAYNE (1948-62)

1948 (Bears)

Opponent	Att	Comp	Pct	Yds	TD	Int
At Green Bay	3	1	33.3	34	1	0
At Chi. Cardinals	2	0	0.0	0	0	0
Los Angeles	1	1	100.0	35	0	0
Detroit	8	2	25.0	3	0	1
At Philadelphia	0	0	0.0	0	0	0
N.Y. Giants	4	0	0.0	0	0	0
At Los Angeles	0	0	0.0	0	0	0
Green Bay	4	2	50.0	47	1	0
At Boston	18	9	50.0	113	1	0
Washington	10	1	10.0	0	0	1
At Detroit	2	0	0.0	0	0	0
Totals	**52**	**16**	**30.8**	**232**	**3**	**2**

1949 (Bulldogs)

Opponent	Att	Comp	Pct	Yds	TD	Int
N.Y. Giants	20	12	60.0	120	0	0
Green Bay	20	11	55.0	97	0	0
At Washington	27	13	48.1	124	0	0
At Pittsburgh	37	17	45.9	226	0	2
Washington	20	11	55.0	157	2	1
At N.Y. Giants	39	23	59.0	333	2	1
Chi. Cardinals	33	14	42.4	213	1	6
At Philadelphia	14	5	35.7	35	0	2
At Los Angeles	15	8	53.3	128	1	1
At Detroit	40	25	62.5	223	3	2
Pittsburgh	34	16	47.1	140	0	3
Totals	**299**	**155**	**51.8**	**1796**	**9**	**18**

1950 (Lions)

Opponent	Att	Comp	Pct	Yds	TD	Int
At Green Bay	18	10	55.6	232	1	1
Pittsburgh	24	10	41.7	78	1	2
At N.Y. Yankees	30	10	33.3	118	0	2
San Francisco	32	15	46.9	205	2	0
Los Angeles	32	13	40.6	205	2	2
At San Francisco	32	13	40.6	218	2	2
At Los Angeles	10	5	50.0	27	0	0
Chi. Bears	45	23	51.1	374	1	1
Green Bay	24	10	41.7	188	2	3
N.Y. Yankees	18	11	61.1	171	2	1
At Baltimore	27	16	59.3	341	3	3
At Chi. Bears	44	16	36.4	166	0	1
Totals	**336**	**152**	**45.2**	**2323**	**16**	**18**

1951

Opponent	Att	Comp	Pct	Yds	TD	Int
Washington	26	20	76.9	310	2	0
At N.Y. Yankees	26	9	34.6	152	3	0
Los Angeles	19	5	26.3	63	1	4
N.Y. Yankees	44	20	45.5	306	1	2
Chi. Bears	31	15	43.4	299	3	3
At Green Bay	16	7	43.8	162	3	2
At Chi. Bears	30	16	53.3	259	4	1
At Philadelphia	24	10	41.7	144	3	3
Green Bay	36	20	55.6	296	4	1
San Francisco	32	11	34.4	112	1	1
At Los Angeles	15	6	40.0	69	0	2
At San Francisco	33	13	39.4	231	1	4
Totals	**332**	**152**	**45.8**	**2403**	**26**	**23**

1952

Opponent	Att	Comp	Pct	Yds	TD	Int
At San Francisco	26	13	50.0	115	0	2
At Los Angeles	26	13	50.0	145	2	3
San Francisco	15	5	33.3	43	0	1
Los Angeles	30	14	46.7	227	1	4
At Green Bay	19	11	57.9	173	3	1
Cleveland	32	15	46.9	193	2	3
At Pittsburgh	14	4	28.6	71	1	0
Dallas	14	7	50.0	162	1	0
At Chi. Bears	26	9	34.6	148	0	2
Green Bay	30	16	53.3	249	3	3
Chi. Bears	35	22	62.9	296	4	0
Dallas	20	10	50.0	177	2	1
Los Angeles (P)	21	9	42.9	144	0	4
At Cleveland (C)	9	7	77.8	68	0	0
Totals	**287**	**139**	**48.4**	**1999**	**19**	**20**
Postseason	**30**	**16**	**53.3**	**212**	**0**	**4**

1953

Opponent	Att	Comp	Pct	Yds	TD	Int
Pittsburgh	34	16	47.1	364	2	0
At Baltimore	8	3	37.5	65	0	3
San Francisco	18	9	50.0	166	1	3
Los Angeles	30	14	46.7	255	2	2
At San Francisco	21	9	42.9	126	2	0
At Los Angeles	17	5	29.4	50	1	3
Baltimore	21	10	47.6	140	2	0
At Green Bay	23	8	34.8	173	2	4
At Chi. Bears	43	21	48.8	241	0	0
Green Bay	13	7	53.8	150	1	2
Chi. Bears	17	6	35.3	146	1	2
At N.Y. Giants	28	17	60.7	212	2	2
Cleveland (C)	25	12	48.0	179	1	2
Totals	**273**	**125**	**45.8**	**2088**	**16**	**21**
Postseason	**25**	**12**	**48.0**	**179**	**1**	**2**

Teams (W-L Record): Chicago Bears, 1948; N.Y. Bulldogs, 1949; Detroit, 1950-57; Pittsburgh, 1958-62 (105-72-7, .590).

Hall of Fame? Yes (1st year eligible)

Honors: All-NFL (2), 1952, '56; Pro Bowl (5), 1951-53, '56, '59.

Records: Most passing yards, career, 26,768*; most touchdown passes, career, 196.*

Lifetime Rankings: 63.2 passer rating (9th/--); 26,768 yards (1st/22nd); 196 TDs (1st/T16th).

300-Yard Games: 10

400-Yard Games: 1

Interception Probability: 6.6% (243/3,700)

Injuries: 1957--injured ankle; 1961--hematoma.

Comment: For a guy who had a reputation for being a money player, Layne sure had some lousy postseason games. He played in four in his career and threw 12 interceptions and one touchdown pass. The TD, however, won the 1953 title game against the Browns. That's the way it was with Layne. He was better than his statistics suggest. He also gave the Steelers a couple of good years late in his career, leading them to a 6-0-1 finish in '58 and going to the Pro Bowl in '59 at the age of 33. A natural athlete, he took over the kicking for the Lions after Doak Walker retired and proceeded to make 68 percent of his field goal attempts (34 of 50). That was better than Lou Groza.

1954

Opponent	Att	Comp	Pct	Yds	TD	Int
Chi. Bears	16	4	25.0	84	0	2
Los Angeles	5	2	40.0	32	0	1
Baltimore	13	10	76.9	133	3	0
At San Francisco	29	17	58.6	212	1	0
At Los Angeles	22	11	50.0	177	1	1
At Baltimore	28	18	64.3	246	1	1
San Francisco	15	8	53.3	165	2	0
At Green Bay	30	19	63.3	230	2	2
Green Bay	26	16	61.5	178	2	1
Philadelphia	26	12	46.2	178	0	4
At Chi. Bears	0	0	0.0	0	0	0
At Cleveland	36	18	50.0	183	2	0
At Cleveland (C)	42	18	42.9	177	0	6
Totals	**246**	**135**	**54.9**	**1818**	**14**	**12**
Postseason	**42**	**18**	**42.9**	**177**	**0**	**6**

1955

Opponent	Att	Comp	Pct	Yds	TD	Int
At Green Bay	19	8	42.1	155	1	1
At Baltimore	42	19	45.2	238	2	2
Los Angeles	45	26	57.8	273	0	3
San Francisco	8	4	50.0	49	0	2
At Los Angeles	0	0	0.0	0	0	0
At San Francisco	45	22	48.9	296	2	2
Baltimore	24	13	54.2	193	1	4
At Pittsburgh	16	10	62.5	109	1	0
Chi. Bears	32	20	62.5	319	2	2
Green Bay	21	11	52.4	92	1	1
At Chi. Bears	18	10	55.6	106	1	0
N.Y. Giants	0	0	0.0	0	0	0
Totals	**270**	**143**	**53.0**	**1830**	**11**	**17**

1956

Opponent	Att	Comp	Pct	Yds	TD	Int
At Green Bay	12	7	58.3	129	0	0
At Baltimore	22	15	68.2	236	2	0
Los Angeles	27	14	51.9	205	1	2
San Francisco	27	15	55.6	155	0	1
At Los Angeles	16	11	68.8	177	0	0
At San Francisco	18	7	38.9	94	0	2
At Washington	40	15	37.5	266	1	4
Baltimore	20	12	60.0	153	1	1
Green Bay	22	9	40.9	147	1	3
Chi. Bears	19	11	57.9	210	2	2
Pittsburgh	14	9	64.3	95	1	2
At Chi. Bears	7	4	57.1	42	0	0
Totals	**244**	**129**	**52.9**	**1909**	**9**	**17**

1957

Opponent	Att	Comp	Pct	Yds	TD	Int
At Baltimore	15	8	53.3	144	0	3
At Green Bay	14	4	28.6	59	0	1
Los Angeles	9	4	44.4	15	0	0
Baltimore	21	8	38.1	139	2	2
At Los Angeles	32	17	53.1	193	0	2
At San Francisco	14	6	42.9	59	0	0
At Philadelphia	13	8	61.5	147	3	0
San Francisco	24	17	70.8	250	1	1
Chi. Bears	25	10	40.0	112	0	1
Green Bay	6	3	50.0	36	0	2
Cleveland	6	2	33.3	15	0	0
At Chi Bears	(did not play)					
At San Francisco (P)	(did not play)					
Cleveland (C)	(did not play)					
Totals	**179**	**87**	**48.6**	**1169**	**6**	**12**

1958 (Lions 2/Steelers 10)

Opponent	Att	Comp	Pct	Yds	TD	Int
At Baltimore	17	7	41.2	103	1	1
At Green Bay	9	5	55.6	68	0	1
Philadelphia	20	10	50.0	81	0	1
At Cleveland	26	14	53.8	133	0	1
At N.Y. Giants	31	13	41.9	184	0	0
Washington	25	13	52.0	265	2	0
At Philadelphia	22	10	45.5	225	4	2
N.Y. Giants	20	9	45.0	179	1	0
At Chi. Cardinals	28	16	57.1	352	1	0
Chi. Bears	15	7	46.7	202	1	0
At Washington	32	18	56.3	309	2	3
Chi. Cardinals	49	23	46.9	409	2	3
Totals	**294**	**145**	**49.3**	**2510**	**14**	**12**

1959

Opponent	Att	Comp	Pct	Yds	TD	Int
Cleveland	20	13	65.0	209	2	2
Washington	41	21	51.2	226	1	2
At Philadelphia	33	18	54.5	209	2	1
At Washington	14	8	57.1	77	0	2
N.Y. Giants	26	9	34.6	165	1	4
At Chi. Cardinals	17	5	29.4	115	1	2
Detroit	27	12	44.4	181	1	3
At N.Y. Giants	30	13	43.3	190	2	3
At Cleveland	20	12	60.0	126	1	0
Philadelphia	28	12	42.9	182	4	1
At Chi. Bears	24	8	33.3	105	1	0
Chi. Cardinals	17	11	64.7	201	4	1
Totals	**297**	**142**	**47.8**	**1986**	**20**	**21**

1960

Opponent	Att	Comp	Pct	Yds	TD	Int
At Dallas	25	16	64.2	288	4	1
At Cleveland	21	14	66.7	296	2	1
N.Y. Giants	21	7	33.3	146	1	4
St. Louis	11	8	72.7	95	1	0
At Washington	0	0	0.0	0	0	0
Green Bay	20	12	60.0	209	2	0
At Philadelphia	16	2	12.5	23	0	2
At N.Y. Giants	22	9	40.9	169	1	2
Cleveland	23	10	43.5	174	0	2
Washington	24	9	37.5	159	0	2
Philadelphia	18	12	66.7	163	1	3
At St. Louis	8	4	50.0	92	1	0
Totals	**209**	**103**	**49.3**	**1814**	**13**	**17**

1961

Opponent	Att	Comp	Pct	Yds	TD	Int
At Dallas	25	16	64.0	252	1	3
N.Y. Giants	19	7	36.8	111	1	2
At Los Angeles	5	1	20.0	11	0	2
At Philadelphia	(did not play)					
Washington	(did not play)					
Cleveland	(did not play)					
San Francisco	(did not play)					
At Cleveland	(did not play)					
Dallas	(did not play)					
At N.Y. Giants	8	6	75.0	100	1	0
St. Louis	25	10	40.0	187	1	4
Philadelphia	29	13	44.8	179	3	3
At Washington	19	13	68.4	226	4	0
At St. Louis	19	9	47.4	139	0	2
Totals	**149**	**75**	**50.3**	**1205**	**11**	**16**

1962

Opponent	Att	Comp	Pct	Yds	TD	Int
At Detroit	10	5	50.0	76	0	0
At Dallas	24	10	41.7	144	2	1
N.Y. Giants	23	12	52.2	166	1	2
Philadelphia	18	11	61.1	132	0	2
At N.Y. Giants	10	5	50.0	72	1	0
Dallas	30	15	50.0	266	2	2
Cleveland	9	3	33.3	44	0	1
Minnesota	28	16	57.1	254	0	1
At St. Louis	14	8	57.1	79	1	0
Washington	23	8	34.8	87	0	3
At Cleveland	23	13	56.5	155	0	1
St. Louis	(did not play)					
At Philadelphia	4	2	50.0	10	0	2
At Washington	17	8	47.1	201	2	2
Totals	**233**	**116**	**49.8**	**1686**	**9**	**17**

14 OTTO GRAHAM (1950-55)

Opponent	1950 Att	Comp	Pct	Yds	TD	Int
At Philadelphia	38	21	55.3	346	3	2
At Baltimore	23	11	47.8	177	1	4
N.Y. Giants	30	12	40.0	127	0	3
At Pittsburgh	17	10	58.8	75	0	0
Chi. Cardinals	35	22	62.9	369	2	3
At N.Y. Giants	18	10	55.6	118	0	3
Pittsburgh	9	5	55.6	157	2	0
At Chi. Cardinals	21	10	47.6	114	0	2
San Francisco	17	7	41.2	74	1	0
Washington	13	6	46.2	65	1	2
Philadelphia	0	0	0.0	0	0	0
At Washington	32	23	71.9	321	4	1
N.Y. Giants (P)	9	3	33.3	43	0	1
Los Angeles (C)	32	22	68.8	298	4	1
Totals	253	137	54.2	1943	14	20
Postseason	41	25	61.0	341	4	2

Opponent	1951 Att	Comp	Pct	Yds	TD	Int
At San Francisco	30	18	60.0	222	1	2
At Los Angeles	19	10	52.6	219	1	2
Washington	15	8	53.3	135	0	0
Pittsburgh	15	9	60.0	67	0	1
N.Y. Giants	24	16	66.7	216	2	3
At Chi. Cardinals	21	15	71.4	210	1	0
Philadelphia	30	14	46.7	192	2	1
At N.Y. Giants	18	8	44.4	162	1	3
Chi. Bears	19	12	63.2	277	2	1
Chi. Cardinals	29	14	48.3	217	4	3
At Pittsburgh	18	12	66.7	128	1	0
At Philadelphia	27	11	40.7	160	2	0
At Los Angeles (C)	40	19	47.5	280	1	3
Totals	265	147	55.5	2205	17	16
Postseason	40	19	47.5	280	1	3

Opponent	1952 Att	Comp	Pct	Yds	TD	Int
Los Angeles	16	10	62.5	138	2	1
At Pittsburgh	49	21	42.9	401	3	4
N.Y. Giants	34	14	41.2	236	0	1
At Philadelphia	30	18	60.0	290	4	2
Washington	29	11	37.9	190	0	1
At Detroit	32	13	40.6	165	0	3
Chi. Cardinals	24	18	75.0	249	2	0
Pittsburgh	40	21	52.5	239	2	2
Philadelphia	36	14	38.9	227	2	2
At Washington	20	9	45.0	195	2	3
At Chi. Cardinals	22	14	63.6	207	1	2
At N.Y. Giants	32	18	56.3	279	2	3
Detroit (C)	35	20	57.1	191	0	1
Totals	364	181	49.7	2816	20	24
Postseason	35	20	57.1	191	0	1

Opponent	1953 Att	Comp	Pct	Yds	TD	Int
At Green Bay	24	18	75.0	292	0	1
At Chi. Cardinals	22	15	68.2	310	3	0
Philadelphia	30	20	66.7	328	1	0
At Washington	32	16	50.0	235	0	1
At N.Y. Giants	5	2	40.0	26	0	1
Washington	19	13	68.4	194	0	1
Pittsburgh	18	12	66.7	218	1	2
San Francisco	24	17	70.8	286	1	0
At Pittsburgh	28	16	57.1	200	2	1
Chi. Cardinals	28	19	67.9	276	0	0
N.Y. Giants	4	4	100.0	116	1	0
At Philadelphia	24	15	62.5	241	1	2
At Detroit (C)	15	2	13.3	20	0	2
Totals	258	167	64.7	2722	11	9
Postseason	15	2	13.3	20	0	2

Opponent	1954 Att	Comp	Pct	Yds	TD	Int
At Philadelphia	23	9	39.1	130	1	1
Chi. Cardinals	18	14	77.8	266	3	0
At Pittsburgh	28	22	78.6	298	3	5
At Chi. Cardinals	24	16	66.7	182	1	1
N.Y. Giants	26	14	53.8	160	1	3
Washington	17	8	47.1	102	1	1
At Chi. Bears	23	11	47.8	120	1	1
Philadelphia	21	11	52.4	192	0	2
At N.Y. Giants	27	16	59.3	238	0	2
At Washington	18	13	72.2	252	0	1
Pittsburgh	9	7	77.8	137	0	0
Detroit	6	1	16.7	15	0	0
Detroit (C)	12	9	75.0	163	3	2
Totals	240	142	59.2	2092	11	17
Postseason	12	9	75.0	163	3	2

Opponent	1955 Att	Comp	Pct	Yds	TD	Int
Washington	9	3	33.3	30	0	2
At San Francisco	11	7	63.6	140	0	0
Philadelphia	21	16	76.2	223	2	0
At Washington	16	9	56.3	138	1	1
Green Bay	12	7	58.3	187	0	0
At Chi. Cardinals	12	4	33.3	62	0	1
N.Y. Giants	10	5	50.0	57	0	1
At Philadelphia	17	7	41.2	150	1	2
Pittsburgh	9	6	66.7	79	2	0
At N.Y. Giants	31	17	54.8	319	3	1
At Pittsburgh	12	4	33.3	95	2	0
Chi. Cardinals	25	13	52.0	241	3	1
At Los Angeles (C)	25	14	56.0	209	2	3
Totals	185	98	53.0	1721	15	8
Postseason	25	14	56.0	209	2	3

Team (W-L Record): Cleveland, 1946-55 (105-17-4, .849).

Hall of Fame? Yes (3rd year eligible)

Honors: UPI NFL Player of the Year, 1953, '55; all-NFL (5), 1951-55; Pro Bowl (5), 1950-54.

Records: 10 championship games in 10 seasons (4 All-America Conference, 6 NFL).

Lifetime Rankings (NFL only): 78.2 passer rating (1st/21st); 13,499 yards (4th/--); 88 TDs (8th/--).

300-Yard Games: 7

400-Yard Games: 1

Interception Probability: 6.0% (94/1,565)

Injuries: None

Comment: Graham's career totals would be higher by 10,085 yards and 86 touchdown passes if his AAFC statistics were counted. But he wasn't playing, for the most part, against NFL-calibre competition. He had 86 TD passes and 41 interceptions in four AAFC seasons, 88 TD passes and 94 interceptions in six NFL seasons. It's hard to see any quarterback ever coming near his won-lost record. What a winner. He bounced back from his worst season in 1952 (49.7 completion percentage) to have his best in '53 (64.7). A tremendous deep thrower who also had touch -- and the mobility that went with being a former all-America basketball player. He rushed for 169 yards in two 1950 postseason games and for five TDs in his last two title games. He tried to retire after the '54 season but agreed to return late in training camp the next year when his replacement, George Ratterman, wasn't doing the job. "We never found another Otto Graham," coach Paul Brown said in his autobiography.

19 JOHNNY UNITAS (1956-73)

Teams (W-L Record): Baltimore, 1956-72; San Diego, 1973 (150-86-6, .632).
Hall of Fame? Yes (1st year eligible)
Honors: Bert Bell Trophy and UPI NFL Player of the Year, 1959, '64 and '67; all-NFL (5), 1958-59, '64-65, '67; Pro Bowl (10), 1957-64, '66-67.
Records: Most passing yards, 40,239,* and touchdown passes, 290,* career.
Lifetime Rankings: 78.2 passer rating (5th/20th); 40,239 yards (1st/3rd); 290 TDs (1st/2nd).
300-Yard Games: 26
400-Yard Games: 1
Interception Probability: 4.9% (253/5,186)
Injuries: 1958--fractured ribs, collapsed lung; 1968--torn right elbow muscle.
Comment: Johnny U. sure fills up a page, doesn't he? Eighteen seasons. We could have lived without the last three except for one memorable duel with Joe Namath in early 1972. The two combined for a then-record 872 passing yards (Namath won, 496-376). Unitas was 39. Imagine the kind of quarterback he was in the late '50s and early '60s.

1956 (Colts)

Opponent	Att	Comp	Pct	Yds	TD	Int
Detroit	2	0	0.0	0	0	1
At Chi. Bears	19	9	47.4	131	1	1
Green Bay	16	8	50.0	128	2	1
At Cleveland	14	5	35.7	21	0	0
At Detroit	30	17	56.7	314	0	1
Los Angeles	24	18	75.0	293	3	1
San Francisco	30	18	60.0	179	0	2
At Los Angeles	29	14	48.3	147	1	1
At San Francisco	16	11	68.8	124	1	1
Washington	18	10	55.6	161	1	1
Totals	**198**	**110**	**55.6**	**1498**	**9**	**10**

1957

Opponent	Att	Comp	Pct	Yds	TD	Int
Detroit	23	14	60.9	241	4	3
Chi. Bears	26	17	65.4	184	2	1
At Green Bay	17	7	41.2	130	2	2
At Detroit	21	16	76.2	239	4	1
Green Bay	31	16	51.6	188	2	2
Pittsburgh	9	3	33.3	56	1	3
At Washington	30	17	56.7	247	2	0
At Chi. Bears	23	11	47.8	245	1	0
San Francisco	25	16	64.0	230	1	0
Los Angeles	30	18	60.0	271	3	1
At San Francisco	37	23	62.2	296	1	2
At Los Angeles	29	14	48.3	223	1	2
Totals	**301**	**172**	**57.1**	**2550**	**24**	**17**

1958

Opponent	Att	Comp	Pct	Yds	TD	Int
Detroit	43	23	53.5	250	2	1
Chi. Bears	23	10	43.5	198	4	1
At Green Bay	35	16	45.7	238	1	1
At Detroit	17	11	64.7	221	1	0
Washington	15	8	53.3	183	2	0
Green Bay	16	5	31.3	99	2	0
Los Angeles	18	12	66.7	218	2	0
San Francisco	33	17	51.5	229	1	1
At Los Angeles	38	23	60.5	214	3	3
At San Francisco	25	11	44.0	157	1	0
At N.Y. Giants (C)	40	26	65.0	361	1	1
Totals	**263**	**136**	**51.7**	**2007**	**19**	**7**
Postseason	**40**	**26**	**65.0**	**361**	**1**	**1**

1959

Opponent	Att	Comp	Pct	Yds	TD	Int
Detroit	30	13	43.3	230	2	0
Chi. Bears	38	17	44.7	221	3	3
At Detroit	25	13	52.0	257	3	2
At Chi. Bears	30	16	53.3	233	2	2
Green Bay	29	19	65.5	206	3	0
Cleveland	41	23	56.1	397	4	3
At Washington	35	15	42.9	265	2	2
At Green Bay	33	19	57.6	324	3	0
San Francisco	19	10	52.6	141	2	1
Los Angeles	24	14	58.3	242	2	1
At San Francisco	36	21	58.3	273	3	0
At Los Angeles	27	13	48.1	110	3	0
N.Y. Giants (C)	29	18	62.1	265	2	0
Totals	**367**	**193**	**52.6**	**2899**	**32**	**14**
Postseason	**29**	**18**	**62.1**	**265**	**2**	**0**

1960

Opponent	Att	Comp	Pct	Yds	TD	Int
Washington	35	17	48.6	232	1	1
Chi. Bears	27	14	51.9	307	4	0
At Green Bay	31	16	51.6	216	1	4
Los Angeles	23	12	52.2	176	1	2
At Detroit	40	20	50.0	253	2	2
At Dallas	16	8	50.0	270	4	0
Green Bay	29	20	69.0	324	4	1
At Chi. Bears	33	16	48.5	266	2	2
San Francisco	30	16	53.3	356	3	5
Detroit	40	22	55.0	357	2	3
At Los Angeles	38	17	44.7	182	0	1
At San Francisco	36	12	33.3	160	1	3
Totals	**378**	**190**	**50.3**	**3099**	**25**	**24**

1961

Opponent	Att	Comp	Pct	Yds	TD	Int
Los Angeles	22	10	45.5	132	1	2
Detroit	16	10	62.5	105	1	1
Minnesota	27	13	48.1	284	2	1
At Green Bay	24	11	45.8	141	0	5
At Chi. Bears	36	19	52.8	278	0	1
At Detroit	36	22	61.1	244	0	4
Chi. Bears	36	20	55.6	302	2	2
Green Bay	35	22	62.9	218	4	1
At Minnesota	31	14	45.2	138	0	2
St. Louis	36	21	58.3	246	1	0
At Washington	33	18	54.5	208	1	3
San Francisco	27	15	55.5	216	1	1
At Los Angeles	27	15	55.5	164	0	1
At San Francisco	34	19	55.9	314	3	0
Totals	**420**	**229**	**54.5**	**2990**	**16**	**24**

1962

Opponent	Att	Comp	Pct	Yds	TD	Int
Los Angeles	35	19	54.3	245	4	2
At Minnesota	21	13	61.9	133	1	2
Detroit	31	14	45.2	166	1	3
San Francisco	15	8	53.3	82	0	0
At Cleveland	31	18	58.1	225	3	1
At Chi. Bears	27	16	59.3	255	2	3
Green Bay	30	18	60.0	161	0	1
At San Francisco	17	9	52.9	156	1	0
At Los Angeles	27	16	59.3	232	0	2
At Green Bay	28	17	60.7	237	1	1
Chi. Bears	24	11	45.8	91	0	1
At Detroit	33	19	57.6	232	2	2
Washington	36	25	69.4	367	4	1
Minnesota	34	19	55.9	385	4	4
Totals	**389**	**222**	**57.1**	**2967**	**23**	**23**

1963

Opponent	Att	Comp	Pct	Yds	TD	Int
N.Y. Giants	33	19	57.6	219	2	2
At San Francisco	44	23	52.3	288	1	0
At Green Bay	30	19	63.3	267	0	2
At Chi. Bears	36	21	58.3	182	0	1
San Francisco	25	11	44.0	159	1	0
At Detroit	24	9	37.5	123	1	1
Green Bay	23	11	47.8	233	2	2
Chi. Bears	18	11	61.1	127	0	1
Detroit	24	17	70.8	376	2	1
At Minnesota	23	14	60.9	248	4	0
At Los Angeles	34	20	58.8	237	0	1
At Washington	37	24	64.9	355	3	0
Minnesota	22	17	77.3	344	3	0
Los Angeles	37	21	56.8	323	1	1
Totals	**410**	**237**	**57.8**	**3481**	**20**	**12**

1964

Opponent	Att	Comp	Pct	Yds	TD	Int
At Minnesota	26	11	42.3	209	2	0
At Green Bay	12	7	58.3	154	2	0
Chi. Bears	13	11	84.6	247	3	1
Los Angeles	18	10	55.6	232	3	0
St. Louis	20	8	40.0	117	1	0
Green Bay	27	14	51.9	157	0	0
At Detroit	24	12	50.0	210	2	2
San Francisco	29	14	48.3	222	1	1
At Chi. Bears	32	16	50.0	241	0	0
Minnesota	31	15	48.4	289	2	0
At Los Angeles	18	6	33.3	142	0	0
At San Francisco	15	8	53.3	135	1	0
Detroit	20	13	65.0	243	0	1
Washington	20	13	65.0	226	2	1
At Cleveland (C)	20	12	60.0	95	0	2
Totals	**305**	**158**	**51.8**	**2824**	**19**	**6**
Postseason	**20**	**12**	**60.0**	**95**	**0**	**2**

1965

Opponent	Att	Comp	Pct	Yds	TD	Int
Minnesota	22	14	63.6	224	2	2
At Green Bay	32	14	43.8	210	1	2
San Francisco	30	18	60.0	236	1	1
Detroit	24	18	75.0	319	3	1
At Washington	18	12	66.7	221	2	1
Los Angeles	27	18	66.7	251	3	0
At San Francisco	34	23	67.6	324	4	0
At Chi. Bears	20	11	55.0	228	2	2
Philadelphia	32	19	59.4	305	2	1
At Detroit	34	14	41.2	188	3	2
Chi. Bears	9	3	33.3	24	0	0
Totals	**282**	**164**	**58.2**	**2530**	**23**	**12**

1966

Opponent	Att	Comp	Pct	Yds	TD	Int
At Green Bay	20	14	70.0	106	0	3
At Minnesota	22	14	63.6	241	4	2
San Francisco	30	14	46.7	225	2	1
At Chicago	38	18	47.4	274	1	2
Detroit	27	18	66.7	218	4	0
Minnesota	28	17	60.7	214	1	0
At Los Angeles	22	13	59.1	252	2	1
Washington	31	22	71.0	342	3	2
At Atlanta	25	10	40.0	121	0	2
At Detroit	19	9	47.4	93	0	5
Los Angeles	11	2	18.2	35	0	1
Chi. Bears	21	13	61.9	148	1	1
Green Bay	24	11	45.8	140	0	3
At San Francisco	30	20	66.7	339	4	1
Philadelphia (PB)	33	19	57.6	193	1	1
Totals	**348**	**195**	**56.0**	**2748**	**22**	**24**
Postseason	**33**	**19**	**57.6**	**193**	**1**	**1**

1967

Opponent	Att	Comp	Pct	Yds	TD	Int
Atlanta	32	22	68.8	401	2	1
At Philadelphia	34	21	61.8	267	2	0
San Francisco	37	22	59.5	353	2	0
At Chi. Bears	37	19	51.4	149	1	3
Los Angeles	34	21	61.8	288	2	1
At Minnesota	34	20	58.8	235	1	1
At Washington	33	19	57.6	242	1	1
Green Bay	32	15	46.9	126	2	1
At Atlanta	20	17	85.0	370	4	0
Detroit	22	12	54.5	157	1	1
At San Francisco	27	16	59.3	211	0	1
Dallas	39	22	56.4	275	1	3
New Orleans	24	10	41.7	148	0	1
At Los Angeles	31	19	61.3	206	1	2
Totals	**436**	**255**	**58.5**	**3428**	**20**	**16**

1968

Opponent	Att	Comp	Pct	Yds	TD	Int
At San Francisco	2	1	50.0	6	1	0
Cleveland	11	1	9.1	12	0	3
Atlanta	10	5	50.0	54	0	0
Los Angeles	9	4	44.4	67	1	1
N.Y. Jets (SB)	24	11	45.8	110	1	0
Totals	**32**	**11**	**34.4**	**139**	**2**	**4**
Postseason	**24**	**11**	**45.8**	**110**	**1**	**0**

1969

Opponent	Att	Comp	Pct	Yds	TD	Int
Los Angeles	42	20	47.6	297	2	3
At Minnesota	22	8	36.4	68	0	1
At Atlanta	24	18	75.0	164	1	1
Philadelphia	34	19	55.9	250	0	2
At New Orleans	28	20	71.4	319	3	0
San Francisco	37	19	51.4	300	2	3
Washington	20	10	50.0	139	0	1
Green Bay	25	15	60.0	145	2	3
At San Francisco	8	2	25.0	14	1	1
At Chi. Bears	3	3	100.0	29	0	0
Atlanta	23	13	56.5	164	0	0
At Dallas	28	12	42.9	193	1	3
At Los Angeles	33	19	57.6	260	0	2
Totals	**327**	**178**	**54.4**	**2342**	**12**	**20**

1970

Opponent	Att	Comp	Pct	Yds	TD	Int
At San Diego	31	15	48.4	202	0	1
Kansas City	15	5	33.3	58	0	2
At Boston	7	3	42.9	64	1	0
At Houston	30	15	50.0	227	2	1
At N.Y. Jets	24	12	50.0	206	1	3
Boston	21	12	57.1	155	3	0
Miami	19	11	57.9	142	1	1
At Green Bay	17	9	52.9	125	0	1
Buffalo	29	15	51.7	221	1	1
At Miami	36	22	61.1	203	2	2
Chi. Bears	40	23	57.5	258	2	5
Philadelphia	18	10	55.6	113	1	1
At Buffalo	31	13	41.9	236	0	0
N.Y. Jets	3	1	33.3	3	0	0
Cincinnati (P)	17	6	35.3	145	2	0
Oakland (P)	30	11	36.7	245	1	0
Dallas (SB)	9	3	33.3	88	1	2
Totals	**321**	**166**	**51.7**	**2213**	**14**	**18**
Postseason	**56**	**20**	**35.7**	**478**	**4**	**2**

1971

Opponent	Att	Comp	Pct	Yds	TD	Int
N.Y. Jets	3	1	33.3	-9	0	0
Cleveland	6	0	0.0	0	0	2
At New England	7	6	85.7	73	0	0
At Buffalo	9	3	33.3	60	0	1
At N.Y. Giants	5	2	40.0	7	0	0
At Minnesota	5	3	60.0	25	0	0
Pittsburgh	15	7	46.7	32	0	1
At N.Y. Jets	21	8	38.1	116	0	0
At Miami	17	9	52.9	78	0	2
At Oakland	16	10	62.5	119	0	0
Buffalo	21	11	52.4	134	1	1
Miami	19	16	84.2	142	0	0
New England	32	16	50.0	165	2	2
At Cleveland (P)	21	13	61.9	143	0	1
At Miami (P)	36	20	55.6	224	0	3
Totals	**176**	**92**	**52.3**	**942**	**3**	**9**
Postseason	**57**	**33**	**57.9**	**367**	**0**	**4**

1972

Opponent	Att	Comp	Pct	Yds	TD	Int
St. Louis	36	22	61.1	257	0	2
N.Y. Jets	45	26	57.8	376	2	0
At Buffalo	28	12	42.9	184	1	2
San Diego	22	14	63.6	130	0	0
Dallas	22	11	50.0	97	0	1
Buffalo	2	2	100.0	64	1	0
At Miami	2	1	50.0	3	0	1
Totals	**157**	**88**	**56.1**	**1111**	**4**	**6**

1973 (Chargers)

Opponent	Att	Comp	Pct	Yds	TD	Int
At Washington	17	6	35.3	55	0	3
Buffalo	18	10	55.6	175	2	0
Cincinnati	31	15	48.4	215	1	2
At Pittsburgh	9	2	22.2	19	0	2
Kansas City	1	1	100.0	7	0	0
Totals	**76**	**34**	**44.7**	**471**	**3**	**7**

9 SONNY JURGENSEN (1957-74)

1957 (Eagles)

Opponent	Att	Comp	Pct	Yds	TD	Int
At Cleveland	10	4	40.0	17	0	1
Cleveland	9	6	66.7	84	1	0
At Pittsburgh	5	1	20.0	12	0	1
At Chi. Cardinals	3	2	66.7	8	0	0
Detroit	4	1	25.0	15	0	1
At N.Y. Giants	1	0	0.0	0	0	0
Washington	14	9	64.3	211	3	2
Pittsburgh	5	4	80.0	56	1	0
At Washington	17	5	29.4	61	0	3
Chi. Cardinals	2	1	50.0	6	0	0
Totals	**70**	**33**	**47.1**	**470**	**5**	**8**

1958

Chi. Cardinals	4	2	50.0	33	0	1
At Washington	18	10	55.6	226	0	0
Totals	**22**	**12**	**54.5**	**259**	**0**	**1**

1959

N.Y. Giants	5	3	60.0	27	1	0
Totals	**5**	**3**	**60.0**	**27**	**1**	**0**

1960

Cleveland	6	5	83.3	57	1	0
Detroit	4	1	25.0	−3	0	0
Pittsburgh	4	2	50.0	25	0	0
At Pittsburgh	19	8	42.1	211	2	1
At Washington	11	8	72.7	196	2	0
Green Bay (C)			(did not play)			
Totals	**44**	**24**	**54.5**	**486**	**5**	**1**

1961

Cleveland	17	11	64.7	183	2	1
Washington	28	11	39.3	210	2	3
St. Louis	36	24	66.7	399	3	2
Pittsburgh	22	11	50.0	109	2	3
At St. Louis	32	17	53.1	233	2	0
At Dallas	15	10	66.7	154	0	0
At Washington	41	27	65.9	436	3	2
Chi. Bears	33	18	54.5	249	1	3
At N.Y. Giants	33	15	45.5	188	2	3
At Cleveland	32	18	56.3	230	2	1
Dallas	23	16	69.6	351	5	2
At Pittsburgh	31	14	45.2	211	2	0
N.Y. Giants	31	16	51.6	367	3	2
At Detroit	42	27	64.3	403	3	2
Detroit (PB)	17	8	47.1	62	0	2
Totals	**416**	**235**	**56.5**	**3723**	**32**	**24**
Postseason	**17**	**8**	**47.1**	**62**	**0**	**2**

1962

St. Louis	25	15	60.0	273	1	2
N.Y. Giants	57	33	57.9	396	1	3
Cleveland	24	18	75.0	265	2	2
At Pittsburgh	33	13	39.4	163	1	2
At Dallas	10	4	40.0	60	0	0
Washington	22	15	68.2	231	3	2
At Minnesota	23	12	52.2	297	2	2
At Cleveland	27	15	55.6	142	1	3
Green Bay	13	4	30.8	35	0	1
At N.Y. Giants	23	8	34.8	119	1	0
Dallas	21	13	61.9	342	1	2
At Washington	19	14	73.7	261	2	1
Pittsburgh	35	17	48.6	258	2	3
At St. Louis	34	15	44.1	419	5	3
Totals	**366**	**196**	**53.6**	**3261**	**22**	**26**

1963

Pittsburgh	26	16	61.5	322	3	2
St. Louis	24	12	50.0	166	0	0
N.Y. Giants	10	5	50.0	50	0	4
Dallas	1	0	0.0	0	0	0
At Washington	29	17	58.6	315	4	2
At Cleveland	13	7	53.8	76	1	1
Washington	37	19	51.4	209	1	1
At St. Louis	18	10	55.6	121	0	1
Minnesota	26	13	50.0	154	2	2
Totals	**184**	**99**	**53.8**	**1413**	**11**	**13**

1964 (Redskins)

Cleveland	30	17	56.7	235	0	0
At Dallas	21	6	28.6	75	0	1
At N.Y. Giants	24	14	58.3	157	1	0
St. Louis	24	12	50.0	170	1	2
Philadelphia	33	22	66.7	385	5	2
At St. Louis	25	11	44.0	159	2	1
Chi. Bears	31	16	51.6	205	4	1
At Philadelphia	18	7	38.9	141	1	1
At Cleveland	36	21	58.3	261	3	1
At Pittsburgh	10	7	70.0	210	2	1
Dallas	33	20	60.6	307	1	1
N.Y. Giants	43	24	55.8	319	4	0
Pittsburgh	35	17	48.6	136	0	1
At Baltimore	22	13	59.1	174	0	1
Totals	**385**	**207**	**53.8**	**2934**	**24**	**13**

Teams (W-L Record): Philadelphia, 1957-63; Washington, 1964-74 (120-114-10, .512).

Hall of Fame? Yes (4th year of eligibility)

Honors: All-NFL (2), 1961, '69; Pro Bowl (5), 1961, '64, '66-67, '69.

Records: Most attempts, 508,* completions, 288,* and yards, 3,747,* season, 1967.

Lifetime Rankings: 82.6 passer rating (1st/10th); 32,244 yards (3rd/7th); 255 TDs (3rd/3rd).

300-Yard Games: 25

400-Yard Games: 5

Interception Probability: 4.4% (189/4,262)

Injuries: 1968--elbow surgery, fractured ribs; 1971--left shoulder injury; 1972--ruptured Achilles tendon.

Comment: Jurgensen's career spanned 18 years, but the first four were spent backing up Norm Van Brocklin and the last four battling injuries or playing behind Billy Kilmer. So his considerable statistics were really compiled in the equivalent of 11 seasons. In his first year as a starting quarterback, in 1961, he set a league record with 3,723 passing yards and tied another with 32 touchdown passes. When he retired, he was the top-rated passer of all time. "If we'd had you in Green Bay," Vince Lombardi told him after taking over the Redskins in '69, "we never would have lost." Amazingly, Jurgensen's last game was his first playoff game.

1965

Cleveland	21	9	42.9	124	0	1
At Dallas	30	13	43.3	206	1	1
At Detroit	11	6	54.5	19	0	4
St. Louis			(did not play)			
Baltimore	40	21	52.5	205	0	2
At St. Louis	14	12	85.7	195	3	0
Philadelphia	35	23	65.7	293	2	1
At N.Y. Giants	20	10	50.0	125	0	1
At Philadelphia	29	16	55.2	177	2	1
At Pittsburgh	23	9	39.1	121	1	1
Dallas	43	26	60.5	411	3	2
At Cleveland	35	18	51.4	155	1	2
N.Y. Giants	34	15	44.1	184	0	0
Pittsburgh	21	12	57.1	152	2	0
Totals	**356**	**190**	**53.4**	**2367**	**15**	**16**

1966

Cleveland	35	17	48.6	240	1	5
At St. Louis	32	18	56.3	197	1	0
At Pittsburgh	33	20	60.6	235	2	2
Pittsburgh	21	14	66.7	262	3	0
Atlanta	26	17	65.4	286	2	0
At N.Y. Giants	20	9	45.0	125	1	2
St. Louis	35	20	57.1	246	2	1
At Philadelphia	31	18	58.1	171	2	2
At Baltimore	32	21	65.6	220	1	2
Dallas	46	26	56.5	347	3	0
At Cleveland	38	27	71.0	178	0	2
N.Y. Giants	16	10	62.5	145	3	0
At Dallas	33	18	54.5	308	3	1
Philadelphia	38	19	50.0	249	4	2
Totals	**436**	**254**	**58.3**	**3209**	**28**	**19**

1967

At Philadelphia	46	25	54.3	324	1	0
At New Orleans	14	9	64.3	148	1	1
N.Y. Giants	36	22	61.1	285	2	1
Dallas	33	20	60.6	260	1	1
At Atlanta	41	28	68.3	326	3	2
At Los Angeles	41	18	43.9	334	4	0
Baltimore	35	25	71.4	226	1	1
St. Louis	18	6	33.3	135	1	1
San Francisco	41	22	53.7	291	3	1
At Dallas	33	23	69.7	265	4	1
At Cleveland	50	32	64.0	418	3	1
Philadelphia	50	30	60.0	366	4	2
At Pittsburgh	32	9	28.1	155	1	3
New Orleans	38	19	50.0	214	2	1
Totals	**508**	**288**	**56.7**	**3747**	**31**	**16**

1968

At Chi. Bears	21	14	66.7	276	4	0
At New Orleans	24	13	54.2	172	2	1
At N.Y. Giants	40	26	65.0	270	2	3
Philadelphia	29	21	72.4	196	1	1
Pittsburgh	29	15	51.7	178	2	1
At St. Louis	23	17	73.9	211	1	0
N.Y. Giants	25	7	28.0	73	0	1
At Minnesota	18	12	66.7	85	0	1
At Philadelphia	6	0	0.0	0	0	0
Dallas	25	12	48.0	228	2	0
Green Bay	29	18	62.1	164	1	0
At Dallas			(did not play)			
Cleveland	23	12	52.2	127	2	3
Detroit			(did not play)			
Totals	**292**	**167**	**57.2**	**1980**	**17**	**11**

1969

At New Orleans	23	10	43.5	229	3	0
At Cleveland	18	14	77.8	121	2	0
At San Francisco	39	27	69.2	258	1	1
St. Louis	34	19	55.9	238	2	0
N.Y. Giants	21	11	52.4	111	0	1
At Pittsburgh	29	14	48.3	155	1	2
At Baltimore	38	28	73.7	339	2	3
Philadelphia	32	22	68.8	252	2	0
Dallas	35	24	68.6	338	4	4
Atlanta	32	26	81.3	300	2	1
Los Angeles	39	21	53.8	206	0	2
At Philadelphia	33	18	54.5	182	2	0
New Orleans	28	15	53.6	167	1	0
At Dallas	41	25	61.0	206	0	1
Totals	**442**	**274**	**62.0**	**3102**	**22**	**15**

1970

At San Francisco	30	16	53.3	141	1	1
At St. Louis	26	12	46.2	114	0	2
At Philadelphia	28	14	50.0	139	2	0
Detroit	20	14	70.0	225	3	1
At Oakland	31	24	77.4	232	2	0
Cincinnati	24	13	54.2	123	2	0
At Denver	17	9	52.9	120	2	0
Minnesota	25	18	72.0	201	1	0
At N.Y. Giants	27	14	51.9	249	1	1
Dallas	26	17	65.4	190	3	0
N.Y. Giants	29	18	62.1	203	3	2
At Dallas	25	14	56.0	110	0	2
Philadelphia	15	10	66.7	161	1	0
St. Louis	14	9	64.3	146	2	1
Totals	**337**	**202**	**59.9**	**2354**	**23**	**10**

1971

At Chi. Bears	6	4	66.7	43	0	0
Dallas	16	9	56.3	76	0	2
At Philadelphia	6	3	50.0	51	0	0
Totals	**28**	**16**	**57.1**	**170**	**0**	**2**

1972

Philadelphia	24	14	58.3	237	1	3
At St. Louis	18	13	72.2	203	0	1
At Dallas	16	11	68.8	180	1	0
At N.Y. Giants	1	1	100.0	13	0	0
Green Bay (P)			(did not play)			
Dallas (P)			(did not play)			
Miami (SB)			(did not play)			
Totals	**59**	**39**	**66.1**	**633**	**2**	**4**

1973

At St. Louis	18	12	66.7	140	1	0
At Philadelphia	29	16	55.2	195	2	1
Dallas	20	14	70.0	140	1	0
At N.Y. Giants	13	8	61.5	52	0	3
At New Orleans	25	13	52.0	110	0	1
San Francisco	1	1	100.0	18	1	0
N.Y. Giants	15	12	80.0	135	1	0
At Dallas	24	11	45.8	114	0	0
At Minnesota (P)			(did not play)			
Totals	**145**	**87**	**60.0**	**904**	**6**	**5**

1974

At N.Y. Giants	4	4	100.0	26	0	0
At Cincinnati	20	12	60.0	104	2	0
Miami	39	26	66.7	303	2	3
N.Y. Giants	30	17	56.7	174	3	1
At St. Louis	29	20	69.0	201	2	1
At Philadelphia	23	14	60.9	172	1	0
Chi. Bears	22	14	63.6	205	1	0
At Los Angeles (P)	12	6	50.0	78	0	3
Totals	**167**	**107**	**64.1**	**1185**	**11**	**5**
Postseason	**12**	**6**	**50.0**	**78**	**0**	**3**

12 JOE NAMATH (1965-77)

1965 (Jets)

Opponent	Att	Comp	Pct	Yds	TD	Int
At Houston	0	0	0.0	0	0	0
Kansas City	23	11	47.8	121	1	0
At Buffalo	40	19	47.5	287	2	2
At Denver	34	18	52.9	152	0	2
Oakland	21	5	23.8	126	1	1
San Diego	5	2	40.0	21	0	0
Denver	6	5	83.3	49	1	0
At Kansas City	16	7	43.8	81	1	0
At Boston	25	10	40.0	180	2	0
Houston	26	17	65.4	221	4	1
Boston	30	16	53.3	284	1	1
At San Diego	34	18	52.9	179	1	3
At Oakland	36	19	52.8	280	2	3
Buffalo	44	17	38.6	239	2	2
Totals	**340**	**164**	**48.2**	**2220**	**18**	**15**

1966

Opponent	Att	Comp	Pct	Yds	TD	Int
At Miami	19	8	42.1	100	0	1
Houston	31	12	38.7	283	5	0
At Denver	35	16	45.7	206	1	2
At Boston	56	28	50.0	338	2	3
San Diego	22	11	50.0	129	1	3
At Houston	37	16	43.2	143	0	4
Oakland	32	19	59.4	272	0	0
Buffalo	53	24	45.3	343	2	5
At Buffalo	36	19	52.8	286	0	1
Miami	30	17	56.7	236	0	0
Kansas City	36	18	50.0	263	2	1
At Oakland	42	20	47.6	327	2	5
At San Diego	21	10	47.6	166	1	2
Boston	21	14	66.7	287	3	0
Totals	**471**	**232**	**49.3**	**3379**	**19**	**27**

1967

Opponent	Att	Comp	Pct	Yds	TD	Int
At Buffalo	23	11	47.8	153	2	0
At Denver	37	22	59.5	399	2	2
Miami	39	23	59.0	415	3	1
Oakland	28	9	32.1	166	0	2
Houston	49	27	55.1	295	1	6
At Miami	15	13	86.7	199	2	0
Boston	43	22	51.2	362	2	2
At Kansas City	40	20	50.0	245	1	3
Buffalo	37	13	35.1	338	1	2
At Boston	23	15	65.2	297	2	1
Denver	60	24	40.0	292	3	4
Kansas City	25	14	56.0	133	0	2
At Oakland	46	27	58.7	370	3	3
At San Diego	26	18	69.2	343	4	0
Totals	**491**	**258**	**52.5**	**4007**	**26**	**28**

1968

Opponent	Att	Comp	Pct	Yds	TD	Int
At Kansas City	29	17	58.6	302	2	1
At Boston	25	13	52.0	196	2	1
At Buffalo	43	19	44.2	280	4	5
San Diego	34	16	47.1	220	0	0
Denver	41	20	48.8	341	0	5
At Houston	27	12	44.4	145	0	0
Boston	18	10	55.6	170	0	2
Buffalo	28	10	35.7	164	0	1
Houston	20	17	85.0	185	0	0
At Oakland	37	19	51.4	381	1	0
At San Diego	31	17	54.8	337	2	1
Miami	14	8	57.1	104	2	0
Cincinnati	23	13	56.5	193	2	1
At Miami	10	6	60.0	120	0	0
Oakland (P)	49	19	38.8	266	3	1
Baltimore (SB)	28	17	60.7	206	0	0
Totals	**380**	**187**	**49.2**	**3143**	**15**	**17**
Postseason	**77**	**36**	**46.8**	**472**	**3**	**1**

1969

Opponent	Att	Comp	Pct	Yds	TD	Int
At Buffalo	13	7	53.8	157	1	3
At Denver	37	19	51.4	283	0	0
At San Diego	51	29	56.9	344	2	2
At Boston	21	15	71.4	145	1	1
At Cincinnati	26	14	53.8	163	1	1
Houston	24	12	50.0	306	2	3
Boston	21	10	47.6	115	0	1
Miami	26	13	50.0	233	3	1
Buffalo	22	10	45.5	169	0	1
Kansas City	40	24	60.0	327	2	3
Cincinnati	20	11	55.0	172	2	0
Oakland	30	10	33.3	169	1	1
At Houston	16	6	37.5	52	2	0
At Miami	8	5	62.5	99	2	0
Kansas City (P)	40	14	35.0	164	0	3
Totals	**361**	**185**	**51.2**	**2734**	**19**	**17**
Postseason	**40**	**14**	**35.0**	**164**	**0**	**3**

Teams (W-L Record): N.Y. Jets, 1965-76; L.A. Rams, 1977 (84-94-4, .473).
Hall of Fame? Yes (3rd year eligible)
Honors: Consensus AFL player of the year, 1968; Super Bowl MVP, 1969; consensus AFL rookie of the year, 1965; all-AFL (2), 1968-69; all-NFL (1), 1972; AFL All-Star Game (4), 1965, '67-69; Pro Bowl (1), 1972.
Records: Most passing yards, season, 4,007, 1967*; most consecutive passes completed, 15, 1967.*
Lifetime Rankings: 65.5 passer rating (--/--); 27,663 yards (10th/20th); 173 TDs (T14th/T26th).
300-Yard Games: 21
400-Yard Games: 3
Interception Probability: 5.8% (222/3,762)
Last Reported Salary: $350,000
Injuries: 1965--torn right knee ligaments, cartilage; 1966--right knee tendon transfer, cartilage removed; 1968--torn left knee tendon; 1970--broken wrist; 1971--torn left knee ligaments; 1973--separated shoulder.
Comment: We left in all the "did not plays" so you'd get the full effect of Namath's physical problems. During one stretch from 1970 to '73, he missed 28 of 50 games -- two seasons. By that time he had the knees of a nonagenarian. His career was excitingly erratic. One week in 1967 he threw six interceptions in the second half against Houston, the next he started a record-tying streak of 15 straight completed passes. Between injuries, Namath made all-NFL in 1972, a fact that tends to be forgotten. What could he have accomplished if he were fully functional?

1970

Opponent	Att	Comp	Pct	Yds	TD	Int
At Cleveland	31	18	58.1	298	1	3
At Boston	20	9	45.0	96	1	0
At Buffalo	26	12	46.2	228	2	0
Miami	40	17	42.5	240	0	3
Baltimore	62	34	54.8	397	1	6
Buffalo	(did not play)					
N.Y. Giants	(did not play)					
At Pittsburgh	(did not play)					
At L.A. Rams	(did not play)					
Boston	(did not play)					
Minnesota	(did not play)					
Oakland	(did not play)					
At Miami	(did not play)					
At Baltimore	(did not play)					
Totals	**179**	**90**	**50.3**	**1259**	**5**	**12**

1971

Opponent	Att	Comp	Pct	Yds	TD	Int
At Baltimore	(did not play)					
At St. Louis	(did not play)					
At Miami	(did not play)					
At New England	(did not play)					
Buffalo	(did not play)					
Miami	(did not play)					
At San Diego	(did not play)					
Kansas City	(did not play)					
Baltimore	(did not play)					
At Buffalo	(did not play)					
San Francisco	27	11	40.7	258	3	2
At Dallas	5	1	20.0	20	0	1
New England	12	7	58.3	95	0	2
Cincinnati	15	9	60.0	164	2	1
Totals	**59**	**28**	**47.5**	**537**	**5**	**6**

1972

Opponent	Att	Comp	Pct	Yds	TD	Int
At Buffalo	14	5	35.7	113	1	1
At Baltimore	28	15	53.6	496	6	1
At Houston	38	18	47.4	301	2	2
Miami	25	12	48.0	156	0	1
At New England	8	5	62.5	63	1	1
Baltimore	16	5	31.3	228	2	3
New England	24	12	50.0	203	0	1
Washington	28	15	53.6	148	1	3
Buffalo	12	6	50.0	106	2	1
At Miami	23	14	60.9	175	2	2
At Detroit	22	9	40.9	165	1	1
New Orleans	40	21	52.5	259	0	2
At Oakland	46	25	54.3	403	1	2
Cleveland	(did not play)					
Totals	**324**	**162**	**50.0**	**2816**	**19**	**21**

1973

Opponent	Att	Comp	Pct	Yds	TD	Int
At Green Bay	33	16	48.5	203	0	1
At Baltimore	4	3	75.0	37	0	0
At Buffalo	(did not play)					
At Miami	(did not play)					
At New England	(did not play)					
At Pittsburgh	(did not play)					
Denver	(did not play)					
Miami	(did not play)					
New England	(did not play)					
At Cincinnati	13	6	46.2	98	0	1
Atlanta	32	15	46.9	191	2	3
Baltimore	21	15	71.4	231	1	1
At Philadelphia	(did not play)					
Buffalo	30	13	43.3	206	2	0
Totals	**133**	**68**	**51.1**	**966**	**5**	**6**

1974

Opponent	Att	Comp	Pct	Yds	TD	Int
At Kansas City	30	14	46.7	210	2	4
At Chicago	23	16	69.6	257	1	0
At Buffalo	18	2	11.1	33	0	3
At Miami	39	17	43.6	290	2	3
New England	21	7	33.3	63	0	2
Baltimore	20	12	60.0	156	2	1
Los Angeles	32	19	59.4	155	0	2
Houston	31	19	61.3	256	2	2
At N.Y. Giants	31	20	64.5	236	2	0
At New England	20	8	40.0	112	2	2
Miami	22	13	59.1	182	2	3
San Diego	27	17	63.0	254	1	0
Buffalo	19	8	42.1	131	2	0
At Baltimore	28	19	67.9	281	2	0
Totals	**361**	**191**	**52.9**	**2616**	**20**	**22**

1975

Opponent	Att	Comp	Pct	Yds	TD	Int
At Buffalo	36	14	38.9	173	2	4
At Kansas City	14	7	50.0	126	1	2
New England	21	15	71.4	218	4	1
At Minnesota	21	12	57.1	195	1	2
Miami	24	8	33.3	96	0	6
Baltimore	28	19	67.9	333	3	1
Buffalo	31	16	51.6	208	2	1
At Miami	28	11	39.3	140	1	2
At Baltimore	26	9	34.6	194	0	2
St. Louis	21	8	38.1	117	0	1
Pittsburgh	21	8	38.1	138	1	4
At New England	18	14	77.8	160	0	0
At San Diego	29	15	51.7	181	0	2
Dallas	8	1	12.5	7	0	0
Totals	**326**	**157**	**48.2**	**2286**	**15**	**28**

1976

Opponent	Att	Comp	Pct	Yds	TD	Int
At Cleveland	31	15	48.4	137	0	1
At Denver	18	11	61.1	106	0	1
At Miami	26	16	61.5	171	0	1
At San Francisco	17	8	47.1	70	0	0
Buffalo	11	3	27.3	21	1	1
At New England	27	16	59.3	135	1	1
Baltimore	29	15	51.7	154	0	2
At Buffalo	(did not play)					
Miami	(did not play)					
Tampa Bay	12	7	58.3	94	1	0
New England	36	16	44.4	176	1	5
At Baltimore	8	3	37.5	6	0	0
Washington	(did not play)					
Cincinnati	15	4	26.7	20	0	4
Totals	**230**	**114**	**49.6**	**1090**	**4**	**16**

1977 (Rams)

Opponent	Att	Comp	Pct	Yds	TD	Int
At Atlanta	30	15	50.0	141	1	0
Philadelphia	23	12	52.2	136	2	1
San Francisco	14	7	50.0	126	0	0
At Chicago	40	16	40.0	203	0	4
New Orleans	(did not play)					
Minnesota	(did not play)					
At New Orleans	(did not play)					
Tampa Bay	(did not play)					
At Green Bay	(did not play)					
At San Francisco	(did not play)					
At Cleveland	(did not play)					
Oakland	(did not play)					
Atlanta	(did not play)					
Washington	(did not play)					
At Minnesota (P)	(did not play)					
Totals	**107**	**50**	**46.7**	**606**	**3**	**5**

12 ROGER STAUBACH (1969-79)

1969

Opponent	Att	Comp	Pct	Yds	TD	Int
St. Louis	15	7	46.7	222	1	0
At New Orleans	(did not play)					
At Philadelphia	8	5	62.5	60	0	1
At Atlanta	1	0	0.0	0	0	0
Philadelphia	8	3	37.5	45	0	1
N.Y. Giants	(did not play)					
At Cleveland	11	6	54.5	74	0	0
New Orleans	(did not play)					
At Washington	(did not play)					
At Los Angeles	(did not play)					
San Francisco	(did not play)					
At Pittsburgh	(did not play)					
Baltimore	4	2	50.0	22	0	0
Washington	(did not play)					
Cleveland (P)	5	4	80.0	44	1	0
Los Angeles (PB)	6	1	16.7	16	0	0
Totals	**47**	**23**	**48.9**	**421**	**1**	**2**
Postseason	**11**	**5**	**45.4**	**60**	**1**	**0**

1970

Opponent	Att	Comp	Pct	Yds	TD	Int
At Philadelphia	15	11	73.3	115	1	1
N.Y. Giants	23	13	56.5	133	1	1
At St. Louis	6	2	33.3	16	0	2
Atlanta	(did not play)					
At Minnesota	16	9	56.3	109	0	3
At Kansas City	(did not play)					
Philadelphia	(did not play)					
At N.Y. Giants	(did not play)					
St. Louis	8	2	25.0	61	0	1
At Washington	5	2	40.0	26	0	0
Green Bay	(did not play)					
Washington	4	3	75.0	66	0	0
At Cleveland	(did not play)					
Houston	5	2	40.0	16	0	0
Detroit (P)	(did not play)					
San Francisco (P)	(did not play)					
Baltimore (SB)	(did not play)					
Totals	**82**	**44**	**53.7**	**542**	**2**	**8**

1971

Opponent	Att	Comp	Pct	Yds	TD	Int
At Buffalo	(did not play)					
At Philadelphia	4	2	50.0	23	0	1
Washington	9	6	66.7	103	0	0
N.Y. Giants	17	8	47.1	106	1	0
At New Orleans	10	7	70.0	117	2	1
New England	21	13	61.9	197	2	0
At Chicago	11	7	63.6	87	0	1
At St. Louis	31	20	64.5	199	1	0
Philadelphia	28	14	50.0	176	0	0
At Washington	21	11	52.4	151	0	0
Los Angeles	14	8	57.1	176	2	0
N.Y. Jets	15	10	66.7	168	3	0
At N.Y. Giants	14	10	71.4	232	3	0
St. Louis	16	10	62.5	147	1	1
At Minnesota (P)	14	10	71.4	99	1	0
San Francisco (P)	18	9	50.0	103	0	0
Miami (SB)	19	12	63.2	119	2	0
Totals	**211**	**126**	**59.7**	**1882**	**15**	**4**
Postseason	**51**	**31**	**60.8**	**321**	**3**	**0**

1972

Opponent	Att	Comp	Pct	Yds	TD	Int
Philadelphia	(did not play)					
At N.Y. Giants	(did not play)					
At Green Bay	(did not play)					
Pittsburgh	(did not play)					
At Baltimore	(did not play)					
At Washington	(did not play)					
Detroit	(did not play)					
At San Diego	(did not play)					
St. Louis	(did not play)					
At Philadelphia	3	1	33.3	16	0	1
San Francisco	5	1	20.0	12	0	0
At St. Louis	3	1	33.3	21	0	0
Washington	(did not play)					
N.Y. Giants	9	6	66.7	49	0	1
At S.F. (P)	20	12	60.0	174	2	0
At Washington (P)	20	9	45.0	98	0	0
Totals	**20**	**9**	**45.0**	**98**	**0**	**2**
Postseason	**40**	**21**	**52.5**	**272**	**2**	**0**

1973

Opponent	Att	Comp	Pct	Yds	TD	Int
At Chicago	22	9	40.9	91	2	2
New Orleans	15	10	66.7	124	1	1
St. Louis	22	17	77.3	276	2	0
At Washington	17	9	52.9	101	1	0
At Los Angeles	25	15	60.0	173	2	3
N.Y. Giants	11	8	72.7	146	2	1
At Philadelphia	38	24	63.2	250	2	2
Cincinnati	18	14	77.8	209	3	0
At N.Y. Giants	16	7	43.8	76	1	0
Philadelphia	16	7	43.8	108	2	3
Miami	24	15	62.5	155	0	1
At Denver	18	14	77.8	240	2	0
Washington	25	16	64.0	223	0	2
At St. Louis	19	14	73.7	256	3	0
Los Angeles (P)	16	8	50.0	180	2	2
Minnesota (P)	21	10	47.6	89	0	4
Totals	**286**	**179**	**62.6**	**2428**	**23**	**15**
Postseason	**37**	**18**	**48.6**	**269**	**2**	**6**

Team (W-L Record): Dallas, 1969-79 (116-41-1, .737).
Hall of Fame? Yes (1st year eligible)
Honors: Bert Bell Trophy, 1971; Super Bowl MVP, 1972; Sporting News NFC Player of the Year, 1971; Pro Bowl (5), 1971, '76-79.
Records: None
Lifetime Rankings: 83.4 passer rating (1st/5th); 22,700 yards (18th/38th); (6th/13th); 153 TDs (22nd/40th).
300-Yard Games: 6
400-Yard Games: None
Interception Probability: 3.7% (109/2,958)
Injuries: 1972--separated shoulder.
Comment: Early in Staubach's career, a teammate said: "If he called his own plays, he would throw 65 passes a game, 80 percent to a double-covered receiver." Fortunately for the Cowboys, Tom Landry called the plays and Staubach became a more discriminating reader of defenses. Staubach doesn't have the whopping career totals of other modern quarterbacks, but there are reasons for that. He started four years late because of a Naval commitment, didn't take the starting job away from Craig Morton until his third season, missed most of 1973 with an injury and then retired after leading the league in passing in '79. He also played for a team that ran the ball well. Consider: Staubach didn't have his first 300-yard passing day until his 72nd NFL game. Heck, Dan Marino had more 300-yard games in his second season (9) than Staubach had in his entire career (6). But when pro football became more of a passing game in the late '70s, Staubach put up bigger numbers. His yardage total in his last regular-season game (336) was his second-highest ever. Because of his mobility, Staubach could play in any era. And he may have been the best at the two-minute drill since Bobby Layne.

1974

Opponent	Att	Comp	Pct	Yds	TD	Int
At Atlanta	27	13	48.1	252	1	0
At Philadelphia	33	19	57.6	217	0	2
N.Y. Giants	37	20	54.1	256	1	3
Minnesota	20	9	45.0	144	2	4
At St. Louis	29	19	65.5	236	1	1
Philadelphia	27	18	66.7	224	0	0
At N.Y. Giants	19	10	52.6	121	1	2
St. Louis	27	15	55.5	154	0	0
San Francisco	14	9	64.3	177	0	0
At Washington	38	16	42.1	174	2	1
At Houston	15	8	53.3	69	0	0
Washington	11	3	27.3	32	0	1
Cleveland	24	14	58.3	230	3	1
At Oakland	39	17	43.6	266	0	0
Totals	**360**	**190**	**52.8**	**2552**	**11**	**15**

1975

Opponent	Att	Comp	Pct	Yds	TD	Int
Los Angeles	23	10	43.5	106	0	0
St. Louis	34	23	67.6	307	3	1
At Detroit	18	11	61.1	212	2	2
At N.Y. Giants	22	8	36.4	87	1	0
Green Bay	31	16	51.6	201	0	1
At Philadelphia	49	27	55.1	314	1	1
At Washington	29	17	58.6	217	2	1
Kansas City	31	17	54.8	243	2	2
At New England	14	10	71.4	190	3	0
Philadelphia	15	11	73.3	155	0	2
N.Y. Giants	22	13	59.1	213	1	2
At St. Louis	41	25	61.0	268	0	3
Washington	19	10	52.6	153	2	1
At N.Y. Jets	(did not play)					
At Minnesota (P)	29	17	58.6	246	1	0
At L.A. (P)	26	16	61.5	220	4	1
Pittsburgh (SB)	24	15	62.5	204	2	3
Totals	**348**	**198**	**56.9**	**2666**	**17**	**16**
Postseason	**79**	**48**	**60.8**	**670**	**7**	**4**

1976

Opponent	Att	Comp	Pct	Yds	TD	Int
Philadelphia	28	19	67.8	242	2	1
At New Orleans	22	15	68.2	239	0	0
Baltimore	28	22	78.6	339	2	0
At Seattle	20	14	70.0	200	2	1
At N.Y. Giants	15	13	86.7	178	1	0
At St. Louis	42	21	50.0	250	2	1
Chicago	21	12	57.1	162	1	0
At Washington	23	13	56.5	152	0	0
N.Y. Giants	25	13	52.0	161	0	1
Buffalo	34	15	44.1	202	1	0
At Atlanta	28	13	46.4	157	0	3
St. Louis	21	10	47.6	83	1	2
At Philadelphia	40	23	57.5	259	1	0
Washington	22	5	22.7	91	1	2
Los Angeles (P)	37	15	40.5	150	0	3
Totals	**369**	**208**	**56.4**	**2715**	**14**	**11**
Postseason	**37**	**15**	**40.5**	**150**	**0**	**3**

1977

Opponent	Att	Comp	Pct	Yds	TD	Int
At Minnesota	30	18	60.0	196	1	0
N.Y. Giants	29	18	62.1	235	1	0
Tampa Bay	24	15	62.5	212	0	1
At St. Louis	29	18	62.1	153	1	0
Washington	28	15	53.6	250	2	0
At Philadelphia	25	15	60.0	172	0	0
Detroit	25	16	64.0	179	3	0
At N.Y. Giants	25	14	56.0	190	1	0
St. Louis	20	11	55.0	102	1	2
At Pittsburgh	36	18	50.0	230	1	2
At Washington	24	10	41.7	138	1	1
Philadelphia	26	13	50.0	183	1	2
At San Francisco	19	14	73.7	220	3	0
Denver	20	15	75.0	160	2	1
Chicago (P)	13	8	61.5	134	1	1
Minnesota (P)	23	12	52.2	165	1	1
Denver (SB)	25	17	68.0	183	1	0
Totals	**361**	**210**	**58.2**	**2620**	**18**	**9**
Postseason	**61**	**37**	**60.7**	**481**	**3**	**2**

1978

Opponent	Att	Comp	Pct	Yds	TD	Int
Baltimore	22	16	72.7	280	4	2
At N.Y. Giants	28	18	64.2	212	2	1
At Los Angeles	46	22	47.8	246	2	4
St. Louis	26	16	61.5	182	1	0
At Washington	30	13	43.3	212	0	1
N.Y. Giants	32	17	53.1	246	3	1
At St. Louis	40	23	57.5	289	3	2
Philadelphia	22	10	45.5	108	1	0
Minnesota	26	12	46.2	148	0	2
At Miami	30	19	63.3	275	1	2
At Green Bay	31	19	61.3	200	2	0
New Orleans	15	9	60.0	141	1	0
Washington	19	9	47.4	218	1	1
New England	27	15	55.6	243	2	0
At Philadelphia	19	13	68.4	190	2	0
At N.Y. Jets	(did not play)					
Atlanta (P)	17	7	41.2	105	0	0
Los Angeles (P)	25	13	52.0	126	2	2
Pittsburgh (SB)	30	17	56.7	228	3	1
Totals	**413**	**231**	**55.9**	**3190**	**25**	**16**
Postseason	**72**	**37**	**51.4**	**459**	**5**	**3**

1979

Opponent	Att	Comp	Pct	Yds	TD	Int
At St. Louis	34	20	58.8	269	0	0
At San Francisco	34	20	58.8	259	2	0
Chicago	31	18	58.1	222	3	0
At Cleveland	39	21	53.8	303	1	2
Cincinnati	25	12	48.0	164	2	1
At Minnesota	23	15	65.2	174	0	0
Los Angeles	18	13	72.2	176	3	0
St. Louis	25	11	44.0	164	2	2
At Pittsburgh	25	11	44.0	113	0	0
At N.Y. Giants	30	20	66.7	266	1	0
Philadelphia	28	17	60.7	308	3	0
At Washington	38	23	60.5	276	1	3
Houston	30	21	70.0	287	2	2
N.Y. Giants	18	10	55.5	164	3	0
At Philadelphia	21	11	52.9	105	1	0
Washington	42	24	57.1	336	3	1
Los Angeles (P)	28	12	42.9	124	1	1
Totals	**461**	**267**	**57.9**	**3586**	**27**	**11**
Postseason	**28**	**12**	**42.9**	**124**	**1**	**1**

12 TERRY BRADSHAW (1970-83)

1970

Opponent	Att	Comp	Pct	Yds	TD	Int
Houston	16	4	25.0	70	0	1
At Denver	26	13	50.0	211	0	1
At Cleveland	29	13	44.8	207	0	3
Buffalo	12	3	25.0	24	0	0
At Houston	17	8	47.1	208	1	3
At Oakland	27	12	44.4	138	1	4
Cincinnati	12	4	33.3	40	0	0
N.Y. Jets	(did not play)					
Kansas City	19	8	42.1	74	1	3
At Cincinnati	19	8	42.1	101	0	3
Cleveland	9	4	44.4	197	2	0
Green Bay	20	3	15.0	110	1	4
At Atlanta	12	3	25.0	30	0	2
At Philadelphia	0	0	0.0	0	0	0
Totals	**218**	**83**	**38.1**	**1410**	**6**	**24**

1971

Opponent	Att	Comp	Pct	Yds	TD	Int
At Chicago	24	10	41.7	129	0	4
Cincinnati	30	18	60.0	249	2	1
San Diego	24	15	62.5	175	0	0
At Cleveland	27	12	44.4	126	2	1
At Kansas City	39	20	51.3	269	0	2
Houston	32	21	65.6	279	0	3
At Baltimore	35	20	57.1	187	1	1
Cleveland	11	4	36.4	70	0	1
At Miami	36	25	69.4	253	3	2
N.Y. Giants	20	12	60.0	75	1	0
Denver	17	6	35.3	68	0	0
At Houston	31	14	45.2	111	0	3
At Cincinnati	13	6	46.2	105	2	0
Los Angeles	34	20	58.8	163	2	4
Totals	**373**	**203**	**54.4**	**2259**	**13**	**22**

1972

Opponent	Att	Comp	Pct	Yds	TD	Int
Oakland	17	7	41.2	124	1	3
At Cincinnati	34	18	52.9	170	0	0
At St. Louis	40	25	62.5	229	1	1
At Dallas	39	12	30.8	166	0	1
Houston	19	9	47.4	70	1	0
New England	11	7	63.6	173	1	0
At Buffalo	17	9	52.9	93	1	1
Cincinnati	20	10	50.0	190	3	0
Kansas City	20	8	40.0	92	0	3
At Cleveland	21	10	47.6	136	1	1
Minnesota	19	7	36.8	93	1	1
Cleveland	17	9	52.9	162	1	0
At Houston	11	4	36.4	37	0	0
At San Diego	23	12	52.2	152	1	1
Oakland (P)	25	11	25.0	175	1	1
Miami (P)	10	5	50.0	82	1	2
Totals	**308**	**147**	**47.7**	**1887**	**12**	**12**
Postseason	**35**	**16**	**45.7**	**257**	**2**	**3**

1973

Opponent	Att	Comp	Pct	Yds	TD	Int
Detroit	23	15	65.2	154	2	1
Cleveland	14	5	35.7	140	1	1
At Houston	17	9	52.9	159	1	2
San Diego	16	7	43.8	99	1	1
At Cincinnati	14	9	64.3	106	0	1
N.Y. Jets	18	8	44.4	119	0	1
Cincinnati	7	3	42.9	37	0	1
Washington	(did not play)					
At Oakland	(did not play)					
Denver	(did not play)					
At Cleveland	(did not play)					
At Miami	35	14	40.0	117	2	3
Houston	20	11	55.0	117	2	4
At San Francisco	16	8	50.0	135	1	0
At Oakland (P)	25	12	48.0	167	2	3
Totals	**180**	**89**	**49.4**	**1183**	**10**	**15**
Postseason	**25**	**12**	**48.0**	**167**	**2**	**3**

1974

Opponent	Att	Comp	Pct	Yds	TD	Int
Baltimore	(did not play)					
At Denver	(did not play)					
Oakland	2	1	50.0	11	0	1
At Houston	(did not play)					
At Kansas City	(did not play)					
Cleveland	(did not play)					
Atlanta	21	9	42.9	130	0	2
Philadelphia	22	12	54.5	146	1	0
At Cincinnati	35	13	37.1	140	0	1
At Cleveland	(did not play)					
At New Orleans	19	8	42.1	80	2	2
Houston	20	6	30.0	60	1	1
At New England	16	10	62.5	86	1	1
Cincinnati	13	8	61.5	132	2	0
Buffalo (P)	19	12	63.2	203	1	0
At Oakland (P)	17	8	47.1	95	1	1
Minnesota (SB)	14	9	64.3	96	1	0
Totals	**148**	**67**	**45.3**	**785**	**7**	**8**
Postseason	**50**	**29**	**58.0**	**394**	**3**	**1**

Team (W-L Record): Pittsburgh, 1970-83 (132-68-1, .659).
Hall of Fame? Yes (1st year eligible)
Honors: Bert Bell Trophy, 1978; AP NFL MVP, 1978; Super Bowl MVP, 1979-80; all-NFL (1), 1978; Pro Bowl (3), 1975, '78-79.
Records: None
Lifetime Rankings: 70.7 passer rating (--/--); 27,989 yards (13th/16th); 212 TDs (T8th/T11th).
300-Yard Games: 4 (plus 3 postseason)
400-Yard Games: None
Interception Probability: 5.4% (210/3901)
Last Reported Salary: $362,500
Injuries: 1983--elbow injury.
Comment: The first time the Steelers won it all, in 1974, Bradshaw was just along for the ride. It was the Steel Curtain's show. But after that he became a star in his own right. His numbers don't jump out at you. The team was so successful running the ball with Franco Harris that Bradshaw had only seven 300-yard passing days (the first wasn't until his 128th game!). Three, however, came in postseason play, two in the Super Bowl. Fine athlete, great arm and tough, too.

1975

Opponent	Att	Comp	Pct	Yds	TD	Int
At San Diego	28	21	75.0	227	2	0
Buffalo	8	3	37.5	69	0	1
At Cleveland	8	7	87.5	151	1	0
Denver	26	16	61.5	191	2	0
Chicago	22	11	50.0	146	0	0
At Green Bay	22	12	54.5	84	0	0
At Cincinnati	24	13	54.2	130	2	2
Houston	28	17	60.7	219	3	1
Kansas City	24	16	66.7	204	2	1
At Houston	16	13	81.3	168	1	2
At N.Y. Jets	22	9	40.9	120	2	0
Cleveland	25	11	44.0	135	2	0
Cincinnati	23	13	56.5	149	1	1
At Los Angeles	10	3	30.0	28	0	1
Baltimore (P)	13	8	61.5	103	0	2
Oakland (P)	25	15	60.0	215	1	3
Dallas (SB)	19	9	47.4	209	2	0
Totals	**286**	**165**	**57.7**	**2055**	**18**	**9**
Postseason	**57**	**32**	**56.1**	**527**	**3**	**5**

1976

Opponent	Att	Comp	Pct	Yds	TD	Int
At Oakland	27	15	55.6	253	1	1
Cleveland	23	7	30.4	77	2	0
New England	39	20	51.3	291	1	0
At Minnesota	22	10	45.5	90	1	4
At Cleveland	18	10	55.6	75	0	1
Cincinnati	(did not play)					
At N.Y. Giants	(did not play)					
San Diego	19	9	47.4	104	1	1
At Kansas City	15	7	46.7	132	1	1
Miami	2	0	0.0	0	0	0
Houston	(did not play)					
At Cincinnati	(did not play)					
Tampa Bay	8	6	75.0	79	2	0
At Houston	19	8	42.1	76	1	0
At Baltimore (P)	18	14	77.8	264	3	0
At Oakland (P)	35	14	40.0	176	0	1
Totals	**192**	**92**	**47.9**	**1177**	**10**	**9**
Postseason	**53**	**28**	**52.8**	**440**	**3**	**1**

1977

Opponent	Att	Comp	Pct	Yds	TD	Int
San Francisco	23	12	52.2	164	1	0
Oakland	32	16	50.0	268	1	3
At Cleveland	17	10	58.8	143	3	2
At Houston	19	7	36.8	149	0	4
Cincinnati	9	6	66.7	117	0	0
Houston	24	16	66.7	227	2	1
At Baltimore	26	11	42.3	234	1	5
At Denver	26	13	50.0	146	1	0
Cleveland	21	13	61.9	283	3	0
Dallas	12	7	58.3	106	2	0
At N.Y. Jets	28	10	35.7	143	2	1
Seattle	21	13	61.9	158	1	1
At Cincinnati	39	20	51.3	246	0	1
At San Diego	17	8	47.1	139	0	1
At Denver (P)	37	19	51.4	177	1	3
Totals	**314**	**162**	**51.6**	**2523**	**17**	**19**
Postseason	**37**	**19**	**51.4**	**177**	**1**	**3**

1978

Opponent	Att	Comp	Pct	Yds	TD	Int
At Buffalo	19	14	73.7	217	2	1
Seattle	33	17	51.5	213	2	0
At Cincinnati	19	14	73.7	242	2	1
Cleveland	32	14	43.8	208	1	2
At N.Y. Jets	25	17	68.0	189	3	1
Atlanta	18	13	72.2	231	1	0
At Cleveland	21	10	47.6	175	2	0
Houston	33	17	51.5	226	2	1
Kansas City	13	7	53.8	109	1	2
New Orleans	23	16	69.6	200	2	1
At Los Angeles	25	11	44.0	125	1	3
Cincinnati	30	12	40.0	117	0	4
At San Francisco	21	13	61.9	195	3	1
At Houston	24	11	45.8	97	1	1
Baltimore	18	11	61.1	240	3	2
At Denver	14	10	71.4	131	2	0
Denver (P)	29	16	55.2	272	2	1
Houston (P)	19	11	57.9	200	2	2
Dallas (SB)	30	17	56.7	318	4	1
Totals	**368**	**207**	**56.3**	**2915**	**28**	**20**
Postseason	**78**	**44**	**56.4**	**790**	**8**	**4**

1979

Opponent	Att	Comp	Pct	Yds	TD	Int
At New England	26	15	57.7	221	1	0
Houston	29	12	41.4	198	2	2
At St. Louis	31	14	45.2	206	2	2
Baltimore	29	19	65.5	249	2	2
At Philadelphia	26	12	46.2	176	1	2
At Cleveland	21	12	57.1	161	3	0
At Cincinnati	40	21	52.5	275	1	2
Denver	24	18	75.0	267	2	1
Dallas	25	11	44.0	126	0	0
Washington	27	15	55.6	311	4	1
At Kansas City	29	17	58.6	232	3	2
At San Diego	36	18	50.0	153	0	5
Cleveland	44	30	68.2	364	1	1
Cincinnati	29	17	58.6	339	2	1
At Houston	29	14	48.3	237	1	2
Buffalo	27	14	51.9	209	1	2
Miami (P)	31	21	67.7	230	2	0
Houston (P)	30	18	60.0	219	2	1
Los Angeles (SB)	21	14	66.7	309	2	3
Totals	**472**	**259**	**54.9**	**3724**	**26**	**25**
Postseason	**82**	**53**	**64.6**	**758**	**6**	**4**

1980

Opponent	Att	Comp	Pct	Yds	TD	Int
Houston	24	12	50.0	254	2	2
At Baltimore	35	20	57.1	282	2	1
At Cincinnati	25	14	56.0	265	3	2
Chicago	19	12	63.2	217	4	1
At Minnesota	28	16	57.1	236	1	1
Cincinnati	35	14	40.0	237	1	1
Oakland	27	18	66.7	299	2	1
At Cleveland	(did not play)					
Green Bay	28	12	42.9	135	2	2
At Tampa Bay	26	11	42.3	100	1	1
Cleveland	35	19	54.3	263	2	4
At Buffalo	31	17	54.8	155	0	0
Miami	31	13	41.9	289	1	1
At Houston	26	10	38.5	138	0	3
Kansas City	22	14	63.6	197	2	2
At San Diego	32	16	50.0	272	1	0
Totals	**424**	**218**	**51.4**	**3339**	**24**	**22**

1981

Opponent	Att	Comp	Pct	Yds	TD	Int
Kansas City	36	21	58.3	319	2	2
At Miami	33	15	45.5	222	1	2
N.Y. Jets	28	14	50.0	225	0	0
New England	30	15	50.0	247	2	0
At New Orleans	28	19	67.9	276	2	0
Cleveland	33	19	57.6	199	1	1
At Cincinnati	27	14	51.9	145	1	0
Houston	28	14	50.0	208	2	1
San Francisco	23	12	52.2	125	1	3
At Seattle	22	13	59.1	212	1	2
At Atlanta	22	14	63.6	253	5	1
At Cleveland	32	17	53.1	223	2	2
Los Angeles	19	10	52.6	204	1	0
At Oakland	9	4	44.4	29	1	0
Cincinnati	(did not play)					
At Houston	(did not play)					
Totals	**370**	**201**	**54.3**	**2887**	**22**	**14**

1982

Opponent	Att	Comp	Pct	Yds	TD	Int
At Dallas	28	17	60.7	246	3	0
Cincinnati	42	29	69.0	298	3	0
At Houston	40	16	40.0	228	3	2
At Seattle	7	5	71.4	67	0	0
Kansas City	20	15	75.0	231	3	1
At Buffalo	13	2	15.4	3	0	2
At Cleveland	39	12	30.8	144	1	4
New England	27	17	63.0	282	2	0
Cleveland	24	14	58.3	269	2	2
San Diego (P)	39	28	71.8	325	2	2
Totals	**240**	**127**	**52.9**	**1768**	**17**	**11**
Postseason	**39**	**28**	**71.8**	**325**	**2**	**2**

1983

Opponent	Att	Comp	Pct	Yds	TD	Int
At N.Y. Jets	8	5	62.5	77	2	0
At Cleveland	0	0	0.0	0	0	0
Totals	**8**	**5**	**62.5**	**77**	**2**	**0**

16 JOE MONTANA (1979-)

1979

Opponent	Att	Comp	Pct	Yds	TD	Int
At Minnesota			(did not play)			
Dallas			(did not play)			
At L.A. Rams	1	1	100.0	8	0	0
New Orleans			(did not play)			
At San Diego			(did not play)			
Seattle			(did not play)			
At N.Y. Giants			(did not play)			
Atlanta	1	1	100.0	-8	0	0
Chicago			(did not play)			
At Oakland			(did not play)			
At New Orleans			(did not play)			
Denver	5	3	60.0	30	1	0
L.A. Rams			(did not play)			
At St. Louis	12	5	41.7	36	0	0
Tampa Bay	4	3	75.0	30	0	0
At Atlanta			(did not play)			
Totals	**23**	**13**	**56.5**	**96**	**1**	**0**

1980

Opponent	Att	Comp	Pct	Yds	TD	Int
At New Orleans			(did not play)			
St. Louis			(did not play)			
At N.Y. Jets	6	4	66.7	60	2	0
Atlanta			(did not play)			
At L.A. Rams	33	21	63.6	253	2	1
At Dallas			(did not play)			
L.A. Rams	37	21	56.8	252	2	2
Tampa Bay	31	24	77.4	200	1	1
At Detroit	11	6	54.5	51	0	0
At Green Bay			(did not play)			
At Miami	4	3	75.0	35	0	0
N.Y. Giants	15	9	60.0	151	1	2
New England	23	14	60.9	123	3	1
New Orleans	36	24	66.7	285	2	0
At Atlanta	41	25	61.0	222	1	2
Buffalo	36	25	69.4	163	1	0
Totals	**273**	**176**	**64.5**	**1795**	**15**	**9**

1981

Opponent	Att	Comp	Pct	Yds	TD	Int
At Detroit	28	18	64.3	195	1	1
Chicago	32	20	62.5	287	3	0
At Atlanta	34	24	70.6	274	2	2
New Orleans	22	16	72.7	175	1	1
At Washington	28	15	53.6	193	0	1
Dallas	29	19	65.5	279	2	0
At Green Bay	32	23	71.9	220	0	0
L.A. Rams	32	18	56.3	287	2	0
At Pittsburgh	37	22	59.5	205	1	2
Atlanta	30	16	53.3	223	2	1
Cleveland	42	24	57.1	213	0	2
At L.A. Rams	30	19	63.3	283	0	1
N.Y. Giants	39	27	69.2	234	0	0
At Cincinnati	36	23	63.9	187	2	1
Houston	26	18	69.2	204	1	0
At New Orleans	11	9	81.8	106	2	0
N.Y. Giants (P)	31	20	64.5	304	2	1
Dallas (P)	35	22	62.9	286	3	3
Cincinnati (SB)	22	14	63.6	157	1	0
Totals	**488**	**311**	**63.7**	**3565**	**19**	**12**
Postseason	**88**	**56**	**63.6**	**747**	**6**	**4**

1982

Opponent	Att	Comp	Pct	Yds	TD	Int
L.A. Raiders	41	21	51.2	244	2	1
At Denver	37	26	70.3	336	2	2
At St. Louis	39	26	66.7	408	3	1
New Orleans	42	27	64.3	334	2	1
At L.A. Rams	37	26	70.3	305	2	0
San Diego	46	31	67.4	356	3	2
Atlanta	31	16	51.6	177	1	1
At Kansas City	35	20	57.1	253	0	2
L.A. Rams	38	20	52.6	200	2	1
Totals	**346**	**213**	**61.6**	**2613**	**17**	**11**

1983

Opponent	Att	Comp	Pct	Yds	TD	Int
Philadelphia	20	10	50.0	118	0	1
At Minnesota	24	17	70.8	230	4	0
At St. Louis	32	20	62.5	341	3	1
Atlanta	32	27	84.4	261	3	2
At New England	38	25	65.8	288	2	0
L.A. Rams	42	28	66.7	316	0	0
At New Orleans	27	17	63.0	145	0	1
At L.A. Rams	39	25	64.1	358	3	0
N.Y. Jets	36	21	58.3	233	1	2
Miami	26	16	61.5	232	1	0
New Orleans	43	26	60.5	283	3	2
At Atlanta	28	21	75.0	182	1	0
At Chicago	43	26	60.5	255	0	2
Tampa Bay	31	21	67.7	227	0	0
At Buffalo	28	18	64.3	218	1	0
Dallas	26	14	53.8	223	4	1
Detroit (P)	31	18	58.1	201	1	1
At Washington (P)	48	27	56.3	347	3	1
Totals	**515**	**332**	**64.5**	**3910**	**26**	**12**
Postseason	**79**	**45**	**57.0**	**548**	**4**	**2**

Team (W-L Record): San Francisco, 1979- (105-61-1, .632).
Hall of Fame? Not eligible
Honors: Consensus NFL MVP/player of the year, 1989; Super Bowl MVP, 1982, '85, '90; all-NFL (2), 1987, '89; Pro Bowl (6), 1981, '83-85, '87, '89.
Records: Highest passer rating, career, 94.0; highest passer rating, season, 112.4, 1989; highest completion percentage, career, 63.9 percent; most consecutive passes completed, 22, 1987.
Lifetime Rankings: 94.0 passer rating (1st); 31,054 yards (9th); 216 TDs (9th).
300-Yard Games: 30
400-Yard Games: 5
Interception Probability: 2.6% (107/4,059)
Last Reported Salary: $1,200,000
Injuries: 1986--ruptured disk.
Comment: Montana is the most accurate passer in NFL history. He has the highest career completion percentage and the second-lowest interception percentage ever. In the 1988 and '89 playoffs, he had 19 touchdown passes, 1 interception and a 133.7 quarterback rating. He has now thrown 122 passes in the Super Bowl without getting one picked off. Is this boring you? Montana is the Wade Boggs of pro football, a man of 1,000 statistics -- all of them mind-boggling. About the only thing he hasn't done is father a boy. Keep tryin', Joe!

1984

Opponent	Att	Comp	Pct	Yds	TD	Int
At Detroit	25	16	64.0	188	1	0
Washington	40	24	60.0	381	2	0
New Orleans	17	10	58.8	128	1	1
At Philadelphia			(did not play)			
Atlanta	25	13	52.0	149	2	0
At N.Y. Giants	24	15	62.5	207	3	0
Pittsburgh	34	24	70.6	241	0	1
At Houston	35	25	71.4	353	3	1
At L.A. Rams	31	21	67.7	365	3	0
Cincinnati	42	27	64.3	301	2	4
At Cleveland	30	24	80.0	263	2	1
Tampa Bay	23	19	82.6	247	0	0
At New Orleans	30	14	46.7	177	2	0
At Atlanta	24	12	50.0	165	2	2
Minnesota	21	15	71.4	246	3	0
L.A. Rams	31	20	64.5	219	2	0
N.Y. Giants (P)	39	25	64.1	309	3	3
Chicago (P)	34	18	52.9	233	1	2
Miami (SB)	35	24	68.6	331	3	0
Totals	**432**	**279**	**64.6**	**3630**	**28**	**10**
Postseason	**108**	**67**	**62.0**	**873**	**7**	**5**

1985

Opponent	Att	Comp	Pct	Yds	TD	Int
At Minnesota	39	24	61.5	265	2	2
Atlanta	26	19	73.1	204	1	1
At L.A. Raiders	24	14	58.3	255	2	0
New Orleans	26	12	46.2	120	0	2
At Atlanta	57	37	64.9	429	5	0
Chicago	29	17	58.6	160	0	0
At Detroit	26	15	57.7	97	0	1
At L.A. Rams	30	22	73.3	306	3	0
Philadelphia			(did not play)			
At Denver	40	17	42.5	222	1	0
Kansas City	34	23	67.6	235	2	0
Seattle	33	17	51.5	237	2	3
At Washington	22	11	50.0	119	1	0
L.A. Rams	36	26	72.2	328	3	2
At New Orleans	38	25	65.8	354	3	1
Dallas	34	24	70.6	322	2	1
N.Y. Giants (P)	47	26	55.3	296	0	1
Totals	**494**	**303**	**61.3**	**3653**	**27**	**13**
Postseason	**47**	**26**	**55.3**	**296**	**0**	**1**

1986

Opponent	Att	Comp	Pct	Yds	TD	Int
At Tampa Bay	46	32	69.6	356	1	1
At L.A. Rams			(did not play)			
New Orleans			(did not play)			
At Miami			(did not play)			
Indianapolis			(did not play)			
Minnesota			(did not play)			
At Atlanta			(did not play)			
At Green Bay			(did not play)			
At New Orleans			(did not play)			
St. Louis	19	13	68.4	270	3	1
At Washington	60	33	55.0	441	0	3
Atlanta	32	21	65.6	233	1	0
N.Y. Giants	52	32	61.5	251	1	1
N.Y. Jets	37	23	62.2	245	0	1
At New England	25	14	56.0	202	0	1
L.A. Rams	36	23	63.9	238	2	1
At N.Y. Giants (P)	15	8	53.3	98	0	1
Totals	**307**	**191**	**62.2**	**2236**	**8**	**9**
Postseason	**15**	**8**	**53.3**	**98**	**0**	**1**

1987

Opponent	Att	Comp	Pct	Yds	TD	Int
At Pittsburgh	49	34	69.4	316	2	3
At Cincinnati	37	27	73.0	250	3	0
At Atlanta	8	5	62.5	63	1	0
St. Louis	39	31	79.5	334	4	2
At New Orleans	32	18	56.3	256	3	0
At L.A. Rams	30	21	70.0	294	3	1
Houston	46	32	69.6	289	3	2
New Orleans	29	16	55.2	144	1	2
At Tampa Bay	45	29	64.4	304	3	1
Cleveland	31	23	74.2	342	4	1
At Green Bay	35	26	74.3	308	2	1
Chicago	8	4	50.0	47	0	0
Atlanta			(did not play)			
L.A. Rams	9	6	66.7	107	2	0
Minnesota (P)	26	12	46.2	109	0	1
Totals	**398**	**266**	**66.8**	**3054**	**31**	**13**
Postseason	**26**	**12**	**46.2**	**109**	**0**	**1**

1988

Opponent	Att	Comp	Pct	Yds	TD	Int
At New Orleans	23	13	56.5	161	3	1
At N.Y. Giants	18	10	55.6	148	1	0
Atlanta	48	32	66.7	343	2	3
At Seattle	29	20	69.0	302	4	1
Detroit	30	19	63.3	182	0	0
Denver	24	12	50.0	191	0	1
At L.A. Rams	31	21	67.7	203	0	1
At Chicago	29	13	44.8	168	1	1
Minnesota			(did not play)			
At Phoenix			(did not play)			
L.A. Raiders	31	16	51.6	160	0	0
Washington	23	15	65.2	218	2	1
At San Diego	22	14	63.6	271	3	0
At Atlanta	34	20	58.8	230	1	0
New Orleans	29	18	62.1	233	1	1
L.A. Rams	26	15	57.7	171	0	0
Minnesota (P)	27	16	59.3	178	3	1
At Chicago (P)	27	17	63.0	288	3	0
Cincinnati (SB)	36	23	63.9	357	2	0
Totals	**397**	**238**	**59.9**	**2981**	**18**	**10**
Postseason	**90**	**56**	**62.2**	**823**	**8**	**1**

1989

Opponent	Att	Comp	Pct	Yds	TD	Int
At Indianapolis	26	15	57.7	233	1	0
At Tampa Bay	39	25	64.1	266	1	2
At Philadelphia	34	25	73.5	428	5	1
L.A. Rams	35	25	71.4	227	0	0
At New Orleans	29	21	72.4	291	3	0
At Dallas			(did not play)			
New England	22	16	72.7	178	1	0
At N.Y. Jets			(did not play)			
New Orleans	31	22	71.0	302	3	0
Atlanta	19	16	84.2	270	3	0
Green Bay	42	30	71.4	325	2	1
N.Y. Giants	33	27	81.8	292	3	0
At Atlanta	13	9	69.2	145	0	1
At L.A. Rams	42	30	71.4	458	3	2
Buffalo			(did not play)			
Chicago	21	10	47.6	106	1	1
Minnesota (P)	24	17	70.8	241	4	0
L.A. Rams (P)	30	26	86.7	262	2	0
Denver (SB)	29	22	75.9	297	5	0
Totals	**386**	**271**	**70.2**	**3521**	**26**	**8**
Postseason	**83**	**65**	**78.3**	**800**	**11**	**0**

13 DAN MARINO (1983-)

1983

Opponent	Att	Comp	Pct	Yds	TD	Int
At Buffalo		(did not play)				
New England		(did not play)				
At L.A. Raiders	17	11	64.8	90	2	0
Kansas City		(did not play)				
At New Orleans	22	12	54.5	150	1	1
Buffalo	29	19	65.5	322	3	2
At N.Y. Jets	30	17	56.7	225	3	0
At Baltimore	18	11	61.1	157	2	0
L.A. Rams	38	25	65.8	279	2	1
At San Francisco	29	15	51.7	194	2	0
At New England	37	14	37.8	141	0	1
Baltimore	21	14	66.7	240	1	0
Cincinnati	29	18	62.1	217	3	0
At Houston	26	17	65.4	195	1	1
Atlanta		(did not play)				
N.Y. Jets		(did not play)				
Seattle (P)	25	15	60.0	193	2	2
Totals	**296**	**173**	**58.4**	**2210**	**20**	**6**
Postseason	**25**	**15**	**60.0**	**193**	**2**	**2**

1984

Opponent	Att	Comp	Pct	Yds	TD	Int
At Washington	28	21	75.0	311	5	0
New England	27	16	59.3	234	2	2
At Buffalo	35	26	74.3	296	3	1
Indianapolis	29	14	48.3	257	2	0
At St. Louis	36	24	66.7	429	3	0
At Pittsburgh	24	16	66.7	226	2	1
Houston	32	25	78.1	321	3	0
At New England	39	24	61.5	316	4	1
Buffalo	28	19	67.9	282	3	3
At N.Y. Jets	42	23	54.8	422	2	2
Philadelphia	34	20	58.9	246	1	1
At San Diego	41	28	68.3	338	2	1
N.Y. Jets	31	19	61.3	192	4	0
L.A. Raiders	57	35	61.4	470	4	2
At Indianapolis	41	29	70.7	404	4	1
Dallas	40	23	57.5	340	4	2
Seattle (P)	34	21	61.8	262	3	2
Pittsburgh (P)	32	21	65.6	421	4	1
San Francisco (SB)	50	29	58.0	318	1	2
Totals	**564**	**362**	**64.2**	**5084**	**48**	**17**
Postseason	**116**	**71**	**61.2**	**1001**	**8**	**5**

1985

Opponent	Att	Comp	Pct	Yds	TD	Int
At Houston	24	13	54.2	159	0	2
Indianapolis	48	29	60.4	329	2	0
Kansas City	35	23	65.7	258	2	1
At Denver	43	25	58.1	390	3	0
Pittsburgh	45	27	60.0	277	1	3
At N.Y. Jets	23	13	56.5	136	0	1
Tampa Bay	39	27	69.2	302	3	1
At Detroit	44	23	52.3	247	2	2
At New England	33	15	51.5	171	0	2
N.Y. Jets	37	21	56.8	362	3	3
At Indianapolis	37	22	59.5	330	1	0
At Buffalo	31	22	70.9	233	2	2
Chicago	27	14	51.9	270	3	1
At Green Bay	44	30	68.2	345	5	1
New England	33	17	51.5	192	1	1
Buffalo	24	15	62.5	136	2	1
Cleveland (P)	45	25	55.6	238	1	1
New England (P)	48	20	41.7	248	2	2
Totals	**587**	**336**	**59.3**	**4137**	**30**	**21**
Postseason	**93**	**45**	**48.4**	**486**	**3**	**3**

Team (W-L Record): Miami, 1983- (67-41-0, .620).

Hall of Fame? Not eligible

Honors: Bert Bell Trophy, 1984; consensus NFL MVP/player of the year, 1984; Sporting News NFL Rookie of the Year, 1983; all-NFL (3), 1984-86; Pro Bowl (5), 1983-87.

Records: Most touchdown passes, season, 48, 1984; most passing yards, season, 5,084, 1984.

Lifetime Rankings: 89.3 passer rating (2nd); 27,853 yards (19th); 220 TDs (8th).

300-Yard Games: 37 (plus 2 postseason)

400-Yard Games: 10 (plus 1 postseason)

Interception Probability: 3.4% (125/3,650)

Last Reported Salary: $1,450,000

Injuries: 1984--sprained knee.

Comments: Here's something you probably didn't know: Marino and Johnny Unitas have the same middle name -- Constantine, no less. Marino's stats speak for themselves. If he stays healthy, he'll probably own most of the passing records when he retires. The question is: Are the Dolphins going to be Super Bowl contenders again while he's still in his prime? His 1988 and '89 seasons were the worst of his career (though far from bad). Maybe he just has less talent around him, or maybe he's beginning to lose interest. Then again, maybe he's just depressed he can't play the Jets every week. He's had games of 521, 448, 427 and 422 yards against them.

1986

Opponent	Att	Comp	Pct	Yds	TD	Int
At San Diego	36	23	63.9	290	3	0
Indianapolis	29	17	58.6	254	1	1
At N.Y. Jets	50	30	60.0	448	6	2
San Francisco	46	27	58.7	301	1	4
At New England	23	13	56.5	167	1	3
Buffalo	41	24	58.5	337	1	1
L.A. Raiders	32	20	62.5	286	3	2
At Indianapolis	42	23	54.8	243	1	0
Houston	29	12	41.4	220	4	2
At Cleveland	39	22	56.4	295	2	1
At Buffalo	54	39	72.2	404	4	0
N.Y. Jets	36	29	80.6	288	4	0
Atlanta	40	20	50.0	303	2	4
At New Orleans	41	27	65.9	241	3	0
At L.A. Rams	46	29	63.0	403	5	1
New England	39	23	59.0	266	3	2
Totals	**623**	**378**	**60.7**	**4746**	**44**	**23**

1987

Opponent	Att	Comp	Pct	Yds	TD	Int
At New England	37	19	51.4	165	3	2
At Indianapolis	32	23	71.9	254	3	0
Buffalo	36	24	66.7	303	4	0
Pittsburgh	31	25	80.6	332	4	2
At Cincinnati	41	26	63.4	262	1	0
Indianapolis	34	14	41.2	194	2	1
At Dallas	39	22	56.4	265	1	1
At Buffalo	28	13	46.4	165	0	3
N.Y. Jets	40	29	72.5	293	1	0
At Philadelphia	39	25	64.1	376	3	1
Washington	50	22	44.0	393	3	1
New England	37	21	56.8	243	1	2
Totals	**444**	**263**	**59.2**	**3245**	**26**	**13**

1988

Opponent	Att	Comp	Pct	Yds	TD	Int
At Chicago	22	9	40.9	113	1	0
At Buffalo	34	22	64.7	221	0	0
Green Bay	33	22	66.7	261	2	2
At Indianapolis	35	22	62.9	276	2	1
Minnesota	37	20	54.1	264	2	3
At L.A. Raiders	36	14	38.9	175	1	1
San Diego	45	26	57.8	329	1	0
N.Y. Jets	60	35	58.3	521	3	5
At Tampa Bay	46	27	58.7	266	2	0
At New England	51	29	56.7	359	1	2
Buffalo	30	19	63.3	224	1	3
New England	29	19	65.5	169	0	0
At N.Y. Jets	35	17	48.6	353	5	0
Indianapolis	32	26	81.3	304	3	1
Cleveland	50	30	60.0	404	4	3
At Pittsburgh	31	17	54.8	195	0	2
Totals	**606**	**354**	**58.4**	**4434**	**28**	**23**

1989

Opponent	Att	Comp	Pct	Yds	TD	Int
Buffalo	38	25	65.8	255	1	2
At New England	28	17	60.7	226	3	3
N.Y. Jets	55	33	60.0	427	3	2
At Houston	29	11	37.9	103	0	2
Cleveland	33	19	57.6	234	1	1
At Cincinnati	33	16	48.5	266	0	1
Green Bay	37	24	64.9	333	2	2
At Buffalo	36	20	55.6	255	1	3
Indianapolis	26	14	53.8	149	2	0
At N.Y. Jets	34	18	52.9	359	3	2
At Dallas	36	21	58.3	255	1	0
Pittsburgh	16	8	50.0	128	1	0
At Kansas City	37	18	48.6	218	3	1
New England	32	21	65.6	300	0	1
At Indianapolis	33	15	45.5	150	0	1
Kansas City	47	28	59.6	339	3	1
Totals	**550**	**308**	**56.0**	**3997**	**24**	**22**

7 JOHN ELWAY (1983-)

1983

Opponent	Att	Comp	Pct	Yds	TD	Int
At Pittsburgh	8	1	12.5	14	0	1
At Baltimore	21	9	42.9	106	0	0
Philadelphia	33	18	54.5	193	1	2
L.A. Raiders	11	6	54.5	71	0	1
At Chicago	10	4	40.0	36	0	1
At Houston			(did not play)			
Cincinnati			(did not play)			
San Diego			(did not play)			
Kansas City			(did not play)			
At Seattle	15	8	55.3	134	1	0
At L.A. Raiders	31	11	35.5	190	0	1
Seattle			(did not play)			
At San Diego	28	14	50.0	147	0	3
Cleveland	24	16	66.7	284	2	1
Baltimore	44	23	52.3	345	3	0
At Kansas City	34	13	38.2	143	0	4
At Seattle (P)	15	10	66.7	123	0	1
Totals	**259**	**123**	**47.5**	**1663**	**7**	**14**
Postseason	**15**	**10**	**66.7**	**123**	**0**	**1**

1984

Opponent	Att	Comp	Pct	Yds	TD	Int
Cincinnati	13	8	61.5	127	1	1
At Chicago	3	2	66.7	11	0	1
At Cleveland	35	15	42.9	170	2	1
Kansas City	29	17	58.6	172	0	2
L.A. Raiders	26	14	53.8	139	0	1
At Detroit	22	16	72.7	210	1	1
Green Bay	20	11	55.0	101	0	1
At Buffalo	23	12	55.2	148	2	0
At L.A. Raiders			(did not play)			
New England	40	26	65.0	315	3	1
At San Diego	35	19	54.3	188	0	0
Minnesota	19	16	84.2	218	5	0
Seattle	27	15	55.6	275	2	1
At Kansas City	36	16	44.4	183	1	1
San Diego	31	18	58.1	193	0	1
At Seattle	21	9	42.9	148	1	4
Pittsburgh (P)	37	19	51.3	184	2	2
Totals	**380**	**214**	**56.3**	**2598**	**18**	**15**
Postseason	**37**	**19**	**51.3**	**184**	**2**	**2**

1985

Opponent	Att	Comp	Pct	Yds	TD	Int
At L.A. Rams	38	18	47.4	229	2	1
New Orleans	43	28	65.1	353	4	1
At Atlanta	38	19	50.0	291	3	2
Miami	37	18	48.6	250	0	1
Houston	35	17	48.6	256	3	3
At Indianapolis	36	17	47.2	239	0	1
Seattle	43	22	51.2	166	0	0
At Kansas City	20	13	65.0	116	0	0
At San Diego	35	20	57.1	222	0	2
San Francisco	42	20	47.6	215	2	1
San Diego	50	28	56.0	261	1	2
At L.A. Raiders	32	19	59.4	164	3	0
At Pittsburgh	41	24	58.5	238	1	1
L.A. Raiders	36	18	50.0	158	1	3
Kansas City	37	22	59.5	301	1	5
At Seattle	42	24	57.1	432	1	0
Totals	**605**	**327**	**54.0**	**3891**	**22**	**23**

1986

Opponent	Att	Comp	Pct	Yds	TD	Int
L.A. Raiders	35	21	60.0	239	2	0
At Pittsburgh	38	21	55.3	243	3	0
At Philadelphia	12	7	58.3	96	1	0
New England	34	18	52.9	188	1	1
Dallas	24	12	50.0	200	3	0
At San Diego	34	20	58.8	242	1	1
At N.Y. Jets	28	13	46.4	145	0	1
Seattle	32	18	56.3	321	1	1
At L.A. Raiders	12	11	91.6	141	1	0
San Diego	31	13	41.9	196	0	3
Kansas City	29	15	51.7	196	0	0
At N.Y. Giants	47	29	61.7	336	0	2
Cincinnati	34	22	64.7	228	3	0
At Kansas City	42	23	54.8	246	1	4
Washington	35	20	57.1	282	1	0
At Seattle	37	20	54.1	186	1	0
New England (P)	32	13	40.6	257	1	2
At Cleveland (P)	38	22	57.9	244	1	1
N.Y. Giants (SB)	37	22	59.5	304	1	1
Totals	**504**	**280**	**55.6**	**3485**	**19**	**13**
Postseason	**107**	**57**	**53.3**	**805**	**3**	**4**

1987

Opponent	Att	Comp	Pct	Yds	TD	Int
Seattle	32	22	68.8	338	4	1
At Green Bay	48	30	62.5	285	0	3
At Minnesota	39	22	56.4	245	2	1
Detroit	30	16	53.3	246	1	0
At Buffalo	30	13	43.3	163	1	0
Chicago	40	21	52.5	341	3	2
At L.A. Raiders	29	16	55.2	298	1	0
At San Diego	32	21	65.6	347	3	1
New England	37	17	45.9	265	2	1
At Seattle	42	21	50.0	335	1	2
Kansas City	31	18	58.1	237	1	0
San Diego	20	7	35.0	98	0	1
Houston (P)	25	14	56.0	259	2	1
Cleveland (P)	26	14	53.8	281	3	1
Washington (SB)	38	14	36.8	257	1	3
Totals	**410**	**224**	**54.6**	**3198**	**19**	**12**
Postseason	**89**	**42**	**47.2**	**797**	**6**	**5**

1988

Opponent	Att	Comp	Pct	Yds	TD	Int
Seattle	45	21	46.7	259	2	2
San Diego	28	17	60.7	259	2	0
At Kansas City	32	15	46.9	213	0	2
L.A. Raiders	28	14	50.0	220	1	4
At San Diego	29	17	58.6	184	0	1
At San Francisco	39	21	53.8	210	1	2
Atlanta	26	16	61.5	235	1	0
At Pittsburgh			(did not play)			
At Indianapolis	27	15	55.6	158	1	0
Kansas City	28	14	50.0	183	1	2
Cleveland	30	21	70.0	207	2	0
At New Orleans	36	18	50.0	166	0	1
L.A. Raiders	36	21	58.3	272	3	1
At L.A. Raiders	49	29	59.2	324	2	3
At Seattle	34	21	61.8	270	1	0
New England	29	14	48.3	149	0	1
Totals	**496**	**274**	**55.2**	**3309**	**17**	**19**

1989

Opponent	Att	Comp	Pct	Yds	TD	Int
Kansas City	28	16	57.1	150	1	2
At Buffalo	28	15	53.6	207	1	2
L.A. Raiders	23	11	47.8	131	2	1
At Cleveland	19	6	31.6	198	1	1
San Diego	35	19	54.3	199	0	1
Indianapolis	25	13	52.0	150	0	1
At Seattle	35	18	51.4	344	2	0
Philadelphia	39	19	48.7	278	2	3
Pittsburgh	21	14	66.7	261	1	2
At Kansas City	22	11	50.0	133	0	1
At Washington			(did not play)			
Seattle	19	10	52.6	217	4	0
At L.A. Raiders	36	23	63.9	197	0	2
N.Y. Giants	47	23	48.9	292	1	0
At Phoenix	29	20	69.0	247	2	2
At San Diego	10	5	50.0	47	1	0
Pittsburgh (P)	20	12	60.0	239	1	1
Cleveland (P)	36	20	55.6	385	3	0
San Francisco (SB)	26	10	38.5	108	0	2
Totals	**416**	**223**	**53.8**	**3051**	**18**	**18**
Postseason	**82**	**42**	**51.2**	**732**	**4**	**3**

Team (W-L Record): Denver, 1983-89 (71-36-1, .730).

Hall of Fame? Not eligible

Honors: AP NFL MVP, 1987; UPI AFC Offensive Player of the Year, 1987; Pro Bowl (2), 1986-87.

Records: None

Lifetime Rankings: 73.6 passer rating (--); 21,195 yards (43rd); 120 TDs (--)

300-Yard Games: 13 (plus 2 postseason)

400-Yard Games: 1

Interception Probability: 3.7% (114/3,070)

Last Reported Salary: $1,425,000

Injuries: None

Comment: Elway was the Fran Tarkenton of the '80s -- three Super Bowls in four years, three one-sided losses. But Tarkenton had nice-enough looking numbers to make the Hall of Fame. The same can't be said for Elway. In seven seasons he has never made all-pro. The only category he has ever led the league in is pass attempts (605 in 1985). He's supposed to be a downfield thrower, but just once has he averaged even 7 yards per pass. This, playing in the Almost Football Conference. The arm, the mobility, the smarts -- everything is there. Except the results.

32 JIM BROWN (1957-65)

Opponent	1957 Att.	Yds.	Avg.	TD
N.Y Giants	21	89	4.2	0
At Pittsburgh	15	39	2.6	0
Philadelphia	10	28	2.8	0
At Philadelphia	12	53	4.4	1
At Chi. Cardinals	22	70	3.2	1
Washington	21	109	5.2	0
Pittsburgh	14	76	5.4	0
At Washington	15	68	4.5	0
Los Angeles	31	237	7.6	4
Chi. Cardinals	10	57	5.7	0
At Detroit	16	38	2.4	0
At N.Y. Giants	15	78	5.2	1
At Detroit (C)	20	69	3.5	1
Totals	202	942	4.7	9
Postseason	20	69	3.5	1

1958				
At Los Angeles	24	171	7.1	2
At Pittsburgh	17	129	7.6	3
Chi. Cardinals	34	182	5.4	3
Pittsburgh	19	153	8.1	1
At Chi. Cardinals	24	180	7.5	4
N.Y. Giants	13	113	8.7	1
Detroit	21	83	4.0	0
At Washington	27	152	5.6	2
Philadelphia	20	66	3.3	0
Washington	11	12	1.1	0
At Philadelphia	21	138	6.6	0
At N.Y. Giants	26	148	5.7	1
At N.Y. Giants (P)	7	8	1.1	0
Totals	257	1527	5.9	17
Postseason	7	8	1.1	0

1959				
At Pittsburgh	19	81	4.3	0
At Chi. Cardinals	37	147	4.0	2
N.Y. Giants	22	86	3.9	0
Chi. Cardinals	27	123	4.6	0
Washington	17	122	7.2	1
At Baltimore	32	178	5.6	5
Philadelphia	29	125	4.3	2
At Washington	16	40	2.5	0
Pittsburgh	15	111	7.4	0
San Francisco	28	114	4.1	2
At N.Y. Giants	15	50	3.3	0
At Philadelphia	33	152	4.6	2
Totals	290	1329	4.6	14

1960				
At Philadelphia	24	153	6.4	1
Pittsburgh	19	87	4.6	1
At Dallas	7	25	3.6	1
Philadelphia	22	167	7.6	1
At Washington	12	60	5.0	1
N.Y. Giants	11	29	2.6	0
St. Louis	28	173	6.2	2
At Pittsburgh	17	86	5.1	0
At St. Louis	24	132	5.5	0
Washington	15	135	9.0	0
Chi. Bears	22	100	4.5	1
At N.Y. Giants	14	110	7.9	1
Detroit (PB)	22	132	6.0	0
Totals	215	1257	5.8	9
Postseason	22	132	6.0	0

1961				
At Philadelphia	19	99	5.2	0
St. Louis	22	94	4.3	0
Dallas	22	98	4.5	1
Washington	17	24	1.4	0
Green Bay	16	72	4.5	0
At Pittsburgh	29	114	3.9	0
At St. Louis	28	109	3.9	0
Pittsburgh	18	110	6.1	1
At Washington	20	133	6.7	0
Philadelphia	34	237	7.0	4
N.Y. Giants	20	68	3.4	1
At Dallas	18	86	4.8	1
At Chi. Bears	18	62	3.4	0
At N.Y. Giants	24	102	4.3	0
Totals	305	1408	4.6	8

Team (W-L Record): Cleveland, 1957-65 (79-34-5, .691).

Hall of Fame? Yes (1st year eligible)

Honors: Bert Bell Trophy, 1963; UPI NFL Player of the Year, 1958, '63, '65; UPI NFL Rookie of the Year, 1957; all-NFL (8), 1957-61, '63-65; Pro Bowl (9), 1957-65.

Records: Most rushing yards, career, 12,312*; most touchdowns, career, 126; most rushing yards, season, 1,863, 1963*; most rushing yards, game, 237, 1957, '61.*

Lifetime Rankings: 2,359 attempts (1st/7th); 12,312 yards (1st/3rd); 106 rushing TDs (1st/2nd).

100-Yard Games: 58 (plus 2 postseason)

200-Yard Games: 4

Avg. Rushing Yards Per Season: 1,368

Avg. Rushing Yards Per Game: 104

Fumble Probability: 2.2% (57/2,650)

Injuries: 1962--severely sprained wrist.

Comment: Brown set a single-game rushing record of 237 yards in 1957 in his ninth NFL game. But it was his '58 season that blew everybody away. At the time, ex-Eagle Steve Van Buren had the league marks of 1,146 rushing yards (1949) and 15 touchdowns (1945, against wartime competition). It took Brown just eight games to break them. If he hadn't retired at 29 to make bad movies, he might still have the career rushing record. But there was no compelling reason to keep playing. He was already the all-time leader by 3,934 yards, nearly 50 percent more than second-place Joe Perry. Only Eric Dickerson has averaged more rushing yards per game -- 107 to 104 -- but Dickerson has played two fewer seasons. We'll see if he's still ahead at the end of 1991.

1962				
N.Y. Giants	17	134	7.9	1
Washington	20	88	4.4	1
At Philadelphia	12	38	3.2	1
Dallas	18	71	3.9	1
Baltimore	14	11	0.8	0
At St. Louis	17	57	3.4	0
At Pittsburgh	21	93	4.4	1
Philadelphia	20	69	3.5	0
At Washington	9	27	3.0	0
St. Louis	19	79	4.2	4
Pittsburgh	19	110	5.8	2
At Dallas	8	29	3.6	0
At N.Y. Giants	14	55	3.9	1
At San Francisco	22	135	6.1	2
Totals	230	996	4.3	13

1963				
Washington	15	162	10.8	2
At Dallas	20	232	11.6	2
Los Angeles	22	95	4.3	1
Pittsburgh	21	175	8.3	1
At N.Y. Giants	23	123	5.3	2
Philadelphia	25	144	5.8	0
N.Y. Giants	9	40	4.4	0
At Philadelphia	28	223	8.0	1
At Pittsburgh	19	99	5.2	0
St. Louis	22	154	7.0	1
Dallas	17	51	3.0	0
At St. Louis	29	179	6.2	2
At Detroit	13	61	4.7	0
At Washington	28	125	4.5	0
Green Bay (PB)	11	56	5.1	0
Totals	291	1863	6.4	12
Postseason	11	56	5.1	0

1964				
At Washington	23	89	3.9	2
St. Louis	21	79	3.8	1
At Philadelphia	25	104	4.2	0
Dallas	23	89	3.9	0
Pittsburgh	8	59	7.4	0
At Dallas	26	188	7.2	0
N.Y. Giants	12	56	4.7	0
At Pittsburgh	23	149	6.5	0
Washington	18	121	6.7	1
Detroit	24	147	6.1	2
At Green Bay	20	74	3.7	1
Philadelphia	22	133	6.0	0
At St. Louis	15	59	3.9	0
At N.Y. Giants	20	99	5.0	0
Baltimore (C)	27	114	4.2	0
Totals	280	1446	5.2	7
Postseason	27	114	4.2	0

1965				
At Washington	21	65	3.1	0
St. Louis	17	110	6.5	0
At Philadelphia	27	133	4.9	3
Pittsburgh	29	168	5.8	1
Dallas	22	85	3.9	1
At N.Y. Giants	24	177	7.4	1
Minnesota	18	39	2.2	1
Philadelphia	20	131	6.6	2
N.Y. Giants	20	156	7.8	3
At Dallas	19	99	5.2	1
At Pittsburgh	20	146	7.3	1
Washington	27	141	5.2	1
At Los Angeles	13	20	1.5	0
At St. Louis	12	74	6.2	0
At Green Bay (C)	12	50	4.2	0
Totals	289	1544	5.3	17
Postseason	12	50	4.2	0

40 GALE SAYERS (1965-71)

1965

Opponent	Att.	Yds.	Avg.	TD
At San Francisco	12	44	3.7	0
At Los Angeles	1	18	18.0	1
At Green Bay	17	80	4.7	1
Los Angeles	12	9	0.8	0
At Minnesota	13	64	4.9	1
Detroit	8	21	2.6	0
Green Bay	16	66	4.1	1
Baltimore	11	17	1.5	0
St. Louis	14	62	4.4	1
At Detroit	10	60	6.0	1
At N.Y. Giants	13	113	8.7	2
At Baltimore	16	118	7.4	1
San Francisco	9	113	12.6	4
Minnesota	14	82	5.9	1
Totals	**166**	**867**	**5.2**	**14**

1966

Opponent	Att.	Yds.	Avg.	TD
At Detroit	17	79	4.6	0
At Los Angeles	18	97	5.4	2
At Minnesota	9	40	4.4	0
Baltimore	18	106	5.9	2
Green Bay	15	29	1.9	0
Los Angeles	16	87	5.4	0
At St. Louis	19	68	3.6	0
Detroit	21	124	5.9	1
San Francisco	14	87	6.2	0
At Green Bay	20	68	3.4	1
Atlanta	19	172	9.1	0
At Baltimore	16	38	2.4	0
At San Francisco	10	39	3.9	1
Minnesota	17	197	11.6	1
Totals	**229**	**1231**	**5.4**	**8**

1967

Opponent	Att.	Yds.	Avg.	TD
At Pittsburgh	7	2	0.3	0
At Green Bay	15	63	4.2	1
At Minnesota	13	73	5.6	0
Baltimore	14	40	2.9	0
Detroit	22	142	6.5	1
At Cleveland		(did not play)		
Los Angeles	13	13	1.0	0
At Detroit	8	64	8.0	0
N.Y. Giants	14	34	2.4	0
St. Louis	12	51	4.3	0
Green Bay	18	117	6.5	1
At San Francisco	11	30	2.7	1
Minnesota	20	131	6.6	1
At Atlanta	19	120	6.3	1
Totals	**186**	**880**	**4.7**	**7**

1968

Opponent	Att.	Yds.	Avg.	TD
Washington	15	105	7.0	0
At Detroit	12	43	3.6	0
At Minnesota	16	108	6.8	1
At Baltimore	15	105	7.0	1
Detroit	12	38	3.2	0
At Philadelphia	15	77	5.1	0
Minnesota	18	143	7.9	0
At Green Bay	24	205	8.5	0
San Francisco	11	32	2.9	0
Atlanta		(did not play)		
Dallas		(did not play)		
At New Orleans		(did not play)		
At Los Angeles		(did not play)		
Green Bay		(did not play)		
Totals	**138**	**856**	**6.2**	**2**

Team (W-L Record): Chicago, 1965-71 (41-54-3, .434).

Hall of Fame? Yes (1st year eligible)

Honors: UPI Rookie of the Year, 1965; all-NFL (5), 1965-69; Pro Bowl (4), 1965-67, '69.

Records: Most touchdowns, game, 6, 1965; Most touchdowns, season, 22, 1965.*

Lifetime Rankings: 991 attempts (32nd/--); 4,956 rushing yards (19th/--), 39 TDs (T21st/--).

100-Yard Games: 20

200-Yard Games: 1

Avg. Rushing Yards Per Season: 708

Avg. Rushing Yards Per Game: 73

Fumble Probability: 2.8% (34/1,222)

Injuries: 1968--right knee surgery; 1970--left knee surgery; 1971--two more operations on left knee.

Comment: The Joe Namath of running backs. But at least Namath got to play in the Super Bowl. Sayers never even made it to the playoffs. (He used to tear up the Pro Bowl, though, winning back-of-the-game honors three times in four years.) In 1969 Sayers became the first NFL back to rush for 1,000 yards the season after undergoing knee surgery. But an injury to his other knee in '70 finished him. He was probably the greatest kick returner of all time. He was also one of the last players to score a touchdown three different ways in a game. It's been done just six times since 1963. Sayers did it twice in '65 and once in '67. What a loss.

1969

Opponent	Att.	Yds.	Avg.	TD
At Green Bay	10	36	3.6	0
At St. Louis	16	76	4.8	0
At N.Y. Giants	20	81	4.1	0
Minnesota	13	15	1.2	0
At Detroit	9	12	0.8	0
Los Angeles	15	109	7.3	1
At Minnesota	20	116	5.8	1
Pittsburgh	28	112	4.0	2
At Atlanta	14	96	6.9	1
Baltimore	19	62	3.3	1
Cleveland	20	126	6.3	1
At San Francisco	12	41	3.4	1
Green Bay	25	90	3.6	0
Detroit	15	60	4.0	0
Totals	**236**	**1032**	**4.4**	**8**

1970

Opponent	Att.	Yds.	Avg.	TD
At N.Y. Giants	17	43	2.5	0
At Philadelphia		(did not play)		
Detroit		(did not play)		
Minnesota	6	9	1.5	0
San Diego		(did not play)		
Detroit		(did not play)		
At Atlanta		(did not play)		
San Francisco		(did not play)		
At Green Bay		(did not play)		
Buffalo		(did not play)		
At Baltimore		(did not play)		
At Minnesota		(did not play)		
Green Bay		(did not play)		
At New Orleans		(did not play)		
Totals	**23**	**52**	**2.3**	**0**

1971

Opponent	Att.	Yds.	Avg.	TD
Pittsburgh		(did not play)		
At Minnesota		(did not play)		
At Los Angeles		(did not play)		
New Orleans	8	30	3.8	0
At San Francisco	5	8	1.6	0
At Detroit		(did not play)		
Dallas		(did not play)		
Green Bay		(did not play)		
Washington		(did not play)		
Detroit		(did not play)		
At Miami		(did not play)		
At Denver		(did not play)		
At Green Bay		(did not play)		
Minnesota		(did not play)		
Totals	**13**	**38**	**2.9**	**0**

32 O.J. SIMPSON (1969-79)

1969 (Bills)

Opponent	Att.	Yds.	Avg.	TD
N.Y. Jets	10	35	3.5	1
Houston	19	58	3.1	0
Denver	24	110	4.6	0
At Houston	13	27	2.1	0
Boston		(did not play)		
At Oakland	6	50	8.3	0
At Miami	10	12	1.2	0
Kansas City	16	41	2.6	0
At N.Y. Jets	14	70	5.0	0
Miami	21	72	3.4	0
At Boston	17	98	5.8	0
Cincinnati	13	35	2.7	0
At Kansas City	11	62	5.6	1
At San Diego	7	27	3.9	0
Totals	**181**	**697**	**3.9**	**2**

1970

Opponent	Att.	Yds.	Avg.	TD
Denver	18	52	2.9	1
Los Angeles	14	24	1.7	0
N.Y. Jets	21	99	4.7	1
At Pittsburgh	14	60	4.3	1
Miami	11	35	3.2	0
At N.Y Jets	15	55	3.7	0
At Boston	17	123	7.2	1
Cincinnati	10	40	4.0	1
At Baltimore		(did not play)		
At Chicago		(did not play)		
Boston		(did not play)		
At N.Y. Giants		(did not play)		
Baltimore		(did not play)		
At Miami		(did not play)		
Totals	**120**	**488**	**4.1**	**5**

1971

Opponent	Att.	Yds.	Avg.	TD
Dallas	14	25	1.8	1
Miami	9	82	9.1	1
At Minnesota	12	45	3.8	0
Baltimore	7	-10	-1.4	0
At N.Y. Jets	18	69	3.8	1
At San Diego	18	106	5.9	0
St. Louis	16	42	2.6	0
At Miami	10	90	9.0	0
At New England	16	61	3.8	0
N.Y. Jets	14	48	3.4	0
New England	14	61	4.4	1
At Baltimore	9	26	2.9	0
Houston	12	29	2.4	1
At Kansas City	14	68	4.9	0
Totals	**183**	**742**	**4.1**	**5**

1972

Opponent	Att.	Yds.	Avg.	TD
N.Y. Jets	14	41	2.9	0
San Francisco	29	138	4.8	0
Baltimore	21	78	3.7	0
New England	13	31	2.4	1
At Oakland	28	144	5.1	0
At Miami	16	57	3.6	0
Pittsburgh	22	189	8.6	1
Miami	13	45	3.5	0
At N.Y. Jets	20	89	4.5	0
At New England	22	103	4.7	1
At Cleveland	27	93	3.4	1
At Baltimore	14	26	1.9	1
Detroit	27	116	4.3	0
At Washington	26	101	3.9	1
Totals	**292**	**1251**	**4.3**	**6**

1973

Opponent	Att.	Yds.	Avg.	TD
At New England	29	250	8.6	2
At San Diego	22	103	4.7	1
N.Y. Jets	24	123	5.1	0
Philadelphia	27	171	6.3	1
Baltimore	22	166	7.5	2
At Miami	14	55	3.9	0
Kansas City	39	157	4.0	2
At New Orleans	20	79	3.9	0
Cincinnati	20	99	5.0	1
Miami	20	120	6.0	0
At Baltimore	15	124	8.3	1
At Atlanta	24	137	5.7	0
New England	22	219	10.0	1
At N.Y. Jets	34	200	5.9	1
Totals	**332**	**2003**	**6.0**	**12**

1974

Opponent	Att.	Yds.	Avg.	TD
Oakland	12	78	6.5	0
Miami	15	63	4.2	0
N.Y. Jets	31	117	3.8	0
At Green Bay	16	62	3.9	0
At Baltimore	23	127	5.5	0
New England	32	122	3.8	1
Chicago	17	62	3.6	0
At New England	19	74	3.9	1
Houston	17	57	3.4	0
At Miami	14	60	4.3	0
At Cleveland	22	115	5.2	1
Baltimore	24	67	2.8	0
At N.Y. Jets	15	48	3.2	0
At Los Angeles	13	73	5.6	0
At Pittsburgh (P)	15	49	3.3	0
Totals	**270**	**1125**	**4.2**	**3**
Postseason	**15**	**49**	**3.3**	**0**

1975

Opponent	Att.	Yds.	Avg.	TD
N.Y. Jets	32	173	5.4	2
At Pittsburgh	28	227	8.1	1
Denver	26	138	5.3	1
At Baltimore	32	159	5.0	1
N.Y. Giants	34	126	3.7	1
Miami	19	88	4.6	0
At N.Y. Jets	21	94	4.5	0
Baltimore	19	123	6.5	1
At Cincinnati	17	197	11.6	2
New England	27	69	2.6	2
At St. Louis	23	85	3.7	1
At Miami	18	96	5.3	1
At New England	21	185	8.8	1
Minnesota	12	57	4.8	1
Totals	**329**	**1817**	**5.5**	**16**

1976

Opponent	Att.	Yds.	Avg.	TD
Miami	5	28	5.6	0
Houston	16	38	2.4	0
At Tampa Bay	20	39	2.0	0
Kansas City	24	130	5.4	2
At N.Y. Jets	15	53	3.5	0
Baltimore	20	88	4.4	0
New England	25	110	4.4	2
N.Y. Jets	29	166	5.7	0
At New England	6	8	1.3	0
At Dallas	24	78	3.3	0
San Diego	25	118	4.7	0
At Detroit	29	273	9.4	2
At Miami	24	203	8.5	1
At Baltimore	28	171	6.1	1
Totals	**290**	**1503**	**5.2**	**8**

1977

Opponent	Att.	Yds.	Avg.	TD
Miami	21	71	3.4	0
At Denver	15	43	2.9	0
At Baltimore	16	52	3.3	0
N.Y. Jets	23	122	5.3	0
Atlanta	23	138	6.0	0
Cleveland	19	99	5.2	0
At Seattle	9	32	3.6	0
At New England		(did not play)		
Baltimore		(did not play)		
New England		(did not play)		
At Oakland		(did not play)		
Washington		(did not play)		
At N.Y. Jets		(did not play)		
At Miami		(did not play)		
Totals	**126**	**557**	**4.4**	**0**

1978 (49ers)

Opponent	Att.	Yds.	Avg.	TD
At Cleveland	22	78	3.5	0
Chicago	27	108	4.0	0
At Houston	7	7	1.0	0
At N.Y. Giants	20	88	4.4	0
Cincinnati	10	35	3.5	0
At Los Angeles	20	83	4.2	0
New Orleans	17	37	2.2	0
Atlanta	18	96	5.3	1
At Washington	15	46	3.1	0
At Atlanta	5	15	3.0	0
St. Louis		(did not play)		
Los Angeles		(did not play)		
Pittsburgh		(did not play)		
At New Orleans		(did not play)		
Tampa Bay		(did not play)		
At Detroit		(did not play)		
Totals	**161**	**593**	**3.7**	**1**

1979

Opponent	Att.	Yds.	Avg.	TD
At Minnesota		(did not play)		
Dallas	14	43	3.1	1
At Los Angeles	18	73	4.1	0
New Orleans	7	25	3.6	0
At San Diego	16	89	5.6	1
Seattle	15	71	4.7	1
At N.Y. Giants	12	24	2.0	0
Atlanta	10	21	2.1	0
Chicago	9	29	3.2	0
At Oakland	3	8	2.7	0
At New Orleans		(did not play)		
Denver		(did not play)		
Los Angeles	5	30	6.0	0
At St. Louis	3	9	3.0	0
Tampa Bay	6	26	4.3	0
At Atlanta	2	12	6.0	0
Totals	**120**	**460**	**3.8**	**3**

Teams (W-L Record): Buffalo, 1969-77; San Francisco, 1978-79 (47-109-2, .304).

Hall of Fame? Yes (1st year eligible)

Honors: Bert Bell Trophy, 1973; UPI AFC Player of the Year, 1972-73, '75; Sporting News AFC Player of the Year, 1973, '75; all-NFL (5), 1972-76; Pro Bowl (5), 1972-76; AFL All-Star Game (1), 1969.

Records: Most rushing yards, season, 2,003, 1973*; most touchdowns, season, 23, 1975*; most rushing attempts, career, 2,404*; most rushing attempts, game, 39, 1973.*

Lifetime Rankings: 2,404 attempts (1st/6th); 11,236 yards (2nd/7th); 61 TDs (7th/17th).

100-Yard Games: 42

200-Yard Games: 6

Avg. Rushing Yards Per Season: 1,021

Avg. Rushing Yards Per Game: 83

Fumble Probability: 2.3% (62/2,640)

Last Reported Salary: $806,668

Injuries: 1970--knee injury; 1977--knee surgery (cartilage); 1978--shoulder injury; 1979--knee surgery (cartilage).

Comment: You forget how bad Simpson's teams were. Six won three or fewer games. We haven't figured it out for everybody, but he could have the worst winning percentage of any Hall-of-Famer. One unusual thing about his career is that, in his first eight seasons, he averaged better than a yard per carry more on the road than at home (5.45 to 4.4). Wonder what that means. His last 100-yard game came against the Bears in early 1978. The Juice got up for Walter Payton and outrushed him, 108-62.

44 JOHN RIGGINS (1971-85)

1971 (Jets)

Opponent	Att.	Yds.	Avg.	TD
At Baltimore	9	32	3.6	0
At St. Louis	9	36	4.0	0
At Miami	6	17	2.8	0
At New England	22	93	4.2	0
Buffalo	9	32	3.6	0
Miami	10	43	4.3	0
At San Diego	10	63	6.3	0
Kansas City	11	63	5.7	0
Baltimore	10	28	2.8	0
At Buffalo	17	74	4.4	0
San Francisco	13	62	4.8	0
At Dallas	13	36	2.8	0
New England	24	91	3.8	1
Cincinnati	17	99	5.8	0
Totals	**180**	**769**	**4.3**	**1**

1972

Opponent	Att.	Yds.	Avg.	TD
At Buffalo	26	125	4.8	1
At Baltimore	21	87	4.1	0
At Houston	12	67	5.6	0
Miami	10	50	5.0	0
At New England	32	168	5.3	1
Baltimore	21	90	4.3	1
New England	0	0	0.0	0
Washington	20	85	4.3	1
Buffalo	14	64	4.6	1
At Miami	18	83	4.6	1
At Detroit	24	105	4.4	1
New Orleans	9	20	2.2	0
At Oakland	(did not play)			
Cleveland	(did not play)			
Totals	**207**	**944**	**4.6**	**7**

1973

Opponent	Att.	Yds.	Avg.	TD
At Green Bay	6	2	0.3	0
At Baltimore	13	36	2.8	0
At Buffalo	12	43	3.6	0
At Miami	8	16	2.0	0
At New England	28	132	4.7	0
At Pittsburgh	15	42	2.8	1
Denver	8	31	3.9	0
Miami	23	79	3.4	2
New England	19	96	5.1	0
At Cincinnati	2	5	2.5	0
Atlanta	(did not play)			
Baltimore	(did not play)			
At Philadelphia	0	0	0.0	0
Buffalo	(did not play)			
Totals	**134**	**482**	**3.6**	**4**

1974

Opponent	Att.	Yds.	Avg.	TD
At Kansas City	22	116	5.3	0
At Chicago	20	63	3.2	0
At Buffalo	15	37	2.5	1
At Miami	13	39	3.0	0
New England	16	100	6.3	0
Baltimore	8	23	2.9	0
Los Angeles	(did not play)			
Houston	(did not play)			
At N.Y. Giants	(did not play)			
At New England	(did not play)			
Miami	22	93	4.2	0
San Diego	18	61	3.4	2
Buffalo	14	41	2.9	0
At Baltimore	21	107	5.1	2
Totals	**169**	**680**	**4.0**	**5**

1975

Opponent	Att.	Yds.	Avg.	TD
At Buffalo	10	61	6.1	0
At Kansas City	27	145	5.4	2
New England	11	36	3.3	0
At Minnesota	15	45	3.0	1
Miami	11	33	3.0	0
Baltimore	11	23	2.1	0
Buffalo	24	108	4.5	0
At Miami	16	90	5.6	0
At Baltimore	8	14	1.8	1
St. Louis	17	92	5.4	0
Pittsburgh	16	69	4.3	0
At New England	20	152	7.6	2
At San Diego	25	75	3.0	1
Dallas	27	62	2.3	1
Totals	**238**	**1005**	**4.2**	**8**

1976 (Redskins)

Opponent	Att.	Yds.	Avg.	TD
N.Y. Giants	8	25	3.1	0
Seattle	17	71	4.2	0
At Philadelphia	15	38	2.5	0
At Chicago	4	20	5.0	0
Kansas City	10	24	2.4	1
Detroit	11	25	2.3	0
St. Louis	8	14	1.8	0
Dallas	5	21	4.2	0
At San Francisco	9	23	2.6	0
At N.Y. Giants	9	48	5.3	0
At St. Louis	18	49	2.7	0
Philadelphia	6	15	2.5	0
At N.Y. Jets	19	104	5.5	1
At Dallas	23	95	4.1	0
At Minnesota (P)	7	30	4.3	0
Totals	**162**	**572**	**3.5**	**3**
Postseason	**7**	**30**	**4.3**	**0**

Teams (W-L Record): N.Y. Jets, 1971-75; Washington, 1976-85 (115-88, .567).

Hall of Fame? Not eligible

Honors: Bert Bell Trophy, 1983; Super Bowl MVP, 1983; all-NFL (1), 1983; Pro Bowl (1), 1975.

Records: Most touchdowns and rushing TDs, season, 24, 1983.

Lifetime Rankings: 2,916 attempts (3rd/4th); 11,352 yards (4th/5th); 104 TDs (2nd/3rd).

100-Yard Games: 29 (plus 6 in postseason)

Avg. Rushing Yards Per Season: 811

Avg. Rushing Yards Per Game: 65

Fumble Probability: 1.8% (58/3,166)

Last Reported Salary: $715,000

Injuries/Absences: 1972--minor knee surgery; 1973-74--shoulder injury; 1977--knee surgery; 1980--sat out season in contract dispute.

Comment: Riggins ran the ball better longer than any back in NFL history. He rushed for more yards in his 30s (5,683) than he did in his 20s (5,663). Only three other players -- John Henry Johnson, MacArthur Lane and Rocky Bleier -- can make that claim. Statistically, Riggins' prime was from 33 to 35. He averaged 1,250 yards a season and 91 a game in that period (counting the 13-game 1982 strike season and postseason as a season). In 1985, at the age of 36, he topped 100 yards three times in four weeks before giving way to George Rogers for the rest of the year. Riggins wasn't indestructible. In fact, he missed 28 games in 14 seasons. But he always came back for more.

1977

Opponent	Att.	Yds.	Avg.	TD
At N.Y. Giants	20	79	4.0	0
Atlanta	8	4	0.5	0
St. Louis	18	47	2.6	0
At Tampa Bay	17	52	3.1	0
At Dallas	5	21	4.2	0
Totals	**68**	**203**	**3.0**	**0**

1978

Opponent	Att.	Yds.	Avg.	TD
At New England	16	60	3.8	0
Philadelphia	21	76	3.6	0
At St. Louis	16	108	6.8	0
N.Y. Jets	21	114	5.4	0
Dallas	19	96	5.1	0
At Detroit	12	44	3.7	0
At Philadelphia	21	97	4.6	1
At N.Y. Giants	18	78	4.3	0
San Francisco	21	61	2.9	2
At Baltimore	20	60	3.0	1
N.Y. Giants	12	29	2.4	0
St. Louis	(did not play)			
At Dallas	12	40	3.3	0
Miami	11	43	3.9	0
At Atlanta	18	64	3.6	1
Chicago	10	44	4.4	0
Totals	**248**	**1014**	**4.1**	**5**

1979

Opponent	Att.	Yds.	Avg.	TD
Houston	12	54	4.5	0
At Detroit	18	80	4.4	0
N.Y. Giants	15	52	3.5	0
At. St. Louis	12	34	2.8	0
At Atlanta	18	56	3.1	1
At Philadelphia	23	115	5.0	1
At Cleveland	14	31	2.2	0
Philadelphia	19	120	6.3	1
New Orleans	12	47	3.9	0
At Pittsburgh	13	56	4.3	1
St. Louis	17	62	3.6	1
Dallas	12	40	3.3	1
At N.Y. Giants	17	72	4.2	0
Green Bay	17	88	5.2	0
Cincinnati	19	95	5.0	2
At Dallas	22	151	6.9	2
Totals	**260**	**1153**	**4.4**	**9**

1981

Opponent	Att.	Yds.	Avg.	TD
Dallas	8	25	3.1	0
N.Y. Giants	6	28	4.7	0
At St. Louis	(did not play)			
At Philadelphia	9	22	2.4	1
San Francisco	13	47	3.6	0
At Chicago	23	126	5.5	2
At Miami	20	77	3.9	1
New England	15	40	2.7	0
St. Louis	14	53	3.8	3
Detroit	12	28	2.3	0
At N.Y. Giants	26	82	3.2	1
At Dallas	9	12	1.3	0
At Buffalo	7	6	0.9	1
Philadelphia	11	61	5.5	0
Baltimore	7	50	7.1	2
At Los Angeles	15	57	3.8	2
Totals	**195**	**714**	**3.7**	**13**

1982

Opponent	Att.	Yds.	Avg.	TD
At Philadelphia	20	66	3.3	1
At Tampa Bay	34	136	4.0	0
At N.Y. Giants	28	70	2.5	1
Philadelphia	20	52	2.6	0
Dallas	9	26	2.9	0
At St. Louis	26	89	3.4	0
N.Y. Giants	31	87	2.8	0
At New Orleans	9	27	3.0	1
St. Louis	(did not play)			
Detroit (P)	25	119	4.8	0
Minnesota (P)	37	185	5.0	1
Dallas (P)	36	140	3.9	2
Miami (SB)	38	166	4.4	1
Totals	**177**	**553**	**3.1**	**3**
Postseason	**136**	**610**	**4.5**	**4**

1983

Opponent	Att.	Yds.	Avg.	TD
Dallas	27	89	3.3	1
At Philadelphia	27	100	3.7	1
Kansas City	21	84	4.0	1
At Seattle	30	83	2.8	1
L.A. Raiders	26	91	3.5	1
At St. Louis	22	115	5.2	3
At Green Bay	25	98	3.9	2
Detroit	(did not play)			
At San Diego	29	93	3.2	2
St. Louis	17	58	3.4	2
At N.Y. Giants	23	61	2.7	2
At L.A. Rams	22	78	3.5	2
Philadelphia	26	99	3.8	2
Atlanta	23	87	3.8	0
At Dallas	27	89	3.3	1
N.Y. Giants	30	122	4.1	1
L.A. Rams (P)	25	119	4.8	3
San Francisco (P)	36	123	3.4	2
L.A. Raiders (SB)	26	64	2.5	1
Totals	**375**	**1347**	**3.6**	**24**
Postseason	**87**	**306**	**3.5**	**6**

1984

Opponent	Att.	Yds.	Avg.	TD
Miami	15	98	6.5	1
At San Francisco	10	12	1.2	2
N.Y. Giants	30	92	3.1	1
At New England	33	140	4.2	1
Philadelphia	28	104	3.7	1
At Indianapolis	19	94	4.9	1
Dallas	32	165	5.2	0
At St. Louis	32	98	3.1	1
At N.Y. Giants	16	51	3.2	1
Atlanta	32	100	3.1	2
Detroit	(did not play)			
At Philadelphia	26	92	3.5	0
Buffalo	3	6	2.0	1
At Minnesota	(did not play)			
At Dallas	24	111	4.6	1
St. Louis	27	76	2.8	1
Chicago (P)	21	50	2.4	2
Totals	**327**	**1239**	**3.8**	**14**
Postseason	**21**	**50**	**2.4**	**2**

1985

Opponent	Att.	Yds.	Avg.	TD
At Dallas	12	44	3.7	1
Houston	16	84	5.3	0
Philadelphia	12	32	2.7	0
At Chicago	11	29	2.6	1
St. Louis	17	103	6.1	0
Detroit	21	114	5.4	3
At N.Y. Giants	11	35	3.2	0
At Cleveland	30	112	3.7	1
Atlanta	(did not play)			
Dallas	7	34	4.9	0
N.Y. Giants	11	7	0.6	1
At Pittsburgh	18	44	2.4	0
San Francisco	10	39	3.9	0
At Philadelphia	(did not play)			
Cincinnati	(did not play)			
At St. Louis	(did not play)			
Totals	**176**	**677**	**3.8**	**8**

32 FRANCO HARRIS (1972-84)

1972 (Steelers)

Opponent	Att.	Yds.	Avg.	TD
Oakland	10	28	2.8	0
At Cincinnati	13	35	2.7	0
At St. Louis	(did not play)			
At Dallas	3	16	5.3	0
Houston	19	115	6.1	1
New England	11	27	2.5	0
At Buffalo	15	138	9.2	2
Cincinnati	15	101	6.7	1
Kansas City	17	134	7.9	1
At Cleveland	12	136	11.3	1
Minnesota	17	128	7.5	1
Cleveland	20	102	5.1	2
At Houston	21	61	2.9	0
At San Diego	15	34	2.3	1
Oakland (P)	18	64	3.6	0
Miami (P)	16	76	4.8	0
Totals	**188**	**1055**	**5.6**	**10**
Postseason	**34**	**140**	**4.1**	**0**

1973

Opponent	Att.	Yds.	Avg.	TD
Detroit	(did not play)			
Cleveland	4	14	3.5	0
At Houston	8	25	3.1	0
San Diego	7	14	2.0	0
At Cincinnati	(did not play)			
N.Y. Jets	25	102	4.1	1
Cincinnati	21	43	2.0	0
Washington	25	90	3.6	0
At Oakland	20	77	3.8	1
Denver	11	53	4.8	0
At Cleveland	22	48	2.2	0
At Miami	15	105	7.0	1
Houston	20	73	3.7	0
At San Francisco	10	54	5.4	0
At Oakland (P)	10	29	2.9	0
Totals	**188**	**698**	**3.7**	**3**
Postseason	**10**	**29**	**2.9**	**0**

1974

Opponent	Att.	Yds.	Avg.	TD
Baltimore	13	49	3.8	1
At Denver	20	70	3.5	0
Oakland	1	6	6.0	0
At Houston	(did not play)			
At Kansas City	(did not play)			
Cleveland	14	81	5.8	1
Atlanta	28	141	5.4	1
Philadelphia	20	70	3.5	1
At Cincinnati	17	75	4.4	0
At Cleveland	23	156	6.8	0
At New Orleans	19	114	6.0	0
Houston	7	29	4.1	0
At New England	29	136	4.7	1
Cincinnati	17	79	4.6	0
Buffalo (P)	24	74	3.1	3
At Oakland (P)	29	111	3.8	2
Minnesota (SB)	34	158	4.7	1
Totals	**208**	**1006**	**4.8**	**5**
Postseason	**87**	**343**	**3.9**	**6**

1975

Opponent	Att.	Yds.	Avg.	TD
At San Diego	17	78	4.6	0
Buffalo	18	84	4.7	2
At Cleveland	17	57	3.4	1
Denver	21	69	3.3	0
Chicago	17	41	2.4	1
At Green Bay	8	16	2.0	0
At Cincinnati	27	157	5.8	0
Houston	19	68	3.6	0
Kansas City	17	119	7.0	0
At Houston	21	149	7.0	2
At N.Y. Jets	14	61	4.4	0
Cleveland	25	103	4.1	2
Cincinnati	20	118	5.9	2
At L.A. Rams	21	126	6.0	0
Baltimore (P)	27	153	5.7	1
Oakland (P)	27	79	2.9	1
Dallas (SB)	27	82	3.0	0
Totals	**262**	**1246**	**4.8**	**10**
Postseason	**81**	**314**	**3.9**	**2**

1976

Opponent	Att.	Yds.	Avg.	TD
At Oakland	18	68	4.3	1
Cleveland	25	118	4.7	1
New England	19	78	4.1	2
At Minnesota	17	34	2.0	0
At Cleveland	13	39	3.0	1
Cincinnati	41	143	3.5	2
At N.Y. Giants	27	106	3.9	2
San Diego	11	32	2.9	0
At Kansas City	23	117	5.1	2
Miami	22	110	5.0	1
Houston	10	37	3.7	0
At Cincinnati	26	87	3.3	1
Tampa Bay	14	55	3.9	0
At Houston	23	104	4.3	1
At Baltimore (P)	18	132	7.3	0
At Oakland (P)	(did not play)			
Totals	**289**	**1128**	**3.9**	**14**
Postseason	**18**	**132**	**7.3**	**0**

Teams (W-L Record): Pittsburgh, 1972-83; Seattle, 1984 (127-53-1, .704).

Hall of Fame? Not eligible

Honors: Super Bowl MVP, 1975; UPI and Sporting News AFC Rookie of the Year, 1972; all-NFL (1), 1977; Pro Bowl (9), 1972-80.

Records: Most rushing attempts, game, 41, 1976.*

Lifetime Rankings: 2,949 attempts (2nd/2nd); 12,120 yards (3rd/4th); 91 TDs (3rd/4th).

100-Yard Games: 47 (plus 5 postseason)

200-Yard Games: None

Avg. Rushing Yards Per Season: 932

Avg. Rushing Yards Per Game: 71

Fumble Probability: 2.8% (90/3,266)

Last Reported Salary: $350,000 (1983)

Injuries: None

Comment: Harris was always catching heck for his unphysical running style. But taking on too many tacklers is what got Earl Campbell early retirement. Four Super Bowl rings, the Immaculate Reception -- except for the sad way it ended with Seattle, there isn't much about Harris' career you'd want to change.

1977

Opponent	Att.	Yds.	Avg.	TD
San Francisco	27	100	3.7	2
Oakland	16	64	4.0	0
At Cleveland	22	72	3.3	0
At Houston	16	55	3.4	0
Cincinnati	16	73	4.6	0
Houston	23	77	3.3	2
At Baltimore	20	85	4.3	2
At Denver	23	62	2.7	0
Cleveland	28	99	3.5	1
Dallas	29	179	6.2	2
At N.Y. Jets	21	83	4.0	1
Seattle	23	103	4.5	0
At Cincinnati	25	95	3.8	1
At San Diego	11	15	1.4	0
At Denver (P)	28	92	3.3	1
Totals	**300**	**1162**	**3.9**	**11**
Postseason	**28**	**92**	**3.3**	**1**

1978

Opponent	Att.	Yds.	Avg.	TD
At Buffalo	27	96	3.6	1
Seattle	18	64	3.6	1
At Cincinnati	16	73	4.6	1
Cleveland	26	84	3.2	0
At N.Y. Jets	20	67	3.3	0
Atlanta	20	104	5.2	0
At Cleveland	15	41	2.7	0
Houston	16	56	3.1	0
Kansas City	25	90	3.6	2
New Orleans	15	57	3.8	0
At L.A. Rams	22	50	2.3	0
Cincinnati	22	64	2.9	0
At San Francisco	12	61	5.1	0
At Houston	27	102	3.8	0
Baltimore	17	52	3.1	2
At Denver	12	21	1.8	1
Denver (P)	24	104	4.4	2
Houston (P)	20	51	2.5	1
Dallas (SB)	20	68	3.4	1
Totals	**310**	**1082**	**3.5**	**8**
Postseason	**64**	**223**	**3.5**	**4**

1979

Opponent	Att.	Yds.	Avg.	TD
At New England	26	74	2.8	0
Houston	14	42	3.0	0
At St. Louis	13	29	2.2	0
Baltimore	(did not play)			
At Philadelphia	11	44	4.0	0
At Cleveland	19	153	8.1	2
At Cincinnati	9	45	5.0	0
Denver	17	121	7.1	2
Dallas	18	102	5.7	2
Washington	15	62	4.1	0
At Kansas City	20	68	3.4	0
At San Diego	20	44	2.2	0
Cleveland	32	151	4.7	2
Cincinnati	20	92	4.6	1
At Houston	12	59	4.9	0
Buffalo	21	100	4.8	2
Miami (P)	21	83	4.0	1
Houston (P)	21	85	4.1	0
Los Angeles (SB)	20	46	2.3	2
Totals	**267**	**1186**	**4.4**	**11**
Postseason	**62**	**214**	**3.5**	**3**

1980

Opponent	Att.	Yds.	Avg.	TD
Houston	20	46	2.3	1
At Baltimore	17	47	2.8	0
At Cincinnati	12	59	4.9	0
Chicago	22	102	4.6	1
At Minnesota	13	47	3.6	0
Cincinnati	(did not play)			
Oakland	(did not play)			
At Cleveland	15	56	3.7	0
Green Bay	(did not play)			
At Tampa Bay	(did not play)			
Cleveland	15	40	2.7	0
At Buffalo	12	57	4.8	1
Miami	28	116	4.1	1
At Houston	15	54	3.6	0
Kansas City	18	62	3.4	0
At San Diego	9	30	3.3	0
Totals	**208**	**789**	**3.8**	**4**

1981

Opponent	Att.	Yds.	Avg.	TD
Kansas City	19	70	3.7	2
At Miami	13	38	2.9	0
N.Y. Jets	13	68	5.2	0
New England	17	63	3.7	2
At New Orleans	13	59	4.5	0
Cleveland	13	80	6.2	0
At Cincinnati	8	24	3.0	0
Houston	17	84	4.9	1
San Francisco	17	104	6.3	0
At Seattle	15	61	4.1	0
At Atlanta	17	54	3.2	0
At Cleveland	20	75	3.8	1
Los Angeles	18	114	6.3	1
At Oakland	11	15	1.4	0
Cincinnati	14	42	3.0	0
At Houston	17	36	2.1	0
Totals	**242**	**987**	**4.1**	**8**

1982

Opponent	Att.	Yds.	Avg.	TD
At Dallas	24	103	4.3	0
Cincinnati	6	3	0.5	0
At Houston	13	59	4.5	0
At Seattle	6	33	5.6	0
Kansas City	18	68	3.8	1
At Buffalo	13	52	4.0	0
At Cleveland	14	65	4.6	0
New England	23	101	4.4	1
Cleveland	23	120	5.2	1
San Diego (P)	10	35	3.5	0
Totals	**140**	**604**	**4.3**	**2**
Postseason	**10**	**35**	**3.5**	**0**

1983

Opponent	Att.	Yds.	Avg.	TD
Denver	14	27	1.9	1
At Green Bay	22	118	5.4	1
At Houston	26	115	4.4	1
New England	25	106	4.2	0
Houston	16	51	3.9	0
At Cincinnati	7	23	3.3	0
Cleveland	15	38	2.5	1
At Seattle	31	132	4.3	1
Tampa Bay	13	37	2.8	0
San Diego	22	70	3.9	0
At Baltimore	19	65	3.4	0
Minnesota	11	33	3.0	0
At Detroit	5	16	3.2	0
Cincinnati	7	17	2.4	0
At N.Y. Jets	26	103	4.0	0
At Cleveland	20	56	2.8	0
At L.A. Raiders (P)	6	33	5.5	0
Totals	**279**	**1007**	**3.6**	**5**
Postseason	**6**	**33**	**5.5**	**0**

1984 (Seahawks)

Opponent	Att.	Yds.	Avg.	TD
San Diego	14	46	3.3	0
At New England	10	13	1.3	0
Chicago	14	23	1.6	0
At Minnesota	9	52	5.8	0
At L.A. Raiders	9	13	1.4	0
Buffalo	3	4	1.3	0
At Green Bay	6	16	2.7	0
At San Diego	3	3	1.0	0
Totals	**68**	**170**	**2.5**	**0**

34 WALTER PAYTON (1975-87)

1975

Opponent	Att.	Yds.	Avg.	TD
Baltimore	8	0	0.0	0
Philadelphia	21	95	4.5	0
At Minnesota	18	61	3.4	0
At Detroit	10	0	0.0	0
At Pittsburgh		(did not play)		
Minnesota	10	44	4.4	0
Miami	7	26	3.7	1
Green Bay	14	49	3.5	0
At San Francisco	23	105	4.6	0
At Los Angeles	4	2	0.5	0
At Green Bay	12	40	3.3	1
Detroit	27	65	2.4	2
St. Louis	17	58	3.4	1
At New Orleans	25	134	5.4	1
Totals	**196**	**679**	**3.5**	**7**

1976

Detroit	25	70	2.8	0
At San Francisco	28	148	5.3	2
Atlanta	23	86	3.7	0
Washington	18	104	5.8	1
At Minnesota	19	141	7.4	2
At L.A. Rams	27	145	5.4	1
At Dallas	17	41	2.4	1
Minnesota	15	67	4.5	1
Oakland	36	97	2.7	3
Green Bay	18	109	6.1	1
At Detroit	17	40	2.4	0
At Green Bay	27	110	4.1	0
At Seattle	27	183	6.8	0
Denver	14	49	3.5	1
Totals	**311**	**1390**	**4.5**	**13**

1977

Detroit	23	160	7.0	2
At St. Louis	11	36	3.3	0
New Orleans	19	140	7.4	2
L.A. Rams	24	126	5.3	0
At Minnesota	24	122	5.1	0
Atlanta	24	69	2.9	0
At Green Bay	23	205	8.9	2
At Houston	18	79	4.4	0
Kansas City	33	192	5.8	3
Minnesota	40	275	6.9	1
At Detroit	20	137	6.9	1
At Tampa Bay	33	101	3.1	1
Green Bay	32	163	5.1	2
At N.Y. Giants	15	47	3.1	0
At Dallas (P)	19	60	3.2	0
Totals	**339**	**1852**	**5.5**	**14**
Postseason	**19**	**60**	**3.2**	**0**

1978

St. Louis	26	101	3.9	1
At San Francisco	21	62	3.0	0
At Detroit	22	77	3.5	1
Minnesota	24	58	2.4	2
Oakland	27	123	4.6	0
At Green Bay	19	82	4.3	0
At Denver	22	157	7.1	0
At Tampa Bay	15	34	2.3	0
Detroit	18	89	4.9	0
Seattle	18	109	6.1	1
At Minnesota	23	127	5.5	2
Atlanta	20	34	1.7	1
Tampa Bay	27	105	3.9	1
At San Diego	17	50	2.9	0
Green Bay	18	97	5.4	1
At Washington	16	90	5.6	1
Totals	**333**	**1395**	**4.2**	**11**

1979

Green Bay	36	125	3.5	0
Minnesota	23	182	7.9	0
At Dallas	22	134	6.1	0
At Miami	15	43	2.9	0
Tampa Bay	15	46	3.1	0
At Buffalo	39	155	4.0	1
New England	15	42	2.8	0
At Minnesota	23	111	4.8	1
At San Francisco	23	162	7.0	3
Detroit	22	113	5.1	2
L.A. Rams	18	41	2.3	1
N.Y. Jets	20	53	2.7	0
At Detroit	18	54	3.0	0
At Tampa Bay	22	77	3.5	1
At Green Bay	25	115	4.6	0
St. Louis	33	157	4.8	2
At Philadelphia (P)	16	67	4.2	2
Totals	**369**	**1610**	**4.4**	**14**
Postseason	**16**	**67**	**4.2**	**2**

Team (W-L Record): Chicago, 1975-87 (109-82-0, .571).

Hall of Fame? Not eligible

Honors: Bert Bell Trophy, 1985; consensus NFL/NFC player of the year, 1977; Sporting News NFC Player of the Year, 1976; all-NFL (7), 1976-80, '84-85; Pro Bowl (9), 1976-80, '83-86.

Records: Most rushing yards career, 16,726; most 100-yard rushing games, career, 77; most rushing touchdowns, career, 110; most rushing yards, game, 275, 1977.

Lifetime Rankings: 3,838 attempts (1st/1st); 16,726 yards (1st/1st); 110 TDs (1st/1st).

100-Yard Games: 77 (plus 1 postseason)

200-Yard Games: 2

Avg. Rushing Yards Per Season: 1,287

Avg. Rushing Yards Per Game: 88

Fumble Probability: 2% (86/4,347)

Last Reported Salary: $1,000,000

Injuries: None

Comment: Payton should donate his knees to science. He ran with the ball 4,347 times in the artificial turf era and missed just one game (in 1975, because of a bruised thigh and knee). The second wind he got from 1983 to '86 was remarkable. He's the only NFL player to have three 1,000-yard rushing seasons in his 30s. We could have listed Payton among the runner/receivers just as easily. His 492 receptions are the most by a back, though Roger Craig figures to pass him in 1990.

1980

At Green Bay	31	65	2.1	0
New Orleans	18	183	10.2	1
Minnesota	16	39	2.4	0
At Pittsburgh	12	60	5.0	0
Tampa Bay	28	183	6.5	0
At Minnesota	23	102	4.4	0
Detroit	27	101	3.7	0
At Philadelphia	17	79	4.6	0
At Cleveland	11	30	2.7	0
Washington	17	107	6.3	1
Houston	18	60	3.3	0
At Atlanta	12	40	3.3	1
At Detroit	18	123	6.8	0
Green Bay	22	130	5.9	3
Cincinnati	18	78	4.3	0
At Tampa Bay	29	130	4.5	0
Totals	**317**	**1460**	**4.6**	**6**

1981

Green Bay	19	81	4.3	1
At San Francisco	27	97	3.6	1
Tampa Bay	21	64	3.0	0
L.A. Rams	17	45	2.6	0
At Minnesota	20	49	2.5	0
Washington	5	5	1.0	0
At Detroit	19	89	4.7	1
San Diego	36	107	3.0	1
At Tampa Bay	22	92	4.2	1
At Kansas City	21	70	3.3	0
At Green Bay	22	105	4.8	1
Detroit	13	37	2.8	0
At Dallas	38	179	4.7	0
Minnesota	33	112	3.4	0
At Oakland	7	28	4.0	0
Denver	19	62	3.3	0
Totals	**339**	**1222**	**3.6**	**6**

1982

At Detroit	14	26	1.9	0
New Orleans	8	20	2.5	0
Detroit	21	87	4.1	0
At Minnesota	12	67	5.6	0
New England	13	70	5.4	0
At Seattle	14	40	2.9	0
St. Louis	20	73	3.7	0
At L.A. Rams	20	104	5.2	1
At Tampa Bay	26	109	4.2	0
Totals	**148**	**596**	**4.0**	**1**

1983

Atlanta	20	103	5.2	0
Tampa Bay	17	45	2.6	0
At New Orleans	28	161	5.8	0
At Baltimore	3	4	1.3	0
Denver	23	91	4.0	0
Minnesota	20	102	5.1	2
At Detroit	15	86	5.7	0
At Philadelphia	30	82	2.7	0
Detroit	20	80	4.0	0
At L.A. Rams	14	62	4.4	0
Philadelphia	23	131	5.7	0
At Tampa Bay	22	106	4.8	2
San Francisco	16	68	4.3	0
At Green Bay	16	58	3.6	0
At Minnesota	17	94	5.5	0
Green Bay	30	148	4.9	0
Totals	**314**	**1421**	**4.5**	**6**

1984

Tampa Bay	16	61	3.8	0
Denver	20	179	9.0	1
At Green Bay	27	110	4.1	0
At Seattle	24	116	4.8	0
Dallas	25	155	6.2	1
New Orleans	32	154	4.8	0
At St. Louis	23	100	4.3	1
At Tampa Bay	20	72	3.6	2
Minnesota	22	54	2.5	0
L.A. Raiders	27	111	4.1	2
At L.A. Rams	13	60	4.6	0
Detroit	29	66	2.3	0
At Minnesota	23	117	5.1	1
At San Diego	23	92	4.0	1
Green Bay	35	175	5.0	1
At Detroit	22	62	2.8	0
At Washington (P)	24	104	4.3	0
At San Francisco (P)	22	92	4.2	0
Totals	**381**	**1684**	**4.4**	**11**
Postseason	**46**	**196**	**4.3**	**0**

1985

Tampa Bay	17	120	7.1	0
New England	11	39	3.5	0
At Minnesota	15	62	4.1	0
Washington	7	6	0.9	0
At Tampa Bay	16	63	3.9	2
At San Francisco	24	132	5.5	2
Green Bay	25	112	4.5	2
Minnesota	19	118	6.2	0
At Green Bay	28	192	6.9	1
Detroit	26	107	4.1	0
At Dallas	22	132	6.0	0
Atlanta	20	102	5.1	1
At Miami	23	121	5.3	0
Indianapolis	26	111	4.3	1
At N.Y. Jets	28	53	1.9	0
At Detroit	17	81	4.8	0
N.Y. Giants (P)	27	93	3.4	0
L.A. Rams (P)	18	32	1.8	0
New England (SB)	22	61	2.8	0
Totals	**324**	**1551**	**4.8**	**9**
Postseason	**67**	**186**	**2.8**	**0**

1986

Cleveland	22	113	5.1	1
Philadelphia	34	177	5.2	1
At Green Bay	18	57	3.2	1
At Cincinnati	10	51	5.1	0
Minnesota	26	108	4.2	1
At Houston	22	76	3.5	1
At Minnesota	9	28	3.1	0
Detroit	21	67	3.2	0
L.A. Rams	19	61	3.2	0
At Tampa Bay	20	139	7.0	0
At Atlanta	20	69	3.5	0
Green Bay	17	85	5.0	0
Pittsburgh	31	90	2.9	1
Tampa Bay	20	78	3.9	1
At Detroit	19	83	4.4	0
At Dallas	13	51	3.9	1
Washington (P)	14	38	2.7	0
Totals	**321**	**1333**	**4.2**	**8**
Postseason	**14**	**38**	**2.7**	**0**

1987

N.Y. Giants	18	42	2.3	0
Tampa Bay	15	24	1.6	1
At Tampa Bay	6	30	5.0	0
Kansas City	8	15	1.9	0
At Green Bay	12	49	4.1	1
At Denver	12	73	6.1	0
Detroit	13	60	4.6	0
Green Bay	8	22	2.8	0
At Minnesota	10	39	3.9	0
At San Francisco	7	18	2.6	0
Seattle	17	79	4.6	2
At L.A. Raiders	20	82	4.1	0
Washington (P)	18	85	4.7	0
Totals	**146**	**533**	**3.7**	**4**
Postseason	**18**	**85**	**4.7**	**0**

33 TONY DORSETT (1977-88)

1977 (Cowboys)

Opponent	Att.	Yds.	Avg.	TD
At Minnesota	4	11	2.8	0
N.Y. Giants	7	62	8.9	2
Tampa Bay	10	72	7.2	0
At St. Louis	14	141	10.1	2
Washington	19	51	2.7	0
At Philadelphia	13	48	3.7	1
Detroit	13	48	3.7	0
At N.Y. Giants	16	39	2.4	1
St. Louis	16	50	3.1	1
At Pittsburgh	17	73	4.3	1
At Washington	19	64	3.4	1
Philadelphia	23	206	9.0	2
At San Francisco	20	92	4.6	1
Denver	17	50	2.9	0
Chicago (P)	17	85	5.0	2
Minnesota (P)	19	71	3.7	1
Denver (SB)	15	66	4.1	1
Totals	**208**	**1007**	**4.8**	**12**
Postseason	**51**	**222**	**4.4**	**4**

1978

Opponent	Att.	Yds.	Avg.	TD
Baltimore	15	147	9.8	0
At N.Y. Giants	24	111	4.6	1
At Los Angeles	19	38	2.0	0
St. Louis	21	154	7.3	1
At Washington	21	61	2.9	0
N.Y. Giants	17	73	4.3	0
At St. Louis	12	24	2.0	0
Philadelphia	7	24	3.4	0
Minnesota	11	38	3.5	0
At Miami	10	49	4.9	0
At Green Bay	23	149	6.5	2
New Orleans	25	152	6.1	1
Washington	21	72	3.4	0
New England	15	49	3.3	0
At Philadelphia	20	63	3.2	1
At N.Y. Jets	29	121	4.2	1
Atlanta (P)	14	65	4.6	0
At Los Angeles (P)	14	101	7.2	1
Pittsburgh (SB)	16	96	6.0	0
Totals	**290**	**1325**	**4.6**	**7**
Postseason	**44**	**262**	**6.0**	**1**

1979

Opponent	Att.	Yds.	Avg.	TD
At St. Louis		(did not play)		
At San Francisco	19	54	2.8	0
Chicago	20	108	5.4	0
At Cleveland	14	64	4.6	0
Cincinnati	20	119	6.0	0
At Minnesota	21	145	6.9	3
Los Angeles	24	103	4.3	1
St. Louis	20	111	5.6	0
At Pittsburgh	19	73	3.8	0
At N.Y. Giants	16	36	2.3	0
Philadelphia	13	53	4.1	0
At Washington	14	43	3.1	0
Houston	12	54	4.5	1
N.Y. Giants	29	108	3.7	1
At Philadelphia	9	36	4.0	0
Washington		(did not play)		
Los Angeles (P)	19	87	4.6	0
Totals	**250**	**1107**	**4.4**	**6**
Postseason	**19**	**87**	**4.6**	**0**

1980

Opponent	Att.	Yds.	Avg.	TD
At Washington	17	66	3.9	1
At Denver	17	62	3.6	0
Tampa Bay	20	100	5.0	0
At Green Bay	22	77	3.5	1
N.Y. Giants	15	26	1.7	0
San Francisco	19	75	3.9	1
At Philadelphia	6	17	2.8	0
San Diego		(did not play)		
At St. Louis	16	43	2.7	1
At N.Y. Giants	24	183	7.6	2
St. Louis	26	122	4.7	1
Washington	17	59	3.5	0
Seattle	24	107	4.5	2
At Oakland	25	97	3.9	1
At Los Angeles	14	77	5.5	0
Philadelphia	16	74	4.6	0
Los Angeles (P)	22	160	7.3	1
At Atlanta (P)	10	51	5.1	0
At Philadelphia (P)	13	41	3.2	1
Totals	**278**	**1185**	**4.3**	**11**
Postseason	**45**	**252**	**5.6**	**2**

Teams (W-L Record): Dallas, 1977-87; Denver, 1988 (118-64, .648).
Hall of Fame? Not eligible
Honors: UPI NFC Player of the Year, 1983; consensus rookie of the year, 1977; all-NFL (1), 1981; Pro Bowl (4), 1978, '81-83.
Records: Longest run from scrimmage, 99 yards, 1983 ('82 season).
Lifetime Rankings: 2,936 attempts (3rd); 12,739 yards (2nd); 77 TDs (7th).
100-Yard Games: 44 (plus 3 postseason)
200-Yard Games: 1
Avg. Rushing Yards Per Season: 1,062
Avg. Rushing Yards Per Game: 74
Fumble Probability: 2.7% (90/3,334)
Last Reported Salary: $500,000
Injuries: 1989--torn knee ligaments (training camp).
Comment: Dorsett was as lucky as he was good. Unlike most franchise backs, he stepped into an ideal situation in the pros. The Cowboys were at their peak when he joined them in 1977. Had he wound up with Seattle, which originally had his pick, or Tampa Bay, as poor Ricky Bell did, it's hard to say what course his career would have taken. But he probably wouldn't have retired No. 2 on the all-time rushing list. We're not down on Dorsett, necessarily. We just think his statistics are a little inflated.

1981

Opponent	Att.	Yds.	Avg.	TD
At Washington	21	132	6.3	0
St. Louis	16	129	8.1	0
At New England	19	162	8.5	1
N.Y. Giants	22	70	3.2	0
At St. Louis	21	99	4.7	1
At San Francisco	9	21	2.3	0
Los Angeles	27	159	5.9	1
Miami	24	122	5.1	0
At Philadelphia	20	78	3.9	1
Buffalo	28	117	4.2	0
At Detroit	15	55	3.7	0
Washington	23	115	5.0	0
Chicago	19	72	3.8	0
At Baltimore	30	175	5.8	0
Philadelphia	28	101	3.6	0
At N.Y. Giants	20	39	2.0	0
Tampa Bay (P)	16	86	5.4	1
At San Francisco (P)	22	91	4.1	1
Totals	**342**	**1646**	**4.8**	**4**
Postseason	**38**	**177**	**4.7**	**2**

1982

Opponent	Att.	Yds.	Avg.	TD
Pittsburgh	11	30	2.7	0
At St. Louis	22	98	4.5	0
Tampa Bay	15	52	3.5	0
Cleveland	20	116	5.8	2
At Washington	26	57	2.2	0
At Houston	18	65	3.6	0
New Orleans	25	105	4.2	2
Philadelphia	24	69	2.9	0
At Minnesota	16	153	9.6	1
Tampa Bay (P)	26	110	4.2	0
Green Bay (P)	27	99	3.7	0
At Washington (P)	15	57	3.4	0
Totals	**177**	**745**	**4.2**	**5**
Postseason	**68**	**266**	**3.9**	**0**

1983

Opponent	Att.	Yds.	Avg.	TD
At Washington	14	151	10.8	0
At St. Louis	12	35	2.9	0
N.Y. Giants	13	49	3.8	0
New Orleans	16	124	7.8	0
At Minnesota	26	141	5.4	0
Tampa Bay	24	68	2.8	0
Philadelphia	19	92	4.8	1
L.A. Raiders	20	65	3.3	0
At N.Y. Giants	22	94	4.3	0
At Philadelphia	16	51	3.2	1
At San Diego	17	58	3.4	0
Kansas City	18	108	6.0	2
St. Louis	17	102	6.0	2
At Seattle	26	117	4.5	2
Washington	14	34	2.4	0
At San Francisco	15	32	2.1	0
L.A. Rams (P)	17	59	3.5	0
Totals	**289**	**1321**	**4.6**	**8**
Postseason	**17**	**59**	**3.5**	**0**

1984

Opponent	Att.	Yds.	Avg.	TD
At L.A. Rams	25	81	3.2	1
At N.Y. Giants	15	95	6.3	0
Philadelphia	22	66	3.0	0
Green Bay	20	44	2.2	1
At Chicago	18	51	2.8	0
St. Louis	14	96	6.9	1
At Washington	18	81	4.5	2
New Orleans	22	80	3.6	1
Indianapolis	24	104	4.3	0
N.Y. Giants	13	78	6.0	0
At St. Louis	19	84	4.4	0
At Buffalo	17	70	4.1	0
New England	19	49	2.6	0
At Philadelphia	22	110	5.0	0
Washington	15	42	2.8	0
At Miami	19	58	3.1	0
Totals	**302**	**1189**	**3.9**	**6**

1985

Opponent	Att.	Yds.	Avg.	TD
Washington	19	70	3.7	1
At Detroit	12	62	5.2	0
Cleveland	15	67	4.5	0
At Houston	23	159	6.9	0
At N.Y. Giants	25	86	3.4	0
Pittsburgh	21	113	5.4	1
At Philadelphia	20	100	5.0	1
Atlanta	16	90	5.6	1
At St. Louis	16	66	4.1	0
At Washington	22	86	3.9	0
Chicago	12	44	3.7	0
Philadelphia	30	86	2.9	2
St. Louis	19	73	3.8	1
At Cincinnati	17	64	3.8	0
N.Y. Giants	19	92	4.8	0
At San Francisco	19	49	2.6	0
At L.A. Rams (P)	17	58	3.4	0
Totals	**305**	**1307**	**4.3**	**7**
Postseason	**17**	**58**	**3.4**	**0**

1986

Opponent	Att.	Yds.	Avg.	TD
N.Y. Giants	8	25	3.1	0
At Detroit	23	117	5.1	1
Atlanta	17	86	5.1	0
At St. Louis		(did not play)		
At Denver		(did not play)		
Washington	18	22	1.2	0
At Philadelphia	11	54	4.9	1
St. Louis		(did not play)		
At N.Y. Giants	10	45	4.5	1
L.A. Raiders	22	101	4.6	1
At San Diego	14	76	5.4	0
At Washington	11	13	1.2	0
Seattle	14	59	4.2	1
At L.A. Rams	11	36	3.3	0
Philadelphia	14	49	3.5	0
Chicago	11	65	5.9	0
Totals	**184**	**748**	**4.1**	**5**

1987

Opponent	Att.	Yds.	Avg.	TD
At St. Louis	18	60	3.3	0
At N.Y. Giants	18	75	4.2	0
At N.Y. Jets		(did not play)		
Philadelphia	4	27	6.8	1
Washington	19	81	4.3	0
At Philadelphia	11	32	2.9	0
N.Y. Giants	14	3	0.2	0
At Detroit	11	29	2.6	0
At New England	1	5	5.0	0
Miami		(did not play)		
Minnesota	7	19	2.7	0
Atlanta	7	33	4.7	0
At Washington	8	40	5.0	0
At L.A. Rams	12	52	4.3	0
St. Louis		(did not play)		
Totals	**130**	**456**	**3.5**	**1**

1988 (Broncos)

Opponent	Att.	Yds.	Avg.	TD
Seattle	9	32	3.6	0
San Diego	23	113	4.9	1
At Kansas City	10	35	3.5	1
L.A. Raiders	32	119	3.7	2
At San Diego	19	46	2.4	0
At San Francisco	5	12	2.4	0
Atlanta	17	86	5.1	0
At Pittsburgh	12	24	2.0	0
At Indianapolis	6	22	3.7	0
Kansas City	10	44	4.4	0
Cleveland	14	42	3.0	0
At New Orleans	2	3	1.5	0
L.A. Rams	7	21	3.0	0
At L.A. Raiders	5	18	3.6	0
At Seattle	0	0	0.0	0
New England	10	86	8.6	1
Totals	**181**	**703**	**3.9**	**5**

34 EARL CAMPBELL (1978-85)

1978 (Oilers)

Opponent	Att.	Yds.	Avg.	TD
At Atlanta	15	137	9.1	1
At Kansas City	22	111	5.0	2
San Francisco	26	76	2.9	1
Los Angeles	13	77	5.9	0
At Cleveland		(did not play)		
At Oakland	26	103	4.0	0
Buffalo	19	105	5.5	0
At Pittsburgh	21	89	4.2	3
At Cincinnati	18	102	5.7	0
Cleveland	19	71	3.7	0
At New England	24	74	3.1	1
Miami	28	199	7.1	4
Cincinnati	27	122	4.5	0
Pittsburgh	7	41	5.9	0
At New Orleans	24	63	2.6	1
San Diego	14	77	5.5	0
At Miami (P)	26	84	3.2	1
At New England (P)	27	118	4.4	1
At Pittsburgh (P)	22	62	2.8	0
Totals	**302**	**1450**	**4.8**	**13**
Postseason	**75**	**264**	**3.5**	**2**

1979

Opponent	Att.	Yds.	Avg.	TD
At Washington	32	166	5.2	2
At Pittsburgh	16	38	2.4	0
Kansas City	32	131	4.1	1
At Cincinnati	34	158	4.6	1
Cleveland	18	76	4.2	3
St. Louis	13	53	4.1	1
At Baltimore	22	149	6.8	3
At Seattle	3	4	1.3	0
N.Y. Jets	11	37	3.4	1
At Miami	32	120	3.8	0
Oakland	32	107	3.3	1
Cincinnati	19	112	5.9	2
At Dallas	33	195	5.9	2
At Cleveland	22	108	4.9	1
Pittsburgh	33	109	3.3	0
Philadelphia	16	134	8.4	1
Denver (P)	16	50	3.1	1
At San Diego (P)		(did not play)		
At Pittsburgh (P)	17	15	0.9	0
Totals	**368**	**1697**	**4.6**	**19**
Postseason	**33**	**65**	**2.0**	**1**

1980

Opponent	Att.	Yds.	Avg.	TD
At Pittsburgh	13	57	4.4	1
At Cleveland	18	106	5.9	0
Baltimore	7	11	1.6	1
At Cincinnati		(did not play)		
Seattle	12	50	4.2	0
At Kansas City	38	178	4.7	1
Tampa Bay	33	203	6.2	0
Cincinnati	27	202	7.5	2
At Denver	36	157	4.4	2
New England	30	130	4.3	2
At Chicago	31	206	6.6	0
At N.Y. Jets	15	60	4.0	0
Cleveland	27	109	4.0	1
Pittsburgh	21	81	3.9	0
At Green Bay	36	181	5.0	2
Minnesota	29	203	7.0	1
At Oakland (P)	27	91	3.4	1
Totals	**373**	**1934**	**5.2**	**13**
Postseason	**27**	**91**	**3.4**	**1**

Teams (W-L Record): Houston, 1978-84; New Orleans, 1984-85 (51-70, .421).

Hall of Fame? Not eligible

Honors: Bert Bell Trophy, 1979; AP NFL MVP, 1979; UPI and Sporting News AFC Player of the Year, 1978; consensus rookie of the year, 1978; all-pro (3), 1978-80; Pro Bowl (5), 1978-81, '83.

Records: Most 200-yard rushing games, season, 4, 1980.

Lifetime Rankings: 2,187 attempts (7th/9th); 9,407 yards (8th/9th); 74 TDs (T7th/T9th).

100-Yard Games: 40 (plus 1 postseason)

200-Yard Games: 4

Avg. Rushing Yards Per Season: 1,176

Avg. Rushing Yards Per Game: 83

Fumble Probability: 1.9% (43/2,308)

Last Reported Salary: $400,000

Injuries: 1984--knee surgery.

Comment: Campbell's physical running style wasn't conducive to a long career, but he was great while he lasted. He averaged 1,614 yards his first four seasons. His top rushing total -- 1,934 yards, third-most in NFL history -- was accomplished in 15 games in 1980. He was a beat-up back, at the end, though. On his last carry, he broke into the clear for what appeared to be a touchdown, but pulled a thigh muscle, was caught from behind and fumbled.

1981

Opponent	Att.	Yds.	Avg.	TD
At Los Angeles	27	122	4.5	0
At Cleveland	17	42	2.5	0
Miami	19	78	4.1	0
At N.Y. Jets	16	88	5.5	1
Cincinnati	37	182	4.9	1
Seattle	39	186	4.8	2
At New England	27	86	3.2	0
At Pittsburgh	23	56	2.4	0
At Cincinnati	14	74	5.3	0
Oakland	31	86	2.8	0
At Kansas City	21	99	4.7	0
New Orleans	25	96	3.8	2
Atlanta	19	81	4.3	1
Cleveland	15	31	2.1	1
At San Francisco	18	45	2.5	1
Pittsburgh	13	24	1.8	1
Totals	**361**	**1376**	**3.8**	**10**

1982

Opponent	Att.	Yds.	Avg.	TD
At Cincinnati	20	82	4.1	0
Seattle	30	142	4.7	1
Pittsburgh	15	66	4.4	0
At New England	16	37	2.3	1
At N.Y. Giants	23	66	2.9	0
Dallas	7	12	1.7	0
At Philadelphia	18	26	1.4	0
Cleveland	17	43	2.5	0
Cincinnati	11	64	5.8	0
Totals	**157**	**538**	**3.4**	**2**

1983

Opponent	Att.	Yds.	Avg.	TD
Green Bay	27	123	4.6	3
At L.A. Raiders		(did not play)		
Pittsburgh	13	40	3.1	1
At Pittsburgh	30	142	4.7	1
At Pittsburgh	26	69	2.7	1
Denver	19	101	5.3	1
At Minnesota	29	130	4.5	1
Kansas City	7	54	7.7	0
At Cleveland		(did not play)		
Cincinnati	17	49	2.9	0
Detroit	28	107	3.8	0
At Cincinnati	15	38	2.5	0
At Tampa Bay	24	87	3.6	2
Miami	28	138	4.9	1
Cleveland	32	130	4.1	0
At Baltimore	27	93	3.4	0
Totals	**322**	**1301**	**4.0**	**12**

1984 (Oilers 6/Saints 10)

Opponent	Att.	Yds.	Avg.	TD
L.A. Raiders	25	92	3.7	0
Indianapolis	15	44	2.9	3
At San Diego	7	8	1.1	0
At Atlanta	17	49	2.9	0
New Orleans	15	38	2.5	1
At Cincinnati	17	47	2.8	0
L.A. Rams	5	19	3.8	0
At Dallas	12	67	5.6	0
At Cleveland	6	9	1.5	0
Green Bay	7	21	3.0	0
Atlanta		(did not play)		
Pittsburgh	5	13	2.6	0
San Francisco	1	5	5.0	0
At L.A. Rams		(did not play)		
Cincinnati	7	32	4.6	0
N.Y. Giants	7	24	3.4	0
Totals	**146**	**468**	**3.2**	**4**

1985

Opponent	Att.	Yds.	Avg.	TD
Kansas City	11	47	4.3	0
At Denver	14	41	2.9	0
Tampa Bay	14	47	3.4	0
At San Francisco	6	26	4.3	0
Philadelphia		(did not play)		
At L.A. Raiders	8	19	2.4	0
At Atlanta	6	23	3.8	0
N.Y. Giants	10	40	4.0	0
At L.A. Rams	3	36	12.0	0
Seattle	6	19	3.2	0
At Green Bay	4	5	1.3	0
At Minnesota	35	160	4.6	1
L.A. Rams	22	74	3.4	0
At St. Louis	11	35	3.2	0
San Francisco	6	20	3.3	0
Atlanta	2	51	25.5	0
Totals	**158**	**643**	**4.1**	**1**

32 OTTIS ANDERSON (1979-)

1979 (Cardinals)

Opponent	Att.	Yds.	Avg.	TD
Dallas	21	193	9.2	1
At N.Y. Giants	31	109	3.5	0
Pittsburgh	16	37	2.3	1
Washington	19	67	3.5	0
At L.A. Rams	17	75	4.4	0
At Houston	16	109	6.8	0
Philadelphia	21	73	3.5	1
At Dallas	20	105	5.3	0
Cleveland	17	68	4.0	1
Minnesota	25	164	6.6	1
At Washington	25	105	4.2	0
At Philadelphia	17	112	6.6	0
At Cincinnati	16	80	5.0	0
San Francisco	27	129	4.8	1
N.Y. Giants	29	140	4.8	2
At Chicago	14	39	2.8	0
Totals	**331**	**1605**	**4.8**	**8**

1980

Opponent	Att.	Yds.	Avg.	TD
N.Y. Giants	12	85	7.1	1
At San Francisco	20	59	3.0	0
At Detroit	15	71	4.7	0
Philadelphia	27	151	5.6	2
At New Orleans	22	126	5.7	0
L.A. Rams	15	62	4.1	0
At Washington	17	43	2.5	0
At Baltimore	20	51	2.6	1
Dallas	22	92	4.2	0
Atlanta	1	8	8.0	1
At Dallas	16	100	6.3	1
Kansas City	16	107	6.7	1
At N.Y. Giants	31	168	5.4	2
Detroit	28	68	2.4	0
At Philadelphia	17	39	2.3	0
Washington	22	122	5.5	0
Totals	**301**	**1352**	**4.5**	**9**

1981

Opponent	Att.	Yds.	Avg.	TD
Miami	20	52	2.6	1
At Dallas	16	80	5.0	0
Washington	20	48	2.4	1
At Tampa Bay	20	97	4.9	0
Dallas	20	72	3.6	0
At N.Y. Giants	18	71	3.9	1
At Atlanta	18	59	3.3	2
Minnesota	23	77	3.3	0
At Washington	18	122	6.8	0
Philadelphia	12	55	4.6	0
Buffalo	27	177	6.6	2
At Baltimore	29	130	4.5	2
At New England	25	95	3.8	1
New Orleans	26	64	2.5	0
N.Y. Giants	18	75	4.2	0
At Philadelphia	19	102	5.4	0
Totals	**329**	**1376**	**4.2**	**9**

1982

Opponent	Att.	Yds.	Avg.	TD
At New Orleans	22	62	2.8	1
Dallas	17	30	1.8	0
San Francisco	15	65	4.3	1
At Atlanta	20	122	6.1	1
At Philadelphia		(did not play)		
Washington	15	109	7.3	0
At Chicago	16	58	3.6	0
N.Y. Giants	30	110	3.7	0
At Washington	10	31	3.1	0
At Green Bay (P)	8	58	7.3	0
Totals	**145**	**587**	**4.0**	**3**
Postseason	**8**	**58**	**7.3**	**0**

1983

Opponent	Att.	Yds.	Avg.	TD
At New Orleans	18	60	3.3	0
Dallas	13	25	1.9	0
San Francisco	4	10	2.5	0
At Philadelphia	29	133	4.6	0
At Kansas City	21	106	5.0	1
Washington	17	60	3.5	0
At Tampa Bay	13	55	4.2	0
N.Y. Giants		(did not play)		
Minnesota	24	136	5.7	1
At Washington	15	73	4.9	0
Seattle	29	130	4.5	0
San Diego	28	113	4.0	1
At Dallas	13	37	2.8	0
At N.Y. Giants	25	57	2.3	0
At L.A. Raiders	24	119	5.0	0
Philadelphia	23	156	6.8	1
Totals	**296**	**1270**	**4.3**	**5**

1984

Opponent	Att.	Yds.	Avg.	TD
At Green Bay	18	51	2.8	1
Buffalo	20	83	4.2	1
At Indianapolis	23	119	5.2	1
At New Orleans	5	22	4.4	0
Miami		(did not play)		
At Dallas	25	110	4.4	0
Chicago	19	82	4.3	1
Washington	16	76	4.8	0
At Philadelphia	18	75	4.2	0
L.A. Rams	16	33	2.1	0
Dallas	19	69	3.6	0
At N.Y. Giants	24	111	4.6	0
Philadelphia	21	92	4.4	0
At New England	30	136	4.5	1
N.Y. Giants	23	91	4.0	1
At Washington	12	24	2.0	0
Totals	**289**	**1174**	**4.1**	**6**

1985

Opponent	Att.	Yds.	Avg.	TD
At Cleveland	17	55	3.2	1
Cincinnati	20	89	4.5	1
At N.Y. Giants	9	51	5.7	0
Green Bay	20	104	5.2	1
At Washington	9	63	7.0	1
At Philadelphia	14	36	2.6	0
At Pittsburgh	16	88	5.5	0
Houston		(did not play)		
Dallas	11	-10	-0.9	0
At Tampa Bay	1	3	3.0	0
Philadelphia		(did not play)		
N.Y. Giants		(did not play)		
At Dallas		(did not play)		
New Orleans		(did not play)		
At L.A. Rams		(did not play)		
Washington		(did not play)		
Totals	**117**	**479**	**4.1**	**4**

1986 (Cardinals 5/Giants 11)

Opponent	Att.	Yds.	Avg.	TD
L.A. Rams	10	31	3.1	1
At Atlanta		(did not play)		
At Buffalo	7	5	0.7	0
Dallas	16	65	4.1	1
N.Y. Giants	18	55	3.1	0
Philadelphia	7	32	4.6	0
At Seattle	0	0	0.0	0
Washington	2	6	3.0	0
Dallas	4	12	3.0	0
At Philadelphia		(did not play)		
At Minnesota		(did not play)		
Denver		(did not play)		
At San Francisco	2	1	0.5	1
At Washington	0	0	0.0	0
St. Louis	3	9	3.0	0
Green Bay	6	21	3.5	0
San Francisco (P)	4	2	0.5	0
Washington (P)	1	3	3.0	0
Denver (SB)	2	1	0.5	1
Totals	**75**	**237**	**3.2**	**3**
Postseason	**7**	**6**	**0.9**	**1**

1987

Opponent	Att.	Yds.	Avg.	TD
At Chicago	0	0	0.0	0
Dallas	2	6	3.0	0
St. Louis	0	0	0.0	0
At Dallas	0	0	0.0	0
New England		(did not play)		
At Philadelphia		(did not play)		
At New Orleans		(did not play)		
At Washington		(did not play)		
Philadelphia		(did not play)		
At St. Louis		(did not play)		
Green Bay		(did not play)		
N.Y. Jets		(did not play)		
Totals	**2**	**6**	**3.0**	**0**

1988

Opponent	Att.	Yds.	Avg.	TD
Washington	0	0	0.0	0
San Francisco	0	0	0.0	0
At Dallas	4	13	3.3	0
L.A. Rams	2	5	2.5	0
At Washington	3	7	2.3	1
At Philadelphia	0	0	0.0	0
Detroit	13	41	3.2	0
At Atlanta	5	10	2.0	1
At Detroit	6	17	2.8	0
Dallas	9	32	3.6	1
At Phoenix	1	1	1.0	1
Philadelphia	0	0	0.0	0
At New Orleans	0	0	0.0	0
Phoenix	11	34	3.1	3
Kansas City	5	14	2.8	1
At N.Y. Jets	6	34	5.7	0
Totals	**65**	**208**	**3.2**	**8**

1989

Opponent	Att.	Yds.	Avg.	TD
At Washington	23	93	4.0	1
Detroit	25	85	3.4	1
Phoenix	21	98	4.7	1
At Dallas	16	45	2.8	1
At Philadelphia	13	25	1.9	0
Washington	25	101	4.0	0
At San Diego	27	96	3.6	2
Minnesota	29	66	2.3	1
At Phoenix	27	89	3.3	0
At L.A. Rams	9	7	0.8	1
Seattle	23	65	2.8	0
At San Francisco	5	8	1.6	1
Philadelphia	16	46	2.9	1
At Denver	18	34	1.9	1
Dallas	25	91	3.6	1
L.A. Raiders	23	74	3.2	2
L.A. Rams (P)	24	120	5.0	1
Totals	**325**	**1023**	**3.1**	**14**
Postseason	**24**	**120**	**5.0**	**1**

Teams (W-L Record): St. Louis, 1979-86; N.Y. Giants, 1986- (82-82-1, .500).

Hall of Fame? Not eligible

Honors: UPI and Sporting News NFC Player of the Year, 1979; consensus NFL rookie of the year, 1979; all-NFL (1), 1979; Pro Bowl (2), 1979-80.

Records: Most rushing yards by a rookie, 1,605, 1979.*

Lifetime Rankings: 2,274 attempts (8th); 9,317 yards (9th); 69 TDs (T12th).

100-Yard Games: 35 (plus 1 postseason)

200-Yard Games: None

Avg. Rushing Yards Per Season: 847

Avg. Rushing Yards Per Game: 65

Fumble Probability: 2.1% (55/2,621)

Last Reported Salary: $475,000

Injuries: 1985--foot injury.

Comment: In 1989 Anderson nearly became the first 1,000-yard back who didn't have a 100-yard game. He eked out 101 against the Redskins in Week 6. No NFL runner broke in with a bigger bang than Ottis, however. He rushed for 193 yards, still his career high, in his debut against the Cowboys. His '89 comeback stopped a downward spiral that began four years earlier with a foot injury. After 5 1/2 seasons of heavy use, he hardly played in '86, '87 and '88. Maybe workhorse backs should take a sabbatical in mid-career to rejuvenate themselves. It worked for John Riggins, too.

20 BILLY SIMS (1980-84)

1980

Opponent	Att.	Yds.	Avg.	TD
At Los Angeles	22	153	7.0	3
At Green Bay	20	134	6.7	1
St. Louis	25	95	3.8	1
Minnesota	27	157	5.8	0
At Atlanta	14	21	1.5	0
New Orleans	23	91	4.0	2
At Chicago	14	53	3.8	0
At Kansas City	28	155	5.5	2
San Francisco	17	37	2.2	0
At Minnesota	9	21	2.3	0
Baltimore	30	126	4.2	0
At Tampa Bay	15	75	5.0	1
Chicago	19	72	3.8	0
At St. Louis	20	43	2.2	1
Tampa Bay	12	16	1.3	1
Green Bay	18	54	3.0	1
Totals	**313**	**1303**	**4.2**	**13**

1981

Opponent	Att.	Yds.	Avg.	TD
San Francisco	21	59	2.8	1
At San Diego	23	98	4.3	1
At Minnesota	27	112	4.1	2
Oakland	21	133	6.3	1
At Tampa Bay	24	75	3.1	0
At Denver	28	185	6.6	2
Chicago		(did not play)		
Green Bay		(did not play)		
At Los Angeles	14	66	4.7	0
At Washington	21	159	7.6	2
Dallas	23	119	5.2	1
At Chicago	22	117	5.3	0
Kansas City	20	64	3.2	1
At Green Bay	20	64	3.2	1
Minnesota	13	110	8.5	1
Tampa Bay	19	76	4.0	0
Totals	**296**	**1437**	**4.9**	**13**

1982

Opponent	Att.	Yds.	Avg.	TD
Chicago	13	33	2.5	1
At Los Angeles	25	119	4.8	0
At Chicago	20	67	3.4	0
N.Y. Giants	26	114	4.4	0
N.Y. Jets	12	43	3.6	0
At Green Bay	29	109	3.8	1
Minnesota	12	22	1.8	1
At Tampa Bay	21	68	3.2	1
Green Bay	14	64	4.6	0
At Washington (P)	6	19	3.2	0
Totals	**172**	**639**	**3.7**	**4**
Postseason	**6**	**19**	**3.2**	**0**

1983

Opponent	Att.	Yds.	Avg.	TD
At Tampa Bay	14	37	2.6	0
Cleveland	11	54	4.9	0
Atlanta	2	4	2.0	0
At Minnesota		(did not play)		
At L.A. Rams		(did not play)		
Green Bay		(did not play)		
Chicago	15	77	5.1	1
At Washington	5	18	3.6	1
At Chicago	19	91	4.8	0
N.Y. Giants	14	86	6.1	1
At Houston	20	105	5.3	1
At Green Bay	36	189	5.3	0
Pittsburgh	26	106	4.1	2
Minnesota	23	137	6.0	0
At Cincinnati	20	80	4.0	0
Tampa Bay	15	56	3.7	1
At San Francisco (P)	20	114	5.7	2
Totals	**220**	**1040**	**4.7**	**7**
Postseason	**20**	**114**	**5.7**	**2**

1984

Opponent	Att.	Yds.	Avg.	TD
San Francisco	17	69	4.1	1
At Atlanta	23	140	6.1	1
At Tampa Bay	11	39	3.5	0
Minnesota	12	66	5.5	0
At San Diego	14	119	8.5	2
Denver	15	51	3.4	0
Tampa Bay	16	100	6.3	0
At Minnesota	22	103	4.7	1
At Green Bay		(did not play)		
At Philadelphia		(did not play)		
At Washington		(did not play)		
At Chicago		(did not play)		
Green Bay		(did not play)		
At Seattle		(did not play)		
L.A. Raiders		(did not play)		
Chicago		(did not play)		
Totals	**130**	**687**	**5.3**	**5**

Team (W-L Record): Detroit, 1980-84 (34-38-1, .473).

Hall of Fame? Not eligible

Honors: Consensus rookie of the year, 1980; all-NFL (1), 1981; Pro Bowl (3), 1980-82.

Records: None

Lifetime Rankings: 1,131 attempts (--/--); 5,106 yards (44th/--); 42 TDs (T34th/T43rd).

100-Yard Games: 24

200-Yard Games: None

Avg. Rushing Yards Per Season: 1,021

Avg. Rushing Yards Per Game: 85

Fumble probability: 3% (40/1,317)

Last Reported Salary: $600,000

Injuries: 1983--broken hand; 1984--torn knee ligaments.

Comment: Sims' per-game rushing average is only three yards less than Walter Payton's. He also could catch the ball, gaining nearly 1,100 yards receiving in his first two seasons. About the only knock on him was that he was a bit of a fumbler. He didn't make out too badly financially, though. He tore up his knee in the first year of a 5-year, $4.5 million guaranteed contract.

29 ERIC DICKERSON (1983-)

1983 (Rams)

Opponent	Att.	Yds.	Avg.	TD
At N.Y. Giants	31	91	2.9	0
New Orleans	18	88	4.9	2
At Green Bay	20	75	3.8	1
At N.Y. Jets	28	192	6.9	2
Detroit	30	199	6.6	3
At San Francisco	22	142	6.5	1
Atlanta	29	64	2.2	2
San Francisco	25	144	5.8	0
At Miami	14	101	7.2	1
Chicago	34	127	3.7	2
At Atlanta	21	146	7.0	2
Washington	12	37	3.1	0
Buffalo	32	125	3.9	1
At Philadelphia	28	103	3.7	0
New England	27	94	3.5	0
At New Orleans	19	80	4.2	0
At Dallas (P)	23	99	4.3	0
At Washington (P)	10	16	1.6	0
Totals	**390**	**1808**	**4.6**	**18**
Postseason	**33**	**115**	**3.5**	**0**

1984

	Att.	Yds.	Avg.	TD
Dallas	21	138	6.6	1
Cleveland	27	102	3.8	0
At Pittsburgh	23	49	2.1	0
At Cincinnati	22	89	4.1	1
N.Y. Giants	22	120	5.5	0
Atlanta	19	107	5.6	2
At New Orleans	20	175	8.8	0
At Atlanta	24	145	7.3	1
San Francisco	13	38	2.9	0
At St. Louis	21	208	9.9	0
Chicago	28	149	5.3	2
At Green Bay	25	132	5.3	0
At Tampa Bay	28	191	6.8	3
New Orleans	33	149	4.5	1
Houston	27	215	8.0	2
At San Francisco	26	98	3.8	1
N.Y. Giants (P)	23	107	4.7	1
Totals	**379**	**2105**	**5.6**	**14**
Postseason	**23**	**107**	**4.7**	**1**

1985

	Att.	Yds.	Avg.	TD
Denver		(did not play)		
At Philadelphia		(did not play)		
At Seattle	31	150	4.8	3
Atlanta	7	26	3.7	0
Minnesota	25	55	2.2	1
At Tampa Bay	25	75	3.0	1
At Kansas City	26	68	2.6	1
San Francisco	12	61	5.1	0
New Orleans	23	108	4.7	1
At N.Y. Giants	24	101	4.2	1
At Atlanta	11	41	3.7	1
Green Bay	31	150	4.8	1
At New Orleans	16	80	5.0	0
At San Francisco	16	97	6.1	0
St. Louis	20	124	6.2	2
L.A. Raiders	25	98	3.9	0
Dallas (P)	34	248	7.3	2
At Chicago (P)	17	46	4.4	0
Totals	**292**	**1234**	**4.2**	**12**
Postseason	**51**	**294**	**5.8**	**2**

1986

	Att.	Yds.	Avg.	TD
At St. Louis	38	193	5.1	2
San Francisco	19	78	4.1	0
At Indianapolis	25	121	4.8	1
At Philadelphia	17	58	3.4	0
Tampa Bay	30	207	6.9	2
At Atlanta	16	73	4.6	1
Detroit	24	130	5.4	1
Atlanta	30	170	5.7	0
At Chicago	29	111	3.8	0
At New Orleans	20	57	2.9	0
New England	24	102	4.3	0
New Orleans	27	116	4.3	1
At N.Y. Jets	31	107	3.5	0
Dallas	28	106	3.8	0
Miami	28	124	4.4	1
At San Francisco	18	68	3.8	1
At Washington (P)	26	158	6.1	0
Totals	**404**	**1821**	**4.5**	**11**
Postseason	**26**	**158**	**6.1**	**0**

Teams (W-L Record): L.A. Rams, 1983-87; Indianapolis, 1987- (63-45, .583).

Hall of Fame? Not eligible

Honors: Sporting News NFL Player of the Year, 1983; UPI NFC Player of the Year, 1983-84; AP Offensive Rookie of the Year and UPI NFC Rookie of the Year, 1983; all-NFL (5), 1983-84; '86-88; Pro Bowl (6); 1983-84; '86-89.

Records: Most rushing yards, season, 2,105, 1984.

Lifetime Rankings: 2,450 attempts (5th); 11,226 yards (6th); 82 TDs (6th).

100-Yard Games: 58 (plus 3 postseason)

200-Yard Games: 3 (plus 1 postseason)

Avg. Rushing Yards Per Season: 1,604

Avg. Rushing Yards Per Game: 107

Fumble Probability: 2.7% (71/2,652)

Last Reported Salary: $1,300,000

Injuries: None

Comment: ESPN's Pete Axthelm says Dickerson is the most overrated player in pro football. That's overstating it a bit. Of course, that's what Ax gets paid to do. Granted Dickerson drops the ball now and then. But so would you if you carried it 350 times a season for seven years. No back in history has handled the load Dickerson has. Never mind his running ability. This guy is durable. He's also taken teams quarterbacked by Jeff Kemp, Dieter Brock, rookie Jim Everett and Jack Trudeau to the playoffs. Dickerson may not be the greatest running back of all time, but he deserves respect.

1987 (Rams 3/Colts 9)

	Att.	Yds.	Avg.	TD
At Houston	27	142	5.3	0
Minnesota	26	90	3.5	0
At Cleveland	7	38	5.4	1
At N.Y. Jets	10	38	3.8	0
San Diego	35	138	3.9	0
At Miami	30	154	5.1	1
At New England	27	117	4.3	0
Houston	27	136	5.0	2
At Cleveland	27	98	3.6	0
Buffalo	11	19	1.7	0
At San Diego	23	115	5.0	0
Tampa Bay	33	196	5.9	2
At Cleveland (P)	15	50	3.3	0
Totals	**223**	**1011**	**4.5**	**6**
Postseason	**15**	**50**	**3.3**	**0**

1988

	Att.	Yds.	Avg.	TD
Houston	24	109	4.5	0
Chicago	24	95	4.0	1
At Cleveland	22	117	5.3	1
Miami	30	125	4.2	0
At New England	29	118	4.1	1
At Buffalo	18	66	3.7	0
Tampa Bay	27	80	3.0	2
At San Diego	30	169	5.6	0
Denver	21	159	7.6	4
N.Y. Jets	19	58	3.1	1
At Green Bay	19	69	3.6	0
At Minnesota	22	72	3.3	0
New England	20	45	2.3	2
At Miami	31	169	5.5	1
At N.Y. Jets	16	42	2.6	1
Buffalo	36	166	4.6	0
Totals	**388**	**1659**	**4.3**	**14**

1989

	Att.	Yds.	Avg.	TD
San Francisco	19	106	5.6	0
At L.A. Rams	21	116	5.5	1
Atlanta	22	80	3.6	0
At N.Y. Jets	18	52	2.9	0
Buffalo	22	92	4.2	2
At Denver	13	35	2.7	0
At Cincinnati	31	152	4.9	1
New England	14	60	4.3	0
At Miami		(did not play)		
At Buffalo	19	79	4.2	0
N.Y. Jets	31	131	4.2	1
San Diego	17	30	1.8	0
At New England	24	80	3.3	0
Cleveland	26	137	5.3	0
Miami	21	107	5.1	2
At New Orleans	16	54	3.4	0
Totals	**314**	**1311**	**4.2**	**7**

24 LENNY MOORE (1956-67)

1956

Opponent	Rushing Att-Yds	Receiving No-Yds	TD	Total Yds
Chi. Bears	7-(-10)	2-9	1	-1
Detroit	5-14	0-0	0	14
At Green Bay	7-66	1-11	2	77
At Chi. Bears	2-78	2-15	1	93
Green Bay	13-185	1-27	2	212
At Cleveland	11-120	0-0	1	120
At Detroit	9-(-14)	2-15	0	1
Los Angeles	2-8	0-0	0	8
San Francisco	8-25	0-0	0	25
At Los Angeles	7-77	1-9	0	86
At San Francisco	8-53	2-16	1	69
Washington	7-47	0-0	1	47
Totals	**86-649**	**11-102**	**9**	**751**

1957

Opponent	Rushing Att-Yds	Receiving No-Yds	TD	Total Yds
Detroit	8-54	3-56	0	110
Chi. Bears	12-83	2-35	1	118
At Green Bay	12-81	1-52	0	133
At Detroit	7-3	6-100	2	103
Green Bay	9-33	6-20	1	53
Pittsburgh	7-35	0-0	0	35
At Washington	2-3	0-0	0	3
At Chi. Bears	5-(-9)	3-70	0	61
San Francisco	12-91	4-57	1	148
Los Angeles	8-50	5-99	3	149
At San Francisco	8-9	6-180	1	189
At Los Angeles	8-55	4-18	1	73
Totals	**98-488**	**40-687**	**10**	**1175**

1958

Opponent	Rushing Att-Yds	Receiving No-Yds	TD	Total Yds
Detroit	7-36	6-59	1	95
Chi. Bears	10-71	6-118	4	189
At Green Bay	6-21	6-108	1	129
At Detroit	12-136	1-15	1	151
Washington	7-60	2-62	1	122
Green Bay	0-0	2-65	1	65
At New York	6-27	6-181	2	208
At Chi. Bears	7-19	4-39	1	58
Los Angeles	6-22	6-157	2	179
San Francisco	8-114	5-38	1	152
At Los Angeles	6-19	6-52	1	71
At San Francisco	7-73	3-44	0	117
At New York (C)	9-24	5-99	0	123
Totals	**82-598**	**50-938**	**14**	**1536**
Postseason	**9-24**	**5-99**	**0**	**123**

1959

Opponent	Rushing Att-Yds	Receiving No-Yds	TD	Total Yds
Detroit	10-24	3-60	0	84
Chi. Bears	6-19	4-44	0	63
At Detroit	11-53	2-78	1	131
At Chi. Bears	7-22	5-90	1	112
Green Bay	8-42	4-41	0	83
Cleveland	5-9	5-115	1	124
At Washington	12-77	4-109	0	186
At Green Bay	11-72	6-95	1	167
San Francisco	11-37	4-51	2	88
Los Angeles	3-47	1-17	0	64
At San Francisco	6-1	6-115	1	116
At Los Angeles	2-19	3-31	0	50
New York (C)	4-7	3-126	1	133
Totals	**92-422**	**47-846**	**6**	**1268**
Postseason	**4-7**	**3-126**	**1**	**133**

1960

Opponent	Rushing Att-Yds	Receiving No-Yds	TD	Total Yds
Washington	12-56	1-23	1	79
Chi. Bears	2-10	4-140	2	150
At Green Bay	8-32	2-36	0	68
Los Angeles	9-118	2-21	0	139
At Detroit	6-(-2)	4-46	0	44
At Dallas	6-31	2-42	1	73
Green Bay	4-15	8-137	0	152
At Chi. Bears	10-36	4-82	2	118
San Francisco	4-4	5-139	1	143
Detroit	8-18	4-139	2	157
At Los Angeles	18-44	3-39	0	83
At San Francisco	4-12	6-92	0	104
Totals	**91-374**	**45-936**	**13**	**1310**

1961

Opponent	Rushing Att-Yds	Receiving No-Yds	TD	Total Yds
Los Angeles	6-70	3-47	2	117
Detroit	9-36	4-7	1	43
Minnesota	4-20	5-143	4	163
At Green Bay	4-19	4-60	1	79
At Chi. Bears	2-11	0-0	0	11
At Detroit	5-40	7-81	2	121
Chi. Bears	9-55	7-155	1	210
Green Bay	7-38	7-75	1	113
At Minnesota	12-77	1-8	1	85
St. Louis	8-51	6-76	1	127
At Washington	6-122	2-11	1	133
San Francisco	11-41	1-43	0	84
At Los Angeles	9-68	2-22	0	90
At San Francisco	0-0	0-0	0	0
Totals	**92-648**	**49-728**	**15**	**1376**

1962

Opponent	Rushing Att-Yds	Receiving No-Yds	TD	Total Yds
Los Angeles	(did not play)			
At Minnesota	(did not play)			
Detroit	(did not play)			
San Francisco	(did not play)			
At Cleveland	(did not play)			
At Chi. Bears	(did not play)			
Green Bay	18-77	4-36	0	113
At San Francisco	16-95	2-17	1	112
At Los Angeles	20-48	1-10	1	58
At Green Bay	13-65	3-11	0	76
Chi. Bears	4-31	3-45	0	76
At Detroit	12-40	4-16	0	56
Washington	9-30	0-0	0	30
Minnesota	14-84	1-80	2	164
Totals	**106-470**	**18-215**	**4**	**685**

1963

Opponent	Rushing Att-Yds	Receiving No-Yds	TD	Total Yds
New York	(did not play)			
At San Francisco	(did not play)			
At Green Bay	0-0	4-68	0	68
At Chi. Bears	1-9	3-36	0	45
San Francisco	0-0	3-25	1	25
At Detroit	1-7	2-11	0	18
Green Bay	0-0	4-69	1	69
Chi. Bears	13-71	4-45	1	116
Detroit	12-49	1-34	1	83
At Minnesota	(did not play)			
At Los Angeles	(did not play)			
At Washington	(did not play)			
Minnesota	(did not play)			
Los Angeles	(did not play)			
Totals	**27-136**	**21-288**	**4**	**424**

1964

Opponent	Rushing Att-Yds	Receiving No-Yds	TD	Total Yds
At Minnesota	6-26	1-70	2	96
At Green Bay	12-34	1-52	2	86
Chi. Bears	10-48	1-17	1	65
Los Angeles	13-86	1-46	2	132
St. Louis	15-72	0-0	1	72
Green Bay	18-71	1-1	2	72
At Detroit	12-40	1-17	1	57
San Francisco	17-40	4-71	2	111
At Chi. Bears	9-9	4-33	1	42
Minnesota	10-34	3-107	1	141
At Los Angeles	9-64	0-0	1	64
At San Francisco	3-3	3-34	1	37
Detroit	10-35	0-0	1	35
Washington	13-22	1-24	2	46
At Cleveland (C)	9-40	2-4	0	44
Totals	**157-584**	**21-472**	**20**	**1056**
Postseason	**9-40**	**2-4**	**0**	**44**

1965

Opponent	Rushing Att-Yds	Receiving No-Yds	TD	Total Yds
Minnesota	10-20	0-0	1	20
At Green Bay	14-69	2-6	0	75
San Francisco	16-32	4-58	2	90
Detroit	11-33	1-21	0	54
At Washington	(did not play)			
Los Angeles	(did not play)			
At San Francisco	11-24	3-56	0	80
At Chi. Bears	14-35	1-19	0	54
At Minnesota	7-34	2-45	1	79
Philadelphia	10-54	7-163	2	217
At Detroit	7-55	3-18	0	73
Chi. Bears	5-11	2-14	0	25
Green Bay	15-42	2-14	1	56
At Los Angeles	13-55	0-0	1	55
At Green Bay (P)	12-33	2-15	0	48
Dallas (PB)	14-56	0-0	1	56
Totals	**133-464**	**27-414**	**8**	**878**
Postseason	**26-89**	**2-15**	**1**	**104**

1966

Opponent	Rushing Att-Yds	Receiving No-Yds	TD	Total Yds
At Green Bay	8-21	2-10	0	31
At Minnesota	3-4	1-(-6)	0	-2
San Francisco	11-52	4-56	0	108
At Chicago	6-8	2-32	0	40
Detroit	(did not play)			
Minnesota	4-27	0-0	0	27
At Los Angeles	4-4	3-58	0	62
Washington	6-18	0-0	0	18
At Atlanta	11-33	5-69	1	102
At Detroit	6-25	2-23	1	48
Los Angeles	1-3	0-0	0	3
Chi. Bears	1-10	0-0	0	10
Green Bay	0-0	2-18	0	18
At San Francisco	2-4	0-0	0	4
Philadelphia (PB)	1-5	0-0	0	5
Totals	**63-209**	**21-260**	**3**	**489**
Postseason	**1-5**	**0-0**	**0**	**5**

1967

Opponent	Rushing Att-Yds	Receiving No-Yds	TD	Total Yds
Atlanta	1-5	0-0	0	5
At Philadelphia	2-4	1-3	1	4
San Francisco	5-9	2-54	0	63
At Chi. Bears	2-1	2-24	0	25
Los Angeles	8-31	1-3	1	34
At Minnesota	3-7	1-9	0	16
At Washington	6-30	2-18	0	48
Green Bay	5-(-1)	1-9	0	8
At Atlanta	0-0	0-0	0	0
Detroit	5-28	0-0	0	28
At San Francisco	2-8	0-0	0	8
Dallas	2-4	1-7	1	11
New Orleans	0-0	0-0	0	0
At Los Angeles	1-6	3-29	0	35
Totals	**42-132**	**13-153**	**4**	**285**

Team (W-L Record): Baltimore, 1956-67 (101-54-3, .649).

Hall of Fame? Yes (3rd year eligible)

Honors: UPI Rookie of the Year, 1956; All-NFL (5), 1958-61, '64; Pro Bowl (7), 1956, '58-62, '64.

Records: Most touchdowns, season, 20, 1964*; most receiving yards by a running back, career, 6,039; most receiving yards by a running back, season, 938, 1958.*

Lifetime Rankings: 5,174 rushing yards (9th/--); 6,039 receiving yards (1st/1st among backs); 11,213 yards from scrimmage (2nd/9th among backs).

100-Yard Games: Rushing, 6; receiving, 17 (plus 1 postseason); combined, 47 (plus 2 postseason).

Avg. Yards Per Season: Rushing, 431; receiving, 503; combined, 934.

Avg. Yards Per Game: 76

Fumble probability: 2.7% (41/1,495).

Injuries: 1962--cracked kneecap; 1963--appendectomy, head injury.

Comment: Moore is a unique player in pro football history. He was an all-pro halfback and flanker wrapped into one, the only NFL player with 5,000 yards rushing and 5,000 receiving. Raymond Berry thought Moore could have been the best receiver ever if he put his mind to it, but Moore's versatility was too valuable to the Colts. In 1958, his best season, he averaged 50 yards rushing (598 total) and 78 receiving (938) a game. Two years later he averaged 77 yards receiving (936) a game. Those are still the two best receiving seasons by a back, based on yards per game. When he was well past his prime, at 31, he set a record with 20 touchdowns. If Moore isn't the greatest player, he's certainly one of the finalists.

26 LYDELL MITCHELL (1972-80)

1972 (Colts)

Opponent	Rushing Att-Yds	Receiving No-Yds	TD	Total Yds
St. Louis	(did not play)			
New York Jets	(did not play)			
At Buffalo	(did not play)			
San Diego	0-0	0-0	0	0
Dallas	0-0	1-3	0	3
At N.Y. Jets	0-0	0-0	0	0
Miami	0-0	0-0	0	0
At New England	0-0	0-0	0	0
At San Francisco	0-0	0-0	0	0
At Cincinnati	2-15	1-5	1	20
New England	14-82	2-17	0	99
Buffalo	10-45	7-69	1	114
At Kansas City	10-31	3-28	0	59
At Miami	9-42	4-25	0	67
Totals	**45-215**	**18-147**	**2**	**362**

1973

Opponent	Rushing Att-Yds	Receiving No-Yds	TD	Total Yds
At Cleveland	0-0	1-8	0	8
New York Jets	4-24	3-24	0	48
New Orleans	22-133	1-5	0	138
At New England	14-42	1-9	0	51
At Buffalo	16-56	0-0	0	56
At Detroit	24-84	1-14	0	98
Oakland	15-57	1-3	1	60
Houston	22-83	1-7	0	90
At Miami	8-31	1-(-1)	0	30
At Washington	17-54	4-22	0	76
Buffalo	22-67	1-4	0	71
At N.Y. Jets	20-86	1-7	1	93
Miami	35-104	1-11	0	115
New England	34-142	0-0	0	142
Totals	**253-963**	**17-113**	**2**	**1076**

1974

Opponent	Rushing Att-Yds	Receiving No-Yds	TD	Total Yds
At Pittsburgh	9-44	1-5	0	49
Green Bay	18-63	5-47	0	110
At Philadelphia	7-2	5-43	0	45
At New England	3-7	6-32	0	39
Buffalo	20-81	3-13	1	94
At N.Y. Jets	40-156	2-6	1	162
At Miami	8-20	3-18	0	38
Cincinnati	16-47	7-64	2	111
Denver	19-38	11-90	0	128
At Atlanta	33-151	1-18	0	169
New England	13-48	5-51	1	99
At Buffalo	11-30	3-20	0	50
Miami	10-44	7-55	0	99
N.Y. Jets	7-26	13-82	1	108
Totals	**214-757**	**72-544**	**7**	**1301**

1975

Opponent	Rushing Att-Yds	Receiving No-Yds	TD	Total Yds
At Chicago	22-50	5-49	0	99
Oakland	16-38	5-34	0	72
At L.A. Rams	17-66	6-57	0	123
Buffalo	19-107	3-53	4	160
At New England	15-45	7-28	0	73
At N.Y. Jets	14-98	3-18	1	116
Cleveland	11-27	4-69	1	96
At Buffalo	27-112	4-25	3	137
N.Y. Jets	9-62	7-91	1	153
At Miami	26-106	1-5	1	111
Kansas City	26-178	4-41	1	219
At N.Y. Giants	23-119	4-15	1	134
Miami	30-87	6-53	1	140
New England	34-98	1-6	1	104
At Pittsburgh (P)	26-63	4-20	0	83
Totals	**289-1193**	**60-544**	**15**	**1737**
Postseason	**26-63**	**4-20**	**0**	**83**

1976

Opponent	Rushing Att-Yds	Receiving No-Yds	TD	Total Yds
At New England	18-73	6-72	1	145
Cincinnati	27-106	5-42	0	148
At Dallas	27-115	0-0	0	115
Tampa Bay	14-98	5-41	1	139
Miami	33-95	2-27	0	122
At Buffalo	22-91	2-13	0	104
At N.Y. Jets	22-82	4-28	0	110
Houston	28-136	7-46	0	182
At San Diego	17-91	8-125	1	216
New England	16-52	3-26	0	78
At Miami	20-80	3-42	1	122
N.Y. Jets	19-93	12-64	1	157
At St. Louis	15-54	0-0	1	54
Buffalo	11-34	3-29	1	63
Pittsburgh (P)	16-55	5-42	0	97
Totals	**289-1200**	**60-555**	**8**	**1755**
Postseason	**16-55**	**5-42**	**0**	**97**

1977

Opponent	Rushing Att-Yds	Receiving No-Yds	TD	Total Yds
At Seattle	32-114	5-31	0	145
At N.Y. Jets	26-68	3-23	0	91
Buffalo	23-90	7-32	0	122
Miami	17-142	5-17	1	159
At Kansas City	28-97	4-14	0	111
At New England	13-29	0-0	0	29
Pittsburgh	26-99	3-23	1	122
Washington	29-111	3-55	0	166
At Buffalo	21-82	3-60	2	142
N.Y. Jets	14-52	9-90	1	142
At Denver	7-14	9-74	1	88
At Miami	20-84	6-62	0	146
Detroit	22-94	9-88	1	182
New England	23-83	5-51	0	134
Oakland (P)	23-67	3-39	0	106
Totals	**301-1159**	**71-620**	**7**	**1779**
Postseason	**23-67**	**3-39**	**0**	**106**

1978 (Chargers)

Opponent	Rushing Att-Yds	Receiving No-Yds	TD	Total Yds
At Seattle	0-0	0-0	0	0
Oakland	9-38	1-(-5)	0	33
At Denver	6-27	5-42	0	69
Green Bay	14-47	4-39	0	86
At New England	8-24	3-22	0	46
Denver	19-65	9-51	0	116
Miami	19-77	6-64	3	141
At Detroit	9-53	1-55	0	108
At Oakland	24-92	5-75	0	167
Cincinnati	28-101	4-25	0	126
Kansas City	29-144	0-0	0	144
At Minnesota	3-4	1-8	0	12
At Kansas City	14-58	6-41	0	99
Chicago	16-36	2-19	1	55
Seattle	8-19	7-49	0	68
At Houston	8-35	3-15	0	50
Totals	**214-820**	**57-500**	**5**	**1320**

1979

Opponent	Rushing Att-Yds	Receiving No-Yds	TD	Total Yds
At Seattle	0-0	0-0	0	0
Oakland	6-20	0-0	0	20
Buffalo	(did not play)			
At New England	(did not play)			
San Francisco	(did not play)			
At Denver	(did not play)			
Seattle	5-14	4-41	1	55
At L.A. Rams	12-48	3-17	0	65
At Oakland	8-17	4-44	0	61
At Kansas City	13-43	5-40	0	83
At Cincinnati	6-22	1-5	0	27
Pittsburgh	4-13	0-0	0	13
Kansas City	6-24	0-0	0	24
Atlanta	0-0	1-3	0	3
At New Orleans	3-10	1-9	0	19
Denver	0-0	0-0	0	0
Houston (P)	8-33	4-26	1	59
Totals	**63-211**	**19-159**	**1**	**370**
Postseason	**8-33**	**4-26**	**1**	**59**

1980 (Rams)

Opponent	Rushing Att-Yds	Receiving No-Yds	TD	Total Yds
Dallas	7-16	1-8	0	24
Atlanta	0-0	1-13	0	13
At Dallas (P)	(did not play)			
Totals	**7-16**	**2-21**	**0**	**37**

Teams (W-L Record): Baltimore, 1972-77; San Diego, 1978-79; L.A. Rams, 1980 (65-53-0, .551).

Hall of Fame? No

Honors: Pro Bowl (3), 1975-77.

Records: Most pass receptions by a running back, season, 72, 1974*; most rushing attempts, game, 40, 1974.*

Lifetime Rankings: 6,534 rushing yards (11th/26th); 3,203 receiving yards (7th/17th among backs); 9,737 yards from scrimmage (8th/15th among backs).

100-Yard Games: Rushing, 18; receiving, 1; combined, 48.

200-Yard Games: Combined, 2.

Avg. Yards Per Season: Rushing, 726; receiving, 356; combined, 1,082.

Avg. Yards Per Game: 88

Fumble Probability: 1.4% (29/2,052)

Injuries: 1979--staph infection in knee.

Comment: Mitchell and Chuck Foreman could have been twins separated at birth. In the six seasons that could be considered his prime (1973-78), he averaged 104 yards rushing and receiving per game (Foreman averaged 106 over the same stretch). And look at that fumble probability! He almost never gave up the ball. When he held out in 1978, the Colts traded him to the Chargers for Joe Washington and a fifth-round draft pick. But he developed a staph infection in his left knee after the season. It was the beginning of the end.

44 CHUCK FOREMAN (1973-80)

1973 (Vikings)

Opponent	Rushing Att-Yds	Receiving No-Yds	TD	Total Yds
Oakland	9-26	6-53	1	79
At Chicago	16-116	4-46	0	162
Green Bay	16-89	5-62	0	151
At Detroit	16-114	2-24	0	138
At San Francisco	22-71	1-6	1	77
Philadelphia	21-68	3-17	1	85
L.A. Rams	23-86	1-9	1	95
Cleveland	(did not play)			
Detroit	(did not play)			
At Atlanta	9-38	3-46	0	84
Chicago	11-39	3-22	1	61
At Cincinnati	11-38	4-28	0	66
At Green Bay	19-100	3-21	1	121
At N.Y. Giants	9-16	2-28	0	44
Washington (P)	11-40	3-23	0	63
At Dallas (P)	19-76	4-28	1	104
Miami (SB)	7-18	5-27	0	45
Totals	182-801	37-362	6	1163
Postseason	37-134	12-78	1	212

1974

Opponent	Rushing Att-Yds	Receiving No-Yds	TD	Total Yds
At Green Bay	22-67	5-32	3	99
At Detroit	13-83	2-(-1)	1	82
Chicago	16-74	5-43	0	117
At Dallas	23-72	5-131	2	203
Houston	16-61	4-63	2	124
Detroit	13-55	3-36	2	91
New England	17-68	7-73	1	141
At Chicago	21-80	1-7	0	87
At St. Louis	13-68	3-20	1	88
Green Bay	10-39	4-51	1	90
At L.A. Rams	12-49	9-88	2	137
New Orleans	19-54	3-25	0	79
Atlanta	4-7	2-18	0	25
At Kansas City	(did not play)			
St. Louis (P)	23-114	5-54	1	168
L.A. Rams (P)	22-80	0-0	0	80
Pittsburgh (SB)	12-22	5-50	0	72
Totals	199-777	53-586	15	1363
Postseason	57-216	10-104	1	320

1975

Opponent	Rushing Att-Yds	Receiving No-Yds	TD	Total Yds
San Francisco	5-8	1-6	1	14
At Cleveland	11-33	7-61	2	94
Chicago	17-56	4-48	1	104
N.Y. Jets	25-96	9-105	3	201
Detroit	22-107	1-(-2)	0	105
At Chicago	26-102	3-34	0	136
At Green Bay	25-72	9-93	1	165
Atlanta	26-102	4-19	3	121
At New Orleans	24-117	8-63	0	180
At San Diego	33-127	4-17	3	144
At Washington	20-77	6-75	3	152
Green Bay	13-64	6-81	1	145
At Detroit	14-24	1-4	0	28
At Buffalo	19-85	10-87	4	172
Dallas (P)	18-56	4-42	1	96
Totals	280-1070	73-691	22	1761
Postseason	18-56	4-42	1	96

1976

Opponent	Rushing Att-Yds	Receiving No-Yds	TD	Total Yds
At New Orleans	14-53	7-106	2	159
L.A. Rams	11-31	6-31	0	62
At Detroit	25-94	3-14	1	108
Pittsburgh	27-148	0-0	2	148
Chicago	23-63	0-0	2	63
N.Y. Giants	23-83	8-118	1	201
At Philadelphia	28-200	6-65	2	265
At Chicago	17-35	8-72	0	107
Detroit	19-51	2-22	2	73
Seattle	17-100	5-61	0	161
At Green Bay	19-84	5-39	0	123
At San Francisco	23-93	3-23	0	116
Green Bay	18-42	1-8	2	50
At Miami	14-78	1-8	0	86
Washington (P)	20-105	0-0	2	105
L.A. Rams (P)	15-118	5-81	1	199
Oakland (SB)	17-44	5-62	0	106
Totals	278-1155	55-587	14	1722
Postseason	52-267	10-143	3	410

Teams (W-L Record): Minnesota, 1973-79; New England, 1980 (79-37-2, .678).

Hall of Fame? No

Honors: Sporting News NFC Player of the Year, 1974; UPI NFC Player of the Year, 1976; Sporting News NFC Rookie of the Year, 1973; all-NFL (2), 1975-76; Pro Bowl (5), 1973-77.

Records: Most receptions by a running back, season, 73, 1975.*

Lifetime Rankings: 5,950 rushing yards (17th/34th); 3,156 receiving yards (10th/20th among backs); 9,106 yards from scrimmage (10th/22nd among backs).

100-Yard Games: Rushing, 17 (plus 4 postseason); receiving, 4; combined, 40 (plus 6 postseason).

200-Yard Games: Combined, 4.

Avg. Yards Per Season: Rushing, 744; receiving, 395; combined, 1,138.

Avg. Yards Per Game: 84

Fumble Probability: 2.7% (52/1,908).

Last Reported Salary: $300,000 (1979)

Injuries: 1978--knee injury; 1979--rib injury.

Comment: If Foreman's body had held up a couple of more years, he'd probably be a Hall-of-Famer. What more could you want? He could run, catch and, in a defensive era, averaged 106 yards from scrimmage per game for six seasons. He won NFC player of the year awards in 1974 and '76, and his best year was '75, when he scored 22 touchdowns and set a record for receptions by a running back with 73. In '76 he had back-to-back 200-yard games (201 rushing and receiving vs. the Giants and 265 vs. the Eagles). Note, though, how much his lifetime rankings have dropped since he retired in 1980. It helps explain why he has been so quickly forgotten. Playing only eight seasons really hurts him.

1977

Opponent	Rushing Att-Yds	Receiving No-Yds	TD	Total Yds
Dallas	22-66	5-56	1	122
At Tampa Bay	14-58	4-52	1	110
Green Bay	19-53	5-40	1	93
Detroit	19-42	1-10	0	52
Chicago	26-150	5-33	1	183
At L.A. Rams	10-35	1-4	0	39
At Atlanta	23-91	1-7	0	98
St. Louis	11-86	7-54	0	140
Cincinnati	29-133	5-30	3	163
At Chicago	14-54	1-5	0	59
At Green Bay	26-101	0-0	0	101
San Francisco	13-39	0-0	0	39
At Oakland	11-48	3-17	0	65
At Detroit	33-156	0-0	2	156
At L.A. Rams (P)	31-101	1-6	1	107
At Dallas (P)	21-59	5-36	0	95
Totals	270-1112	38-308	9	1420
Postseason	52-160	6-42	1	202

1978

Opponent	Rushing Att-Yds	Receiving No-Yds	TD	Total Yds
At New Orleans	18-122	5-35	1	157
Denver	22-59	4-28	0	87
Tampa Bay	12-25	7-33	0	58
At Chicago	17-73	0-0	0	73
At Tampa Bay	(did not play)			
At Seattle	(did not play)			
L.A. Rams	9-17	0-0	0	17
Green Bay	24-46	7-47	1	93
At Dallas	22-101	5-33	1	134
Detroit	20-35	2-(-2)	0	33
Chicago	18-54	5-34	2	88
San Diego	13-42	9-76	0	118
At Green Bay	24-52	5-35	0	87
Philadelphia	18-69	6-31	0	100
At Detroit	7-13	2-20	0	33
At Oakland	13-41	4-26	0	67
At L.A. Rams (P)	13-31	3-38	0	71
Totals	237-749	61-396	7	1145
Postseason	13-31	3-38	0	71

1979

Opponent	Rushing Att-Yds	Receiving No-Yds	TD	Total Yds
San Francisco	11-33	1-10	0	43
At Chicago	11-13	1-21	0	34
Miami	12-38	3-13	0	51
Green Bay	6-11	1-12	0	23
At Detroit	11-40	1-22	1	62
Dallas	10-19	1-8	0	27
At N.Y. Jets	8-13	8-44	1	57
Chicago	6-28	0-0	0	28
Tampa Bay	2-3	0-0	0	3
At St. Louis	0-0	2-12	0	12
At Green Bay	4-9	1-5	0	14
Detroit	6-16	0-0	0	16
At Tampa Bay	(did not play)			
At L.A. Rams	(did not play)			
Buffalo	(did not play)			
At New England	(did not play)			
Totals	87-223	19-147	2	370

1980 (Patriots)

Opponent	Rushing Att-Yds	Receiving No-Yds	TD	Total Yds
Cleveland	5-13	2-9	0	22
Atlanta	3-18	2-15	0	33
At Seattle	0-0	2-17	0	17
Denver	0-0	0-0	0	0
At N.Y. Jets	0-0	2-9	0	9
Miami	8-24	0-0	0	24
At Baltimore	3-0	0-0	1	0
At Buffalo	0-0	1-1	0	1
N.Y. Jets	2-3	1-10	0	13
At Houston	0-0	1-18	0	18
L.A. Rams	0-0	0-0	0	0
Baltimore	0-0	1-6	0	6
At San Francisco	0-0	0-0	0	0
At Miami	2-5	2-14	0	19
Buffalo	0-0	0-0	0	0
At New Orleans	0-0	0-0	0	0
Totals	23-63	14-99	1	162

31 WILLIAM ANDREWS (1979-86)

1979

Opponent	Rushing Att-Yds	Receiving No-Yds	TD	Total Yds
At New Orleans	30-167	3-22	1	189
At Philadelphia	24-121	1-3	0	124
Denver	20-41	5-35	1	76
At Detroit	7-22	1-34	0	56
Washington	15-59	0-0	1	59
Green Bay	13-60	2-17	0	77
At Oakland	(did not play)			
At San Francisco	12-36	6-41	0	77
Seattle	11-50	3-19	0	69
Tampa Bay	15-49	4-16	0	62
At N.Y. Giants	11-73	0-0	0	73
At L.A. Rams	16-80	1-5	0	85
New Orleans	12-43	3-11	1	54
At San Diego	21-131	4-38	1	169
L.A. Rams	13-28	2-18	0	46
San Francisco	19-63	4-50	0	113
Totals	**239-1023**	**39-309**	**5**	**1332**

1980

Opponent	Rushing Att-Yds	Receiving No-Yds	TD	Total Yds
At Miami	7-35	5-36	0	71
At New England	19-124	4-30	1	154
Miami	6-21	3-23	0	44
At San Francisco	20-98	3-15	0	113
Detroit	13-78	1-17	1	95
N.Y. Jets	7-31	7-56	0	87
At New Orleans	14-64	2-18	1	82
L.A. Rams	20-111	2-22	0	133
At Buffalo	20-87	2-30	0	117
At St. Louis	20-115	6-28	0	143
New Orleans	19-79	3-29	0	108
Chicago	19-70	2-20	2	90
Washington	24-111	2-34	0	145
At Philadelphia	18-101	0-0	0	101
San Francisco	18-105	7-62	0	167
At L.A. Rams	21-78	2-36	0	114
Dallas (P)	14-43	2-19	1	62
Totals	**265-1308**	**51-456**	**5**	**1764**
Postseason	**14-43**	**2-19**	**1**	**62**

1981

Opponent	Rushing Att-Yds	Receiving No-Yds	TD	Total Yds
New Orleans	18-86	2-14	0	100
At Green Bay	19-87	1-9	1	96
San Francisco	12-85	4-37	0	122
At Cleveland	16-97	2-9	0	106
At Philadelphia	21-84	5-56	0	140
L.A. Rams	21-119	4-35	2	154
St. Louis	9-25	8-132	2	157
N.Y. Giants	21-92	4-40	0	132
At New Orleans	17-79	4-39	1	118
At San Francisco	18-61	6-31	1	92
Pittsburgh	12-36	15-124	0	160
Minnesota	22-91	2-12	0	103
At Houston	25-101	3-47	1	148
At Tampa Bay	17-80	13-98	2	178
At L.A. Rams	23-115	2-3	0	118
Cincinnati	18-63	6-49	2	112
Totals	**289-1301**	**81-735**	**12**	**2036**

Team (W-L): Atlanta, 1979-83, '86 (44-44-1, .500).

Hall of Fame? Not eligible

Honors: All-NFL (1), 1983; Pro Bowl (4), 1980-83.

Records: None

Lifetime Rankings: 5,986 rushing yards (26th/32nd); 2,647 receiving yards (31st/32nd among backs); 8,633 yards from scrimmage (23rd/30th among backs).

100-Yard Games: Rushing, 21; receiving, 3; combined, 45.

200-Yard Games: Combined, 3.

Avg. Yards Per Season: Rushing, 998; receiving, 441; combined, 1,439.

Avg. Yards Per Game: 99

Fumble Probability: 1.9% (30/1,596)

Last Reported Salary: $530,000

Injuries: 1984--torn knee ligaments, damaged cartilage and nerve (missed two seasons).

Comment: Andrews was just beginning to move up among the all-time leaders when he suffered a knee injury that essentially ended his career. He could run, catch and block with the best of them. Feast your eyes on his 1981 season. He missed by 12 yards becoming the only back in NFL history to gain 100 yards from scrimmage in every game. The Packers "held" him to 96 and the 49ers to 92. The one-back offense installed by Falcons coach Dan Henning in '83 was made for Andrews. He gained a career-high 2,176 yards that year. Gerald Riggs might never have gotten his chance if Andrews had stayed healthy. Strange stat: Andrews averaged an excellent 4.6 yards a carry for his career even though his longest run was 33 yards.

1982

Opponent	Rushing Att-Yds	Receiving No-Yds	TD	Total Yds
At N.Y. Giants	18-64	2-16	1	80
L.A. Raiders	10-25	5-94	1	119
L.A. Rams	21-119	7-88	1	207
St. Louis	11-25	5-41	0	66
At Denver	16-73	3-106	3	179
New Orleans	14-61	3-1	0	62
At San Francisco	24-108	4-68	0	176
Green Bay	11-41	11-77	1	118
At New Orleans	14-57	2-12	0	69
At Minnesota (P)	11-48	0-0	0	48
Totals	**139-573**	**42-503**	**7**	**1076**
Postseason	**11-48**	**0-0**	**0**	**48**

1983

Opponent	Rushing Att-Yds	Receiving No-Yds	TD	Total Yds
At Chicago	22-95	3-43	1	138
N.Y. Giants	16-55	4-61	0	116
At Detroit	32-150	4-34	0	184
At San Francisco	28-126	2-26	0	152
Philadelphia	25-150	1-10	0	160
New Orleans	25-77	3-6	1	83
At L.A. Rams	18-82	2-19	0	101
At N.Y. Giants	12-50	8-82	1	132
New England	25-125	3-52	0	177
At New Orleans	17-45	3-14	1	59
L.A. Rams	14-52	1-6	0	58
San Francisco	16-38	5-45	0	83
Green Bay	20-129	5-54	3	183
At Washington	12-74	3-46	0	120
At Miami	21-161	5-62	1	223
Buffalo	28-158	7-49	3	207
Totals	**331-1567**	**59-609**	**11**	**2176**

1986

Opponent	Rushing Att-Yds	Receiving No-Yds	TD	Total Yds
At New Orleans	5-28	0-0	0	28
St. Louis	2-8	0-0	1	8
At Dallas	0-0	0-0	0	0
At Tampa Bay	1-3	1-2	0	5
Philadelphia	0-0	0-0	0	0
L.A. Rams	3-13	0-0	0	13
San Francisco	5-29	0-0	0	29
At L.A. Rams	0-0	0-0	0	0
At New England	3-5	0-0	0	5
N.Y. Jets	0-0	0-0	0	0
Chicago	(did not play)			
At San Francisco	1-1	0-0	0	1
At Miami	4-23	1-6	0	29
Indianapolis	8-23	1-14	0	37
New Orleans	2-5	1-9	0	14
At Detroit	18-76	1-4	0	80
Totals	**52-214**	**5-35**	**1**	**249**

32 MARCUS ALLEN (1982-)

1982

Opponent	Rushing Att-Yds	Receiving No-Yds	TD	Total Yds
At San Francisco	23-116	4-64	1	180
At Atlanta	12-56	4-39	2	95
San Diego	18-87	5-37	1	124
At Cincinnati	8-0	6-54	0	54
Seattle	24-156	2-14	2	170
At Kansas City	18-47	1-1	0	48
L.A. Rams	25-93	8-61	3	154
Denver	12-16	5-91	2	107
At San Diego	20-126	3-40	2	166
Cleveland (P)	17-72	6-75	2	147
N.Y. Jets (P)	15-36	6-37	1	73
Totals	**160-697**	**38-401**	**14**	**1098**
Postseason	**32-108**	**12-112**	**3**	**220**

1983

Opponent	Rushing Att-Yds	Receiving No-Yds	TD	Total Yds
At Cincinnati	17-47	3-19	2	66
Houston	17-96	4-29	0	125
Miami	22-105	1-10	0	115
At Denver	15-45	4-20	0	65
At Washington	(did not play)			
Kansas City	21-53	6-58	0	111
At Seattle	18-86	5-25	1	111
At Dallas	15-55	7-67	0	122
Seattle	13-30	8-104	1	134
At Kansas City	21-64	3-31	1	95
Denver	18-84	6-49	1	133
At Buffalo	26-89	8-68	1	157
N.Y. Giants	13-64	4-19	1	83
At San Diego	16-38	1-7	0	45
St. Louis	18-86	3-35	1	121
San Diego	16-72	5-49	2	121
Pittsburgh (P)	13-121	5-38	2	159
Seattle (P)	25-154	7-62	1	216
Washington (SB)	20-191	2-18	2	209
Totals	**266-1014**	**68-590**	**11**	**1604**
Postseason	**58-466**	**14-118**	**5**	**584**

1984

Opponent	Rushing Att-Yds	Receiving No-Yds	TD	Total Yds
At Houston	22-83	5-38	1	121
Green Bay	20-81	3-13	1	94
At Kansas City	22-69	6-46	0	115
San Diego	18-47	6-62	4	109
At Denver	13-66	4-44	0	110
Seattle	15-40	4-173	2	213
Minnesota	17-54	6-42	1	96
At San Diego	19-107	5-40	1	147
Denver	16-70	6-63	2	133
At Chicago	15-42	4-53	0	95
At Seattle	15-57	5-37	2	94
Kansas City	16-95	3-21	0	116
Indianapolis	18-110	1-9	0	119
At Miami	20-155	1-10	3	165
At Detroit	17-56	3-93	1	149
Pittsburgh	13-38	2-14	0	52
At Seattle (P)	17-61	5-90	1	151
Totals	**276-1170**	**64-758**	**18**	**1928**
Postseason	**17-61**	**5-90**	**1**	**151**

1985

Opponent	Rushing Att-Yds	Receiving No-Yds	TD	Total Yds
N.Y. Jets	20-76	2-30	2	106
At Kansas City	14-50	6-27	0	77
San Francisco	12-59	8-53	0	112
At New England	21-98	3-30	0	128
Kansas City	29-126	3-24	0	150
New Orleans	28-107	3-51	2	158
At Cleveland	20-81	3-41	1	122
San Diego	30-111	3-24	3	135
At Seattle	19-101	5-49	0	150
At San Diego	28-119	5-30	1	149
Cincinnati	31-135	6-54	1	189
Denver	24-173	4-49	1	222
At Atlanta	28-156	2-42	1	198
At Denver	25-135	5-21	1	156
Seattle	27-109	1-5	1	114
At L.A. Rams	24-123	8-25	0	148
New England (P)	22-121	3-8	1	129
Totals	**380-1759**	**87-555**	**14**	**2314**
Postseason	**22-121**	**3-8**	**1**	**129**

1986

Opponent	Rushing Att-Yds	Receiving No-Yds	TD	Total Yds
At Denver	24-102	6-102	2	204
At Washington	23-104	5-33	0	137
N.Y. Giants	15-40	5-86	0	126
San Diego	(did not play)			
At Kansas City	(did not play)			
Seattle	6-11	1-11	0	22
At Miami	21-96	3-20	3	116
At Houston	(did not play)			
Denver	22-71	4-19	0	90
At Dallas	7-29	1-5	0	34
Cleveland	13-56	1-3	0	59
At San Diego	21-88	4-19	1	107
Philadelphia	24-59	5-91	0	150
At Seattle	9-12	2-14	0	26
Kansas City	13-60	6-38	1	98
Indianapolis	10-31	3-12	0	43
Totals	**208-759**	**46-453**	**7**	**1212**

1987

Opponent	Rushing Att-Yds	Receiving No-Yds	TD	Total Yds
At Green Bay	33-136	2-0	1	136
Detroit	22-79	3-6	1	85
Seattle	11-29	3-14	0	43
At New England	16-41	5-60	1	101
At Minnesota	11-50	4-12	0	62
At San Diego	13-82	3-21	0	103
Denver	11-44	4-60	0	104
At Seattle	18-76	3-20	0	96
Buffalo	15-47	5-58	1	105
At Kansas City	18-60	3-53	1	113
Cleveland	14-35	10-84	0	119
Chicago	18-75	6-22	0	97
Totals	**200-754**	**51-410**	**5**	**1164**

1988

Opponent	Rushing Att-Yds	Receiving No-Yds	TD	Total Yds
San Diego	28-88	1-9	2	97
At Houston	22-70	2-22	2	92
L.A. Rams	14-53	5-54	1	107
At Denver	22-56	2-16	1	72
Cincinnati	11-53	5-32	0	85
Miami	(did not play)			
At Kansas City	11-20	1-7	1	27
At New Orleans	20-102	3-26	0	128
Kansas City	21-70	2-20	1	90
At San Diego	17-67	0-0	0	67
At San Francisco	14-58	1-9	0	67
Atlanta	7-18	3-30	0	48
At Seattle	8-75	1-17	0	92
Denver	13-57	3-25	0	82
At Buffalo	11-37	3-31	0	68
Seattle	4-7	2-5	0	12
Totals	**223-831**	**34-303**	**8**	**1134**

1989

Opponent	Rushing Att-Yds	Receiving No-Yds	TD	Total Yds
San Diego	13-51	2-(-1)	1	50
At Kansas City	18-58	3-44	0	102
At Denver	10-45	6-63	0	108
Seattle	11-65	3-31	0	96
At N.Y. Jets	10-43	4-34	0	77
Kansas City	(did not play)			
At Philadelphia	(did not play)			
Washington	(did not play)			
Cincinnati	(did not play)			
At San Diego	(did not play)			
At Houston	(did not play)			
New England	(did not play)			
Denver	(did not play)			
Phoenix	4-10	1-9	1	19
At Seattle	1-8	0-0	0	8
At N.Y. Giants	2-13	1-11	0	24
Totals	**69-293**	**20-191**	**2**	**484**

Team (W-L Record): L.A. Raiders, 1982- (70-47, .598).

Hall of Fame? Not eligible

Honors: Consensus MVP/player of the year, 1985; Super Bowl MVP, 1984; consensus rookie of the year, 1982; all-NFL (2), 1982, '85; Pro Bowl (5), 1982, '84-87.

Records: Most yards gained from scrimmage, season, 2,314, 1985.

Lifetime Rankings: 7,275 rushing yards (17th); 3,661 receiving yards (5th among backs); 10,936 yards from scrimmage (10th among backs).

100-Yard Games: Rushing, 22 (plus 4 postseason); receiving, 3; combined, 59 (plus 6 postseason).

200-Yard Games: Combined, 3 (plus 2 postseason).

Avg. Yards Per Season: Rushing, 909; receiving, 458; combined, 1,367.

Avg. Yards Per Game: 105

Fumble Probability: 2.2% (47/2,169)

Last Reported Salary: $1,100,000

Injuries: 1989--knee injury.

Comment: Allen's 1985 might have been the best all-around season ever by an NFL back. He averaged 144.6 yards from scrimmage per game and was held under 100 only once. He started out the next year with a rare double-triple -- 102 yards rushing and 102 receiving against Denver -- but the Raiders were going downhill and his statistics began to suffer. In 1989 he missed eight games with a knee injury and was no longer the team's best back (Bo knows football). Despite playing just six full seasons and two half-seasons, though, Allen ranks in the top 10 all-time in yards from scrimmage.

33 ROGER CRAIG (1983-)

1983

Opponent	Rushing Att-Yds	Receiving No-Yds	TD	Total Yds
Philadelphia	14-42	3-24	0	66
At Minnesota	15-36	0-0	1	36
At St. Louis	2-6	0-0	0	6
Atlanta	7-44	1-12	0	56
At New England	18-54	2-18	0	72
L.A. Rams	14-52	3-27	1	79
At New Orleans	8-87	1-0	0	87
At L.A. Rams	11-55	2-28	1	83
N.Y. Jets	8-27	7-67	1	94
Miami	18-85	5-44	1	129
New Orleans	3-7	1-10	0	17
At Atlanta	8-38	5-49	0	87
At Chicago	10-21	7-57	0	78
Tampa Bay	15-71	4-37	3	108
At Buffalo	15-47	2-10	1	57
Dallas	10-53	5-44	2	97
Detroit (P)	7-13	7-61	1	74
At Washington (P)	3-3	3-15	0	18
Totals	176-725	48-427	12	1152
Postseason	10-16	10-76	1	92

1984

Opponent	Rushing Att-Yds	Receiving No-Yds	TD	Total Yds
At Detroit	8-15	3-32	0	47
Washington	17-57	3-37	0	94
New Orleans	10-47	3-22	0	69
At Philadelphia	10-39	4-58	1	97
Atlanta	10-44	1-6	0	54
At N.Y. Giants	9-33	7-95	1	128
Pittsburgh	6-29	7-43	0	72
At Houston	8-31	7-61	0	92
At L.A. Rams	10-24	2-83	2	107
Cincinnati	12-34	7-44	0	78
At Cleveland	9-45	8-49	2	94
Tampa Bay	16-86	4-22	1	108
At New Orleans	7-25	2-24	1	49
At Atlanta	8-36	4-42	1	78
Minnesota	7-45	4-31	0	76
L.A. Rams	8-59	5-26	0	85
N.Y. Giants (P)	10-34	4-31	0	65
Chicago (P)	8-44	0-0	0	44
Miami (SB)	15-58	7-77	3	135
Totals	155-649	71-675	10	1324
Postseason	33-136	11-108	3	244

1985

Opponent	Rushing Att-Yds	Receiving No-Yds	TD	Total Yds
At Minnesota	13-78	7-72	3	150
Atlanta	11-107	6-77	2	184
At L.A. Raiders	10-34	5-61	1	95
New Orleans	8-37	3-24	1	61
At Atlanta	3-15	12-167	1	182
Chicago	4-42	1-14	0	56
At Detroit	16-80	6-43	1	123
At L.A. Rams	14-63	6-132	2	195
Philadelphia	18-91	7-76	0	167
At Denver	22-117	3-21	0	138
Kansas City	15-55	8-70	1	125
Seattle	15-54	6-76	0	130
At Washington	15-61	2-10	0	71
L.A. Rams	19-56	7-41	1	97
At New Orleans	18-88	8-82	1	170
Dallas	13-72	5-50	1	122
At N.Y. Giants (P)	9-23	2-18	0	41
Totals	214-1050	92-1016	15	2066
Postseason	9-23	2-18	0	41

1986

Opponent	Rushing Att-Yds	Receiving No-Yds	TD	Total Yds
At Tampa Bay	14-42	9-76	2	118
At L.A. Rams	15-44	2-4	0	48
New Orleans	19-42	7-29	0	71
At Miami	11-69	4-24	1	93
Indianapolis	2-22	0-0	0	22
Minnesota	17-32	6-75	0	107
At Atlanta	12-51	3-12	1	63
At Green Bay	12-39	5-24	0	63
At New Orleans	6-9	3-25	0	34
St. Louis	6-38	3-56	0	94
At Washington	9-47	5-42	0	89
Atlanta	17-101	5-15	0	116
N.Y. Giants	10-43	12-75	0	118
N.Y. Jets	17-85	7-43	2	128
At New England	16-86	6-89	1	175
L.A. Rams	21-80	4-35	0	115
At N.Y. Giants (P)	5-17	4-22	0	39
Totals	204-830	81-624	7	1454
Postseason	5-17	4-22	0	39

Team (W-L Record): San Francisco, 1983- (81-28-1, .741).

Hall of Fame? Not eligible

Honors: AP NFL Offensive Player of the Year and UPI NFC Offensive Player of the Year, 1989; All-NFL (2), 1985, '88; Pro Bowl (4), 1985, '87-89.

Records: Most receptions by a running back, season, 92, 1985.

Lifetime Rankings: 6,625 rushing yards (24th); 4,241 receiving yards (3rd among backs); 10,866 yards from scrimmage (11th among backs).

100-Yard Games: Rushing, 14 (plus 2 postseason); receiving, 2 (plus 1 postseason); combined, 48 (plus 7 postseason).

Avg. Yards Per Season: Rushing, 946; receiving, 606; combined, 1,552.

Avg. Yards Per Game: 99

Fumble probability: 1.7% (35/2,030)

Last reported salary: $650,000

Injuries: None

Comment: It was Craig's pass-catching ability that stood out initially. In 1985, he and the Chargers' Lionel James became the first backs to gain 1,000 yards receiving in a season. But in 1988 he emerged as a first-rate runner, too, rushing for 1,502 yards. His versatility makes him almost impossible to shut down. And he turns it up a notch in the playoffs, averaging 133 yards a game in '88 and '89. By the time he's through he may well be in the top five all-time in yards gained from scrimmage. He also could become only the second NFL player to gain 5,000 yards both rushing and receiving. The first: Lenny Moore. Rapidly closing in on Canton.

1987

Opponent	Rushing Att-Yds	Receiving No-Yds	TD	Total Yds
At Pittsburgh	10-16	10-61	0	77
At Cincinnati	12-35	4-23	0	58
At Atlanta	17-91	1-12	1	103
St. Louis	17-71	7-99	2	170
At New Orleans	15-55	5-50	0	105
At L.A. Rams	23-104	2-19	0	123
Houston	16-68	8-51	0	119
New Orleans	17-65	10-43	0	108
At Tampa Bay	15-60	5-28	0	88
Cleveland	13-26	3-23	0	49
At Green Bay	14-48	6-46	0	94
Chicago	12-51	1-3	0	54
Atlanta	19-69	2-29	0	98
L.A. Rams	15-56	2-5	1	61
Minnesota (P)	7-17	9-78	0	95
Totals	215-815	66-492	4	1307
Postseason	7-17	9-78	0	95

1988

Opponent	Rushing Att-Yds	Receiving No-Yds	TD	Total Yds
At New Orleans	18-67	5-43	1	110
At N.Y. Giants	18-110	9-69	0	179
Atlanta	13-57	10-61	0	118
At Seattle	21-107	6-38	0	145
Detroit	18-90	5-31	0	121
Denver	26-143	2-18	0	161
At L.A. Rams	22-190	5-12	3	202
At Chicago	10-31	6-39	0	70
Minnesota	19-56	3-37	1	93
At Phoenix	26-162	1-0	0	162
L.A. Raiders	17-58	5-29	0	87
Washington	24-75	5-37	0	112
At San Diego	17-87	2-8	3	95
At Atlanta	23-103	7-73	0	176
New Orleans	22-115	2-7	1	122
L.A. Rams	16-51	3-32	0	83
Minnesota (P)	21-135	3-26	0	161
At Chicago (P)	18-68	2-33	0	101
Cincinnati (SB)	17-74	8-101	0	175
Totals	310-1502	76-534	10	2036
Postseason	56-277	13-160	0	437

1989

Opponent	Rushing Att-Yds	Receiving No-Yds	TD	Total Yds
At Indianapolis	24-131	1-0	2	131
At Tampa Bay	16-36	3-30	0	66
At Philadelphia	8-14	4-20	0	34
L.A. Rams	18-67	2-10	0	77
At New Orleans	18-70	4-37	0	107
At Dallas	18-61	3-23	1	84
New England	22-66	3-55	1	121
At N.Y. Jets	17-78	6-85	0	163
New Orleans	17-51	3-24	0	75
Atlanta	17-109	2-15	0	124
Green Bay	8-41	5-76	1	117
N.Y. Giants	20-49	4-13	0	62
At Atlanta	17-97	3-32	0	129
At L.A. Rams	16-48	4-31	1	79
Buffalo	25-105	1-12	1	117
Chicago	10-31	1-10	0	41
Minnesota (P)	18-125	0-0	1	125
L.A. Rams (P)	23-93	3-40	1	133
Denver (SB)	20-69	5-34	1	103
Totals	271-1054	49-473	7	1527
Postseason	61-287	8-74	3	361

14 DON HUTSON (1935-45)

1935

Opponent	No.	Yds.	Avg.	TD
Chi. Cardinals	0	0	0.0	0
Chi. Bears	1	83	83.0	1
New York	0	0	0.0	0
Pittsburgh	4	109	27.3	2
Chi. Cardinals	1	4	4.0	0
Detroit	4	38	9.5	0
At Chi. Bears	5	103	20.6	2
Detroit	3	83	27.7	1
At Detroit	0	0	0.0	0
At Pittsburgh	0	0	0.0	0
At Chi. Cardinals	0	0	0.0	0
At Philadelphia	0	0	0.0	0
Totals	**18**	**420**	**23.3**	**6**

1936

Opponent	No.	Yds.	Avg.	TD
Chi. Cardinals	0	0	0.0	0
Chi. Bears	0	0	0.0	0
Chi. Cardinals	0	0	0.0	0
Boston	3	87	29.0	1
Detroit	5	51	10.2	0
Pittsburgh	5	84	16.8	2
At Chi. Bears	3	41	13.7	1
At Boston	6	83	13.8	1
At Brooklyn	3	52	17.3	2
At New York	3	41	13.7	0
At Detroit	6	97	16.2	1
Boston at N.Y. (C)	5	76	15.2	1
Totals	**34**	**536**	**15.8**	**8**
Postseason	**5**	**76**	**15.2**	**1**

1937

Opponent	No.	Yds.	Avg.	TD
Chi. Cardinals	2	8	4.0	0
Chi. Bears	1	21	21.0	0
Detroit	3	38	12.7	0
Chi. Cardinals	1	20	20.0	0
At Cleveland	5	94	18.8	3
Cleveland	3	20	6.7	0
At Detroit	6	56	9.3	0
At Chi. Bears	5	140	28.0	1
Philadelphia	5	69	13.8	2
At New York	3	37	12.3	0
At Washington	7	49	7.0	1
Totals	**41**	**552**	**13.5**	**7**

1938

Opponent	No.	Yds.	Avg.	TD
Cleveland	5	65	13.0	3
Chi. Bears	1	11	11.0	0
Chi. Cardinals	2	35	17.5	0
At Chi. Cardinals	3	34	11.3	1
Detroit	5	92	18.4	0
Brooklyn	4	59	14.8	1
Pittsburgh	2	43	21.5	0
At Cleveland	6	148	24.7	3
At Chi. Bears	1	20	20.0	1
At Detroit	3	41	13.7	0
At New York		(did not play)		
At New York (C)	0	0	0.0	0
Totals	**32**	**548**	**17.1**	**9**
Postseason	**0**	**0**	**0.0**	**0**

1939

Opponent	No.	Yds.	Avg.	TD
Chi.Cardinals	2	70	35.0	0
Chi. Bears	2	27	13.5	0
Cleveland	4	74	18.5	0
Chi. Cardinals	3	126	42.0	2
Detroit	2	111	55.5	2
Washington	1	28	28.0	0
At Chi. Bears	5	97	19.4	1
At Philadelphia	5	112	22.4	0
At Brooklyn	3	149	49.7	1
At Cleveland	3	21	7.0	0
At Detroit	4	31	7.8	0
New York (C)	2	21	10.5	0
Totals	**34**	**846**	**24.9**	**6**
Postseason	**2**	**21**	**10.5**	**0**

Team (W-L Record): Green Bay, 1935-45 (87-29-4, .742).

Hall of Fame? Yes (charter member)

Honors: Bert Bell Trophy, 1941-42; all-NFL (9), 1936, '38-45; NFL All-Star Game (4), 1939-42.

Records: All the season and career records for receptions, yards and TDs, plus the mark for the shortest TD catch -- 4 inches from Cecil Isbell, 1942.*

Lifetime Rankings: 488 receptions (1st/30th); 7,991 yards (1st/23rd); 99 TDs (1st/2nd).

100-Yard Games: 24

200-Yard Games: 4

Avg. Yards Per Season: 726

Avg. Yards Per Game: 68

Injuries: 1938--injured knee (sat out last game and virtually all of title game).

Comment: Hutson was a great player, no question. But his statistics are somewhat padded because he played during World War II, when the talent in the NFL was way down. His 1942 season -- 74 receptions, 1,211 yards and 17 touchdowns, all records -- was outrageous. No other receiver in the league had more than 27 catches, 571 yards or 8 TDs. His TD mark wasn't broken until 1984. If Hutson had produced statistics over his last four years (1942-45) comparable to his first seven, he would have retired with 412 receptions, 6,763 yards and 83 TDs. In other words, playing against wartime competition may have added 76 catches, 1,228 yards and 16 TDs to his career totals. That changes things. A career TD record of 83 would have lasted until 1968. Hutson's record of 99 stood until 1989.

1940

Opponent	No.	Yds.	Avg.	TD
Philadelphia	2	32	16.0	0
Chi. Bears	5	86	17.2	1
Chi. Cardinals	4	76	19.0	1
Cleveland	5	86	17.2	1
Detroit	6	89	14.8	0
Pittsburgh	3	36	12.0	1
At Chi. Bears	8	96	12.0	1
At Chi. Cardinals	2	60	30.0	1
At New York	4	43	10.8	0
At Detroit	3	28	9.3	1
At Cleveland	3	32	10.7	1
Totals	**45**	**664**	**14.8**	**7**

1941

Opponent	No.	Yds.	Avg.	TD
Detroit	6	61	10.2	1
Cleveland	0	0	0.0	0
Chi. Bears	4	74	18.5	1
Chi. Cardinals	5	40	8.0	0
Brooklyn	8	126	15.8	1
At Cleveland	6	71	11.8	0
At Chi. Bears	7	69	9.9	2
Chi. Cardinals	4	43	10.8	0
At Chi. Cardinals	2	47	23.5	1
At Pittsburgh	7	72	10.3	1
At Washington	9	135	15.0	3
At Chi. Bears (P)	1	19	19.0	0
Totals	**58**	**738**	**12.7**	**10**
Postseason	**1**	**19**	**19.0**	**0**

1942

Opponent	No.	Yds.	Avg.	TD
Chi. Bears	7	143	20.4	2
At Chi. Cardinals	3	23	7.7	1
Detroit	5	149	29.8	2
Cleveland	13	209	16.1	2
Chi. Bears	5	88	17.6	0
Chi. Cardinals	5	207	41.4	3
At Cleveland	9	96	10.7	3
At Chi. Bears	10	117	11.7	1
At New York	14	134	9.6	2
At Philadelphia	2	38	19.0	1
Pittsburgh	1	7	7.0	0
Totals	**74**	**1211**	**16.4**	**17**

1943

Opponent	No.	Yds.	Avg.	TD
Chi. Bears	2	40	20.0	1
At Chi. Cardinals	3	46	15.3	0
Detroit	3	38	12.7	0
Washington	1	17	17.0	1
At Detroit	6	84	14.0	1
At New York	8	103	12.9	2
At Chi. Bears	4	69	17.3	0
Chi. Cardinals	6	86	14.3	2
At Brooklyn	8	237	29.6	2
At Phil-Pitt	6	56	9.3	2
Totals	**47**	**776**	**16.5**	**11**

1944

Opponent	No.	Yds.	Avg.	TD
Brooklyn	5	74	14.8	1
Chi. Bears	3	57	19.0	1
Detroit	9	88	9.8	1
Card-Pitt	11	207	18.8	2
Cleveland	7	87	12.4	0
At Detroit	3	37	12.3	0
At Chi. Bears	6	82	13.7	0
At Cleveland	5	107	21.4	2
At New York	4	31	7.8	0
At Card-Pitt	5	96	19.2	2
At New York (C)	2	46	23.0	0
Totals	**58**	**866**	**14.9**	**9**
Postseason	**2**	**46**	**23.0**	**0**

1945

Opponent	No.	Yds.	Avg.	TD
Chi. Bears	3	69	23.0	0
Detroit	6	144	24.0	4
Cleveland	7	110	15.7	0
Boston	6	169	28.2	2
Chi. Cardinals	7	141	20.1	2
At Chi. Bears	3	42	14.0	0
At Cleveland	5	44	8.8	0
At Boston	5	60	12.0	1
At New York	1	15	15.0	0
At Detroit	4	40	10.0	0
Totals	**47**	**834**	**17.7**	**9**

82 RAYMOND BERRY (1955-67)

1955

Opponent	No.	Yds.	Avg.	TD
Chi. Bears		(did not play)		
Detroit	1	19	19.0	0
At Green Bay		(did not play)		
At Chi. Bears	1	15	15.0	0
Washington		(did not play)		
Green Bay		(did not play)		
At Detroit	3	36	12.0	0
At N.Y. Giants	4	78	19.5	0
Los Angeles	1	12	12.0	0
San Francisco	1	18	18.0	0
At Los Angeles	1	14	14.0	0
At San Francisco	1	13	13.0	0
Totals	**13**	**205**	**15.8**	**0**

1956

	No.	Yds.	Avg.	TD
Chi. Bears	2	20	10.0	0
Detroit	3	69	23.0	0
At Green Bay	3	37	12.3	0
At Chi. Bears	3	24	8.0	0
Green Bay	3	70	23.3	1
At Cleveland		(did not play)		
At Detroit	6	155	25.8	0
Los Angeles	6	73	12.2	0
San Francisco	6	83	13.8	0
At Los Angeles		(did not play)		
At San Francisco	2	40	20.0	1
Washington	3	30	10.0	0
Totals	**37**	**601**	**16.2**	**2**

1957

	No.	Yds.	Avg.	TD
Detroit	1	35	35.0	1
Chi. Bears	4	55	13.8	0
At Green Bay	1	2	2.0	0
At Detroit	1	13	13.0	0
Green Bay	4	98	24.5	1
Pittsburgh	3	56	18.7	1
At Washington	12	224	18.7	2
At Chi. Bears	2	25	12.5	0
San Francisco	3	62	20.7	0
Los Angeles	6	57	9.5	1
At San Francisco	3	27	9.0	0
At Los Angeles	7	146	20.9	0
Totals	**47**	**800**	**17.0**	**6**

1958

	No.	Yds.	Avg.	TD
Detroit	10	149	14.9	2
Chi. Bears	4	63	15.8	1
At Green Bay	5	54	10.8	0
At Detroit	4	95	23.8	0
Washington	4	92	23.0	2
Green Bay	2	25	12.5	0
At N.Y. Giants	4	49	12.3	1
At Chi. Bears	3	38	12.7	1
Los Angeles	3	37	12.3	0
San Francisco	9	114	12.7	1
At Los Angeles	8	78	9.8	1
At San Francisco		(did not play)		
At N.Y. Giants (C)	12	178	14.8	1
Totals	**56**	**794**	**14.2**	**9**
Postseason	**12**	**178**	**14.8**	**1**

1959

	No.	Yds.	Avg.	TD
Detroit	2	44	22.0	1
Chi. Bears	8	123	15.4	1
At Detroit	6	96	16.0	1
At Chi. Bears	3	48	16.0	0
Green Bay	10	117	11.7	2
Cleveland	11	156	14.2	1
At Washington	4	59	14.8	0
At Green Bay	4	36	9.0	2
San Francisco	3	48	16.0	1
Los Angeles	7	168	24.0	1
At San Francisco	5	41	8.2	2
At Los Angeles	3	23	7.7	2
N.Y. Giants (C)	5	68	13.6	0
Totals	**66**	**959**	**14.5**	**14**
Postseason	**5**	**68**	**13.6**	**0**

1960

	No.	Yds.	Avg.	TD
Washington	4	60	15.0	0
Chi. Bears	7	113	16.1	1
At Green Bay	5	85	17.0	0
Los Angeles	5	86	17.2	0
At Detroit	11	186	16.9	1
At Dallas	4	195	48.8	3
Green Bay	10	137	13.7	3
At Chi. Bears	6	104	17.3	0
San Francisco	9	181	20.1	1
Detroit	10	117	11.7	0
At Los Angeles	1	11	11.0	0
At San Francisco	2	23	11.5	0
Totals	**74**	**1298**	**17.5**	**10**

1961

	No.	Yds.	Avg.	TD
Los Angeles		(did not play)		
Detroit		(did not play)		
Minnesota	6	96	16.0	0
At Green Bay	4	71	17.8	0
At Chi. Bears	6	80	13.3	0
At Detroit	8	94	11.8	0
Chi. Bears	5	50	10.0	0
Green Bay	8	72	9.0	0
At Minnesota	8	86	10.8	0
St. Louis	5	48	9.6	0
At Washington	7	89	12.7	0
San Francisco	8	71	8.9	0
At Los Angeles	6	48	8.0	0
At San Francisco	4	68	17.0	0
Totals	**75**	**873**	**11.6**	**0**

1962

	No.	Yds.	Avg.	TD
Los Angeles	5	93	18.6	1
At Minnesota	5	36	7.2	0
Detroit	4	91	22.8	0
San Francisco	1	8	8.0	0
At Cleveland	1	7	7.0	0
At Chi. Bears	5	55	11.0	0
Green Bay	3	36	12.0	0
At San Francisco	0	0	0.0	0
At Los Angeles	2	26	13.0	0
At Green Bay	0	0	0.0	0
Chicago	0	0	0.0	0
At Detroit	6	82	13.7	1
Washington	11	122	11.1	0
Minnesota	8	131	16.4	1
Totals	**51**	**687**	**13.5**	**3**

Team (W-L Record): Baltimore, 1955-67 (106-60-4, .635).

Hall of Fame? Yes (1st year eligible)

Honors: All-NFL (3), 1958-60; Pro Bowl (5), 1958-59, '61, '63-64.

Records: Most receptions, career, 631*; most receiving yards, career, 9,275.*

Lifetime Rankings: 631 receptions (1st/7th); 9,275 yards (1st/8th); 68 TDs (3rd/16th).

100-Yard Games: 22 (plus 1 postseason)

200-Yard Games: 1

Avg. Yards Per Season: 713

Avg. Yards Per Game: 60

Injuries: 1961--knee surgery; 1963--dislocated shoulder.

Comment: Knee surgery in 1961 turned Berry into a completely different receiver. The previous season had been his greatest -- 74 receptions, 1,298 yards, 10 touchdowns. In '61 he caught 75 passes, but for 873 yards and no TDs. It's still the most catches a wide receiver has ever had without scoring. Little-known fact: Berry's 178-yard receiving day against the Giants in 1958 was an NFL championship game record for 29 years. The Redskins' Ricky Sanders finally broke it in the '87 Super Bowl when he had 191 yards. It's little-known because, for some strange reason, the NFL keeps Super Bowl marks separate from pre-Super Bowl (1932-65) title game marks. Come on, a title game is a title game.

1963

	No.	Yds.	Avg.	TD
N.Y. Giants	4	33	8.3	0
At San Francisco	1	11	11.0	0
At Green Bay		(did not play)		
At Chi. Bears		(did not play)		
San Francisco		(did not play)		
At Detroit		(did not play)		
Green Bay		(did not play)		
Chi. Bears	4	42	10.5	0
Detroit	5	148	29.6	1
At Minnesota	3	74	24.7	0
At Los Angeles	7	95	13.6	0
At Washington	5	43	8.6	1
Minnesota	8	127	15.9	1
Los Angeles	7	130	18.6	0
Totals	**44**	**703**	**16.0**	**3**

1964

	No.	Yds.	Avg.	TD
At Minnesota	1	8	8.0	0
At Green Bay	2	16	8.0	0
Chi. Bears	4	98	24.5	1
Los Angeles	2	19	9.5	0
St. Louis	5	78	15.6	1
Green Bay	7	78	11.1	0
At Detroit	4	25	6.3	1
San Francisco	5	96	19.2	1
At Chi. Bears		(did not play)		
Minnesota		(did not play)		
At Los Angeles	2	52	26.0	0
At San Francisco	2	48	24.0	1
Detroit	4	56	14.0	0
Washington	5	89	17.8	1
At Cleveland (C)	3	38	12.7	0
Totals	**43**	**663**	**15.4**	**6**
Postseason	**3**	**38**	**12.7**	**0**

1965

	No.	Yds.	Avg.	TD
Minnesota	5	56	11.2	0
At Green Bay	5	62	12.4	1
San Francisco	5	49	9.8	0
Detroit	2	19	9.5	0
At Washington	2	14	7.0	0
Los Angeles	7	75	10.7	1
At San Francisco	5	62	12.4	1
At Chi. Bears	3	60	20.0	1
At Minnesota	4	85	21.3	1
Philadelphia	7	89	12.7	0
At Detroit	1	13	13.0	0
Chi. Bears	2	30	15.0	0
Green Bay	10	125	12.5	1
At Los Angeles		(did not play)		
At Green Bay (P)	0	0	0.0	0
Dallas (PB)	3	41	13.7	0
Totals	**58**	**739**	**12.7**	**7**
Postseason	**3**	**41**	**13.7**	**0**

1966

	No.	Yds.	Avg.	TD
At Green Bay	5	40	8.0	0
At Minnesota	1	40	40.0	1
San Francisco	1	6	6.0	0
At Chi. Bears	6	84	14.0	0
Detroit	5	66	13.2	1
Minnesota	5	87	17.4	1
At Los Angeles	2	42	21.0	0
Washington	10	131	13.1	2
At Atlanta	3	29	9.7	0
At Detroit	4	45	11.3	0
Los Angeles	3	40	13.3	0
Chi. Bears	3	52	17.3	1
Green Bay	4	59	14.8	0
At San Francisco	4	65	16.3	1
Philadelphia (PB)	4	49	12.3	1
Totals	**56**	**786**	**14.0**	**7**
Postseason	**4**	**49**	**12.3**	**1**

1967

	No.	Yds.	Avg.	TD
Atlanta	4	60	15.0	0
At Philadelphia	2	27	13.5	0
San Francisco	0	0	0.0	0
At Chi. Bears		(did not play)		
Los Angeles		(did not play)		
At Minnesota	2	52	26.0	0
At Washington		(did not play)		
Green Bay		(did not play)		
At Atlanta		(did not play)		
Detroit		(did not play)		
At San Francisco		(did not play)		
Dallas	1	5	5.0	0
New Orleans	1	12	12.0	0
At Los Angeles	1	11	11.0	0
Totals	**11**	**167**	**15.2**	**1**

13 DON MAYNARD (1958-73)

1958 (Giants)

Opponent	No.	Yds.	Avg.	TD
Chi. Cardinals	2	47	23.5	0
At Cleveland	2	29	14.5	0
At Pittsburgh	1	8	8.0	0
Baltimore (C)	0	0	0.0	0
Totals	**5**	**84**	**16.8**	**0**
Postseason	**0**	**0**	**0.0**	**0**

1960 (Titans/Jets)

Opponent	No.	Yds.	Avg.	TD
Buffalo	4	116	29.0	0
Boston	5	76	15.2	0
Denver	5	93	18.6	0
At Dallas	6	85	14.2	1
At Houston	11	174	15.8	0
At Buffalo	6	82	13.7	0
Houston	7	156	22.3	1
Oakland	4	57	14.3	1
Los Angeles	4	41	10.3	0
At Boston	5	100	20.0	1
Dallas	10	179	17.9	1
At Denver	2	57	28.5	0
At Oakland	0	0	0.0	0
At Los Angeles	3	49	16.3	0
Totals	**72**	**1265**	**17.6**	**6**

1961

Opponent	No.	Yds.	Avg.	TD
At Boston	7	86	12.3	1
At Buffalo	9	107	11.9	2
Denver	4	84	21.0	2
Boston	6	87	14.5	1
San Diego	5	80	16.0	0
At Denver	0	0	0.0	0
At Oakland	0	0	0.0	0
At San Diego	0	0	0.0	0
Oakland	0	0	0.0	0
At Houston	4	37	9.3	1
Buffalo	3	41	13.7	0
Dallas	1	23	23.0	0
Houston	1	45	45.0	1
At Dallas	3	39	13.0	0
Totals	**43**	**629**	**14.6**	**8**

1962

Opponent	No.	Yds.	Avg.	TD
At Oakland	3	85	28.3	1
At San Diego	3	47	15.7	0
At Buffalo	1	13	13.0	0
Denver	5	83	16.6	1
Boston	5	117	23.4	1
At Houston	3	35	11.7	0
At Dallas	4	102	25.5	0
San Diego	6	157	26.2	2
Oakland	5	86	17.2	1
Dallas	0	0	0.0	0
At Denver	4	105	26.3	1
At Boston	8	113	14.1	1
Buffalo	7	83	11.9	0
Houston	2	15	7.5	0
Totals	**56**	**1041**	**18.6**	**8**

1963

Opponent	No.	Yds.	Avg.	TD
At Boston	4	32	8.0	0
Houston	4	71	17.8	0
Oakland	2	45	22.5	0
Boston	3	51	17.0	2
At San Diego	2	59	29.5	0
At Oakland	2	32	16.0	0
Denver	5	159	31.8	3
San Diego		(did not play)		
At Houston		(did not play)		
At Denver	3	99	33.0	1
Kansas City	4	46	11.5	1
At Buffalo	5	85	17.0	1
Buffalo	3	98	32.7	1
At Kansas City	1	3	3.0	0
Totals	**38**	**780**	**20.5**	**9**

1964

Opponent	No.	Yds.	Avg.	TD
Denver	4	101	25.3	1
At Boston	4	64	16.0	0
San Diego	4	113	28.3	1
Oakland	0	0	0.0	0
Houston	4	102	25.5	2
At Buffalo	4	53	13.3	2
Boston	6	109	18.2	1
Buffalo	5	100	20.0	0
At Denver	3	45	15.0	0
At Oakland	4	75	18.8	1
Kansas City	5	45	9.0	0
At San Diego	2	27	13.5	0
At Houston	1	13	13.0	0
At Kansas City	0	0	0.0	0
Totals	**46**	**847**	**18.4**	**8**

Teams (W-L Record): New York Giants, 1958; N.Y. Titans/Jets, 1960-72; St. Louis, 1973 (97-93-6, .510).

Hall of Fame? Yes (9th year eligible)

Honors: All-AFL (1), 1969; AFL All-Star Game (4), 1965, '67-69.

Records: Most receptions, career, 633*; most receiving yards, career, 11,834.*

Lifetime Rankings: 633 receptions (1st/6th); 11,834 yards (1st/3rd); 88 TDs (2nd/3rd).

100-Yard Games: 50 (plus 1 postseason)

200-Yard Games: 3

Avg. Yards Per Season: 789

Avg. Yards Per Game: 64

Injuries: 1969--fractured foot; 1970--muscle/knee injuries.

Comment: Maynard had to wait a while to get into Canton. He'd caught more than half his passes in the AFL's early years, you see. But there's no doubt he belongs there. He was one of the most dangerous receivers in pro football in the late '60s. In 1968, the season the Jets won the Super Bowl, he had 200-yard games against the two best teams in the league, the Raiders and Chiefs. Pulled leg muscles plagued him throughout his career, but he kept his speed to the end.

1965

Opponent	No.	Yds.	Avg.	TD
At Houston	2	43	21.5	1
Kansas City	4	83	20.8	1
At Buffalo	4	81	20.3	0
At Denver	7	76	10.9	0
Oakland	6	149	24.8	2
San Diego	4	36	9.0	0
Denver	1	14	14.0	1
At Kansas City	1	31	31.0	1
At Boston	6	122	20.3	2
Houston	7	87	12.4	2
Boston	5	121	24.2	0
At San Diego	5	83	16.6	1
At Oakland	7	112	16.0	1
Buffalo	9	180	20.0	2
Totals	**68**	**1218**	**17.9**	**14**

1966

Opponent	No.	Yds.	Avg.	TD
At Miami	3	41	13.7	0
Houston	7	156	22.3	2
At Denver	5	101	20.2	0
At Boston	2	17	8.5	0
San Diego	1	18	18.0	0
At Houston	2	15	7.5	0
Oakland	3	66	22.0	0
Buffalo	2	69	34.5	1
At Buffalo	2	39	19.5	0
Miami	3	29	9.7	0
Kansas City	2	54	27.0	0
At Oakland	5	50	10.0	0
At San Diego	5	56	11.2	0
Boston	6	129	21.5	2
Totals	**48**	**840**	**17.5**	**5**

1967

Opponent	No.	Yds.	Avg.	TD
At Buffalo	5	106	21.2	2
At Denver	4	141	35.3	0
Miami	4	121	30.3	0
Oakland	4	86	21.5	0
Houston	10	157	15.7	1
At Miami	4	51	12.8	1
Boston	5	132	26.4	0
At Kansas City	5	60	12.0	0
Buffalo	4	103	25.8	0
At Boston	5	164	32.8	1
Denver	0	0	0.0	0
Kansas City	1	13	13.0	0
At Oakland	12	159	13.3	2
At San Diego	8	141	17.6	3
Total	**71**	**1434**	**20.2**	**10**

1968

Opponent	No.	Yds.	Avg.	TD
At Kansas City	8	203	25.4	2
Boston (Birmingham)	1	39	39.0	1
At Buffalo	3	114	38.0	1
San Diego	4	59	14.8	0
Denver	7	140	20.0	0
At Houston	1	16	16.0	0
Boston	2	21	10.5	0
Buffalo	2	29	14.5	0
Houston	1	19	19.0	0
At Oakland	10	228	22.8	1
At San Diego	6	166	27.7	0
Miami	7	160	22.9	3
Cincinnati	5	103	20.6	1
At Miami		(did not play)		
Oakland (C)	6	118	19.7	2
Baltimore (SB)	0	0	0.0	0
Totals	**57**	**1297**	**22.8**	**10**
Postseason	**6**	**118**	**19.7**	**2**

1969

Opponent	No.	Yds.	Avg.	TD
At Buffalo	3	118	39.3	1
At Denver	4	44	11.0	0
At San Diego	5	76	15.2	0
At Boston		(did not play)		
At Cincinnati	4	35	8.8	0
Houston	7	212	30.3	2
Boston	1	20	20.0	0
Miami	4	121	30.3	2
Buffalo	2	38	19.0	0
Kansas City	9	137	15.2	1
Cincinnati	8	137	17.1	0
Oakland		(did not play)		
At Houston		(did not play)		
At Miami		(did not play)		
Kansas City (P)	1	18	18.0	0
Totals	**47**	**938**	**20.0**	**6**
Postseason	**1**	**18**	**18.0**	**0**

1970

Opponent	No.	Yds.	Avg.	TD
At Cleveland	4	69	17.3	0
At Boston	0	0	0.0	0
At Buffalo		(did not play)		
Miami		(did not play)		
Baltimore	9	148	16.4	0
Buffalo	3	29	9.7	0
N.Y. Giants	3	48	16.0	0
At Pittsburgh	3	48	16.0	0
At Los Angeles	3	102	34.0	0
Boston	2	33	16.5	0
Minnesota	3	32	10.7	0
Oakland		(did not play)		
At Miami	1	16	16.0	0
At Baltimore		(did not play)		
Totals	**31**	**525**	**16.9**	**0**

1971

Opponent	No.	Yds.	Avg.	TD
At Baltimore	1	7	7.0	0
At St. Louis	5	51	10.2	0
At Miami	1	11	11.0	0
At New England	0	0	0.0	0
Buffalo	1	44	44.0	0
Miami	1	32	32.0	0
At San Diego	1	5	5.0	0
Kansas City	2	24	12.0	0
Baltimore	0	0	0.0	0
At Buffalo	2	49	24.5	1
San Francisco	2	43	21.5	0
At Dallas	1	20	20.0	0
New England	1	8	8.0	0
Cincinnati	3	114	38.0	1
Totals	**21**	**408**	**19.4**	**2**

1972

Opponent	No.	Yds.	Avg.	TD
At Buffalo	0	0	0.0	0
At Baltimore	1	28	28.0	1
At Houston	3	35	11.7	0
Miami	2	26	13.0	0
At New England	1	10	10.0	0
Baltimore	1	26	26.0	0
New England	3	58	19.3	0
Washington	2	33	16.5	1
Buffalo	1	18	18.0	0
At Miami	1	41	41.0	0
At Detroit	2	38	19.0	0
New Orleans	5	66	13.2	0
At Oakland	7	131	18.7	0
Cleveland	0	0	0.0	0
Totals	**29**	**510**	**17.6**	**2**

1973 (Cardinals)

Opponent	No.	Yds.	Avg.	TD
At Philadelphia	1	18	18.0	0
Washington	0	0	0.0	0
Totals	**1**	**18**	**18.0**	**0**

19 LANCE ALWORTH (1962-72)

1962 (Chargers)

Opponent	No.	Yds.	Avg.	TD
At Denver	1	17	17.0	0
New York	2	90	45.0	2
Houston	4	53	13.3	0
At Oakland	3	66	22.0	1
Totals	**10**	**226**	**22.6**	**3**

1963

	No.	Yds.	Avg.	TD
Buffalo	2	37	18.5	0
Boston	4	76	19.0	1
Kansas City	2	16	8.0	0
At Denver	4	114	28.5	1
New York	4	54	13.5	1
At Kansas City	9	232	25.8	2
Oakland	3	50	16.7	1
At New York	5	180	36.0	1
At Boston	13	210	16.2	1
At Buffalo	4	79	19.8	1
Houston	4	56	14.0	1
At Oakland	3	71	23.7	1
Denver	1	4	4.0	0
At Houston	3	28	9.3	0
Boston (C)	4	77	19.3	1
Totals	**61**	**1205**	**19.8**	**11**
Postseason	**4**	**77**	**19.3**	**1**

1964

	No.	Yds.	Avg.	TD
Houston	6	119	19.8	1
Boston	5	67	13.4	1
At Buffalo	(did not play)			
At New York	(did not play)			
At Boston	8	124	15.5	2
Denver	5	44	8.8	1
At Houston	5	76	15.2	0
Oakland	8	203	25.4	2
At Denver	4	54	13.5	1
At Kansas City	5	168	33.6	1
Buffalo	4	185	46.3	2
New York	3	101	33.7	1
Kansas City	6	80	13.3	1
At Oakland	2	14	7.0	0
Totals	**61**	**1235**	**20.2**	**13**

1965

	No.	Yds.	Avg.	TD
Denver	7	211	30.1	1
At Oakland	4	71	17.8	1
Kansas City	2	21	10.5	0
Houston	4	145	36.3	2
At Buffalo	8	168	21.0	2
At Boston	3	109	36.3	1
At New York	7	142	20.3	1
Boston	5	59	11.8	0
At Denver	2	47	23.5	1
At Kansas City	6	181	30.2	1
Buffalo	7	127	18.1	0
New York	7	147	21.0	2
At Houston	2	14	7.0	1
Oakland	5	160	32.0	1
At Buffalo (C)	4	82	20.5	0
Totals	**69**	**1602**	**23.2**	**14**
Postseason	**4**	**82**	**20.5**	**0**

1966

	No.	Yds.	Avg.	TD
Buffalo	5	46	9.2	1
Boston	5	97	19.4	1
At Oakland	2	50	25.0	0
Miami	6	119	19.8	2
At New York	10	149	14.9	0
At Buffalo	3	56	18.7	0
At Boston	6	177	29.5	2
Denver	5	47	9.4	0
At Kansas City	6	101	16.8	2
Oakland	(did not play)			
At Denver	6	111	18.5	2
At Houston	4	147	36.8	2
New York	7	127	18.1	0
Kansas City	8	156	19.5	1
Totals	**73**	**1383**	**18.9**	**13**

1967

	No.	Yds.	Avg.	TD
Boston	3	36	12.0	0
Houston	10	121	12.1	1
At Buffalo	4	99	24.8	0
Boston	4	62	15.5	1
Kansas City	5	95	19.0	2
At Denver	5	142	28.4	1
At Oakland	10	213	21.3	1
Miami	4	125	31.3	1
At Kansas City	1	2	2.0	1
Denver	(did not play)			
Oakland	4	86	21.5	1
At Miami	(did not play)			
At Houston	(did not play)			
New York	2	29	14.5	0
Totals	**52**	**1010**	**19.4**	**9**

1968

	No.	Yds.	Avg.	TD
Cincinnati	4	58	14.5	0
Houston	8	183	22.9	1
At Cincinnati	1	11	11.0	0
At New York	8	137	17.1	1
At Oakland	9	182	20.2	1
Denver	4	131	32.8	1
At Kansas City	6	169	28.2	0
Miami	5	60	12.0	2
At Boston	1	29	29.0	0
At Buffalo	2	29	14.5	0
New York	3	33	11.0	0
At Denver	9	171	19.0	4
Kansas City	3	39	13.0	0
Oakland	5	80	16.0	0
Totals	**68**	**1312**	**19.3**	**10**

1969

	No.	Yds.	Avg.	TD
Kansas City	4	94	23.5	0
At Cincinnati	2	18	9.0	0
New York	4	33	8.3	1
Cincinnati	8	125	15.6	0
At Miami	3	55	18.3	0
At Boston	7	95	13.6	0
Oakland	6	96	16.0	1
At Denver	2	13	6.5	0
At Kansas City	3	43	14.3	0
At Oakland	3	25	8.3	0
Denver	2	52	26.0	0
At Houston	7	85	12.1	0
Boston	6	147	24.5	1
Buffalo	7	122	17.4	1
Totals	**64**	**1003**	**15.7**	**4**

1970

	No.	Yds.	Avg.	TD
Baltimore	0	0	0.0	0
Oakland	1	37	37.0	1
At Los Angeles	0	0	0.0	0
Green Bay	1	6	6.0	0
At Chicago	6	96	16.0	0
Houston	2	124	62.0	1
At Cleveland	4	76	19.0	1
Denver	4	51	12.8	0
At Boston	4	51	12.8	1
At Oakland	2	17	8.5	0
At Kansas City	3	44	14.7	0
Cincinnati	4	50	12.5	0
At Denver	4	56	14.0	0
Kansas City	0	0	0.0	0
Totals	**35**	**608**	**17.4**	**4**

1971 (Cowboys)

	No.	Yds.	Avg.	TD
At Buffalo	(did not play)			
At Philadelphia	(did not play)			
Washington	1	24	24.0	0
N.Y. Giants	0	0	0.0	0
At New Orleans	5	46	9.2	0
New England	2	38	19.0	0
At Chicago	5	67	13.4	0
At St. Louis	8	89	11.1	0
Philadelphia	4	59	14.8	0
At Washington	1	25	25.0	0
Los Angeles	2	34	17.0	1
N.Y. Jets	3	54	18.0	0
At N.Y. Giants	2	26	13.0	0
St. Louis	1	25	25.0	0
At Minnesota (P)	2	33	16.5	0
San Francisco (P)	1	17	17.0	0
Miami (SB)	2	28	14.0	1
Totals	**34**	**487**	**14.3**	**2**
Postseason	**5**	**78**	**15.6**	**1**

1972

	No.	Yds.	Avg.	TD
Philadelphia	3	46	15.3	1
At N.Y. Giants	1	3	3.0	0
At Green Bay	4	55	13.8	0
Pittsburgh	0	0	0.0	0
At Baltimore	0	0	0.0	0
At Washington	1	16	16.0	0
Detroit	0	0	0.0	0
At San Diego	1	8	8.0	0
St. Louis	0	0	0.0	0
At Philadelphia	0	0	0.0	0
San Francisco	1	12	12.0	0
At St. Louis	3	41	13.7	0
Washington	1	14	14.0	0
N.Y. Giants	0	0	0.0	0
At San Francisco (P)	2	40	20.0	1
At Washington (P)	1	15	15.0	0
Totals	**15**	**195**	**13.0**	**2**
Postseason	**3**	**55**	**18.3**	**1**

Teams (W-L Record): San Diego, 1962-70; Dallas, 1971-72 (90-55-9, .614).

Hall of Fame? Yes (1st year eligible; 1st AFL player)

Honors: All-AFL (7), 1963-69; AFL All-Star Game (7), 1963-69.

Records: Most consecutive games with a reception, 96, 1962-69*; most 200-yard games, career, 5.

Lifetime Rankings: 542 receptions (4th/15th); 10,266 yards (2nd/7th); 85 TDs (3rd/T4th).

100-Yard Games: 41

200-Yard Games: 5

Avg. Yards Per Season: 933

Avg. Yards Per Game: 74

Injuries: 1962--torn thigh muscle.

Comment: Alworth averaged 100 yards a game three straight seasons -- in 1964 (102.9 in 12 games), '65 (114.4) and '66 (106.4 in 13). No other receiver in AFL-NFL history has done it even two years in a row. If he hadn't missed three games in 1967, he probably would have caught 10 or more touchdown passes in six consecutive seasons instead of just five out of six, which is still the best such streak of all time. Al Davis, Mr. Vertical Passing Game himself, loved Alworth. Davis scouted him at Arkansas, coached him as a rookie, then moved to Oakland and watched in dismay as Alworth had games of 213, 203, 182 and 160 yards against the Raiders. What probably hurt Al more than anything was that the second-round pick San Diego used to draft Alworth originally belonged to Oakland. He got over it in time, though, to present Alworth at his Hall of Fame induction in 1978. Alworth's 18.9-yard per-catch average is sixth-highest among players with 300 or more receptions. He didn't fumble in his last seven seasons.

42 CHARLEY TAYLOR (1964-75, '77)

1964

Opponent	No.	Yds.	Avg.	TD
Cleveland	8	88	11.0	0
At Dallas	1	16	16.0	0
At N.Y. Giants	4	36	9.0	0
St. Louis	3	33	11.0	0
Philadelphia	3	92	30.7	2
At St. Louis	3	81	27.0	0
Chicago	4	9	2.3	0
At Philadelphia	1	34	34.0	0
At Cleveland	7	77	11.0	0
At Pittsburgh	1	80	80.0	1
Dallas	7	86	12.3	0
N.Y. Giants	3	54	18.0	1
Pittsburgh	4	34	8.5	0
At Baltimore	4	94	23.5	0
Totals	**53**	**814**	**15.4**	**5**

1965

Opponent	No.	Yds.	Avg.	TD
Cleveland	2	41	20.5	0
At Dallas		(did not play)		
At Detroit	3	60	20.0	0
St. Louis	3	21	7.0	0
Baltimore	5	22	4.4	0
At St. Louis	3	61	20.3	1
Philadelphia	3	81	27.0	1
At N.Y. Giants	2	32	16.0	0
At Philadelphia	5	44	8.8	0
At Pittsburgh	1	24	24.0	0
Dallas	7	139	19.9	1
At Cleveland	3	25	8.3	0
N.Y. Giants	2	20	10.0	0
Pittsburgh	1	7	7.0	0
Totals	**40**	**577**	**14.4**	**3**

1966

Opponent	No.	Yds.	Avg.	TD
Cleveland	5	94	18.8	1
At St. Louis	0	0	0.0	0
At Pittsburgh	5	52	10.4	1
Pittsburgh	3	80	26.7	1
Atlanta	3	105	35.0	1
At N.Y. Giants	2	17	8.5	0
St. Louis	5	51	10.2	0
At Philadelphia	3	7	2.3	0
At Baltimore	8	111	13.9	1
Dallas	11	199	18.1	2
At Cleveland	9	60	6.7	0
N.Y. Giants	6	124	20.7	2
At Dallas	4	145	36.3	1
Philadelphia	8	74	9.3	2
Totals	**72**	**1119**	**15.5**	**12**

1967

Opponent	No.	Yds.	Avg.	TD
At Philadelphia	8	144	18.0	0
At New Orleans	3	45	15.0	1
N.Y. Giants	7	106	15.1	0
Dallas	7	73	10.4	1
At Atlanta	7	73	10.4	1
At L.A. Rams	3	148	49.3	1
Baltimore Colts		(did not play)		
St. Louis	2	29	14.5	0
San Francisco		(did not play)		
At Dallas	5	25	5.0	0
At Cleveland	11	123	11.2	2
Philadelphia	6	58	9.7	1
At Pittsburgh	3	75	25.0	1
New Orleans	8	91	11.4	1
Totals	**70**	**990**	**14.1**	**9**

1968

Opponent	No.	Yds.	Avg.	TD
At Chicago	4	81	20.3	0
At New Orleans	3	18	6.0	0
At N.Y. Giants	8	74	9.3	0
Philadelphia	6	75	12.5	1
Pittsburgh	3	27	9.0	0
At St. Louis	6	58	9.7	0
N.Y. Giants	1	11	11.0	0
At Minnesota	2	38	19.0	0
At Philadelphia	0	0	0.0	0
Dallas	5	114	22.8	2
Green Bay	5	51	10.2	0
At Dallas	3	59	19.7	1
Cleveland	2	44	22.0	1
Detroit	0	0	0.0	0
Totals	**48**	**650**	**13.5**	**5**

1969

Opponent	No.	Yds.	Avg.	TD
At New Orleans	5	92	18.4	2
At Cleveland	2	19	9.5	0
At San Francisco	8	92	11.5	0
St. Louis	4	51	12.8	0
N.Y. Giants	1	14	14.0	0
At Pittsburgh	5	55	11.0	1
At Baltimore	5	52	10.4	1
Philadelphia	6	67	11.2	1
Dallas	6	155	25.8	1
Atlanta	5	43	8.6	0
Los Angeles	3	36	12.0	0
At Philadelphia	10	87	8.7	1
New Orleans	5	60	12.0	0
At Dallas	6	60	10.0	0
Totals	**71**	**883**	**12.4**	**8**

1970

Opponent	No.	Yds.	Avg.	TD
At San Francisco	3	22	7.3	0
At St. Louis	5	54	10.8	0
At Philadelphia	2	25	12.5	1
Detroit	6	124	20.7	2
At Oakland	7	102	14.6	1
Cincinnati	5	70	14.0	2
At Denver	3	34	11.3	0
Minnesota	4	26	6.5	0
At N.Y. Giants	5	100	20.0	1
Dallas	2	36	18.0	0
N.Y. Giants		(did not play)		
At Dallas		(did not play)		
Philadelphia		(did not play)		
St. Louis		(did not play)		
Totals	**42**	**593**	**14.1**	**8**

1971

Opponent	No.	Yds.	Avg.	TD
At St. Louis	2	11	5.5	0
At N.Y. Giants	6	125	20.8	2
At Dallas	2	17	8.5	0
Houston	4	59	14.8	0
St. Louis	3	33	11.0	0
At Kansas City	7	125	17.9	2
New Orleans		(did not play)		
Philadelphia		(did not play)		
At Chicago		(did not play)		
Dallas		(did not play)		
At Philadelphia		(did not play)		
N.Y. Giants		(did not play)		
At L.A. Rams		(did not play)		
Cleveland		(did not play)		
At San Francisco (P)		(did not play)		
Totals	**24**	**370**	**15.4**	**4**

1972

Opponent	No.	Yds.	Avg.	TD
At Minnesota	2	9	4.5	0
St. Louis	5	39	7.8	0
At New England	7	134	19.1	2
Philadelphia	4	60	15.0	0
At St. Louis	5	52	10.4	0
Dallas	2	26	13.0	0
At N.Y. Giants	1	13	13.0	0
At N.Y. Jets	2	75	37.5	1
N.Y. Giants	2	50	25.0	0
Atlanta	4	37	9.3	0
Green Bay	5	53	10.6	1
At Philadelphia	5	75	15.0	1
At Dallas	5	50	10.0	0
Buffalo	0	0	0.0	0
Green Bay (P)	2	16	8.0	0
Dallas (P)	7	146	20.9	2
Miami (SB)	2	20	10.0	0
Totals	**49**	**673**	**13.7**	**7**
Postseason	**11**	**182**	**16.5**	**2**

1973

Opponent	No.	Yds.	Avg.	TD
San Diego	3	60	20.0	1
At St. Louis	9	132	14.7	1
At Philadelphia	7	69	9.9	2
Dallas	4	29	7.3	1
At N.Y. Giants	5	48	9.6	0
St. Louis	7	153	21.9	1
At New Orleans	1	16	16.0	0
At Pittsburgh	0	0	0.0	0
San Francisco	7	72	10.3	0
Baltimore	2	31	-15.5	0
At Detroit	5	34	6.8	1
N.Y. Giants	3	73	24.3	0
At Dallas	3	48	16.0	0
Philadelphia	3	36	12.0	0
At Minnesota (P)	4	56	14.0	0
Totals	**59**	**801**	**13.6**	**7**
Postseason	**4**	**56**	**14.0**	**0**

1974

Opponent	No.	Yds.	Avg.	TD
At N.Y. Giants	2	15	7.5	0
St. Louis	4	48	12.0	0
Denver	6	59	9.8	2
At Cincinnati	4	78	19.5	0
Miami	3	43	14.3	0
N.Y. Giants	6	59	9.8	0
At St. Louis	3	57	19.0	0
At Green Bay	3	46	15.3	0
At Philadelphia	9	155	17.2	1
Dallas	3	34	11.3	0
Philadelphia	3	51	17.0	0
At Dallas	1	13	13.0	0
At Los Angeles	3	39	13.0	0
Chicago	4	41	10.3	2
At L.A. Rams (P)	4	79	19.8	0
Totals	**54**	**738**	**13.7**	**5**
Postseason	**4**	**79**	**19.8**	**0**

1975

Opponent	No.	Yds.	Avg.	TD
New Orleans	6	58	9.7	2
N.Y. Giants	5	51	10.2	1
At Philadelphia	1	24	24.0	0
St. Louis	2	42	21.0	0
At Houston	4	93	23.3	0
At Cleveland	3	49	16.3	0
Dallas	7	69	9.9	1
At N.Y. Giants	4	49	12.3	0
At St. Louis	3	70	23.3	1
Oakland	6	61	10.2	1
Minnesota	3	59	19.7	0
At Atlanta	5	65	13.0	0
At Dallas	2	38	19.0	0
Philadelphia	2	16	8.0	0
Totals	**53**	**744**	**14.0**	**6**

1977

Opponent	No.	Yds.	Avg.	TD
At N.Y. Giants	2	18	9.0	0
Atlanta	3	39	13.0	0
At St. Louis	1	11	11.0	0
At Tampa Bay	2	26	13.0	0
Dallas	2	32	16.0	0
N.Y. Giants	2	27	13.5	0
Philadelphia		(did not play)		
At Baltimore		(did not play)		
At Philadelphia	0	0	0.0	0
At Green Bay	0	0	0.0	0
Dallas	0	0	0.0	0
At Buffalo	0	0	0.0	0
At St. Louis	0	0	0.0	0
L.A. Rams	2	5	2.5	0
Totals	**14**	**158**	**11.3**	**0**

Team (W-L Record): Washington, 1964-75, '77 (99-77-6, .560).

Hall of Fame? Yes (2nd year eligible)

Honors: UPI NFL Rookie of the Year, 1964; all-NFL (1), 1967; Pro Bowl (8), 1964-67, '72-75.

Records: Most receptions, career, 649.*

Lifetime Rankings: 649 receptions (1st/4th); 9,140 yards (4th/10th); 79 TDs (7th/T8th).

100-Yard Games: 22

200-Yard Games: None

Avg. Yards Per Season: 703

Avg. Yards Per Game: 55

Injuries: 1970--broken collarbone; 1971--fractured ankle; 1976--shoulder injury.

Comment: Taylor gave the Redskins in the '60s and '70s what Art Monk gives them now: a big (6'3", 210), rugged receiver who could make the tough catch in traffic. Both were originally running backs. Taylor didn't make the switch until mid-1966, his third NFL season. He wound up leading the league in receptions that year. Injuries in '70 and '71 cost him 13 games and the chance to be the first receiver with 700 catches. An absolutely devastating downfield blocker.

42 PAUL WARFIELD (1964-77)

1964 (Browns)

Opponent	No.	Yds.	Avg.	TD
At Washington	0	0	0.0	0
St. Louis	3	63	21.0	1
At Philadelphia	6	97	16.2	1
Dallas	5	123	24.6	1
Pittsburgh	3	34	11.3	0
At Dallas	2	36	18.0	0
N.Y. Giants	3	33	11.0	1
At Pittsburgh	2	24	12.0	0
Washington	3	82	27.3	1
Detroit	5	92	18.4	1
At Green Bay	7	126	18.0	2
Philadelphia	2	16	8.0	1
At St. Louis	6	91	15.2	0
At N.Y. Giants	5	103	20.6	1
Baltimore (C)	1	13	13.0	0
Totals	**52**	**920**	**17.7**	**9**
Postseason	**1**	**13**	**13.0**	**0**

1965

	No.	Yds.	Avg.	TD
At Washington	(did not play)			
St. Louis	(did not play)			
At Philadelphia	(did not play)			
Pittsburgh	(did not play)			
Dallas	(did not play)			
At N.Y. Giants	(did not play)			
Minnesota	(did not play)			
Philadelphia	(did not play)			
N.Y. Giants	(did not play)			
At Dallas	(did not play)			
At Pittsburgh	(did not play)			
Washington	(did not play)			
At L.A. Rams	3	30	10.0	0
At St. Louis	(did not play)			
At Green Bay (C)	2	30	15.0	0
Totals	**3**	**30**	**10.0**	**0**
Postseason	**2**	**30**	**15.0**	**0**

1966

	No.	Yds.	Avg.	TD
At Washington	4	59	14.8	1
Green Bay	3	54	18.0	0
St. Louis	3	79	26.3	0
At N.Y. Giants	2	17	8.5	0
Pittsburgh	2	41	20.5	0
Dallas	3	39	13.0	1
At Atlanta	3	78	26.0	1
At Pittsburgh	1	12	12.0	0
Philadelphia	3	64	21.3	1
Washington	2	36	18.0	0
At Dallas	1	23	23.0	0
N.Y. Giants	0	0	0.0	0
At Philadelphia	3	78	26.0	0
At St. Louis	6	161	26.8	0
Totals	**36**	**741**	**20.6**	**5**

1967

	No.	Yds.	Avg.	TD
Dallas	3	46	15.3	0
At Detroit	2	48	24.0	1
At New Orleans	4	107	26.8	2
Pittsburgh	3	45	15.0	1
St. Louis	1	28	28.0	0
Chicago	1	33	33.0	0
At N.Y. Giants	5	126	25.2	2
At Pittsburgh	3	61	20.3	0
At Green Bay	2	24	12.0	0
Minnesota	2	28	14.0	0
Washington	3	96	32.0	1
N.Y. Giants	0	0	0.0	0
At St. Louis	2	57	28.5	1
At Philadelphia	1	3	3.0	0
At Dallas (P)	3	99	33.0	1
Totals	**32**	**702**	**21.9**	**8**
Postseason	**3**	**99**	**33.0**	**1**

1968

	No.	Yds.	Avg.	TD
At New Orleans	3	65	21.7	0
At Dallas	3	85	28.3	1
L.A. Rams	1	57	57.0	1
Pittsburgh	5	70	14.0	1
St. Louis	3	93	31.0	1
At Baltimore	5	46	9.2	0
Atlanta	4	80	20.0	1
At San Francisco	4	63	15.8	0
New Orleans	5	107	21.4	1
At Pittsburgh	4	68	17.0	1
Philadelphia	3	54	18.0	2
N.Y. Giants	6	137	22.8	1
At Washington	1	38	38.0	1
At St. Louis	3	104	34.7	1
Dallas (P)	4	86	21.5	0
Baltimore (P)	2	30	15.0	0
Totals	**50**	**1067**	**21.3**	**12**
Postseason	**6**	**116**	**19.3**	**0**

Teams (W-L Record): Cleveland, 1964-69, '76-77; Miami, 1970-74 (131-48-3, .728).

Hall of Fame? Yes (1st year eligible)

Honors: All-NFL (5), 1964, '68-69, '71-72; Pro Bowl (8), 1964, '68-74.

Records: None

Lifetime Rankings: 427 receptions (T17th/T46th); 8,565 yards (6th/16th); 85 TDs (T3rd/T4th).

100-Yard Games: 22 (plus 2 postseason)

200-Yard Games: None

Avg. Yards Per Season: 659

Avg. Yards Per Game: 55

Injuries/Absences: 1965--broken collarbone; 1975--World Football League.

Comment: In another few years Warfield won't even be in the top 50 in career receptions. But then, he was a quality not a quantity receiver. He averaged 20 yards a catch and a touchdown every five catches. No other player with 400 or more receptions can make that claim. The Dolphins didn't throw to him that much, only enough to keep defenses honest. But he still got his TDs -- 10 in 31 catches in the first nine games of 1971, 11 in 29 catches in '73. He didn't play on a losing pro team until his 14th and last season.

1969

	No.	Yds.	Avg.	TD
At Philadelphia	1	9	9.0	0
Washington	4	69	17.3	0
Detroit	7	106	15.1	1
At New Orleans	5	93	18.6	0
Pittsburgh	0	0	0.0	0
St. Louis	4	88	22.0	1
Dallas	3	84	28.0	2
At Minnesota	1	27	27.0	0
At Pittsburgh	5	132	26.4	1
N.Y. Giants	1	30	30.0	1
At Chicago	1	10	10.0	1
Green Bay	2	44	22.0	1
At St. Louis	4	119	29.8	2
At N.Y. Giants	4	75	18.8	1
At Dallas (P)	8	99	12.4	0
At Minnesota (P)	4	47	11.8	0
Totals	**42**	**886**	**21.1**	**10**
Postseason	**12**	**146**	**12.2**	**0**

1970 (Dolphins)

	No.	Yds.	Avg.	TD
At Boston	1	19	19.0	0
At Houston	3	64	21.3	0
Oakland	3	120	40.0	2
At N.Y. Jets	5	122	24.4	1
At Buffalo	4	89	22.3	1
Cleveland	3	69	23.0	0
At Baltimore	1	30	30.0	0
At Philadelphia	2	67	33.5	1
New Orleans	4	73	18.3	0
Baltimore	2	50	25.0	1
At Atlanta	0	0	0.0	0
Boston	(did not play)			
N.Y. Jets	(did not play)			
Buffalo	0	0	0.0	0
At Oakland (P)	4	62	15.5	1
Totals	**28**	**703**	**25.1**	**6**
Postseason	**4**	**62**	**15.5**	**1**

1971

	No.	Yds.	Avg.	TD
At Denver	6	146	24.3	1
At Buffalo	4	65	16.3	1
N.Y. Jets	4	104	26.0	1
At Cincinnati	4	92	23.0	1
New England	3	68	22.7	2
At N.Y. Jets	2	48	24.0	1
At L.A. Rams	3	108	36.0	1
Buffalo	2	12	6.0	1
Pittsburgh	3	158	52.7	3
Baltimore	1	13	13.0	0
Chicago	2	47	23.5	0
At New England	2	46	23.0	0
At Baltimore	3	28	9.3	0
Green Bay	4	61	15.3	0
At Kansas City (P)	7	140	20.0	0
Baltimore (P)	2	125	62.5	1
Dallas (SB)	4	39	9.8	0
Totals	**43**	**996**	**23.2**	**11**
Postseason	**13**	**304**	**23.4**	**1**

1972

At Kansas City	2	49	24.5	0
Houston	3	67	22.3	0
At Minnesota	2	15	7.5	0
At N.Y. Jets	5	71	14.2	1
San Diego	2	38	19.0	1
Buffalo	2	33	16.5	0
At Baltimore	2	35	17.5	0
At Buffalo	0	0	0.0	0
New England	2	42	21.0	0
N.Y. Jets	(did not play)			
St. Louis	(did not play)			
At New England	3	89	29.7	0
At N.Y. Giants	4	132	33.0	1
Baltimore	2	35	17.5	1
Cleveland (P)	2	50	25.0	0
At Pittsburgh (P)	2	63	31.5	0
Washington (SB)	3	36	12.0	0
Totals	**29**	**606**	**20.9**	**3**
Postseason	**8**	**149**	**18.6**	**0**

1973

San Francisco	4	39	9.8	1
At Oakland	0	0	0.0	0
New England	2	26	13.0	1
N.Y. Jets	2	43	21.5	2
At Cleveland	1	33	33.0	0
Buffalo	2	50	25.0	0
At New England	2	25	12.5	0
At N.Y. Jets	3	61	20.3	1
Baltimore	0	0	0.0	0
At Buffalo	4	59	14.8	1
At Dallas	1	45	45.0	1
Pittsburgh	1	10	10.0	0
At Baltimore	1	20	20.0	0
Detroit	6	103	17.2	4
Cincinnati (P)	4	95	23.8	1
Oakland (P)	1	27	27.0	0
Minnesota (SB)	2	33	16.5	0
Totals	**29**	**514**	**17.7**	**11**
Postseason	**7**	**155**	**22.1**	**1**

1974

At New England	5	104	20.8	0
At Buffalo	5	52	10.4	0
At San Diego	1	17	17.0	0
N.Y. Jets	(did not play)			
At Washington	(did not play)			
Kansas City	(did not play)			
Baltimore	(did not play)			
Atlanta	4	71	17.8	1
At New Orleans	2	27	13.5	0
Buffalo	4	139	34.8	1
At N.Y. Jets	3	68	22.7	0
Cincinnati	2	50	25.0	0
At Baltimore	1	8	8.0	0
New England	(did not play)			
At Oakland (P)	3	47	15.7	1
Totals	**27**	**536**	**19.9**	**2**
Postseason	**3**	**47**	**15.7**	**1**

1976 (Browns)

N.Y. Jets	3	32	10.7	1
At Pittsburgh	2	49	24.5	0
At Denver	1	11	11.0	0
Cincinnati	0	0	0.0	0
Pittsburgh	3	65	21.7	0
At Atlanta	4	69	17.3	1
San Diego	5	76	15.2	0
At Cincinnati	2	36	18.0	0
At Houston	1	20	20.0	0
Philadelphia	5	47	9.4	1
At Tampa Bay	4	79	19.8	1
Miami	4	60	15.0	1
Houston	2	50	25.0	0
At Kansas City	2	19	9.5	1
Totals	**38**	**613**	**16.1**	**6**

1977

At Cincinnati	0	0	0.0	0
New England	0	0	0.0	0
Pittsburgh	0	0	0.0	0
Oakland	0	0	0.0	0
At Houston	1	3	3.0	0
At Buffalo	1	52	52.0	1
Kansas City	1	11	11.0	0
Cincinnati	3	19	6.3	0
At Pittsburgh	4	52	13.0	0
At N.Y. Giants	2	33	16.5	1
L.A. Rams	3	46	15.3	0
At San Diego	1	11	11.0	0
Houston	2	24	12.0	0
At Seattle	0	0	0.0	0
Totals	**18**	**251**	**13.9**	**2**

17 HAROLD CARMICHAEL (1971-84)

1971 (Eagles)

Opponent	No.	Yds.	Avg.	TD
At Cincinnati	2	46	23.0	0
Dallas	1	11	11.0	0
San Francisco	2	40	20.0	0
Minnesota	5	67	13.4	0
At Oakland	1	7	7.0	0
N.Y. Giants	2	12	6.0	0
Denver	2	25	12.5	0
At Washington	1	6	6.0	0
At Dallas	4	74	18.5	0
At St. Louis	(did not play)			
Washington	(did not play)			
At Detroit	(did not play)			
St. Louis	(did not play)			
At N.Y. Giants	(did not play)			
Totals	**20**	**288**	**14.4**	**0**

1972

Opponent	No.	Yds.	Avg.	TD
At Dallas	1	4	4.0	0
Cleveland	0	0	0.0	0
N.Y. Giants	0	0	0.0	0
At Washington	1	21	21.0	0
Los Angeles	3	31	10.3	0
At Kansas City	(did not play)			
At New Orleans	1	8	8.0	0
St. Louis	1	34	34.0	0
At Houston	2	20	10.0	0
Dallas	1	1	1.0	0
At N.Y. Giants	1	16	16.0	0
Washington	2	10	5.0	1
Chicago	2	31	15.5	0
At St. Louis	5	100	20.0	1
Totals	**20**	**276**	**13.8**	**2**

1973

Opponent	No.	Yds.	Avg.	TD
St. Louis	5	51	10.2	1
At N.Y. Giants	5	103	20.6	1
Washington	4	62	15.5	0
At Buffalo	2	49	24.5	0
At St. Louis	12	187	15.6	2
At Minnesota	6	52	8.7	0
Dallas	4	54	13.5	2
New England	3	50	16.7	0
Atlanta	6	105	17.5	1
At Dallas	3	24	8.0	0
N.Y. Giants	2	33	16.5	0
At San Francisco	6	89	14.8	1
N.Y. Jets	5	146	29.2	1
At Washington	4	111	27.8	0
Totals	**67**	**1116**	**16.7**	**9**

1974

Opponent	No.	Yds.	Avg.	TD
At St. Louis	5	49	9.8	0
Dallas	2	45	22.5	0
Baltimore	5	89	17.8	0
At San Diego	3	27	9.0	0
N.Y. Giants	8	79	9.9	1
At Dallas	5	85	17.0	1
At New Orleans	6	39	6.5	1
At Pittsburgh	1	29	29.0	0
Washington	3	32	10.7	2
St. Louis	3	26	8.7	0
At Washington	4	32	8.0	1
Green Bay	6	66	11.0	0
At N.Y. Giants	1	12	12.0	0
Detroit	4	39	9.8	1
Totals	**56**	**649**	**11.6**	**8**

1975

Opponent	No.	Yds.	Avg.	TD
N.Y. Giants	6	89	14.8	1
At Chicago	6	75	12.5	1
Washington	2	85	42.5	1
At Miami	2	7	3.5	0
At St. Louis	1	15	15.0	1
Dallas	3	26	8.7	2
Los Angeles	4	67	16.8	0
St. Louis	3	21	7.0	0
At N.Y. Giants	2	15	7.5	0
At Dallas	3	49	16.3	0
San Francisco	6	83	13.8	1
Cincinnati	5	52	10.4	0
At Denver	2	22	11.0	0
At Washington	4	33	8.3	0
Totals	**49**	**639**	**13.0**	**7**

1976

Opponent	No.	Yds.	Avg.	TD
At Dallas	2	43	21.5	0
N.Y. Giants	3	48	16.0	1
Washington	3	40	13.3	0
At Atlanta	3	36	12.0	1
St. Louis	2	16	8.0	0
At Green Bay	5	60	12.0	0
Minnesota	3	16	5.3	1
At N.Y. Giants	5	58	11.6	0
At St. Louis	2	14	7.0	0
At Cleveland	2	15	7.5	0
Oakland	3	26	8.7	1
At Washington	2	29	14.5	0
Dallas	3	37	12.3	0
Seattle	4	65	16.3	0
Totals	**42**	**503**	**12.0**	**5**

Teams (W-L Record): Philadelphia, 1972-83; Dallas, 1984 (85-101-3, .458).

Hall of Fame? Not eligible

Honors: All-NFL (1), 1973; Pro Bowl (4), 1973, '78-80.

Records: Most consecutive games with a reception, 127, 1972-80.*

Lifetime Rankings: 590 receptions (5th/9th); 8,985 yards (7th/11th); 79 TDs (T7th/T8th).

100-Yard Games: 20 (plus 1 postseason)

200-Yard Games: None

Avg. Yards Per Season: 642

Avg. Yards Per Game: 49

Last Reported Salary: $250,000

Injuries: None

Comment: Carmichael's season totals aren't that sensational. He had only one big year, in 1973 when he led the league in receptions (67) and receiving yards (1,116). During a 64-game stretch from 1974 to mid-'78 he had just one 100-yard day. But he was durable, played a lot of years, and had a 127-game receiving streak, which was the record for a while. He also scored 79 touchdowns. Around the goal line, Eagles quarterbacks liked to look for Harold, who, at 6'8", wasn't hard to find.

1977

Opponent	No.	Yds.	Avg.	TD
Tampa Bay	4	30	7.5	0
At Los Angeles	2	11	5.5	0
At Detroit	4	67	16.8	1
At N.Y. Giants	4	59	14.8	0
St. Louis	3	99	33.0	1
Dallas	1	7	7.0	0
At Washington	4	116	29.0	1
New Orleans	3	20	6.7	2
Washington	3	30	10.0	0
At St. Louis	6	85	14.2	1
At New England	3	72	24.0	0
At Dallas	4	25	6.3	1
N.Y. Giants	3	28	9.3	0
N.Y. Jets	2	16	8.0	0
Totals	**46**	**665**	**14.5**	**7**

1978

Opponent	No.	Yds.	Avg.	TD
Los Angeles	1	32	32.0	0
At Washington	4	81	20.3	0
At New Orleans	5	95	19.0	2
Miami	3	50	16.7	0
At Baltimore	2	58	29.0	0
At New England	3	54	18.0	1
Washington	1	28	28.0	0
At Dallas	3	45	15.0	0
St. Louis	7	126	18.0	1
Green Bay	3	38	12.7	0
N.Y. Jets	3	45	15.0	2
At N.Y. Giants	5	105	21.0	0
At St. Louis	5	52	10.4	0
At Minnesota	4	115	28.8	2
Dallas	3	91	30.3	0
N.Y. Giants	3	57	19.0	0
At Atlanta (P)	5	45	9.0	1
Totals	**55**	**1072**	**19.5**	**8**
Postseason	**5**	**45**	**9.0**	**1**

1979

Opponent	No.	Yds.	Avg.	TD
N.Y. Giants	4	98	24.5	2
Atlanta	9	127	14.1	0
At New Orleans	2	16	8.0	0
At N.Y. Giants	4	29	7.3	0
Pittsburgh	1	18	18.0	0
Washington	2	55	27.5	0
At St. Louis	3	35	11.7	1
At Washington	1	26	26.0	0
At Cincinnati	5	54	10.8	1
Cleveland	5	95	19.0	1
At Dallas	4	69	17.3	2
St. Louis	1	0	0.0	0
At Green Bay	3	71	23.7	2
Detroit	5	96	19.2	1
Dallas	1	34	34.0	0
At Houston	2	49	24.5	0
Chicago (P)	6	111	18.5	2
At Tampa Bay (P)	3	92	30.7	1
Totals	**52**	**872**	**16.8**	**11**
Postseason	**9**	**203**	**22.6**	**3**

1980

Opponent	No.	Yds.	Avg.	TD
Denver	3	135	45.0	1
At Minnesota	5	95	19.0	1
N.Y. Giants	4	59	14.8	1
At St. Louis	5	108	21.6	0
Washington	4	63	15.8	1
At N.Y. Giants	3	30	10.0	0
Dallas	3	45	15.0	1
Chicago	2	29	14.5	0
At Seattle	3	31	10.3	0
At New Orleans	5	89	17.8	3
At Washington	1	11	11.0	0
Oakland	3	18	6.0	0
At San Diego	1	23	23.0	0
Atlanta	4	66	16.5	1
St. Louis	2	13	6.5	0
At Dallas	0	0	0.0	0
Minnesota (P)	7	84	12.0	1
Dallas (P)	1	7	7.0	0
Oakland (SB)	5	83	16.6	0
Totals	**48**	**815**	**17.0**	**9**
Postseason	**13**	**174**	**13.4**	**1**

1981

Opponent	No.	Yds.	Avg.	TD
At N.Y. Giants	1	19	19.0	0
New England	5	70	14.0	0
At Buffalo	4	61	15.3	1
Washington	3	49	16.3	0
Atlanta	2	55	27.5	0
At New Orleans	4	88	22.0	0
At Minnesota	8	109	13.6	1
Tampa Bay	1	20	20.0	0
Dallas	5	151	30.2	1
At St. Louis	5	103	20.6	2
Baltimore	7	93	13.3	0
N.Y. Giants	2	14	7.0	0
At Miami	4	61	15.3	0
At Washington	2	47	23.5	0
At Dallas	2	21	10.5	0
St. Louis	6	67	11.2	1
N.Y. Giants (P)	2	43	21.5	1
Totals	**61**	**1028**	**16.9**	**6**
Postseason	**2**	**43**	**21.5**	**1**

1982

Opponent	No.	Yds.	Avg.	TD
Washington	5	72	14.4	1
At Cleveland	6	100	16.7	0
Cincinnati	5	57	11.4	0
At Washington	6	109	18.2	0
St. Louis	2	37	18.5	0
At N.Y. Giants	4	57	14.3	1
Houston	2	38	19.0	0
At Dallas	2	17	8.5	1
N.Y. Giants	3	53	17.7	0
Totals	**35**	**540**	**15.4**	**4**

1983

Opponent	No.	Yds.	Avg.	TD
At San Francisco	2	25	12.5	0
Washington	9	108	12.0	0
At Denver	1	16	16.0	0
St. Louis	1	7	7.0	0
At Atlanta	1	29	29.0	1
At N.Y. Giants	3	54	18.0	0
At Dallas	2	22	11.0	0
Chicago	1	9	9.0	0
Baltimore	3	42	14.0	1
Dallas	1	12	12.0	0
At Chicago	0	0	0.0	0
N.Y. Giants	0	0	0.0	0
At Washington	2	24	12.0	0
Los Angeles Rams	4	51	12.8	0
New Orleans	3	14	4.7	1
At St. Louis	5	102	20.4	0
Totals	**38**	**515**	**13.6**	**3**

1984 (Cowboys)

Opponent	No.	Yds.	Avg.	TD
At Chicago	0	0	0.0	0
Indianapolis	1	7	7.0	0
Totals	**1**	**7**	**7.0**	**0**

80 STEVE LARGENT (1976–1989)

1976

Opponent	No.	Yds.	Avg.	TD
St. Louis	5	86	17.2	0
At Washington	2	34	17.0	0
San Francisco	7	128	18.3	1
Dallas	4	26	6.5	1
At Green Bay	5	39	7.8	0
At Tampa Bay	3	49	16.3	0
Detroit	2	52	26.0	0
At L.A. Rams	2	14	7.0	0
Atlanta	3	22	7.3	0
At Minnesota	2	0	0.0	0
New Orleans	6	101	16.8	1
At N.Y. Giants	2	9	4.5	0
Chicago	4	47	11.8	0
At Philadelphia	7	98	14.0	1
Totals	**54**	**705**	**13.1**	**4**

1977

Baltimore	4	73	18.3	0
At Cincinnati	3	41	13.7	0
Denver	3	71	23.7	1
At New England	0	0	0.0	0
Tampa Bay	4	44	11.0	2
At Miami	2	28	14.0	1
Buffalo	4	134	33.5	2
At Oakland	1	15	15.0	0
At N.Y. Jets	0	0	0.0	0
Houston	1	4	4.0	0
San Diego	4	116	29.0	2
At Pittsburgh	4	71	17.8	1
At Kansas City	2	31	15.5	0
Cleveland	1	15	15.0	1
Totals	**33**	**643**	**19.5**	**10**

1978

San Diego	6	127	21.2	1
At Pittsburgh	4	88	22.0	0
At N.Y. Jets	7	53	7.6	0
Detroit	4	85	21.3	1
At Denver	3	39	13.0	0
Minnesota	1	13	13.0	0
At Green Bay	6	127	21.2	1
Oakland	4	67	16.8	0
Denver	1	11	11.0	0
At Chicago	6	126	21.0	2
Baltimore	4	57	14.3	0
At Kansas City	6	89	14.8	0
At Oakland	5	51	10.2	1
Cleveland	8	108	13.5	1
At San Diego	3	46	15.3	0
Kansas City	3	81	27.0	1
Totals	**71**	**1168**	**16.5**	**8**

1979

San Diego	2	45	22.5	0
At Miami	1	13	13.0	0
Oakland	5	139	27.8	2
At Denver	6	110	18.3	0
Kansas City	2	43	21.5	0
At San Francisco	4	83	20.8	0
At San Diego	1	12	12.0	0
Houston	6	135	22.5	2
At Atlanta	6	127	21.2	0
L.A. Rams	2	25	12.5	0
At Cleveland	3	93	31.0	0
New Orleans	9	146	16.2	2
N.Y. Jets	7	68	9.7	1
At Kansas City	9	120	13.3	0
Denver	3	78	26.0	0
At Oakland		(did not play)		
Totals	**66**	**1237**	**18.7**	**9**

1980

San Diego	5	62	12.4	0
At Kansas City	3	31	10.3	0
New England	6	127	21.2	0
At Washington	1	24	24.0	0
At Houston	2	50	25.0	0
Cleveland	2	9	4.5	0
At N.Y. Jets	5	53	10.6	0
At Oakland	4	142	35.5	1
Philadelphia	6	101	16.8	1
Kansas City	3	31	10.3	0
Oakland	5	68	13.6	0
At Denver	4	83	20.8	0
At Dallas	2	19	9.5	0
N.Y. Giants	8	139	17.4	1
At San Diego	5	55	11.0	1
Denver	5	70	14.0	0
Totals	**66**	**1064**	**16.1**	**6**

Team (W-L Record): Seattle, 1976-89 (102-108, .486).

Hall of Fame? Not eligible

Honors: All-NFL (2), 1985, '87; Pro Bowl (7), 1978-79, '81, '84-87.

Records: Most receptions, 819; receiving yards, 13,089; and TD receptions, 100, career; most consecutive games with a reception, 177, 1977-89.

Lifetime Rankings: 819 receptions (1st); 13,089 yards (1st); 100 TDs (1st).

100-Yard Games: 40 (plus 2 postseason)

200-Yard Games: 1

Avg. Yards Per Season: 935

Avg. Yards Per Game: 65

Last Reported Salary: $1,300,000

Injuries: 1989--fractured elbow.

Comment: In every full season from 1978 to '86, Largent caught at least 66 passes and gained over 1,000 yards. Some prime.

1981

At Cincinnati	8	114	14.3	1
Denver	5	45	9.0	0
At Oakland	6	92	15.3	0
Kansas City	4	52	13.0	0
At San Diego	5	118	23.6	1
At Houston	4	65	16.3	1
N.Y. Giants	4	40	10.0	0
At N.Y. Jets	6	80	13.3	1
At Green Bay	3	45	15.0	0
Pittsburgh	4	82	20.5	0
San Diego	3	44	14.7	0
At Kansas City	4	63	15.8	1
Oakland	3	63	21.0	1
N.Y. Jets	7	169	24.1	1
At Denver	3	72	24.0	0
Cleveland	6	80	13.3	2
Totals	**75**	**1224**	**16.3**	**9**

1982

Cleveland	6	71	11.8	0
At Houston		(did not play)		
At Denver	3	59	19.7	1
Pittsburgh	5	109	21.8	0
At L.A. Raiders	2	11	5.5	1
Chicago	8	111	13.9	0
New England	3	45	15.0	1
At Cincinnati	4	51	12.8	1
Denver	3	36	12.0	0
Totals	**34**	**493**	**14.5**	**3**

1983

At Kansas City	4	55	13.8	0
At N.Y. Jets	3	35	11.7	0
San Diego	8	116	14.5	2
Washington	8	130	16.3	2
At Cleveland	2	30	15.0	0
At San Diego	3	21	7.0	0
L.A. Raiders		(did not play)		
Pittsburgh	2	67	33.5	1
At L.A. Raiders	4	45	11.3	0
Denver	4	48	12.0	1
At St. Louis	8	155	19.4	3
At Denver	7	84	12.0	0
Kansas City	4	66	16.5	0
Dallas	5	60	12.0	0
At N.Y. Giants	3	29	9.7	1
New England	7	133	19.0	1
Denver (P)	4	76	19.0	1
At Miami (P)	2	56	28.0	1
At L.A. Raiders (P)	2	25	12.5	0
Totals	**72**	**1074**	**14.9**	**11**
Postseason	**8**	**157**	**19.6**	**2**

1984

Cleveland	2	17	8.5	0
San Diego	2	27	13.5	0
At New England	3	38	12.7	0
Chicago	1	29	29.0	0
At Minnesota	8	130	16.3	1
At L.A. Raiders	4	66	16.5	1
Buffalo	5	106	21.2	2
At Green Bay	7	129	18.4	1
At San Diego	4	51	12.8	3
Kansas City	1	11	11.0	0
L.A. Raiders	1	6	6.0	0
At Cincinnati	5	65	13.0	1
At Denver	12	191	15.9	1
Detroit	8	104	13.0	2
At Kansas City	4	98	24.5	0
Denver	7	96	13.7	0
L.A. Raiders (P)	0	0	0.0	0
At Miami (P)	6	128	21.3	1
Totals	**74**	**1164**	**15.7**	**12**
Postseason	**6**	**128**	**21.3**	**1**

1985

At Cincinnati	5	81	16.2	0
At San Diego	6	99	16.5	1
L.A. Rams	6	88	14.7	0
At Kansas City	6	92	15.3	0
San Diego	5	69	13.8	1
Atlanta	8	103	12.9	1
At Denver	1	9	9.0	1
At N.Y. Jets	2	44	22.0	0
L.A. Raiders	3	47	15.7	0
At New Orleans	5	110	22.0	0
New England	8	138	17.3	0
At San Francisco	4	91	22.8	0
Kansas City	7	101	14.4	1
Cleveland	5	89	17.8	0
At L.A. Raiders	4	61	15.3	0
Denver	4	65	16.3	0
Totals	**79**	**1287**	**16.3**	**6**

1986

Pittsburgh	7	65	9.3	1
Kansas City	5	62	12.4	0
At New England	1	9	9.0	0
At Washington	3	44	14.7	1
San Diego	4	78	19.5	1
At L.A. Raiders	4	60	15.0	0
N.Y. Giants	2	20	10.0	0
At Denver	3	37	12.3	1
N.Y. Jets	7	108	15.4	0
At Kansas City	4	72	18.0	1
At Cincinnati	7	102	14.6	0
Philadelphia	3	65	21.7	0
At Dallas	3	75	25.0	1
L.A. Raiders	5	76	15.2	1
At San Diego	6	96	16.0	2
Denver	6	101	16.8	0
Totals	**70**	**1070**	**15.3**	**9**

1987

At Denver	4	73	18.3	0
Kansas City	2	17	8.5	0
At Detroit	15	261	17.4	3
At L.A. Raiders	5	56	11.2	0
Minnesota	2	29	14.5	1
At N.Y. Jets	4	88	22.0	1
Green Bay	5	79	15.8	0
San Diego	5	84	16.8	1
L.A. Raiders	2	25	12.5	0
At Pittsburgh	2	26	13.0	1
Denver	3	43	14.3	0
At Chicago	3	36	12.0	0
At Kansas City	6	95	15.8	1
At Houston (P)	7	132	18.9	2
Totals	**58**	**912**	**15.7**	**8**
Postseason	**7**	**132**	**18.9**	**2**

1988

At Denver	2	21	10.5	0
Kansas City	2	34	17.0	0
At San Diego	4	71	17.8	0
San Francisco	1	9	9.0	0
At Atlanta	3	59	19.7	0
At Cleveland	1	9	9.0	0
New Orleans	7	85	12.1	0
At L.A. Rams	2	14	7.0	0
San Diego	3	37	12.3	0
Buffalo	2	56	28.0	0
Houston	2	46	23.0	0
At Kansas City	1	11	11.0	0
L.A. Raiders	4	67	16.8	1
At New England		(did not play)		
Denver	3	76	25.3	0
At L.A. Raiders (P)	2	50	25.0	1
At Cincinnati (P)	2	17	8.5	0
Totals	**39**	**645**	**16.5**	**2**
Postseason	**2**	**17**	**8.5**	**0**

1989

At Philadelphia	1	23	23.0	1
Phoenix		(did not play)		
At New England		(did not play)		
At L.A. Raiders		(did not play)		
Kansas City		(did not play)		
At San Diego		(did not play)		
Denver		(did not play)		
San Diego	2	32	16.0	0
At Kansas City	3	47	15.7	0
Cleveland	4	33	8.3	0
At N.Y. Giants	4	39	9.9	0
At Denver	5	83	16.6	1
Buffalo	1	24	24.0	0
At Cincinnati	5	68	13.6	1
L.A. Raiders	1	13	13.0	0
Washington	2	41	20.5	0
Totals	**28**	**403**	**14.4**	**3**

81 ART MONK (1980-)

1980

Opponent	No.	Yds.	Avg.	TD
Dallas	5	55	11.0	0
At N.Y. Giants	2	20	10.0	0
At L.A. Raiders	2	25	12.5	0
Seattle	1	45	45.0	0
At Philadelphia	2	44	22.0	0
At Denver	6	47	7.8	1
St. Louis	6	85	14.2	0
New Orleans	5	75	15.0	0
Minnesota	4	54	13.5	0
At Chicago	8	124	15.5	0
Philadelphia	3	16	5.3	0
At Dallas	2	7	3.5	0
At Atlanta	4	62	15.5	0
San Diego	0	0	0.0	0
N.Y. Giants	3	43	14.3	0
At St. Louis	5	95	19.0	2
Totals	**58**	**797**	**13.7**	**3**

1981

Opponent	No.	Yds.	Avg.	TD
Dallas	3	38	12.7	0
N.Y. Giants	7	74	10.6	0
At St. Louis	4	128	32.0	1
At Philadelphia	4	33	8.3	0
San Francisco	4	42	10.5	0
At Chicago	2	30	15.0	0
At Miami	4	42	10.5	0
New England	2	38	19.0	0
St. Louis	3	77	25.7	2
Detroit	3	45	15.0	1
At N.Y. Giants	3	20	6.7	0
At Dallas	1	13	13.0	0
At Buffalo	6	60	10.0	1
Philadelphia	1	8	8.0	0
Baltimore	7	148	21.1	1
At L.A. Rams	2	98	49.0	0
Totals	**56**	**894**	**16.0**	**6**

1982

Opponent	No.	Yds.	Avg.	TD
At Philadelphia	8	134	16.8	1
At Tampa Bay	4	41	10.3	0
At N.Y. Giants	6	42	7.0	0
Philadelphia	1	10	10.0	0
Dallas	7	100	14.3	0
At St. Louis	0	0	0.0	0
N.Y. Giants	4	60	15.0	0
At New Orleans	5	60	12.0	0
St. Louis	0	0	0.0	0
Detroit (P)	(did not play)			
Minnesota (P)	(did not play)			
Dallas (P)	(did not play)			
Miami (SB)	(did not play)			
Totals	**35**	**447**	**12.8**	**1**

1983

Opponent	No.	Yds.	Avg.	TD
Dallas	(did not play)			
At Philadelphia	(did not play)			
Kansas City	(did not play)			
At Seattle	(did not play)			
L.A. Raiders	3	59	19.7	0
At St. Louis	3	38	12.7	1
At Green Bay	5	105	21.0	0
Detroit	3	43	14.3	1
At San Diego	7	106	15.1	0
St. Louis	4	71	17.8	0
At N.Y. Giants	1	5	5.0	0
At L.A. Rams	5	80	16.0	0
Philadelphia	2	28	14.0	1
Atlanta	3	19	6.3	1
At Dallas	6	119	19.8	1
N.Y. Giants	3	73	14.6	0
L.A. Rams (P)	4	60	15.0	2
San Francisco (P)	3	35	11.7	0
L.A. Raiders (SB)	1	26	26.0	0
Totals	**47**	**746**	**15.9**	**5**
Postseason	**8**	**121**	**15.1**	**2**

1984

Opponent	No.	Yds.	Avg.	TD
Miami	3	54	18.0	0
At San Francisco	10	200	20.0	0
N.Y. Giants	8	78	9.8	0
At New England	5	37	7.4	0
Philadelphia	5	80	16.0	1
At Indianapolis	8	141	17.6	3
Dallas	4	67	16.8	0
At St. Louis	6	87	14.5	0
At N.Y. Giants	4	104	26.0	0
Atlanta	5	45	9.0	0
Detroit	5	34	6.8	0
At Philadelphia	8	80	10.0	1
Buffalo	11	104	9.5	1
At Miami	6	45	7.5	0
At Dallas	7	80	11.4	0
St. Louis	11	136	12.4	2
Chicago (P)	10	122	12.2	0
Totals	**106**	**1372**	**12.9**	**7**
Postseason	**10**	**122**	**12.2**	**0**

Team (W-L Record): Washington, 1980- (94-55, .631).
Hall of Fame? Not eligible
Records: Most receptions, season, 106, 1984.
Lifetime Rankings: 662 receptions (3rd); 9,165 yards (9th); 47 TDs (--).
100-Yard Games: 28 (plus 2 postseason)
200-Yard Games: 2
Avg. Yards Per Season: 917
Avg. Yards Per Game: 65
Last Reported Salary: $800,000
Injuries: 1982--broken foot; 1983--sprained knee; 1987--torn knee ligaments.
Comment: Monk has enough receptions and yards to get into the Hall of Fame right now. It's his touchdown total that might give the selection committee pause. He's scored less often than any wide receiver in the all-time top 20 (7.1 percent of the time). In one 20-game stretch in 1984 and '85, he had two TDs in 120 catches. Part of the explanation is that he runs a lot of short and underneath routes that gain ground but usually don't get you in the end zone. If he stays healthy, however, he could break Steve Largent's career reception record. Then the Canton question would be moot.

1985

Opponent	No.	Yds.	Avg.	TD
At Dallas	5	51	10.2	0
Houston	5	35	7.0	0
Philadelphia	7	73	10.4	0
At Chicago	4	14	3.5	0
St. Louis	4	44	11.0	0
Detroit	8	73	9.1	0
At N.Y. Giants	(did not play)			
At Cleveland	2	10	5.0	0
At Atlanta	6	106	17.7	1
Dallas	5	103	20.6	0
N.Y. Giants	7	130	18.6	0
At Pittsburgh	6	65	10.8	0
San Francisco	8	150	18.8	0
At Philadelphia	7	109	15.6	0
Cincinnati	13	230	17.7	1
At St. Louis	4	33	8.3	0
Totals	**91**	**1226**	**13.5**	**2**

1986

Opponent	No.	Yds.	Avg.	TD
Philadelphia	4	37	9.3	0
L.A. Raiders	4	48	12.0	0
At San Diego	7	174	24.9	0
Seattle	5	103	20.6	0
At New Orleans	7	80	11.4	1
At Dallas	4	30	7.5	0
St. Louis	5	79	15.8	1
At N.Y. Giants	3	59	19.7	0
Minnesota	6	102	17.0	1
At Green Bay	1	3	3.0	0
San Francisco	6	57	9.5	0
Dallas	3	64	21.3	0
At St. Louis	3	24	8.0	0
N.Y. Giants	5	40	8.0	0
At Denver	6	129	21.5	1
At Philadelphia	4	39	9.8	0
L.A. Rams (P)	5	34	6.8	0
At Chicago (P)	5	81	16.2	2
At N.Y. Giants (P)	8	126	15.8	0
Totals	**73**	**1068**	**14.6**	**4**
Postseason	**18**	**241**	**13.4**	**2**

1987

Opponent	No.	Yds.	Avg.	TD
Philadelphia	3	53	17.7	2
At Atlanta	2	12	6.0	1
N.Y. Jets	3	70	23.3	0
At Buffalo	5	38	7.6	0
At Philadelphia	5	81	16.2	1
Detroit	4	39	9.8	0
L.A. Rams	5	93	18.6	2
N.Y. Giants	8	74	9.3	0
At St. Louis	3	23	7.7	0
Dallas	(did not play)			
At Miami	(did not play)			
At Minnesota	(did not play)			
At Chicago (P)	(did not play)			
Minnesota (P)	(did not play)			
Denver (SB)	1	40	40.0	0
Totals	**38**	**483**	**12.7**	**6**
Postseason	**1**	**40**	**40.0**	**0**

1988

Opponent	No.	Yds.	Avg.	TD
At N.Y. Giants	2	32	16.0	0
Pittsburgh	9	86	9.6	0
Philadelphia	2	34	17.0	0
At Phoenix	6	92	15.3	1
N.Y. Giants	1	38	38.0	0
At Dallas	2	29	14.5	0
Phoenix	4	82	20.5	2
At Green Bay	4	40	10.0	1
At Houston	3	50	16.7	0
New Orleans	3	61	20.3	0
Chicago	6	91	15.2	0
At San Francisco	9	89	9.9	1
Cleveland	2	30	15.0	0
At Philadelphia	6	37	6.2	0
Dallas	7	103	14.7	0
At Cincinnati	6	52	8.7	0
Totals	**72**	**946**	**13.1**	**5**

1989

Opponent	No.	Yds.	Avg.	TD
N.Y. Giants	4	38	9.5	1
Philadelphia	4	87	21.8	1
At Dallas	6	114	19.0	0
At New Orleans	5	94	18.8	0
Phoenix	8	102	12.8	1
At N.Y. Giants	3	25	8.3	1
Tampa Bay	8	97	12.1	0
At L.A. Raiders	2	29	14.5	0
Dallas	8	98	12.3	0
At Philadelphia	1	8	8.0	0
Denver	2	16	8.0	0
Chicago	9	152	16.9	2
At Phoenix	6	45	7.5	0
San Diego	9	81	9.0	0
At Atlanta	6	131	21.8	2
At Seattle	5	69	13.8	0
Totals	**86**	**1186**	**13.8**	**8**

80 JERRY RICE (1985-)

1985

Opponent	No.	Yds.	Avg.	TD
At Minnesota	4	67	16.8	0
Atlanta	2	35	17.5	0
At L.A. Raiders	3	94	31.3	0
New Orleans	0	0	0.0	0
At Atlanta	3	42	14.0	1
Chicago	3	37	12.3	0
At Detroit	1	3	3.0	0
At L.A. Rams	2	17	8.5	0
Philadelphia	3	70	23.3	1
At Denver	4	67	16.8	0
Kansas City	1	19	19.0	0
Seattle	2	42	21.0	0
At Washington	0	0	0.0	0
L.A. Rams	10	241	24.1	1
At New Orleans	4	82	20.5	0
Dallas	7	111	15.9	0
At N.Y. Giants (P)	4	45	11.3	0
Totals	**49**	**927**	**18.9**	**3**
Postseason	**4**	**45**	**11.3**	**0**

1986

Opponent	No.	Yds.	Avg.	TD
At Tampa Bay	5	54	10.8	0
At L.A. Rams	6	157	26.1	1
New Orleans	7	120	17.1	0
At Miami	3	76	25.3	2
Indianapolis	6	172	28.6	3
Minnesota	7	144	20.5	2
At Atlanta	3	58	19.3	0
At Green Bay	4	49	12.2	1
At New Orleans	4	44	11.0	0
St. Louis	4	156	39.0	3
At Washington	12	204	17.0	0
Atlanta	4	47	11.7	1
N.Y. Giants	9	86	9.5	1
N.Y. Jets	5	97	19.4	0
At New England	4	35	8.7	1
L.A. Rams	3	71	23.6	1
At N.Y. Giants (P)	3	48	16.0	0
Totals	**86**	**1570**	**18.3**	**15**
Postseason	**3**	**48**	**16.0**	**0**

1987

Opponent	No.	Yds.	Avg.	TD
At Pittsburgh	8	106	13.2	1
At Cincinnati	4	86	21.5	2
At New Orleans	6	89	14.8	1
At L.A. Rams	3	70	23.3	1
Houston	7	77	11.0	1
New Orleans	4	108	27.0	2
At Tampa Bay	7	103	14.7	3
Cleveland	7	126	18.0	3
At Green Bay	4	90	22.5	1
Chicago	8	75	9.3	3
Atlanta	4	58	14.5	2
L.A. Rams	3	90	30.0	2
Minnesota (P)	3	28	9.3	0
Totals	**65**	**1078**	**16.6**	**22**
Postseason	**3**	**28**	**9.3**	**0**

Team (W-L Record): San Francisco, 1985- (54-21-1, .717).

Hall of Fame? Not eligible

Honors: Bert Bell Trophy, 1987; consensus NFL MVP/player of the year, 1987; Super Bowl MVP, 1989; all-NFL (4), 1986-89; Pro Bowl (4), 1986-89.

Records: Most touchdown receptions, season, 22, 1987; most consecutive games with a TD reception, 13, 1986-87.

Lifetime Rankings: 346 receptions (--); 6,364 yards (--); 66 TDs (T19th).

100-Yard Games: 25 (plus 4 postseason)

200-Yard Games: 2 (plus 1 postseason)

Avg. Yards Per Season: 1,273

Avg. Yards Per Game: 84

Last Reported Salary: $850,000

Injuries: None

Comment: Let's compare Rice's first five seasons against those of Steve Largent, the all-time leader in receptions, yards and touchdowns. Largent had 290 catches (56 fewer than Rice), 4,817 yards (1,547 fewer) and 37 TDs (29 fewer) at that point in his career. Or what about Paul Warfield, who, stylistically, probably compares closest to Rice? After five years, Warfield had 173 catches, 3,460 yards and 34 TDs -- about half as many of everything. Rice's statistics are so extraordinary they're beginning to have a numbing effect. Why, he caught 17 scoring passes in 1989 and nobody much noticed because he'd grabbed 22 two years before. In case you'd forgotten, 17 was the NFL record until 1984. His postseason play has been no less spectacular. In the '88 and '89 playoffs he had 40 receptions for 726 yards and 11 TDs. Over a 16-game season, that projects to 107 receptions, 1,936 yards and 29 TDs. How high can he go?

1988

Opponent	No.	Yds.	Avg.	TD
At New Orleans	2	41	20.5	0
At N.Y. Giants	4	109	27.2	1
Atlanta	8	163	20.3	0
At Seattle	6	163	27.2	3
Detroit	2	35	17.5	0
Denver	3	78	26.0	0
At L.A. Rams	4	65	16.2	0
At Chicago	4	86	21.5	1
Minnesota	1	22	22.0	0
At Phoenix	3	37	12.3	0
L.A. Raiders	5	61	12.2	0
Washington	3	105	35.0	1
At San Diego	6	171	28.5	2
At Atlanta	5	63	12.6	1
New Orleans	6	78	13.0	0
L.A. Rams	2	29	14.5	0
Minnesota (P)	5	61	12.2	3
At Chicago (P)	5	133	26.6	2
Cincinnati (SB)	11	215	19.5	1
Totals	**64**	**1306**	**20.4**	**9**
Postseason	**21**	**409**	**19.4**	**6**

1989

Opponent	No.	Yds.	Avg.	TD
At Indianapolis	6	163	27.2	1
At Tampa Bay	8	122	15.3	1
At Philadelphia	6	164	27.3	2
L.A. Rams	2	36	18.0	0
At New Orleans	7	149	21.3	1
At Dallas	2	28	14.0	1
New England	6	112	18.7	2
At N.Y. Jets	5	95	19.0	1
New Orleans	6	93	15.5	2
Atlanta	3	81	27.0	2
Green Bay	9	106	11.8	1
N.Y. Giants	7	117	16.7	1
At Atlanta	3	32	10.7	0
At L.A. Rams	5	38	7.6	1
Buffalo	3	46	15.3	1
Chicago	4	101	25.3	1
Minnesota (P)	6	114	19.0	2
L.A. Rams (P)	6	55	9.2	0
Denver (SB)	7	148	21.1	3
Totals	**82**	**1483**	**18.1**	**17**
Postseason	**19**	**317**	**16.7**	**5**

35 PETE PIHOS (1947-55)

1947

Opponent	No.	Yds.	Avg.	TD
Washington	5	89	17.8	2
New York	1	14	14.0	0
At Pittsburgh	2	61	30.5	2
Los Angeles	1	10	10.0	0
At Washington	2	14	7.0	1
At New York	1	1	1.0	0
Boston	0	0	0.0	0
At Boston	1	9	9.0	0
Pittsburgh	2	17	8.5	0
Chi. Cardinals	4	59	14.8	1
Green Bay	4	108	27.0	1
At Pittsburgh (P)	1	18	18.0	0
At Chi. Cardinals (C)	3	27	9.0	0
Totals	**23**	**382**	**16.6**	**7**
Postseason	**4**	**45**	**11.3**	**0**

1948

Opponent	No.	Yds.	Avg.	TD
At Chi. Cardinals	2	75	37.5	1
At Los Angeles	3	90	30.0	2
New York	4	61	15.3	1
At Washington	3	38	12.7	1
Chi. Bears	2	34	17.0	0
At Pittsburgh	5	37	7.4	0
At New York	5	128	25.6	2
Boston	3	46	15.3	1
Washington	3	66	22.0	1
Pittsburgh	7	112	16.0	1
At Boston	3	27	9.0	0
Detroit	6	52	8.7	1
Chi. Cardinals	1	0	0.0	0
Totals	**46**	**766**	**16.7**	**11**
Postseason	**1**	**0**	**0.0**	**0**

1949

Opponent	No.	Yds.	Avg.	TD
At N.Y. Bulldogs	1	22	22.0	0
At Detroit	7	86	12.3	0
Chi. Cardinals	3	75	25.0	0
At Chi. Bears	5	29	5.8	1
Washington	5	68	13.6	0
At Pittsburgh	3	50	16.7	1
Los Angeles	4	87	21.8	1
At Washington	3	43	14.3	1
N.Y. Bulldogs	1	11	11.0	0
Pittsburgh	1	15	15.0	0
At N.Y. Giants		(did not play)		
N.Y. Giants	1	-2	-2.0	0
At Los Angeles (C)	1	31	31.0	1
Totals	**34**	**484**	**14.2**	**4**
Postseason	**1**	**31**	**31.0**	**1**

1950

Opponent	No.	Yds.	Avg.	TD
Cleveland	4	51	12.8	1
At Chi. Cardinals	3	32	10.7	1
Los Angeles	3	26	8.7	1
At Baltimore	1	16	16.0	1
At Pittsburgh	3	17	5.7	0
Washington	2	45	22.5	1
Pittsburgh	5	63	12.6	0
At Washington	5	59	11.8	0
Chi. Cardinals	3	32	10.7	1
At N.Y. Giants	5	43	8.6	0
At Cleveland	1	6	6.0	0
N.Y. Giants	3	57	19.0	0
Totals	**38**	**447**	**11.8**	**6**

Team: Philadelphia, 1947-55 (63-41-4, .602).

Hall of Fame? Yes (8th year eligible)

Honors: All-NFL (6), 1948-49, '52 (defensive end); '53-55; Pro Bowl (6), 1950-55.

Records: None

Lifetime Rankings: 373 receptions (3rd/--); 5,619 yards (2nd/--); 61 TDs (2nd/26th).

100-Yard Games: 15

200-Yard Games: None

Avg. Yards Per Season: 624

Avg. Yards Per Game: 53

Injuries: None

Comment: The Eagles became a passing team after Steve Van Buren retired, and Pihos' catches increased dramatically late in his career. He led the league in receptions his last three seasons, a feat that may never be duplicated. In his final three games, he caught 27 passes for 344 yards and two touchdowns. Here was a player who knew how to make an exit. By getting out at the age of 32, however, he passed up a shot at Don Hutson's career reception record of 488. Note that Pihos' catches dropped to 12 in 1952. He was an all-pro defensive end that year.

1951

Opponent	No.	Yds.	Avg.	TD
At Chi. Cardinals	1	19	19.0	1
San Francisco	6	91	15.2	0
At Green Bay	5	65	13.0	1
At N.Y. Giants	4	73	18.3	0
Washington	1	8	8.0	0
At Pittsburgh	3	36	12.0	1
At Cleveland	2	26	13.0	0
Detroit	5	98	19.6	1
Pittsburgh	4	68	17.0	1
At Washington	2	25	12.5	0
N.Y. Giants	2	27	13.5	0
Cleveland	0	0	0.0	0
Totals	**35**	**536**	**15.3**	**5**

1952

Opponent	No.	Yds.	Avg.	TD
At Pittsburgh	3	83	27.7	1
N.Y. Giants	1	10	10.0	0
Pittsburgh	1	9	9.0	0
Cleveland	0	0	0.0	0
At N.Y. Giants	1	28	28.0	0
At Green Bay	0	0	0.0	0
Washington	3	52	17.3	0
Chi. Cardinals	1	13	13.0	0
At Cleveland	0	0	0.0	0
At Chi. Cardinals	1	13	13.0	0
Dallas	0	0	0.0	0
At Washington	1	11	11.0	0
Totals	**12**	**219**	**18.3**	**1**

1953

Opponent	No.	Yds.	Avg.	TD
At San Francisco	5	61	12.2	1
Washington	5	68	13.6	2
At Cleveland	4	64	16.0	0
Pittsburgh	6	91	15.2	1
At Chi. Cardinals	8	156	19.5	1
At Pittsburgh	4	77	19.3	1
N.Y. Giants	7	145	20.7	2
Baltimore	7	118	16.9	1
Chi. Cardinals	7	113	16.1	0
At N.Y. Giants	3	38	12.7	0
At Washington	2	38	19.0	0
Cleveland	5	80	16.0	1
Totals	**63**	**1049**	**16.7**	**10**

1954

Opponent	No.	Yds.	Avg.	TD
Cleveland	6	86	14.3	1
At Chi. Cardinals	5	86	17.2	0
Pittsburgh	1	13	13.0	1
At Washington	9	132	14.7	3
At Pittsburgh	7	111	15.9	1
Green Bay	1	4	4.0	0
Chi. Cardinals	4	50	12.5	1
At N.Y. Giants	6	89	14.8	0
At Cleveland	2	18	9.0	0
Washington	6	81	13.5	1
At Detroit	5	83	16.6	1
N.Y. Giants	8	119	14.9	1
Totals	**60**	**872**	**14.5**	**10**

1955

Opponent	No.	Yds.	Avg.	TD
New York	4	68	17.0	0
Washington	7	84	12.0	1
At Cleveland	3	26	8.7	0
At Pittsburgh	1	16	16.0	0
At Chi. Cardinals	5	96	19.2	1
Pittsburgh	4	65	16.3	1
At Washington	8	119	14.9	1
Cleveland	3	46	15.3	0
At N.Y. Giants	0	0	0.0	0
Los Angeles	6	103	17.2	1
Chi. Cardinals	10	127	12.7	1
At Chi. Bears	11	114	10.4	0
Totals	**62**	**864**	**13.9**	**7**

89 MIKE DITKA (1961-72)

1961 (Bears)

Opponent	No.	Yds.	Avg.	TD
At Minnesota	1	18	18.0	0
At Los Angeles	5	130	26.0	1
At Green Bay	3	47	15.7	0
At Detroit	5	120	24.0	1
Baltimore	1	22	22.0	0
San Francisco	4	107	26.8	2
At Baltimore	4	61	15.3	1
At Philadelphia	1	76	76.0	1
Green Bay	9	190	21.1	3
At San Francisco	5	98	19.6	1
Los Angeles	0	0	0.0	0
Detroit	6	70	11.7	0
Cleveland	4	35	8.8	0
Minnesota	8	102	12.8	2
Totals	**56**	**1076**	**19.2**	**12**

1962

Opponent	No.	Yds.	Avg.	TD
At San Francisco	1	3	3.0	0
At Los Angeles	1	19	19.0	0
At Green Bay	1	12	12.0	0
At Minnesota	4	69	17.3	0
San Francisco	8	132	16.5	0
Baltimore	4	100	25.0	1
At Detroit	2	20	10.0	0
Green Bay	5	79	15.8	0
Minnesota	7	59	8.4	1
At Dallas	7	133	19.0	1
At Baltimore	4	40	10.0	1
N.Y. Giants	3	32	10.7	1
Los Angeles	6	155	25.8	1
Detroit	5	51	10.2	0
Totals	**58**	**904**	**15.6**	**5**

1963

Opponent	No.	Yds.	Avg.	TD
At Green Bay	1	12	12.0	0
At Minnesota	8	124	15.5	2
At Detroit	4	49	12.3	1
Baltimore	1	14	14.0	0
At Los Angeles	9	110	12.2	4
At San Francisco	5	37	7.4	0
Philadelphia	4	59	14.8	0
At Baltimore	1	6	6.0	0
Los Angeles	7	62	8.9	0
Green Bay	2	32	16.0	0
At Pittsburgh	7	146	20.9	0
Minnesota	5	76	15.2	0
San Francisco	2	27	13.5	0
Detroit	3	40	13.3	1
N.Y. Giants (C)	3	38	12.7	0
Totals	**59**	**794**	**13.5**	**8**
Postseason	**3**	**38**	**12.7**	**0**

1964

Opponent	No.	Yds.	Avg.	TD
At Green Bay	7	74	10.6	1
At Minnesota	6	62	10.3	0
At Baltimore	6	106	17.7	0
At San Francisco	6	48	8.0	0
Los Angeles	6	81	13.5	2
Detroit	6	78	13.0	0
At Washington	13	168	12.9	0
Dallas	3	45	15.0	0
Baltimore	2	17	8.5	1
At Los Angeles	4	44	11.0	1
San Francisco	7	85	12.1	0
At Detroit	4	35	8.8	0
Green Bay	4	30	7.5	0
Minnesota	1	24	24.0	0
Totals	**75**	**897**	**12.0**	**5**

1965

Opponent	No.	Yds.	Avg.	TD
At San Francisco	1	26	26.0	0
At Los Angeles	3	26	8.7	0
At Green Bay	3	23	7.7	0
Los Angeles	5	68	13.6	0
At Minnesota	0	0	0.0	0
Detroit	4	48	12.0	1
Green Bay	0	0	0.0	0
Baltimore	6	76	12.7	0
St. Louis	3	20	6.7	0
At Detroit	1	4	4.0	0
At N.Y. Giants	5	80	16.0	0
At Baltimore	1	11	11.0	0
San Francisco	2	45	22.5	1
Minnesota	2	27	13.5	0
Totals	**36**	**454**	**12.6**	**2**

1966

Opponent	No.	Yds.	Avg.	TD
At Detroit	1	5	5.0	0
At Los Angeles	2	17	8.5	0
At Minnesota	3	41	13.7	1
Baltimore	2	17	8.5	0
Green Bay	2	26	13.0	0
Los Angeles	2	22	11.0	0
At St. Louis	2	29	14.5	0
Detroit	2	35	17.5	0
San Francisco	1	6	6.0	0
At Green Bay	3	29	9.7	0
Atlanta	1	10	10.0	0
At Baltimore	7	95	13.6	1
At San Francisco	3	32	10.7	0
Minnesota	1	14	14.0	0
Totals	**32**	**378**	**11.8**	**2**

1967 (Eagles)

Opponent	No.	Yds.	Avg.	TD
Washington	5	42	8.4	0
Baltimore	3	32	10.7	0
Pittsburgh		(did not play)		
At Atlanta	3	30	10.0	1
San Francisco	3	43	14.3	1
At St. Louis	3	31	10.3	0
Dallas	5	52	10.4	0
At New Orleans	2	26	13.0	0
At Los Angeles		(did not play)		
New Orleans		(did not play)		
At N.Y. Giants		(did not play)		
At Washington		(did not play)		
At Dallas	1	13	13.0	0
Cleveland	1	5	5.0	0
Totals	**26**	**274**	**10.5**	**2**

Biography

Teams (W-L Record): Chicago, 1961-66; Philadelphia, 1967-68; Dallas, 1969-72 (97-65-6, .595).

Hall of Fame? Yes (11th year eligible)

Records: Most receptions by a tight end, season, 75, 1964*; most touchdown receptions by a tight end, 12, 1961.

Honors: UPI NFL Rookie of the Year, 1961; all-NFL (4), 1961-64; Pro Bowl (5), 1961-65.

Lifetime Rankings: 427 receptions (13th overall/6th among tight ends); 5,812 yards (30th/5th); 43 TDs (--/6th).

100-Yard Games: 14

Avg. Yards Per Season: 484

Avg. Yards Per Game: 37

Injuries: 1965--foot injury; 1967--partially torn knee ligament.

Comment: For four seasons, Ditka defined the tight end position. He averaged 62 receptions, 993 yards and 8 touchdowns a year from 1961 to '64 -- in addition to being a relentless blocker. Richie Petitbon, who had to cover him in practice with the Bears, said, "I have never met a player who had more desire." Injuries diminished Ditka's offensive skills (he didn't have a 100-yard game after the age of 25), but he remained a useful player until 1972 and caught 30 passes for the Cowboys' '71 title team.

1968

Opponent	No.	Yds.	Avg.	TD
At Green Bay	0	0	0.0	0
N.Y Giants	0	0	0.0	0
Dallas	3	25	8.3	0
At Washington	1	8	8.0	0
At Dallas	3	28	9.3	1
Chicago	4	28	7.0	1
At Pittsburgh	2	22	11.0	0
St. Louis		(did not play)		
Washington		(did not play)		
At N.Y. Giants		(did not play)		
At Cleveland	0	0	0.0	0
At Detroit	0	0	0.0	0
New Orleans	0	0	0.0	0
Minnesota	0	0	0.0	0
Totals	**13**	**111**	**8.5**	**2**

1969 (Cowboys)

Opponent	No.	Yds.	Avg.	TD
St. Louis	1	28	28.0	0
At New Orleans	2	20	10.0	0
At Philadelphia	2	17	8.5	1
At Atlanta	2	42	21.0	0
Philadelphia	0	0	0.0	0
N.Y. Giants	0	0	0.0	0
At Cleveland	3	34	11.3	0
New Orleans	3	82	27.3	1
At Washington	1	7	7.0	0
At Los Angeles	2	32	16.0	1
San Francisco	0	0	0.0	0
At Pittsburgh		(did not play)		
Baltimore		(did not play)		
Washington	1	6	6.0	0
Cleveland (P)	0	0	0.0	0
Los Angeles (PB)	0	0	0.0	0
Totals	**17**	**268**	**15.8**	**3**
Postseason	**0**	**0**	**0.0**	**0**

1970

Opponent	No.	Yds.	Avg.	TD
At Philadelphia	0	0	0.0	0
N.Y. Giants	0	0	0.0	0
At St. Louis	4	80	20.0	0
Atlanta	1	12	12.0	0
At Minnesota	0	0	0.0	0
At Kansas City	0	0	0.0	0
Philadelphia	0	0	0.0	0
At N.Y. Giants	0	0	0.0	0
St. Louis	0	0	.0	0
At Washington	0	0	0.0	0
Green Bay	0	0	0.0	0
Washington	2	-2	-1.0	0
At Cleveland	1	8	8.0	0
Houston	0	0	0.0	0
Detroit (P)	0	0	0.0	0
At San Francisco (P)	1	5	5.0	0
Baltimore (SB)	0	0	0.0	0
Totals	**8**	**98**	**12.3**	**0**
Postseason	**1**	**5**	**5.0**	**0**

1971

Opponent	No.	Yds.	Avg.	TD
At Buffalo	2	35	17.5	0
At Philadelphia	3	34	11.3	0
Washington	4	45	11.3	0
N.Y. Giants	0	0	0.0	0
At New Orleans	2	23	11.5	0
New England	2	20	10.0	0
At Chicago	4	52	13.0	0
At St. Louis	3	13	4.3	1
Philadelphia	2	28	14.0	0
At Washington	1	8	8.0	0
Los Angeles	0	0	0.0	0
N.Y. Jets	4	64	16.0	0
At N.Y. Giants	2	32	16.0	0
St. Louis	1	6	6.0	0
At Minnesota (P)	2	18	9.0	0
San Francisco (P)	1	5	5.0	0
Miami (SB)	2	28	14.0	1
Totals	**30**	**360**	**12.0**	**1**
Postseason	**5**	**51**	**10.2**	**1**

1972

Opponent	No.	Yds.	Avg.	TD
Philadelphia	1	14	14.0	0
At N.Y. Giants	0	0	0.0	0
At Green Bay	1	8	8.0	0
Pittsburgh	2	36	18.0	0
At Baltimore	1	13	13.0	0
At Washington	2	20	10.0	0
Detroit	1	6	6.0	0
At San Diego	4	36	9.0	1
St. Louis	0	0	0.0	0
At Philadelphia	0	0	0.0	0
San Francisco	3	24	8.0	0
At St. Louis	1	15	15.0	0
Washington	0	0	0.0	0
N.Y. Giants	1	26	26.0	0
At San Francisco (P)	1	9	9.0	0
At Washington (P)	1	4	4.0	0
Totals	**17**	**198**	**11.6**	**1**
Postseason	**2**	**13**	**6.5**	**0**

1978

Opponent	No.	Yds.	Avg.	TD
San Francisco	1	6	6.0	0
Cincinnati	3	42	14.0	0
At Atlanta	4	19	4.8	1
At Pittsburgh	2	19	9.5	0
Houston	2	11	5.5	0
At New Orleans	4	35	8.8	1
Pittsburgh	3	47	15.7	0
At Kansas City	1	12	12.0	0
Buffalo	4	96	24.0	0
At Houston	4	124	31.0	0
Denver		(did not play)		
At Baltimore	2	38	19.0	0
L.A. Rams	3	73	24.3	0
At Seattle	3	19	6.3	0
N.Y. Jets	1	29	29.0	0
At Cincinnati	1	19	19.0	0
Totals	**38**	**589**	**15.5**	**2**

1979

	No.	Yds.	Avg.	TD
At N.Y. Jets	3	31	10.3	1
At Kansas City	6	77	12.8	1
Baltimore	3	84	28.0	1
Dallas	3	53	17.7	1
At Houston	2	21	10.5	0
Pittsburgh	6	97	16.2	1
Washington		(did not play)		
Cincinnati	5	90	18.0	1
At St. Louis	4	19	4.8	0
At Philadelphia	2	23	11.5	1
Seattle	3	61	20.3	0
Miami	4	76	19.0	2
At Pittsburgh	5	77	15.4	0
Houston	4	42	10.5	0
At Oakland	2	14	7.0	0
At Cincinnati	3	16	5.3	0
Totals	**55**	**781**	**14.2**	**9**

1980

	No.	Yds.	Avg.	TD
At New England	3	32	10.7	0
Houston	2	12	6.0	0
Kansas City	6	55	9.2	0
At Tampa Bay	2	25	12.5	0
Denver	4	37	9.3	0
At Seattle	2	60	30.0	0
Green Bay	5	60	12.0	1
Pittsburgh	4	55	13.8	0
Chicago	5	97	19.4	0
At Baltimore	2	13	6.5	0
At Pittsburgh	3	42	14.0	1
Cincinnati	1	14	14.0	0
At Houston	1	7	7.0	0
N.Y. Jets	3	28	9.3	0
At Minnesota	3	27	9.0	0
At Cincinnati	5	30	6.0	0
Oakland (P)	4	51	12.8	0
Totals	**51**	**594**	**11.6**	**3**
Postseason	**4**	**51**	**12.8**	**0**

1981

	No.	Yds.	Avg.	TD
San Diego	6	87	14.5	0
Houston	6	57	9.5	0
At Cincinnati	5	42	8.4	1
Atlanta	6	78	13.0	1
At L.A. Rams	2	56	28.0	1
At Pittsburgh	5	120	24.0	1
New Orleans	7	65	9.3	0
Baltimore	5	85	17.0	1
At Buffalo	3	52	17.3	1
At Denver	3	89	29.7	0
At San Francisco	3	36	12.0	0
Pittsburgh	5	61	12.2	0
Cincinnati	4	58	14.5	0
At Houston	3	26	8.7	0
N.Y. Jets	5	79	15.8	0
At Seattle	1	11	11.0	0
Totals	**69**	**1002**	**14.5**	**6**

1982

	No.	Yds.	Avg.	TD
At Seattle	2	22	11.0	0
Philadelphia	8	122	15.3	2
New England	1	10	10.0	0
At Dallas	2	40	20.0	0
San Diego	10	140	14.0	1
At Cincinnati	10	88	8.8	0
Pittsburgh	4	42	10.5	0
At Houston	3	46	15.3	0
At Pittsburgh	9	123	13.7	0
Oakland (P)	4	51	12.8	0
Totals	**49**	**633**	**12.9**	**3**
Postseason	**4**	**51**	**12.8**	**0**

Team (W-L Record): Cleveland, 1978- (99-82-1, .547).

Hall of Fame? Not eligible

Honors: All-NFL (2), 1979, '84; Pro Bowl (3), 1981, '84-85.

Records: Most receptions by a tight end, career, 639.

Lifetime Rankings: 639 receptions (5th overall/1st among tight ends); 7,740 yards (28th/2nd); 45 TDs (--/T4th).

100-Yard Games: 9 (plus 1 postseason)

200-Yard Games: None

Avg. Yards Per Season: 645

Avg. Yards Per Game: 43

Last Reported Salary: $450,000

Injuries: None

Comment: Newsome is a steady, unspectacular type who has caught a lot of passes for a lot of yards playing for a team that likes to throw to its tight end. His 150-game receiving streak, snapped in 1989, is the second-longest in history. He also hasn't fumbled the last 534 times he's had the ball, going back to '80. But he has only nine 100-yard games in 12 seasons, just one in his last five, and his 12.1-yard average is low. Unless Hall of Fame voters become less picky about tight ends, he probably won't make it.

1983

	No.	Yds.	Avg.	TD
Minnesota	5	35	7.0	0
At Detroit	3	33	11.0	1
Cincinnati	5	50	10.0	1
At San Diego	7	65	9.3	1
Seattle	5	55	11.0	0
N.Y. Jets	5	57	11.4	0
At Pittsburgh	9	103	11.4	0
At Cincinnati	7	69	9.9	2
Houston	4	41	10.3	0
At Green Bay	8	90	11.3	0
Tampa Bay	3	81	27.0	0
At New England	1	4	4.0	0
Baltimore	8	108	13.5	1
At Denver	8	78	9.8	0
At Houston	7	71	10.1	0
Pittsburgh	4	30	7.5	0
Totals	**89**	**970**	**10.9**	**6**

1984

	No.	Yds.	Avg.	TD
At Seattle	2	22	11.0	0
At L.A. Rams	8	65	8.1	1
Denver	2	12	6.0	0
Pittsburgh	6	99	16.5	0
At Kansas City	7	74	10.6	0
New England	6	55	9.2	0
N.Y. Jets	14	191	13.6	0
At Cincinnati	4	20	5.0	0
New Orleans	4	42	10.5	2
At Buffalo	4	53	13.3	0
San Francisco	2	56	28.0	0
At Atlanta	5	97	19.4	1
Houston	10	102	10.2	1
Cincinnati	8	62	7.8	0
At Pittsburgh	5	33	6.6	0
At Houston	2	18	9.0	0
Totals	**89**	**1001**	**11.2**	**5**

1985

	No.	Yds.	Avg.	TD
St. Louis	6	79	13.2	1
Pittsburgh	4	27	6.8	0
At Dallas	4	40	10.0	0
At San Diego	1	6	6.0	0
New England	6	73	12.2	1
At Houston	1	7	7.0	0
L.A. Raiders	4	49	12.3	0
Washington	9	92	10.2	1
At Pittsburgh	2	21	10.5	0
At Cincinnati	7	94	13.4	0
Buffalo	3	17	5.7	1
Cincinnati	2	7	3.5	0
At N.Y. Giants	3	52	17.3	0
At Seattle	4	31	7.8	0
Houston	4	85	21.3	1
At N.Y. Jets	2	31	15.5	0
At Miami (P)	2	22	11.0	0
Totals	**62**	**711**	**11.5**	**5**
Postseason	**2**	**22**	**11.0**	**0**

1986

	No.	Yds.	Avg.	TD
At Chicago	1	14	14.0	0
At Houston	2	19	9.5	0
Cincinnati	2	9	4.5	0
Detroit	1	10	10.0	0
At Pittsburgh	2	18	9.0	0
Kansas City	4	47	11.8	1
Green Bay	3	21	7.0	0
At Minnesota	2	10	5.0	0
At Indianapolis	3	49	16.3	1
Miami	7	94	13.4	0
At L.A. Raiders	1	4	4.0	0
Pittsburgh	2	32	16.0	1
Houston	1	3	3.0	0
At Buffalo	4	48	12.0	0
At Cincinnati	2	32	16.0	0
San Diego	2	7	3.5	0
N.Y. Jets (P)	6	114	19.0	0
Denver (P)	0	0	0.0	0
Totals	**39**	**417**	**10.7**	**3**
Postseason	**6**	**114**	**19.0**	**0**

1987

	No.	Yds.	Avg.	TD
At New Orleans	5	43	8.6	0
Pittsburgh	1	6	6.0	0
At New England		(did not play)		
Houston		(did not play)		
At Cincinnati	4	29	7.3	0
L.A. Rams	2	7	3.5	0
At San Diego	2	10	5.0	0
Atlanta	3	33	11.0	0
Buffalo	3	70	23.3	0
At Houston	2	47	23.5	0
At San Francisco	1	6	6.0	0
Indianapolis	1	11	11.0	0
Cincinnati	3	18	6.0	0
At L.A. Raiders	1	1	1.0	0
At Pittsburgh	6	94	15.7	0
Indianapolis (P)	4	65	16.3	0
At Denver (P)	3	35	11.7	0
Totals	**34**	**375**	**11.0**	**0**
Postseason	**7**	**100**	**14.3**	**0**

1988

	No.	Yds.	Avg.	TD
At Kansas City	3	31	10.3	0
N.Y. Jets	2	26	13.0	0
Indianapolis	3	20	6.7	1
At Cincinnati	5	72	14.4	0
At Pittsburgh	2	11	5.5	0
Seattle	2	27	13.5	0
Philadelphia	1	6	6.0	0
At Phoenix	1	5	5.0	0
Cincinnati	1	5	5.0	0
At Houston	5	65	13.0	1
At Denver	1	8	8.0	0
Pittsburgh	1	8	8.0	0
At Washington	1	5	5.0	0
Dallas	2	18	9.0	0
At Miami	4	23	5.8	0
Houston	1	13	13.0	0
Houston (P)	0	0	0.0	0
Totals	**35**	**343**	**9.8**	**2**
Postseason	**0**	**0**	**0.0**	**0**

1989

	No.	Yds.	Avg.	TD
At Pittsburgh	1	8	8.0	0
N.Y. Jets	4	31	7.8	1
At Cincinnati	2	32	16.0	0
Denver	3	21	7.0	0
At Miami	3	40	13.3	0
Pittsburgh	2	28	14.0	0
Chicago	2	26	13.0	0
Houston	0	0	0.0	0
At Tampa Bay	0	0	0.0	0
At Seattle	1	7	7.0	0
Kansas City	0	0	0.0	0
At Detroit	4	53	13.3	0
Cincinnati	2	16	8.0	0
At Indianapolis	3	43	14.3	0
Minnesota	1	18	18.0	0
At Houston	1	1	1.0	0
Buffalo (P)	4	35	8.8	0
At Denver (P)	0	0	0.0	0
Totals	**29**	**324**	**11.2**	**1**
Postseason	**4**	**35**	**8.8**	**0**

33 SAMMY BAUGH (1937-52)

BAUGH'S BEST YEAR, 1947

Opponent	Att	Comp	Pct	Yds	TD	Int
At Philadelphia	34	21	61.8	364	5	2
Pittsburgh	28	13	46.4	275	3	2
N.Y. Giants	19	13	68.4	214	1	1
At Green Bay	39	19	48.7	234	1	2
Chi. Bears	26	17	65.4	220	1	1
Philadelphia	21	12	57.1	142	1	1
At Pittsburgh	19	10	52.6	183	1	0
At Detroit	31	21	67.7	172	2	1
Chi. Cardinals	33	25	75.8	355	6	2
At N.Y. Yanks	29	20	69.0	278	1	0
At N.Y. Giants	34	14	41.2	158	0	2
N.Y. Yanks	41	25	61.0	343	3	1
Totals	**354**	**210**	**59.3**	**2938**	**25**	**15**

Team (W-L Record): Washington, 1937-52 (99-73-7, .573).

Hall of Fame? Yes (charter member)

Honors: All-NFL (6), 1937, '40, '43, '45, '47-48; NFL All-Star Game (5), 1938, '40-42, '51.

Records: Most passing yards, 21,886, and touchdown passes, 186, career; highest single-season completion rate, 70.3%, 1945.

Lifetime Rankings: 72.0 passer rating (--); 21,886 yards (41st); 186 TDs (21st).

Interception Probability: 6.8%

Comment: One year Baugh went on Bill Stern's radio show to announce the famous sportscaster's all-America team. During a run-through, however, he had trouble pronouncing with his Texas accent the name of Chuck Bednarik, the Penn center. Stern solved the problem by dropping Bednarik from the squad and replacing him with Paul Duke of Georgia Tech. Or so the story goes. No pro football legend is larger than Baugh's. His 1947 statistics show you why. They're good enough to win the passing title *today*. He threw for 2,938 yards that year, a record that survived the wide-open '50s. Sonny Jurgensen finally beat it in '61. Baugh had his biggest games against the two division winners, the Eagles (364 yards, 5 touchdowns) and Cardinals (355, 6).

16 GEORGE BLANDA (1949-58, '60-75)

Teams (W-L Record): Chicago Bears, 1949-58; Houston (AFL), 1960-66; Oakland, 1967-75 (213-121-10, 634).

Hall of Fame? Yes (3rd year eligible)

Honors: Bert Bell Trophy, 1970; Sporting News AFL Player of the Year, 1961; AFL All-Star Game (4), 1961-63, '67.

Records: Just about all the longevity marks; most points, career, 2,002.

Lifetime Rankings: 60.8 passer rating (--); 26,920 yards (21st), 236 TDs (7th)

Interception Probability: 6.9%

Comment: You'll notice Blanda didn't play in two games in 1961. He was benched after the defending AFL champion Oilers started slowly. Then there was a coaching change, and he won back his job. Thus Blanda actually threw his record-setting 36 touchdown passes in *12* games. Dan Marino had the same number of TDs at the same point in '84, the year he "broke" Blanda's mark with 48. We're not suggesting Blanda's feat compares to Marino's. He did it, after all, in the AFL's rag days. We just felt like busting Marino's chops. Besides, it's impossible to feel sentimental about an ornery cuss like Blanda, who routinely blew off autograph seekers and reporters. His season is more of a curiosity. He tied another record with seven TD passes against the New York Titans and led Houston to 10 victories in a row and its second-straight title.

BLANDA'S BEST YEAR, 1961

Opponent	Att	Comp	Pct	Yds	TD	Int
Oakland	24	11	45.8	233	3	1
At San Diego	29	15	51.7	131	0	4
At Dallas	36	15	41.7	275	3	2
Buffalo	(did not play)					
At Boston	(did not play)					
Dallas	24	11	45.8	215	3	0
At Buffalo	32	18	56.3	464	4	4
At Denver	35	17	48.6	263	3	1
Boston	25	9	36.0	134	1	2
N.Y. Titans	32	20	62.5	418	7	1
Denver	28	15	53.6	209	1	3
San Diego	33	20	60.6	351	4	1
At N.Y. Titans	33	18	54.5	287	3	1
At Oakland	31	18	58.1	350	4	2
At San Diego (C)	40	18	45.0	160	1	5
Totals	**362**	**187**	**51.7**	**3330**	**36**	**22**
Postseason	**40**	**18**	**45.0**	**160**	**1**	**5**

12 JOHN BRODIE (1957-73)

BRODIE'S BEST YEAR, 1965

Opponent	Att	Comp	Pct	Yds	TD	Int
Chicago	20	14	70.0	269	4	0
Pittsburgh	20	16	80.0	236	1	0
At Baltimore	36	18	50.0	268	2	3
At Green Bay	38	21	55.3	198	1	1
At Los Angeles	26	18	69.2	215	3	2
Minnesota	29	19	65.5	264	3	1
Baltimore	28	20	71.4	289	2	0
At Dallas			(did not play)			
At Detroit	32	20	62.5	196	1	2
Los Angeles	37	23	62.2	214	2	2
At Minnesota	19	10	52.6	209	5	0
Detroit	35	18	51.4	209	1	1
At Chicago	37	19	51.4	250	2	1
Green Bay	34	26	76.5	295	3	3
Totals	**391**	**242**	**61.9**	**3112**	**30**	**16**

Team (W-L Record): San Francisco, 1957-73 (110-111-9, .498).

Hall of Fame? No

Honors: UPI and Sporting News Player of the Year, 1970; all-NFL (1), 1970; Pro Bowl (2), 1965, '70.

Records: None

Lifetime Rankings: 72.3 passer rating (--); 31,548 yards (8th); 214 TDs (10th).

Interception Probability: 5% (224/4,491)

Comment: What's unusual about this season is that Brodie led the league in passing yards, completion percentage and touchdown passes -- the quarterback's triple crown. Nobody, not even Dan Marino in 1984 or Joe Montana in '89, has done it in the quarter century since. In fact, only two others have accomplished the feat: Sammy Baugh in 1940 and '47 and the Giants' Ed Danowski in '35. Brodie was a near Hall-of-Famer who had two sensational years, the second being 1970. He'd be appreciated more if he hadn't played at a time when there were so many great QBs.

16 LEN DAWSON (1957-75)

Teams (W-L Record): Pittsburgh, 1957-59; Cleveland, 1960-61; Dallas/Kansas City (AFL), 1962-75 (150-94-14, .609).

Hall of Fame? Yes (7th year eligible)

Honors: Sporting News AFL Player of the Year, 1962; Super Bowl MVP, 1970; AFL All-Star Game (6), 1962, '64, '66-69; Pro Bowl (1), 1971.

Records: Highest career completion percentage, AFL, 56.8.

Lifetime Rankings: 82.6 passer rating (11th); 28,711 yards (13th); 239 TDs (6th).

Interception Probability: 4.9% (179/3,601)

Comment: Dawson's Chiefs teammates called him Ajax -- after the cleanser, not the Greek warrior. He hated to get his uniform dirty and rarely did. His 19-year career is longer than any quarterback's except George Blanda, but it started slowly. He threw only 45 passes his first five seasons, washed out with two NFL teams and was said to have a bad arm. Hooking up with former college coach Hank Stram in the AFL saved him. It's hard to get a read on just how good he was because he was 35 when the leagues merged. He won one Super Bowl and played well in another, but was he any better than John Brodie?

DAWSON'S BEST YEAR, 1966

Opponent	Att	Comp	Pct	Yds	TD	Int
At Buffalo	11	8	72.7	129	2	0
At Oakland	16	7	43.8	89	3	0
At Boston	32	20	62.5	291	5	1
Buffalo	15	5	33.3	143	2	1
Denver	20	11	55.0	123	1	0
Oakland	15	9	60.0	118	0	0
At Denver	20	12	60.0	215	2	1
Houston	17	7	41.2	184	2	0
San Diego	24	12	50.0	153	2	2
Miami	14	10	71.4	256	3	1
Boston	38	25	65.8	324	2	1
At N.Y. Jets	23	13	56.5	260	1	0
At Miami	24	11	45.8	121	1	2
At San Diego	15	9	60.0	121	0	1
Buffalo (P)	24	16	66.7	227	2	0
Green Bay (SB)	27	16	59.3	211	1	1
Totals	**284**	**159**	**56.0**	**2527**	**26**	**10**
Postseason	**51**	**32**	**62.8**	**438**	**3**	**1**

10 FRAN TARKENTON (1961-78)

TARKENTON'S BEST YEAR, 1975

Opponent	Att	Comp	Pct	Yds	TD	Int
San Francisco	26	14	53.8	165	1	2
At Cleveland	27	17	63.0	170	2	2
Chicago	30	19	63.3	250	3	1
N.Y. Jets	28	18	64.3	244	2	1
Detroit	24	15	62.5	148	2	0
At Chicago	30	16	53.3	234	1	0
At Green Bay	30	24	80.0	285	3	1
Atlanta	22	11	50.0	47	1	0
At New Orleans	39	25	64.1	310	3	2
At San Diego	32	24	75.0	201	1	2
At Washington	37	27	73.0	357	1	0
Green Bay	30	20	66.7	211	3	0
At Detroit	34	18	52.9	156	0	2
At Buffalo	36	25	69.4	216	2	0
Dallas (P)	26	12	46.2	135	0	1
Totals	**425**	**273**	**64.2**	**2994**	**25**	**13**
Postseason	**26**	**12**	**46.2**	**135**	**0**	**1**

Teams (W-L Record): Minnesota, 1961-66, '72-78; N.Y. Giants, 1967-71 (131-117-6, .528).
Hall of Fame? Yes (3rd year eligible)
Honors: Consensus NFL MVP/player of the year, 1975; all-NFL (2), 1973, '75; Pro Bowl (9), 1964-65, '67-70, '74-76.
Records: Most of the career marks -- yards, 47,003; TDs, 342; attempts, 6,467; and completions, 3,686.
Lifetime Rankings: 80.4 passer rating (15th); 47,003 yards (1st); 342 TDs (1st).
Interception Probability: 4.1% (266/6,467)
Comment: Tarkenton wasn't a great passer, which is probably why he had to wait three years to get in the Hall of Fame. You'd think, given his mediocre arm, there'd be *more* appreciation for what he accomplished. Three lopsided Super Bowl losses didn't help him any, but the Vikings were never the better team. People forget how good he was at an early age. He had a terrific rookie season for an expansion club and made the Vikes respectable in a hurry.

12 KEN STABLER (1970-84)

Teams (W-L Record): Oakland, 1970-79; Houston, 1980-81; New Orleans, 1982-84 (137-74-6, .645).
Hall of Fame? No
Honors: Bert Bell Trophy and AP Player of the Year, 1974; Sporting News Player of the Year, 1974, '76; all-NFL (1), 1974; Pro Bowl (4), 1973-74, '76-77.
Records: Highest completion percentage, career, 59.9.*
Lifetime Rankings: 75.1 passer rating (--); 27,938 yards (17th); 194 TDs (19th).
Interception Probability: 5.9% (222/3,793)
Comment: Stabler didn't become a starter until he was 27, so he had a short prime. But in the mid-'70s there was no one better. He could throw accurately -- he had the highest completion percentage in history until Joe Montana and Dan Marino came along -- *and* deep. He also was a renowned clutch player, even though he made it to the Super Bowl just once. The Raiders were in five straight conference title games from 1973-77, but those Dolphins and Steelers were hard to beat.

STABLER'S BEST YEAR, 1976

Opponent	Att	Comp	Pct	Yds	TD	Int
Pittsburgh	38	21	55.3	342	3	4
At Kansas City	28	22	78.6	224	3	1
At Houston			(did not play)			
At New England	35	20	57.1	225	1	1
At San Diego	26	20	76.9	339	3	1
At Denver	20	16	80.0	175	1	1
Green Bay	21	13	61.9	220	3	1
Denver	27	16	59.3	245	1	2
At Chicago	17	11	64.7	234	3	0
Kansas City	18	10	55.6	138	2	4
At Philadelphia	18	14	77.8	133	1	0
Tampa Bay	23	15	65.2	245	2	1
Cincinnati	20	16	80.0	217	4	1
San Diego			(did not play)			
New England (P)	32	19	59.4	233	1	0
Pittsburgh (P)	16	10	62.5	88	2	0
Minnesota (SB)	19	12	63.2	180	1	0
Totals	**291**	**194**	**66.7**	**2737**	**27**	**17**
Postseason	**67**	**41**	**61.2**	**501**	**4**	**0**

14 KEN ANDERSON (1971-86)

ANDERSON'S BEST YEAR, 1982

Opponent	Att	Comp	Pct	Yds	TD	Int
Houston	40	29	72.5	354	2	0
At Pittsburgh	38	27	71.1	323	0	3
At Philadelphia	32	19	59.4	215	1	2
L.A. Raiders	26	14	53.9	210	1	0
At Baltimore	29	22	75.9	206	3	0
Cleveland	28	18	64.3	183	0	1
At San Diego	56	40	71.4	416	2	1
Seattle	29	22	75.9	265	1	2
At Houston	31	27	87.1	323	2	0
N.Y. Jets (P)	35	26	74.3	354	2	3
Totals	**309**	**218**	**70.6**	**2495**	**12**	**9**
Postseason	**35**	**26**	**74.3**	**354**	**2**	**3**

Team (W-L Record): Cincinnati, 1971-86 (123-112, .523).

Hall of Fame? Not eligible

Honors: Consensus Player of the Year, 1981; all-NFL (1), 1981; Pro Bowl (4), 1975-76, '81-82.

Records: Highest completion percentage, season, 70.6, 1982.

Lifetime Rankings: 81.9 passer rating (12th); 32,838 yards (6th); 197 TDs (T15th).

Interception Percentage: 3.6% (160/4,475)

Comment: Anderson was a great quarterback when he had a great offensive coordinator. He won his first two passing titles in 1974-75 under Bill Walsh and his second two in 1981-82 under Lindy Infante. In between, however, he had some tough times. After Walsh left, his completion percentage dropped from 60.5 to 53.0 to 51.4 the next two years. Infante's arrival spurred an Anderson revival. During the strike-shortened '82 season, Anderson completed 70.6 percent of his passes to break Sammy Baugh's 37-year-old record.

14 DAN FOUTS (1973-87)

Team (W-L Record): San Diego, 1973-87 (100-118-1, .459).

Hall of Fame? Not eligible

Honors: Sporting News Player of the Year, 1979; all-NFL (2), 1978, '81; Pro Bowl (6), 1979-83, '85.

Records: Most 3,000-yard passing seasons, career, 6; most 300-yard passing games, career, 51.

Lifetime Rankings: 80.2 passer rating (17th); 43,040 yards (2nd); 254 TDs (4th).

Interception Probability: 4.3% (242/5,604)

Comment: The Sonny Jurgensen of his era -- pure passer, great receivers, big numbers, no championships. Fouts blossomed in 1978 when Don (Air) Coryell took over as head coach. For eight seasons he averaged 3,729 yards and 24 touchdowns. But all that firepower couldn't put the Chargers in the Super Bowl. They lost in the AFC title game in 1981 (Ice Bowl II) and '82. No one hung tougher in the pocket.

FOUTS' BEST YEAR, 1981

Opponent	Att	Comp	Pct	Yds	TD	Int
At Cleveland	25	19	76.0	330	3	0
Detroit	25	18	72.0	316	1	1
At Kansas City	43	22	51.2	284	3	3
At Denver	47	26	55.3	298	2	3
Seattle	41	30	73.2	302	3	0
Minnesota	38	20	52.6	310	2	0
At Baltimore	43	26	60.5	298	3	0
At Chicago	43	13	30.2	295	2	2
Kansas City	39	24	61.5	297	0	1
Cincinnati	40	20	50.0	352	2	2
At Seattle	34	20	58.8	252	1	1
At Oakland	44	28	63.6	296	6	1
Denver	29	19	65.5	256	1	0
Buffalo	42	28	66.7	343	2	1
At Tampa Bay	49	33	67.4	351	1	2
Oakland	27	14	51.9	222	1	0
At Miami (P)	53	33	62.3	433	3	1
At Cincinnati (P)	28	15	53.6	185	1	2
Totals	**609**	**360**	**59.1**	**4802**	**33**	**17**
Postseason	**81**	**48**	**59.3**	**618**	**4**	**3**

15 STEVE VAN BUREN (1944-51)

VAN BUREN'S BEST YEAR, 1949

Opponent	Att.	Yds.	Avg.	TD
At N.Y. Bulldogs	25	58	2.3	0
At Detroit	33	135	4.1	2
Chi. Cardinals	22	98	4.4	2
At Chi. Bears	15	18	1.2	0
Washington	12	39	3.3	1
At Pittsburgh	17	103	6.1	2
Los Angeles	21	71	3.4	0
At Washington	18	96	5.3	1
N.Y. Bulldogs	35	174	5.0	2
Pittsburgh	27	205	7.6	0
At N.Y. Giants	17	53	3.1	0
N.Y. Giants	21	96	4.4	1
At Los Angeles (C)	31	196	6.3	0
Totals	**263**	**1146**	**4.4**	**11**
Postseason	**31**	**196**	**6.3**	**0**

Team (W-L Record): Philadelphia, 1944-51 (58-30-3, .654).
Hall of Fame? Yes (third year eligible)
Honors: All-NFL (5), 1944-45, '47-49.
Records: Most rushing yards, career, 5,860; most rushing yards, season, 1,146, 1949.
Lifetime Rankings: 1,320 attempts (T42nd); 5,860 rushing yards (37th); 69 TDs (T12th).
Avg. Rushing Yards Per Season: 733
Avg. Rushing Yards Per Game: 71
Fumble Probability: 2.5% (34/1,377)
Comment: Van Buren was the worst driver in NFL history. He once cracked up three cars in 24 hours. Years later he remarked: "I never got in an accident for going too *fast*." He was a flyer on the field, a 9.8 100 man in college. He was also a workhorse until injuries struck in the '50s. The Eagles rode him to three straight championship games and won the last two. In the '49 title game he sloshed through the rain and mud for a record 196 yards in a 14-0 victory over the Rams. Roommate Alex Wojciechowicz says Van Buren played in a rage because commissioner Bert Bell allowed the game to be played under such conditions. The players' purse was determined by the attendance, and only 27,000 showed up at L.A. Coliseum -- after 90,000 had been expected.

34 JOE PERRY (1948-63)

Teams (W-L Record): San Francisco, 1948-60, '63; Baltimore, 1961-62 (108-89-3, .548).
Hall of Fame? Yes (first year eligible)
Honors: All-NFL (2), 1953-54; Pro Bowl (3), 1952-54.
Records: Most rushing yards, career, 8,378.*
Lifetime Rankings (NFL only): 1,737 attempts (15th); 8,378 rushing yards (11th); 53 TDs (20th).
Avg. Rushing Yards Per Season: 598
Avg. Rushing Yards Per Game: 55
Fumble Probability: 3.3% (66/2,010)
Comment: Perry was the NFL's all-time leading rusher for several years, even though he never had a 200-carry season. The problem was that the 49ers had four Hall-of-Famers in the backfield -- Y. A. Tittle, Hugh McElhenny and John Henry Johnson were the others -- and only one ball. Perry was a halfback-sized fullback who brought rare speed (9.7) to the position. He had prodigious thighs, though, and put up with the pounding for 16 years. Joe the Jet's engine ran hot. He sweated so much he had to change jerseys every quarter. On a 100-degree day in Dallas in 1952 he went through eight.

PERRY'S BEST YEAR, 1954

Opponent	Att.	Yds.	Avg.	TD
Washington	12	90	7.5	2
At Los Angeles	4	47	11.8	1
At Green Bay	23	100	4.4	1
At Chi. Bears	11	119	10.8	0
Detroit	13	51	3.9	0
Chi. Bears	10	39	3.9	0
Los Angeles	12	124	10.3	1
At Detroit	13	86	6.6	0
At Pittsburgh	21	122	5.8	1
At Baltimore	16	92	5.8	0
Green Bay	20	137	6.9	1
Baltimore	18	42	2.3	1
Totals	**173**	**1,049**	**6.1**	**8**

31 JIM TAYLOR (1958-67)

TAYLOR'S BEST YEAR, 1962

Opponent	Att.	Yds.	Avg.	TD
Minnesota	17	75	4.4	0
St. Louis	23	122	5.3	0
Chicago	17	126	7.4	3
Detroit	20	95	4.8	0
At Minnesota	17	164	9.6	0
San Francisco	17	160	9.4	2
At Baltimore	16	68	4.3	1
At Chicago	25	124	5.0	4
At Philadelphia	25	141	5.6	4
Baltimore	19	46	2.4	0
At Detroit	13	47	3.6	1
Los Angeles	16	71	4.4	2
At San Francisco	24	79	3.3	1
At Los Angeles	23	156	6.8	1
At N.Y. Giants (C)	31	85	2.7	1
Totals	**272**	**1474**	**5.4**	**19**
Postseason	**31**	**85**	**2.7**	**1**

Teams (W-L Record): Green Bay, 1958-66; New Orleans, 1967 (84-46-4, .642).
Hall of Fame? Yes (4th year eligible)
Honors: All-NFL (2), 1961-62; Pro Bowl (5), 1960-64.
Records: Most rushing touchdowns, season, 19, 1962.
Lifetime Rankings: 1,941 attempts (10th); 8,597 yards (10th); 83 TDs (5th).
Avg. Rushing Yards Per Season: 860
Avg. Rushing Yards Per Game: 65
Fumble Probability: 1.6% (34/2,173)
Comment: 1962 was the only season of his career Jim Brown didn't win the NFL rushing title. Taylor, who was always finishing second to him (1960, '61, '63 and '64), ran wild that year. His 1,474 yards were second-best all-time, and he set records for touchdowns and rushing touchdowns with 19. The mark for rushing TDs didn't fall until '83. Taylor was one tough sumbitch. Giants linebacker Sam Huff recalled: "He'd kick you, gouge you, spit at you, whatever it took. . . . He ran hard and he loved to kick you in the head with those knees." Huff claims Taylor dented his helmet that way in the '62 championship game. Taylor played out his option in '66 and signed with the expansion New Orleans Saints in his native Louisiana. He took the money and ran, playing one more season before retiring.

44 LEROY KELLY (1964-73)

Team (W-L Record): Cleveland, 1964-73 (92-44-4, .671).
Hall of Fame? No
Honors: Bert Bell Trophy, 1968; all-NFL (1), 1966; Pro Bowl (6), 1966-71.
Records: None
Lifetime Rankings: 1,727 attempts (16th); 7,274 yards rushing (16th); 74 TDs (T9th).
Avg. Rushing Yards Per Season: 727
Avg. Rushing Yards Per Game: 53
Fumble Probability: 1.7% (35/2,087)
Comment: Kelly had three almost identical 1,000-yard seasons from 1966 to '68. 1968 was his best for yards and touchdowns. The year before he led the NFL in those two categories *and* rushing average. Only seven backs in NFL/AFL history have achieved such a triple crown -- Jim Brown (1963), O. J. Simpson ('75), Walter Payton ('77) and Earl Campbell ('80) among them. Kelly's celebrated flatfooted running style made him especially effective on muddy fields. He also was incredibly quick off the ball. In his first year as a starter, the Browns kept getting illegal-motion penalties because officials thought he was beating the snap count. The team sent films to the league office to prove he wasn't.

KELLY'S BEST YEAR, 1968

Opponent	Att.	Yds.	Avg.	TD
At New Orleans	20	107	5.4	1
At Dallas	13	58	4.5	0
Los Angeles	11	49	4.5	0
Pittsburgh	25	128	5.1	1
St. Louis	11	5	0.5	0
At Baltimore	30	130	4.3	1
Atlanta	19	112	5.9	2
At San Francisco	27	174	6.4	1
New Orleans	17	127	7.5	1
At Pittsburgh	11	19	1.7	1
Philadelphia	20	108	5.4	2
N.Y. Giants	16	56	3.5	4
At Washington	18	99	5.5	1
At St. Louis	10	67	6.7	1
Dallas (P)	20	87	4.4	1
Baltimore (C)	13	28	2.2	0
Totals	**248**	**1239**	**5.0**	**16**
Postseason	**33**	**115**	**3.5**	**1**

39 LARRY CSONKA (1968-74, '76-79)

CSONKA'S BEST YEAR, 1972

Opponent	Att.	Yds.	Avg.	TD
At Kansas City	21	118	5.6	1
Houston	17	79	4.6	1
At Minnesota	10	66	6.6	0
At N.Y. Jets	18	102	5.7	0
San Diego	13	70	5.4	0
Buffalo	18	107	5.9	1
At Baltimore	19	93	4.9	2
At Buffalo	17	72	4.2	0
New England	5	32	6.4	1
N.Y. Jets	17	72	4.2	0
St. Louis	16	114	7.1	0
At New England	15	91	6.1	0
At N.Y. Giants	9	30	3.3	0
Baltimore	18	71	3.9	0
Cleveland (P)	13	32	2.5	0
At Pittsburgh (P)	24	68	2.8	0
Washington (SB)	15	112	7.5	0
Totals	**213**	**1117**	**5.2**	**6**
Postseason	**52**	**212**	**4.1**	**0**

Teams (W-L Record): Miami, 1968-74; '79; N.Y. Giants, '76-'78 (85-70-3, .548).
Hall of Fame? Yes (3rd year eligible)
Honors: Super Bowl MVP, 1974; all-NFL (1), 1970; Pro Bowl (5), 1970-74.
Records: None
Lifetime Rankings: 1,891 attempts (11th); 8,081 yards (12th); 64 TDs (14th).
Avg. Yards Per Season: 735
Avg. Yards Per Game: 55
Fumble Probability: 1.1% (21/1,997)
Comment: Csonka gave America the finger on a Sports Illustrated cover. The historic date was Aug. 7, 1972. The guy belongs in the Hall of Fame on the basis of that alone. He made it instead on the strength of three 1,000-yard seasons during the Dolphins' glory days in the early '70s. His punishing running style was influenced by Marion Motley, one of his boyhood heroes. He'd rank a lot higher on the all-time rushing list if he hadn't jumped to the World Football League in '75 and then wasted three years with the godawful Giants. By the way, he appeared on another SI cover (July 28, 1975) along with Miami teammates Jim Kiick and Paul Warfield after they signed with the WFL. His pose was the same as in '72, sitting against the goal post, one leg crossed over the other. This time he displayed two fingers, his right index and middle.

42 GERALD RIGGS (1982-)

Teams (W-L Record): Atlanta, 1982-88; Washington, 1989- (44-72-1, .380).
Hall of Fame? Not eligible
Honors: Pro Bowl (3), 1985-87.
Records: None
Lifetime Rankings: 1,788 attempts (13th); 7,465 yards (13th); 52 TDs (T22nd).
Avg. Yards Per Season: 933
Avg. Yards Per Game: 72
Fumble Probability: 1.8% (35/1,998)
Comment: Riggs' most impressive statistic in 1985 doesn't show up in his game-by-game. He carried 397 times, the third-highest total in league history, and didn't fumble. Note also that he gained 110 yards against a Bears defense that was practically impenetrable that season. What a man! His emergence the year before, after two seasons of spot duty, helped the Falcons withstand the loss of William Andrews. He's a fullback in the classic mow-'em-down mold. In training camp with the Redskins in '89, he ran out of bounds into a parked pickup truck. Riggs returned to the huddle; the truck went to the shop for $1,500 in repairs.

RIGGS' BEST YEAR, 1985

Opponent	Att.	Yds.	Avg.	TD
Detroit	31	131	4.2	1
At San Francisco	21	92	4.4	0
Denver	21	77	3.1	1
At L.A. Rams	18	61	3.4	0
San Francisco	13	43	3.3	0
At Seattle	23	139	6.0	0
New Orleans	26	97	3.7	1
At Dallas	24	127	5.3	0
Washington	22	127	5.8	0
At Philadelphia	27	129	4.8	1
L.A. Rams	41	123	3.0	3
At Chicago	30	110	3.7	0
L.A. Raiders	25	95	3.8	1
At Kansas City	26	197	7.6	1
Minnesota	10	13	1.3	0
At New Orleans	39	158	4.1	1
Totals	**397**	**1719**	**4.1**	**10**

28 CURT WARNER (1983-)

WARNER'S BEST YEAR, 1983

Opponent	Att.	Yds.	Avg.	TD
At Kansas City	12	93	7.8	0
At N.Y. Jets	24	128	5.3	2
San Diego	22	109	5.0	0
Washington	15	34	2.3	0
At Cleveland	24	94	3.9	2
At San Diego	19	73	3.8	2
L.A. Raiders	22	75	3.4	1
Pittsburgh	12	48	4.0	1
At L.A. Raiders	23	101	4.4	1
Denver	25	134	5.4	0
At Phoenix	21	83	4.0	0
At Denver	20	70	3.5	0
Kansas City	32	207	6.5	3
Dallas	12	22	1.8	1
At N.Y. Giants	26	62	2.4	0
New England	26	116	4.5	0
Denver (P)	23	99	4.3	0
At Miami (P)	29	113	3.9	2
At L.A. Raiders (P)	11	26	2.4	0
Totals	**335**	**1449**	**4.3**	**13**
Postseason	**63**	**238**	**3.8**	**2**

Team (W-L Record): Seattle, 1983-89 (51-42, .548).
Hall of Fame? Not eligible
Honors: UPI Rookie and Player of the Year, 1983; UPI AFC Offensive Player of the Year, 1986; Pro Bowl (3), 1983, '86-87.
Records: None
Lifetime Rankings: 1,649 attempts (T19th); 6,705 rushing yards (21st); 55 TDs (18th).
Avg. Rushing Yards Per Season: 958
Avg. Rushing Yards Per Game: 72
Fumble Probability: 1.2% (36/2,986)
Comment: Warner's rookie rushing total of 1,449 is one of the six highest in league history. He was at his best then, a lethal cutback runner, and carried the Seahawks to the AFC championship game. But what he did in 1986 may have been even more extraordinary. He came virtually all the way back from a serious knee injury that wiped out his '84 season, gaining a career-high 1,481 yards. We say virtually because no back, especially one with Warner's style, is ever quite the same.

5 PAUL HORNUNG (1957-62, '64-66)

176 POINTS IN A SEASON, 1960

Opponent	Pts	How He Scored (Yds)
Bears	8	run (2 yards), 2 PAT
Lions	16	reception (16), run (11), 4 PAT
Colts	5	5 PAT
49ers	23	2 runs (1,1), 2 FG (47,32), 5 PAT
At Steelers	13	4 FG (35,35,45,17), PAT
At Colts	18	2 runs (10,2), FG (21), 3 PAT
Cowboys	17	run (4), 2 FG (21,21), 5 PAT
Rams	19	2 runs (2,2), FG (12), 4 PAT
At Lions	10	run (8), FG (12), PAT
At Bears	23	reception (17), run (10), 2 FG (21,41), 5 PAT
At 49ers	13	run (28), 2 FG (38,23), PAT
At Rams	11	run (1), 5 PAT
Totals	**176**	**15 TD, 15 FG, 41 PAT**

Teams (W-L Record): Green Bay, 1957-62, '64-66 (73-42-3, .631).
Hall of Fame? Yes (15th year eligible)
Honors: Bert Bell Trophy, 1961; all-NFL (2), 1960-61; Pro Bowl (2), 1959-60.
Records: Most points, season, 1976, 1960; most points in a championship game, 19, 1961.
Lifetime Rankings: 3,711 rushing yards (--); 1,480 receiving yards (--); 5,191 yards from scrimmage (--).
Avg. Yards Per Season: 577
Avg. Yards Per Game: 50
Fumble Probability: 2.1% (22/1,033).
Comment: Hornung's record 176 points in 1960 just might be unreachable. It was set in 12 games but hasn't been seriously challenged even in 16. His big advantage was that he played *and* kicked, something no one does anymore. Twice that season he scored all the Packers' points. The closest anyone has come to him since is 161 by the Redskins' Mark Moseley in 1983. Moseley had 47 field-goal and 63 extra-point tries -- 110 kicks -- and still couldn't do it. If anybody does threaten Hornung's record, he has this as a final line of defense: He also threw two touchdown passes, meaning he had a hand in 188 points.

22 TIMMY BROWN (1959-68)

Teams (W-L Record): Green Bay, 1959; Philadelphia, 1960-67; Baltimore, 1968 (60-72-4, .456).
Hall of Fame? No
Honors: Pro Bowl (3), 1962-63, '65.
Records: Most kickoff returns for a touchdown, game, 2, 1962.
Lifetime Rankings: 3,862 rushing yards (--); 3,399 receiving yards (12th among backs); 7,261 yards from scrimmage (--).
Avg. Yards Per Season: Rushing, 386; receiving, 340; combined, 726.
Avg. Yards Per Game: 67
Fumble Probability: 3% (41/1,380)
Comment: Pro football doesn't appreciate versatility anymore. Only backs who were great *runners* make the Hall of Fame these days. Players like Timmy Brown, Chuck Foreman, Lydell Mitchell and James Brooks -- good-to-very-good runners who also excelled in other areas -- are left out in the cold. It's not just that these guys aren't or won't be in the Hall, it's that they don't seem to get serious consideration. Something's wrong. Brown may have been the most well-rounded of the bunch. He was the best receiving back in pro football from 1962 to '65, had two 800-yard rushing seasons and was a first-class kick returner. He even recorded a couple of records and did some acting. Nobody ever gained as many yards in back-to-back years as he did in '62

BROWN'S 2,306-YARD YEAR, 1962

Opponent	Rush.	Rec.	Punt	KO	Total	TD
Cardinals	22	25	0	43	90*	2
Giants	11	160	16	97	284	1
Browns	72	42	9	19	142	0
At Steelers	23	44	0	21	88	0
At Cowboys	41	70	18	88	217	0
Redskins	17	-2	0	0	15	0
At Vikings	23	174	0	66	263	1
At Browns	30	44	38	72	184	1
Packers	3	0	0	54	57	0
At Giants	65	11	0	117	193	1
Cowboys	107	37	0	63	207	2
At Redskins	46	24	0	99	169	2
Steelers	35	21	0	0	56	0
At Cardinals	50	199	0	92	341	2
Totals	**545**	**849**	**81**	**831**	**2306***	**13**

*Doesn't include 99-yard missed field goal return for a touchdown.

and '63 (4,734). He was a bigger, faster, better Terry Metcalf. The knock on him was that he fumbled, and the statistics bear that out. But he also brought plenty of excitement to the game. Doesn't that count for anything?

25 JOE WASHINGTON (1977-85)

WASHINGTON'S BEST YEAR, 1979

Opponent	Rushing Att–Yds	Receiving No–Yds	TD	Total Yds
At Kansas City	16-63	13-130	0	193
Tampa Bay		(did not play)		
At Cleveland	19-59	5-33	0	92
At Pittsburgh	21-65	3-19	0	84
Buffalo	14-37	4-27	0	64
N.Y. Jets	7-18	7-29	0	47
Houston	18-86	5-53	0	139
At Buffalo	14-49	2-34	0	83
New England	14-53	3-19	3	72
Cincinnati	22-106	2-52	1	158
At Miami	18-56	10-121	0	177
At New England	14-68	6-62	0	130
Miami	16-47	2-12	1	59
At N.Y. Jets	11-68	10-57	1	125
Kansas City	21-51	6-70	1	121
At N.Y. Giants	17-58	4-32	0	90
Totals	**242–884**	**82–750**	**7**	**1634**

Teams (W-L Record): San Diego, 1977; Baltimore, 1978-80; Washington, 1981-84; Atlanta, 1985 (69-66, .511).
Hall of Fame? Not eligible
Honors: Pro Bowl (1), 1979.
Records: None
Lifetime Rankings: 4,839 rushing yards (--); 3,413 receiving yards (11th among backs); 8,252 yards from scrimmage (38th among backs).
Avg. Yards Per Season: Rushing, 538; receiving, 379; combined, 917.
Avg. Yards Per Game: 69
Fumble Probability: 2.6% (42/1,618)
Comment: When healthy, Washington was a productive multi-purpose player. Unfortunately knee injuries cost him his rookie season and half of two others. In 1979, the only time he went to the Pro Bowl, he became the second player to gain 750 yards both rushing and receiving. Charley Taylor was the first, and Marcus Allen and Roger Craig have done it since. Washington also led the NFL in receptions that year. But what he did in '78 might have been even tougher. He carried 240 times, gaining 956 yards, without scoring a touchdown -- a record.

21 JAMES BROOKS (1981-)

Teams (W-L Record): San Diego, 1981-83; Cincinnati, 1984- (70-63, .526).
Hall of Fame? Not eligible
Honors: Pro Bowl (3), 1986, '88-89.
Records: None
Lifetime Rankings: 6,343 rushing yards (28th); 3,005 receiving yards (25th among backs); 9,348 yards from scrimmage (19th among backs).
Avg. Yards Per Season: Rushing, 705; receiving, 334; combined, 1,039.
Avg. Yards Per Game: 75
Fumble Probability: 2.3% (42/1,805)
Comment: Only in the last couple of years have people begun to realize how good this guy is. Brooks started out as an undersized (5'10", 182) situation player in San Diego. But in 1985 he became an undersized every-down player in Cincinnati. He was still producing in '89 at age 30, rushing for a career-high 1,239 yards and making his third Pro Bowl in four seasons. Going into 1990 he needed 652 yards to become the 15th NFL player to gain 10,000 from scrimmage. He was already one of just eight backs with 2,500 yards in three categories -- rushing, receiving and returning.

BROOKS' BEST YEAR, 1986

Opponent	Rushing Att–Yds	Receiving No–Yds	TD	Total Yds
At Kansas City	13-40	3-22	0	62
Buffalo	8-29	1-9	0	38
At Cleveland	14-118	3-40	0	158
Chicago	7-15	3-18	1	33
At Green Bay	20-94	2-29	2	123
Pittsburgh	14-69	3-26	0	95
Houston	18-133	6-62	2	195
At Pittsburgh	11-48	6-69	0	117
At Detroit	15-120	2-16	0	136
At Houston	9-26	3-55	2	81
Seattle	12-42	4-90	0	132
Minnesota	12-41	1-8	1	49
At Denver	7-27	3-55	0	82
At New England	18-163	6-101	1	264
Cleveland	12-43	7-75	0	118
N.Y. Jets	15-79	1-11	0	90
Totals	**205–1087**	**54–686**	**9**	**1773**

42 JAMES WILDER (1981-)

WILDER'S BEST YEAR, 1984

Opponent	Rushing Att–Yds	Receiving No–Yds	TD	Total Yds
At Chicago	16-73	2-56	0	129
At New Orleans	21-75	2-17	0	92
Detroit	22-89	8-56	1	145
At N.Y. Giants	24-112	4-65	1	177
Green Bay	43-172	4-44	1	216
Minnesota	25-89	6-40	2	129
At Detroit	30-72	9-60	0	132
Chicago	13-44	2-12	0	56
At Kansas City	25-91	7-44	0	135
At Minnesota	30-146	4-46	2	192
N.Y. Giants	34-99	0-0	1	99
At San Francisco	18-89	5-35	0	124
L.A. Rams	20-77	10-80	2	157
At Green Bay	27-88	11-48	0	136
Atlanta	28-125	2-22	1	147
N.Y. Jets	31-103	9-60	2	163
Totals	**407–1544**	**85–685**	**13**	**2229**

Teams (W-L Record): Tampa Bay, 1981-89; Washington, 1990- (38-95, .286).
Hall of Fame? Not eligible
Honors: Pro Bowl (1), 1984.
Records: Most rushing attempts, season, 407, 1984; most rushing attempts, game, 43, 1984.*
Lifetime Rankings: 5,957 rushing yards (34th); 3,492 receiving yards (10th among backs); 9,449 yards from scrimmage (18th among backs).
Avg. Yards Per Season: Rushing, 662; receiving, 388; combined, 1,050.
Avg. Yards Per Game: 84
Fumble Probability: 2.2% (44/2,008)
Comment: What must it be like to be tackled 479 times in a season? Only James Wilder knows. In 1984 he had a record 407 carries plus 85 receptions. Subtract his 13 touchdowns and you get 479, which is a conservative estimate. He probably got the hell beat out of him on a couple of TDs because they all came on the ground. He didn't score on any of his 85 catches. That's another mark. (The next year he had 53 catches without a TD.) All kidding aside, Wilder's '84 is a monument to human endurance.

34 HERSCHEL WALKER (1986-)

Teams (W-L Record): USFL, 1983-85; Dallas, 1986-89; Minnesota, 1989 (22-38, .367).
Hall of Fame? Not eligible
Honors: Pro Bowl (2), 1987-88.
Records: None
Lifetime Rankings: 4,057 rushing yards (--); 2,480 receiving yards (--); 6,537 yards from scrimmage (--).
Avg. Yards Per Season: Rushing, 1,014; receiving, 620; combined, 1,634.
Avg. Yards Per Game: 109
Fumble Probability: 1.8% (22/1,213)
Comment: Walker's a great *athlete*, not a great football player. A quarterback could hand him a piano instead of the ball and he'd probably still gain 4.2 yards. He has speed, size, strength, hands, everything you'd look for in a back -- except the slightest hint of instinctive running ability. Even so, he's had some awesome games. Against the Eagles in 1986 he touched the ball 15 times and gained 292 yards from scrimmage. That's probably the biggest day any NFL running back has ever had.

WALKER'S BEST YEAR, 1988

Opponent	Rushing Att–Yds	Receiving No–Yds	TD	Total Yds
At Pittsburgh	19-79	6-56	0	135
At Phoenix	29-149	3-22	1	171
N.Y Giants	19-78	5-80	1	158
Atlanta	25-96	5-27	1	123
At New Orleans	26-124	4-23	0	147
Washington	15-51	5-92	0	143
At Chicago	21-88	4-47	0	135
At Philadelphia	25-85	4-42	0	127
Phoenix	17-87	0-0	0	87
At N.Y. Giants	20-96	6-40	0	136
Minnesota	21-86	0-0	0	86
Cincinnati	27-131	2-16	1	147
Houston	22-69	4-20	1	89
At Cleveland	25-134	3-7	1	141
At Washington	27-98	2-33	0	131
Philadelphia	23-63	0-0	1	63
Totals	**361–1514**	**53–505**	**7**	**2019**

49 JIM BENTON (1938-40, '42-47)

BENTON'S BEST YEAR, 1945

Opponent	No.	Yds.	Avg.	TD
Chi. Cardinals	1	9	9.0	0
Chi. Bears		(did not play)		
At Green Bay	5	85	17.0	1
At Chi. Bears	7	151	21.6	1
At Philadelphia	4	77	19.3	1
At N.Y. Giants	5	111	22.2	0
Green Bay	1	84	84.0	1
At Chi. Cardinals	4	128	32.0	2
At Detroit	10	303	30.3	1
N.Y. Yanks	8	119	14.9	1
Washington (C)	9	125	13.9	1
Totals	**45**	**1067**	**23.7**	**8**
Postseason	**9**	**125**	**13.9**	**1**
10-Game Totals	**54**	**1192**	**22.1**	**9**

Teams (W-L Record): Cleveland/L.A. Rams, 1938-42, '44-47; Chicago Bears, 1943 (51-42-4, .546).
Hall of Fame? No
Honors: All-NFL (2), 1945-46; NFL All-Star Game (1), 1939.
Records: Most receiving yards, game, 303, 1945.*
Lifetime Rankings: 288 receptions (--); 4,801 yards (--); 45 TDs (--).
Avg. Yards Per Season: 533
Avg. Yards Per Game: 55
Comment: You never hear much about the season Benton had in 1945. Strange, because the man in whose shadow he played, Don Hutson, had only one year that was better. Despite missing a game with an injury, Benton caught 45 passes for 1,067 yards and eight touchdowns, an average of 118.6 a game. Just three receivers have ever averaged more. And he played for a team that led the league in *rushing*. He had his biggest game Thanksgiving Day at Detroit with the division championship at stake: 10 receptions, 303 yards and one TD in a 28-21 Cleveland victory. His yardage total broke Hutson's league record by 66 yards. The mark stood for 40 years. This was wartime, of course, but Benton was a legitimate talent. The next year he won the receiving title with 63 catches. When he retired he was second only to Hutson in career receptions, yards and touchdowns. A distant second, however, which may be why he's not in Canton.

40 ELROY HIRSCH (1946-57)

Teams (W-L Record): AAFC, 1946-48; Los Angeles, 1949-57 (73-69-8, .513).
Hall of Fame? Yes (6th year eligible)
Honors: All-NFL (2), 1951, '53; Pro Bowl (3), 1951-53.
Records: Most receiving yards, season, 1,495, 1951*; most touchdown receptions, season, 17, 1951*; consecutive games with a TD reception, 11, 1950-51.*
Lifetime Rankings (NFL only): 343 receptions (--); 6,299 yards (--); 53 TDs (T38th).
Avg. Yards Per Season: 700
Avg. Yards Per Game: 61
Comment: Hirsch's 1951 season gets our vote as the greatest ever by a receiver. Unlike many other pass-catching feats, it didn't happen in wartime or the bombs-away early AFL. The NFL was as competitive then as it's ever been. "During that period of time, the late 1940s and 1950s, there were more superstars in pro football than at any other time," says the Patriots' Bucko Kilroy. Hirsch just played on another level that year. In tying Don Hutson's 1942 record of 17 touchdowns, he *averaged* 47.8 yards per TD. His yardage total of 1,495 wasn't topped by an NFL receiver for 33 years, and only then in a 16-game season. Hirsch's numbers were so off the charts that even he, a Hall-of-Famer, never came within 500 yards or eight TDs of duplicating them.

HIRSCH'S BEST YEAR, 1951

Opponent	No.	Yds.	Avg.	TD
N.Y. Yankees	9	173	19.2	4
Cleveland	4	69	17.3	1
At Detroit	7	147	21.0	1
At Green Bay	3	111	37.0	1
At San Francisco	7	163	23.3	1
San Francisco	4	103	25.8	1
Chi. Cardinals	6	195	32.5	2
N.Y. Yankees	4	97	24.3	1
At Washington	7	104	14.9	1
At Chi. Bears	3	106	35.3	1
Detroit	6	81	13.5	0
Green Bay	6	146	24.3	3
At Cleveland (C)	4	66	16.5	0
Totals	**66**	**1495**	**22.7**	**17**
Postseason	**4**	**66**	**16.5**	**0**

25 TOMMY McDONALD (1957-68)

McDONALD'S BEST YEAR, 1961

Opponent	No.	Yds.	Avg.	TD
Cleveland	4	53	13.3	1
Washington	2	36	18.0	1
St. Louis	11	187	17.0	0
Pittsburgh	3	23	7.7	0
At St. Louis	4	43	10.8	1
At Dallas	3	36	12.0	1
At Washington	7	141	20.1	1
Chicago	6	109	18.2	1
At N.Y. Giants	3	26	8.7	0
At Cleveland	2	25	12.5	1
Dallas	5	131	26.2	3
At Pittsburgh	1	7	7.0	0
N.Y. Giants	7	237	33.9	2
At Detroit	6	90	15.0	1
Detroit (PB)	3	53	17.7	0
Totals	**64**	**1144**	**17.9**	**13**
Postseason	**3**	**53**	**17.7**	**0**

Teams (W-L Record): Philadelphia, 1957-63; Dallas, 1964; L.A. Rams, 1965-66; Atlanta, 1967; Cleveland, 1968 (66-88-6, .431).
Hall of Fame? No
Honors: Pro Bowls (6), 1958-62, '65.
Records: Most consecutive games with a reception, 93, 1957-64.*
Lifetime Rankings: 495 receptions (T24th); 8,410 yards (18th); 84 TDs (6th).
Avg. Yards Per Season: 701
Avg. Yards Per Game: 55
Comment: Why isn't Tommy McDonald in the Hall of Fame? He caught 495 passes and scored 84 touchdowns, sixth-most in history. That's one TD every 5.9 receptions. Jerry Rice, Mr. Touchdown, averages one every 5.2. Here's what controversial cornerback Johnny Sample had to say about McDonald: "He could catch the ball better than any receiver I have ever known . . . was the only man I ever really feared going into a ballgame. He would make my shoes rattle because he would never quit, never give up. . . . And he didn't mind running across the middle, the toughest area to play because you always get hit hard there. Most receivers, even the really great ones, don't like to run across the middle. Tommy's best pattern was a cross-pattern." This, at 5'9", 176 pounds. McDonald was *at least* as good as Fred Biletnikoff.

49 BOBBY MITCHELL (1958-68)

Teams (W-L Record): Cleveland, 1958-61; Washington, 1962-68 (69-72-7, .490).
Hall of Fame? Yes (10th year eligible)
Honors: All-NFL (3), 1962-64; Pro Bowl (4), 1960, '62-64.
Records: Longest pass reception, 99 yards, 1963.
Lifetime Rankings: 521 receptions (19th); 7,954 yards (25th); 65 TDs (21st).
Avg. Yards Per Season: 723
Avg. Yards Per Game: 54
Comment: First off, Mitchell *galloped* when he ran. Nobody gallops anymore. Because of that, you'd remember him even if he wasn't much good. And he was much good, among the most exciting all-around players the game has known. 1962 was a crucial year for him. It would have been enough that he was playing a new position, flanker, for a new team, the Redskins. But he also was one of three players chosen to integrate the team, the last in the league to sign blacks. He responded with 872 receiving yards and 10 touchdowns in the first seven games en route to a 1,384-yard season. In '63 he gained 1,436 yards. They were the second- and third-highest totals of all time. And he was still learning the position.

MITCHELL'S BEST YEAR, 1962

Opponent	No.	Yds.	Avg.	TD
At Dallas	6	135	22.5	2
At Cleveland	3	94	31.3	1
St. Louis	7	147	21.0	2
Los Angeles	3	33	11.0	0
At St. Louis	7	158	22.6	1
At Philadelphia	8	147	18.4	2
At N.Y. Giants	5	158	31.6	2
Dallas	5	86	17.2	0
Cleveland	2	14	7.0	0
At Pittsburgh	2	25	12.5	0
N.Y. Giants	5	76	15.2	1
Philadelphia	8	114	14.3	0
At Baltimore	7	107	15.3	0
Pittsburgh	4	90	22.5	0
Totals	**72**	**1384**	**19.2**	**11**

25 FRED BILETNIKOFF (1965-78)

BILETNIKOFF'S BEST YEAR, 1971

Opponent	No.	Yds.	Avg.	TD
At New England	3	34	11.3	0
At San Diego	5	93	18.6	2
At Cleveland	2	60	30.0	0
At Denver	3	28	9.3	0
Philadelphia	8	148	18.5	1
Cincinnati	1	16	16.0	0
Kansas City	7	128	18.3	1
At New Orleans	3	74	24.7	2
Houston	1	11	11.0	0
San Diego	7	80	11.4	0
Baltimore	7	87	12.4	2
At Atlanta	6	86	14.3	1
At Kansas City	6	52	8.7	0
Denver	2	32	16.0	0
Totals	**61**	**929**	**15.2**	**9**

Team (W-L Record): Oakland, 1965-78 (144-45-9 .750).

Hall of Fame? Yes (5th year eligible)

Honors: Super Bowl MVP, 1977; All-NFL (2), 1972-73; Pro Bowls (4), 1970-71, '73-74; all-AFL (1), 1969; AFL All-Star Game (2), 1967, '69.

Records: None

Lifetime Rankings: 589 receptions (10th); 8,974 yards (12th); 76 TDs (T10th).

Avg. Yards Per Season: 641

Avg. Yards Per Game: 47

Comment: With Biletnikoff it's difficult to determine where the stickum ended and the hands began. He kept huge gobs of the stuff on his socks and used to load up between plays. Some passes he didn't even catch; they just adhered to him. Maybe we're being too hard on Freddie, but Gaylord Perry isn't in the Baseball Hall of Fame. Biletnikoff was a real character. He used to throw up before every game (hopefully *before* he put on the stickum) and supposedly slept with his eyes open during team meetings. Forgotten is the 190-yard receiving day he had against the Jets in the 1968 AFL title game, one of the greatest clutch performances ever. He had cornerback Johnny Sample turned around so bad that Sample was benched.

29 HAROLD JACKSON (1968-83)

Teams (W-L Record): L.A. Rams, 1968, '73-77; Philadelphia, 1969-72; New England, 1978-81; Minnesota, 1982; Seattle, 1983 (120-94-6, .559).

Hall of Fame? No

Honors: All-NFL (1), 1973; Pro Bowl (5), 1969, '72-73, '75, '77.

Records: None

Lifetime Rankings: 579 receptions (11th); 10,372 yards (5th); 76 TDs (T10th).

Avg. Yards Per Season: 691

Avg. Yards Per Game: 50

Comment: Jackson proved it was possible to have a *quiet* 579 receptions. He did it by: (1) never catching more than 48 passes in his last 11 seasons; (2) changing teams five times during his career; (3) not playing in the Super Bowl; and (4) being only 5'10" (if that), 175 pounds. But he made five Pro Bowls and hung onto his speed long enough to gain over 1,000 yards and average 22.5 a catch at the age of 33. His 238-yard game against Dallas in 1973 was the second-best by a receiver in the '70s. He scored four touchdowns that day and turned Cowboys cornerback Charlie Waters into a safety.

JACKSON'S BEST YEAR, 1973

Opponent	No.	Yds.	Avg.	TD
At Kansas City	2	22	11.0	0
Atlanta	3	34	11.3	1
At San Francisco	2	45	22.5	1
At Houston	2	84	42.0	2
Dallas	7	238	34.0	4
At Green Bay	2	55	27.5	1
At Minnesota	2	31	15.5	0
At Atlanta	3	66	22.0	0
New Orleans	3	75	25.0	0
San Francisco	4	117	29.3	3
At New Orleans	1	10	10.0	0
Chicago	2	10	5.0	0
N.Y. Giants	4	39	9.8	0
Cleveland	3	48	16.0	1
At Dallas (P)	1	40	40.0	0
Totals	**40**	**874**	**21.9**	**13**
Postseason	**1**	**40**	**40.0**	**0**

18 CHARLIE JOINER (1969-86)

JOINER'S BEST YEAR, 1981

Opponent	No.	Yds.	Avg.	TD
At Cleveland	6	191	31.8	0
Detroit	7	166	23.7	0
At Kansas City	2	23	11.5	0
At Denver	3	32	10.7	0
Seattle	3	34	11.3	2
Minnesota	6	97	16.2	1
At Baltimore	6	82	13.7	1
At Chicago	5	124	24.8	1
Kansas City	3	48	16.0	0
Cincinnati	2	14	7.0	0
At Seattle	2	13	6.5	0
At Oakland	3	38	12.7	1
Denver	2	27	13.5	0
Buffalo	7	106	15.1	0
At Tampa Bay	7	99	14.1	0
Oakland	6	94	15.7	1
At Miami (P)	7	108	15.4	0
At Cincinnati (P)	3	41	13.7	0
Totals	**70**	**1188**	**17.0**	**7**
Postseason	**10**	**149**	**14.9**	**0**

Teams (W-L Record): Houston, 1969-72; Cincinnati, 1972-75; San Diego, 1976-86 (138-121-4, .532).
Hall of Fame? Not eligible
Honors: All-NFL (1), 1980; Pro Bowl (3), 1976, '79, '80.
Records: Most receptions, career, 750*; most receiving yards, career, 12,146.*
Lifetime Rankings: 750 receptions (2nd); 12,146 yards (2nd); 65 TDs (T21st).
Avg. Yards Per Season: 675
Avg. Yards Per Game: 51
Comment: Joiner is one of only four NFL receivers who had better statistics in their 30s than in their 20s. He had 1,000-yard seasons at 32, 33 and 34 and just missed at 36 and 38. But despite his huge numbers, he never led the league in any category. Most of his time with the Chargers he was the team's third-best receiver. He'll be an interesting test case. Hall of Fame selectors are big on longevity which, when you stop and think about it, has a lot to do with luck. Joiner played 18 seasons and was virtually injury-free the last 13. He had 750 catches but made only three Pro Bowls. Does being good a long time make you great?

86 STANLEY MORGAN (1977-)

Team (W-L Record): New England, 1977- (105-90, .538).
Hall of Fame? Not eligible
Honors: Pro Bowl (4), 1979-80, '86-87.
Records: None
Lifetime Rankings: 534 receptions (17th); 10,352 yards (6th); 67 TDs (T17th).
Avg. Yards Per Season: 796
Avg. Yards Per Game: 56
Comment: Morgan had a career year in 1986 at the age of 31. He caught 26 more passes for 462 more yards than ever before. And defenses knew the Patriots were going to throw; they finished last in the league in rushing. Morgan's lifetime receiving average of 19.4 is the best among players with 500 catches. His totals would be even higher if he hadn't had to share the ball earlier in his career with Harold Jackson and Russ Francis. Some have questioned his willingness to go over the middle.

MORGAN'S BEST YEAR, 1986

Opponent	No.	Yds.	Avg.	TD
Indianapolis	7	116	16.6	1
At N.Y. Jets	8	104	13.0	0
Seattle	7	161	23.0	3
At Denver	2	14	7.0	1
Miami	6	125	20.8	1
N.Y. Jets	7	162	23.1	1
At Pittsburgh	2	45	22.5	0
At Buffalo	3	49	16.3	0
Atlanta	3	36	12.0	0
At Indianapolis	5	89	17.8	0
At L.A. Rams	7	118	16.9	0
Buffalo	3	45	15.0	0
At New Orleans	3	51	17.0	0
Cincinnati	5	107	21.4	0
San Francisco	8	121	15.1	1
At Miami	8	148	18.5	2
At Denver (P)	3	100	33.3	2
Totals	**84**	**1491**	**17.8**	**10**
Postseason	**3**	**100**	**33.3**	**2**

80 JAMES LOFTON (1978-)

LOFTON'S BEST YEAR, 1984

Opponent	No.	Yds.	Avg.	TD
St. Louis	7	134	19.1	0
At L.A. Raiders	0	0	0.0	0
Chicago	4	89	22.3	0
At Dallas	1	8	8.0	0
At Tampa Bay	3	70	23.3	0
San Diego	5	158	31.6	1
At Denver	11	206	18.7	1
Seattle	5	162	32.4	2
Detroit	5	80	16.0	1
At New Orleans	3	63	21.0	0
Minnesota	4	119	29.8	1
L.A. Rams	6	129	21.5	0
At Detroit	1	24	24.0	0
Tampa Bay	0	0	0.0	0
At Chicago	2	28	14.0	0
At Minnesota	5	91	18.2	1
Totals	**62**	**1361**	**22.0**	**7**

Teams (W-L Record): Green Bay, 1978-86; L.A. Raiders, 1987-88; Buffalo, 1989 (79-99-3, .445).
Hall of Fame? Not eligible
Honors: All-NFL (4), 1980-81, '83-84; Pro Bowl (7), 1978, '80-85.
Records: None
Lifetime Rankings: 607 catches (8th); 11,251 yards (4th); 57 TDs (T33rd).
Avg. Yards Per Season: 938
Avg. Yards Per Game: 66
Comment: The greatest deep threat in the '80s. Only the '82 strike kept Lofton from having six straight 1,000-yard seasons, a remarkable feat considering the talent around him. He had some problems with the law, though, that could hurt his Hall of Fame chances.

89 WES CHANDLER (1978-88)

Teams (W-L Record): New Orleans, 1978-81; San Diego, 1981-87; San Francisco, 1988 (64-90, .416).
Hall of Fame? Not eligible
Honors: All-NFL (1), 1982; Pro Bowl (4), 1979, '82-83, '85.
Records: None
Lifetime Rankings: 559 receptions (13th); 8,966 yards (13th); 56 TDs (T35th).
Avg. Yards Per Season: 815
Avg. Yards Per Game: 60
Comment: Chandler had the most amazing *half-season* in pro football history. It's one of the few things worth remembering about 1982. In the nine games that were squeezed in around the player strike he had 1,032 receiving yards. He didn't even play one week. He also had nine touchdown catches, tops in the NFL and the second-best total of his career. Too bad nobody gave a damn.

1,032 YARDS IN EIGHT GAMES, 1982

Opponent	No.	Yds.	Avg.	TD
At Denver	4	120	30.0	0
At Kansas City	6	69	11.5	1
At L.A. Raiders	7	118	16.9	0
Denver		(did not play)		
At Cleveland	5	84	16.8	0
At San Francisco	7	125	17.9	3
Cincinnati	10	260	26.0	2
Baltimore	4	118	29.5	2
L.A. Raiders	6	138	23.0	1
At Pittsburgh (P)	9	124	13.8	0
At Miami (P)	2	38	19.0	0
Totals	**49**	**1032**	**21.1**	**9**
Postseason	**11**	**162**	**14.7**	**0**

87 CHARLEY HENNIGAN (1961)

1,762 YARDS RECEIVING

Opponent	No.	Yds.	Avg.	TD
Oakland	4	113	28.3	1
At San Diego	6	109	18.2	0
At Dallas	3	101	33.7	1
Buffalo	4	109	27.3	0
At Boston	13	272	20.9	1
Dallas	4	108	27.0	1
At Buffalo	9	232	25.8	2
At Denver	6	78	13.0	0
Boston	0	0	0.0	0
New York	8	123	15.4	1
Denver	4	82	20.5	1
San Diego	10	214	21.4	3
At N.Y. Titans	6	82	13.7	1
At Oakland	5	123	24.6	0
At San Diego (C)	5	43	8.6	0
Totals	**82**	**1,746**	**21.3**	**12**
Postseason	**5**	**43**	**8.6**	**0**

Comment: Hennigan was a deity in the early days of the AFL. He caught 101 passes in 1964, and it wasn't even his best season. That would have been 1961, when he had 1,746 receiving yards to set a record that remains intact. Now, the AFL in '61 wasn't much more than USFL quality, but 1,746 yards is 1,746 yards, especially in a 14-game schedule. The closest anyone's come in the NFL is 1,570 yards by Jerry Rice in '86, and that was in 16 games. Hennigan was actually shut out one week. He made up for it, though, with three 200-yard games, one against the second-best team in the league, the Chargers. Halfway through the season he had 1,044 yards.

10 BOBBY DOUGLASS (1972)

Comment: There's never been a running quarterback like Douglass. He was a *runner*, not a scrambler. A big (6'4", 225) runner. A big, fast runner. Trying to tackle him in the open field was like taking on a tight end or fullback. In 1972 he led the Bears with 968 rushing yards, easily the most ever by a quarterback. He had 30 runs of 10 yards or more. Against the Eagles he hit only 1 of 9 passes but ran for touchdowns of 32 and 19 yards in a 21-12 win. His inaccuracy ultimately put him on the bench, however. Though he had a strong arm, he completed just 37.9 percent in '72 and 43 percent for his 10-year career. There was talk about moving him to running back, but coach Abe Gibron decided against it because of Douglass' upright running style.

968 YARDS RUSHING BY A QB

Opponent	Att.	Yds.	Avg.	TD
Atlanta	9	68	7.6	0
Los Angeles	7	82	11.7	0
Detroit	12	97	8.1	1
At Green Bay	12	45	3.8	1
At Cleveland	11	117	10.6	1
Minnesota	11	66	6.0	0
At St. Louis	9	29	3.2	1
At Detroit	7	52	7.4	0
Green Bay	12	68	5.7	1
San Francisco	12	79	6.6	1
Cincinnati	5	40	8.0	0
At Minnesota	5	23	4.6	0
At Philadelphia	15	75	5.0	2
At Oakland	14	127	9.1	0
Totals	**141**	**968**	**6.9**	**8**

88 JOHN MACKEY (1963-72)

MACKEY'S BEST YEAR, 1966

Opponent	No.	Yds.	Avg.	TD
At Green Bay	4	34	8.5	0
At Minnesota	6	143	23.8	2
San Francisco	3	76	25.3	1
At Chicago	2	89	44.5	1
Detroit	4	53	13.3	1
Minnesota	5	52	10.4	0
At L.A. Rams	5	132	26.4	2
Washington	2	13	6.5	0
At Atlanta	2	23	11.5	0
At Detroit	4	91	22.8	1
L.A. Rams	0	0	0.0	0
Chicago	4	38	9.5	0
Green Bay	2	15	7.5	0
At San Francisco	7	70	10.0	1
Philadelphia (PB)	4	42	10.5	0
Totals	**50**	**829**	**16.6**	**9**
Postseason	**4**	**42**	**10.5**	**0**

Teams (W-L Record): Baltimore, 1963-71; San Diego, 1972 (96-38-6, .707).
Hall of Fame? No
Honors: All-NFL (3), 1966-68; Pro Bowl (5), 1963, '65-68.
Records: None
Lifetime Rankings: 331 receptions (18th among tight ends); 5,236 yards (9th among tight ends); 38 TDs (14th among tight ends).
Avg. Yards Per Season: 524
Avg. Yards Per Game: 37
Comment: Mike Ditka, the first tight end to make the Hall of Fame, wondered why Mackey wasn't already there. The answer, of course, was Mackey's union militancy. He was certainly a good enough *player*. He was a killer blocker and almost impossible to bring down one-on-one in the open field. The latter is reflected in his 16-yard career average, unusually high for a tight end. In '63 and '65 he averaged 20-plus yards per catch.

81 JACKIE SMITH (1963-78)

Teams (W-L Record): St. Louis, 1963-77; Dallas, 1978 (120-96-10, .553).
Hall of Fame? No
Honors: All-NFL (1), 1967; Pro Bowl (5), 1966-70.
Records: Most receptions by a tight end, career, 480*; most receiving yards by a tight end, career, 7,918.
Lifetime Rankings: 480 receptions (31st overall/3rd among tight ends); 7,918 yards (26th/1st); 40 TDs (--/T12th)
Avg. Yards Per Season: 495
Avg. Yards Per Game: 38
Comment: It's Smith's cursed fate to be remembered for the pass he dropped -- in Super Bowl 13 with the Cowboys -- and not the 480 he caught. More than a decade after his retirement he still has more yards than any tight end in history. His 1967 stats look like a deep receiver's. Tight ends just don't average 21.5 yards a catch; some of today's stars average barely half that much. Just as impressive is his yardage total of 1,205, which is really the record for tight ends if you go by yards per game. Smith was big (6'4", 232), fast and ran with abandon. If he'd played for a better team or in a bigger market, he might be in the Hall of Fame.

SMITH'S BEST YEAR, 1967

Opponent	No.	Yds.	Avg.	TD
N.Y. Giants	3	86	28.7	0
At Pittsburgh	0	0	0.0	0
Detroit	3	83	27.7	1
At Minnesota	4	83	20.8	0
At Cleveland	3	90	30.0	0
Philadelphia	4	116	29.0	2
Green Bay	5	97	19.4	0
At Washington	4	103	25.8	0
Pittsburgh	3	31	10.3	1
At Chicago	7	61	8.7	0
At Dallas	4	116	29.0	1
New Orleans	2	96	48.0	2
Cleveland	6	91	15.2	1
At N.Y. Giants	8	152	19.0	1
Totals	**56**	**1205**	**21.5**	**9**

87 JERRY SMITH (1965-77)

SMITH'S BEST YEAR, 1967

Opponent	No.	Yds.	Avg.	TD
At Philadelphia	8	81	10.1	1
At New Orleans	2	38	19.0	0
N.Y. Giants	4	73	18.3	1
Dallas	3	39	13.0	0
At Atlanta	6	45	7.5	1
At L.A. Rams	7	102	14.6	3
Baltimore	1	16	16.0	0
St. Louis		(did not play)		
San Francisco	9	101	11.2	2
At Dallas	5	66	13.2	2
At Cleveland	4	63	15.8	0
Philadelphia	9	145	16.1	2
At Pittsburgh	4	44	11.0	0
New Orleans	5	36	7.2	0
Totals	**67**	**849**	**12.7**	**12**

Team (W-L Record): Washington, 1965-77 (103-73-6, .582).
Hall of Fame? No
Honors: All-NFL (1), 1969; Pro Bowl (2), 1967, '69.
Records: Most touchdown passes, tight end, career, 60.
Lifetime Rankings: 421 receptions (T50th overall/8th among tight ends); 5,496 yards (7th among tight ends); 60 TDs (T27th overall/1st among tight ends).
Avg. Yards Per Season: 423
Avg. Yards Per Game: 33
Comment: Smith was built more like a wide receiver at 6'3", 208 pounds. But he was a better blocker than given credit for -- and what hands! Unfortunately he played in the shadow of Charley Taylor and Bobby Mitchell (later Roy Jefferson). He scored more touchdowns than any tight end -- 60 -- and most fans don't even know it.

87 DAVE CASPER (1974-84)

Teams (W-L Record): Oakland/L.A. Raiders, 1974-80, '84; Houston, 1980-83; Minnesota, 1983.
Hall of Fame? Not eligible
Honors: All-NFL (4), 1976-79; Pro Bowl (5), 1976-80.
Records: Most touchdown receptions in a playoff game, 3, 1977.
Lifetime Rankings: 378 receptions (12th among tight ends); 5,216 yards (10th); 52 TDs (T40th overall/2nd among tight ends).
Avg. Yards Per Season: 474
Avg. Yards Per Game: 35
Comment: Casper was the best tight end in football from 1976 to '80. He averaged 55 receptions, 739 yards and six touchdowns a year over that stretch and was a playoff terror. But he was a hard guy to figure out. He'd show up on the practice field without socks and punt the ball over the fence for no apparent reason. Even the counter-culture Raiders ran out of patience with him. He was traded to the Oilers in the middle of a 56-catch season in '80 and bounced around his last few years. Teammate Bob Chandler thought he had a self-destructive personality.

CASPER'S BEST YEAR, 1978

Opponent	No.	Yds.	Avg.	TD
At Denver	2	35	17.5	0
At San Diego	5	100	20.0	1
At Green Bay	3	41	13.7	1
New England	4	55	13.8	1
At Chicago	2	40	20.0	0
Houston	4	33	8.3	1
Kansas City	5	51	10.2	1
At Seattle	1	8	8.0	0
San Diego	4	43	10.8	1
At Kansas City	7	112	16.0	0
At Cincinnati	3	75	25.0	1
Detroit	5	65	13.0	1
Seattle	5	90	18.0	1
Denver	7	56	8.0	0
At Miami	3	19	6.3	0
Minnesota	2	29	14.5	0
Totals	**62**	**852**	**13.7**	**9**

80 KELLEN WINSLOW (1979-87)

WINSLOW'S BEST YEAR, 1980

Opponent	No.	Yds.	Avg.	TD
At Seattle	2	41	20.5	0
Oakland	9	132	14.7	1
At Denver	3	60	20.0	0
At Kansas City	6	74	12.3	2
Buffalo	3	26	8.7	1
At Oakland	7	91	13.0	0
N.Y. Giants	6	102	17.0	0
At Dallas	5	110	22.0	2
At Cincinnati	9	153	17.0	1
Denver	4	32	8.0	0
Kansas City	5	57	11.4	0
At Miami	7	53	7.6	0
Philadelphia	6	89	14.8	2
At Washington	1	42	42.0	0
Seattle	6	57	9.5	0
Pittsburgh	10	171	17.1	0
Buffalo (P)	1	5	5.0	0
Oakland (P)	3	42	14.0	0
Totals	**89**	**1290**	**14.5**	**9**
Postseason	**4**	**47**	**11.8**	**0**

Teams (W-L Record): San Diego, 1979-87 (69-64, .519).

Hall of Fame? Not eligible

Honors: All-NFL (3), 1980-82; Pro Bowl (5), 1980-83, '87.

Records: Most touchdown receptions, game, 5, 1981; most receptions by a tight end, season, 89, 1980*; most receiving yards by a tight end, season, 1,290, 1980.

Lifetime Rankings: 541 receptions (15th overall/2nd among tight ends); 6,741 yards (3rd among tight ends); 45 TDs (T4th among tight ends).

Avg. Yards Per Season: 749

Avg. Yards Per Game: 62

Comment: Winslow was a phenomenon until he blew out his knee. He caught 374 passes in the equivalent of four seasons from 1980 to '84. Pro football had never seen anything like him. He was 6'5", 250 pounds, had speed, soft hands and even blocked kicks. The injury could have ended his career, but he returned a year later and made the Pro Bowl in 1987. Scouts are still looking for another one like him.

46 TODD CHRISTENSEN (1979-88)

Teams (W-L Record): N.Y. Giants, 1978; Oakland, 1978-88 (89-60, .597).

Hall of Fame? Not eligible

Honors: All-NFL (3), 1983, '85-86; Pro Bowls (5), 1983-87.

Records: Most receptions by a tight end, season, 95, 1986; most touchdown receptions by a tight end, season, 12, 1983.

Lifetime Rankings: 461 receptions (37th overall/4th among tight ends); 5,872 yards (4th among tight ends); 41 TDs (T8th among tight ends).

Avg. Yards Per Season: 587

Avg. Yards Per Game: 42

Comment: Christensen, an aspiring poet, showed the media some of his stuff during Super Bowl week 1984. Walt Whitman he wasn't. Fortunately he had football to fall back on. From 1983 to '86, he averaged 87 receptions, 1,099 yards and 8 TDs a year, despite a revolving quarterbacks situation. His 95 catches in '86 set a record for tight ends, and his 12 TDs in '83 tied one. Not bad for a failed running back who didn't catch his first pass until his third season.

CHRISTENSEN'S BEST YEAR, 1983

Opponent	No.	Yds.	Avg.	TD
At Cincinnati	3	35	11.7	0
Houston	6	58	9.7	1
Miami	6	95	15.8	1
At Denver	1	9	9.0	0
At Washington	5	70	14.0	1
Kansas City	5	32	6.4	1
At Seattle	11	152	13.8	3
At Dallas	7	90	12.9	1
Seattle	4	60	15.0	0
At Kansas City	3	46	15.3	0
Denver	8	114	14.3	0
At Buffalo	7	86	12.3	1
N.Y. Giants	4	46	11.5	0
At San Diego	8	140	17.5	3
St. Louis	6	78	13.0	0
San Diego	8	136	17.0	0
Pittsburgh (P)	7	88	12.6	0
Seattle (P)	3	14	4.7	0
Washington (SB)	4	32	8.0	0
Totals	**92**	**1247**	**13.6**	**12**
Postseason	**14**	**134**	**9.6**	**0**

STUFF YOU CAN NEVER LAY YOUR HANDS ON

NUMBERS

Nobody's into football numbers like CBS analyst John Madden. "I've always felt that you can put a number on a person that tells about that person," he says in his book *One Size Doesn't Fit All*. "Certain numbers have certain characteristics. It's not always something you can explain."

Number 12 is "a leader with charisma"; 16 has "a certain softness about it"; 22 is "a speed number"; 32 is "a skills number, but it also fits people with some hardness."

Madden always fancied himself a 74. But in his only NFL training camp, with the Eagles in 1959, he was issued 77 (we looked it up). In the book he assigns numbers to famous people. The 74s were Franklin Delano Roosevelt, George Foreman and Byron Nelson. The 77s were Johnny Cash and Lee Iacocca.

Only nine numbers from 0 and 00 to 99 have never been worn by a Pro Football Hall-of-Famer—23, 43, 48, 58, 65, 67, 68, 69 and 85. Aside from the numbers in the 90s, 69 is probably least popular among well-known players.

Some of the following players wore other numbers than the ones they're listed for. A few of them wore other numbers longer than the ones they're listed for. *You* try putting together a list like this sometime.

0 George Plimpton ('63 Lions training camp), Johnny Olszewski, Obert Logan

00 Jim Otto, Ken Burrough

1 Jim Thorpe, Paddy Driscoll, Fritz Pollard, Curly Lambeau, Jimmy Conzelman, Noland Smith, Garo Yepremian

2 Walt Kiesling, Father Lumpkin, Cookie Gilchrist, Doug Flutie

3 Bronko Nagurski, Glenn Presnell, Tony Canadeo, Pete Gogolak, Jan Stenerud, Rohn Stark

4 Ernie Nevers, Tuffy Leemans, Joey Sternaman, Reggie Roby

5 George McAfee, Paul Hornung, Ace Gutowsky, Sean Landeta

6 Benny Friedman, Rolf Benirschke, Kevin Butler

7 George Halas, Dutch Clark, Mel Hein, Ace Parker, Bob Waterfield, Jim Finks, Ed Sprinkle, John Elway, Boomer Esiason, Morten Andersen

8 Larry Wilson, Two Bits Homan, Archie Manning, Ben Agajanian, Ray Guy, Nick Lowery

9 Sonny Jurgensen, Jim McMahon, Pug Manders, Duke Osborn

10 Fran Tarkenton, Bobby Douglass

11 Norm Van Brocklin, Joe Guyon, Link Lyman, Joe Kapp, Phil Simms, Jim Turner

12 Joe Namath, Roger Staubach, Terry Bradshaw, Bob Griese, Ken Stabler, Don Cockroft

13 Dan Marino, George Trafton, Guy Chamberlin, Fats Henry, Joe Stydahar, Kenny Washington, Don Maynard, Jake Scott, Ken Riley

14 Don Hutson, Otto Graham, Y. A. Tittle, Ken Anderson, Dan Fouts, Duke Slater, George Christensen, Dick Plasman, Willie Thrower, Eddie LeBaron, Fred Cox

15 Steve Van Buren, Bart Starr, Jack Kemp, Earl Morrall, Jim Barber

16 George Blanda, Joe Montana, Frank Gifford, Ed Healey, George Musso, Len Dawson, Warren Beatty (in the movie *Heaven Can Wait*)

17 Don Meredith, Charlton Heston (*Number One*), Turk Edwards, Cecil Isbell, Harold Carmichael, Joe Gilliam, Doug Williams, Richie Petitbon

18 Charlie Joiner, Roman Gabriel, Gene Washington (49ers), Emmitt Thomas, Tobin Rote, Swede Youngstrom

19 Johnny Unitas, Lance Alworth, Tom Dempsey, Lance Rentzel, Bull Behman

20 Cliff Battles, Billy Cannon, Billy Sims, Don

Rogers, Ox Emerson, Buster Ramsey, Mel Renfro, Lem Barney, Louis Wright, Jimmy Patton, Gino Cappelletti

21 Danny Fortmann, John Hadl, Cliff Branch, Terry Metcalf, James Brooks, Mike Nelms, Jim Kiick

22 Bobby Layne, Buddy Young, Bob Hayes, Mercury Morris, Lavie Dilweg, Ed Danowski, Paul Krause, Roger Wehrli, Keith Lincoln, Timmy Brown

23 Travis Williams, Gus Sonnenberg, Jim Poole, Goose Gonsoulin

24 Lenny Moore, Whizzer White, Luke Johnsos, Jack Christiansen, Willie Wood, Willie Brown, Everson Walls, Fred "The Hammer" Williamson, Johnny Sample, Tommie "Jet" Smith ('69 Bengals camp)

25 Bruiser Kinard, Fred Biletnikoff, Tommy McDonald, Jim David, Jim Bakken

26 Herb Adderley, Lydell Mitchell, Shipwreck Kelly, George Saimes, Jack McBride

27 Ken Houston, R. C. Owens, Irv Cross

28 Yale Lary, Ahmad Rashad, Darrell Green, Curt Warner

29 Eric Dickerson, Harold Jackson, Stan Kopcha, Charlie Brock

30 Clarke Hinkle, Bill Willis, Dan Reeves, Ron Johnson, Lawrence McCutcheon

31 Jim Taylor, Mike Michalske, Gaynell Tinsley, Nate Barrager, Joe Fortunato, William Andrews, Wilbert Montgomery

32 Jim Brown, O. J. Simpson, Franco Harris, Deacon Dan Towler, Jack Tatum, Joe Don Looney, Mike Curtis, Jack Pardee, Marcus Allen, Ottis Anderson, Hoyle Granger

33 Sammy Baugh, Ollie Matson, Tony Dorsett, Roger Craig, Hardy Brown, Duane Thomas, Charles White

34 Walter Payton, Earl Campbell, Joe Perry, Bo Jackson, Pat Harder, Cornell Green, Andy Russell, Don Chandler

35 Bill Dudley, Pete Pihos, John Henry Johnson, Tank Younger, Alan Ameche, Rick Casares, Pete Gent

36 Marion Motley, Clem Daniels, Willie Wilkin

37 Doak Walker, Lester Hayes, Jimmy Johnson, Pat Fischer

38 Arnie Herber, Bob Tucker, Sam Baker

39 Hugh McElhenny, Larry Csonka

40 Gale Sayers, Crazylegs Hirsch, Mike Haynes,

Wayne Millner, Bobby Joe Conrad, Tom Brookshier, Abe Woodson, Bobby Boyd, Dick Anderson

41 Cal Hubbard, Brian Piccolo, Jerry Norton, Jimmy Hill, Tom Matte

42 Paul Warfield, Charley Taylor, Sid Luckman, Charley Conerly, Ronnie Lott, Johnny Robinson, John Gilliam

43 Larry Brown, Don Perkins, Gerald Riggs, George Atkinson, Cliff Harris, Will Sherman

44 John Riggins, Leroy Kelly, Chuck Foreman, Floyd Little, John David Crow, Charlie Tolar, Pete Retzlaff, Baby Ray, Lou Rymkus, Bert Rechichar, Bobby Dillon, Don Doll, Dick LeBeau, Jerrel Wilson

45 Em Tunnell, Homer Jones, Speedy Duncan, Ernie Davis

46 Chuck Muncie, Todd Christensen, Verne Lewellen, Russ Letlow, Doug Plank

47 Mel Blount, Johnny Morris, Dennis Quaid (*Everybody's All-American*)

48 Beattie Feathers, Les Richter

49 Bobby Mitchell, Tom Landry, Jim Benton, Erich Barnes

50 Alex Wojciechowicz, Ken Strong

51 Dick Butkus, Jim Ringo, Ken Kavanaugh, Carl Weathers

52 Frank Gatski, Robert Brazile, Randy Gradishar

53 Mick Tinglehoff, Alyn Beals, Bob Matheson

54 Randy White, Wahoo McDaniel, Chuck Howley, Tom Banks

55 Steve Owen, Ray Wietecha, Paul Maguire, Maxie Baughan, Wayne Walker

56 Lawrence Taylor, Joe Schmidt, Bill Hewitt, Andre Tippett, Rickey Jackson, Bill Walsh

57 Johnny Blood, Dwight Stephenson, Steve Nelson, Reggie Williams

58 Jack Lambert, Mike Stratton, Dan Currie

59 Jack Ham, Horace Gillom

60 Chuck Bednarik, Dave Meggysey, Dale Dodrill, Tommy Nobis, Larry Grantham, Len Younce

61 Bill George, Dick Barwegan, Duane Putnam, Bob DeMarco, Bob Talamini

62 Charley Trippi, Jim Langer, Ed White

63 Gene Upshaw, Willie Lanier, Lee Roy Selmon, Frankie Albert, Dick Stanfel, Bruno Banducci

64 Jerry Kramer, Abe Gibron, Ted Fritsch, Ken

Gray, Jim Ray Smith, Bud McFadin, Dave Wilcox

65 Les Bingaman, Dave Butz, Chuck Noll, Tom Mack, Elvin Bethea, Houston Antwine

66 Bulldog Turner, Ray Nitschke, Larry Little, Billy Shaw, Gene Hickerson, Harley Sewell

67 Bob Kuechenberg, Art Still

68 L. C. Greenwood, Joe DeLamielleure

69 Tim Krumrie, Woody Peoples, R. C. Thielemann, Conrad Dobler

70 Sam Huff, Art Donovan, Ernie Stautner, Jim Marshall, Charlie Krueger, Rayfield Wright, Russ Washington, Leon Gray, Tom Sestak, Al Wistert, Don Colo

71 Alex Karras, George Connor, Ed Budde, Bill Forester

72 Refrigerator Perry, John Matuszak, Too Tall Jones, Dexter Manley, Dan Dierdorf, Bob Vogel, Jess Richardson

73 Leo Nomellini, John Hannah, Arnie Weinmeister, Ron Yary, Ernie McMillan, Thurman McGraw

74 Merlin Olsen, Bob Lilly, Ron Mix, Mike McCormack, Henry Jordan, Bob Toneff

75 Mean Joe Greene, Deacon Jones, Forrest Gregg, Howie Long, George Kunz, Winston Hill, Jerry Mays, Jim Katcavage

76 Lou Groza, Big Daddy Lipscomb, Rosey Grier, Bucko Kilroy, Lou Creekmur, Bob Brown, John Niland, Don Reese

77 Red Grange, Jim Parker, Lyle Alzado, Ernie Ladd, Jim Tyrer, Dick Schafrath, John Madden ('59 Eagles camp)

78 Bubba Smith, Bobby Bell, Art Shell, Stan Jones, Walt Sweeney

79 Rosey Brown, Bob St. Clair, Bob Gain, Harvey Martin, Sherman Plunkett, Vic Sears

80 Tom Fears, Len Ford, Jerry Rice, Steve Largent, Kellen Winslow, Jack Butler, Andy Nelson, Gene Brito, Cloyce Box, Rick Upchurch

81 Night Train Lane, Andy Robustelli, Doug Atkins, Carl Eller, Jackie Smith, Art Monk, Roy Green, Jerry Philbin, Spec Sanders

82 Raymond Berry, Ozzie Newsome, Ray Bray, Gordie Soltau, Ted Kwalick, Mike Quick, Jim Houston

83 Ted Hendricks, Mark Clayton, Renaldo Nehemiah, George Sauer, Bobby Walston, Flipper Anderson

84 Billy "White Shoes" Johnson, Darryl Sting-

ley, Bob Trumpy, Billy Wilson, Art Powell, Carroll Dale, Bill Stanfill

85 Jack Youngblood, Nick Buoniconti, Del Shofner, Mel Gray

86 Dante Lavelli, Bud Grant, Billy Howton, Gary Collins, Boyd Dowler, Stanley Morgan, Buck Buchanan

87 Willie Davis, Claude Humphrey, Dave Casper, Jerry Smith, Nick Nolte (*North Dallas Forty*), Dwight Clark, Harlon Hill, Charley Hennigan, Lionel Taylor

88 Alan Page, Pat Summerall, John Mackey, Ron Kramer, Lynn Swann, Drew Pearson, Sonny Randle, Mac Speedie

89 Gino Marchetti, Mike Ditka, Otis Taylor, John Havlicek ('62 Browns camp), Dave Robinson, Fred Dryer

90 George Webster, Bob Hoernschemeyer

91 Dub Jones, Johnny Strzykalski, Brad Van Pelt, Leslie O'Neal

92 Reggie White

93 George Taliaferro

94 Louie Kelcher, Charles Haley, Pepper Martin

95 Richard Dent, Michael Carter, Glenn Dobbs

96 Don Shula

97 Tim Harris, Gary "Big Hands" Johnson

98 Tom Harmon

99 Dan Hampton, Mark Gastineau, Marshall Goldberg, Perry Schwartz, Jim Hines

■ ■ ■

THE REAL RECORD BOOK

Part of the reason so much of pro football's past has disappeared is the NFL's record-keeping philosophy. It gives quantity precedence over quality. If a player in a 12-game season rushed for 1,999 yards, and a player in 16-game season rushed for 2,000, the player who played four more games and gained one more yard would be listed first in the record book. Ridiculous.

Equally ridiculous is including records from the pre–Super Bowl AFL (1960–65) and the World War II period (1942–45), when the caliber of play wasn't up to NFL standards. Any marks from the 1982 strike (half-)season should be thrown out, too, except for Mark Moseley's consecutive field-goal streak. What's more important, consistency or fairness?

In that spirit, we offer you the *real* record book. It recognizes the best single-season performances based on *per-game averages* and shows you what the player would have done if he'd played 16 games instead of 14 or 12. Records from the early AFL, the war years and '82 aren't counted. It also shows you which records achieved in 16-game seasons are legitimate and which are merely the product of an expanded schedule.

		TOP 3 IN NFL RECORD BOOK	THE REAL TOP 3 (TOTAL/GAMES)	16-GAME EQUIVALENT
MOST POINTS	176	Paul Hornung, Green Bay, 1960	Hornung, 1960 (176/14)	235
	161	Mark Moseley, Washington, 1983	Doak Walker, Detroit, 1950 (128/12)	171
	155	Gino Cappelletti, Boston, 1964	Hornung, 1961 (146/14)	167
MOST TOUCHDOWNS	24	John Riggins, Washington, 1983	Rice, 1987 (23/12)	31
	23	O. J. Simpson, Buffalo, 1975	Simpson, 1975 (23/14)	26
		Jerry Rice, San Francisco, 1987	Gale Sayers, Chicago, 1965 (22/14)	25
MOST FIELD GOALS	35	Ali Haji-Sheikh, N.Y. Giants, 1983	Turner, 1968 (34/14)	39
	34	Jim Turner, N.Y. Jets, 1968	Marcol, 1972 (33/14)	38
	33	Chester Marcol, Green Bay, 1972	Turner, 1969 (32/14)	37
		Mark Moseley, Washington, 1983		
		Gary Anderson, Pittsburgh, 1985		
MOST RUSHING YARDS	2,105	Eric Dickerson, L.A. Rams, 1984	Simpson, 1973 (2,003/14)	2,289
	2,003	O. J. Simpson, Buffalo, 1973	Jim Brown, Cleveland, 1963 (1,863/14)	2,129
	1,934	Earl Campbell, Houston, 1980	Walter Payton, Chicago, 1977 (1,852/14)	2,117

		TOP 3 IN NFL RECORD BOOK	THE REAL TOP 3 (TOTAL/GAMES)	16-GAME EQUIVALENT
MOST RUSHING TOUCHDOWNS	24	John Riggins, Washington, 1983	Riggins, 1983 (24/16)	24
	21	Joe Morris, N.Y. Giants, 1985	Jim Brown, Cleveland, 1958 (17/12)	23
	19	Jim Taylor, Green Bay, 1962	Taylor, 1962 (19/14)	22
		Earl Campbell, Houston, 1979		
		Chuck Muncie, San Diego, 1981		
MOST PASSING YARDS	5,084	Dan Marino, Miami, 1984	Marino, 1984 (5,084/16)	5,084
	4,802	Dan Fouts, San Diego, 1981	Fouts, 1981 (4,802/16)	4,802
	4,746	Dan Marino, Miami, 1986	Marino, 1986 (4,746/14)	4,746
MOST TOUCHDOWN PASSES	48	Dan Marino, Miami, 1984	Marino, 1984 (48/16)	48
	44	Dan Marino, Miami, 1986	Marino, 1986 (44/16)	44
	36	George Blanda, Houston, 1961	Johnny Unitas, Baltimore, 1959 (32/12)	43
		Y. A. Tittle, N.Y. Giants, 1963		
MOST INTERCEPTIONS THROWN	42	George Blanda, Houston, 1962	Sid Luckman, Chicago Bears, 1947 (31/12)	41
	35	Vinny Testaverde, Tampa Bay, 1988	Y. A. Tittle, San Francisco, 1955 (28/12)	37
	34	Frank Tripucka, Denver, 1960	John Hadl, San Diego, 1968 (32/14)	37
MOST RECEPTIONS	106	Art Monk, Washington, 1984	Tom Fears, L.A. Rams, 1950 (84/12)	112
	101	Charley Hennigan, Houston, 1964	Johnny Morris, Chicago, 1964 (93/14)	106
	100	Lionel Taylor, Denver, 1961	Monk, 1984 (106/16)	106

	TOP 3 IN NFL RECORD BOOK		THE REAL TOP 3 (TOTAL/GAMES)	16-GAME EQUIVALENT
MOST RECEIVING YARDS	1,746	Charley Hennigan, Houston, 1961	Crazylegs Hirsch, L.A. Rams, 1951 (1,495/12)	1,993
	1,602	Lance Alworth, San Diego, 1965	Raymond Berry, Baltimore, 1960 (1,298/12)	1,731
	1,570	Jerry Rice, San Francisco, 1986	Billy Howton, Green Bay, 1952 (1,231/12)	1,641
			Bobby Mitchell, Washington, 1963 (1,436/14)	1,641
MOST RECEIVING TOUCHDOWNS	22	Jerry Rice, San Francisco, 1987	Rice, 1987 (22/12)	29
	18	Mark Clayton, Miami, 1984	Hirsch, 1951 (17/12)	23
	17	Don Hutson, Green Bay, 1942	Cloyce Box, Detroit, 1952 (15/12)	20
		Crazylegs Hirsch, L.A. Rams, 1951		
		Bill Groman, Houston, 1961		
MOST INTERCEPTIONS	14	Night Train Lane, Detroit, 1952	Lane, 1952 (14/12)	19
	13	Don Sandifer, Washington, 1948	Sandifer, 1948 (13/12)	17
		Spec Sanders, N.Y. Yanks, 1950	Sanders, 1950 (13/12)	17
		Lester Hayes, Oakland, 1980		
MOST COMBINED YARDS (RUSHING, RECEIVING, RETURNING)	2,535	Lionel James, San Diego, 1985	Metcalf, 1975 (2,462/14)	2,814
	2,462	Terry Metcalf, St. Louis, 1975	Herron, 1974 (2,444/14)	2,793
	2,444	Mack Herron, New England, 1974	Timmy Brown, Philadelphia, 1963 (2,428/14)	2,775

U.S. PRO FOOTBALL CITIES,
1920 TO PRESENT

(Includes: American Professional Football Association, 1920–21; NFL, 1922–;
American Football League, 1926; AFL, 1936–37; AFL, 1940–41; All-America
Football Conference, 1946–49; AFL, 1960–69; World Football League, 1974–75;
U.S. Football League, 1983–85.)

AKRON, OHIO
Pros, 1920–25 (APFA/NFL)
Indians, 1926 (NFL)

ANAHEIM, CALIF.
Southern California Sun, 1974–75 (WFL)

ATLANTA
Falcons, 1966– (NFL)

BALTIMORE
Colts, 1947–50 (AAFC/NFL)
Colts, 1953–83 (NFL)
Stars, 1985 (USFL)

BIRMINGHAM, ALA.
Americans, 1974 (WFL)
Vulcans, 1975 (WFL)
Stallions, 1983–85 (USFL)

BOSTON
Bulldogs, 1926 (AFL)
Bulldogs, 1929 (NFL)
Braves, 1932 (NFL)
Redskins, 1933–36 (NFL)
Shamrocks, 1936–37 (AFL)
Bears, 1940 (AFL)
Yanks, 1944–48 (NFL)
Patriots, 1960–70 (AFL/NFL)
New England Patriots, 1971– (NFL)
Breakers, 1983 (USFL)

BROOKLYN
Horsemen, 1926 (AFL)
Lions, 1926 (NFL)
Dodgers, 1930–43 (NFL)
Tigers, 1936 (AFL)
Tigers, 1944 (NFL)
Dodgers, 1946–48 (AAFC)

BUFFALO
All-Americans, 1921–23 (APFA/NFL)
Bisons, 1924–25 (NFL)
Rangers, 1926 (NFL)
Bisons, 1927, '29 (NFL)
Indians, 1940–41 (AFL)
Bisons, 1946 (AAFC)
Bills, 1947–49 (AAFC)
Bills, 1960– (AFL/NFL)

CANTON, OHIO
Bulldogs, 1920–23, '25–26 (APFA/NFL)

CHARLOTTE, N.C.
Hornets, 1974–75 (WFL)

CHICAGO
Cardinals, 1920–59 (APFA/NFL)
Tigers, 1920 (APFA)
Staleys, 1921 (APFA)
Bears, 1922– (NFL)
Bulls, 1926 (AFL)
Rockets, 1946–48 (AAFC)
Hornets, 1949 (AAFC)
Fire, 1974 (WFL)
Winds, 1975 (WFL)
Blitz, 1983–84 (USFL)

CINCINNATI
Celts, 1921 (APFA)
Reds, 1933–34 (NFL)
Bengals, 1937 (AFL)
Bengals, 1940–41 (AFL)
Bengals, 1968– (AFL/NFL)

CLEVELAND
Tigers, 1920–21 (APFA)
Indians, 1923 (NFL)
Bulldogs, 1924–25, '27 (NFL)
Panthers, 1926 (AFL)
Indians, 1931 (NFL)
Rams, 1936–42, '44–45 (AFL/NFL)
Browns, 1946– (AAFC/NFL)

COLUMBUS, OHIO
Panhandles, 1920–22 (APFA/NFL)

COLUMBUS *(cont'd)*
Tigers, 1923–26 (NFL)
Bullies, 1940–41 (AFL)

DALLAS
Texans, 1952 (NFL)
Cowboys, 1960– (NFL)
Texans, 1960–62 (AFL)

DAYTON, OHIO
Triangles, 1920–29 (APFA/NFL)

DECATUR, ILL.
Staleys, 1920 (APFA)

DENVER
Broncos, 1960– (AFL/NFL)
Gold, 1983–85 (USFL)

DETROIT
Heralds, 1920–21 (APFA)
Panthers, 1925–26 (NFL)
Wolverines, 1928 (NFL)
Lions, 1934– (NFL)
Wheels, 1974 (WFL)
Michigan Panthers, 1983–84 (USFL)

DULUTH, MINN.
Kelleys, 1923–25 (NFL)
Eskimos, 1926–27 (NFL)

EAST RUTHERFORD, N.J.
New Jersey Generals, 1983–85 (USFL)

EVANSVILLE, IND.
Crimson Giants, 1921–22 (APFA/NFL)

FRANKFORD, PA.
Yellow Jackets, 1924–31 (NFL)

GREEN BAY
Packers, 1921– (APFA/NFL)

HAMMOND, IND.
Pros, 1920–26 (APFA/NFL)

HARTFORD, CONN.
Blues, 1926 (NFL)

HONOLULU
Hawaiians, 1974–75 (WFL)

HOUSTON
Oilers, 1960– (AFL/NFL)
Texans, 1974 (WFL)
Gamblers, 1984–85 (USFL)

JACKSONVILLE, FLA.
Sharks, 1974 (WFL)
Express, 1975 (WFL)
Bulls, 1984–85 (USFL)

KANSAS CITY
Blues, 1924 (NFL)
Cowboys, 1925–26 (NFL)
Chiefs, 1963– (AFL/NFL)

KENOSHA, WIS.
Maroons, 1924 (NFL)

LOS ANGELES
Buccaneers, 1926 (NFL)
Wildcats, 1926 (AFL)
Bulldogs, 1937 (AFL)
Dons, 1946–49 (AAFC)
Rams, 1946– (NFL)
Chargers, 1960 (AFL)
Raiders, 1982– (NFL)
Express, 1983–85 (USFL)

LOUISVILLE, KY.
Brecks, 1921–23 (APFA/NFL)
Colonels, 1926 (NFL)

MARION, OHIO
Oorang Indians, 1922–23 (NFL)

MEMPHIS
Southmen, 1974–75 (WFL)
Showboats, 1984–85 (USFL)

MIAMI
Seahawks, 1946 (AAFC)
Dolphins, 1966– (AFL/NFL)

MILWAUKEE
Badgers, 1922–26 (NFL)
Chiefs, 1940–41 (AFL)

MINNEAPOLIS–ST. PAUL
Minneapolis Marines, 1922–24 (NFL)
Minneapolis Redjackets, 1929–30 (NFL)
Minnesota Vikings, 1961– (NFL)

MUNCIE, IND.
Flyers, 1920–21 (APFA)

NEW ORLEANS
Saints, 1967– (NFL)
Breakers, 1984 (USFL)

NEW YORK
Brickley's Giants, 1921 (APFA)
Giants, 1925– (NFL)
Yankees, 1926–28 (AFL/NFL)
Yankees, 1936–37 (AFL)
Yankees, 1940 (AFL)
Americans, 1941 (AFL)
Bulldogs, 1949 (NFL)
Yankees, 1946–49 (AAFC)
Yanks, 1950–51 (NFL)
Titans, 1960–62 (AFL)
Jets, 1963– (AFL/NFL)
Stars, 1974 (WFL)

NEWARK, N.J.
Bears, 1926 (AFL)
Tornadoes, 1930 (NFL)

OAKLAND
Raiders, 1960–81 (AFL/NFL)
Invaders, 1983–85 (USFL)

ORANGE, N.J.
Tornadoes, 1929 (NFL)

ORLANDO, FLA.
Florida Blazers, 1974 (WFL)
Renegades, 1985 (USFL)

PHILADELPHIA
Quakers, 1926 (AFL)
Eagles, 1933– (NFL)
Bell, 1974–75 (WFL)
Stars, 1983–84 (USFL)

PHOENIX
Arizona Wranglers, 1983–85 (USFL)
Cardinals, 1988– (NFL)

PITTSBURGH
Pirates, 1933–39 (NFL)
Americans, 1936–37 (AFL)
Steelers, 1940– (NFL)
Maulers, 1984 (USFL)

PORTLAND, ORE.
Storm, 1974 (WFL)
Thunder, 1975 (WFL)
Breakers, 1985 (USFL)

PORTSMOUTH, OHIO
Spartans, 1930–33 (NFL)

POTTSVILLE, PA.
Maroons, 1925–28 (NFL)

PROVIDENCE, R.I.
Steam Roller, 1925–31 (NFL)

RACINE, WIS.
Legion, 1922–24 (NFL)
Tornadoes, 1926 (NFL)

ROCHESTER, N.Y.
Jeffersons, 1920–25 (APFA/NFL)
Tigers, 1936–37 (AFL)

ROCK ISLAND, ILL.
Independents, 1920–26 (APFA/NFL/AFL)

SAN ANTONIO, TEXAS
Wings, 1975 (WFL)
Gunslingers, 1984–85 (USFL)

SAN DIEGO
Chargers, 1961– (AFL/NFL)

SAN FRANCISCO
49ers, 1946– (AAFC/NFL)

SEATTLE
Seahawks, 1976– (NFL)

SHREVEPORT, LA.
Steamer, 1974–75 (WFL)

STAPLETON, N.Y.
Staten Island Stapletons, 1929–32 (NFL)

ST. LOUIS
All-Stars, 1923 (NFL)
Gunners, 1934 (NFL)
Cardinals, 1960–87 (NFL)

TAMPA
Tampa Bay Buccaneers, 1976– (NFL)
Tampa Bay Bandits, 1983–85 (USFL)

TOLEDO, OHIO
Maroons, 1922–23 (NFL)

TONAWANDA, N.Y.
Kardex, 1921 (APFA)

TULSA, OKLA.
Oklahoma Outlaws, 1984 (USFL)

WASHINGTON
Senators, 1921 (APFA)
Redskins, 1937– (NFL)
Federals, 1983–84 (USFL)

■ ■ ■

COACH VS. COACH

How the League's Best Fared Against Each Other (Postseason Included)

GEORGE HALAS vs. CURLY LAMBEAU
Years competed: 1921–29, '33–42, '46–53.
Halas' teams: Bears; 265–106–25, .701.
Lambeau's teams: Packers, Cardinals, Redskins; 230–135–22, .623.
One-on-one: Halas, 30–17–3 (1–0 in playoffs).
Comment: A bitter, intense rivalry—54 meetings and they never once shook hands.

GEORGE HALAS vs. JIMMY CONZELMAN
Years competed: 1921–23, '25–29, '40–42, '46–48.
Halas' teams: Bears; 127–41–15, .735.
Conzelman's teams: Rock Island Independents, Milwaukee Badgers, Detroit Panthers, Providence Steam Roller, Chicago Cardinals; 82–58–18, .576.
One-on-one: Halas, 11–6–4.
Comment: When Conzelman had good teams, he gave Halas fits. He was 4–2 against the Bears from 1946 to '48.

GEORGE HALAS vs. GUY CHAMBERLIN
Years competed: 1922–27.
Halas' teams: Bears; 54–15–14, .735.

Chamberlin's teams: Canton and Cleveland Bulldogs, Frankford Yellow Jackets, Chicago Cardinals; 58–16–7, .759.
One-on-one: Chamberlin, 4–3.
Comment: The underrated Chamberlin has the highest career winning percentage of any coach in NFL history.

STEVE OWEN vs. RAY FLAHERTY
Years competed: 1936–42.
Owen's teams: Giants; 48–26–7, .636.
Flaherty's teams: Redskins; 56–23–3, .701.
One-on-one: Owen, 8–5–1.
Comment: Stout Steve's defense shut out the 'Skins three times and allowed them more than two TDs only twice in 14 games.

GREASY NEALE vs. STEVE OWEN
Years competed: 1941–50.
Neale's teams: Eagles; 66–44–5, .596.
Owen's teams: Giants; 59–50–7, .539.
One-on-one: Neale, 10–9–1.
Comment: Known more for their friendship than rivalry. Owen actually helped Neale with draft information in Greasy's early years in Philadelphia. The better team almost always won the season series.

PAUL BROWN vs. BUDDY PARKER
Years competed: 1950–62.
Brown's teams: Browns; 115–48–5, .699.
Parker's teams: Lions, Steelers; 97–64–5, .599.
One-on-one: Brown, 9–8 (1–2 in NFL championships).
Comment: Brown made up a lot of ground after Parker jumped to the Steelers in '57. Counting exhibitions, Parker's Lions teams were 10–1–1 vs. the Browns.

PAUL BROWN vs. JIM LEE HOWELL
Years competed: 1954–60.
Brown's record: Browns; 58–27–3, .676.
Howell's record: Giants; 55–29–4, .648.
One-on-one: 7–7–1.
Comment: Brown won six of the first eight games; Howell six of the last seven.

PAUL BROWN vs. BUCK SHAW
Years competed: 1946–54, '58–60.
Brown's teams: Browns; 130–27–4, .820.
Shaw's teams: 49ers, Eagles; 91–55–5, .619.

One-on-one: Brown, 14–4.

Comment: "Four years ago, I'd never even met Paul Brown," Shaw said in 1949. "Now I scheme to beat him, dream of beating him and wind up screaming because I haven't beaten him." Shaw's only consolation was that two of his four victories cost Brown undefeated seasons ('51, '53).

TOM LANDRY vs. VINCE LOMBARDI

Years competed: 1960–67, '69.

Landry's teams: Cowboys; 56–66–6, .461.

Lombardi's teams: Packers, Redskins; 98–30–6, .754.

One-on-one: Lombardi, 5–2 (2–0 in NFL championships).

Comment: Lombardi's two title-game victories give him a huge edge.

TOM LANDRY vs. GEORGE ALLEN

Years competed: 1966–77.

Landry's teams: Cowboys; 134–50–3, .725.

Allen's teams: Rams, Redskins; 119–54–4, .684.

One-on-one: Allen, 9–8 (1–0 in NFC championship).

Comment: Extremism gains a narrow victory; Allen once told his Redskins he'd cut off an arm to beat Landry.

VINCE LOMBARDI vs. DON SHULA

Years competed: 1963–67, '69.

Lombardi's teams: Packers, Redskins; 64–21–6, .736.

Shula's teams: Colts; 58–24–4, .698.

One-on-one: Lombardi, 7–4.

Comment: 1965 was the difference. The Packers won both regular-season games as well as a playoff for the Western Division title.

SID GILLMAN vs. AL DAVIS

Years competed: 1963–69, '71, '73–74 (Davis had the title of head coach from 1963–65, but we don't think he's ever really given it up).

Gillman's teams: Chargers, Oilers; 73–60–6, .547.

Davis' teams: Raiders; 102–40–8, .707.

One-on-one: Davis, 12–6.

Comment: Gillman begat Davis, hiring him to bird-dog talent in the early AFL. When Davis moved to Oakland, he beat the master regularly.

SID GILLMAN vs. HANK STRAM

Years competed: 1960–69, '71, '73–74.

Gillman's teams: Chargers, Oilers; 99–78–6, .557.

Stram's teams: 114–68–8, .621.

One-on-one: Stram, 14–9–1.

Comment: Stram won the last eight as Gillman's teams grew progressively worse.

HANK STRAM vs. AL DAVIS

Years competed: 1960–74, '76–77.

Stram's teams: Chiefs, Saints; 115–92–10, .553.

Davis' teams: Raiders; 161–58–11, .724.

One-on-one: Davis 16–10–2 (1–1 in postseason).

Comment: Stram won the biggest game, though, for the last AFL championship in 1969. A Chiefs fan saw Raiders quarterback Daryle Lamonica diagramming some new plays in a restaurant and presented Stram with the placemat Lamonica used. It may have been the only time Davis got skunked.

TOM LANDRY vs. DON SHULA

Years competed: 1963–88.

Landry's teams: Cowboys; 261–150–3, .634.

Shula's teams: Colts, Dolphins; 277–124–6, .688.

One-on-one: Shula, 5–3 (0–1 in the Super Bowl).

Comment: Met only eight times in 26 years.

DON SHULA vs. BUD GRANT

Years competed: 1967–83, '85.

Shula's teams: Colts, Dolphins; 200–78–5, .716.

Grant's teams: Vikings; 168–108–5, .607.

One-on-one: Shula, 6–2–1 (2–0 in postseason).

Comment: Shula's big edge includes a victory in Super Bowl VIII.

BUD GRANT vs. TOM LANDRY

Years competed: 1967–83, '85.

Grant's teams: Vikings; 168–108–5, .607.

Landry's teams: Cowboys; 209–84–1, .713.

One-on-one: Landry, 7–5 (3–1 in postseason).

Comment: Landry's average margin of victory was 10 points.

GEORGE ALLEN vs. BUD GRANT

Years competed: 1967–77.

Allen's teams: Rams, Redskins; 111–48–4, .693.

Grant's teams: Vikings; 116–52–4, .686.

One-on-one: Grant, 5–4 (3–0 in postseason).

Comment: Allen couldn't beat Grant when it counted—the playoffs. The Vikings, at home each time, knocked his teams out in '69, '73 and '76.

CHUCK NOLL vs. JOHN MADDEN

Years competed: 1969–78.
Noll's teams: Steelers; 99–57–1, .634.
Madden's teams: Raiders; 112–39–7, .731.
One-on-one: Madden, 6–5 (2–3 in postseason).
Comment: A draw if you count Noll's win over George Atkinson in the "criminal element" lawsuit.

JOE GIBBS vs. TOM LANDRY

Years competed: 1981–88.
Gibbs' teams: Redskins; 92–42, .687.
Landry's teams: Cowboys; 69–58, .543.
One-on-one: 8–8 (Gibbs 1–0 in NFC championship).
Comment: You could tell it was Dallas Week in Washington because Gibbs looked at the ground and talked through his teeth when he answered reporters' questions.

BILL WALSH vs. JOE GIBBS

Years competed: 1981–88.
Walsh's teams: 49ers; 94–39–1, .705.
Gibbs' teams: Redskins; 92–42, .687.
One-on-one: Walsh, 4–2 (0–1 in NFC championship).
Comment: The most successful coaches in the '80s, and each was acutely aware of the other's record.

■ ■ ■

NFL OWNERS

(The figures cited were obtained from a variety of sources—news accounts, books, interviews and Pro Football Hall-of-Fame records. Most are approximations but give a reasonable idea of what was paid.)

Atlanta Falcons

- **1965**—Rankin Smith, Sr., awarded new franchise for $8.5 million. Team remains in family's control.

Buffalo Bills

- **1959**—Ralph Wilson awarded franchise in new AFL for $25,000. Team remains in his control.

Chicago Bears

- **1920**—Decatur Staleys, bankrolled by starch maker A. E. Staley and run by George Halas, join new professional league.
- **1921**—Team moves to Chicago. Halas runs team with partner Dutch Sternaman.
- **1922**—A. E. Staley gives up franchise. Halas and Sternaman awarded it at January league meeting. Rename it "Bears."
- **1932**—Halas buys out Sternaman for $38,000.
- **1983**—Halas dies. Control passes to son-in-law Edward McCaskey and grandson Michael McCaskey.

Cincinnati Bengals

- **1967**—Group headed by Paul Brown awarded AFL franchise for $8.5 million. Team remains in family's control.

Cleveland Browns

- **1945**—Mickey McBride gets franchise in new All-America Football Conference for $10,000. (Also might have posted $100,000 bond.)
- **1953**—David R. Jones purchases team from McBride for $600,000.
- **1961**—Art Modell and Donald Schaeffer buy it from Jones for $3,925,000.
- **1965**—Modell pays Schaeffer $1.5 million for his 25 percent. Team remains in his control.

Dallas Cowboys

- **1959**—Clint Murchison, Jr., gets new NFL franchise for $600,000 ($50,000 franchise fee and $550,000 for veteran players in dispersal draft).
- **1984**—Eleven-person limited partnership led by H. R. "Bum" Bright buys team and Texas Stadium from Murchison estate for $80 million.
- **1989**—Jerry Jones buys team, Texas Stadium and outstanding debts for $140 million from Bright.

Denver Broncos

- **1959**—Bob and Lee Howsam awarded franchise in new AFL for $25,000.
- **1961**—Cal Kunz and Gerald Phipps buy Bob Howsam's share of team for between $100,000 and $200,000 and become majority owners.
- **1965**—Gerald Phipps and brother Allan buy out Kunz for $1.5 million. Two now own 99 percent of team.
- **1981**—Edgar Kaiser, Jr., buys team from the Phippses for $30 million.
- **1984**—Patrick Bowlen buys team from Kaiser for $73 million.

Detroit Lions
- **1933**—George Richards buys Portsmouth Spartans franchise for $15,000 plus assumption of $6,500 in debts.
- **1934**—Moves team to Detroit, renames it "Lions."
- **1940**—Fred Mandel buys team from Richards for $225,000.
- **1948**—Group led by Edwin Anderson and D. Lyle Fife buy team from Mandel for $185,000.
- **1964**—William Clay Ford becomes sole owner by buying up outstanding stock for $6.5 million. Team remains in his control.

Green Bay Packers
- **1921**—J. E. Clair awarded franchise.
- **1922**—Clair turns franchise back to league after Packers caught using college players. Group led by Curly Lambeau pays league $50 fee plus $1,000 bond to get franchise back.
- **1934**—Team reorganized and 600 shares of public stock are sold to raise money. Stock has no par value. All profit turned back into team.
- **1950**—More stock sold, raising $118,000. Packers remain league's only publicly owned team.

Houston Oilers
- **1959**—K. S. "Bud" Adams awarded franchise in new AFL for $25,000. Team remains in his control.

Indianapolis Colts
- **1953**—Carroll Rosenbloom heads group that pays league $250,000 for defunct Dallas Texans and puts team in Baltimore. (Rosenbloom paid very little out of pocket. Most of money came from season-ticket sales, a precondition to his buying team.)
- **1964**—Rosenbloom buys up 31 percent of outstanding stock for $1 million and becomes sole owner.
- **1972**—Robert Irsay trades Los Angeles Rams franchise to Rosenbloom for Colts and $3 million.
- **1984**—Irsay moves team to Indianapolis.

Kansas City Chiefs
- **1959**—Lamar Hunt founds AFL and establishes his own franchise in Dallas for $25,000. Team named "Texans."
- **1963**—Hunt moves team to Kansas City. Renames it "Chiefs." Franchise remains in his control.

Los Angeles Raiders
- **1960**—Group of eight headed by Chet Soda, Ed McGah, Wayne Valley and Robert Osborne awarded AFL franchise in Oakland for $25,000.
- **1961**—Valley, McGah and Osborne buy out other partners.
- **1966**—Al Davis buys 10 percent of the club for $18,500 and is named managing general partner. Bitter legal fight eventually develops for control of team. Davis wins.
- **1976**—Valley sells out, further consolidating Davis' power.

Los Angeles Rams
- **1937**—Homer Marshman awarded franchise in Cleveland for $10,000. Team called "Rams."
- **1941**—Dan Reeves and Fred Levy, Jr., buy out Marshman for $100,000.
- **1946**—Reeves moves team to L.A.
- **1962**—Feud among partners becomes so bad that league intervenes. Control of franchise determined by sealed bids. Reeves wins with bid of $7.1 million.
- **1971**—Reeves dies. Team run by associate William Barnes.
- **1972**—Robert Irsay buys franchise for $19 million, trades it to Carroll Rosenbloom for Baltimore Colts and $3 million.
- **1979**—Rosenbloom dies. Widow Georgia assumes control.
- **1981**—Georgia (last name Frontiere) becomes sole owner by purchasing 700 shares of stock held in trust for son Dale Carroll Rosenbloom, Jr. Price is $1.25 million.

Miami Dolphins
- **1965**—Joe Robbie and Danny Thomas awarded AFL franchise for $7.5 million.
- **1966**—Joe Robbie and W. H. Keland buy out Thomas.
- **1969**—Robbie becomes majority owner.
- **1989**—Robbie dies. Team remains in family's control.

Minnesota Vikings
- **1959**—Group headed by Max Winter and Bill Boyer awarded franchise in new AFL for $25,000.
- **1960**—Group drops out of AFL when NFL awards franchise in January. Price is $600,000 ($50,000 for franchise and $550,000 for veteran players to stock it). "Vikings" to begin play in '61.

■ **1984**—Court battle starts when Winter tries to sell his share of team (one-third of voting stock, 48 percent of equity) to Carl Pohlad and Irwin Jacobs for $25 million. Objecting are John Skoglund and Jack Steele, who control other two-thirds of team's voting stock.

■ **1987**—Minnesota Supreme Court clears way for Winter's sale to Pohlad and Jacobs.

New England Patriots

■ **1959**—Billy Sullivan and nine partners awarded franchise in new AFL for $25,000.

■ **1974**—Sullivan forced out as president; Bob Marr elected to replace him.

■ **1975**—Sullivan regains control by buying outstanding stock for $5.3 million.

■ **1988**—Sullivan family sells team to Victor Kiam for $90 million.

New Orleans Saints

■ **1966**—Franchise awarded to group headed by John Mecom, Jr., for $8.5 million. Team to begin play in '67.

■ **1985**—Tom Benson buys franchise from Mecom for $70.2 million.

New York Giants

■ **1925**—Franchise awarded to Tim Mara for $2,500.

■ **1930**—Ownership turned over to Mara's sons Jack and Wellington.

■ **1959**—Tim Mara dies.

■ **1965**—Jack Mara dies and Wellington takes over as team president. Team remains in family's control.

New York Jets

■ **1959**—Harry Wismer awarded franchise in new AFL for $25,000. Team called "Titans."

■ **1962**—Wismer goes bankrupt in November. Team run by league rest of season.

■ **1963**—Sonny Werblin, Don Lillis, Phil Iselin, Leon Hess and Townsend Martin buy team from league for $1 million. Rename it "Jets."

■ **1965**—Werblin bought out by partners for $2 million. Lillis named president but dies shortly thereafter. Iselin assumes team presidency.

■ **1976**—Iselin dies; Hess takes over.

■ **1984**—Hess buys up final 25 percent of franchise and becomes sole owner. Team remains in his control.

Philadelphia Eagles

■ **1933**—Franchise awarded to Bert Bell and Lud Wray for at least $2,500. (Franchise fee is unknown. $2,500 was a guarantee to protect league in case team folded during season. Bell and Wray also assumed $11,000 in debts owed by the defunct Frankford Yellow Jackets franchise to the Packers, Bears, and Giants.)

■ **1940**—Art Rooney buys half interest in team after selling Pittsburgh franchise to Alexis Thompson for $165,000.

■ **1941**—Bell and Rooney trade Philadelphia franchise to Thompson for Pittsburgh franchise.

■ **1949**—Group headed by James Clark buys team from Thompson for $250,000.

■ **1962**—Clark dies.

■ **1964**—Jerry Wolman buys team from Clark's representatives for $5.05 million.

■ **1969**—Leonard Tose buys team from Wolman for $16.1 million.

■ **1985**—Norman Braman buys team from Tose for $65 million.

Phoenix Cardinals

■ **1920**—Club owned by Chris O'Brien joins new professional league.

■ **1929**—Dr. David Jones buys team from O'Brien for $25,000.

■ **1933**—Charles Bidwill buys team from Jones for $50,000.

■ **1947**—Bidwill dies. Ownership falls to wife Violet and sons Charles Jr. and William.

■ **1949**—Violet Bidwill marries Walter Wolfner, who assumes day-to-day operation of team.

■ **1960**—Team moves to St. Louis.

■ **1962**—Violet Bidwill Wolfner dies. Legal fight for control of franchise develops between Wolfner and two Bidwill boys.

■ **1965**—Legal battle settled in Bidwills' favor.

■ **1972**—William Bidwill buys out Charles Jr. for $6.5 million.

■ **1988**—Team moves to Phoenix.

Pittsburgh Steelers

■ **1933**—Art Rooney awarded franchise for at least $2,500. Team called "Pirates." (Franchise fee is unknown. $2,500 was a guarantee to protect league in case team folded during season.)

■ **1940**—Alexis Thompson buys team, renamed "Steelers," from Rooney for $165,000. Rooney buys half interest in Philadelphia franchise.

- **1941**—Rooney and Bert Bell trade franchises with Thompson.
- **1946**—Bell named NFL commissioner. Rooney and his sister's family (the McGinleys) buy Bell's half interest.
- **1989**—Rooney dies. Team remains in family's control.

San Diego Chargers
- **1959**—Barron Hilton awarded Los Angeles franchise in new AFL for $25,000.
- **1961**—Team moves to San Diego.
- **1966**—Group led by Gene Klein and Sam Shulman buys team for $10 million.
- **1972**—Klein buys out Shulman.
- **1984**—Alex Spanos, a minority partner, buys Klein's 56 percent share of the team for $40 million.

San Francisco 49ers
- **1946**—Tony Morabito awarded franchise in new AAFC for $10,000. (Also might have posted $100,000 bond.)
- **1950**—Team joins NFL following merger of two leagues.
- **1957**—Tony Morabito dies. Brother Vic takes over.
- **1964**—Vic Morabito dies. Morabito family remains in control of team.
- **1977**—Eddie DeBartolo, Jr., buys franchise from Morabito family for $18.2 million. Team remains in his control.

Seattle Seahawks
- **1974**—Group headed by Lloyd Nordstrom awarded franchise for $16 million.
- **1976**—Lloyd Nordstrom dies and is succeeded by brother Elmer.
- **1988**—Ken Behring buys team from Nordstrom family for $80 million.

Tampa Bay Buccaneers
- **1974**—Hugh Culverhouse awarded franchise for $16 million. Team to begin play in 1976. Franchise remains in Culverhouse's control.

Washington Redskins
- **1932**—Boston franchise awarded to group headed by George Preston Marshall. Group puts up $1,500 guarantee. Franchise fee unknown. Team called "Braves" (renamed Redskins in '33).
- **1937**—Team moves to Washington.

- **1963**—Court appoints minority partners Leo DeOrsey, Edward Bennett Williams and Milton King conservators of team when illness incapacitates Marshall.
- **1965**—DeOrsey dies. Williams assumes presidency.
- **1969**—Marshall dies.
- **1974**—Last of Marshall's stock (originally 52 percent) bought by team and retired. Jack Kent Cooke, who bought minority interest (25 percent) in 1960 for $350,000, becomes majority stockholder. Williams remains team president and runs day-to-day operation.
- **1979**—Cooke assumes control of the franchise. Team remains his.

■ ■ ■

100 REASONS WHY FOOTBALL IS BETTER THAN BASEBALL

1. Rainouts.
2. Rain delays followed by rainouts.
3. Rain delays followed by 4½-inning "official" games called on account of the weather.
4. Rain checks good for games against the Seattle Mariners.
5. You can just *watch* football. You don't have to "celebrate" it.
6. There are no Cubs fans.
7. Norm Cash won the 1961 American League batting title with a bat that had cork in it. Gale Sayers won the 1969 NFL rushing title with a knee that had no cartilage in it.
8. Most baseball players are mediocre athletes. Wade Boggs, Don Mattingly, Cal Ripken, Jr., Keith Hernandez, and countless other "stars" couldn't outrun your average offensive lineman at 40 yards.
9. You have to be in shape to play football. In baseball love handles are practically a prerequisite. Pitchers are our favorites. When was the last time you saw Sid Fernandez, Rick Reuschel or any middle reliever advertise for Holiday Spas?
10. Because Paul Hornung is in the Hall of Fame and Shoeless Joe Jackson ain't.

11. Football games in September mean something. Baseball games in April, May, June, July and August mean nothing.
12. Fall afternoons are better than summer afternoons.
13. Baseball players go entire games without getting dirt on their uniforms, much less blood. And whenever they do—after sliding, for instance—they immediately call time and brush it off.
14. There's no such thing as a Chinese touchdown. All football fields have the same dimensions. It isn't any easier to score at Schaefer Stadium than it is at Giants Stadium. A homer into the left-field screen at Fenway Park, though, would often be an out at Yankee Stadium. Don't tell us about the sanctity of baseball statistics.
15. You'll see NFL wide receivers make catches like the one Willie Mays made in the '54 World Series several times a season. And Mays didn't have Ronnie Lott or Jack Tatum to worry about. He also had a glove.
16. You can't have a mouthful of sunflower seeds when you're wham-blocking Keith Millard.
17. The NFL draft is a gas. Chiefs owner Lamar Hunt calls it "the single most fascinating aspect of pro football for the fan." ESPN televises it. Local radio stations provide regular updates. Most newspapers give it a lot of space. Baseball's *two* drafts are nonevents.
18. Baseball has one individual matchup—pitcher vs. batter. Football has eleven. On a given play you can choose from an assortment of subplots, Chris Doleman vs. Jimbo Covert, Jerry Gray vs. Jerry Rice, Jay Hilgenberg vs. Michael Carter. Or you can just watch the quarterback. When was the last time you isolated on the right fielder?
19. If baseball umpires are so good, why do they increase the crews from four to six for postseason play? Football officials have it much tougher. They have to chase the play more. In baseball most of the plays come to the umpire. Imagine what life would be like for an ump if he had to worry about whether the fielder had one foot or two on the base when he made the putout.
20. Good NFL coaches are imaginative. Great ones are frequently innovative—Clark Shaughnessy and George Halas redesigned the T-formation; Tom Landry pioneered the 4-3 defense; Sid Gillman gave us the modern passing game; Joe Gibbs made the one-back offense popular. We could go on and on. Football strategy is constantly evolving. The last baseball manager to make an original move was Zack Taylor in 1951. He sent a midget to bat for the St. Louis Browns.
21. Football is better on artificial surfaces than baseball is. Nothing changes but the players' shoes. Baseball's a different game on the rug.
22. Ted Kluszewski's 15-inch biceps were four inches smaller than Randy White's.
23. The most-watched baseball game ever was Game 6 of the 1980 World Series. Eighteen Super Bowls and the 1982 NFC Championship have had higher television ratings.
24. Washington, D.C., has a football team but not a baseball team. What does that say about the nation's priorities?
25. You can't intentionally walk Joe Montana.
26. Baseball fans are forever reaching over the railing to scoop up fair balls and interfering with fielders trying to catch foul balls. They also use outfielders for target practice. Football fans almost never affect the game that way. They influence the outcome in a more positive manner—by making noise.
27. Name one NFL player that 165-pound Billy Martin could have intimidated.
28. When a baseball player hits a home run he jogs around the bases. When a football player scores a touchdown he runs for his life.
29. Baseball players go on the disabled list for pulled hamstrings, sore elbows and stiff backs. Rams defensive end Jack Youngblood played in the 1980 playoffs with a broken leg.
30. Football is governed by a game clock. Time has relevance and adds to the drama of the contest. Baseball games, theoretically, can go on forever. All too often they seem to.
31. At least football has legitimate reasons for the time it takes between plays. The next play has to be called, and near the end of longer drives the players might need to catch their breath. The delays between pitches in baseball are mostly due to preening. The batter steps out of the box. The batter fiddles with his helmet, his wrist bands, the religious medal around his neck. The batter checks the label on his bat. The batter gets back in the box. The bat-

ter digs in again. The pitcher adjust his cap, goes to the resin bag, cleans the mud out of his spikes, smooths the dirt in front of the mound. The pitcher scuffs the ball against his belt buckle. The pitcher *toes the rubber*. Play resumes.

32. Baseball has the San Diego Chicken. Football has the Dallas Cowboys cheerleaders.

33. Quarterbacks make their reputations in the final minutes of close games. Starting pitchers usually give way to relievers.

34. The defense can score in football.

35. On the night after he received a lifetime suspension from baseball, Pete Rose went on a cable television shopping network to sell autographs and personal memorabilia. Charlie Hustle indeed.

36. George Steinbrenner's football career peaked at the assistant-college-coach level. As a baseball owner he'd won four pennants and two World Series at last count.

37. Bad football teams play 16 games. Bad baseball teams play 162.

38. Pat Summerall and John Madden.

39. John Facenda's voice.

40. Fourth-and-one.

41. How can you respect a game that classifies a *walk* as an offensive category?

42. Or a game that, for years, credited the batter with a hit on catcher's interference?

43. Spitting. Baseball players do it every time they exhale. Football players aren't known for their couth, but you don't have to hose down the bench area after a game.

44. Crotch scratching. What is it with baseball players and their groins?

45. There are no 1–0 games.

46. You don't have to wait two days to read the statistics of West Coast games.

47. Baseball can't draw a decent TV audience until the playoffs. But don't take our word for it. Ask CBS, which paid roughly $270 million for exclusive rights in 1990 and planned to broadcast only 16 regular-season games, none in prime time.

48. You can chant "Defense, defense" and not have the yuppie in the next seat give you a funny look.

49. Football doesn't need promotions. Baseball teams will do just about anything to attract fans. There are bat days, ball days, hat days, helmet days, team picture days, resin bag days, drinking cup days, kids days, halter-top days, even nuns days. There was a time in the mid-'70s when the Phillies lineup included Mike Schmidt, Greg Luzinski and Dick Allen, and the team felt compelled to hire "Kiteman" to fly around Veterans Stadium.

50. Passing a football is much more difficult than pitching a baseball. A quarterback has to throw varying distances to moving targets who are usually defended by at least one person. He has to throw over, around and sometimes through linemen and linebackers who make extra money for knocking him down. A pitcher stands by himself on a well-groomed mound, winds leisurely and throws to a stationary target roughly 20 yards away. Over and over and over again. No comparison.

51. Roger Kahn once wrote that baseball has a pace like "a Schubert andante." We couldn't have put it any better ourselves.

52. Dan Jenkins once wrote: "Baseball mainly attracts two demographic groups: boys under 14 and men over 60. Boys under 14 like it because their daddies make them play catch in the yard. Men over 60 like it because they have to piss a lot and they can do this while watching baseball on TV and not miss anything." He left out Rotisserie-league nimrods, but we forgive him.

53. The reason there's so much good baseball fiction is that the real thing isn't very interesting.

54. Football has the offensive coordinator, who devises game plans and calls plays. Baseball has the first-base coach, who pats fannies and reminds players that second base is that-away (as if it's moved in the last 100 years).

55. Our Pop Warner teams can beat Taiwan's any day.

56. Football is "war without death." To which we add: And baseball is mah-jongg with statistics.

57. Bears vs. Packers, any place, any time.

58. In 1989 the average major league baseball player batted .254 and was paid $490,829. (Stop, thief!)

59. There's no balk rule to explain.

60. Aging players don't hang on in football the way they do in baseball. The sport takes too great a physical toll—and is too competitive.

Almost every big baseball star plays three or four years longer than he should, and it's painful to watch. Mickey Mantle hit .237 in his final season, Hank Aaron .229 and Mays .211.

61. Football has "Mouse" [Davis]. Baseball has "The White Rat" [Whitey Herzog].

62. NFL commissioners have names like Bert, Pete and Paul. Baseball's go by Bowie, Bartlett and Fay.

63. Interconference play.

64. Mike Singletary's eyes.

65. Regarding three of the most exciting plays in baseball: For every triple there are nearly four double plays; for every home run about eight strikeouts; and the chances of successfully stealing a base are better than 2 to 1.

66. Football offers a purer form of competition. Within the framework of team play, it comes down to one man trying to beat another physically. Sissy intellectuals can wax poetic about the pastoral qualities of baseball, but football's appeal is basic. Anyone who's ever landed on his butt during a Saturday afternoon game of touch understands it. "Let's face it," says ex–Cowboys guard John Niland, "most people in our society enjoy watching one guy knock down another one."

67. You've got to love a game that requires you to wear a chin strap.

68. You've got to love a game that requires you to have a chin.

69. Lawrence Taylor on third-and-eight.

70. What kind of sport allows its participants to carry on like spoiled children when an umpire's call goes against them? Temper tantrums are kept to a minimum in football because nothing kills a drive like a 15-yard penalty. Baseball considers them part of the show, as if watching a grown man kick dirt on an ump is anyone's idea of a good time.

71. Football arguments, few as they are, offer one thing baseball arguments don't: Sometimes, when the referee forgets to turn off his microphone, you can actually hear what they're saying.

72. Monday nights.

73. Ninety-nine-yard drives.

74. Football teams have names like Bears, Lions, Rams, Buccaneers, Vikings and Raiders.

Baseball teams have names like Cubs, Padres, Phillies, Angels, Twins and Socks misspelled.

75. As boneheaded as football owners can be, they've never been found guilty of collusion.

76. If someone made the argument that the 1926 Frankford Yellow Jackets could have kicked the tar out of the '78 Steelers or '89 49ers, you'd assume he was on some kind of medication. Not so with baseball. A good case can be made for the '27 Yankees as the greatest team ever. In fact the game may never have been better than it was in the '20s. Think about that.

77. Burt Lancaster played Jim Thorpe. William Bendix played Babe Ruth.

78. There were four blacks in pro football before there was one in major league baseball.

79. They buried Jimmy Hoffa under a football field.

80. In a football game the best players "bat" more often. Dan Marino throws 40 passes; Eric Dickerson carries the ball 30 times. Talk about value for your dollar. You'd have to buy a 10-game plan to see your favorite baseball player that much.

81. The first pro athlete to have a 900 number was a baseball player.

82. Jim Brown carried the ball 2,359 times in his career and never missed a game. Babe Ruth got indigestion in 1925 and missed half the season.

83. In baseball they make such a big deal about players who sacrifice themselves by putting down bunts or hitting behind the runner. In football nine players sacrifice themselves on every play to try to keep the defense from tackling the man with the ball.

84. Baseball fans are fantasists. Football fans are realists. Tommy Lasorda says, "Managing is like holding a dove in your hand. Squeeze too hard and you kill it; not hard enough and it flies away," and baseball fans get all weak-kneed and think: What a lovely thought. Football fans smirk and think: When did Tommy Lasorda ever hold a *dove* in his *hand?*

85. When the wind is whipping and Reggie Roby punts one to the clouds, there's no infield fly rule that can help the returner.

86. Rain-shortened six-inning "no hitters."

87. The instant-replay system may have its faults, but at least football admits its officials make

mistakes and tries to correct them. Baseball would rather have the Royals win the 1985 World Series because of a blown call than acknowledge that.

88. What can you say about a game that expends so little of the players' energy that they're able to play doubleheaders?

89. Football players don't play golf the morning of a night game, either.

90. Softball is played with a bloated baseball your bespectacled grandmother could poke out of the park. Touch football uses a real football.

91. Football coaches don't wear uniforms.

92. Baseball has the Phillie Phanatic; football has the Los Angeles Raiders cheerleaders.

93. Football players are, almost without exception, college educated.

94. Batters get hit by a pitch and charge the mound; running backs get hit by 11 angry men on every square inch of their bodies—

sometimes after the whistle—and go back to the huddle.

95. Baseball players don't like contact of any kind. The middle man on a double play often isn't anywhere near the second-base bag. And heaven forbid that a baserunner should bowl over the catcher—the only player on the field wearing armor—on a play at the plate.

96. Steve O'Neal wasn't punting a rabbit ball when he got off his 98-yarder.

97. NFL quarterbacks had a .351 completion percentage in 1933. American League batters had a .238 average in 1968.

98. In football, as in life, the ball doesn't always bounce predictably.

99. Even in West Germany, which doesn't have an NFL franchise, they're electing chancellors named Helmut.

100. Because the Gallup Poll has said so since 1972.

BIBLIOGRAPHY

(Dedicated to New York Giants general manager George Young, who, when asked if he'd read Lawrence Taylor's controversial 1987 autobiography, LT: Living on the Edge, remarked, "I never read a book without a bibliography.")

BOOKS

American Football League Official Guide. St. Louis: The Sporting News, 1962–69.

American Football League Official History. St. Louis: The Sporting News, 1970.

Beckett, James. *The Sport Americana Football, Hockey, Basketball and Boxing Card Price Guide.* Cleveland, Ohio: Edgewater Book Co., 1988–89.

Bergan, Ronald. *Sports in the Movies.* New York: Proteus, 1982.

Bisheff, Steve. *Los Angeles Rams* (Great Teams' Great Years). New York: Macmillan, 1973.

Blount, Roy, Jr. *About Three Bricks Shy of a Load.* Boston: Little, Brown, 1974.

Brown, Jimmy, with Myron Cope. *Off My Chest.* New York: Doubleday, 1964.

Brown, Paul, with Jack Clary. *PB: The Paul Brown Story.* New York: Atheneum, 1979.

Carroll, Bob, Pete Palmer and John Thorn. *The Hidden Game of Football.* New York: Warner, 1988.

Chandler, Bob, with Norm Fox. *Violent Sundays.* New York: Simon and Schuster, 1984.

Christl, Cliff, and Don Langenkamp. *Sleepers, Busts and Franchise-Makers.* Seattle: Preview Publishing, 1983.

Clary, Jack. *Cleveland Browns* (Great Teams' Great Years). New York: Macmillan, 1973.

———. *Topps Football Cards.* New York: Warner, 1986.

———. *Washington Redskins* (Great Teams' Great Years). New York: Macmillan, 1974.

Cope, Myron. *Broken Cigars.* Englewood Cliffs, N.J.: Prentice Hall, 1968.

———. *The Game That Was.* New York: World Publishing, 1970.

Curran, Bob. *Pro Football's Rag Days.* Englewood Cliffs, N.J.: Prentice Hall, 1969.

Danzig, Allison, with Joseph Reichler. *History of American Football.* Englewood Cliffs, N.J.: Prentice Hall, 1956.

Didinger, Ray. *Pittsburgh Steelers.* (Great Teams' Great Years.) New York: Macmillan, 1974.

Donovan, Art, and Bob Drury. *Fatso.* New York: Morrow, 1987.

Erb, Charles, Jr. *The Lost Art of Kicking.* Adohr Milk Farms, 1939.

Eskenazi, Gerald. *There Were Giants in Those Days.* New York: Grosset and Dunlap, 1976.

Football Guide. St. Louis: The Sporting News, 1970–89.

Football Register. St. Louis: The Sporting News, 1966–89.

Friedman, Benny. *The Passing Game.* New York: Steinfeld Inc., 1931.

Gent, Pete. *North Dallas Forty.* New York: Morrow, 1973.

Gogolak, Pete, and Joseph Carter. *Nothing to Kick About.* New York: Dodd, Mead, 1973.

Griffith, Corinne. *My Life with the Redskins.* New York: A. S. Barnes and Co., 1947.

Grosscup, Lee. *Fourth and One.* New York: Harper and Row, 1963.

Gunther, Marc, and Bill Carter. *Monday Night Mayhem.* New York: Morrow, 1989.

Halas, George, with Gwen Morgan and Arthur Veysey. *Halas by Halas.* New York: McGraw-Hill, 1979.

Harris, David. *The League.* New York: Bantam, 1986.

Herskowitz, Mickey. *The Golden Age of Pro Football.* New York: Macmillan, 1974.

Holovak, Mike, and Bill McSweeny. *Violence Every Sunday.* New York: Coward-McCann, 1967.

Hornung, Paul, with Al Silverman. *Football and the Single Man.* New York: Doubleday, 1965.

Horrigan, Jack. *The Other League: The Story of the AFL.* Chicago: Follett Co., 1970.

Huff, Sam, with Leonard Shapiro. *Tough Stuff.* New York: St. Martin's Press, 1988.

Johnson, Chuck. *The Green Bay Packers.* New York: Thomas Nelson and Sons, 1961.

Johnson, Pearce. *Professional Football in Rhode Island.* Providence, R.I.: Pearce Johnson, 1989.

Karras, Alex, with Herb Gluck. *Even Big Guys Cry.* New York: Holt, Rinehart and Winston, 1977.

Klein, Gene, and David Fisher. *First Down and a Billion.* New York: Morrow, 1987.

Kopay, Dave, and Perry Young. *The David Kopay Story.* New York: Arbor House, 1977.

Kowet, Don. *Golden Toes.* New York: St. Martin's Press, 1972.

Kramer, Jerry. *Instant Replay.* Edited by Dick Schaap. Cleveland: World Publishing, 1968.

Leuthner, Stuart. *Iron Men.* New York: Doubleday, 1988.

Levy, Bill. *Return to Glory: The Story of the Cleveland Browns.* Cleveland: World Publishing, 1965.

Mandell, Arnold J. *The Nightmare Season.* New York: Random House, 1976.

March, Harry. *Pro Football: Its Ups and Downs.* Albany, N.Y.: J.B. Lyon, 1934.

Markbreit, Jerry, and Alan Steinberg. *Born to Referee.* New York: Morrow, 1988.

Matuszak, John, with Steve Delsohn. *Cruisin' with the Tooz.* New York: Franklin Watts, 1987.

Meggyesy, Dave. *Out of Their League.* Berkeley, Calif.: Ramparts Press, 1970.

Moldea, Dan. *Interference.* New York: Morrow, 1989.

Names, Larry. *The History of the Green Bay Packers.* Wautoma, Wis.: Angel Press, 1987.

National Football League Media Information Book. New York: Workman Publishing, 1970–83.

Neft, David, and Richard Cohen. *The Sports Encyclopedia: Pro Football (The Modern Era).* New York: St. Martin's Press, 1989.

Neft, David, Richard Cohen et al. *The Sports Encyclopedia: Pro Football (The Early Years).* Ridgefield, Conn.: Sports Products Inc., 1987.

NFL Official Rules for Professional Football. National Football League, 1974–.

Newcombe, Jack, ed. *The Fireside Book of Football.* New York: Simon and Schuster, 1964.

Official National Football League Record (& Roster) Manual. National Football League, 1941–83.

Official National Football League Record & Fact Book. New York: Workman Publishing, 1984–89.

Official Rules for Professional Football. National Football League, 1939–73.

Olderman, Murray. *The Defenders.* Englewood Cliffs, N.J.: Prentice Hall, 1973.

Owen, Steve, with Joe King. *My Kind of Football.* New York: David McKay, 1952.

Parrish, Bernie. *They Call It a Game.* New York: Dial Press, 1971.

Plimpton, George. *Mad Ducks and Bears.* New York: Random House, 1973.

Plimpton, George, and Bill Curry. *One More July.* New York: Harper and Row, 1977.

Porter, David L., ed. *Biographical Dictionary of American Sports: Football.* New York: Greenwood Press, 1987.

Pro Football Weekly Almanac. Chicago: Pro Football Weekly, 1980–84.

Rentzel, Lance. *When All the Laughter Died in Sorrow.* New York: Saturday Review Press, 1972.

Riffenburgh, Beau. *The Official NFL Encyclopedia.* New York: New American Library, 1986.

Roberts, Howard. *The Chicago Bears.* New York: G. P. Putnam's Sons, 1947.

Robustelli, Andy, with Jack Clary. *"Once a Giant, Always . . ."* Boston: Quinlan Press, 1987.

St. John, Bob. *Tex!* Englewood Cliffs, N.J.: Prentice Hall, 1988.

Sample, Johnny, with Fred J. Hamilton and Sonny Schwartz. *Confessions of a Dirty Ballplayer.* New York: Dial Press, 1970.

Smith, Myron. *The Pro Football Bio-Bibliography.* West Cornwall, Conn.: Locust Hill Press, 1989.

Spalding's National Football League Professional Football Rules. New York: Professional Sports Publishing Co., 1935–40.

Stabler, Ken, and Berry Stainback. *Snake.* New York: Doubleday, 1986.

Stingley, Daryle. *Happy to Be Alive.* New York: Beaufort Books, 1983.

Stram, Hank, with Lou Sahadi. *They're Playing My Game.* New York: Morrow, 1986.

Strong, Ken, and Emil Brodbeck. *Football Kicking Techniques.* New York: McGraw-Hill, 1950.

Tatum, Jack, with Bill Kushner. *They Call Me Assassin.* New York: Everest House, 1979.

Telander, Rick. *Joe Namath and the Other Guys.* New York: Holt, Rinehart and Winston, 1976.

Thomas, Duane, and Paul Zimmerman. *Duane Thomas and the Fall of America's Team.* New York: Warner, 1988.

Toomay, Pat. *The Crunch.* New York: Norton, 1975.

Torinus, John. *The Packer Legend.* Neshkoro, Wis.: Laranmark Press, 1982.

Treat, Roger. *The Encyclopedia of Football.* New York: A. S. Barnes and Co., 1952, 1959, 1961, 1964, 1967, 1974.

Twombly, Wells. *Blanda, Alive and Kicking.* Los Angeles: Nash Publishing, 1972.

Vass, George. *George Halas and the Chicago Bears.* Chicago: Henry Regnery Co., 1971.

Ward, Arch. *The Green Bay Packers.* New York: G. P. Putnam's Sons, 1946.

Whittingham, Richard. *What a Game They Played.* New York: Harper and Row, 1984.

Whittingham, Richard, ed. *The Fireside Book of Pro Football.* New York: Simon and Schuster, 1989.

Wismer, Harry. *The Public Calls It Sport.* Englewood Cliffs, N.J.: Prentice Hall, 1965.

Zimmerman, Paul. *A Thinking Man's Guide to Pro Football.* New York: E. P. Dutton and Co., 1971.

———. *The New Thinking Man's Guide to Pro Football.* New York: Simon and Schuster, 1984.

Zucker, Harvey Marc, and Lawrence J. Babich. *Sports Films: A Complete Reference.* Jefferson, N.C.: McFarland and Co., 1987.

UNPUBLISHED MATERIAL

Governali, Paul. "The Professional Football Player: His Vocational Status." Doctoral thesis, Teacher's College, Columbia University, 1951.

Langhammer, Jay. "Across the Border: U.S. College-Trained Players in the CFL." 1983.

NEWSPAPERS

Akron, Ohio *Beacon Journal*

Albany, N.Y. *Evening News, Times-Union*

Atlanta, Ga. *Constitution, Journal*
Baltimore, Md. *Evening Sun, News-American, News Post, Sun*
Boston, Mass. *Evening Transcript, Evening Globe, Globe, Herald, Herald American, Post*
Buffalo, N.Y. *Courier-Express, Morning Express, News*
Canton, Ohio *Evening Repository*
Chicago, Ill. *Daily News, Herald & Examiner, Journal, Tribune, Sun-Times*
Childress, Texas *Daily Index*
Cincinnati, Ohio *Enquirer*
Cleveland, Ohio *Plain Dealer, Press*
Dallas, Texas *Morning News, Times Herald*
Decatur, Ill. *Herald*
Denver, Colo. *Post, Rocky Mountain News*
Detroit, Mich. *Free Press, News*
Fort Worth, Texas *Star-Telegram*
Green Bay, Wis. *Press-Gazette*
Hartford, Conn. *Courant, Times*
Houston, Texas *Chronicle, Post*
Indianapolis, Ind. *News, Star*
Jacksonville, Fla. *Florida Times-Union*
Kansas City, Mo. *Star, Times*
Los Angeles, Calif. *Herald-Examiner, Herald-Express, Times*
Louisville, Ky. *Courier-Journal*
Memphis, Tenn. *Commercial Appeal*
Miami, Fla. *Herald*
Milwaukee, Wis. *Journal, Leader, Post, Sentinel*
Minneapolis, Minn. *Journal, Star and Tribune, Tribune*
Montreal, Que. *Star*
Newark, N.J. *Evening News, Star-Ledger*
New Orleans, La. *Times-Picayune*
New York, N.Y. *American, Brooklyn Eagle, Daily Mirror, Daily News, Evening Journal, Herald Tribune, Journal American, Newsday* (Long Island), *Post, Sun, Times, World, World-Telegram*
Oakland, Calif. *Tribune*
Philadelphia, Pa. *Evening Bulletin, Inquirer, Public Ledger, Record*
Pittsburgh, Pa. *Post-Gazette, Press*
Portland, Ore. *Oregonian*
Providence, R.I. *Evening Bulletin, Journal*
Reno, Nev. *Nevada State Journal*

Rochester, N.Y. *Democrat & Chronicle, Times-Union*
Rock Island, Ill. *Argus*
St. Louis, Mo. *Globe-Democrat, Post-Dispatch*
St. Petersburg, Fla. *Times*
Sacramento, Calif. *Bee*
San Diego, Calif. *Union*
San Francisco, Calif. *Chronicle, Examiner*
Santa Rosa, Calif. *Press Democrat*
Seattle, Wash. *Times*
Tampa, Fla. *Tribune*
Toronto, Ont. *Globe & Mail*
Tulsa, Okla. *Daily World*
Washington, D.C. *Daily News, Herald, Post, Star, Times, Times-Herald*

MAGAZINES

American Heritage
American Scholar
Coffin Corner
Collier's
Ebony
Esquire
Gameday
Inside Sports
Kick-Off
Liberty
Life
Literary Digest
Look
M
Newsweek
The New Yorker
Playboy
Pro!
Pro Football
Pro Football Stars
Saturday Evening Post
Sport
Sporting News
Sports Heritage
Sports Illustrated
Time
True Detective

INDEX

Page numbers in *italics* indicate illustrations.